D1270705

THE BRETHREN
IN THE NEW NATION

THE BRETHREN IN THE NEW NATION

A Source Book on the Development
of the Church of the Brethren,
1785-1865

Compiled and edited with an introduction by
ROGER E. SAPPINGTON

THE BRETHREN PRESS
ELGIN, ILL.

Copyright © 1976, The Brethren Press
Printed in the United States of America

The author and publisher are grateful to the
owners of copyright materials who have granted permission for their use in this sourcebook. Specific information as to source of all quoted selections is indicated in the Notes, beginning on page 473.

Library of Congress Cataloging in Publication Data

Main entry under title:

The Brethren in the new nation.

    Includes bibliographical references and index.
    1.   Church of the Brethren—History—Sources.
I. Sappington, Roger Edwin, 1929-
BX7816.B74   286'.5   76-13641
ISBN O-87178-113-1

This Volume Is Dedicated
to My Three Sons:
David
Paul
Mark

CONTENTS

INTRODUCTION

The new United States of America in 1785 was in a state of political, economic, and social transition. The War of Independence with Great Britain had just been completed, and most new patterns of life had not yet developed. However, the American people were ingenious and resourceful, and they were able to create new political, economic, and social institutions suited to their particular needs. One of the earliest of these new institutions to be implemented was a new form of government based on the Constitution of 1787. Among the many compromises written into this document was the very important compromise between the large states and the small states regarding their representation in the national congress. This compromise made it possible for all of the states to work together in one united nation—at least until 1861, when other factors became involved. A very important transition took place during the years following 1785 in the change from a weak, divided, and unstable government under the Articles of Confederation in 1785 to a strong, united, and stable government after 1787. It was indeed a new nation!

One of the advantages of this strong and united new nation was that it was able to hold military action with its disturbing results to a minimum. The War of 1812 in the decade of the 1810s and the Mexican War in the decade of the 1840s were both relatively brief; because there was no national conscription and because there was very little fighting on United States soil, the effects on most people were quite limited. Thus, from the end of the American War of Independence in 1783 to the advent of the Civil War in 1861 or throughout most of the period from 1785 to 1865, the people of the United States were able to live in peace.

Although the United States government after 1787 was generally peaceful, strong, and stable, it provided for change in order to meet the changing needs of the American people. In 1788 when the first President and Congress were elected, the number of people who were qualified to vote was very limited. The franchise was controlled by the states and was generally determined by an individual's wealth. Thus, this government might well be called an oligarchy, or a government by the few. By 1865 many political changes had occurred, including the modification of state electoral laws, the development of the two-party system, the election of stronger Presidents such as Andrew Jackson, the convention system of nominating candidates for President, and the longer ballot by which more public officials were elected by the people. All of these changes combined to convert the United States government from an oligarchy to a democracy, or a "government of the people, by the people, for the people," as Lincoln so enduringly described it. This type of government placed pressure on every citizen to participate in some way.

In addition to all of the internal political changes taking place, the United States was also changing its external boundaries in a significant way during the years from 1785 to 1865. The Louisiana Purchase in 1803, the Florida Purchase in 1819, the annexation of Texas in 1845, the Oregon boundary settlement with Great Britain in 1846, the treaty ending the war with Mexico in 1848, and the Gadsden Purchase in 1853 more than doubled the territory of the United States and included all of the land that composed the first forty-eight states. Although the heaviest settlement of these new areas generally came after 1865, many pioneers were establishing farms before 1865. The eminent American historian, Frederick Jackson Turner, argued that the settlement of the frontier, more than any other factor, shaped American life. In spite of the fact that Turner's "Frontier Thesis" has been examined critically by later historians, it is still true that the frontier provided many opportunities for the American people.

The availability of all of this land contributed to economic prosperity in the United States, because the overwhelming majority of the American people earned their living in agriculture in the years down in 1865. American agriculture was undergoing a significant transition during these years from the largely self-sufficient farmer of the frontier who produced a large proportion of his daily needs to the specialized farmer who concentrated on producing large amounts of one crop to be sold on the market and who then purchased many of his daily needs from other specialists. In the lower South the crop was cotton, in the upper South it was tobacco, in the East it was dairy and vegetable products, and in the West it was grain. Many of the surplus agricultural products, especially cotton, tobacco, and grain, were sold overseas in Europe. Contributing to this agricultural specialization was the introduction of new and expensive machinery; a good illustration was the wheat harvester, which was invented in the 1830s and which enabled farmers to plant larger amounts of wheat because they could harvest it more quickly when it was ripe. By 1856 Cyrus Hall Mc-Cormick was producing four thousand harvesters a year in a factory in Chicago. In order to compete with other farmers, a farmer needed to invest a considerable amount of capital in land and in machinery, and thus he became involved in supporting the rapidly growing American industry.

Some Americans were dissatisfied with the way in which American political and economic life was changing, and the result was the development of a series of reform movements which proposed to modify American society. For example, the growth of American cities, where most industries were located, encouraged the settlement of immigrants who provided workers in the factories. Some of these immigrant groups seemed to consume alcoholic beverages more freely than other Americans, and the result was the organization of the temperance movement. At any rate, much of the activity of the temperance reformers was centered in the cities.

Another reform movement which drew most of its support from the cities was the abolitionist movement, even though its goal was the freeing of the Negroes who were being held in slavery in the Southern states. The abolitionists created very strong emotions, pro and con, because of the racial issues involved. For example, the three largest American churches, Baptist, Methodist, and Presbyterian, all split into Northern and Southern divisions primarily over the issue of Negro slavery. Reform movements might be either constructive or destructive, depending on one's particular point of view.

The division of the three largest American denominations not only reflected the seriousness of the abolition movement, it also reflected the significance of religion in American life. None of the three was destroyed by the division because each one had succeeded in putting its roots deep into American life. Although each one had a European background, it had adapted its message to the demands of the American milieu in such a way that it had been abundantly successful. In addition to these and other religious groups with a European background, a significant development in American religious life was the organization of a number of new indigenous religious groups, including the Latter Day Saints or Mormons, the Seventh Day Adventists, and the Disciples of Christ. The first two of these were somewhat unorthodox, as measured by traditional American religious patterns. The Disciples of Christ, which had Baptist and Presbyterian roots, was more orthodox than the other two groups.

The arrival of a number of new religious movements and the continued presence of a number of older groups with European backgrounds led to the development of an intense sectarian rivalry among them. No one group had a monopoly on the truth in this rivalry—even though it may have thought so. One of the smaller, old-line European religious groups which became involved in this competition for men's souls was the Brethren, frequently known as the Dunkers (from the German, *tunken,* to dip) from their pattern of baptizing adult believers by three separate complete immersions forward. They are distinctly different from other groups which use the term Brethren, including the Moravians, the Plymouth Brethren, the United Brethren, and the Brethren in Christ or River Brethren. In 1836 they became known officially as the Fraternity of German Baptists, which was changed in 1871 to the German Baptist Brethren and in 1908 to the Church of the Brethren. In this volume, they will be known simply as the Brethren.

As described in more detail in previous volumes in this series,[1] these Brethren had been organized in Germany in 1708 under the leadership of Alexander Mack, a young German miller. They were influenced by the Pietistic movement of the late seventeenth and early eighteenth centuries and by the earlier Anabaptist movement, which was currently represented in Germany by the group known as Mennonites. Beginning in 1719 and for about the next fifteen years almost all of the Brethren emigrated to America, landing in William Penn's city of Philadelphia. From that port they moved west and south, primarily into the mountain valleys of Pennsylvania, Maryland, Virginia, and the Carolinas, all of which had settlements of Brethren before 1785. They shared the German fame for agricultural skill, generally settling on limestone soil and building large bank barns to take care of their livestock. The Germans developed the Conestoga (from a stream in Pennsylvania) workhorse and the Conestoga wagon (the famed covered wagon of the American frontier). Both horse and wagon were among the finest in America. Although relatively small in total membership, these Brethren were already making a contribution to American life.

Another means of identifying these Brethren is by a statistical examination. Unfortunately, however, the statistical evidence regarding the Brethren between 1785 and 1865 is very limited, which was evidently the way the Brethren intended that it should be. David Benedict, who included the Brethren in his volume on American Baptists in 1813, noted: "I am informed by Dr. Rogers of Philadelphia, and others, that 'it is, at present, a fixed principle with them, to make no communication; and that they feel hurt when interrogated respecting their society.' Indeed, they have always been shy of the English, and suspicious of encroachment and exposure."[2]

Toward the end of this period, Joseph Belcher, writing in 1859, observed: "It is a matter of regret that the German Baptist Brethren altogether neglect any records of their proceedings, and are opposed even to publishing their numbers, lest it should seem to savor of pride; on this account it is very difficult to give the information which might be desired."[3]

The earliest source of statistical information regarding the Brethren in the years following 1785 was published by Morgan Edwards, a well-known Baptist minister and historian, in his history of the Baptists in New Jersey in 1792. After describing the only Brethren church in New Jersey, he also wrote that there were fifteen Brethren churches in Pennsylvania, seven in Maryland, and ten in the states south of Maryland.[4] Benedict, who had access to Edwards' writings, reported that this was five more churches than Edwards had described in his earlier writings in 1772. Now, writing about twenty years after Edwards' account of the Baptists in New Jersey, Benedict could only state: "But what has been their progress since the last-mentioned date, or what is their present situation as to numbers, &c., I have not been able to learn.... Many of the churches mentioned by him have become extinct, and others have suffered great diminutions, and it is generally believed that their society is declining; but still they are considerably numerous in Pennsylvania and Maryland, and small detachments of them are to be found in most of the southern and western States. While they have declined in some places, and become extinct in others, they have emigrated to remoter regions, and formed new establishments some of which are very large.... These people have also become adventurers to the western States of Ohio and Kentucky; and some of them, I have been informed, have settled not far from Detroit, in the Michigan Territory."[5]

Two secular sources, Timothy Flint, writing in 1833,[6] and Frederick von Raumer, writing in 1846[7] each listed a figure of thirty thousand for the Brethren in a compilation of membership of American churches. This figure is almost certainly too large. Flint did qualify his statistics by indicating that thirty thousand was total population, while three thousand would be the number of actual communicants. In addition, his evidence indicated that there were forty ministers and forty congregations.

David Benedict, writing in a revised edition of his history of American Baptists in 1848 with the Brethren minister, Philip Boyle, as a source, reported that there were forty-six congregations in Ohio, forty in Pennsylvania, and about twenty in Virginia and in Indiana. "Maryland, next to Pennsylvania, probably contains more of them than any other Atlantic

State." In addition, there were a "few congregations" in Illinois, Kentucky, and Tennessee, "and a few scattered members in Iowa." Benedict included a summary statistical statement of the Brethren:

"Congregations and churches . . . . 145 to 150
Ministers of all grades, about 300
Communicants, say . . . . 10,000 or upwards."[8]

Another Baptist source, "The Baptist Almanac for 1854," gave very similar statistics for the Brethren: one hundred fifty churches, two hundred ministers, and eight thousand members.[9]

Finally, the United States Government Census during these years provided information on the location and number of church buildings. According to the Census of 1850, the Brethren had fifty-two churches, which could accommodate 35,075 worshipers.[10] By the time of the Census of 1860, the Brethren had one hundred sixty-three churches, which could accommodate 67,995 worshipers.

A further analysis of the Census of 1860 indicated that the Brethren were located in seventy-eight counties in nine states. Pennsylvania had the largest number of churches, forty-six, Virginia had thirty, Indiana had twenty-seven, Ohio had twenty-three, and Maryland had thirteen.[11] Although there was undoubtedly a considerable number of Brethren congregations which had not yet built a church, the number of churches already built according to the Census of 1860 probably gives an accurate indication of the number of Brethren living in each of these states. It seems very doubtful if Benedict's information in 1848 that Maryland had more Brethren than Virginia or that Ohio had more than Pennsylvania was accurate. However, these government statistics do not reveal how many members of the church were living in each state. That information is simply unavailable. Very probably, when the Civil War began in 1861, most of the Brethren were living on the Northern side of the line.[12]

Because most of the Brethren lived in the Northern states, most of the available material describing the history of the Brethren between 1785 and 1865 has been found in those states. And most of it has become located in a relatively small number of centers. Fortunately, two of the most extensive collections are now located within a few miles of each other; one at the Brethren Historical Library at the church's general offices in Elgin, Illinois, and the other at the church's only seminary, Bethany Theological Seminary, at Oak Brook, Illinois. Much of the material in this book has been found in these two collections, and I am deeply indebted to the staffs of these two institutions for their generous assistance. Quite a bit of the material in the Brethren Historical Library was collected by J. H. Moore, who had served for nearly forty years down to 1915 as the editor of the church's weekly periodical, the *Gospel Messenger*. The collection at the seminary has a valuable part of the material collected by the greatest of all of the Brethren collectors, Abraham Harley Cassel.[13]

Additional material from the Cassel collection is located at Juniata College in Huntingdon, Pennsylvania, and at the Historical Society of Pennsylvania in Philadelphia. Unfortunately, neither of these collections was adequately studied in the preparation of this volume, because of lack of time. There are a few items from the Cassel collection at Juniata which were located and provided by my colleagues. Perhaps it is just as well that I did not utilize these Cassel collections more completely, because in order to meet the authorized number of pages for this book I had to abridge or omit entirely a number of documents.

The one major collection of manuscript material relating to the Brethren which is not located in the Northern states and which has been used extensively in this volume is located at Duke University in Durham, North Carolina. Altogether four different collections from the Manuscript Division of the Perkins Library have been utilized. Permission has been secured to use this material in this book. For this permission and for the extensive assistance provided by the staff of the Manuscript Division, I am deeply grateful.

I am also deeply grateful to a number of others who have provided assistance in the preparation of this volume. I have lost track of all of the Bridgewater College students who have spent countless hours typing manuscript and printed documents, but they have collectively been a great help in preparing this material for publication. To the staff of The Brethren Press of Elgin, Illinois, especially Ora W. Garber and Kenneth I. Morse, I am very much indebted. Mr. Garber, who served for many years as book editor prior to his retirement in 1969, was responsible for my beginning to collect material for this book in the early 1960s. Mr. Morse, the present book editor, has guided this book through the process of preparation for the press, as well as its actual publication.

Finally, my wife, LeVerle, and my four children have sacrificed in many ways in order that I might have the time to do the research and writing involved in the completion of this book. For their support, I am always thankful.

Roger E. Sappington

Bridgewater, Virginia
September 1, 1975

I. GEOGRAPHICAL EXPANSION

INTRODUCTION

During the years from 1785 to 1865 one of the major activities in which Brethren were engaged was emigrating from their homes in the Atlantic seaboard states to the new territory of the United States that was being opened to settlement on the west side of the Appalachian Mountains. The pressures to move, as in all human migration, were essentially of two types: the dissatisfaction with one's status in the present location and the call to move to new areas because "the grass might be greener on the other side of the fence."

The first type of pressure was illustrated in a letter written by a member of the church in Maryland.

McKinstrys Mills, Maryland
August 26, 1865

last Sunday there was a big meeting at Sams creek near Clemsons & a wonderful turn out   our youngsters were there and brought about 30 home with them to supper   they had a big time among them   I am getting quite tired of these gatherings and dont know how to stop them unless we go west where we will not have so many acquaintances   that would stop it a while any how   we have been talking pretty strong about selling and going west this last week again and may be we may get there by next spring yet   Howard talks like he will go west in the Spring wheather we move out or not and I have not much notion of going into the work myself so I think we had as well sell   Granville will never be able to do much hard work   as soon as he does something a little hard he is complain[in]g   of   head   ache   or   his   nose   bleeding   or   something wrong   hands are scarce and wages too high for the crops we are now raising   our grain is poor this year   we have threshed the wheat grown on about 18 acres land and I dont think it will make over 250 bu wheat and that not so overly good that it is rather discouraging to farm   with as expensive a family as we have it is getting to be hard work to make both ends meet[1]

Although several types of pressure were mentioned in this letter, the most important in this case, as in most instances, was the economic factor. There was always the hope that a family could achieve greater prosperity by moving to the west. Incidentally, this family did move to Iowa within the next year, and their report is included in the section of this chapter which describes the Brethren settlements west of the Mississippi River.

The other type of pressure, the call from the west, is illustrated in a number of letters included in this chapter. One interesting appeal which some Brethren may have seen was written in the 1830s by the famous preacher, Lyman Beecher, who personally moved to the west and liked it.

It is equally plain that the religious and political destiny of our nation is to be decided in the West. There is the territory, and there soon will be the population, the wealth, and the political power. The Atlantic commerce and manufactures may confer always some peculiar advantages on the East. But the West is destined to be the great central power of the nation, and under heaven, must affect powerfully the cause of free institutions and the liberty of the world.

The West is a young empire of mind, and power, and wealth, and free institutions, rushing up to a giant manhood, with a rapidity and a power never before witnessed below the sun. And if she carries with her the elements of her preservation, the experiment will be glorious—the joy of the whole earth, as she rises in the majesty of her intelligence and benevolence, and enterprise, for the emancipation of the world.

It is equally clear, that the conflict which is to decide the destiny of the West, will be a conflict of institutions for the education of her sons, for purposes of superstition, or evangelical light; of despotism, or liberty.[2]

Certainly, many Brethren heeded the "call of the West," from whatever source they had heard the call, and migrated westward. One interesting case was that of Daniel Leedy, who traveled all the way across the continent from Virginia to Oregon.

Bro. Daniel Leedy was born in Rockingham County, Va., March 13, 1818. In his youth he moved to his father's family to Ohio, and settled near Eaton. In 1840 he was married to Miss Mary Huston, of Oxford, Ohio. In 1841 he moved with his young family to Huntington, Ind., and made himself a home in that then new country, covered with thick timber. There he gave his heart and life to the Master, and accepted Christ as his Savior. He and his companion united with the Church of the Brethren at that place.

In 1848 they moved with their five small children to Jefferson County, Iowa, where he was soon called to the ministry, and assisted older ministers to conduct the public services in God's house.[3]

In 1854 Daniel Leedy and his family migrated to Oregon, where he was for a number of years the only Brethren minister. His work in that territory is described later in this chapter.

The material in this chapter is arranged primarily by geographical areas. The first of these areas is North Carolina, which was in some ways a frontier area for the Brethren even though it was not a part of the West.

NORTH CAROLINA

Although there were Brethren living in North Carolina at least as early as the 1740s and 1750s and three of these early settlements were described in Morgan Edwards' account,[4] none of these settlements became the basis of a permanent Brethren congregation. They usually came to an end as the result of the loss of leadership, either by death or by emigration. By the end of the eighteenth century, however, Brethren had established settlements in two areas which would survive across the years and become permanent congregations. The older of these settlements probably began in the 1770s in an area south of the present-day city of Winston-Salem. The Moravians had purchased a large piece of property on which they established several different communities, including Salem. They were also willing to sell their property as indicated in the following references from the very excellent records which the Moravians maintained.

From the Salem Diary, February 12, 1772:

The great needs of Salem received special help today when quite unexpectedly, three Dunkards came and asked to buy 1000 acres of land in Wachovia; which was promised them when they had seen it.[5]

From the Bethabara Diary, February 26, 1772:

Br. Reuter left day before yesterday, already, as this week he is to survey 800 acres on the Ens, near Peter Pfaff, for Schutz and Tanner, two Baptists from the Huwaren [Ewarrie].[6]

From the Friedberg Diary, July 23, 1772:

Johann Nicholas Boeckel told me that he had sold his plantation on the Reedy Creek to a Dunkard, and has taken 250 acres in Wachovia from Br. Marshall.[7]

In addition to Brethren moving into this area from other Brethren settlements in North Carolina, such as the Ewarry (Huwaren) congregation, the Brethren were also emigrating into this area from Pennsylvania.

From the Salem Diary, May 22, 1773:

At the end of the week four more families came from Pennsylvania to settle in Wachovia. — Brendle, Beroth, Rothrock, and a Dunkard.[8]

At least as early as 1774 Brethren in this area which later became known as the Fraternity congregation had become numerous enough to have worship services.

From the Friedberg Diary, May 1, 1774:

Only preaching was held today, not many being present. Some had gone to the English service at Salem; others out of curiosity were at the

Dunkard meeting; still others had gone to buy the wares which Jacob and John Rothrock recently brought from Yorktown.[9]

From the Friedberg Diary, August 26, 1775:

Last Sunday Christian Frey attended a Dunkard meeting, in which three persons were baptised.[10]

When baptisms took place, it normally indicated both the presence of an ordained minister and the establishment of an organized congregation. The ordained minister was Jehu Burkhart who had come to this area from Frederick County, Maryland, in 1775, and whose land grant for two hundred thirty-five acres was registered by the state of North Carolina in November, 1778. The Moravians also learned to know Burkhart.

From the Salem Diary, May 9, 1791:

The wagon of our neighbor Jehu Burkart, which went to Pennsylvania in March, has returned and brought us letters and Nachrichten, for which we were grateful for we have received none since October.[11]

From the Friedberg Diary, December 2, 1800:

I attended two meetings held by the Tunkers at the home of Jehu Barkhart. Two or three preachers from Virginia were present, and among other things they spoke much about the sufferings of Jesus. Their guide, George Giersch, a Tunker from Pattitat [Botetourt] County, came to me and referred with pleasure to his childhood, when he spent two years in the school of the Brethren [Moravians] two miles from Quithopehill [Pennsylvania].[12]

From the Friedberg Diary, June 13, 1807:

We had a pleasant visit from the Dunkard bishop, Jehu Burkhart. He inquired about a number of Brethren [Moravians] whom he knew, and especially about Br. John Gambold and the mission to the Cherokees.[13]

From the Salem Diary, July 20, 1808:

This morning, Br. Rude held the funeral of a boy, aged fifteen years, Friedrich Muller, who was killed five miles fron Friedberg . . . . At the funeral Br. Rude spoke to the numerous company on the need to be ever ready, for no one could know in what hour he would be called from this earth. The Dunkard bishop, Jehu Burkardt, who was present, followed with an address to the company.[14]

From the Friedberg Diary, August 12, 1810:

The old Tunker bishop, Jehu Burkhart, attended the preaching service.[15]

Jehu Burkhart moved to southern Ohio sometime before 1810. From the wording of the last three references, his move might have been completed by 1807. The man who took over the leadership of the Fraternity congregation after Burkhart's departure was his son-in-law, Isaac Faw, who had married Magdalene Burkhart on August 10, 1791. Isaac had come to North Carolina as a young boy with his father, Jacob, in the late 1770s. In the 1790s Isaac Faw purchased land from the Moravians. He evidently liked what he had and decided to stay in North Carolina. When his father-in-law departed he accepted the responsibility for the Fraternity congregation and continued as its minister until his death in 1835. He was evidently the only Brethren minister in the original area of settlement along the Yadkin River who did not emigrate to the west with the tide of the frontier. The Moravians also learned to know "the Dunkard preacher, Faw."

From the Salem Diary, June 1, 1823:

By request, Br. Denke went to the home of the Dunkard preacher, Faw, near Hope, and married his daughter, Maria Faw, to the Single Br. Thomas Hanes. The wedding festivities which followed were conducted in a Christian fashion, accompanied by prayer and the singing of hymns.[16]

Years later, when the four Hanes' children were growing up, the Moravian minister visited the home.

From the Hope Diary, January 28, 1839:

I visited Thos. Hanes and had a thorough discussion with him in regard to his merely nominal membership with us. He seems to hold with the principles of the Baptists and that is the reason none of his children are baptized. Since his views on baptism as it is practiced by the Baptists seem really only superficial, I dared to offer some points against the principles and advised him to read the holy scriptures with a request for enlightenment of the Holy Spirit and before all things to ask for the baptism of the Spirit, without which no water baptism can avail for bliss.[17]

Actually, this case of inter-marrying between the Brethren and the Moravians was not the first time such a thing had happened, for as early as 1783 the Moravians had reported in the Salem Board Minutes, May 30, 1783:

Kastner has chosen to marry the daughter of a Dunkard. It will not be wise publicly to turn him out, but the newly elected Friedland committee,—the Brn. Peter Kroen and Jacob Ried as Stewards, and the four Brn. Friedrich Muller, John Heyn, Johann Lanius, and Friedrich Kunzel,—can be asked whether they will recognize such a man as a Society Brother, and then they can tell the settlement of their decision.[18]

As illustrated in these instances of inter-marrying, the relations between the two sects were sometimes not so good, especially in situations involving preaching and baptizing.

From the Friedberg Diary, on a journey to Reedy Creek and Stinking Quarter, late in the evening of May 25, 1776:

Another unmarried woman, daughter of a Dunkard, and herself unbaptised, asked concerning the baptism of her child. I replied that so long as she did not believe on the Savior, and did not seek baptism for herself, her child also might not be baptised.

May 26. On the way to the church, which was a mile from our lodging, an old Dunkard, father of the above mentioned woman, asked whether I was going to baptise his daughter's child today? I answered that if his daughter should come to me, acknowledging her sin, and showing faith in the Savior, and asking baptism for herself and her child, I would baptise both, but otherwise I would baptise neither. Then he wanted to discuss with me the subject of the baptism of children. I replied that faith is a matter of the heart, not of great knowledge and wisdom, and therefore that the Holy Ghost could not only influence children as well as adults, but He could do far more with children, teaching them true faith in the Savior and leading them the right way. Then I went into the church, and after a hymn preached on John XIV, 23.[19]

From the Salem Board Minutes, May 3, 1782:

The so-called Dunkards, and especially the Methodists, seem to be trying hard to take over our people in their *persuasion.* The latter become constantly more busy in the neighborhood of Hope, but the last speaking with the members of that Society did not show that any harm had been done. The best thing, under the circumstances, is for our preachers to set forth the gospel, and leave the doctrines of Jesus, committed to us, to approve themselves to the hearts of men as the power of God.[20]

From the Salem Diary, June 23, 1799:

Br. Kramsch reported from Hope that today, two miles from there, the Dunkers held a great gathering, on which occasion various ministers preached, prayed and sang, alternately in German and English. Then three persons were immersed in the South Fork. Altogether the meeting lasted more that four hours. As this seldom happens, more than three hundred persons gathered, standing on both banks of the creek.[21]

From the Friedberg Diary, June 23, 1799:

I attended the baptism of three Tunkers on the South Fork near the home of Rudy Heuer.[22]

From the Salem Diary, October 10, 1819:

In Hope few attended the meetings because a Tunker preacher was baptizing in Muddy Creek, two miles from there.[23]

From the Bethania Diary, October 3, 1828:

A Free Dunker (or Bearded Man) preached on Salem Square; did not win approbation. The church had been refused him, although some members seemed to want him to use it.[24]

From the Bethania Diary, May, 1835:

(Brother Bahnson reports:) On the 14th I preached, following a Tunker preacher, in Conrad's schoolhouse a mile distant from Bethania. This preacher, Friedr. Hauser, (Houser), declared in the beginning that he was not in the habit of taking a text for his sermon because, as he said, from a single passage of scripture almost anything could be proved, and his congregation could be misled; but he would choose today Hebrews 1:1, a text that gave him opportunity to pass from book to book through the Bible, displaying his truly wonderful knowledge of the passages of scripture, so that an adult member of the congregation said: "He told us everything he knew by heart out of the Bible.[25]

From the Friedberg and Hope Diary, November 29, 1835:

This month in Hope a member of the Dunkard Church, who was baptized by her Uncle Faw, asked to become a member of our congregation.[26]

From the Minutes of the LAC, July 6, 1843:

Br. Hubener reports that the Tunkers have appeared in the neighborhood of Friedberg and preached, whereupon a long discussion about baptism and related subjects ensued.[27]

The final reference in 1843 occurred after the death of Isaac Faw in 1835, which caused a crisis in the life of the Fraternity congregation, for there was no minister prepared to take his place. After several years of uncertainty, Isaac Faw's youngest son, Jacob, finally became convinced that he should accept the call of God to undertake the leadership of the congregation. However, he was not even baptized and there was no minister in the immediate area to baptize him. He did remember that there were Brethren ministers in Virginia and so he tried writing to one of them. What happened has been described by Daniel Peters, who witnessed some of the events.

At one time a man from North Carolina, by the name of Jacob Faw, not knowing Bro. [John] Bowman's given name or address, but wishing to learn something from him of the Brethren church, wrote a letter, addressed to Preacher Bowman, Rocky Mountain, Va., the countyseat of Franklin County. After receiving a reply from Bro. Bowman, he came to his home on Friday evening, talked with him on Saturday, making known all of his wishes. On Sunday morning he accompanied Bro. Bowman to his preaching point. After the services he was baptized into Christ, I being one of the witnesses of this impressive scene. After Bro. Faw's baptism, he returned to his home in North Carolina.

Soon afterward the Brethren of this county began preaching down there, going two or three times a year, on horseback. In a short time, Bro. Faw was called to the ministry, and soon to the eldership. During his administration, with the assistance of others, the church in North Carolina prospered.[28]

Jacob Faw himself had an opportunity to describe his life in North Carolina in a letter written in 1853.

Forsyth Co., N.C.
April 25th, 1853

We received your friendly and pleasing letter dated March 15 which gives us much satisfaction to hear from you again and with pleasure I comply with your request by writing you this letter at this time thanks be to God the father of all mercies for His many blessings to us His poor unworthy children. We hope our letter may find you all well, our friends and few relatives are all well as far as I know and enjoying peace and plenty. Our last year's crop of all kinds were very plentiful and the present prospect for wheat is very fair. . . . As to stock and chattels I deem it unnessary to relate as my affections is not altogether here. I would rather seek a country that is a Heavenly country although we cannot partake of so many blessings of our kind and heavenly parent without regard especially for the sake of Him who giveth us richly all things to enjoy has a powerful influence upon the inhabitants of this country. Our church here is not increasing but we still indevor to be faithful over a few things; sometimes I am almost inclined to contemplate about going to a free state where the brethren is more prosperous but it don't seem like I can ever leave this country as long as there is any church here, and as long as I am here. . . . When I got your letter I learne that you had moved and yet you enjoyed the blessed hope of a church which is more to be desired than all other advantages in this life. I rejoice whenever I can hear of any of our brethren in our country. As for our prospects in church matters here is not good on account of the numerous sects that is more popular and pleasing to carnal minds and the pride of life and fashions of the day; now least I should weary you I shall draw my letter to a close; We remember our love to you and your family and all the friends and brethren that you may have the convenience of communication; We remain your unworthy but well wishing brother and sister.[29]

Finally, his contributions to the church and his life were summarized in a tribute by a non-Brethren leader in the community after Faw's death in 1887.

I am told that the church had declined in numbers during the interval between his father's death and his ordination to the ministry, and that by his personal efforts new life was infused into it, so that it was soon brought up to its former prosperous condition having built several years ago a neat house of worship. It is a matter of history that, under his ministry, they steadily gained in numbers, till they have grown to be a large and influential part of the community, maintaining their distinctive individuality as a church by their piety and simplicity of life, as manifested by their friendly manners and plainess, through scrupulous neatness of dress without change, through all the visisitudes and oft-changing fashions of these latter times. . . .

He was a model farmer, the principles of his church making it necessary that he should earn his own living as well as preach. He had everything around him arranged to more convenience than any farm house in all the surrounding country. He disposed of the products of his farm in Salem, where his customers took whatever he had to sell at his own weight or measure, an exception to a rule very probably not made in behalf of any other man who trades in Winston-Salem, thus paying tribute by their confidence to his sterling honesty and truthfulness. It is true that honesty and truthfulness were conspicuous traits of his character, but no more honest truthful and moral man ever commanded the public confidence to the extent that he did, and therefore we must look for the explanation of the general esteem in which he was held in his faithful and unwavering discharge of duty, as he saw it, to God and man. It is then as a model man of God, especially, that he is known and revered. For half a century he has been a prominent figure in the community, towering far above all other men as a model for Christian living.[30]

In addition to the Brethren settlement known as the Fraternity con-
gregation which developed on the south side of the Moravian territory, the
Brethren also put down permanent roots before 1800 in the mountainous
northwestern corner of North Carolina in Ashe County. When the first
Brethren arrived in this area is not known, but certainly they were there by
the 1780s, for numerous Brethren names were reported in this area in the
census of 1790. The number of Brethren in the settlement increased during
the 1790s, and in 1801 many of them placed their names on a petition to
the government of North Carolina dealing with land problems.

To the Honourable House of the General Assembly

The distressed Situation in which your humble petitioners by the late
Act of Assembly for the Year 1801 in the Second Section, in respect to the
Land Law's is reduced: it is impossible without flowing Tears the
Grievances thereof to prescribe! it is evident, that the County of Wilkes
before its division, that part of it, which is called now the County of Ashe,
being first inhabited with Hunters, made their living by Hunting game. Ul-
rick Kessler, a Dunkard Preacher coming from the North, was the first inhabitance of the Germans who bought his land for 300 £ and paid for it,
and by his persuasion, drawing his congregation hither, till this Wild Country became inhabited with industrious farmers, Purchasing their land, and
give their Money, Horses, Waggons and nearly all their living for their
Possessions. then this part of the Country being Granted by the Legislature
unto a party of Speculators, who by their granted Authority, oppressed
this people very much, to make themselves rich of their Labour. The first
Settlers and Hunters could not endure to live amongst Labouring and industrious farmers, Sold their rights, moving to the West Country's,
Cumberland, Kentucky, etc. The Germans who had bought their
Possessions, labouring with industry, clearing Land, building Houses,
Barns, planting Orchards, made Meadows, raising Stock, building Gear
Mills, Saw Mills, fulling mills; that this Wild Country became fertile of
Utility, by the blessing of the Supreme being, who made all things; paying
their Taxes annually, and living peaceably and quietly in their Possessions,
under the Protection of the legislature of the State; till this present juncture
of the above mentioned late Act, when the Speculators Grants and Rights
was broke, and the Land Office for to make Entry's upon Land was establish'd. Some of them made Entry's upon Vacant Treasury, getting their
Grants, improved it by their family's, without hearing of any other Claim
of any other person of persons, of their possessions till now. at the time
when Wilkes County was divided, and this Country became the Name the
County of Ashe, the Commissioners faithfully Purchasing Fifty Acres of

Land, laying it out in Lot's, Sold them, and Builded a Court House, made a Contract for to Build the Prison, out of the Surplus of that Money, which gave the date to Conceive and bring forth a New-Birth of the infernal part of Self Interested party Speculators. Robert Nall, Surveyor who had undoubtedly a View of this Speculation, for the former Benefit, made him Sure of the New, that by his influence, to the Committee of this County, under a Cloak that it was beneficial for the poor inhabitance, to petition for that Law; no Sooner that Law came in existence; than he had a Store of Old Warrants, which was bought for a trifle, having the Books of Fletcher, forming a Body of party Speculators, claiming the Town Land and all the plantations within Six Miles round, near the Court House, Surveyes the Land and especially where a German lives without distinction. For this Speculators Say, they had the Oldest Warrant, it was their Right and Title, and in any Court of justice and Equity they could keep it, for the Word: previous of that date give it to them by the Said Act. and not in one clause of Said Act is left a iota of reserve, for the defence of a Labouring industrious Citizen; it is impossible that your humble petitioners can believe, that the Legislature could be so Tyrannical to pass Such Act and Law, with an intent; that Honest Citizen should be cheated and defrauded out of their property and Possessions for the Cause of a few Speculating individuals. Therefore your Humble petitioners beg the Honourable House of Assembly to take the Grievances of the foregoing Circumstances into Consideration; and Consider at *first* That the Established Land paid into the Treasury, and that the Grants for said Land is Lawfull and Ought to be protected. *Secondly* That the Warrants, with which the Speculators will Cheat and Defraud, to drive honest Citizens out of their Possessions; if they had not be revived by the late Act, being all Dead and out of date, and then to make a Conclusion for a remedy of redress. *Thirdly* That an Additional Act, that it the meaning of the Legislature not is, that honest Citizen should be cheated, defrauded and deprived out of their Possessions by the said Act, and that the Older Grant should be protected in any Court of justice and equity for ever in which hopes your humble petitioners is in duty bound, and will for ever pray.

Michajah Pennington	John Byrket	Moses Toliver
Wm hubbart	Andrew Fouts	George Eberly
Peter Hart	Jacob May	Allen Noulin
Jos Rowland	Christian Byrket	William Pennington
James Mulkey Capt	Wm May	G Koons
David Connelson	George Grubb	John Phillips
John Johnson	William Migapha	Henry Miller

George Miller
Henry Dulheur
John Kessler
David Engrum
Lewis Bonner
Andrew Sheets
Peter Dick
John Dick jr
Conrad Grubb
Luke White
John Koons
Daniel Miller
Leonard Baumgarner
James Shasser
Michael Stocker
Jacob Fouts
Wm Shepperd
Emmanuel Croster

Henry Michel
Andrew Rowland
Jonathan Miller
Wilm Henson Junr
Jacob Grimes
benja manhubbire
Woller Weaver
Jacob Reese
John Ford
John Norris
Gilbirt Norris
Barnet Owen
Henry Graybeal
John Whit
Jacob Eller
Peter Eller
John Maxwell

Zacariah Harwood
James Rowrick
Jacob Pfau
Samuel Wilcocken
John Sturgin
Charles Williams
John Miller
Jas Bunyard
Samuel Taylor
Isaac Weaver
Id manhubbire
Landrine Eggers
John Ress
Henry agrer
Wm Morris
Ephrim Norris
Wm Owen

The presence of Brethren in this area along the New River was also confirmed at about this same time by a Moravian missionary.

Report of Br. Abraham Steiner of his visit to Deep Creek in Surry County, and to the Mountains in Ashe County, in the month of May, 1804.

Going further into the country I crossed New River with difficulty and toward evening reached a settlement of Dunkards, and spent the night with a Mr. Bauer, of that persuasion, a mile from the Courthouse. This man is an exhorter among his people, and during the evening spoke much about religious matters, but in such a way and in such a strain that I must admit I did not understand him.[32]

Still a third Brethren minister in Ashe County, and one who contributed significantly to the permanence of the Brethren settlement by spending his mature life in this area, was Jonathan Miller. In a letter which he received from his brother Henry in Missouri in 1842, Henry commented on the prosperity of Zion in North Carolina, which has been interpreted as a reference to the church in Ashe County.

State of Missouri, Newton County
July 3, 1842
After a long delay I take this opportunity of writing to you and hope

these lines will find you and yours and all Connection Well which Lines leave us all here Enjoying that Inestimable Blessing for which We feel Thankful for. I received your Letter Dated Nov. 28th 1840. And was happy to hear of you all being Well & Rejoiced to hear of the Prosperity of Zion in your Land and hope that the Lord will continue to bring in such as should be saved and pour out his Spirit as a rain on thirsty Land. I am still well satisfied with this Country and Expect to end my last Days where I am settled. I feel thankful to God the giver of all good. He still smiles upon my Endeavors and has blest me with Plenty of this world's good and hope he will bless me with that Religion that will stand when this world shall cease to be. I still have an Eye to the great Recompense of Reward and know if I prove faithful I shall one Day reap the benefit a Crown of Glory laid up for them that prove faithful and I hope if we should meet here no more I hope to meet you all in that Land where pleasures flow forevermore. All connection well here and would be glad to hear from you all and how you are doing with regard to Religion it appears to be measurably cold in this section but hope there will be a change for the better— Produce Rates here Wheat 75 cents Corn 37½ Bui Cows and calves $10 each Sheep $2 Flour $3 per 100lb Crops likely to be good. Considerable wheat raised here this year I have about 60 acres in grain wheat rye Oats & Corn.[33]

By 1865 the Brethren had active congregations in North Carolina in the Fraternity area near Winston-Salem and in the Ashe County area, both of which were old and well-established settlements.

TENNESSEE

By 1800 Brethren from Virginia and North Carolina were moving into the eastern part of Tennessee along the North Carolina border. Among the earliest families were the Shanks, the Simmons, the Krouses, and the Bowmans. During a visit to the area, Samuel Garber, a minister from Rockingham County, Virginia, organized the Brethren settlers as a congregation. The date is not known, but it was probably very early in the nineteenth century. He is described as "our dear brother" in an invitation to come to Tennessee to live signed by six Brethren in 1818.

Jonesboro, Tenn.
June 6, 1818

Our most hearty greeting from us the undersigned to you dear brothers,

Abram and Joel Krumbacker and (your) both families; and (we) wish heartily that this letter finds you all well.

What concerns us so far as we know we are all well for which we have God especially to thank.

Dear brothers we have resolved to write to you, of which we have often spoken, and much more since our dear brother Samuel Gerber was here whose troubles you will have heard of by this time.

He has advised us likewise to visit you since we ascertained that you sold ... your land and thought of going elsewhere. However if you have not yet decided where to go, if it pleases God to direct you to come this way and visit us you might then determine [with] satisfaction that you can settle as you wish.

David Bauman	Nicholas Eisenberg
Michael Kraus	Joseph Bauman
John Bauman	Christian Zetty[34]

Whether or not the Krumbackers came to Tennessee to settle is not known. In addition to the Brethren who settled permanently, primarily in Washington County and in Hawkins County in eastern Tennessee, Brethren ministers traveled widely and preached wherever there was opportunity. Such a person was Joseph Roland, who spent his young life in North Carolina and who later moved to Kentucky. On one occasion as he traveled between the two states, he preached in Wilson County, Tennessee. A young man named Isham Gibson heard him, and after meditating on Roland's message for several months, decided to ride some distance, probably into Kentucky, to be baptized by Joseph Roland. Five years later, in 1826, he was ordained as a bishop by the same Joseph Roland.

To all to whom these presants shall come greeting
Know ye that Isham Gibson was ordained a Bishop of the Church of the Fraternity of Baptist by the laying on of hands by the presbytry on the West fork of Stones river—Rutherford County Tennessee   Given under my hand this 28th of May in the [year] of our Lord 1826

Joseph Roland

Attest
Abraham Welty[35]

Rutherford County adjoined Wilson County on the south side. Evidently, there was little challenge for a Brethren minister in this area, and in 1830 he and his father relocated in Illinois, where he served as a minister for more than forty years.

The center of Brethren activity in Tennessee continued to be in the Washington County area. Two letters written by Brethren in this area indicated some of the human problems of that day as well as some of the activities of the church.

Limestone Creek, Washington County, Tenn.
August 12, 1838

old Brother Michal Garver and his wife Catherine Came to see us the 2 satterday in June   they Live about 15 miles from us on Brush Creek not far from wattaga river   she is a verry large fresh Stout Looking woman she took the fever and the 11 day she died   that was the 7 of August she had a daughter maried 2 monts ago   she is very Low   no Life Expected   her son samuel the preacher is got the fever to and some more of the familly has the fever   the peopel about hear are all well as far as I know with the Exception of severl Children   they have the gray flux   one of Isic Mcphersons Children Died and one more so Low that their is no hopse for it   he was gone to Baltimore and gust Came home a few days before his Child died   old Brother Joseph Beckner and his nephew Joseph Beckner a step son to Christena amen Came to us and staid all night with us the first friday in this month and on satter day Christena step son was Baptised and tomeses wife preacher Crouses daughter she was baptised the same day   their was 2 days meeting at the meeting hous then   I think their was about 20 aded to our Church since we Came hear   7 Baptisde and the oathers movd heare   their has Been 9 men from rockingham [Va.] this spring on the hunt of Land   the one was old unkel John florys son

this day 3 weeks ago their was a young man kild in hawkins by the Lightning   his name was simmons a brothers son to the simmons that Lives near to John Brubaker   his Brother and Brothers in law are boath preachers in our Church[36]

Washington County, Tennessee
January 5, 1863

And now I must inform you of the prosperity of the church   there has bin a considerable increase since you had left but most in the Pleasent Valley church   thanks be to God for his abundent Mercy that the Cause of Christs Kingdom might prosper   And we had an Election on the 4th of this inst   there was two placed to the word Brother Samuel S. Sherfey & George Bowman   two Deacons Peter Bashor & Joel Sherfy and hoping the good will of the Lord may continue and may prosper here and every where that all things we undertake and do may be to the Honor and Glory of God and for the salvation of our immortal and never dying Souls.

Brother J. Nead departed this life on 5th of December and old Sister Himes the same day   there ware great many deaths through our country but knowing this is our Common lot prepared or unprepard dust thou art and to dust thou shalt return then   wisdom would say let us prepare to meet our God in peace then   Dear Brother & Sister I desire your prayers to God in my behalf.[37]

As in North Carolina, the Brethren had put down permanent roots in this section of Tennessee by 1865.

KENTUCKY

When Joseph Roland, who baptized and ordained Isham Gibson, preached in Tennessee about 1820, he was traveling between North Carolina and Kentucky. He was one of a number of Brethren who moved to Kentucky over a considerable span of years before and after 1800. In fact, when the Brethren first began to move to Kentucky is unknown. Certainly, there were quite a number of Brethren in the state by 1800, as demonstrated by an examination of Shelby County tax lists and marriage records.

Tax list, 1792-1795
Hostedler, Abram, 110 on Buck Creek (Beech)
Hostedler, Christian, 287 on Beech Creek
Hartman, Abm., 468 on Gist, 108 on Snake Run, 185 on Beech Creek
Hartman, Anthony, 71 on Bresheares Creek
Letherman, Peter, 150 on Buck Creek
Letherman, Nancy, 370 on Buck Creek
Ruble, Jacob, 71 on Gist
Ruble, Adam, 80 on Buck Creek
Ritchie, Jacob
Ritchie, Thomas, 148 on Jepsey Creek
Snider, Peter, 200 on Buck Creek
Shively, Henry
Ullery, Jacob, 100 on Brasheres Creek

Marriage records, 1792-1800
Cline, John—Elizabeth Yunt, Jan. 15, 1799
Cline, Nicholas—Elizabeth Favours, March 4, 1794
Gassaway, Nicholas—Dorothy Leatherman, Oct. 28, 1800
Houghstatler, Adam—Hannah Hartman, June 20, 1797
Jacobs, Thomas—Elizabeth Cline, June 28, 1796
Leatherman, Christian—Barbary Hostidler, Aug. 4, 1798
Leatherman, Frederick—Polly Lastly, Aug. 21, 1797
Leatherman, John—Betsy Graves, Feb. 3, 1797
Ritchie, Jacob—Mary Martin, Aug. 25, 1794
Ruble, Jonathan—Hanna Letherman, June 10, 1797
Taylor, George—Betsy Leatherman, Feb. 4, 1797[38]

One of the very prominent Brethren families in this area was the Hostetler (spelled many different ways) family. A very excellent biographical study of one of the younger members of this family, Joseph Hostetler, was written in the 1860s. It describes many aspects of life in this area in the early 1800s.

JOSEPH HOSTETLER

The subject of this sketch was born in Shelby county, Kentucky, February 27th, 1797. His father and grandfather were natives of Pennsylvania; but his great-grandfather was born in Germany, near the Rhine. His mother, Agnes, was the daughter of Anthony Hardman, about whose ancestry nothing is known.

About the year 1795 his parents emigrated from Pennsylvania, and settled in Shelby county, Kentucky. Though no longer in a German settlement, they still retained in their family the German language; and Elder Hostetler distinctly remembers the difficulties he encountered in acquiring the rudiments of the English.

When in his seventh year he entered a common school, kept by a queer little Englishman of strong Roman Catholic proclivities, though a member of the Episcopal church. Intoxicating beverages were then freely used by people of both sexes; and, in this particular, the school-master was wholly conformed to the world. Yet he maintained inviolate the *form* of godliness; and, on every Friday afternoon, required his pupils to form in a circle about him and repeat after him, with great solemnity, the Lord's Prayer and the Apostles' Creed!

To this school he was sent three months each year until he was twelve years old. By this means he acquired the arts of reading and penmanship; and also completed the arithmetical course, which extended only to "the Single Rule of Three." Except the medical lectures, which he subsequently attended, this was all the instruction he ever received at school.

His parents were both exemplary members of the German Baptist or Tunker church, which, even at that early period, had adopted the New Testament as its only book of discipline. It was their chief care to bring up their children in the nurture and admonition of the Lord; and the mother, especially, spared no pains in teaching her little ones to pray; and in instructing them in what she conceived to be the doctrine of Christ.

Under her teaching, Joseph became greatly interested in reading the scriptural account of patriarchs and prophets; and often did he pray to be like little Samuel, or like faithful Abraham, who "was called the friend of God."

Along with these wholesome lessons, many superstitious notions were inculcated by an old German woman, who came frequently to his father's house and related frightful stories about ghosts, witches, hobgoblins, etc. Each of these served "to point a moral"; and all together deeply impressed him with the reality of a future state and the awful penalties visited upon evil-doers.

It was to be supposed that one brought up under such circumstances would readily walk in the way of the righteous. But he was naturally of a very mischievous disposition; at times highly passionate; and "as prone to evil as the sparks to fly upward." When, therefore, he grew older and became less in the presence of his parents, he often set at naught all their counsel to walk in the counsel of the ungodly.

In the winter of 1810-11 there occurred, in his native county, a great revival, which, beginning among the Calvinistic Baptists, soon extended to the Methodists and Tunkers. His grandfather and his uncle Adam Hostetler were the principal Tunker preachers, the former speaking in German, the latter in English. Under their earnest preaching and the excitement that generally prevailed, his early religious feelings were revived; and, but for the intervention of his parents, he would have convenanted to walk in a new life. They, however, thought him too young; and prevailed upon him to postpone for a brief period his union with the church. . . .

Subsequently, through the efforts of his uncle Adam, he was induced to "ponder the path of his feet." He grew more serious; read the Bible through; and became convinced that his skepticism was based, not on the Scriptures, but on the contradictory theories and absurd speculations of professed Christians.

This conclusion reached, he again became a seeker; but the "whisper of peace," as formerly, strangely delayed its coming.

Finally he discovered by his own reading what the believer must do to be saved. He revealed his discovery to his uncle, who at once accepted his views and on the next Lord's day taught the people openly that they should repent; confess the Lord Jesus; and be baptized in His name "for the remission of sins." On that day Elder Hostetler—then in his nineteenth year—made the good confession and was immersed into the "one body." . . .

Immediately after his immersion he began to take part with his brethren in prayer and exhortation, and to labor for the reformation of his wicked associates, some of whom are indebted to him, under God, for their hope of eternal life. . . .

Shortly after [his marriage on July 20, 1816] he was authorized, by the congregation of which he was a member, to preach the gospel and baptize believers according to the custom of the Tunker church. His uncle being absent for the most part, he at once assumed the principal care of the home church; and in a short time he accompanied his kinsman on a preaching tour through the counties of Nelson, Franklin, Washington, Mercer, Casey, Nicolas, and Fleming.

His ministry was fruitful from the very first, on which account, as well as by the expressions of his friends, he was greatly encouraged.[39]

More of the story of Joseph Hostetler will be found in the section on Indiana, because he moved to that state and continued his ministry there.

Another individual who spent some years in a Brethren home in Kentucky was Jacob Bower, although during his early life he had lived in Pennsylvania. Late in his life he wrote a short autobiography, which described in fascinating detail the life of a child in a Brethren home and also the process of conversion and of becoming a church member.

JACOB BOWER

I was born in Manheim Township, Lancaster county in the State of Pennsylvania, on the 26. day of September in the year of our Lord 1786. When I was about three years old my Father emigrated to what was then called the back woods in Westmorland county. Early in the month of May before I was six years old. I was sent to a German school, and by the time I was six years old, I could read the New Testament.

Thank God for pious parents

I had a sister too young to go to school with me. My parents belonged to the denomination of christians called Tunkers, as early as I can recollect, my Father kept the regular morning and evening worship in the family. Commonly he would read a chapter in the German Testament, then sing a hymn in German, then say a prayer in the same language, and [we] were taught to sing with them. We were instructed in such lessons as we were able to understand such as this. Be good children, all good children when they die will go to a good place, where Jesus is, and many pretty Angels and they would be happy forever. Bad children when they die will go to a bad place, where there is a great fire, and the Devil and his Angels tormenting the wicked forever. These instructions were ingraven on my mind, I have never forgotten them, and were a means of continual restraint from being wicked. In January after I was six years old, the Lord took my good Mother home to Heaven, and I wished very much to go withe her to the good place she had gon to. I was yet unconcious of sin in myself, and my anxiety to die and go to the good place wher Mother was, greatly increased. . . .

[When I was a young man,] I fel into a snare of the fowler. One day a company was collected to repave the highway; and a certain individual who professed himself to be a Universalist, he and the old Judge had a long argument on the subject, each of them made two or three speaches in turn. I began to think that if Universalism was true, there is no need of being so much concerned about my situation, I hoped that all would be well enough at last, and began to grow more careless about religion. About this time, I went in company with some eight or ten others about thirty miles to a Universalist love feast, as it was called, I stayed among them (I think) three days & nights, the result was that I imbraced their sentiments more fully. I was taught to believe that "God so loved the world that he gave his only begotten Son, who taisted death for every man, he came not to condemn the world, but to save the world, and that he would do it, and he would not louse one of Adams race, but he would save all." I came to the conclusion that, if all the world are to be saved, I certainly would be included, therefore I was sure of Salvation. This kind of wind blew off my convictions and trouble about my unhappy state. I was rocked to sleep in the cradle of Universalism for a little more than five years. . . .

My Father had previous to this emigrated to Sheby county K—y about 160 miles from where I resided in Muhlenberg county. About the first of October. 1811. I and my wife paid them a visit—stayed with them about ten days. A universalist Minister resided in the vicinity, and I made him several visits, who strengthened me some in the faith, I was verry fond of his company.

But when the time arived that we must lieve for hom, I felt unusually solemn. My Father accompanied us about four miles to a large creek, and now the time came that we must take the parting hand. I put on as chearful a 'countinance as posible, and said, Well Father, come let us take a parting *dram,* perhaps it may be the last time we shall ever drink together. I dont want to drink a drop, said he, I have something to say to you, Jacob, Well Father, said I, what is it? "I want you to promise me,' said he, 'that you will serve God & keep out of bad company." Well Father I will, said I, Farewell, Farewell. I started to go accross the creek, which was about thirty yards accross, and as my horse steped out of the water to rise the bank, instantly my promise staired me in the face. Although he had given me the same council, and in the same words, perhaps an hundred times before, Yet it never produced such an impression on my mind as now. To serve God and keep out of bad company wrung in my ears all day long, I had promised my Father, and God heard it, that I would do it, but alas how can I, and he expects that I will do it. I began to feal in a way quite different from what I had ever done before. . . .

Early the next morning before it was quite light, we were on the road. But not without the good mans benediction. Soon we met large companies of Negro-s, we passed several companies, at length we met an old man walking by himself, I stoped him, and enquired of him, where they were all going so early this morning. The old negro said, "we are all going to Beards Town to see a fellow servent hung to day for killing his fellow servent." I started on with this thought, how does that man feal, knowing that he must die to day. Suddenly, as if some one had asked me. And how do you feal? You dont know but that you may die before he does. All of a sudden, (ah I shall never forget it) as if a book had been opened to me, the inside of which I had never seen: I got a sight of the wretchedness of my heart—a cage of every unclean and hateful thing. (ah thought I. here lies the root of bitterness, the fountain from whence all my sinful actions have flowed. My mind & heart have always been enmity against God, who is so holy that he cannot allow of no sin, however small it may appear in the sight of men. How can I ever be admited into Heaven with such a heart? it is uterly imposible. Lost, lost forever lost. Right here, and at this time my crumbly foundation of Universalism gave way. I discovered a just God, who, I thought, could not save me and remain just. I could see no way of escaping eternal punishment. . . .

But the ever memerable morning of the 17th day of December 1811. About 2 oclock A. M. when most people were in their beds sound asleep. There was an Earthquake, verry violent indeed. I and my wife both awoke about the same time, she spoke first, and said, Lord have mercy upon us, what is it shaking the house so? From a discription given of an Earthquake in Germany by a Tunkard preacher in a sermon when I was about ten years old, I immediately recognized it, and replied, it is an Earthquake. The Lord have mercy upon us, we shall all be sunk & lost, and I am not prepared. O God have mercy upon us all. I expected immediate distruction, had no hope of seeing the dawn of another day. Eternity, oh Eternity was just at hand, and all of us unprepared; just about the time the sun arose, as I supposed, for it was a thick, dark and foggy morning, there was another verry hard shock—lasted several minutes terible indeed. To see everything touching the earth, shakeing—quivering, trembling; and mens hearts quaking for fear of the approaching judgment. Many families ran together and grasped each other in their arms. One instance near to where I lived, the women & five children, all gathered around her husband, crying O my husband pray for me, The children crying, Father, pray for me, O pray for me, for the day of Judgment is come, and we are unprepared! The people relinquished all kinds of labour for a time, except feeding stock, and eat only enough to support nature a fiew days. Visiting from house to house, going to meeting Singing—praying, exoting, and once in a while ketch a sermon from a travelling Minister. Men, Women and children, everywhere were heard enquiering what they must do to be saved. This shaking continued more or less for near two years, sometimes just percievable. . . .

For several days past, I had been thinking about giving up to God, and resign myself into his hands, for I can do nothing to save myself, and all I do is so sinful in his sight that he disregards my cries & prayers. But a follish thought suggested itself to my mind, that I must not give up to God to do with me as he pleased, for I thought that the moment I did that, he would kill me and send me instantly to hell, and although I had long ago confessed that he would be just in so doing, Yet I was willing that Justice should be executed, and I thought that as long as I was not willing, he would not do it. My toung never can till, not my pen discribe, the struglings & anxities I passed through about this time. . . .

Suddenly my thoughts turned to the sufferings of Christ, and what he endured on the cross. That he suffered in soul & body, his soul was exceeding sorrowful even unto death. sweting as it had been drops of blood falling to the ground; and all his painful sufferings for the space of three hours on the cross, and that not for himself; it was for sinners that he thus suffered that they mite be saved. The next thought that passed through my mind was. If it was done for sinners, it was done for me. I believed it. The storm calmed off, My troubled soul was easy. I felt as light as a fether, and all was quiet—pieceful—tranquil and serene. This transpired about midnight, and I had not slept for several nights previous, for fear that if I went to sleep, I would awake in hell. I thought of lying down. I first walked out of doors, and everything I could see, appeared intierly new. The trees (I thought) lifted their hands up toards Heaven as if they were praising God. I cast my eyes upward, and beheld the bright twinkling stars shining to there makers praise. They appeared as so many holes through which I could look & see the glory of Heaven. Glory to God. Thank God. Bless the Lord O my soul, was busily runing throug my mind— What is the matter with me. I never felt so strange before, strange wonderful—wonderful indeed. A little while ago I felt as if I were hanging by a slender thread over the pit of ruin. God would not have mercy on me—Hell was my portion. God was just in sending me there—This was the last call—the last time, and the last moment with me on Eerth. Before morning I shall lift up my eyes in hell. My burdin—my distress of soul was too heavy to be bourn any longer. And now all of a sudden I feal so light—so easy—so happy, so full of glory, and so full of love to everything I see. And so full of love to God. What is it, what can all this mean? It did not then enter my mind that this was religion; or that this was salvation. But in this calm and piecful state of fealing, I laid myself down to sleep, when I awoke, the sun was just then rising, and a bright streak of light shone against the wall, which was the first thing I saw, and the first thought I had was, O the glory of heaven. I arose—walked out, and I never saw the gees—ducks—hogs and every living creature praising God so before. The birds were singing God's praise, and invited me to unite with them in singing the praise of God, for he is good and his mercy endureth forever.

This was the Lords day morning, and the 8th day of February, 1812 I recollected an appointment for a prayermeeting about six miles off, and I had to pass my house to get there. I made arrangments for my wife to come on after the day got some warmer.

I started verry early and got to the meeting just as the people were singing. I thought that I had never heard such heavenly music; all their singing—praying—exhortation, shakeing of hands accompanied with singing, was certainly the sweetest exercise I had ever witnessed. I wept all the time, the people seamed more like Angels than human beings, O how I loved them and their religious exercises. I had a faint hope that perhaps I would soon get religion. But a great desire to be a christian. . . .

In those halceon days, the following hymn expressed the sentiment of my heart & fealings.

> Saved by Grace, I live to tell
> What the love of Christ hath done,
> He redeem'd my soul from hell,
> Of a rebel made a son.

Sporting on distruction's brink,
Yet preserved from falling in.

In a kind propitious hour,
To my heart the saviour spoke,
Oh! I tremble still to think
How secure I lived in sin,
And my dangerous slumber broke
Then I saw and own'd my guilt:
Soon my gracious Lord replied,
Fear not, I my blood have spilt,
Twas for such as thee I died.

Shame and Wonder, joy and love,
All at once possess'd my heart:
Can I hope thy grace to prove,
After acting such a part?
Thou hast greatly sinn'd, he said,
Touch'd me by his spirit's power,
But I freely all forgive.
I myself the debt have paid,
Now I bid thee rise and live.

Come my fellow sinners, try:
Jesus' heart is full of love:
O, that you, as well as I,
May his wondrous mercy prove
He has sent me to declare,
All is ready, all is free:
Why should any soul despair,
When he saved a wretch like me?

I was feasting on the love of God, and contemplating on what he had done for me, oh, I had heaven on Earth, not a cloud, not a temptation, not a single cross met me. . . .

About this time I had a great desire to be united with some society of christians. And in those days there were no societies in that part of Kentucky but Baptistst, Tunkars, and some Methodists, and for a time I could not decide which of them to offer myself to for membership. I felt quite unworthy to be united with any, for I verily thought with myself, that if I was a child of grace at all, I was less than the least of all saints, and unworthy the name of a christian. I first thought of Uniting with the Tunkars. And if Mr. Hendrix (their preacher) had come into the vicinity, I would have been baptized by him. (by trine immersion) I thought that it must be the right way, or Father would not have been baptized that way. But I could not arrive at any decission on the subject. I therfore resolved to read the new Testament, and go the way it pointed out to me, and unite with that church which practised, and walked nearest to the divine rule. I commenced at the first chapter of Mathew, determined to read the Testament through and through again & again till I could be able to decide. I had a German Testament, and when I could not well understand the English, the German would explain it to me. It was just three weeks from the time I obtained a hope in the saviour, till Hazle Creek Baptist Church Meeting; of an eavning I would gather dry brush (sticks) to make a fire, light enough to see to read by. I read on and soon came to the conclusion that according to the book. Baptism must be recieved by immersion I could not tell what Baptism must be received by immersion I could not tell what Baptism ment. But the German Testament said *Taufen,* and this I knew was to dip, Diping &c. But here arose another difficulty, to know whether this Taufen ment once, or thrice. When I read to Rom. 6-4. Being buried with Christ in Baptism &c. I supposed that baptism must in some way resemble a burial. When I read Colos. 2-12 the words repeeted, I paused, and began to reason on this point—Lord teach me that I may understand thy word aright. lead me in the path thou wilt have me to walk. I thought that Baptism was a sign of a death—a burial and a resorection. And as the dead are buried only once, so baptism is to be performed only once, one immersion to represent a deth to sin, a planting, or buri-ing with Christ, and rise to walk in newness of life.

I became perfectly satisfied in relation to Baptism. But I could not be satisfied as to myself being a proper subject. I resolved, however, that I would go to meeting, and I would tell the Church exactly, or as near as I could recollect, all how I had been exercised in my mind, and ask them to give me council, but I did not believe that they would receive me, for if they thought of me, as I did of myself, they would be sure not to receive me. Council was what I wanted. I went to meeting, and after a sermon by their pastor, Eld. Benjamin Talbert. the fellowship of the church was enquired for: a door was opened for to hear expeariences. I had not heard an experience related at that place for four years. But I ventured forward—told my tale, then asked for council. The moderator said. "Can any person forbid water?" In a moment I was threwn into the strongest kind of temptation. He extended to me the hand of fellowship for the water. I first thought of refusing my hand. Thinking that he was jesting—making sport of me. But old Brother David Rhoads gathered me into his arms, and all members rushed forward to give me their hands, som wept aloud for joy, my jealously was removed—singing and shaking of hands all through the crowd. That afternoon 16 persons were recieved for Baptism, and two came who wer rejected. The next day, being the first Lords day in March, 1812, I, with fifteen others were Baptized. And like one of old, for a time, I went on my way rejoicing. During that revival, 76 persons were aded to Hazle Creek Church, by baptism.[40]

Jacob Bower eventually served for many years as a Baptist pastor in Illinois.
A final insight into the life of the Brethren in Kentucky was provided by two travelers who visited in areas where Brethren lived. The first was James Weir, identified as a school teacher from South Carolina, who spent some time in a Brethren settlement in Muhlenberg County about 1800.

Having tarried there a few days in a friend's house, I passed over into the state of Kentucky and travelled through some of the lower parts, viz., on Green River and Red River. This country is for the most part newly settled, their buildings and farms but small. Some live by hunting only, which explore the solitary retreats of the wild bear and buffalo. Others, being more industrious, cultivate the soil, though not as properly as they might for want of implements. The land yields exceedingly well, corn, wheat, cotton and all other grains and plants common to the southern states. The latitude is nearly the same as that of North Carolina.

The range for cattle is good in the summer and for hogs I suppose it is equal to any in the world. There are low flats and marshes which overflow at certain seasons which after the water is departed make excellent range for hogs. I saw a gentleman here who from four of a stock raised 200 head in three years. These flats lie along on Green River and up some of the creeks that empty into it. . . .

Here I made a stop again, and kept school six months in Muhlenberg county on this River, in a Dutch settlement. Some of them are of distinguished kindness. Their profession is Dunkards and Baptists. They appear to be very sincere, God only knows their hearts.[41]

The second traveler was a Frenchman, Andre Michaux, who evidently found himself one night quite by accident in a Brethren home. It was a very poor home and he was not too favorably impressed. It may have been an isolated settlement.

On the following day, the 26th [of August, 1802], I went twenty-eight miles, and stopped at the house of Mr. Jacob Kesly, belonging to the Dunker sect, which I discovered by his long beard. About ten miles from Dripping Spring I forded Big-Barren River, which appeared to be one third broader than Green River, the plantation of one Macfiddit, who plies a ferry-boat when the waters are high; and another, belonging to one Chapman. About three miles farther are the two oldest settlements on the road, both of them having been built upwards of fourteen years. When I was at this place, a boat laden with salt arrived from St. Genevieve, a French village situated upon the right bank of the Mississippi, about a hundred miles beyond the mouth of the Ohio.

My landlord's house was as miserably furnished as those I had lodged at for several days preceding, and I was again obliged to sleep on the floor. The major part of the inhabitants of Kentucky have been there too short a time to make any great improvements; they have a very indifferent supply of any thing except Indian corn and forage.

On the 27th of August, I set off very early in the morning; and about thirteen miles from Mr. Kesley's I crossed the line that separates the State of Tennessee from that of Kentucky. There also terminates the Barrens; and to my great satisfaction I got into the woods. Nothing can be more tiresome than the doleful uniformity of these immense meadows where there is nobody to be met with; and where, except a great number of partridges, we neither see nor hear any species of living beings, and are still more isolated than in the middle of the forests.

Editor's note: Michaux passed from General Adair's, through Mercer and Marion counties, and over the range of Muldrow's Hills, which until about 1785 formed the southern boundary of Kentucky settlement. The "barrens," lying south and west, were so called from their lack of trees. The road led through Green, Barren, and Allen counties, and entered Tennessee in Sumner County, about forty miles northeast of Nashville.[42]

By the early years of the nineteenth century, the Brethren had developed about six different settlements in Kentucky, although the exact number is still the subject of historical investigation. One of the major problems in determining the exact number and the location of these settlements is that none of these early settlements became the basis of a permanent congregation. Many of the Brethren, like Joseph Hostetler, moved on to other areas. And a number of Brethren were put out of the church in a serious division which developed between the Brethren moving west from the more conservative areas of Virginia and Pennsylvania and the Brethren who had already arrived in the area from the Carolinas. This difficulty is often noted in references to the "Far Western Brethren."

INDIANA

Many historians who have examined the beginnings of the Church of the Brethren in Indiana have concluded that the first settlement was in Union County in southeastern Indiana along the Ohio border. Recent studies have revealed the existence of an earlier settlement in Clark County along the Ohio River across from Louisville, Kentucky. One of the earliest ministers in this area was Jacob Stutzman, who had previously been identified as a Brethren minister in North Carolina by Morgan Edwards, the Baptist historian.[43] One of the most prominent Brethren ministers in this general area of southern Indiana was Joseph Hostetler, whose early life in Kentucky has already been described.

In the fall of 1817, he removed to Washington county, Indiana. Settling upon a tract of uncleared land, he devoted the most of his time and energies to the opening out of a farm; yet on Lord's-days, and usually on two evenings each week, he proclaimed all he knew of the gospel. Being yet in his minority he was denominated "the boy preacher." This appellation usually attracted a large audience; and, even at that early period, his influence as a preacher began to be felt.

In the Spring of 1819, he removed to Orange county, near Orleans, and again settled in the woods. Here also he worked hard by day; and at night was equally diligent in the study of the Bible and an English dictionary, which two volumes made up the greater part of his library.

Though he occasionally went into Lawrence county, yet his labors were for the most part confined to Orange; and in the fall of 1819 he and Elder John Ribble organized in his neighborhood, and on the foundation of apostles and prophets, a church of some thirty members. This was the origin of what is now known as Old Liberty church—one of the oldest, firmest, and most flourishing [Disciples of Christ Churches] in the state.

One night in August of the next year he dreamed that he saw on the farther side of a river, a large field of wheat and several persons importuning him to come over and help them harvest. As dreams were then of great significance in matters of religion, he inferred from this one that God had called him to preach the gospel in the region beyond White River. He was not disobedient unto what he supposed "the heavenly vision," but set out straightway for the field indicated.

The first man—a blacksmith—to whom he revealed the object of his mission, said to him, "Sir, you have come to a poor place for your business. I have not been to meeting in four years." Yet, commencing at that man's house he preached at several points in that imaginary

Macedonia, everywhere relating his dream, which made a deep and solemn impresssion upon the people; because it led them to believe that God had been mindful of them and had sent his servant to warn them. Having immersed eight persons and left appointments to preach again at each point in four weeks, he returned home.

On his next visit he immersed about twenty, among whom were the smith's wife and daughter; and a short time afterward a church was organized near Abraham Kern's, in Lawrence county.

This year (1820) the Tunker churches in Indiana and Kentucky determined to form a separate Association, being unwilling to conform to all the rules observed by the brethren in Ohio, Pennsylvania and other states. On a specified day the delegates met, organized, and proceeded to enact new laws for the government of the church. Against this action Elder Hostetler, John Ribble of Salem, and Peter Hon of Kentucky, solemnly, but vainly, protested. "Old men for counsel, young men for war," said the venerable controllers of that ecclesiastical body.

The following year this Association met at Old Liberty, at which session Elder Hostetler was regularly ordained as a minister of the grace of God.

As a part of the ceremony his uncle Adam presented him a small Bible, saying *"Preach and practice only what you find in this Holy Book."* This remark, made at that solemn moment when he was on his knees before his Maker, deeply impressed him with a sense of his responsibility. Hitherto he had humbly submitted to the dictum of those who had the rule over him, and had felt that they were chiefly responsible for his ministerial action. But now he realized for the first time that it was his duty to *study* to show himself a workman approved *unto God,* and that to his own Master he should stand or fall. Hence he applied himself more closely than ever before to the study of the Scriptures; and he was not long in discovering radical differences between the church described by the apostles and the various religious organisms by which he was surrounded.

Pursuing the subject of creeds, he perceived that their number constantly decreased in each preceding age, until, arriving at the apostolic period, he found but *"one* Lord, and the *name one."* By this fact his confidence in the popular systems of religion was greatly shaken; yet he quietly adhered to the church of his father for two or three years, during which period he baptized about as many hundred persons.

But the eyes of his understanding were being gradually opened; and his preaching was becoming more and more in accordance with the oracles of God; so much so, indeed, that, at the session of the Association in 1825, he was accused, by some of his brethren, of disseminating heterodox opinions. No decisive action, however, was then taken against him; and he continued to preach during another year, with more and more freedom from all human authority.[44]

The conclusion of the story of Joseph Hostetler in Indiana will be included in the later discussion of the relation between the Brethren and the Disciples of Christ.

By the 1830s Brethren churches in southern Indiana had come to an end and the Brethren were establishing permanent settlements in central and northern Indiana. One of these areas was in Montgomery County, from which the Harshbarger family reported to their friends in Virginia.

Cornstock Grove, Montgomery County, Indiana
August 27, 1843

This is to inform you that we are all well at this time, also hope that these lines will find you enjoying good health, heappiness, and prosperity. Tho as for being contented in mind I dont think you can be for this reason, our country is so much superior to that of yours. our Country is not infested with Slaves, nor with those bald bleak red hills   Dear brother and sister the corn fields before our house if you recollect is now a wilderness of corn   we have excellent corn crops this Season   I think it would be prudent for you to Secure Some of our good land hear for your children even if you did not Sell out and come your selves but this I think you will do as I know you and Sister Susan liked our Country so well that when you got to Va. the hills looked so much higher and regeder than they did before that you will take the Indiana fever, if you have not alredy got it.

Yesterday the Meting was at the widow Stoners   there was a great menny people thare   Daniel Miller, Jacob Garber, Fraces Myers, and Jonathan Myers preached   Jonathan is franks Father   he is what they call the Kentucky Dunkards

On the 4th Sunday of September the Communion meting will be at our house. if you could be with us then how happy I would be and old friend Peter Nead is wanted hear badly. I want you to encourage Nead to come to See this country   I know he will be pleasd with it and he will find friends hear too   land hear is cheap and we will have a good Market hear after a little   I think as good as Lynchburg if not better in a few years as hear we have a chance of the Orleands Market or New York

I was at Wm. Gishes to day   they are well   Wm. Gish is well pleasd with the Country   he said he ought of come hear long ago   he thinks he can do much better hear than he could whare he come from[45]

According to the Harshbargers, there were many good reasons for moving to Indiana, including the lack of slavery, the excellent land, and the active church program.

William Gish was a Brethren minister, who was working diligently to promote a strong church program, according to later letters.

Cornstock, Montgomery County, Indiana
November 16, 1852

I seen a letter quite lately that Brother George Bare rote to Brother Wm Gish   I was truly glad to lern in it that he had Some Idea of the west and more than likely he will come hear in our part of the world   the harvest is great, and the labourers are few   I will now inform you that Brother Wm has no help at this time at all. Old Brother D. Miller at this time is on his way to the Arkanses Country   he says the Osark Mountains is the best climate he knows of. Frank Myers is gone to Iowa and Jeramiah Wootden to the Misouri   So you See Br. William has all to do at this time. Wm. has had a hard time hear but now he is alone   him and Old Brother Daniel got along fine after Frank left   now we begin to see the fruits of Br. Williams labours   our communion on last year waeon the 6th November and Since then there was 19 added to the church by Baptism and one by recantation   Joseph Robertson and his wife Eliza Carrell used to be, and Mathias Frantz and his wife ware the last that come, and on the last Sunday in this month Brother Wm. and Brother John Metsgar on Potato creak have an appointment some 24 miles from hear North East from hear whare their will be 2 reformers baptised to our church   at our last meeting at our meeting house there was an Election held for 2 brethern to be put to the word and 2 for visiting Breathern and for Speaker it fell upon Brother Daniel Himes, Brother Jacob Soninglaw, and Brother Wesley Burket. Both of the men are very worthy men, but I dont think will speak soon. and for visiting Breathern it fell on Brother John Pefley, and your Humble Servent who is one of the unworthiest of all and who would of been well Satisfyde to live a private member

And now you See if brother George Bare should come hear he would be neaded bad to help Brother William   we See the neadcesity of another good Speker hear   no doubt but his labours would be crownd

dear brother we See the Sects Send of[f] their Missionary to forreign Nations to preach the gospel, and leave So much undone at home. if there was no more to do at home then I would be with them but the harvest is truly great hear and why Send them of[f] when the work is not done at home.[46]

Cornstock, Montgomery County, Indiana
September 15, 1853

gish family are all well   Brother William has a hard tower   he has
to do all the preaching hear himself. we ware at meeting on Ramp Creak
yesterday   Brother William Baptised one by the name of Henry Myers a
strange to me   I think there will be Some more come before long.
Brother Alexander Smith Starts for Iowa this weak a moving   he sold
out and also Jonathan Beard Sold   both going to move to Iowa   the
Kentuckyens are coming in and buying out the hoosiers   Some has sold
at as high as $40 per acre and some $30.[47]

*One of the Kentucky families that moved from Shelby County, Ken-
tucky, where Joseph Hostetler had been reared, to Montgomery County,
Indiana, where the Harshbargers were living, was the Miller family.
Whether they had had any contact with the Brethren in Shelby County is
not clear, for they were Baptists when they arrived in Indiana. It is clear
that they had contact with both the Gishes and the Harshbargers in Indiana. One of the Miller boys was named Robert Henry, more frequently
known to the Brethren as R. H. One day Miller, as a budding young
lawyer and debater, tangled with William Gish.*

Elder William Gish was born April 6, 1810, and was married to Ann
Sell on July, 1832. . . . He was well versed in the Bible. He had few other
books. On an argument he had few equals. It is said after he moved to Ind.
that R. H. Miller wanted to have some fun once by trying to down him in a
crowd in a scriptural argument, but he was so badly whipped that he said,
if a man with no learning could down him, there was more in the Bible
than he thought there was, and he would study the Bible in the future. This
led him to the church.[48]

*Another factor which undoubtedly contributed to Miller's interest in
the Brethren was his marriage in 1846 to Sarah Harshbarger, the daughter
of the Harshbargers whose letters from Cornstock Grove have been
quoted. However, Miller was not one to rush into things, and it was not
until 1858 that he and his wife were baptized as Brethren. In addition to
William Gish, one of the Brethren ministers who contributed to Miller's
conversion and to his call to the ministry was Samuel Murray, who later
described his acquaintance with R. H. Miller and his own experiences as an
itinerant minister in the 1850s.*

I got acquainted with Bro. R. H. Miller, perhaps three years before he united with the church. He lived in Montgomery county, about one hundred miles from where I lived, when I lived on Pipe Creek, Medina county, Indiana. They, having no one that could preach for them, asked me to preach for them, which I did for five years as often as I could, at least four or five times a year. As they were situated in four counties it made very laborious work, sometimes preaching one week, and sometimes as much as three weeks at a time. I thank the Lord that he blessed my labors; I baptized some each time I went among them, at one time fourteen were baptized, and these came without any special invitations, only by singing. We were only allowed to preach three times at the same place, then we had to move to another place. All that I ever received for this work was my car fare, and what the railroad gave me was counted out. . . .

Brother Robert was not in the church long until he was elected to the ministry; in a short time he was advanced to the second degree, then ordained to the eldership. I was present when he was elected, also when he was advanced to the second degree. I preached for them perhaps a year after that. Robert began preaching from the very start; it seemed to be no trouble for him to deliver a sermon as he had a good deal of experience as a pettifogger in law; he was also a political stump speaker. One good feature about him was that he laid all that aside and took hold of the Gospel.[49]

Six months after he was baptized, R. H. Miller was called to the ministry, according to the following document.

Montgomery County, Ind., Aug. 16, 1858

This day there is a church meeting held in the Raccoon Creek church for the purpose of electing two brethren to the ministry to serve in said church. The votes were given as annexed to each brother's name:

Robert H. Miller, ...46
Daniel Stoner, ...25
William Frume, ...10
Saml. Harshberger, ...2
Joseph Robinson, ...2
Andrew Peffley, ...4
John Williams, ...1
John Britts, ...1

This is to certify that Bro. Robert H. Miller and Bro. Daniel Stoner were this day called to the ministry.

Given under our hands the day above written. Signed,
Hiel Hamilton.
Samuel Murray.
Matthias Frantz.
Daniel Himes.
Wesley Burkett.[50]

*R. H. Miller seemed to enjoy the new challenge of preaching in
Brethren meetinghouses, and he quickly became a very successful preacher.
At least that was the contemporary evaluation of a fellow minister, John
Click, writing in 1860.*

Carpentersville, Putnam County, Indiana
December 26, 1860
I have thought of you all meneyatime Since I left Botetourt and when
I go to meetting it appears Sorter Strange when I take my Seat at the
Stand and look around over the congregation and can see none of the
Botetourt members amongst them and espesially the ministering Brethren
but notwithstanding we have some strong men here too espesially your
cousin Robert Miller   he is a real Dan Thomas of a preacher   I never
fear when I have him by my side   yet I never herd him preach a full sermon   he always starts me out before when I am thare and then he follow
after me and gathers up what I leave and straiten matters &c. the members
here are tolerably smart scattering   our church district extends some fifty
miles   it is truly so the harvest is great but the labourers are few   I
would like to see you out here in this Hoosier country to help us fight the
good fight of faith and to convert sinners to repentance   thare has been
five added to the church Since we have landed here and thare is a good
prospect for more.[51]

*Miller's father-in-law, Samuel Harshbarger, who was a deacon in the
church, added his evaluation a month later.*

Cornstock, Montgomery County, Indiana
January 21, 1861
the friends and relations are all generaly well, except Aunt Salome
Harshbarger   She has been very feble this winter   She was not able to
do any thing a part of the time and sometimes in bed   She is better
again   She was at meeting yesterday a weak ago about 1 mile from where

they live at Henry Myers school house. Henry Gish was hear with us at meeting from Carrol County. he will make a tolerable good speaker, if he should live long. he is only put to the word last fall   he is very zelous in the cause of Christ   yesterday we had meeting down in Putnam County   we had a fine meeting   Robert Miller has nearly all the labour to do   Br Frantz he is willing to help but cant git along. Soon lacks words and gives it up. Br. Click says but little. then we have others wont do a thing nor never did and one of them will take a Seat behind the table in the way of other preachers   Sometimes, this one would like to lead the church in our church meetings if he could, but thank God, there is brethren hear that knows the order of the breathern too. Robert Miller goes at the work like an old brother that has been at the work for 40 years preaching nearly evry Sunday, and to larg congregations generly on the 3rd Sunday in February 18 miles from home at Sister Etters in putnam Co. he has an appointment   he is requested to preach on Baptism. he baptised 7 in that neighbourhood this last Summer and winter the 2 last was baptised in December   the ice was cut 4 inches thick to baptise a man and his wife   a reformer preacher wants Robert to preach on baptism   he offered his meetinghouse to the brethern for that occation. he is a taking the Methodist and reformers in in that neighbourhood   they can hear a plain dunkard discourse and it costs them nothing, but they say if they hear the Methodist or Kampellite they have to pay from $10 to $20 evry meeting   he baptised 3 methodist and one reformer thare   Now brother David, Robert is agoing to prove the Trine Immersion rite by history, then by Grammer, and then by Scripture, and then lastly by common good sence, and then prove by Scripture that the forward motion is nearer rite than the backward motion. they think he cant. he will deceave them bad when they hear him. he is an able debater in Scripture. if you should ever hear him you will see.

Now the breathern in Putnam say there will be 5 applicants for baptism at their next meeting the 3rd Sunday in February, 3 of them Methodist and one reformer   how this is I do not know myself   the harvest is truly great, but the labourers few.[52]

In the remaining years of his life down to his death in 1892, R. H. Miller became one of the outstanding leaders of the Church of the Brethren. He was an able defender of the beliefs of the church and participated in a number of debates. Also, by his writing, including such books as "The Doctrines of the Brethren Defended," he explained for the layman the basic beliefs of the church. And finally, as indicated in these letters, he was an able preacher who appeared in Brethren meetinghouses and schools across the country.

R. H. Miller

When the Brethren did not have meetinghouses, they found other places to have worship services, including their own houses and the schoolhouses which were becoming more widespread during these years. A letter from another section of Indiana in Wabash County described the use of such facilities.

Sumer Set, Wabash County, Indiana
January 27, 1866

Now I will say something about our arm of the Church   We have no Meeting house in our arm of the church but Stil think we will have if the Lord is willing and I [k]now he will be if it is built for his honor and for the good of prescious & never dying Souls   We have verry good & warm School houses in this country & plenty of them that the Breathern preach in & Some of them hav [m]eet[ings] in ther houses   We have Church

Meeting Evry Six weeakes   We hav three Speakers & three Visiting breathern and one bishop ... We have preaching Everry Sunday on one Side of the River or the other if we want to go but the Grate trubble is now Since the war began is to get the peple to See the Eavel of ther way and turn to God & live   those that are willing to step down in to the watter & acknoledge Christ to bee the Saveure is few & far between but ther is one thing Sure   if tha will not hear & obey the consequence must be with them for in the day of Jugement tha can not Say tha was not warned to flee the rath to come for I know the word is Spokeing in its purrity and meny are gowing contrary to there better jugment and under Standing I my Self for one but I know God is merciful to those that will repent.[53]

In addition to Brethren settlements in southern Indiana, where the Stutzmans and the Hostetlers lived, and in central Indiana where the Harshbargers and the Millers lived, the Brethren also established a number of permanent settlements in the northern part of the state around Goshen. Henry Kurtz, the editor of the "Gospel Visiter," visited these Brethren in the winter of 1853-1854 and commented on the method of settlement used in that area by the Brethren.

About the planting of new churches. In this respect the churches about Goshen, as perhaps many more in Indiana and the West generally, are patterns. Instead of moving one by one into the wilderness, each seeking a home for himself, without considering, whether he or his family ever may enjoy convenient church-fellowship, the first brethren settling in Elkhart co. had in a manner moved there in a body, preachers, deacons and members, and thus planted a church in the wilderness at once, and they and their children, while they possess goodly homes, enjoyed from the first the privileges and benefits of all the means of grace. Thus the children grew up in the nurture and admonition of the Lord, and came soon to the conclusion, to serve their Lord, like their parents, in apostolic simplicity, and such was the increase of the two churches in the vicinity of Goshen, that we have reason to believe that they are now not far behind the largest churches in the older states in number.[54]

Whether they arrived in groups, as Kurtz suggested, or individually, a large number of Brethren had emigrated to Indiana by 1865, and they had established a number of permanent congregations, especially in the central and the northern parts of the state. Also, the Brethren in Indiana had produced some outstanding leaders, including R. H. Miller.

ILLINOIS

As in Indiana, the earliest Brethren evidently arrived in Illinois during the first decade of the nineteenth century. In 1808, George Wolfe, Jr., his brother, Jacob, and Abram Hunsaker emigrated with their families to Union County, Illinois, according to the report of George's son, John.

In October, 1808, my father moved from Logan Co., Kentucky, to what is now Union Co., Ill. He never lived in Missouri but there were Brethren who had settled in Missouri about the same time father moved to Illinois. Father joined the church in the year 1812 in Union Co., Ill. about forty miles north of the city of Cairo. It is situated at the mouth of the Ohio river. He and my mother with six other brethren and their wives, were baptized at the same time by old Elder John Henricks, of Kentucky, and among the number baptized at that time was his brother Jacob Wolf, father of Eld. Geo. Wolf of California. That same season, father was elected to the ministry, and the next Spring they sent to Kentucky for Elders, and Hostettler and Rowland came, and father was ordained to the full ministry and eldership by Hostettler.[55]

John Clingingsmith, who was writing at about the same time as John Wolfe, added some details to the story.

Now we will notice the church in Union County, Illinois, for a while. There were some brethren that had moved there before this John Hendricks visited that place. George Hunsaker, and I think he was from Pennsylvania.

Old Greatgrandfather Wolfe

In the year 1787, old senior Eld. George Wolfe, father of the late Elder George Wolfe, of Liberty, Ill., moved from Lancaster County Pennsylvania, crossing the Alleghany Mountains, to Fayette County, Pa., and in the year 1800, he moved to Logan County, Kentucky, and in the year 1809, when on a preaching tour to Southeastern Missouri, Cape Girardeau County, on his return homeward through Illinois, he, this senior Eld. George Wolfe, took sick at the old town of Kaskaskia, and died and was buried there in 1809. This, in all probability, was the first Dunker brother that ever was buried in Illinois. And in all probability the late junior Eld. Geo. Wolfe, and his brother Jacob were then living in Union County, Illinois.

Now this elder John Hendricks of Kentucky, frequently visited the friends and Brethren in Union County, Illinois, and had many interviews with them and some a little sharp and warm from the late Eld. George Wolfe, and Geo. Davis and others. This was on the subject of the restitution. In the year 1812, this Hendricks baptized the said Geo. Wolfe and his wife, and his brother Jacob Wolfe and his wife, and Geo. Davis and his wife, and four other brethren and their wives, being fourteen in all, in Clear Creek, Union County, Illinois.

These were the first Dunker Brethren that were ever baptized in Illinois, and in all probability, the said Geo. Wolfe was the first of them. In the same year, 1812, this said Geo. Wolfe was elected to the ministry, and his brother, Jacob Wolfe and Geo. Davis, were elected to the deacon's office. It is likely that this was done under the superintendency of Eld. John Hendricks. Then in the spring this Eld. John Hendricks died, as we will see further on.

Then in that year, 1813, the before-named Adam Hostetle and [Peter] Haun, of Kentucky, came and ordained the late Eld. Geo. Wolfe to the eldership, in Union County, Ill. This was the first ordination that ever was made by the brethren in Illinois, but both of these elders, Hostetle and Haun, soon afterward began to preach strange doctrine, and denied the faith of the Brethren, and were expelled.

But now the church in Union County, Ill., prospered and increased under the care and superintendency of the late Eld. Geo. Wolfe, until about the year 1827, when a good share of the members of this church moved from Union County to Adams County, Ill. But we propose to leave this part of the subject until we more properly come to it. This was near the end of the church in Union County.[56]

J. H. Moore, who was prominent in the Church of the Brethren for many years as an editor and writer, spent a few years as a youth on the farm adjoining the farm on which George Wolfe was living in retirement with his son, David. Thus, Moore learned to know George Wolfe personally. Also, he later spent much time interviewing those who had known Wolfe in his prime, and he also read extensively about early Illinois history. His biographical sketch of Wolfe, written in 1893, added to Clingingsmith's account at a number of points.

It was in the year 1800 that Eld. George Wolfe landed in Kentucky with his family. Three years after this,—March 3 1803,—His son George, the subject of this sketch, was married to Anna Hunsicker, who was to him a noble Christian companion. It is related that there were but few single women in the West in those days, and that young George, then twenty-three years old, had little chance of making another choice, as Anna was the only young, unmarried lady in the community. A young lawyer claimed the hand of the young lady, and threatened to severely punish the young farmer for winning the heart of the expected bride. George reasoned with him, telling him the lady had her choice, and made the selection of her own free will; that the "knot was tied," and there was no use in making trouble over it. Reason would not satisfy the young attorney, and, in regular western parlance, he told Wolfe that he could prepare himself for a good "thrashing."

Seeing that the lawyer could not be satisfied with reason and good common sense, George,—who was a man of large bodily proportions, great strength, and inured to the hardships of a frontier life,—told him plainly that he had married the woman in good faith, and if he thought a little, spindling lawyer could handle a strong, robust farmer like himself, he was at liberty to have his satisfaction. . . .

In the year 1811 occurred the remarkable earthquake in the Mississippi Valley, which lasted six months. The convulsions of the earth were so great as to create lakes and islands. Deep chasms were formed in the earth, from which vast volumes of water, sand, and even coal, were thrown to the height of nearly one hundred feet. It was a year of intense excitement and great religious awakening in the West. The Methodists held a revival in the Wolfe neighborhood, and George being of a religious turn of mind, united with them, there being ten others who professed conversion at the same time. Bro. Wolfe was appointed their class-leader. He had a good knowledge of the Brethren and their doctrine, but up to this time had made no profession.

He had taken his conversion and appointment as class-leader quite seriously, and the first time the class met, he took his place as their leader, and addressed the members of his class about as follows: "Brethren and sisters, we are now organized into a class. I have pondered and prayed over this matter, and have come to the conclusion that if John Wesley is the Savior, we are all right, but if Jesus Christ is the Savior then we are all wrong."

This speech from the bold young class-leader sent a thrill of horror through the hearts of the members of the newly-formed class. They said, "Christ is our Savior," and in amazement they asked, "But what shall we do?" Bro. Wolfe said, "Let us send to Kentucky for a Dunkard preacher to come and baptize us." He remembered the instructions of Peter to the Pentecostians, to "repent and be baptized every one of you in the name of Jesus Christ for the remission of sins." Acts 2:38. A young man by the name of Hunsicker, Wolfe's brother-in-law, was immediately started to Kentucky, a distance of about 150 miles. On the road he met Eld. John Hendricks, who was on a visit of love to his friends in Union County. His arrival was hailed with joy, for the harvest was fully ripe. He held meetings and baptized the entire class in Clear Creek, there being about fourteen in all, including the two Wolfe brothers and their wives. Bro. George was the first one to enter the water. He was probably the first person ever baptized by the Brethren in the State. This was in the year 1812, at which time George was thirty-two years old.

The same year the little band was called together to be organized and elect the necessary officers, and a proposition was made to that effect. Bro. Wolfe opposed the election, saying, "I have looked over the brethren carefully and come to the conclusion that there is no one of us qualified for the ministry." Eld. Hendricks replied, "May be the Lord has a choice." Not till then had the thought occurred to Bro. Wolfe that he might be the man, and he was so affected that he wanted to leave before the election was held. But a few words from Eld. Hendricks, concerning Jonah's experience, quieted him and the election proceeded, resulting in selecting George for the ministry and his brother Jacob and another brother for the deacon's office. Bro. George entered earnestly upon the active duties of the ministry, being the only minister at that time in either Illinois or Missouri. . . .

Eld. Wolfe continued his labors in Union County for about nineteen years, traveling and preaching much, and became widely known. Many remarkable things are related of him, only one of which we have space to mention in this brief sketch. He held a public debate with a Roman Catholic priest in the town of Kaskaskia. It was here that his father was buried, as mentioned before. The place had been a Catholic stronghold for more that a hundred years. The debate created a wonderful excitement. It was attended by the Governor of the State, who afterwards said of Eld. Wolfe, "He is the profoundest man, for an illiterate man, I ever heard." So crushing were Bro. Wolfe's arguments against Catholicism, so powerful were his appeals for primitive Christianity, so complete was his victory over his opponent, and so thoroughly did he arouse the Catholic hatred that his life was greatly in jeopardy. At that time a company of soldiers was stationed at Kaskaskia and the Governor, unknown to Bro. Wolfe, had detailed a number of the soldiers to protect him in his homeward journey. When he mounted his horse to leave the place, he was greatly surprised to find himself surrounded by a band of cavalry, with drawn swords, whose officer explained to Eld. Wolfe that he had orders to accompany and protect him on his journey. After guarding him to a safe distance from the town, the soldiers returned. . . .

I first met him in the fall of 1861. He was then quite old and had seen his best days. A few years before his wife had passed into the other world. In appearance he was almost a giant, being nearly six feet and a half tall, and weighing about 275 pounds. He was a man as finely built as any I ever met. He had a very large head, arched eyebrows, a high, broad forehead, and wore a long white beard. A powerful and erect form contributed to his commanding appearance. In manners he was a gentle as a child, and yet as bold as a lion. He was a man who knew no fear. Though a man of very limited education, he was a great reader, and possessed a wonderful stock of information, which was always at his command. As a profound reasoner his resources seemed almost unlimited. Col. Richardson, of Quincy, one time said that he regarded Eld. Wolfe as one of the profoundest thinkers the State of Illinois ever had.

Speaking of him, Eld. D. B. Gibson says: "His manner of preaching, like his presence, was commanding, yet as gentle as a child. His language was simple, easily understood by a child, and yet a philosopher would listen to it spell-bound. I have often heard him preach two hours but never knew any one to leave the congregation because he was not interested. In some respects he was the grandest preacher I ever heard. His great theme was the love of God. I never saw the man who sat under his artless eloquence but what rose up with the feeling that 'I will be a better man.' He seemed so uniform in personage and deportment that no one who once saw him ever forgot him. His coming was looked for by old and young, and from all he received the most cordial and affectionate greeting. He was the most highly-revered man I ever saw. No man ever swore in his presence. He impressed with awe his every beholder.

"In 1864, near the close of his life and the last time I ever heard him,— it was at the District Meeting of Southern Illinois,—Bro. Javan Gibson and myself helped him to the stand and to his feet. He said: 'Why do I wear the Brethren's garb? I answer: When in 1812 I came to the church—the church did not come to me—I weighed well her doctrine, her rules and her order. I joined her communion because I loved her. I became one of her number. I turned away from the world; in fact, I withdrew from it. I reasoned, that I do not love the world, but I do love the church. I will not be like the world which I hate but like the church that I love.' He thus spoke while his limbs trembled with age, his voice became husky with emotion, and his eyes filled with tears."

In one of his last sermons he said: "I have preached the Gospel for over fifty years. I labored much when Illinois was a wilderness. My work is now nearly done. I have, like Paul, finished my course, and if, when eternity shall dawn, and as I gaze with enraptured vision on the mighty hosts of the redeemed, if, in that mighty throng, one soul shall be numbered with the blest, because I worked, prayed and preached, I shall be fully repaid for all my labors here."[57]

The famous Methodist circuit-preacher, Peter Cartwright, on one occasion heard something about the Brethren in Union County. Evidently, he was not too pleased by what he heard, but he was living in a day of intense sectarian rivalry, and it is not surprising, consequently, that he was quite critical of the Brethren. At the same time, however, he provided an interesting insight into the life of the Brethren in Illinois.

I will relate an incident that occurred in the Legislature. After we were sworn in as members of that body, there was a flippant, loquacious lawyer, elected from Union County. He was a pretty speaker, but not very profound, and had a very high opinion of his own tact and talent. He was also a great aspirant, and had a thirst for popularity, and there were several congregations of Dunkers, or Seventh-day Baptists, in the district. This lawyer represented that they kept Saturday for the Christian Sabbath, and thought, or professed to think, it was altogether wrong that they should pay taxes, work on roads, perform military duty, or serve on juries, etc., etc., etc.

He wanted to have a law passed, favoring them in all these particulars, and thus exclusively legislating for their particular benefit, thereby making a religious test, and making a sectarian distinction, and legislating for their pretended scruples of conscience. He accordingly introduced a bill for their special benefit. I opposed the passage of the bill, and briefly remarked, that as a nation, we all acknowledged Sunday as the Christian Sabbath, and that there ought to be no distinction in Churches, or among the people; and as to bearing arms, that the people who were unwilling to take up arms in the defense of their country, were unworthy of the protection of government; and as for not working on roads, if there were any unwilling to work on roads, they should not be allowed the privilege of traveling them; as to serving on juries, if anybody was unwilling to serve on them, he ought to be deprived the privilege of having the right of trial by jury; and if there were any unwilling to pay taxes to support government, they should be declared outlaws, and denied the protection of government. The representative from Union, at this, flew into a mighty rage, and, instead of arguing the case, began to eulogize the Dunkers and drew a contrast between them and the Methodists. He said the Dunkers were an honest, industrious, hard-working people; their preachers worked for their own support; there was no hypocritical begging among them; no carrying the hat round in the

George Wolfe   Daniel B. Sturgis

congregation, and hypocritical whining among them for support, as was to be seen among Methodist preachers. Thus he laid on thick and fast. It was my good fortune to know, that a few years before, this lawyer was a candidate for Congress, and the lamented S. H. Thompson was the presiding elder, and his district covered the congressional district this lawyer desired to represent; and as Brother Thompson was very popular among the people, and had a number of camp and quarterly meetings in the bounds of this congressional district, this said lawyer had pretended to be serious on the subject of religion; and here he followed Brother Thompson from appointment to appointment, appearing to be very much concerned about religion, threw in liberally at every public collection, offering to carry the hat round himself when collection was taken.

When he closed his tirade of abuse, I rose and said, "Mr. Speaker, I award to the gentleman from the Union the honor of being one of the best judges of hypocrisy in all the land" and then narrated the above facts. He rose and called me to order; but the speaker said I was in order, and directed him to sit down. Presently, he rose again, and said if I was not called to order, he would knock me down at the bar. The speaker again pronounced me in order, and bade me proceed. I finished my speech, and left my mark on this belligerent son of the law.[58]

The John Clingingsmith narrative pointed ost that the Brethren did not restrict their activity in Illinois to Union County.

Elders Wolfe and Hendricks also planted a church in Monroe County, Ill., and there was a nice little group of members there, but they having no pastures, some of them moved away among them were John McIntock and his brother James, and several of the Inmans and others, and the rest grew cold and dwindled away.

As we have said about the year 1827, a goodly number of the members of the church in Union County moved to Adams County, Ill. Among them were John Wigle and all his family, including sons and son-in-law and their families, and several of the Hunsakers, also having families, that were members and others. In a year or two there was another lot of the members followed, among them being William Lierle. This was the present W. R. Lierle's father. In 1831 Eld. George Wolfe also moved. These all moved from Union County, Ill., to Adams County, Ill., probably about thirty members in all. This took about one-half of the members in Union County, and I believe the balance about all dwindled away to nothing.

Meantime there were several families moved from Cape Girardeau Co., Missouri to Adams County, Ill., among them were William and Abraham and Henry Hendricks. These were brothers to Elder James Hendricks. Then in the fall of 1831, they had a love feast at the house of John Wigle. This was the first love feast ever held in Adams County by the Brethren.

Now this church in Adams County prospered under the care of Eld. Wolfe. He also went round to other places and preached, and in Pike County, near the place now called New Canton, he had several meetings, and baptized some six or eight, among them being Joseph Jackson, a leading man. He also went over into Iowa, where there were some Brethren. Eld. James Hendricks also visited this church in Adams County, a time or two, and in the round these Elders (Wolfe and Hendricks) found Isham Gibson in Morgan County, Ill.

Isham Gibson was ordained on Stoner River, Rutherford County, Tenn., May 28, 1826, by Joseph Roland, attest, Abraham Welty. Joseph Roland was ordained April 1, 1800, in South Carolina, by Gasper Roland.

Now when Eld. Wolfe and Eld. Isham Gibson became familiar with each other, they operated together considerable. They also went round to different places together.[59]

As Clingingsmith indicated, the Brethren eventually decided to move further north in Illinois into Adams County.

At about the same time that George Wolfe, Jr., was moving to Adams County, Isham Gibson was moving from Tennessee to Morgan County, Illinois, in the same general area of the central part of the state. One of the interesting individuals who came into the church as the result of the ministry of Isham Gibson was D. B. Sturgis. His son, John Sturgis, provided the details of their meeting and of D. B. Sturgis' contribution to the church.

Eld. D. B. Sturgis was born June 17, 1811, in East Tennessee, and died at Mulberry Grove, Ill., March 17, 1896, aged 85 years and 9 months.

His father was a wealthy farmer but lost his property and wealth by going security for others, and being cowed by his reduced circumstances he determined to leave his acquaintances and locality which had known him under better circumstances. Consequently with one horse and a cart he moved from Maryland to East Tennessee, where D. B. Sturgis was born. The tide of emigration being westward soon brought those of former acquaintance into the new country and he determined to move again. This move took him to Montgomery County, Ohio, when Dayton, the county seat, was a small village, and when D. R. Sturgis was three years old. Again those of his acquaintances located near him, and caused him to move again, this time eighty miles northwest of Vandalia, Ill., to Green County, near the McCoupin County line, when D. B. Sturgis was eleven years old. Vandalia was the nearest post office, and mail was obtained twice a year, to which the capital was removed in 1820.

The country was very sparsely settled at this time. There were no school privileges to be had for the lad who grew sturdy of frame and health, inured to privations and hardships. His father died when he was fourteen years old, leaving a very meager estate and a mother and two sisters for him to support. The nearest mill was twelve miles away, run by horse power which ground nothing but corn. In order for him to reach the mill and return home again the same day it was necessary for him to start long before day, with what was called a grist, or one sack with two bushels of corn, carried across the back of the horse he rode while he lead another to help on the power to do the grinding. I have often heard him say that all the opportunities he had in school would not amount to more than nine months, and that in irregular intervals. His thirst for education was such that he borrowed when he could, and by a light made in the fireplace with chips or bark, he would read after the day's work was done, not being able to procure a candle or tallow dip, or even the grease lamp of these primitive times. He was his own teacher and applied himself in the rudimentary branches of penmanship, arithmetic, geography, grammar, etc., till he was capable of teaching school. His services as such were in demand, and still he pursued his studies. On account of there being a derth of physicians he now took up the study of medicine and was soon in demand as a physician. He used the simple remedies afforded by nature's laboratory, the woods and the prairie, which were sufficient for the simple diseases incident to a new country. He practiced some before he was able to attend a medical college.

Being naturally of a devotional turn he read the Bible a great deal, and was a regular attendant at church services until he came to the conclusion that no church obeyed the Gospel, and began to look upon preachers and church members as being a set of hypocrites, pretending to something they neither believed nor practiced. About this time one Sunday morning when nineteen years old, he was out hunting his mothers horses, riding barebacked, barefooted, wearing a pair of tow linen pants and a shirt of the same material and crowned with a broken straw hat, he met with Isham Gibson. After the usual salutation he said, "I believe you are a preacher." Being answered in the affirmative the following conversation took place:

"Well, I presume you are like all other preachers."

"In what way?"

"Neither believe nor practice what the Gospel teaches."

"What part of the Gospel do you refer to?"

"That part that teaches feet-washing, the salutation of the kiss, nonresistence, etc."

"We believe it, teach it and practice it, too."

"I am surprised to hear you say that."

"Why?"

"Because I had fully concluded that there were none that did."

Further illucidation of the Scriptures by the reverend gentleman so interested the young man that before he was aware of it they were at the place of meeting where Bro. Gibson was to preach. The young man thought to keep in the background and hear the sermon. He became so absorbed that he unwittingly moved nearer and nearer until at the close of the sermon he was standing close in front of the preacher. Realizing his grotesque appearance he beat a hasty retreat. As a result he often sought the company of Bro. Gibson in order that he might learn more about the teaching and practice of the new church. His mother, a good Baptist woman, was anxious that her son should embrace religion in the Baptist church. He very promptly told her that he wouldn't join a church that did not teach and practice all that the Gospel taught. She endeavored to show him that he was wrong, but failing called on her preachers to aid her. The result was that it only whetted an already keen appetite for discussion, which grew in him until he became an able defender of his views and opinions of what the Gospel required. He often sought the company of Eld. Gibson and found in him a man to sympathize with him in his thirst for knowledge of the Scriptures, and was ready at all time to give him aid and instruction until he became thoroughtly satisfied that at last he had found a people that in the face of a gainsaying world held steadfastly to the Word of God. He announced to his young wife, who was yet a bride, that he was going to join the church. She thought it could not be that he should join the church without her. As she had observed the teaching of the churches with which she was acquainted, on the subject of pardon of sins, she began to exercise herself in prayer to work herself to that frenzy she had so often seen in revival and campmeetings. Her husband informed her that that was all unnecessary: that pardon came through faith in the Lord Jesus Christ. Repentance of sins committed and baptism into his name for the remission of sins brought pardon and was obtained in no other way. She told him to go on and join the church and she would come too, when she had learned more of what her duty was. It was not long after he identified himself with the church that she came also.

D. B. Stugis was called to the ministry at about the age of twenty-five and was ordained to the eldership at about thirty. He made the double calling to the ministry and the practice of medicine his life work which he pursued faithfully until the weight of years actively and well spent, warned him to seek the quietude of retirement.

The doctrine of the church was quite new to the people and met with fierce opposition, but found in young Sturgis a bold and ready champion and an able defender. He took part in a number of debates, among which was one with two Mormon preachers. One was Sidney Rigdon, one of the Mormon apostles, and the other, Eld. Jaques. These debates took place when Mormonism was at its zenith at Nauvoo, Ill. The result of this one was the breaking of the influence of Mormons in the vicinity where the discussion was held. Eld. Sturgis was challenged to debate the question of baptism, by a Mr. Yates, of the M. E. church, which he accepted. However, the debate never was held for the reason that Mr. Yates was drowned in the Mississippi River prior to the time set for the discussion. It was believed by many that he committed suicide rather than risk defeat in the coming debate.

About the year 1849 or 1850 he located in Bond County, Ill., where there were a few members of the Brethren church. He soon gathered a large congregation into the church, due in part to help given unwillingly by an old Baptist minister. This minister went just one time to hear him preach, after which he told the people not to hear Sturgis preach for he was a very dangerous man. This made the people all the more anxious to hear him, thereby giving him large congregations to preach to.

The congregation he built up was finally divided into what are now the Hurricane Creek and Mulberry Grove congregations.[60]

D. B. Sturgis was ordained as an elder by George Wolfe and Isham Gibson in 1841 at Gibson's home in Illinois.

To whom these presents may come, greeting:

This is to certify that, at a meeting appointed at the house of Brother Isham Gibson, at Apple Creek, Morgan County, Illinois, at the request of the church, Brother Daniel B. Sturgis was ordained a bishop of the church or fraternity of Baptists, by laying on of hands of the presbytery, on the 11th day of September, in the year of our Lord 1841. Given under our hand, day and date above written.

George Wolfe
Isham Gibson[61]

In the same general area of west-central Illinois some miles northeast of Adams County, a group of Brethren moved into Fulton County in the 1840s. Eventually, they began to hold worship services and quite by accident they made contact with George Wolfe. It was probably this group of Brethren from Pennsylvania who first discovered that George Wolfe and his followers were doing some things differently, and that led to the Far Western Brethren controversy.

In the fall of 1844, I [Jacob Negley] with my family, came to Fulton Co., Ill., not knowing of any members here. In the Spring of 1845 my brother-in-law, David Zuck, and his family came. He was in the second degree of the ministry. After settling down, we held social meetings at our houses every two weeks. At first we had small congregations, but after our neighbors heard of it, our congregations increased. During our meetings we became acquainted with three or four members from Ohio, of whom were Brother John Markley and his wife, who had been here several years when we came. In the fall of 1847, Brother Daniel Martin and his family came. He was an ordained elder. (We all emigrated from Welsh Run, Franklin Co., Pa.) We then commenced holding meetings in the school-houses regularly. We had then a small organized body of about eight or nine members.

About a year or less afterward, one Sunday morning, a man by the name of Ensign called at my house to shelter from a storm. After some conversation, he asked me to what denomination we belonged. I answered that we belonged to the German Baptists, but we were probably more commonly known by the name of "Dunkards." He said, "Then you belong to the soup people." "Yes," I said, "we have soup at our communion meetings." Then he said, "I know a man by the name of Wolfe, in Adams Co., an able preacher, who belongs to your church." I asked for his first name and his address, but he could give neither. He, however, said he had a brother-in-law living in the same county, who also belonged to the same church, whose address was Liberty, Adams Co., Ill. I made a note of this.

A short time after the above occurred, I wrote to Brother Wolfe, in care of Brother Bushnel. In about two weeks after I wrote, Brother Bushnel came up to see us. I was not at home when he came, and did not get to see him; but my wife and he had a conversation and concluded that they had the same faith. Through that visit we got Brother Wolfe's name and address. I then opened up a correspondence with him, and gave him several invitations to visit us. As nearly as I can recollect, in the fall of 1849 we appointed.

OUR FIRST LOVE-FEAST

Brother Samuel Garber and several brethren from Ogle Co., Ill., were with us. Brother Wolfe was also invited, and he came. At our meeting, our being strangers to each other, of course, led to some inquiry. After counseling we all concluded to commune, and to wash feet in the single mode (as it is called).

At the next Annual Meeting Brother Garber, I think, introduced Brother Wolfe, and was probably reproved for what he had done. Afterward Brother Wolfe visited us frequently, and was known to the Brotherhood in general.[62]

Much farther north in Ogle County, Illinois, near the Wisconsin border, a considerable settlement of Brethren had arrived by the 1840s. One of these, Daniel Long, described life on the northern Illinois frontier in 1847.

Agust 14th 1847

Deer Children   thank be to god that I am onst more pirmited to set mysetf to rite you a few lines in anser to your letter wich I recievd some time in June   in the first place I will inform you of our helth   we are all well at presant and hav been so eversens I rote you the last letter and thanks be to god for his kind mercis that is shown to words us from time to time and I hope when this come to hand it will find you and family enjoying good helth wich is one of the gratest blesings that we can hav in this world and we oute to be carefull of the time when we are in good helth then is the time to make preparations for the world to come I will also inform you that all the rest of the friends are all in good helth at presant or they was last sunday they were all at meeting near one at Rices scoolhouse and they all went with me home and took dinner with me except William and Nancy   they went to Daniel Wolfs and took dinner there   your unkle Jacob Long and nearly all his family was with me that day but how often I hav to wish you was here to come to our meeting to here the preaching and see the number of people that comes to geder   you could hardly believ that their was so many people in the contry and they all appear to be desirous to hear and to know what will be benifishal to their sole salvation   there was twelv or fourteen added to the church this spring, yes beloved I do wish from the bottom of my hart that you was hear too with you brothers and sisters but I hope and trust in the lord that I will see you all meet again in this world and to injoy each other presants but if we dont meet any more in this world I hope that we will meet in a better world were no parting will be   But dear Children if you were all here to gather their would still be one awanting that would not be here wich is your deer mother   she is not more with us   if I could tell you of the lonesome hours that I hav to pass away no one can tell but them that had the trile of it   for my part I cant tell you my feelings and sadness at hart   when I went from home and came home she would meet me with a smileing fase but now she is no more   we must giv all things over to him that knows all things best and to giv ourselvs up under his holy will and prepare and be ready when we are cald uppon so that we can meet in the rellems above of plesure pese and love were I hope she is at rest to prase her god and redeamer for ever and with out end   I will now inform you off our crops and the wether   our winter crop was not verry good in my nieghbourhood but still there was much more then was expected   I think there was a full half a crop and in some plases they had much more but the sommer crop is in a bandanc   the spring whet is first rate   some thinks they will get forty bushels to the acar   I seen some that was sowd early stood better on the ground then I ever saw wheat stand in Maryland and the oats is as good as I ever saw and the corn is good accoring to the season   we had verry dry wether   we had no rain sens the first of June of any account   the dry wether has not the same affect in this contry as it in maryland   the corn dos not rinkle up in dry wether   I must also inform you that our harvest was verry late this year   there is a good deal of wheat to haul in yet   I weill giv you as much satisfaction how the contry is as I can and tell you of the bad as well as the good and will tell you now that we had a frost in low ground about the twentieth of July and fros all the corn

And I hope the late harvest and frost will not discorrage you of coming to this contry   I think you could do much better here then you can in maryland and liv with more satisfaction in every way   the land is as good as can be and everything that we sow or plant produces in a bundanc and the land is so easy to farm that a boy that knows any thing about horses can plough   my little John can plough as good as a man   he helped to do all the ploughing last spring and farming is done with so little exspens   I put about fifty acars in corn and oats and hav the first time to go to the blacksmith shop to hav any thing done to my plough iron and I dont think I will for two years more   the gratest exspens is harvest   the hands are not plenty but I think that harvesting will go better and hands plenty   the farmers are giting the cuting meschene   they say that they can cut twenty acars pr day at fifty cents per acar but I think it will soon be much lower in price   if I onely could rite to intice you to come to this contry and not bild any more dams to be taken away with high water   with the money that you pay for bilding a dam you can by a good farm that wont wash away and tell your near neighbours to come out from the rocks and red clay and come to a land that can be farmd with all eas and plesure   I must begin to come to a close with my riting   Cathran rote in her last letter that I should come in their but I dont know wether I will or not as we know not how short our time may be but if it is the lords will and I am spard and blesd health I will be in next summer some time to see all my old neighbours once more for the last time but if you sell of[f] and come to this contry I will. try to come sooner and come with you. I wish you would go to Bell and tell him to send my paper to Mount Morris and send them more regular then what he did. I wish you would collect the ballanc of my money and send it on as I stand in need of some at this time I wont to hav some repares done to my huse and I most hav some money do it with. try to get if some if possible and send it on   this and no more at presant   we all join sending our sincere love to you all and all inquireing friends

Daniel Long
to Abraham Miller

Solemn if we meat no more
to glad Each others heart
I hope to meet on canians shore
And never more to part[63]

Brethren life in the same area was described in a diary kept by a young man, John J. Emmert, in the late 1850s.

June 27, 1857—The love feast at Arnolds Grove commences today at 2 o'clock, when Bro. Spogle addressed us.

June 28, 1857—Preaching again at 9 o'clock this morn   very large turn out   listened to an excellent sermon   Kate Stoner baptized

June 29, 1857—Attended an appointed meeting in the court house where I listened to a powerful sermon by Bro. Spogle from 1 Tim chap 16

July 11, 1857—Working some today and as usual went to town getting ready for Camp meeting

July 12, 1857—Went to Camp meeting in dutch hollow rain & wind blowed tent over   got a good thorough drenching   however very good time of it

October 31, 1857—Love feast commenced   able preaching by Bro. Lehman and others   Bros John Buck and Michael Sisler elected to the ministry   Mary C. Slifer reced by baptism

November 1, 1857—Assembled this morn for public worship—a very happy time of it—pleasant weather   house not large enough to contain all the folks

November 22, 1857—Attended meeting at the Grove. Text by C. Long from Matt. 24 chap. after which baptism was administered to Miss I. Hopson—snowing   lively afternoon

January 17, 1858—Went to meeting at the Grove. w[h]ere we were very ably addressed from 16th chap of St. John by James Quinter. Also the eve

January 18, 1858—Meeting again at the Grove. Bro. Quinter addressed us from the 1st Chap of Phillipians. Also this eve Very affectionately

January 19, 1858—Attended meeting in town this eve. Bro Quinter preached us a good lesson from the V chapter St. James very ably

January 20, 1858—We were again very affectionately addressed this eve by Bro. James Quinter

January 21, 1858—Bro. Quinter preached an excellent discourse in Mt. Carroll this eve from Eph. 1. 13, 14

February 26, 1858—A series of meetings commenced at the Grove. Bro. E. Eby preached an excellent sermon from St. John, 1 chap. 12 vs.

February 27, 1858—Preaching again at the Grove by Bro. Eby and Fry. Also this eve from xx chap St. Matthew

February 28, 1858—Assembled for worship. text from Mat 24 chap after which there were nine received by baptism   also preaching this eve from 1 Cor 2nd chap.

March 1, 1858—Meeting at Rittenhouse School House tonight

March 2, 1858—Five souls were rec'd by Baptism today   preaching again tonight

April 10, 1858—Church met at the Grove to set forth four Deacons, viz. N. R. Strickler, S. Musselman, John Rowland & Daniel Kingely were elected

January 13, 1859—A Series of meetings commences at the Grove this evening. Sermon by Bro. Long from Isaiah

January 14, 1859—Also this eve [John] Forney preached to us

January 15, 1859—Assembled today at ten o'clock also this eve- when E. Eby & Fry were present   Eby took a text from the viii Psalm

January 16, 1859—Text by Bro. Eby from XV chap St. Luke   very ably followed by Fry   Eby also spoke tonight from xii chap Romans followed by Rittenhouse   large turn-out

January 17, 1859—Very pleasant tonight   not a very large congregation   nevertheless a very good time   Bro Eby preached to us taking the "prodigal son" for a subject

January 18, 1859—Tonight the meetings break up and Eby preached his farewell sermon from Pauls letter to the Corrinthians- "Finally brethren farewell &c" 2nd Corin xiii, 11

January 19, 1859—Went over to Aunt Susan Emert's tonight to a social meeting- very good time- chapter under consideration xvi chap St. Luke

May 16, 1859—Pike Peak fever rather on the decrease- owing to late not very encourageing news

May 17, 1859—Some teams going and some returning from Pike's Peak

May 19, 1859—Pike Peak generally considered a HUMBUG in full

June 4, 1859—Met John Bohn returning from Pike's Peak

June 7, 1859—The-Love feast at the Grove commences this P. M. at 1 o'clock. plenty of speakers present among which was Joseph Emmert, Enoch Eby, Fry, Garber and others

June 8, 1859—Bro. Eby addressed us very ably this morn. very large congregation. fine weather. good order, and withall a very good and profitable meeting-

June 9, 1859—Uncle Joseph Emmert preached at our house this eve from the words-The word of God is quick and powerful &c Heb IV. xii

June 11, 1859—Attended a Love feast in Stephenson county commencing at 1 o'clock today- excellent meeting Bro. Sprogle arrived this eve from Pa.

June 12, 1859—Assembled this morn at IX o'clock when Sprogle spoke to us from Acts 2nd   came home this P. M.

June 16, 1859—Went to Ogle Co. to Love feast, large assembly. four(4) souls received in the church by immersion

July 4, 1859—Celebrations in every neighborhood. I not feeling it my duty to mix went to plowing corn, and I dare say feel better than if I had spreed.

July 31, 1859—Preaching by C. Long at the Grove from vi chap St. Matthew   Sunday School this afternoon
October 13, 1859—Bros. Wolf and Gibson present   very good speakers   two persons rec'd by Baptism   very excellent meeting
October 16, 1859—Bro. Gibson addressed us from St. Matthew xi chap very ably
December 9, 1859—A discussion on the mode of immersion. John G. Fillmore in favor of trine immersion, Robert Moffett for single[64]

By the time Emmert was writing in his diary in the late 1850s, the Brethren were concentrating their efforts in both Illinois and Indiana in the central and northern parts of the two states. Exactly why that happened is not clear. The availability of leadership was certainly one factor; for example, the decision of Joseph Hostetler to leave the Church of the Brethren and the decision of George Wolfe, Jr., to emigrate to a different section of the state. Another factor was the probability of better farming land which was not as hilly as one moved farther from the Ohio River. Also, it is possible that the Brethren were looking for areas of settlement which were not as strongly pro-slavery and pro-Confederacy as the territory in southern Illinois and in southern Indiana along the Ohio River was in the 1850s and the 1860s. The result has been that almost all of the permanent Brethren settlements in these two states have been in the central and northern sections.

THE FAR WESTERN BRETHREN

In attempting to understand the discussions regarding the "Far Western Brethren," it is necessary first of all to make clear that there were two different periods of time involved. The first period occurred between 1815 and 1820 and took place in Kentucky. The evidence concerning this period is very limited. The second period occurred some forty years later in the 1850s and has been much more satisfactorily described.

The best evidence that has been found concerning the events of the 1810s in Kentucky comes from George Wolfe of Illinois who participated in the Kentucky decisions and who wrote letters to the editor of the "Gospel Visiter" in the 1850s, describing some of the developments of the 1810s as a preparation for the unification of the Far Western Brethren and the main body of the church, which took place later in the 1850s.

After the perusal of your letter, I regarded it as the production of a Christian spirit and a manifestation of brotherly love, which I consider worthy of great regard, especially as it has come from a brother I have never seen. I will endeavor to comply with your request for your satisfaction.

But before I commence to state in a brief manner the difference, I can assure you, the difference did not take place with the design to create a discord in the Brotherhood, neither had we a desire of dissenting from the Brotherhood, but the change was produced by a conviction that it was our duty to do so. The change was produced by a correspondence with Br. Samuel Arnold and Daniel Gerber on the subject of feetwashing, which took place after an association was held in Muhlenberg co., Ky. The same association put Adam H[ostetle]r and his party under a censure, and the next year they were excommunicated in O. Br. H[endrick]s of Mo. and myself was at meeting held in Ky. We were received by the old brethren and sat with them in council, and we agreed in all things that were cancelled, excepting feetwashing. The Western Brotherhood washed feet after supper, which was a subject that was discussed, but not decided. And it was agreed on, that a correspondence should be kept up; the first letter that we received put an end to the difference existing in feetwashing. Those dear brethren cited different portions of Scripture in Mark 14, 22. and that reads as follows: "And as they did eat, Jesus took bread and blessed it and brake it." And in Matth. 26, 26. "And as they were eating, Jesus took bread and broke &c." From these passages they argued, that when Jesus was the administrator, he left no room for feet-washing to come between the supper and the breaking of Bread. From that fact we knew we erred in the time of washing feet, and from that time we changed the washing. We saw, to take our divine Master for an example, we must not put anything between the supper and breaking of bread, and being convinced, if we followed the example, we must break bread as soon as the supper is eaten, or while some are yet eating.

Being through with the cause that produced the change, I will relate our mode of proceeding. The day before the communion we take up in preaching. When the evening comes on, while the supper is preparing, we read the 11 chapter of 1 Cor. and lecture on the necessity of an examination. By early candlelight we have the table furnished with the supper. We then invite the members to take their seats at the table. The brethren occupy one end and the sisters the other end of the table. The administrators place themselves between the brethren and sisters at the table. There the bread and wine is placed on the table, and the aprons and water is put in reach of the administrators. We then sing a hymn and offer up praise. Then the 13 chapter of John is read, and when that part is read "He riseth from supper," the administrator rises to his feet, he lays aside his garment and girds himself with an apron, then commences feet-washing; and when the feet are washed, he wipes them with the apron, wherewith he is girded. When the brother's feet are wiped, he embraced him with a kiss. An elder sister by his side commences in the same way to wash the sisters feet. By the time they have washed two or three members feet, they are released and so change as often as convenient. The members remain at the table and the water is carried around, until all their feet are washed.

While there is washing, an Elder generally lectures all the time on feet-washing and also on the nature of the supper. Then the administrator concludes with speaking on the sufferings and death of our Saviour and the emblem of his mangled body set before them. When this is done thanksgiving and prayer is offered up for the gospel-feast that is before them. This done, they all commence eating and some of the deacons will warm the soup with hot broth. The supper is composed of meat, bread and soup; and while some are yet eating, the administrator takes bread and offers up thanksgiving and prayer, and after the bread is broken, they administer it to each other, as they do on Rock river, and the sisters receive it from the administrator. In feet-washing we have never made any change from what we have seen practiced. But you will see in the supper and breaking of bread we think we are not authorized to unjoint the limbs of the Lamb of God.[65]

Henry Kurtz, the editor of the "Gospel Visiter," prepared a lengthy reply in which he differed with Wolfe in certain aspects of the Love Feast service. Wolfe wrote a lengthy letter in response, a part of which dealt with the earlier problems in Kentucky. That part is included in this section.

Illinois
March 23, 1851

Thirdly, You made an allusion of the housekeeping, that the brethren should perform under the written Gospel, that is to say we should labour together to keep up a oneness and a union in the house-hold of faith, which is an idea I have ever considered to be a duty, and have performed as much labour as any other brother likely in the fraternity, to accomplish that object. I may say through me or my labour caused the association to be held in Kentucky, occasioned by H[ostetle]r and his party; and since that I have not been idle in labouring for the peace and harmony, with all these brethren that I had a correspondence with.

I will venture to say, there has been as much union and harmony in the brotherhood in Illinois, Missouri and Iowa, as in any of the old states. But as to a yearly meeting or conference, I had no knowledge of until of late years. Though I was raised among the brethren in Pennsylvania and my father moved to the southern part of Kentucky among the brethren that emigrated from Pa., and they built up large churches, I never heard a word said about a yearly meeting among them. Strange as you may think it, dear Brother. When we parted with Br. Samuel Arnold and Daniel Garber in Kentucky at the meeting that I named in my last, they gave Br. H[endrick]s and myself a charge, to have a watchful eye over the brotherhood in the west, and if we found distrubance arise among them, we should labour to bring things to a reconciliation, and if we could not succeed to send for them, or any other brethren to our assistance. We promised them we would. But they never named the yearly meeting. The circumstance we were placed in, was this: the southern part of the brotherhood was not included in that, that was disowned, though there was some uneasiness what the result would be, whether they would turn to the H[ostetle]r party, or whether they would remain with the brethren, which was the occasion of those instructions.

I will now turn to some circumstances that took place among us. A disturbance took place in Missouri on account of slave-holding brethren. We laboured to reconcile matters, but we failed, We concluded that Br. H[endrick]s should write to the different churches, as he was a ready scribe, for instructions. We received three letters, they were read in the presence of the brethren; they were called on to say, whether they would be in subjection to those instructions, and they all consented but one, and he was excommunicated. Brother H[endrick]s again called on some of the Ohio brethren for assistance, to settle a dispute between us and some brethren that moved from Kentucky to Sangamon co. Ill. These brethren had not changed the custom of feet-washing. We were charged of leaving the ancient order. We received a letter, and it was not such as I expected or wished to receive. But in the conclusion we were directed to appear at the conference, which was the first knowledge I ever got of such a thing, though we met and things were settled to our satisfaction. So you may see, dear Br. myself and others have laboured near forty years. We kept our eye directed to the word, which was our standard; and if the testimony from foreign brethren can be received, I have never heard them express their mind, but they gave it in our favour. But to be short, I acknowledge the necessity of a conference, in order to come to a decision, whether the example of Christ is to guide us at the communion, or whether some other power is to overrule it. I am much pleased at your acknowledgement, dear Br., that you disown perfection. But is not infallibility ascribed to the old brethren in the Minutes of the last year's conference the 25th question? Was it not for my age and the distance to the next conference I would endeavor to be at it. But if I should be spared and there is one near enough, I am anxious to be at.[66]

In addition to the description by George Wolfe, two other accounts of the events of the 1810s in Kentucky were written in the 1880s by individuals who were close to the event. John Wolfe was a son of George Wolfe, and claimed to have access to written records from the 1810s.

At that time, 1813, [Adam] Hostettler and [Peter] Hawn were in good standing and in full fellowship with the churches. About the year 1815, they commenced practicing heresies in their churches, about as the apostate Hamm did.[67]

In the Spring 1816, there was a committee of elders sent to investigate the matter. They were Samuel and John Leatherman of Virginia, father from Illinois, and James Henricks from Missouri. The result was Hostettler and Hawn were cut off. [Joseph] Rowland's members plead so hard for him, and he making acknowledgement, was held in fellowship, though he was relieved from part of his office, for the time being, but afterwards it was restored back to him again.

I get this knowledge from a copy of the Minutes of that council meeting, which father preserved as long as he lived, but in the last few years they have been destroyed or lost, I rather think the former, as they burned a great many of his old papers a few years ago.[68]

The second account was written by John Clingingsmith, whose father had been one of the earliest Brethren settlers in Missouri and who had moved to Illinois where he had known George Wolfe well and had heard his description of events in Kentucky.

These two elders, Wolfe and Hendricks, also visited the Kentucky Brethren occasionally. But it seems there was trouble among the Kentucky Brethren, and there was a conference or council called. This was bout the year 1820. At that council Elders Wolfe and Hendricks met with some of the eastern elders, probably from Eastern Pennsylvania. What their trouble was I cannot tell, but they adjusted the matter as well as they could. I think I heard some one say, that they (the Eastern Brethren) left the Kentucky church or Brethren, under the care and oversight of Wolfe and Hendricks, but it seems that these Kentucky Brethren finally all went astray, probably followed Hostetle and Haun.

This meeting was probably the last interview that the eastern brethren had with the Far Western Brethren, for many years, but they had some correspondence by letter for awhile, as we shall presently see. In Kentucky I suppose the subject of feet-washing came up between the Wolfe and Hendricks, and the eastern Brethren, but Wolfe and Hendricks were very firmly of the opinion that feet-washing was done by the Savior after supper, from the fact that we read,"and supper being ended," and again, "he riseth from supper, etc." John 13:2-4. When the eastern Brethren saw that they could not convince Wolfe and Hendricks they said to them, "go on in your way till you see better, and then change." To this they agreed, and so they parted, each to his respective place of abode.

In a few weeks Eld. Geo. Wolfe received a letter from the eastern Brethren. He looked over this letter, and the quotations to which it cited, and carefully compared the Scriptures. He became convinced that the eastern Brethren were right, that they should wash feet before supper. Now Wolfe would not send this letter to Hendricks, in Missouri, but he got on his horse, and rode over and carried it to Hendricks himself. After the usual talk Wolfe addressed Hendricks: "Well, I received a letter from the eastern Brethren, and I believe they are right." Hendricks said, "It struck me with astonishment. Thinks I to myself, is it possible that you are also going astray?" Then when they read the letter and the quotations to which it cited, and carefully compared them, Hendricks also became convinced that they (the eastern Brethren) were right.

This I remember hearing Hendricks tell. But the point at issue, I don't remember. But from all other circumstances, I am satisfied that it was this subject of feet-washing. Now these two elders, Wolfe and Hendricks, were convinced that there was no room for feet-washing between the supper and the communion. Each of them laid the question before their church, and they all said that there was no room between the supper and the communion for feet washing, so they changed and washed feet before supper. At the same time, they also agreed, that there was no room there, for the reading of a chapter, and lecturing and the salutation of the holy kiss. So they left off all of these things and took the Scriptures for their guide. And well do I remember of often hearing father Wolfe, when he would rise to break the bread, quote like this: "And while some were yet eating he took bread and blessed and break it"(this would probably be appropriate), but the reading is "and as they did eat he took bread," etc. Now this is the way that these churches in Cape County, Mo., and Union County, Ill. practiced from my first memory, until there was a reunion formed between the Far Western Brethren and the eastern Brethren.

But some one would say, How did they get that practice of feet washing into these churches? I think this may easily be accounted for. When in the year 1813 Wolfe was ordained to the eldership in Union County, Ill., it soon became necessary that the ordinance of the household of faith should be practiced, and he (Wolfe) having no intercourse with the eastern Brethren, so he and Hendricks thought that was the way the Scriptures taught, as we have already seen. This is no more strange then than it was with our forefathers, when they first started the church at Schwarzenau. They washed feet after supper, and the communion, but when they saw better they changed.[69]

The number of Brethren who left the church with Adam Hostetler and Peter Hon cannot be determined from the evidence available today. Estimates by Brethren historians range from several hundred to more than a thousand. Either figure would represent a severe loss in a day when the total membership of the church probably did not exceed several thousand. Probably, the best thing about the difficulty was that a number of Brethren who were put out of the church at this time refused to accept such an action and simply moved to new frontier areas and established Brethren settlements.

By the 1840s these so-called Far Western Brethren were coming in contact with numerous groups of Brethren settlers emigrating to the western states from the more orthodox congregations of the eastern states, and the two groups realized that they were practicing certain aspects of the Love Feast service in different ways. George Wolfe, the leader of the Far Western Brethren, described this contact in the "Gospel Visiter."

About 12 or 14 years ago there had a few members moved to Iowa; they soon became a small church; they appointed a love-feast, and they called for us from Adams co. to assist them; we obeyed their call, and for the first time, there were ten or twelve Eastern members that attended with us.

Previous to this meeting they had become acquainted with the brethren, their daily walk and the principles they maintained, they acknowledged each other brethren, and they communed after the Western custom, they have had communions in succession every year since. They are about equally divided in number, the Eastern and Western members, it is a growing church. There is no jar between the Eastern and Western members there. They live in peace and enjoy each in love.

Our next call was to Fulton county, Illinois. There was a small church from Maryland, some of us attended their call, there was a number of the Rock river brethren in attendance, and after an interview with each other we acknowledged each other brethren in the same faith, and we communed with each other in brotherly love. There the practice of the East is in part carried out, and we have in succession visited each other. We have once attended on Rock-river, and communed with each other, under the compromise that is asked for in the third "proposition."

There is another church in Bond co. Illinois. The members moved from O. They are entirely influenced under the Western practice. In all these places named there has been no jar or confusion. They meet in love, labor together for the building each other up in the faith of the Gospel. And besides these places named there are some moving to themselves at a distance from the churches, and will attend our meetings and partake with us in good faith.[70]

Eventually, the problem that had arisen from the differences was taken to the Annual Meeting of 1850, which decided that the differences were great enough that the two groups could not commune together.

Y. M. 1850. Art. 25. There is a body of people or brethren in the far West, whose doctrine and practice is somewhat different from ours. Some of our brethren live near or almost among them. Now the question arises, are the brethren privileged, according to the gospel, to hold communion with them under existing circumstances? Considered, that according to the gospel and the constant practice of the church, it would not be advisable for brethren to commune with them until a union is effected, and they are agreed to practice according to the ancient order of the church, 1 Cor. 4: 17.[71]

The next step was the introduction of the subject in the pages of the "Gospel Visiter," which arrived on the scene at a strategic time in April, 1851. The editor introduced the subject with the following note:

The following letter was written by a member of that Brotherhood in the "Far West." alluded to in the Minutes of our last Yearly Meeting Art. 25. Some of these were originally members of our fraternity, but being cut off from us by distance, and having no intercourse with us perhaps for more than 30 years, and on the other hand increasing in number, some changes from the ancient order took place among them. Of late years many of our Eastern Brethren have moved to the same country, and come in contact with them. Hence the desire to be One people with us, hence the query before last Yearly Meeting, and hence this present correspondence.[72]

Quite a number of Brethren from both sides became involved in the written debate that took place in the pages of the "Visiter." The two major issues seemed to be the exact pattern of events followed at the Love Feast

service and the authority of the Annual Meeting as opposed to the authori-
ty of the Bible. Undoubtedly, some of the discussion involved a quibbling
over terms, but in the context of the 1850s terms could be of great impor-
tance. Perhaps the first two letters in the debate will be sufficient to il-
lustrate the spirit of the discussion.

Yours of the 8th inst., is duly received with the minutes inclosed and I heartily give thanks to God the giver of all blessings, for your safe arrival home after your long journey, and I have read the minutes through, and it affords me much comfort to find that the questions in them decided on by the council correspond with the ideas we have ever entertained on matters of the same kind. But I was not a little astonished to find such questions brought before the general council from old churches. It appears, many of them are not acquainted with the principles and doctrines of Christ, or, if acquainted, not established in them. I assure you, dear brother, the most of those questions that were cancelled will never be carried from the Western brotherhood to the council, for they are already settled among us, and my own opinion is, every housekeeper ought to have those things settled at home. I consider there was but two important questions cancelled. The first on the subject of deaconship. That is a subject that has caused me some trouble, which has never been settled fairly to the satisfaction of some of our brethren. But I rejoice to find that the conclusion of the council has decided in favor of my practice. I have not had time to thoroughly examine the justification of the reasons they give to establish the practice of the Old or Ancient Brethren. But I intend as soon as I have leisure to take the ideas they have given under a thorough examination. I am much pleased with the ideas given, and I hope they may satisfy them that are dissatisfied, as they appear dissatisfied with the course we have ever pursued.

The second subject that I had reference to is the difference that is stated in the brethren in the "far West" as it is stated that we differ in point of doctrine and practice. If we differ in doctrine I have no knowledge of it. And I will venture to say, dear brother, from the knowledge you had of us in the spring, that you will not say, that there is a difference. But I confess there is a difference in our feetwashing and the supper and communion. And how that difference will be disposed of God only knows. But it is a matter of great weight. While we were thrown out separate from the old brethren, there was no trouble amongst us about it. As we profess to look to no one for instruction but our blessed Redeemer, and taking the examples he gave us to obey those ordinances in the way that he administered them. And after the service was over and an inquiry was made why you did so, we would present the manner and practice of our divine Master, who said, "he had given us an example to go by,"—and again he said, "Learn of me,"—and again—"Follow me."—When these questions (?) are answered, there can be no more objections raised. But an acknowledgement is made, that we are the people we profess to be in following Christ and obeying his command in the way he has given us the example. But now the understanding is amongst us, that the old brethren whom we have ever acknowledged to be our preceptors, they teach to observe Christ's commands and ordinances. But they overlook his example. These things have a very striking effect on the minds of the brethren that come from the old states;— none that comes among us, scruples a moment to go with us. They say at once, "It is not departing from the old brethren, who teach, that we must take Christ for our example as well as our lawgiver."

Now, dear brother, you will see with me that this is a weighty matter, as the old states are moving rapidly to the West, and seeing the examples of Christ practised, they regard it as a great privilege to practise it. If these things are not disposed of in general council to the satisfaction of the brethren in the West as well as in the East, it will amount to a very serious matter. I would write more, but the limit of one sheet will not admit of it.

Dear brother. We live at a distance from each other that we may never have the opportunity of conversing with each other; but we may have a correspondence by way of writing, which may afford us much satisfaction. Be free therefore in writing to me. News of any of you will be a welcome message to me, as my sincere desire is to strive to keep up the unity of the spirit in the brotherhood that is in Christ Jesus. You may expect to hear from me again as soon as I get word from you.

After a considerable delay we feel enabled, to address you at this time. Your letter dated Aug. 21st came to hand. We postponed answering your very friendly letter, until we should be able to notify you of the shipping of your books. Now we can inform you, that they were shipped on the sixth inst. at Pittsburg with the steamer Mt. Vernon to St. Louis, and we hope they will be forwarded to you in due time.

We were much rejoiced to find, that the questions, as they were decided in our last annual meeting met your approbation as corresponding with the ideas you have ever entertained on matters of the same kind. This encourages us to consider you as a brother in the spirit, though we are strangers yet in the body, in a twofold sense, not without hope, and oh how we desire to see it accomplished! that we may yet be brethren in the full sense of the word. This hope and a love, which would fainly embrace you and your brethren, and all the world beside, in brotherly affection, induces us to speak to you, not with enticing words of flattery, but plain and truthful, as brother ought to do with brother.

That you are yet somewhat unacquainted with our brotherhood, appears from the following sentence in your friendly epistle: "But I was not a little astonished to find such questions brought before the council from old churches." True,—the old brethren in council are sometimes a little astonished at the simplicity of questions brought before them; but when they reflect how the apostles, who were endowed with power and wisdom from on high, and having labored for years in preaching the Gospel and establishing the churches, had cause to say to their brethren, "For when for the time ye ought to be teachers, ye have need that one teach you again which be the first principles of the oracles of God &c;—when they reflect further on the actual condition of our churches, their astonishment subsides. They would remember and tell you too, that it would be an error to consider them all as old churches, while in fact there are a great many new or young churches, consisting of members lately received, and not yet so fully established.

With regard to the existing differences between your brethren of the "Far West," and our old brethren, we could have wished you to have stated them explicitly, and not in a general way only, so as to enable us to understand your doctrine and practice perfectly. While you seem not to be aware of any difference in doctrine, you admit there is a difference in practice. Now we believe, that doctrine and practice goes hand in hand, or to speak more distinctly, doctrine must always go before practice, and it appears to us, that there is evidence in your letter of your teaching differently, which we might easily point out, but leave it to your own sagacity, and pass it over at this time.

We agree with you, that this difference is a weighty matter, yes an awful weighty matter, if it does not only divide you and us from each other, but is making still more of a division in our brotherhood by the hasty joining in with you of some of our members. Indeed it is highly necessary to consider this matter seriously, and if you wish our assistance, we will try by the grace of God to examine with you the merits of the case, as impartially as we can. If you write again, please, describe your mode of proceeding in those matters of difference as distinctly as possible, and let us try to humble ourselves as poor erring mortals before a God of unerring wisdom, whenever we shall engage in the discussion of the matter, and ask him for such hearts, that will not seek their own, but should always be willing to give up to better light and knowledge.[73]

The question of the difference between the two sides was not discussed at the Annual Meeting of 1851. The Far Western Brethren wanted to have an opportunity to clarify their own position, and for that purpose they called a special meeting for November 22, 1851 at the meetinghouse in Adams County, Illinois. They drew up a report which included three recommendations.

Extract of a letter from our former Correspondent of the FAR-WEST Brethren.

Feeling it my duty to give you satisfaction on the subject of our not appearing at the last Yearly Meeting, which was occasioned for the want of a general understanding with the brethren. We that were anxious to take some action to obtain a reconciliation, did not wish to act without the general consent of all concerned, which we were unable to accomplish last year. But we have brought the matter so far to a conclusion, that an appointment is made for a meeting on the fourth Saturday in November; the meeting to be at our meetinghouse in Adams county, and the ministering part of the brotherhood in the West are requested to attend, in order to consult on the propriety of sending our grievances to the next Yearly meeting for consideration.[74]

The brethren known as the Western brethren, met in council Nov. 22d, 1851, in Adams county, Illinois.

To take in consideration the difference in practice existing in the administration of the *Lord's supper* and *feet-washing* between us and the Eastern churches. It was unanimously agreed as follows. It was proposed, 1. Can we submit to the Eastern practice? Answer not without a proof from divine authority that we are in error. It was then proposed secondly can we ask the Eastern brethren to submit to our practice? Answer from the sincerity and love which we believe to exist, and the long-continued practice of the Eastern brethren, we cannot.

It was then proposed thirdly, that we use forbearance with each other, and unite in the following manner, (to wit,) When the Eastern brethren commune with us, submit to our practice, and when we commune with them, we will submit to their practice; and so hold a union and communion until we as a united body, can have more light, through the goodness and blessing of almighty God.

The above consideration we unanimously submit to the brethren in conference, for your serious consideration, hoping your forbearance and long-suffering will be exercised toward us, until we can see more clearly where the difficulty exists, as we are always willing to be directed and corrected by the word of God.

Signed by order of the brethren.

GEORGE WOLFE [of Illinois]
DANIEL HENDRICKS
GEORGE WOLFE, jun. [of California][75]

When Henry Kurtz read the report in the "Gospel Visiter" office, he was not particularly pleased, because he had been hoping that the Far Western Brethren would simply change their ideas and practices to bring them into line with the main body of the church which he represented.

Both your letter and the proceedings of your council-meeting bear the marks of a conciliating and loving spirit, which cannot be otherwise but pleasing to me and every reader; yet allow me in candor to confess, that it is not a little mortifying to me, and no doubt to many of our readers, to see in your third proposition, that after all correspondence and labor spent for nearly two years we are just as far apart, than when we set out. I merely state this as a fact, and refrain from making any comments on it, more than this, that it is certainly necessary for us all to examine ourselves as before Him "whose eyes are like unto a flame of fire," in order to see whether we ourselves are not in the fault. This is the more necessary, since you contemplate to meet us at our Annual Meeting next, and it would really be a pity, if a personal interview, (perhaps the first & last between some of us,) should be of no better success, than our correspondence for the purpose of a *Union.*[76]

The leaders of the church who made the decisions at the Annual Meeting of 1852 agreed with Kurtz that the time for the union of the two groups had not yet arrived.

Y. M. 1852. Art. 1. Proceedings of a council meeting held Nov. 22, 1851, in Adams county, Illinois, by the brethren known as the Western brethren, with propositions for a re-union with the body of our brotherhood, represented in this meeting. After the differences having been stated, and considerable conversation had on the subject, it was finally concluded, that this meeting does not feel satisfied, how a full and true union can be obtained on the propositions made by the Western brethren, and that therefore this matter should be postponed until the dear brethren in the West become better acquainted with the grounds of our practice, and meanwhile we should exercise charity and Christian love toward them. —

Art. 2. A letter from Jefferson county, Iowa, referring to the differences existing between the brethren called the Western brethren, and those of our brethren settled around and among them from the East, and wishing to be guided in their intercourse with them by the council of this meeting. Considered, and answered by the foregoing decison.[77]

After 1852 it became clear that both sides would need to do some compromising, and in order to bring about such concessions, a mediator would be needed. The evidence suggests that the individual who succeeded in bringing the two sides together was D. B. Sturgis, who had been brought into the church in the 1830s in Illinois by Isham Gibson of the Far Western Brethren.

He undertook to affect a union between the eastern and western churches (which had long existed as two separate churches or organizations, not recognizing each other as brethren of the same faith). He had not investigated far until he became convinced that the division was based on a misconception and not on facts. He soon enlisted such able brethren in the cause as Isham Gibson and George Wolf on the part of the far Western brethren, and Ellias Dickey, Henry Davy, John Kline and James Tracy on the part of the eastern brethren. The result was a lasting reconcilliation which was affected in or about the year 1858. . . . He often referred to this work as being the crowning work of his life.[78]

At any rate, the Annual Meeting of 1855 heard and accepted the request for the appointment of a committee to confer with the Far Western Brethren and to report on the differences between the two groups.

Y. M. 1855. Art. 29. Request for a committee to (go to) Illinois to confer with the Far Western brethren or a committee of them, to investigate the differences in doctrine and practice existing between them and us, and report to next annual meeting. Granted, and brother A. Mass, Christian Long, John Metzger, Samuel Lehman, James H. Tracey, David Hardman, John Bowman, Daniel Fry, D. P. Sayler, John H. Umstad and James Quinter, appointed for this business.[79]

In 1856 the committee presented a lengthy four-point report to the Meeting.

Y. M. 1856. Art. 14. The committee appointed last annual meeting to visit and confer with the Far Western brethren or a committee of them to investigate the differences in doctrine and practice existing between them and us, submitted the following.

REPORT

May 8, 1856. We, the brethren who constitute the committee appointed by the German Baptist church at our last annual meeting to visit the Western brethren (who recognize brother Wolfe, of Illinois, as their bishop), by the grace and favor of God, were permitted to meet at their meeting house, where we were received on the most friendly and Christianlike terms, and after different queries were proposed for our deliberation, the three (or four) following being considered the most important, we proceeded to make our report accordingly as follows:

1. The question concerning the reality of a devil (which seems to have been doubted by some of them) was considered, and after comparing opinions and sentiment on the subject of the reality of such a being and his nature, we agreed upon the following view, that the Scriptures recognize a devil or an evil spirit, that manifests itself in the flesh.

2. On the doctrine of universal salvation, which denies punishment hereafter (a doctrine which never obtained foothold in our brotherhood, and while a good many of our ancient faithful brethren may have held the doctrine of restoration, and many of our dearly beloved brethren may still hold it, the preaching of such doctrine was, as far as our information extends, never countenanced in our church), we cordially agreed with brother Wolfe, "that all shall receive hereafter according to the deeds done in the body, whether they be good or bad."

3. On the subject of feet washing, brother Wolfe is firm in the opinion that one person should both wash and wipe the feet of a number of brethren (or among the female part of the congregation, one sister the feet of several sisters), and then another, and so on, until all are washed; but he is willing to conform to the practice of the brethren in general when in communion meeting with them, and begs for forbearance on the part of the brethren in general until they shall all come to see alike.

4. Brother Wolfe is likewise strongly of the opinion, that no time should be spent between the eating of the supper and the breaking of the bread in the communion, but that the whole ceremony should be prosecuted without intermission or delay.

It is the sincere desire of brother Wolfe, that however these sentiments may clash with the general practice of the brethren, they may not be considered a sufficient cause why they should not be received in communion and fellowship with the brethren, with which views we, the committee, unanimously agree, and present this our report to the brethren in general council met, for their deliberation and concurrence. Signed by David Hardman, J. H. Umstad, J. H. Tracey, A. Mass., John Metzger, S Lehman, C. Long. (Thus it was entered upon the minutes without note or comment.)[80]

Although the two sides seemed to agree that union was desirable and possible, the final agreements did not come for another three years until the Annual Meeting of 1859, when the Far Western Brethren submitted letters to the Meeting in Pennyslvania which were accepted by the Meeting as the basis of union.

Y. M. 1859. Art. 35. Several communications were sent to this annual meeting from the brethren hitherto distinguished as Western brethren. From these communications we shall give some extracts, as we have not room upon the minutes to give them entire.

"Beloved brethren: We, the brethren in Adams county, Illinois, met together in council, to take into consideration the course we had best adopt in respect to the yearly meeting. On account of the great distance we are from the place of meeting, and none of us being in a situation suitable to take up such a journey, we have concluded to send you these lines, to inform you that after we received the minutes of last conference, held in Indiana, we called a church council, and we concluded for the sake of union in the brotherhood to adopt the minutes of last Y. M., and we intend to carry them out as near as circumstances will admit of . . . We further state, that we are willing to counsel and be counseled by the Y. M." Signed by elder George Wolfe and others, by order of the church.

The following extract is from a letter from Sugar Creek church, Sangamon county, Ill: "We have unanimously agreed to be fully united with our beloved elder brethren, to counsel and be counseled. And we have put in practice the order of receiving and baptizing members, non-swearing, and non-comformity to the world." Signed by elder Isham Gibson and others, by order of the church.

From the brethren in Hurricane Creek district, Bond county, Ill.:

"Dear brethren in the Lord: Considering your love and care for us as manifested by your kind forbearance and long-suffering to usward, we in love to you and all saints, thought it good to send to you this epistle, and also brother Daniel B. Sturgis, delegate from this district, witnessing that we desire full fellowship and union. And we unanimously agree to be counseled by the brethren, and submit to all the decisions of our beloved brethren in conference. We believe the best good of all is maintained by a full subjection to the decisions of the yearly meetings published in the minutes." Signed by Daniel B. Sturgis and others, by order of the church.

The following is the expression of this annual meeting upon the subject referred to in the above communications:

"Whereas, it is known that what have been called the Western brethren have not heretofore been in perfect union with our churches in observing the ordinances and regulations in the house of God; and, whereas, a number of communications have come before this council meeting from said brethren, expressing a strong desire to be in full fellowship with our brotherhood, and promising to submit to and to be governed by the rules by which we think the house of God should be governed, therefore, considered, that we have cause to thank God that the efforts made to bring about a union have been so successful, and we are now happy to recognize them as being in full fellowship with us."[81]

The John Clingingsmith account provided some additional details on the negotiations in the 1850s and summarized the events that made possible the complete union in 1859.

When the eastern Brethren began to move out west into Illinois, they were cautioned against the far western Brethren, knowing that there still did exist some of the so-called Brethren in the far west, but supposing that they had all strayed off from the truth of the Bible.

But they continued to come west until finally some of them met with some of the far western Brethren. This then began to open up an inquiry and a correspondence.

Now the question to the far western Brethren was: "Who are you? and where did you come from. We thought you had all gone astray with or like Haun and Hostetle and others." But Eld. Geo. Wolfe told them, no, we are not of that party. Then after a year or two of correspondence, more or less, this question called for an action in general conference. And in the year 1855 there was a committee of eleven appointed to go to the far western Brethren and investigate this matter, and see who they were and their authority and what the difference was in faith and practice.

So on May 22, 1856 there were seven of this committee met the far western Brethren, who also had been notified and were collected in Adams County, Ill., at their meetinghouse. And after considerable discussion Wolfe told them that our authority is as good as yours, and that we had never strayed away from the Bible. The western Brethren were also accused with Universalism, because they sometimes preached the final restitution. Wolfe told them that the Universalists had done everything they could to draw us from the practice of the Bible, but we stood firm on that.

This committee made their report to the ensuing conference in 1856 and Eld. Wolfe went there also, and there was a compromise or an agreement affected. See Brethren Encyclopedia, page 117, but some one may want to know what the difference was in practice. The eastern Brethren practices of reading of a chapter and lecturing on the suffering of Christ and the salutation of the holy kiss between the supper and the communion, which the western Brethren had left off for many years. But the eastern Brethren insisted that the western Brethren should do this, to which they finally agreed.

There was also another difference. The western Brethren practiced for one to wash feet and wipe the feet he had washed. The eastern Brethren practiced, for one to wash feet and another one to follow and wipe them. To this the western Brethren would not agree, but the compromise was, that when we, the western Brethren, went among them that we should do as they did, and when they came among us that they should do as we did, and that this should make no bar between the eastern and western. Moreover there was an old brother in this committee, named John Umlstead; he was from Germantown, Pa., where the Brethren first commenced in America, and he said that they did and always had practiced for one to wash and wipe the feet he had washed. This was a damper to the eastern Brethren on this subject, but it took many years for this to become reconciled.[82]

On several occasions in the history of the Church of the Brethren there have been schisms which led to the establishment of different churches, all of which claimed the same beginning. However, the union of the eastern and western wings of the church in 1859 was one happy occasion in which two separate groups were successful in overcoming their differences and in uniting.

SETTLEMENTS WEST OF THE MISSISSIPPI RIVER

By 1865, the Brethren had established a number of widely scattered settlements in the large territory of the United States west of the Mississippi River. The earliest of these settlements was evidently in Missouri, where the Brethren had arrived in the 1790s while the territory was controlled by

Spain. John Clingingsmith, whose father, Daniel, was one of the earliest Brethren settlers in Missouri, recounted some of the details of this settlement.

Now we want to notice the Brethren and church in Cape Girardeau County, Mo. In all probability there were several families of Brethren moved here sometime before there was any stopped in Illinois. Now this afore-named Eld. John Hendricks also went to Cape Girardeau Co., Mo. and found these Brethren there. Old Bro. Daniel Hendricks, John's youngest son, says "The first Dunkers that ever moved to Cape Girardeau, Mo., were Peter Baker, John Miller, Joseph Niswanger, these came from North Carolina, and Daniel Clingingsmith," who came from Pennsylvania. "I think," says he, "they moved there about the year 1790." Now this may not be the precise time; but it was not far from that time when these brethren moved there. But be that as it may. My father, Daniel Clingingsmith, moved there while that country belonged to Spain, and he got a Spanish grant of land there.[89]

According to J. H. Moore's account in "Some Brethren Pathfinders," these Brethren were encouraged to emigrate to Missouri by Major George F. Bollinger, a land speculator who had secured a large grant of land from the Spanish. Some years later, about 1818, Bollinger was visited by John Mason Peck, a prominent Baptist minister who traveled extensively as a missionary in Illinois and Missouri. Peck's account of his visit provided some corroboration of Moore's account and added some details.

I was now about to leave Cape Girardeau county, in a northwesterly direction, for St. Michael. The first prominent settlement was Bollinger's, the name of the leading patriarch. Mr. Bollinger and a number of other German families made their pitch here, under the Spanish Government, about the commencement of the present century. They were nominal Lutherans, but being destitute of a pastor, and without schools, they degenerated in religion, but were industrious farmers. Mr. Bollinger was a member of the first Legislature under the State government, and subsequently either he or his son has been repeatedly a member. A few years since a new county was laid off from Cape Girardeau and adjacent counties, and named after him.[84]

Perhaps some of these German settlers in Missouri were Lutherans, as Peck indicated, but some of them were Brethren, and they were taking steps to organize a Brethren congregation, according to Clingingsmith's account.

Daniel Hendricks also says that this old "Elder John Hendricks was the first Dunker preacher of any note that ever preached in Missouri or Illinois." And that "Peter Baker was the first brother that ever was buried in Missouri." This was probably not far from 1810. And that "Isaac Miller was the first brother that was ever baptized there. And the first communion that was ever held there was about the year 1810, at the home of Joseph Niswanger, superintended by Eld. John Hendricks, of Kentucky."

Now this Eld. John Hendricks lived in Kentucky, but intended to move to Cape Girardeau County, Mo. He sold out in Kentucky for that purpose, and was making preparations to move, but before he could do so he took sick and died. From other circumstances, judge that he must have died in the spring of 1813. But his family moved to Missouri. Some of his children having families of their own. There his son James was put to the ministry, and in proper time on the 17th day of October, 1818, he was ordained to the eldership in Cape County, Mo., on White Water Creek, by the late Eld. George Wolfe, of Illinois. This was the first ordination ever made by the Brethren in Missouri. This church also prospered and increased under the care and superindency of Eld. James Hendricks.

In my first memory about 1824 or '23, there was at this place, a nice little church of humble followers of the meek and lowly Jesus—probably between thirty and fifty members,—and it continued in a prosperous condition as long as Eld. James Hendricks lived. We will notice this church further after while.

Now this church, under the care of Eld. James Hendricks, and the church across the river, in Illinois, under the care of Eld. Geo. Wolfe, about forty miles apart, were in peace and harmony, and the ministers frequently visited and assisted each other. And oh, how these pioneers of the West loved each other! Far more so than Brethren usually do now. I heard Jacob Wiggle say, that in these churches, they washed feet after supper, but before the communion. The present John Wolfe, of Liberty, Ill., says that was so. We will come to this subject again after little. . . .

But now again to the church in Cape County, Missouri. Eld. James Hendricks died June 5, 1844, after a long spell of sickness, which started from the prod of an awl in his finger. Eld. Geo. Wolfe, of Adams County, Ill., was called on to preach his funeral and other funerals there and set in order the things wanted in the church.

When Wolfe was called on to preach Hendricks' funeral he said he did not know whether he could or not, for says he: "Hendricks thought as I thought and I thought as he thought." Thus we can see how these old pioneers of the west loved each other.

But in the fall of 1844 Wolfe went to Cape County, Mo. Wife and I accompanied him. He preached these funerals. Then Isham Gibson came there also, and when the church was called together, there had been a choice made for a speaker, it was Daniel Hendricks, James' youngest brother. He was forwarded more fully to the work. Another young man, John H. Miller, was called to his assistance.

About two years after Daniel Hendricks was ordained to the eldership by Isham Gibson, and a while after that Daniel Hendricks moved to Adams County, Ill. Afterward John H. Miller, was ordained to the eldership by Isham Gibson.[85]

Clingingsmith understood that this Brethren congregation in Cape Girardeau County, Missouri, came to an end, when the long-standing Brethren interest in Universalism came to a climax in this area and the Brethren became Universalists. His statement will be quoted in the section dealing with the relation of the Brethren and the Universalists.

As a result of the ending of this Brethren congregation in Missouri, the oldest permanent Brethren settlement west of the Mississippi River was established in Iowa in Jefferson County in southeastern Iowa. One of the pioneers in Iowa was George Wolfe, the nephew of the George Wolfe of Illinois. Late in his life he prepared a brief autobiographical sketch for Abram Cassel. Here is the story of still another member of the pioneering Wolfe family, one who also traveled widely.

My knowledge of my progeneters, paternaly and maternaly is very limited. My father, Jacob Wolfe, died when I was young. Father was Born & raised to manhood in Lancaster Co. Pa. My Mother's Maden Name was Barbara Houser. [She was] Born and raised in Fredericksburg, Maryland. My Mother was raised in the Lutheran faith. Father & Mother was Married March 4th 1799. both being very poor, [they] moved to Kentucky on the green River, when it was a wilderness cuntry. my Father & Eld. Geo. Wolfe, Fathers Brother, lost their land there in the days of instalments & moved to the then teritory of Ills. in that part of the state called Egypt. June 25, 1809 I was born in Union Co. near Jonesboro, Illinois. Sept 18th 1831 I married my Wife. . . . in the Spring of 1833 we was both Baptised by Eld Charles Daugherty in a stream of water caled the north prong of clear Creek. in 1836 I was caled or Chosen to the ministry by the Brethren in that vicinity. Elder James Hendricks of Jackson, Cape Jirardau Co. Mo. presiding. . . . in 1842 or 3 I was ordained by Eld.

George Wolfe Sen & Eld Charles Daugherty in Lee Co. Iowa. helped establish the Churches in Lee, Jefferson, Desmoine, & other counties in Iowa. was the only Elder there was in Iowa for several years. in 1848 moved back to Hancock Co. Ills. laboured there in connection with other Brethren till 1856.[86]

One of the major problems of the Brethren as they emigrated to Iowa and the other western states developed because there was so much available land. Consequently, many of them spread out in all directions with no conscious effort to settle in communities. As a result many Brethren were lost to the church in this way; but on the other hand, many of them were loyal enough to the church that they persuaded ministers from the East to emigrate and begin congregations. Among the isolated families were the Brubakers in Story County, Iowa.

Story County, Iowa
December 4, 1853

i suppose you would like to know how wee like our new home   wee like it verry well   as to the country wee could not got to a richer country in the world   the land is as black as a hat and the soil is from 3 to 6 feet deep   we have some off the pertiest potaters and turnips you ever saw   all kinds off vegitation groes fine hear   when wee first came hear wee livd in a Blacksmith shop 2 months and Built us a new house 13 by 22 and a shed off 9 feet at the end off the house   our well is under the shed at the End off the house   it is 30 feet deep   wee have it fixt with a Endless Chain in it   wee Can se all arounds us 4 and 5 miels over the parares   it is about 2 miels to indian Creek   their is some off the pertiest fish you Ever saw in that Creek   father has a nice farm on the Creek with some verry larg timber some Black walnut and white walnut and . . . Burr oake and white oake   their is no Beach nor sasefras hear   father has enterd and Bought 12 hundred and 60 acres   some timber land   he give 5 dollars pre acre and some not so much . . . too years ago their was noboddy Livd on indian Creek nor near it   the peopel are comming in verry fast   the avrige sum for the Last 3 years of people was one hundred an fifty thousand Emmegrants that has movd to this state   i like this country far Better then i ever did tennesee for severel reassons   i have often wishd that our old Brother helten and solomon garver was out her   their is no Breathren in our settelment   But some must be the first and i hope some will soon come   wee would be glad if some would Come   whie not Come hear whear [you] can get Land for one dollar and 25 cents per acre and i do Certenly know that you never saw as rich Land in your life as this state is and thoes that have thier Land and Live in a slav state   i have not seen a Coullerd person since i am in the State   if anny off the Brethren in tends to move to the new Country now is their time and wee think this Country will have all the things first   in one year or too years   Cattel are verry hie hear   wee Bought one heiffer   she was not quite 2 years old with a young calf for 25 Dollers in gold and that is all wee have got yet   work Cattel sells from sixty to one hundred dollars pr yoke   their is a heap off game hear such as Dear and some bear and turkeys and prarie Chickens and lots of squerrels   the peopel are in a greate way for rail roads   they have one laide out from the massesippee rivver to fort Desmoins and that one will come about 15 miels south of us and one from paduck to rock iland that goes 7 or 8 miels north of us   the one to the fort is to be made in a short time and the steam Boats runns their to   that is about 24 miels from hear   6 years ago their [was] scearly a house their and now it is a Large town and Land sells for forty Dollers pr acre   in that settlement   our nearest mill is their but their is a fine grist mill and saw mill a Building over on skunk river about 7 or 8 miels from hear and the best kind of road[87]

Story County, Iowa
August 20, 1854

    wee Live within 3 miels of the senter of the state of iowa and their is a town Laid off their and it has the name off Iowa Senter that Lays on the nort off us and peora an oather town Lays 3 miles rather south from us   this is one of the most fertield and Beutifullest Countries in the world   our corn feilds and wheat feilds shoes what strong rich Land their is and wee have the Best garden that wee Ever had since wee keep house   their is no Clods and poor Land to Encounter with hear   it can rain hard hear one day and the next day wee can go right to ploughing again   father had 40 acres pararia broake for us and Henry had 40 broake for him and that Cost 2 hundred dollars   wee movd hear the first Day of may whear wee now live   father give Catherine the place whear wee first livd on when wee first Came to this County   father give 12 hundred Dollers for this place   their was 30 acres Broake and fencd and 25 acres in sod Corn   he got the Corn with the Land and a small house on it   wee Built a gud hewd Log house hear 20 wide and 36 long and a seller 20 feet by 18 feet deep and by diging 2 or 3 feet more on the one side wee Can have a nice stream of running watter in the Celler   wee have a nice gravley bottom Clear spring 50 steps from the house and first rate water ... your sister was hear to day and Eat watter mellongs and plums with us   our mellens wais from 20 to 50 pounds hear and the Best kind   wee have a Larg pach of mellons   i want to make some wattermellen butter if i Can   wee have wild fruit hear in abundence gooes berry by the bushels and the Largest i Ever saw in my life and straw berrys by the thousands and raseberys and wild graps and red and yellow plums   i have eate more gud pie this spring and summer then i ever did in that Lenth of time before and wee are all highly pleasd with the Country and our home   one off our old neighbours from tennesee Came to see us   he was hear weeke before Last   you have seen him   it was John Blair that ust to wagon to Linchburg   he says he Cant Content him self in tennesee no Longer   he is a going to sell as soon as he Can and move right hear   he says he studied all the way out hear how wee was fixt and what kind off a home wee had but he found it all so much better then he had anny ideia that he wants to Come and settel hear in a free Country   wee have not seen the first negro since wee are in the state   Evey thing groes hear in abundance and Beese does better hear then i Ever saw   they make a greadeal off honney to the stand   their has been from 75 to 80 pounds taken out off one stand in one season   the whitesd pertiest Comb i ever saw   father found a bee tree Last spring   he put them in a gum that holds a Bushel and a half and i think they will fill it full   their was a man not far from hear cut a bee tree   it was fild 6 feet Clear nice honney Comb and fish in abundens picke hear in indian Creeck 3 feet Long and their is a greate manny wild turkeys and Dear and about 40 miels from hear their are a great manny Elk   their horns wais from 35 to 40 pounds   you have no idie how th[e]y lock with such powerfull horns on their heads and their is some Buffelows up their to and now i must tell you something about the religion   their is some new Lites and some Cammelites some Baptist some united breathren and some methodist   they preach a greadeal   it is Low hear and Low their------ and wee are quite By our selvs and wee have not that Blessing yet that wee Can hear our Dear Belovd breathren preach the gospel in its purity   But wee hope that the time will come when some off our Dear Breathren will move hear and some preachers that will teach the peopel the right way   wee want some to move hear to spread the glad tidings of salvation and teach the peopel the nesesity off observing the Commadments: that our Lord and master taught his desipels to observe   But wee have a sivel neighbourhood and Clever freindly peopel hear   a greadeal more so then i thought wee would find and some wishes verry much to hear the Breathren preach and wee still want you to send Brother george Bear out hear and their is so manny preachers Living in franklin County that one or the oather ought to Come out hear and Build up a Church hear Dear Brother and sister—verry Lonesome and lost on that acount   our prayers is that the Lord will make Evry thing right yet[88]

Another Brethren family that moved from the East to Iowa was the B. E. Plaine family; his letter describing some of the economic problems of Brethren farmers in Maryland and the resulting pressure to move to the West was quoted in the introduction to this chapter. In the spring of 1866, the family made the decision to sell out in Maryland and emigrated to the village of Panora in Guthrie County, Iowa. Plaine wrote a long letter to his brother, David, who was a minister in the Roanoke, Virginia, area, telling about life in Iowa.

Panora, Iowa
July 15, 1866

We have torn up and moved all the way here with the calculation of bettering our condition and I fear in the end we will have worst it as Hannah seems to think she never will feel at Home here although I think we could not [have] moved to a much prettyer one anywhere   the country is not too level or too roling but seems to be just right   our farm lies in a very healthy situation   no sloughs around or about it to taint the atmosphere   a part of the farm is nearly level and a part some rolling and good constant running watter on this part but not at the House but we have 1 well ... of the best of watter and another about 100 yrds from the House we will if we stay sink a well at the barn   we can dig a well in a day or so   we can dig one with a spade   in walling up [the well] we get stone 1½ miles off for 15 cents a load   we quarry them   we can haul 5 loads a day ... we could make this one of the prettiest of farms if all were satisfied and content to stay   I still hope when we fix up a little that mother will be better contented   if only some of our friends would come and settle around us I think we would feel more at home   a farm can be bought just wherever wanted   any person will sell and all at the same price   the price of land improved is selling from 25 to 35 Dols   prairie from 3 to 10 according to location   I could have as much land as I want a[t] fair prices if we were fairly settled down but under the circumstances I have not bot any   I have loaned some money and am buying up soldier bounties   they are selling them at 80 Dols in the one hundred and draw 6 per cent interest as soon as presented to the clerk for his signature   I think there is no harm in taking them as we buy them at their offer and can get thousands dollars at that   they will pay a part back this fall a part in the spring of 67 and a part in a year from this   the money being paid in small dribs they will sooner take less than wait on the payments   75 and 80 is all they can get from any one and buying land at tax sales is another business that pays well though I have not bot any yet   the lands that tax is not payed up on is put up at public sale and sold for the amount of tax   this draws 10 per cent interest and the owner has to pay 30 per cent on the sale to redeem his land   make about 40 per cent and some times the owner never comes and the land is held by the one that buys it   in 3 years after the sale if the land is not redeemed the county make a deed to the purchaser

You dont know how glad I was to hear you say you intended to come to Iowa. *O do come* you have no Ideah what amount of good you may accomplish by coming here   we [have] a small congregation here of brethren   had only one speaker here at first but have elected another since we are here   I think there has been a great reform started in the church since we came   every one appeared to be going his own way but I have tried to bring about a different state of things and I am glad the Anual Meeting has made it obligatory on the over seers of churches to have their rules enforced among their members   it will be a good thing for us   we will have them to back us in what we preach   our speaker is not very popular and but few come to hear him   I dont know how the new one will do as we had not the chance to hear him yet   we had a small lovefeast 3 weeks ago   about 21 or 2 members communed   a large congregation assembled and seemed to pay great attention to the preaching the[y] seem here like sheep without a shepherd   they seem to want to do something and they hardly know in what   *do come out . . .*

Just now Bro. Ozias Ferree & wife & Bro. Jno Diehl our newly elected speaker are driving up and want Hannah & I to go along to meeting 2 miles South of Panora & over 3 miles from here   we are going along

Well we went to meeting and are back again   we went in Ozias Ferree's waggon   all ride in waggons here   they stopt when we returned and took a plate of Ice cream with us but would not stay to dinner   we had 2 good sermons preached to us   Bro. Jacob Haughtailin appeared to be very emty as he said when he arose but the longer he spoke the more seemed to be given him and he seemed loth to quit   Bro. Diehl followed with very appropriate remarks Bro. Ozias Ferree is our Deacon Elected the same time Bro. Diehl was elected Speaker. . . . come & stay here this winter and we will all go [to] the meeting together next spring   the people especially our members are anxious you would come here   we have no Elder in this district   our preachers are both young or rather middle aged men   no bishop nearer than 150 miles I think & no other church within 100 m. so we dont often hear strange preachers   our children under present circumstances I fear will not come in very soon as it suits their convenience best to go to other meetings and mingle in other society   as they are choice in their company they will be with such as dont take an interest in coming to our meetings[89]

By 1865 the Brethren had established a number of permanent settlements in Iowa and in several other areas along the west bank of the Mississippi River. In addition to these settlements, a number of particularly courageous Brethren had crossed the Rocky Mountains and settled along the Pacific Coast. Jacob W. Wigle, a nephew of George Wolfe of Illinois and a member of a particularly significant Brethren pioneering family, was one of the early Brethren settlers in the Oregon territory in the 1850s. Fortunately, he wrote letters to the editor of the "Gospel Visiter," two of which are included in this section because they provide a good description of early pioneer life in Oregon.

Calapoosa, Linn Co. Oregon Terr.
August 8th, 1853

I have thought it necessary to drop you a few lines for the Visiter, rather as a short history of my life. My father and mother in an early day settled in Cape Girardeau County, Missouri, where they become to be members in the church of Christ under the protection of John Hendricks. I was also born in that County in the year 1807.

From thence my father moved to Illinois, ever remained in good standing in that church under the protection of George Wolf. George Wolf is my mother's brother; so I was brought up under the protection of the Gospel, and in an early day of my life I thought it fit, to join myself to the body. So in the year of our Lord 1827 I was baptized by George Wolf in the month of September. Since that time I remained a member of the body, and not as boasting of myself, but feeling myself bound to the truth, I never had a charge brought up against me before the church, but have traveled to and fro with father Wolf about every year visiting the churches in our reach. . . .

But in the spring of 1852, on account of circumstances taken place, I and two of my brothers set out for Oregon Territory. I was told before I started by father Wolf, that our crossing the plains was a denial of the faith, because we would have to travel under military form. Which we did not do; for we found no need of it, but the Indians were no hindrance to us, and rather were entirely friendly to us.

Through much affliction we all got through, and once more restored to good health. . . .

But I can blame no one with my separate condition from the body but myself. I only set out for the purpose of finding a milder climate, which I have found, as every thing we can raise, more than we can eat, is for sale, as our stock needs no feed at no season of the year, only such as we want to keep and work. But this does not satisfy my desire. . . .

On our return home [from attending a Baptist worship service], we were conversing on our condition, and we came to the conclusion to come together, to drop a few lines to you for you to put it in the Visiter, so that if any member should come to this Territory, they might know where to find us. I will describe this place, 80 miles above Oregon City in Linn co., 7 miles above Calapooia Post-office on the East side of the valley of Williamette. I request of you or any other brother that knows of any brethren, that have moved to this Territory, to let me know, what part they are in, that I may have a correspondence with them, and if any should move from the States here, I would like for them to come to us, as I feel lost in our present condition.

Now I would have written, what I have, without further consultation with what few members there are here.

But it is a raining, that I did not care about going out to work. We are 7 in number, 3 brothers and 4 sisters, there were 3 more crossed the plains, but settled about one hundred miles from us. Now we have no one among us with any church office but myself. The church appointed me in the office of a Deacon; so I will write no more, until I see the balance of the members. . . .[90]

Wigle asked the editor of the "Visiter" some questions about holding meetings if there was no minister present, which the editor answered by suggesting that a deacon had certain authority to hold meetings. On that basis, Wigle took the initiative in trying to get something started among the Brethren in Oregon. However, he was pleased to have a minister arrive in Oregon, as he indicated in his next letter written in the winter of 1854-1855.

In love I drop you a few lines informing you, that we are all well, and hoping that this may reach you and find you enjoying the same blessing. When I wrote that letter to you before, I did not know of another member more than I mentioned. But soon afterwards I found a company of emigrants from Indiana, which had nine members in them. I found that there were some 30 come in in 1850. I've seen no more of them until last June; then I took my horse and turned out to see, how many members I could find.

Brother William Carey had just paid me a visit; so I and him started to see how many members we could find. We visited all of them, we found there 16 Indiana Brethren, William Carey being one of the number. Likely you will have some knowledge of Benjamin Hardman's and Joshua Hardman's families. We were kindly entertained, while we were among them.

Daniel Leedy   George Wolfe, Jr.

We tarried with them one night and part of two days; then we took our leave and departed, so that day I went home with brother William Carey.

The next morning we started for Marion Co. to visit brother Peebler; we found where he lived, but he was not at home, yet his wife was at home, and we were happily entertained there again one night. Here we found 4 members, and in the morning we started for home. Reflecting on the prospect before us, I got the Visiter that had the letter in, that I wrote to you, and the answer to it, and read my letter and your answer wherever we stopped amongst the brethren, and trying to see whether we could assemble ourselves together according to your instructions. They all approved of the course, but none willing to step forward to take the lead. I found 3 other deacons besides myself.

By this time we had heard of Daniel Leedy, that he had started from Iowa to Oregon. He was appointed unto the ministry, and we concluded, we would wait until he came, and being in great hopes, that he would be advanced, before he left the body, the church. I frequently heard of him on the way, but he appeared to be so long a getting in, it appeared to me I could wait no longer. So I started to meet him. I only went about 30 miles, and met him; and it was a joyful meeting to me. He landed in the valley the last day of August. So I took him to my house, and he staid with me 3 weeks.

In this time he bought a claim in a mile and half from me; he was only appointed to the ministry, and therefore he was very backward. He was not even willing to make an appointment, but we must do it for him. So we appointed a meeting on the first Sunday of October, when we all met together, and we consulted the matter and concluded, that we were too many to do nothing. We considered ourselves just as much in duty bound to be obedient to the requirements of the Gospel, our number now is 9 in our neighborhood. We were all here. Brother Samuel Hardman was with us. The question was asked, whether we should remain as we had been, or meet together once every two weeks for the purpose of worship? and so took a vote on it. It was a clear vote, all expressed a warm desire, that we would manifest our love in meeting together, exercising the gifts that God has given to us. I think I may safely say it was the first meeting of Brethren, that was ever held in Oregon.

The meeting was at my house, and brother Daniel Leedy was the preacher. We have met together once since, and had a meeting amongst the Hardmans. So our intention is to keep up meeting; we are in hopes, that brother Peter Lutz will come across the plains next season from Iowa. We wish for him or some other bishop. For all the members here express a warm desire to manifest their love in commemorating the death of our Lord and Saviour Jesus Christ.

Now we want you to take our case in consideration, and represent us to the annual meeting. We want to know, whether there is any way provided for us, to meet in communion, provided we get no more help? Daniel Leedy is only appointed into the ministry, just merely to preach the word, and nothing more. Now what are we to do? The distance is too great for us, to ask the brotherhood to send some one to us, and life is uncertain; for us to remain so. In the multitude of council there is safety. We wish for you therefore to not forget us. Brother Peter Lutz is not yet ordained a bishop, though he has the right to administer the Lord's supper; but we have written to the Iowa members, that if he sets out for Oregon next spring, that they should recollect our condition, and ordain him for our sakes. But his arrival here is yet uncertain, and we want to know, whether Daniel Leedy could have the authority to baptize, where no help could be had?[91]

Daniel Leedy, whose earlier life was told in the introduction of this chapter, became a leading spirit in the organization of the Church of the Brethren in Oregon, because for quite a number of years he was the only Brethren minister in the territory. He labored diligently and conscientiously to establish the church in the area, as the following brief sketch makes clear.

[In 1854] he and his then growing family of six children took their long journey across the plains by ox team to Oregon. Starting on April 3, they arrived Sept. 24, where they were given a hearty welcome by some members who had made the journey a year or more before. There he found a new country fast settling up, and truly the harvest was great, but the laborers were few. He was young in the ministry, and only in the first degree, and there was no other minister of the same faith in all the vast Northwest Pacific Coast. The faithful ones here urged him to serve them in conducting public worship. They were hungering for the Bread of Life, and to hear the Gospel preached as in their home church, in the far-away Eastern States. So, meetings were held in schoolhouses, and in residences, or any other available place,—often in groves. The people were glad to hear the blessed Gospel, and used to come for miles around. Never then did the minister have to preach to a mere "handful," or to empty benches.

Soon a few members were found twenty-five miles away, and others were located fifty miles in an adjoining county, and regular meetings were started at both places. Other places called for the minister to preach for them, and when we consider the lack of modern transportation, then you can know how the first minister was kept in his saddle fully half of his time making the long rides from place to place.

In 1856 a congregation was organized in the central part of the large field near Albany, Oregon. The members were then met with the dilemma of having a church without any one who had the power to administer the ordinances. So they called for help from the mother church, and the church here was given power to advance Bro. Leedy to the second degree in the ministry. Thus he labored on alone nearly seventeen years, always praying for the Lord of the harvest to send forth more laborers into his vineyard, in this far-away land. His labors were blessed, and a goodly number were received by his faithful ministry.[92]

Thus was the Church of the Brethren established in Oregon. South of Oregon in California, a Brethren settlement was being established in the 1850s. One of the pioneers was Jacob Wigle's cousin, George Wolfe, whose earlier career as a Brethren minister was described in connection with Iowa. Like Jacob Wigle, George Wolfe also traveled widely.

After paying a visit to the Brethren & friends in Iowa & Southern parts of Ills. in the fall of 1856, on the 16th day of Nov. 1856, we bid farewell to our native State Brethren & friends never expecting to see them more in this life, but hope to meet them in a better land them this. on the 20th of Nov. we left New York on the Steamer George Law for Cal.   landed in San Francisco on the 16th of December 1856.   after two day stay in the City took stage for Watsonville in Santa Cruz Co., Pajaro Valey on the Bay of Montera, Cal. Since then till now 1872 I have traveled & tried to preach far & near Christ the Lord, the Saviour & Redemer of a wanting world, that men and women should repent & turn to God.   menny times there was not a brother or sister in 50 miles of where duty caled me to preach.   numbers have been brought to the faith of the Gospel that never heard there was a people calling them selves Brethren.[93]

California was just one of the many places in the United States in which the Gospel according to the Brethren was being preached to people who had never before heard of the Brethren. In fact, the geographical expansion of the Brethren in the years from 1785 to 1865 was one of the very significant activities in the life of the church, because it led to an increase in the witness of the Christian religion and to an increase in the membership of the Church of the Brethren. The increase in the area of witness and of the membership helped to guarantee the permanence of the church in American life.

II. RELATIONS WITH OTHER RELIGIOUS GROUPS

INTRODUCTION

This period was characterized by intense rivalry and competition among the many different religious groups in the United States, and the Brethren were not immune to such competition. Clearly, the Brethren lived in contact with other religious groups, and they were influencing and being influenced by these other groups. For example, in North Carolina, as has already been pointed out, Brethren and Moravians were living as next-door neighbors in a somewhat uneasy relationship. Both groups were German-speaking, which provided a kinship that did not exist with most other groups. Also, in North Carolina, Brethren made contact with Universalism, as has already been explained in a previous volume in this series. This relationship continued for many years into the nineteenth century. Also, Brethren were particularly influencing the development of two new groups on the American religious scene, the Brethren in Christ in Pennsylvania and the Disciples of Christ in the Ohio River Valley. This chapter includes some of the evidence regarding the relationship between Brethren and each of the latter three groups.

UNIVERSALISM

A good general statement of the relationship between the Brethren and Universalism from the Brethren viewpoint was written in the 1840s by Philip Boyle.

In connection with what has been said in the commencement of our account, concerning their doctrines, &c., we will only add, by way of conclusion, that they believe that God is no respecter of persons, but in every nation, he that feareth him and worketh righteousness, is accepted with him; and that God so loved the world that he gave his only begotten Son, that whosoever believeth on him should not perish, but have everlasting life: and that God sent his Son into the world, to seek and to save that which was lost, believing that he is able to save to the uttermost all that come unto God through a crucified Redeemer, who tasted death for every man, and was manifested to destroy the works of the devil. And although it has herein been testified, that they hold general redemption as a doctrine, still it is not preached among them in general, as an article of faith. It has probably been held forth by those who felt themselves, as it were, lost in the love of God; and, perhaps, on this account, they have been charged with holding the sentiments of the Universalists, which they all deny. They conceive it their duty to declare the whole counsel of God, and therefore they feel themselves bound to proclaim his threatenings and his judgments against the wicked and ungodly; yet in accordance with their general principles which are Love and Good Will, they are more frequently led to speak of the love and goodness of God towards the children of men.

Geographically, Universalism made a significant impact on Brethren in the state where the Brethren had first settled in America—Pennsylvania. Richard Eddy, a Universalist historian, described the experience of Timothy Banger in transferring his membership from the Universalists to the Brethren in Philadelphia.

Rev. Timothy Banger was born in London in 1773, and came to Philadelphia twenty years later, bearing a letter of introduction to Dr. Benjamin Rush from Rev. Elhanan Winchester, which contained the following: "Mr. Banger, who will give this to you, is one of our young men who has sat under my preaching several years, and for two years past has occasionally exercised his gifts in public; I have not heard him, except just in the beginning, but am told by those who have, that he is a promising young man." He was a firm believer in the Trinity; and withdrew from the Philadelphia Church at the time that body embraced Unitarian views, about 1818. The late Rev. A. C. Thomas said of him:—

"He never had a pastorate, but was eminently useful as a preacher, especially during the many unsettled eras of our cause in Philadelphia. His attendance on public worship in Lombard St. Church ceased when the

Trinitarian theory was superseded by the Unitarian, namely, on the settlement of Mr. Kneeland in 1818; yet Mr. Kneeland, writing respecting him (January, 1821), pronounced 'Mr. Banger a worthy and amiable brother, who has always rendered his services gratuitously, and who has supplied the desk when otherwise it would have been vacant (excepting what time it was thought best that the doors of the church should be closed) for more than twenty years.' The same was true of him, to my knowledge, as late as 1839."

On ceasing to worship with the Universalists, Mr. Banger affiliated with the German Baptists (Dunkers), with whom he was elected an "Elder" in April, 1824, and was for a long time associated with Peter Keyser and James Lynd in their ministry at the meetings in Crown Street, Philadelphia, and Germantown. The bodies of the three lie near each other in the Society's burial-ground in Germantown. Mr. Banger died on the first of June, 1847, and his funeral services were conducted by Harriet Livermore, a noted writer and preacher, of whom he had been very considerate in her misfortunes and poverty. This remarkable woman is the "Stranger Guest" described in Whittier's poem entitled "Snowbound."[2]

Eddy's story of Timothy Banger was confirmed by the records of the Philadelphia Church of the Brethren.

At the Church Meeting held in Germantown April 2nd, 1826, all the members present, our Brother Timothy Banger, was duly acknowledged and approved as a Minister of the Gospel in the Church of German Baptist. And on the following Sabbath evening the Church in Philadelphia, in convention ratified the proceedings of the Church at Germantown, and acknowledged and approved in like manner Timothy Banger as a minister and helper in the Gospel of Christ.

Signed on behalf of the Church, Peter Keyser, Secr'y.[3]

Finally, Thomas Whittemore, a Universalist historian writing about 1830, recognized the presence of what he called "Winchesterian Universalists" in Philadelphia. His identification of "a Mr. Keyzer" as the pastor made it clear that he was really describing the Dunkers.

There is, at this day, a regular congregation of Winchesterian Universalists, who have a Meeting House of considerable size in the Northern Liberties [in Philadelphia]. They have never joined the Universalists as a denomination. Their pastor is a Mr. Keyzer, a respectable merchant.[4]

Another Brethren settlement in Pennsylvania which felt the impact of Universalism was Lancaster County. Whittemore also described the developments in that area.

Lancaster county deserves particular notice in the history of Universalism in Pennsylvania. In the borough of Marietta there were a few Universalists of wealth and influence, who, in the year 1827, invited Mr. Smith, the pastor of the Callow-hill-street society in Philadelphia, to visit them. Subsequently, Mr. Fisk, then preaching in that city, went out into the same region, and gave several discourses. Their labors were crowned with great success. Mr. Jacob Meyers, a highly respected preacher among the German Baptists, embraced Universalism, and soon began, with great zeal, to preach it. Two or three young men, of unusual ability, arose simultaneously, to defend the doctrine. In August, 1828, G. Grosh and J. Meyers, issued proposals for publishing a Universalist journal in the German language, in hopes it would be useful in spreading a knowledge of the universal love of God, among the multitudes of Germans, in the middle States. The first number was issued in the month of May following. It is published monthly, in a pamphlet of sixteen octavo pages, and is entitled "DER FROHLICHE BOTSCHAFTER," or the Messenger of Good Tidings. Besides well written articles by the editors, it has consisted of translations from the writings of Ballou, Balfour, &c. and of extracts from other Universalist publications. It is conducted with ability, and has the prayers of the whole Universalist community for its continuance. In January, 1829, a society was regularly formed in Marietta, called "the First Society of Universalists in Lancaster County," and in a few months after, another at East Hempfield, called the *second* society of that faith in the same county. A small building is being erected in Leacock township, which will be dedicated as a place of worship for Universalists.[5]

In response to a questionnaire from Whittemore, A. B. Grosh of Marietta, Pennsylvania, replied:

Persons who *call* themselves Universalists, believe, I compute, from one fiftieth to one twentieth part in punishment after death; but if we include others, (i.e., the Universalists among other denominations) then those who believe in a state of punishment after death, are more than one half of the whole number. For I find many Restorationists among the German Baptists, the Lutherans, and the Reformed Churches; the old Mennonists are nearly all such; and there are a few among the English people, particularly among those who are attached to no society. But very few will care publicly to own this *faith,* since the *name* is attached to it. I am also told that among the German Methodists, some believe in a final Restitution. In answering as to the trinity, I shall class the Arians among the believers in the divine unity. Of those who call themselves Universalists, I have found but one believer in the trinity, and he was a Rellyan.[6]

Richard Eddy, writing later in the nineteenth century, summarized the impact of Universalism in Lancaster County.

PENNSYLVANIA. About 1829, through the indefatigable zeal of Rev. Messrs, A. C. Thomas and A. B. Grosh, Universalism was also carried to the interior of the State, and churches were organized in Marietta and Reading. Rev. Jacob Myers, of Lancaster County, a preacher among the German Baptists, embraced Universalism, and began to preach it in the German tongue in 1828. Shortly after Rev. Samuel Longenecker joined Mr. Myers, and as both spoke equally well in the German and the English, they did a good work among the German population. At Wolmensdorf, Marietta, and Reamstown, they gathered congregations and formed temporary organizations.[7]

From Pennsylvania the ideas of Universalism spread to the Brethren in the Carolinas, although there is some evidence to indicate that the Brethren in the Carolinas developed the ideas of Universalism on their own without the influence of the Pennsylvanians. However it happened, it is clear that Brethren ministers in the Carolinas such as John Ham, David Martin, and Giles Chapman accepted and preached the doctrines of Universalism. The result was that the Brethren church in North Carolina was split and the Brethren church in South Carolina became Universalist.[8]
From the Carolinas the Brethren carried the ideas of Universalism to Kentucky. David Benedict, a Baptist historian writing in 1848 on the basis of material supplied by Philip Boyle, a Brethren minister, commented on Universalism in the Church of the Brethren and noted that some of Ham's followers moved to Kentucky. The material in quotation marks was taken by Benedict from Boyle.

"The German B. Brethren have been charged with holding the sentiments of the Universalists, which they all deny, and often testify against them."

This statement, I suppose, refers to the no-future-punishment system, as he admits that by some of this community "the writings and reasonings of Elhanan Winchester have been well received." He also mentions a schism in this body in 1790, when a party of decided Universalists drew off under the ministry of one John Ham, a man of great talents and popular address. Some of his followers afterward moved into the Green river country, Ky., and caused great confusion among the brotherhood there as well as in North Carolina, where Ham himself lived at the time of the division. "Those who have imbibed his opinions are thought to be in union and fellowship with the German Baptist Brethren, which has not been the case since the Yearly Meeting which was held in Franklin County, Virginia, 50 years ago, or upwards."

This class of Tunkers, at present, reside in Kentucky, in the southern part of Illinois, in Missouri and Iowa.[9]

In the autobiography of Jacob Bower, quoted in a previous chapter, there were a number of references to his contact with Universalism in Kentucky. In particular, he reported attending "a Universalist love feast, as it was called," which carried implications of Brethren influence. Also, he visited a Universalist minister in Muhlenberg County, which was the location of a Brethren settlement. Quite clearly, Bower, who had grown up in a Brethren home, was particularly susceptible to the appeals of Universalism in Kentucky.

Thomas Whittemore in his study of Universalism commented on developments by 1830 in Kentucky.

In Kentucky our friends are not so numerous. I have heard of but one society in that State, who believe in the restoration of all things. It is in the neighborhood of Lexington. Brother John Rice, a German, is the pastor, and I have been told he is a man of many virtues. I have been informed also, that there are two preachers of our order, living in the lower part of the state.[10]

Although Whittemore was not too favorably impressed or too well informed about Kentucky, his statement about the two ministers in the lower part of the state is especially interesting, because that was the territory of Muhlenberg County and of the Green River country, identified by Benedict.

Whittemore had also learned that there were Universalists in the state of Indiana. Very little is known about the relation of the Brethren and the Universalists in Indiana, but there is a brief reference in the records of the Silver Creek Baptist Church in southern Indiana indicating that in 1808 a member was excommunicated for associating with the "Universalist Dunkards."[11] *Undoubtedly, some of the Universalist sentiment had been taken along with the Brethren who were emigrating from the Carolinas to Indiana.*

Next door in Illinois the relation between Brethren and Universalists was much more specific. Eddy was quite concise when he wrote:

The first preacher of Universalism in Illinois was the Rev. George Wolf, a Dunker, in 1812. The doctrine of the final salvation of all souls was always prominent in his preaching.[12]

At another point in his history, Eddy quoted an incident in the life of John A. Gurley, a Universalist minister and editor of the "Star in the West," who visited the Illinois Brethren in 1839.

On the day following the one I spent in Quincy, I attended an appointment about fifteen miles distant, and delivered a discourse to a very large congregation of Dunkards. I was much pleased with the visit and with the people. Here I became acquainted with Father Wolf, a preacher of the above order, but of our faith in all things relating to the doctrine of the Bible. He is a remarkable man for his powers of reasoning, and is esteemed by those best acquainted with him, as possessing natural powers of mind equal to any in the State. He has preached Universalism more than twenty-five years, and has been the means of converting hundreds, and perhaps thousands. His success in the southern part of the State has been great, and his talents and character command the highest esteem and respect wherever he is known. He preaches to a regular society where he resides, statedly; and his congregations are uniformly large. Great anxiety was manifested by him and his society to hear an eastern preacher; for although old in the faith, they had never listened to one connected with our denomination. They desired to hear for themselves, that they might know of a certainty whether we agreed with them in sentiment. I delivered therefore a doctrinal sermon, to which was given the most fixed attention; and, as I proceeded, I was wonderfully pleased at the appearance of the assembly. Not a word was lost, and each one seemed to say, "There, that is just what we believe; that is our doctrine. How singular! He preaches precisely like our preachers, and uses the same arguments." And at the close of the services all seemed satisfied with the sentiments put forth; and Father Wolf assured me that what I had advanced was in perfect harmony with his own belief, and that of his denomination.[13]

Very likely, George Wolfe also had an impact on Brethren in the neighboring state of Missouri where they were influenced by Universalism and at the same time were having an influence on the development of Universalism in that state. Eddy did not know of Wolfe's influence, but he was convinced that the Brethren had played a role in getting Universalism started in Missouri.

MISSOURI. Who were the pioneers of Universalism in this State, is unknown. As early as 1837 or 1838, Rev. J. P. Fuller organized a church in Troy; and from the fact that the members were admitted by immersion, we infer that it was in a Dunkard community,—as many Dunkards believed and openly practiced the doctrine of Universalism.[14]

John Clingingsmith, the Brethren pioneer, added some details as well as a Brethren perspective to the development of Universalism in the Brethren settlement in Missouri.

Now in these western churches the Brethren had been in the habit of preaching the restitution, and especially in the church there in Cape County, Mo. And this called for some universalist preachers to come in there and preach for them, but Eld. Miller stood firm to the practice of the household of faith as practiced by the Brethren. But after while he was overcome by so much opposition, and left off the ordinances of the house of God. And then they soon went into the broad ways of the world. But some of the members would not go with them but these could not help themselves. While the church was all right they chose a minister, Andrew Miller. He is pretty sharp, and he still preaches for them. This is now the only minister that they have, since the death of John H. Miller, about 1865. They call themselves Universalists, but I cannot see any difference between them and the world. So ends the church in Cape County, Mo.[15]

Finally, the whole issue of Universalism was important enough in the life of the church that it was discussed by the Annual Meeting on several different occasions. The first time was in 1849.

Y. M. 1849. Art. 30. Whether it is advisable for a brother to preach universal redemption publicly; that is, that all men, however vile they may have been, shall share alike in the fruition of happiness with the saints? Considered, that we could not approve, by any means, of such proceeding.[16]

The second occasion was in 1856 in connection with the Far Western Brethren controversy and the leadership of George Wolfe. A committee composed of some of the most important leaders of the Annual Meeting met with a group of Far Western Brethren, including Wolfe. They drew up a report, the second point of which read as follows:

2. On the doctrine of universal salvation, which denies punishment hereafter (a doctrine which never obtained foothold in our brotherhood, and while a good many of our ancient faithful brethren may have held the doctrine of restoration, and many of our dearly beloved brethren may still hold it, the preaching of such doctrine was, as far as our information extends, never countenanced in our church), we cordially agreed with brother Wolfe, "that all shall receive hereafter according to the deeds done in the body, whether they be good or bad."[17]

Two years later, the issue was discussed again by the Annual Meeting.

RESTORATION, THE DOCTRINE OF

Y. M. 1858. Art. 2. Is it according to the gospel of Christ, for brethren, especially bishops, in speaking on the final destinies of the ungodly, to preach publicly that they shall be punished with everlasting destruction from the presence of the Lord, and privately teach that all will be restored everlastingly, whether they know God and obey the gospel of our Lord Jesus Christ or not; and if asked the question by an alien, whether the devil himself will be saved, make no reply? Answer.—We think brethren should be careful not to contradict privately what they preach publicly. Art. 3. Is it consistent to preach eternal punishment, and at the same time to peddle Winchester's Dialogues on Restoration? Tell us how it is. Answer. If a brother preaches endless punishment, it would be inconsistent for him to distribute Winchester's Dialogues on Restoration.[18]

Probably, the Brethren policy with regard to Universalism was not entirely consistent, for on the one hand they seemed to believe in many of the basic ideas, but on the other hand they did not want to be known publicly as Universalists. Richard Eddy seems to have understood the Brethren pretty well when he told the following story.

"If I were to say to my neighbors," said a Dunker preacher, whom the writer once visited, "I have a Universalist preacher stopping at my house, they would say, 'How do you dare to have such a character under your roof?' but if I should say, 'I have a friend with me who preaches Universal Restoration,' they would say, 'Have you? I am glad; I would like to come in and see him!' "[19]

BRETHREN IN CHRIST

The historians of the Church of the Brethren and of the Brethren in Christ are generally agreed that there was a close relationship between the two groups at the time when the Brethren in Christ was founded in America in the 1780s. However, that relationship is very difficult to describe specifically, because there is virtually no material available from the time when the Brethren in Christ began. Consequently, historians have been forced to rely largely on the recollections of various participants or their descendants, which were written down many years after the events described. Two of these accounts, both from Church of the Brethren sources, are valuable enough to be included in this discussion. To make these accounts intelligible, it is necessary to know that a small group of Pennsylvania Germans, some of whom had been Mennonites, were aroused emotionally and spiritually by the preaching of Martin Boehm, who later became one of the founders of the United Brethren in Christ. Based on their study of the Bible, they wanted to be baptized by trine immersion and the only way to secure such a baptism was from a Church of the Brethren minister. The first account is from the "History of the Church of the Brethren in Eastern Pennsylvania," published in 1915.

Jacob Nissley, a minister of the River Brethren, who is dead for some time, told the writer, that a delegation of those dissatisfied ones went to the vicinity of Manheim, to confer with Elder C. Longenecker, with a view of uniting with the Church of the Brethren, but that Elder Longenecker told them that the Brethren Church was not any more on the true foundation, that they have the form, but lack life and spirit, and advised them to start a church for themselves, and build on the true foundation. Mr. Nissley said he had his information from the founders of the River Brethren Church. The delegation as abovesaid were: Jacob Engle, Hans Engle, C. Rupp, Hans Stern, a Mr. Heiges, and Schaeffer. . . .

Abraham Gibbel told the writer that Hans Stern, one of the delegation of six, as aforesaid, unhesitatingly told him, that after they went home from Elder Longenecker, they consulted and concluded that they would take the advice, but none of them being baptized, they went across the Blue Ridge, to Elder George Miller, in the Swatara Church; and asked him to baptize them, but told him that they would then organize for themselves, upon which he refused. . . .

From this evidence, the editor of the volume drew this conclusion.

It is reasonable to suppose that if Elder Longenecker had been at peace with the church, and the church with him, and he had done his duty, the River Brethren Church would never have been organized; that is, if they had been honest, and sincere, and the presumption is that they were.[20]

The second account of the founding of the Brethren in Christ, or the River Brethren as they are commonly known, was written by Moses Miller, the grandson of George Miller, in 1881 by the request of Abram Cassel, the Brethren antiquarian and bibliophile.

From circumstances connected with the start of this people. They may have started near one hundred years ago. There were eight persons that united in the organization the names of those I remember and as I noted down some years ago were Jacob and Hans Engel, Stern, Sheaffer, Back [?] and Hikes [Heiges]. I have heard old brethren tell that sometimes it looked as if they would unite with the united brethren but not agreeing with them in Baptism and some other points of doctrine, they came to my grand father George Miller who was ordained in 1780 Bishop of the old brethren in the big Swatara Church Pa. and desired him to baptize them but wished not to unite with the brethren but start a church themselves. Grandfather Miller refused saying that he had no gospel to baptize but to receive them into the church and that they would be willing to take and give admonition according to the scriptures. They made the second effort for grand father to baptize them when he said if you want to begin something of your own you would better baptize your selves. So they met at the Susquehanna river between Bainbridge and Marietta Lancaster County Pa. and the lot fell on Sheaffer who baptized one and then he baptized the other seven and as they baptized in the river and living in its locality they obtained the name river brethren and as Sheaffer was their first baptist they were in some instances called sheafferites and as they numbered 8 they sometimes called themselves Noahs children, and the idea that some hold that they went out from us is incorrect . . .

In doctrine they differ with the Brethren generally preaching the forgiveness of sins and the reception of the Holy Spirit before baptism. 45

or 46 years ago they had a supper or full meal connected with their communion and I remember that one of their ministers then said that they
would not practice any thing but what they had scripture for but they have
long since done away their supper. they have their experience meetings and
some are good in telling what they have experienced. they are plain and
like the Brethren contend for self denial.[21]

*It is clear in conclusion that the group called the Brethren in Christ
was never a part of the Church of the Brethren; thus, no schism or division
was involved. At the same time, the founders of the Brethren in Christ were
influenced by the ideas of the Church of the Brethren and by its leaders. In
fact, the beginnings of the two groups provide some interesting parallels.
One of the differences was that they began some three-quarters of a century
apart. More important was their differing interpretation of the significance
of baptism in terms of its relation to the coming of the Holy Spirit in particular and of salvation in general. Each group was evidently the result of
the pietistic, emotional revival of its own day and age.*

DISCIPLES OF CHRIST

*A second indigenous American religious movement which the
Brethren influenced in its early development was the Disciples of Christ,
which represented a combination of the efforts of Barton W. Stone and
Alexander Campbell. The Brethren influence was greater in southern Indiana than at any other geographical location, and two individuals were
primarily responsible for that influence. The first was John Wright, who
came from a Brethren home in North Carolina, although evidently the
Brethren roots did not extend very far nor were they too strong in some
ways. But a number of Brethren ideas can be discerned in a careful reading
of this biographical account.*

Elder John Wright was born in Rowan County, North Carolina,
December 12th, 1785. His mother was of German descent. His ancestors on
his father's side came from England in very early times, and settled on the
eastern shore of Maryland. From that place they were scattered abroad,
some making their way to the Carolinas. His father was brought up among
the Quakers or Friends; and, singularly enough, he turned away from that
fraternity, who baptized *none,* to the Tunkers, who practiced *trine immersion.* He afterwards cast in his lot with the Dependent Baptists, among
whom he became a preacher.

Elder Wright remained in North Carolina until he was about twelve years of age. His father then removed with him to Powel's Valley, Virginia, where he grew up to manhood. . . .

From Virginia the whole family emigrated to the West, and settled in Wayne county, Kentucky . . .

Late in the year 1807—which was very soon after his second marriage—he removed from Kentucky to Clark's grant, Indiana Territory.

In August, 1808, he and his wife were immersed in the Ohio river, by William Summers, of Kentucky. He immediately united with the Baptist Church, and in the latter part of the same year he began to preach. . . .

In January, 1810, he removed to the Blue River, four miles south of Salem, in what was then Harrison, but now Washington county. There he entered a beautiful tract of land; and, by much hard labor, opened an excellent farm. In a short time his father moved into the same neighborhood; where, in 1810, they organized a congregation of Dependent or Free Will Baptists. . . . He was assisted by his father, and a younger brother, Peter, who was begining to preach with considerable success. The three Wrights exerted quite an influence in the favor of Christianity, and it was not long until they had organized ten Baptist churches, which they formed into what is known as the Blue River Association.

From the very first, John Wright was of the opinion that all human creeds are heretical and schismatical. He was perhaps the first man in Indiana that took his position on the *Bible alone;* and there was not to come after him a more persistent contender for the word of God as the only sufficient guide in religious matters. He labored to destroy divisions, and promote union among all the children of God; and in this difficult yet most important service he made his indelible mark. Though at first he tolerated the term "Baptist"—it being natural to condemn ourselves last—yet he afterwards waged a war against *all* party names. This war was declared in the year 1819, when he offered, in the church at Blue River, a resolution in favor of discarding *their* party name, and calling themselves some name authorized in the Scriptures. As individuals, he was willing that they should be called "Friends," "Disciples," or "Christians;" and as a body, "the Church of Christ," or "the Church of God." He opposed the term "Christian," as applied to the Church, because it was not so applied in the writings of the apostles.

The resolution was adopted with more unanimity that was expected; and the *Baptist* church has since been known as the Church of Christ at Blue River. Having agreed, also, to lay aside, as far as possible, their speculative opinions and contradictory theories, they presumed that they were prepared to plead consistently for Christian union, and to invite others to stand with them upon the one broad and sure foundation. They then began in earnest the work of reformation, and with such success that by the year 1821 there was scarcely a Baptist church in all that region. They all took upon them "that worthy name," and converted their Association into an Annual Meeting.

About this time a spirited controversy on the subject of Trine Immersion, was going on among the Tunkers, of whom there were some fifteen congregations in that section of the country. The leading spirits in opposition to that doctrine were Abram Kern of Indiana, and Peter Hon of Kentucky. At first they contended against great odds, but so many of their opponents came over to their side that they finally gained a decisive victory in favor of one immersion.

At the close of the contest, while both parties were exhausted by the war, Elder Wright recommended to the Annual Meeting that they should send a letter to the Annual Conference of the Tunkers, proposing a union of the two bodies on the Bible alone. The letter was written, and John Wright, his brother Peter, and several others, were appointed as messengers to convey it to the Conference and there advocate the measures it proposed. So successful was the expedition that at the first meeting the union was permanently formed, the Tunkers being persuaded to call themselves Christians.

At the same annual meeting Elder Wright proposed a correspondence with the Newlights [followers of Barton W. Stone], for the purpose of forming with them a more perfect union. He was appointed to conduct the correspondence on the part of his brethren, which he did with such ability and discretion, that a joint convention was assembled near Edinburg, where the union was readily formed. Only one church in all the vicinity refused to join the coalition, and it soon died of *chronic sectarianism.*

A few years subsequent to this, the work of Reformation began to progress rapidly among the Regular Baptists of the Silver Creek Association. . . . Through the influence of [John Wright], his brother Peter, Abram Kern, and others, on the part of what was called the Annual Meeting of the Southern District, which was composed of those who had been Baptists, Tunkers and Newlights; and through the efforts of Mordecai Cole and the Littells, on the part of the Silver Creek Association, a permanent union was formed between those two large and influential bodies of believers. In consequence of this glorious movement, more than *three thousand struck hands in one day*—not in person, but through their legal representatives, all agreeing to stand together on the one foundation and to forget all minor differences in their devotion to the great interests of the Redeemer's kingdom. This was, perhaps, the greatest achievement of Elder Wright's long and eventful life; and he deserves to be held in everlasting remembrance for his love of *truth* rather than of *party*, for his moral courage in carrying out his convictions of right, and for such power in uniting opposing sects and cementing them in love.

To the happy effects of this obliteration of party lines he testified a few years afterward. In a communication to the October number of the Christian Record for 1845, he wrote as follows: . . .

"So it was in Southern Indiana: formerly we had Regular Baptists, separate Baptists, German or Dunkard Baptists, free will Baptists, christian connexion, or Newlights. These societies in some respects were like the Jews and Samaritans of old; but the old gospel was preached among these warring sects with great power and success. Much of the partyism that existed was removed, and most of their party names were done away with. . . . Formerly we all had in our respected churches much that was purely human; but now, in the church of God, we have no need of the "mourning bench," "the anxious seat," or any other institution of man's device; but in the church is the place where the solemn feast of the Lord's body is celebrated, and sincere worship is offered to the Father in spirit and in truth."[22]

Consider alongside the story of John Wright the story of Joseph Hostetler, whose earlier life in Kentucky and in Indiana has been described in another chapter and who by 1820 was living in Orange County, some twenty miles from the residence of John Wright in Washington County.

In the mean time, the first volume of the Christian Baptist fell into his [Hostetler] hands. This he read with eagerness though not entire approbation; for being yet identified with a sect he felt that the blows descended too fast and too heavily. But still the light entered; the faith once delivered to the saints and long obscured by the traditions of men, became more and more apparent; objections to creeds and sects continued to be multiplied; until he found it impossible longer to refrain from a full and public avowal of his sentiments. Accordingly in the spring of 1826, he gave notice that, on a certain day, he would preach at Orleans on the subject of primitive Christianity. The news was carried far and wide; expectation was on tiptoe; and on the appointed day about a thousand persons, including several of the preachers of that section, assembled to hear the promised discourse. He spoke for an hour and a half from that proposition which affirms that "the disciples were called Christians first in Antioch," discussing,

I. The Name
II. The Manner of becoming a Disciple.
III. Creeds.

It was a day of great excitement. After he concluded the people were seen in groups earnestly discussing the merits of the anomalous discourse. Though many doubted, not a few were convinced that Elder Hostetler had shown them a "more excellent way." The preachers present attempted no reply; but adopted a policy which was then, and still is, more effective than a manly opposition. "Oh," said they, "what a great pity that one so young, so useful, and so promising, should thus destroy his influence by bringing in damnable heresies and attempting to change the customs of our fathers." "You ought," said they to his brethren, "to talk to him; and unless he recant you should bring him before the proper authorities and expel him." This advice was listened to; and he was accordingly notified that at the next meeting of the Association he would be required to answer to the charge of heresy.

In the mean time, desiring that all his brethren should understand clearly the things whereof he was accused, he visited all the churches that were to have a voice at his trial; proclaimed to them the ancient gospel; and baptized about a hundred, who gladly received the word.

Thus did God cause even the wrath of man to praise him.

When the day of this trial came he made an able defense, showing that he opposed no practice for which the word of God furnished either precept or example; that he had taught only what was clearly expressed in words which the Holy Spirit teacheth; that he had exhorted to no duty not enjoined by the apostles; and that he had only repeated to the people the exceeding great and precious promises of God, assuring them that He is faithful that promised. In conclusion he referred to the intolerance of all creed-makers, and to the long list of martyrs that have been "beheaded for the witness of Jesus," asking his brethren, if, actuated by the same spirit, they were willing to give their voices against him. "No, no," was the audible response; and a vote being taken, all but five were found to be in his favor. Thus he escaped excommunication; and, in escaping, he made more proselytes to primitive Christianity than he had ever before done in one day.

So great was the confidence reposed in him that his brethren appointed him to deliver the annual sermon at the convening of the next Association. Seeing this, he said to himself, "This day death passed upon this ecclesiastical body. About this time next year it will breathe its last; and my discourse shall be its funeral."

Such was, indeed, the case. Public sentiment rapidly underwent a change in favor of the Bible as the only platform on which all Christians could and should unite; and when the Association came together there were present delegates from the Dependent Baptists and the Old Christian

Body, or Newlights, duly empowered to co-operate with them, the Tunkers, in forming a union of the three parties upon the foundation of apostles and prophets.

In this important movement they were successful. With few exceptions, all the churches of each sect throughout south-eastern Indiana, came promptly into the Reformation. Party names, and unauthorized assemblies such as were their Conferences and Associations, were dispensed with; and Christ became "all and in all."

From this date (1828) Elder Hostetler is to be reckoned among the public advocates of the current Reformation.

The year 1828 was fixed in his memory by other and sadder events. He was brought to death's door by a fever which seized upon him while on a preaching tour to Kentucky. He recovered; but two of his brothers were suddenly cut down, each leaving a widow and three children who became, to some extent, dependent upon him.

Depressed by these afflictions of Providence, and to better provide for his family and, if need be, for the families of his deceased brothers, he turned his attention to the study of medicine. During the year, therefore, he travelled but little and enlisted but few soldiers in the army of the Lord.

During the summer of 1829 he and Elder Peter Hon travelled extensively and preached the gospel with great success. They visited Oldham, Nicolas, Bourbon, Montgomery, and Fleming counties, Kentucky; Highland county, Ohio; and Lawrence, Harrison, Clarke, and Jackson counties, Indiana. There were frequently engaged in protracted meetings and they closed their labors for that year with about four hundred additions to the rapidly-increasing number of the disciples.

The next year he and Elder Hon revisited nearly all the churches for which they had preached the year before; held meetings at several other points; and brought, in all, about five hundred persons to the obedience of the faith.[23]

One of the crucial events in the transition from Brethren to Disciples of Christ was the Edinburg meeting in July, 1828, mentioned by John Wright, which brought together the Blue River Baptist-Brethren group, led by Wright and Hostetler with the New Light followers of Barton W. Stone, who were led at Edinburg by Jesse Hughes. This combination was one of the early events in the development of the group that took more definite form in the 1830s as the Disciples of Christ. From the standpoint of the Brethren, it may be interpreted either as the loss of some fifteen congregations in southern Indiana or as the transferring of such Brethren ideas as believers' baptism to the Disciples of Christ movement.

Alexander Campbell was one of the most prominent leaders of the Disciples of Christ movement as it developed in the 1830s. One of his goals in establishing this group was to unite all Christians in one church. In this context, Campbell is said to have visited the Church of the Brethren in Philadelphia and conferred with one of its leaders, Timothy Banger, about the possibility of the Brethren's joining the Disciples.

About fifty years ago, Alexander Campbell, founder of the sect known as the Disciples, visited Philadelphia, and attempted to induce the Dunker church in that city to enroll themselves among his disciples, and thus form the nucleus of a larger movement. His proposition was made to Timothy Banger, one of the preachers in the church, an avowed and outspoken believer in Universal Restoration. Mr. Banger replied:

"We are both for baptism by immersion, and I do not see any reason why *we* should join *you,* that would not equally require *you* to join *us!*"

Mr. Campbell answered, *"You* celebrate the Lord's Supper twice a year, whereas *we* celebrate it every Lord's day."

"That," replied Mr. Banger, "is only increasing the number of times, but does not touch the principle. What do you say concerning the washing of feet? *We* do *that:* do *you? Besides, we* hold to the restitution of all things: do *you?"*

Negative replies sealed the conclusion: *"Our* testimony is altogether the largest and grandest; and vainly you try to argue us into relinquishment of it."[24]

Philadelphia was not the only place that the Brethren made contact with the Disciples of Christ who were followers of Alexander Campbell. In other parts of Indiana, as indicated in the discussion of that state, R. H. Miller was bringing "Reformers," as they were called, into the Church of the Brethren. In Tennessee, some of the Brethren were leaving the Church of the Brethren to become Disciples or Campbellites, as they were often known. The following letter predicted dire consequences of such action.

Limestone Creek, Washington County, Tenn
August 12, 1838
we receive a Letter from father and Mother this Last week for the first one   he wroate that ware all well and that they Move to Brother Samuel on his place in new house that father Bilt   the Land that father Bought and samuel's Land Joins samuel frankebarger   he still is Lame and has went to the College 5 monts and now has Joind the Cammel Lits and

Dresses altogether in Black ... I suppose the next we will hear that he is a Cammel Lite preacher and old george stover and his wife and young samuel peflys wife they all Joind the Cammel Lits to   I for my part was not so Much surprised when I thought of the Expression that I heard old anne stover make the Last time that I saw her about some of the Breathren   I realy thought if they ware sounded to the Bottom their was something their that was far from Being right according to what they profest at that time   Dear Brother and sister what will be the Consequence when Breathren thus falls off when the scripture Declares unto us that Cursed is he that Lays his hands to the gospel plough and then turns Back for it is impossibel those who ware once enlightened and have tasted of the heavenly gift and ware made pertakers of the holy gost and have tasted the good word of god and the powers of the world to Come if they shall fall away to renew them again unto repentance seeing they crucify to themselves the son of god afresh.

Dear friends Let us try with the help of god and praying to him for assistance try to hold out faithfull unto our Ends for we know not how soon we shall be cald of to stand before the hand of almighty god their to give an account of all the deeds done in the boddy[25]

A major similarity between the Brethren and the Disciples which facilitated the exchange of members which was undoubtedly taking place in some areas was the emphasis on adult baptism by immersion, although the Disciples only immersed once while the Brethren went under three times. This characteristic at least distinguished them from the Methodists and the Presbyterians, both of which baptized infants by sprinkling. For this reason, the Brethren who were well established in much of the north side of the Ohio River before the Disciples were organized were in a position to influence the development of the Disciples Church, as they did in southern Indiana under the leadership in particular of Joseph Hostetler. And of course, some Brethren were attracted by the spirit and enthusiasm of a new movement on the frontier and became Disciples; after all, the Disciples emphasized the unity of all Christians and that goal seemed to be important to a Christian!

It is hardly surprising that the Brethren in these years interacted with a number of other religious groups, both in the old and well-established settlements like Pennsylvania, where the Brethren in Christ were getting started, and in the newer, frontier settlements like the Ohio River Valley, where the Universalists and the Disciples were establishing churches. Also, it should be understood that these three groups were not the only churches with which the Brethren had close contact. The Baptists, especially the group called the Separate Baptists, evidently had a number of close con-

tacts with the Brethren in North Carolina and in Kentucky, especially. The relation between the Brethren and the Separate Baptists merits further study. The Methodists, too, were expanding rapidly, becoming ubiquitous, and the Brethren rubbed shoulders with them at many places. What perhaps seems remarkable is that a small religious group like the Brethren came through this period in good condition without being swallowed by some larger church.

III. ORDINANCES AND BELIEFS

INTRODUCTION

During the years from 1785 to 1865 the Brethren were emphasizing their distinctive beliefs, such as the two sacraments, or ordinances as they usually called them, of baptism and communion. The way in which Brethren performed these ordinances made them distinctive, rather than their belief that they ought to be practiced. The Brethren were forced to debate other Protestant churches who observed these ordinances in other ways and who defended their contrasting views. During much of this period Brethren were engaged in a written debate with Mennonites, who resembled the Brethren in many ways, including their common use of the German language; also, they had settled in many of the same areas, especially in Pennsylvania and in Virginia. Toward the end of the period Brethren became more active in spoken debates in public, which often drew large crowds of people and which were sometimes later published to appeal to an even larger audience.

To say that Brethren were primarily interested in defending their distinctive ordinances implies correctly that they were not very much interested in the orthodox theological positions, such as Arminianism and Calvinism, which were of the utmost importance to some churches, including the Presbyterians. Consequently, it is difficult to categorize the Brethren theologically. They probably tended to be more Arminian than Calvinistic.

The most complete theological work written and published by a Brethren during these years was Peter Nead's "Primitive Christianity" which appeared in 1834; it was expanded with additional material and republished in 1850 as "Theological Writings on Various Subjects." Nead had been born in 1796 in a Lutheran home in Hagerstown, Maryland. However, the religion of his parents did not seem to satisfy the young man and he turned to the Methodist Church. With some education and some speaking ability, he soon became a class leader with the privilege of preaching wherever he was invited. Since his family had moved to the Winchester, Virginia, area, he traveled extensively in the mountain valleys of Virginia, including parts of present-day West Virginia. During his travels, he met the Brethren and evidently was favorably impressed. He was keeping a diary at this time, a part of which is extant. Selections are included in this chapter.

[July, 1823] . . . I scarcely know which way to go. . . . My Friend Price advises me to take a trip through Ham[p]shire and call and see Brother Arnold, and I appear to give my consent to go if the Lord will; . . .

July 28th. Passed through Romney and about 3 o'clock p m arrived at the home of Daniel Arnold who received me into his house very friendly. i made knowen my business to him immediately. i told him i wanted to conform to the ordinances of Christ church i therefore wanted to be baptised. he spoke a great deal on the subject and told me on tomorrow i must call and see his brother, we both held evening worship —

July 29th. Accordingly i went to see Saml Arnold. he, as well as his Brother appears to be a true Servant of Christ. i made knowen my mind to him. After some conversation he told me that there would be no meeting in the neighborhood for some time. Therefore i would have to wate, that it was contrary to there order to baptise any person, until they had the council of the church. i told him i could not conveniently Tarry, as i thought it rong to be burdensome to the Brethren. He told me, that it would not be any but i thought it would not answer. i told him that it was impressed upon my mind that i ought to labour in the vinyard of the Lord, and that when i left home i promised to obey the call. he allowed i ought to have the council of the church, he therefore gave the following advice, and told me as i intended to travel through Rockingham to stop in the neighborhood of Daniel Garver, as there was a large church in that place; and that if i would stop there that he would give me a letter to Garver that he might try to get me a school in that place where i would have an opportunity of being better acquainted with the Brethren and they of me, and if the Lord had designed me to preach that I certainly could then labour with more success. I thanked him for his friendly advice but did not know whether i could comply with the same or not but that i would try and be obedient. O lord have mercy upon me and reveal thyself unto me, more fully. . . .

October 19th   Attended a meeting held by the Dunkerds, at night the washing of feet and the Lords supper was celebrated and to my great satisfaction it was performed according to the Scriptures. i was invited by the Brethren to speak to the people i suppose it was then pass 12 oclock at night and the people appeared to be very uneasy. i did not think proper to detain them—

October 20th. Past about 6 miles from Amsterdam and 4 from Fincastel. Preached at the Mill creek meeting house from Revelations XVIII. chapter 4 verse. and at this meeting got acquainted with Abraham Crumbaker a Preacher of the Dunkerd Persuation. and invited home by John Amen were i was treated very affectionately....

April 13th 1824 on this Day I have entered into a covenant with my God, Wherein I do promise that I will endeavor by His assistance to be more faithful to Him, and Take up my Dayly cross of denying myself all ungodliness and worldly lust, liveing a Sober and godly life, and o may the Lord of Infinite mercy Print this covenant on my heart, that I may not forget my vows but keep them in rememberance performing them, to the Glory and honor of His name to whom they are made — ...

Monday June 14th this Being the Day on which I was Baptised in the Potomac River by Elder Daniel Arnold, and at night the washing of each others feet, the Lords Supper and the communion was observed by the Brethren —[1]

The Belief in Jesus Christ

In addition to his baptism as a Brethren in June 1824, a significant event in Nead's life was his marriage on December 20, 1825, to Elizabeth Yount, a Brethren girl from the Linville Creek congregation, near Broadway, Virginia. The young couple settled down for the next fifteen years on her parents' farm, although Nead evidently made his living as a tanner and a schoolteacher. More important, he was called to the ministry by the Brethren in 1827 and soon became known as "the English preacher," because of his ability to preach in the English language at a time when the Brethren were making a gradual transition from German to English. Most important, he had the ability and the time to put many of his ideas into writing, and the result was the publication in 1834 of "Primitive Christianity," the first book written in English by a Brethren minister. In this book, he came as close as any Brethren writer of this period to a discussion of the major aspects of the Christian theology, such as the doctrine of Jesus Christ.

THE CONCEPTION, BIRTH, LIFE, DEATH, RESURREC-
TION, AND ASCENSION OF JESUS CHRIST.

The Evangelist St. Luke, is very particular in giving us a history of the conception and birth of Emanuel, God with us. He tells us, that the angel Gabriel was commissioned by the Almighty, to inform the Virgin Mary that she would be the Mother of our Lord Jesus Christ. The dazzling appearance of the angel, as well as the message he delivered, was so strange and came so unexpectedly, that the mind of this holy woman became troubled, upon which the angel charged her not to fear. Fear not, Mary, for behold thou shalt conceive in thy womb, and bring forth a son, and shall call his name Jesus; he shall be great, and shall be called the son of the highest, and the Lord God shall give unto him the throne of his father David, and he shall reign over the house of Jacob forever, and of his kingdom there shall be no end. Mary took courage and asked the angel for more information concerning this strange and wonderful news. Then said Mary unto the angel; "How shall this be, seeing I know not a man. And the angel answered and said unto her; The Holy Ghost shall come upon thee, and the power of the Highest shall overshadow thee; therefore, that holy thing which shall be born of thee, shall be called the Son of God." Mary believed in the word delivered by the angel, or she would not have conceived, and said, "Behold the handmaid of the Lord—be it unto me according unto thy word." (See Luke i. 26-39.)

As respects the body of Jesus Christ, it is generally acknowledged that he had a human body, a body like unto the children of men; but whether he derived his body, that is, took flesh and blood, from the Virgin Mary is a disputed point by some. However, it is plainly revealed, that the body of Christ was conceived in the womb of the Virgin Mary, Luke i. 31; and that he took flesh and blood, Heb. ii. 14. The apostle does not say whether he did, or did not derive his body from Mary. It may be, that the apostle was not so inquisitive as we are, to pry into such matters, the knowledge of which would have no influence upon our soul's salvation; and, lastly, that he proceeded from the Virgin Mary; "Therefore, also, that holy thing which shall be born of thee shall be called the Son of God." Luke i. 35. Let this knowledge suffice for us, as it respects from whence Christ derived his body. When the full time was come that the Messiah should make his appearance in the world, Mary and Joseph were in Bethlehem, in compliance with a decree which had been ordered by Caesar Augustus. Bethlehem, being crowded with people, it was with difficulty that lodging could be procured. Joseph and Mary being poor, had to take up their abode in a stable, and that was the place where our King Emanuel first made his appearance. O, how different from the proceedings of the human family! Men of honor and opulence take great pains in rendering their natural situation as comfortable as possible. But not so with the Son of God—he was pleased to be born of a poor, unnoticed virgin; in a manger his infant body is seen; he denies himself of the many comforts of life, or those temporal blessings which nature may crave; they have not the means to obtain them; therefore, their situation is not wondered at. But when we see a wealthy man denying himself of the blessings which make nature comfortable, we say the man must be beside himself, or he is a very singular character. Now it was so with Jesus Christ. He could have had all that human nature could crave or enjoy;—yes, he could have come with all that pomp and splendor which is so much admired by the great and honorable of this world. But this would have been contrary to his holy nature, and would not have answered the purpose for which he came into the world. The apostle tells us that "He was rich, but for our sakes he became poor; that we through his poverty might become rich." 2 Cor. viii. 9. Here we learn why it was that Jesus Christ assumed the character of a poor man—that we, through his poverty, might be made rich. Yes, the human family had fallen to so great a depth, that, in order to their recovery, required all that humiliation, life, and death of the immaculate Lamb of God. It was a high and proud mind that plunged Adam, and his posterity, into the horrible pit of human woe;—it is a meek and low mind that saves man from the pit of destruction. Marvel not at this, ye rich and lofty sons of the earth. Behold the King of Kings and Lord of Glory lying in a manger, wrapt in swaddling bands! Behold his mother at that critical time! We do not read that she was favored with that attendance so common upon such occasions. Again, behold Joseph, the husband of Mary, a poor but honest man, a carpenter by profession, and be wise and learn a lesson—for here it is that you have a complete pattern of self-denial and humiliation—here it is that a cloud covers human glory.

"Go worship at Emanuel's feet,
See in his face what wonders meet;
Earth is too narrow to express
His worth, his glory, or his grace."

Christ was circumcised according to the law, Luke ii. 21. It became him to fulfil the law in every point. At the age of twelve, he was in the temple, in the midst of the Doctors, both hearing them and asking them questions. He was subject to his parents, and no doubt but that he wrought with Joseph at his occupation—and when the time had arrived, that Christ should enter upon his ministry, he left his place of nativity, and came unto Jordan where John was baptizing, to be baptized of John, his forerunner. John at first refused to comply with his request; he considered himself too unworthy to stoop down and unloose his shoe latchets. But when Christ told John that it becometh us to fulfill all righteousness, he consented, and after his baptism, he was led up of the Spirit into the wilderness, to be tempted of the devil; and when he had fasted forty days and forty nights, he became an hungered—and then it was a combat took place between Jesus Christ and the devil that great enemy of both God and man. The devil presents three temptations to the mind of Jesus, which are the chief of all temptations. You can read them at your leisure, in the fourth chapter of Matthew. Had the devil succeeded in overcoming Jesus, then the human family could never have been saved. But glory, praise, and honor, be ascribed to his most holy name, for the victory he obtained over this arch enemy! He put him to flight—he could not stand before him. Yea, it was made manifest, that the power which was in him, was far superior—that he was a more powerful being than the devil—the enemy could but tempt him, and that was all he could do. This was the greatest engagement that ever took place in the world; and when the devil left Jesus, then it was that he came down from the mountain, and selected twelve men to be his witnesses. He called them apostles; they accompanied him while he prosecuted his mission; they saw the miracles he performed; they heard the doctrine he taught—thus they were in every respect qualified to bear testimony to his Messiahship. And when he had given a revelation of his Father's will, then he gave himself into the hands of sinners, that they might put him to death. They did so; and when he had suffered that punishment which was due to him, he proclaimed, It is finished—my suffering time is ended—man's redemption is accomplished. He bowed his head and gave up the ghost. His body was taken down from the cross, embalmed, and laid in a new sepulchre—the third day he rises from the dead—forty days after his resurrection, he ascended into heaven—he took his seat at the right hand of the Majesty on high—and now, he ever lives, to make intercession for the children of men.

Dear reader the life of Jesus Christ, our dear Redeemer, was spent in obedience to the will of his Father. Hear his own words upon this matter: "For I came down from heaven not to do my own will, but the will of him who sent me." John, vi. 38. "Jesus saith unto them, My meat is to do the will of Him that sent me, and to finish His work." John iv. 34. And the apostle tells us, that he was obedient unto death, even the death of the cross. "And being found in fashion as a man, he humbled himself and became obedient unto death, even the death of the cross." Phil. ii. 9. It was through the disobedience of Adam that the fall was occasioned; and it is through the obedience of the second Adam, our Lord Jesus Christ, the children of men can be saved, and restored to the favor and friendship of

God. See him travelling from place to place, from city to city, doing good to the souls and bodies of the children of men! and, notwithstanding he was the Messiah, he never boasted, or endeavored thereby to bring himself into notice; that is, he did not proclaim aloud in every place he went, that he was the Messiah, the Son of the Highest, though he never denied the fact, but when interrogated told the people plainly that he was the Messiah—but would rather have his works to testify of him. The prophet Isaiah prophesied of the spirit which dwelt in the Lord Jesus Christ, which prophecy was quoted by Christ himself; "Behold my servant, whom I have chosen! I will put my Spirit upon him, and he will shew judgment to the Gentiles. He shall not strive, nor cry; neither shall any man hear his voice in the streets. A bruised reed shall he not break, and smoking flax shall he not quench, till he send forth judgment unto victory. And in his name shall the Gentiles trust." Matthew xii. 18, 21.

Jesus Christ is our exampler, and it becometh us to pattern after him—to walk in his footsteps; if so, we shall be careful, and never boast of our state, and not make a public song of our conversion, by telling every person we meet with, that we are the salt of the earth, the children of God. If we have the spirit of Christ, we shall be meek and lowly of heart; and then it is, that our walk and conduct will testify that we are the children of God. But should we at any time be interrogated concerning the hope which is in us, we are then at liberty to give an answer in meekness—as the apostle tells us. "But sanctify the Lord in your hearts, and be ready always to give an answer to every man that asketh you, a reason of the hope that is in you, with meekness and fear." I Peter, iii. 15. Dear reader let us be careful, and guard against every spirit which differs from the spirit of our Lord Jesus Christ; for Christ is the way, the truth, and the life.[2]

THE BELIEF IN MAN

An important aspect of Peter Nead's total understanding of Christian theology was the nature of man. In three chapters he described the condition of human beings and the possibilities available to them through the Christian religion.

THE FALL OF MAN.

That Man is a fallen and depraved creature, cannot be disputed by any, who have a knowledge of his primeval and present state. Solomon, the wise man, declares that God "made man upright; but they have sought out many inventions." Eccl. vii. 29. This solemn truth is plainly delineated in

Peter Nead

the book of God. Moses, that divinely inspired man, gives us not only a history of man's creation but also of his fall. He tells us that "God created man in His own image, in the image of God created He him, male and female created He them." Gen. i. 27. The image of God, understand, righteousness and true holiness: as St. Paul says, "And that ye put on the new man, which after God (or after the image of God,) is created in righteousness, and true holiness." Eph. iv. 24. And in the ii ch. 7 v., he rehearses the matter and informs us of what his body was created, and how he became a living soul. "And the Lord God formed man of the dust of the ground, and breathed into his nostrils the breath of life, and man became a living soul." This is so plain, it needs no explanation. At this time, man was in a state of innocency, pure, and harmless, resembling his Creator, and for the continuation of man in a state of purity, the Lord God planted a garden eastward in Eden, and there He put the man whom He had formed. It was a delightful garden, stored with every thing calculated to promote his eternal felicity. There stood the fair tree of life, a sacred pledge of immortality! Behold the happy pair! No angry passions disturb their peaceful minds; for their passions and appetites were subject to, and controled by that spirit, which they received in their creation. And being filled with love, and clothed with humility, they could see their Creator, and converse with Him, face to face. Oh! what a union of peace and pleasure existed between the creature and Creator; but lamentable to say—that union and communion only lasted for a short time, owing to the transgression of Adam.

God, for wise purposes, put Adam under restrictions, and thereby gave him to know, that notwithstanding his noble extraction and extensive dominion, he was not as yet at the summit of happiness, but in a progressive state or condition, and that in order to his preservation and advancement in glory and happiness, obedience to his will would be indispensably necessary. The law given to Adam, was a fair trial of his love and obedience. It was said to Adam, "of every tree thou mayest freely eat, but of the tree of the knowledge of good and evil, thou shalt not eat of it for in the day that thou eatest thereof thou shalt surely die." Gen. ii. 16 17. The reasonableness of this law will appear quite obvious when we reflect that Adam was created a moral agent—endowed with understanding and will, and of course free and capable of obeying. Adam being the head and representative of his progeny, or human family, acted not only for himself, but also for his posterity, which according to the will of the Creator should be very numerous, consequently his conduct would determine the future condition of himself and descendants.[3]

THE BELIEF IN BAPTISM

According to Peter Nead, the repentance and faith of man should lead to baptism, which he discussed at considerable length. However, Peter Nead was certainly not the first Brethren writer, even during this period, to discuss the Brethren viewpoint on baptism. For example, Christian Longenecker, a Brethren minister in Pennsylvania, wrote a short book of some seventy-five pages on baptism which was published in 1806, probably at Ephrata. He was responding to the Mennonite position on baptism which had just been explained in 1804 in a book by Christian Burkholder; the Mennonites believed in adult baptism, like the Brethren, but they did not believe that immersion was necessary. Their position was further defended in answer to Longenecker by M. Brenneman, in a book published in Lancaster, Pennsylvania, in 1808.

The next act in the continuing debate between the Mennonites and the Brethren took place in Virginia and began when Peter Burkholder published a book in 1816 in Harrisonburg, defending the Mennonite position on baptism. The Brethren respondent was Peter Bowman, whose answer was published by the same printer the following year, 1817. Bowman's book of less than one hundred pages was evidently widely read, for it was reprinted the next year, 1818, in the original German in Chambersburg, Pennsylvania, and in 1831 it was translated into English and printed in Baltimore. About fifteen percent of the English translation of 1831 is included here.

A TESTIMONY ON BAPTISM, AS PRACTISED BY
THE PRIMITIVE CHRISTIANS, FROM THE TIME OF
THE APOSTLES: AND ON THE LORD'S SUPPER,
ACCORDING TO THE INSTITUTION OF CHRIST AND
HIS APOSTLES, AND ON THE WASHING OF FEET,
WITH REGARD TO THE RIGHT MANNER, IN WHICH
THE SAME OUGHT TO BE PERFORMED, AND ALSO,
ON THE LEPROSY AND THE SPRINKLE-WATER,
AND THE SIGNIFICATION THEREOF.

Written by a Lover of the Divine Truth, and submitted to the
reflection of all those who seek their eternal welfare. "But
sanctify the Lord God in your hearts; and be ready always to
give an answer to every man, that asketh you a reason of the
hope that is in you, with meekness and fear." 1 Pet. 3.15.

PREFACE

The motive for writing this, is, to exhibit, according to the dictates of
truth, the institutions of God, as given to his Church, shewing, how we
ought, in conformity to them, to serve God and obey him, chiefly, as we
have reason to believe, that we have arrived to those afflicting times, described Rev. 3: 10, in which the Spirit speaks thus to the Church of
Philadelphia: "Because thou hast kept the word of my patience, I also will
keep thee from the hour of temptation, which shall come upon all the
world, to try them that dwell upon the earth."-Now it is is to be believed
that this "hour of temptation" means nothing else than the power of
darkness, striving to do away entirely the institutions of God, as given by
him to his Church, sanctified by Christ, and confirmed by his example; and
thus to give free scope to the will and regulations of men; but as this cannot be done all at once, but gradually (in the same manner as the all-wise
God, through his servant John, began by establishing his ordinances into
his Church, in the new Covenant of the Gospel, which the Son of God has
confirmed and to which the Father bore testimony, by a voice from
heaven) the enemy will endeavor, in this "hour of temptation," to do away
those ordinances, and will therefore also begin at the same point, to wit: at
the Baptism of St. John, trying to put the same under the law, and thus to
obscure and invalidate it; and because Christ has suffered himself to be
baptized by John, to deem it imperfect, as a work of the Law, and finally,
like all the Ordinances of God, to deem it imperfect, and therefore un-

necessary, and at last to do it away entirely, under the pretext of worshipping Christ in the Spirit only. Now the Spirit of God has given the promise to the Philadelphia Church, in reward of its faithfulness. "Behold I have set before thee an open door, and no man can shut it; for thou hast a little strength, and has kept my word and hast not denied my name." from which may be inferred, that this open door was an emblem of the door of liberty, there having been at that time, in the five primitive churches, a great deal of compulsion and persecution in matters of conscience; but now by the providence and dispensation of God, liberty of conscience has been established, and thus this noble door of conscience has been erected, and has, thanks be to God remained open, even unto the present time, which may be considered as the last time of the Church, as the Church of the Laodiceans, when the Lord complains thus: "I would thou wert cold or hot. So then, because thou art lukewarm, and neither cold nor hot, I will spew thee out of my mouth: Because thou sayest I am rich and increased with goods, and have need of nothing, and knowest not that thou art wretched, and miserable, and poor, and blind, and naked: I counsel thee to buy of me gold, tried in the fire, that thou mayest be rich, and white raiment that thou mayest be clothed, and that the shame of thy nakedness do not appear; and anoint thine eyes with eye salve, that thou mayest see." Now it is thought that in this time of liberty, slothfulness and security are increasing, and "because iniquity abounds, love has waxed cold"-and yet many pretend to say, "I am rich and increased with goods," and don't know that they are wretched, and miserable, blind and naked. Now here the gold is wanting, that is to say, the true belief in God, and in his holy word, and in his ordinances; as also the white garments, to wit: the garment of innocence, which consists in withdrawing one's self from all evil things, and from all iniquity, and in walking unspotted through this world. On the contrary, the love of this world, the pride and haughtiness and the spirit of this world, governs all: all flesh has corrupted its ways, and nearly all are taken with the fashion, and manners of the world. At this period, it is to be feared, that even anointed eyes, may not perceive the danger in its whole extent, the following of Christ may be lukewarm, and that strong delusions will be sent, because the love of truth is not adopted, and thus will christianism be finally spewn out.

As every sect worships according to its own pleasure, it may be presumed, that the temptation, before spoken of has made it appearance, and that the door is opened to antichrist, that he may go into the temple of God, and seating himself on the throne, exalt himself above all that is called God, or that is worshipped—2 Thes. 2. Dan. 11. 36. From this it may be inferred, that the door of liberty will be shut again, and the time of the great tribulation will begin, of which Christ prophesied, saying, that "except those days should be shortened, there should no flesh be saved." Now the intention of this humble composition is, to make a small opposition against the impending great calamity, which is fast approaching, and to offer a warning to the consideration of all those who fear God.

Written the 27th May, A.D. 1817.

A TESTIMONY, &c.

I have been much troubled in my mind, since having been at a certain meeting, on account of several matters set forth there, which has induced me to write my opinion and knowledge of the same. The first subject introduced there was concerning Baptism. . . .

Now we shall mention something on Baptism. When a man becomes enlightened, through the light of the mercy of God, so that he becomes convinced of his sins and in particularly becomes thoroughly convinced of his sinful nature, how he has hitherto been a slave to sin, and loved the follies and the vanity of the world, and therefore, "brought forth fruit unto death." And if, moreover, the guilt of sins is revealed unto him, by the law of God in the conscience, that, as the Apostle says, "sin, by the commandment, might become exceedingly sinful." If such a man perceives his condition, a change will be wrought in his soul, which will make him form a resolution not to sin any more, because he is convinced that sin will plunge him into eternal death and damnation; he is also convinced that he must obtain grace and forgiveness of his sins from God, that otherwise he cannot be saved, nor make his appearance before God. Now his soul has become an afflicted soul and will also be a seeking soul, seeking in full earnest after his salvation: such a soul will also search the scriptures, and the promises of God, and will then find in the saving gospel, how, according to the promise of God, the Heavenly Father, has sent his beloved son into the world, to save sinners, and to seek what is lost; who, through the sacrifice of his life and blood on the cross, has found an eternal propitiation for our sins, in whom mercy and forgiveness of sins are promised unto us. He is the true high priest ordained by God, and his hands is filled to reconcile us, and pronounce us clean from our sins. . . .

And by shedding his innocent blood for us, he has procured for us the propitiation and remission of sins, and has promised unto us the gift of the Holy Ghost. Herewith agrees also what the Apostle Peter said, on the day of Pentecost, when by the preaching of Peter, they were pricked in their hearts, and being convicted of their sins, cried "Men and brethren, what shall we do?" "Peter said unto them, Repent, and be baptized every one of you, in the name of Jesus Christ, for the remission of sins, and ye shall receive the gift of the Holy Ghost. For the promise is unto you, and to your children, and to all that are afar off, even, as many as the Lord our God shall call." Now here not only remission of sins is promised by Baptism but also the gift of the Holy Ghost. For the same reason, Jesus Christ, the heavenly High Priest, also sent to the running water, and caused himself to be baptized by his servant John in the Jordan, by which he has consecrated and confirmed this bath, and God has bore testimony thereto, for the Holy Ghost descended upon him, and a voice came from heaven, saying "Thou art my beloved Son, in whom I am well pleased." . . .

Very lately . . . some friend . . . has written and caused to be printed, and to be published to this world, a treatise, setting forth that the baptism by immersion, is no command of the Lord. Now it is to be wondered at in our friend, (his own practise of baptising being founded only upon his own judgment) that he should take the liberty to accuse others, and that he should set forth as though the Baptists (Untertaeufer) were a sort of people who made a command for themselves to baptize by immersion, and also, that neither Christ nor his apostles had set an example before us, much less had given us a command to do so. Now, it might be thought, that friend ought to know better, for it appears that he formerly entertained some doubts himself, whether the baptism by pouring, was founded in the word of God. Now I say that the Baptists (Untertaeufer) have no privilege to make any command, and nobody else, no human creature whatever has any right to alter the least thing of that which God has commanded and ordained; but in this case there is no need for making a command, because the great king Jesus Christ, the son of God, has made it himself, by causing himself to be baptized by John in the Jordan, and has sanctified this bath and this will ever remain so; therefore we are altogether willing to subject ourselves, and to be obedient therein to this king and we will not take any thing off, nor add any thing to it. I think, for my part, it would be good if that friend was of the same mind, and would relinquish all of his own, for all we have of our own will be of no value before God. Moreover we find it clearly written in the sacred scripture, Mat. chap. 3. how Christ caused himself to be baptized by his servant John, and when he was baptized, went up straightway out of the water; now it is plain, that if any person comes up out of the water, he must before have went down and been immersed in the water, before he can go up out of the water, and when Christ went up, the Holy Ghost lighted upon him, and a voice was heard from Heaven, saying: "This is my beloved Son, in whom I am well pleased." Now a body should think that this would be a sufficient testimony, how baptism ought to be performed to all those who bear a true love to their Redeemer. But we have another testimony, Acts 8. 33. "And he commanded the chariot to stand still; and they went down both into the water, both Philip and the eunuch; and he baptized him. And when they were come up out of the water, the spirit of the Lord caught away Philip, that the eunuch saw him no more, and he went on his way rejoicing."

This shews in what manner the apostles baptized, and how they followed the footsteps of their master. But the said friend may say, this is no certain proof that they baptized by immersion; my reply is: if the word baptism was rightly understood, or if people were willing to understand it, the matter would explain itself, for the meaning of baptism is immersion, or diving into water, as Jeremiah Felbinger has, in his New Testament, translated the word baptism "immersion," and in the original language it means nothing else. But this may perhaps appear contemptible to said friend, because the translation of J. Felbinger is considered invalid by his party, for I have overheard a certain friend myself, saying, that it was only a marginal note. In such a manner they would wish to reject it and undertake to do more than ever any learned man has undertaken, or any government has been able to do, for, by the Providence of God, it was, at the time of the Reformation, when the sacred scriptures were translated into all languages, strongly prohibited by the government, even under penalty of death, not to interpolate any thing, in any translation of the holy scripture, wherefore all translations were closely examined by persons who understood the original languages, in order that no human wisdom should be intermingled with the sacred scriptures, and thus the holy scripture, under the protection of the Most High, has been preserved unadulterated unto our time. It is evident therefore, that, if the translation of Jeremiah Felbinger had been incorrect, it would have been rejected, but it has been pronounced correct, and remained so unto our time. But it is not this translation only, which explains the word baptism by "immersion," but John H. Reitz in his Testament explains the word baptism by immersion, and the Berleburg translation, which takes a great deal of pains to explain the holy scripture, runs thus: "By baptism there ought never to be understood any thing else than immersion," and Froschauer says, Act 10. "Can any man forbid water, that these should not be baptized in water, who have received the Holy Ghost?" And Martin Luther also, who, as is well known, was a translator of the holy scriptures, gives us a fine explanation of the word baptism, saying, first, baptism is called in Greek, baptismas; in Latin, mersio, meaning any thing that is altogether immersed into water, (see history of baptism, page 924) in such a manner that the water joins over it. And also the pious and serious Menno Simon says in his book, written in the low Dutch tongue, page 767, "For though we may by night and by day seek with ever so much earnest, we shall not find more than one baptism in water, which is pleasing to God, expressed and contained in the word of God, to wit: the baptism in faith, commanded by Christ Jesus, preached and practised by his holy apostles, being practised and understood as a taking away and absolution from sin." From this it appears plainly, how far those authors agreed with one another on this head, to wit: that the word "baptism" means immersion.

It might be thought that this testimony would be sufficient to take away every doubt, and that an upright soul that seeks its salvation, can find a firm and sure foundation, and can also plainly perceive, provided it don't shut its eyes upon it, that immersion is the true baptism commanded by God, and established in his church. To this may be added the writings of the apostles, for instance, St. Paul to the Romans, says chap 6. 3. "Know ye not that so many of us as were baptized into Jesus Christ, were baptized into his death; therefore we are buried with him by baptism into death, that like as Christ was raised up from the dead by the glory of the father; even so we also should walk in newness of life." Here the apostle writes about being buried and being raised up in baptism, which our friend however takes and wants to have understood, in a spiritual sense only; but it ought to be taken in an external as well as a spiritual sense. The external part—the being baptized and immersed into water, being an emblem of an external burying, in order to show that our old man, with his sinful works, must absolutely be buried; we rise out of the water, to show that we now must rise up into a new life, and walk therein. . . .

Our friend has also referred to the holy martyrs who were not baptized by water, and yet had remained constant. As to this I say we shall not attempt to deprive even the martyrs of early times, of any of the credit due to them. I believe with all my heart, that for their true love of their Redeemer, and for their leaving all for his sake, and sacrificing their lives for him, they have been magnificently rewarded, and have obtained the crown of life. But I have never found that the martyrs of early times opposed the baptism by immersion, on the contrary they have used it in their defence, and for their protection, and if said friend had acted the same way, I should have never thought about writing against him. The martyrs never also placed baptism under the law but ranked it always foremost in proving their baptism, nor did they ever place baptism among the dead works, as some person wrote and caused to be printed, as though Paul had counted baptism among the dead works. This is certainly a great misconception, for if baptism be a dead work, faith is a dead work also, for they are both connected together, instead of which Paul says Heb. 11. 6. "But without faith it is impossible to please God: for he that cometh to God must believe that he is, and that he is a rewarder of them that diligently seek him." . . .

Said friend treats also on the many different ways of baptizing. Some, he says, baptize this way, others another; some immerse three times into water and others only once backwards, some pour water on the person to be baptized, and others again baptize babes; and are thus divided in their opinions about the right way of baptizing. In answer to this I say, that that is the right baptism only, which is performed according to the pattern of Christ, and his doctrine, and according to the manner in which the primitive Christians did baptize; that is to say: in running waters and wells, renouncing the fiend and all iniquity, and being immersed three times into water.

It is probable that because the first Christians have described their baptism so clearly and minutely they must have celebrated it in full assurance, and that it has remained unchanged from the time of the apostles. I shall here introduce a few remarks on the immersing three times in baptizing. We find that when the Lord revealed himself to Moses in the bush, he spake in this manner—"I am the God of Abraham, and the God of Isaac, and the God of Jacob." Now here the Lord revealed himself already among the old people of Israel, under a threefold name, and in the new covenant, as Father, Son, and Holy Ghost; these three are the one and true God, the Holy Trinity.—And because the first man was created after the image of God, man is also a three-fold man, consisting of spirit, soul and body, and yet is but one man. The true conversion of man is also effected in the same manner; first, the Father shows to the sinner his sins, by his holy law, that he may become acquainted with God in his righteousness, and with himself in his sinful state, and may be humbled; then the Father delivers him over to the Son, and reveals him to him as his Redeemer, who has made a perfect offering of propitiation for him, who now reconciles him as his high priest, and remits his sins; and the Holy Ghost sanctifies man in the truth, and makes him subject unto God. For this reason also, honor is due to each name in particular, wherefore the Lord Jesus has also commanded to baptize in the name of these three Most High, in the name of the Father, and of the Son, and of the Holy Ghost, and these three are the one true God. It is, therefore, to be believed in truth, that the immersing three times, in the name of these three Most High, is the only and true baptism, commanded by God, and founded in the word of God, of which Hironimus writes in his history of baptism, page 324, "for we are all baptized in the same manner, in the name of the Father, and of the Son, and of the Holy Ghost, and are immersed three times, to shew that there is but the one secret of the Trinity, &c." . . .

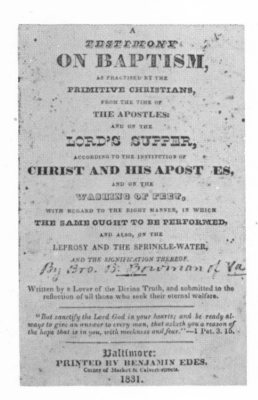

Title page of book
by Benjamin Bowman

And if said friend had not with so much boldness, undertaken to annul the true order of baptism, which no learned man ever undertook nor has been able to do, viz: to reject the baptism by immersion, ... I should have never thought of writing at all. But for the sake of God and his truth and in order to defend the institutions of God, I have considered it my duty and have thought it necessary, to write these few lines, which I commit to the reflection of every one, and recommend them to the examination of all impartial souls, according to the word of the Lord.

There is no doubt but this and that will be said about this treatise. But I say with the Apostle, "With me it is a very small thing that I should be judged of men, or of men's judgment; for truth is always powerful enough to defend itself: and the truth shall obtain the victory and finally conquer all. Glory be to the God of truth in all eternity. Amen."

Written in simplicity by a lover of the divine truth, for the consideration of all those who fear God.[4]

The third act in the written debate between Mennonites and Brethren on the subject of baptism occurred in the 1830s and began with the publication of Nead's "Primitive Christianity" in 1834.

THE LAW OF BAPTISM, AND OF THE SELECTION OF A RELIGIOUS DENOMINATION, PROFESSING TO BE THE CHURCH OF CHRIST.

I have stated, that according to the order of the New Testament, the sinner must observe the doctrine of repentance and faith, and thirdly to be born of the water or to be baptized in order to the promise of the forgiveness of sins—and then it is, that he has the promise of the forgiveness of sins. Repentance towards God and faith in our Lord Jesus Christ—these are the means appointed to constitute us fit subjects for this institution. The two first points have been already proven. I shall now proceed to call the attention of the reader to the subject of Baptism. Upon examining the Gospel, the reader will find that Baptism follows faith and repentance, and that Baptism is binding upon the believer to observe, in order to salvation. We can no where find in the Gospel, that Baptism is enjoined upon an unbeliever, or upon an impenitent character; of course then, it must follow faith and repentance—and as there are all sorts of believers in the world, I shall have to particularize. Among the number are such as do not believe that Baptism is a command of the New Testament—others are to be found who acknowledge that Baptism is a command, but not essential to salvation; and as it respects my faith, I do believe, that baptism is not only a command, but also essential to salvation. Our divine master declared unto Nicodemus, that "Except a man be born of the water and of the Spirit, he cannot enter into the kingdom of God." John, iii. 5. And after his resurrection from the dead, and just before his ascension to heaven, he gave the following charge to his apostles: "Go ye, therefore, and teach all nations, baptizing them in the name of the Father, and of the Son, and of the Holy Ghost." Mat. xxviii. 19; Mark, xvi. 15, 16—"Go ye into all the world and preach the Gospel to every creature. He that believeth not shall be damned." Who that has ever read these verses—who that has ever seriously meditated upon them, can say, in truth, that Baptism is no commandment? If Baptism be no commandment, the apostles misunderstood the Saviour, and of course, were ignorant of their commission—which is too absurd for a disciple of the New Testament to believe. The apostle Peter, at the day of Pentecost, charged those persons to be baptized who inquired the way of salvation—"Men and brethren, what must we do? Then said Peter unto them, repent and be baptized, every one of you, in the name of

Jesus Christ, for the remission of sins, and ye shall receive the gift of the Holy Ghost." Acts, ii. 37, 38.

The above is sufficient to convince the enquirer after the will of God; that Baptism is a commandment, which follows faith and repentance. As you have read, Christ charged his apostles first to preach the Gospel, and thereby teach the nations, and then baptize the believer; and Peter preached that they should repent and be baptized. . . .

I have been at times, very much troubled about some whom I was led to believe, were very sincere in prosecuting their soul's salvation; and after proceeding as far as to Baptism, did not push their inquiries as far as they ought to have done, or if they did, they made a bad choice. Our motives must be pure in selecting and uniting ourselves with any denomination professing to be the church of Christ. It is to be feared that many persons, in uniting themselves to certain denominations professing christianity, do it against their better light and understanding. Some for instance, will unite themselves to a sect in order to please a father or mother, a husband or wife, a son or daughter, a brother or sister, or some great man or persons, for whom they have a great regard, or because they were trained up to such a sect. This is being born of blood, or of the will of man, which will be of no spiritual advantage to them, and for which they will be ranked with that class, which are unworthy of Jesus Christ, and of course, will be disowned by him when he comes to make up his jewels. . . .

But it is a stubborn fact—and what a pity that there are such a diversity of sects!—that persons are to be accommodated just as they desire, or please. If you wish to be a fashionable character, and also bear the name of a christian, you can be accommodated; for there are sects, professing christianity, which admit of, and countenance, all that pomp and grandeur which Lucifer is capable of inventing. . . .

This society believe in anything, and everything, and in nothing at last. By this, I mean that they have no established principles among them; their sole aim is to become numerous. One great reason why many sincere and well disposed persons are led to believe that they must be well founded, is because they appear to be so very zealous for the cause of religion, and devote so much time for praying, singing, preaching, and that for days and weeks in succession. And during their protracted meetings they enlist great numbers in their ranks. . . . Dear reader, reflect well on this subject, it is your privilege and becomes your duty to distinguish between a true and wrong zeal. . . .

It is the duty of the church to attend to the request of the applicant, and as there is an order in the excommunication of disobedient members from the church, so is there also an order in the reception of persons into the church. Therefore the applicant for membership, must be visited and heard on the doctrines of repentance and faith, and if he professes those principles, the church will be counciled on his reception. That this course of procedure with the candidate, is in good keeping with the word of God, is very evident. For example, we have no account in the Testament of the apostles and first preachers of the Gospel baptising persons who made no profession of those principles. When the Eunuch wished to know what would hinder him from being baptised, Philip replied.—"If thou believest with all thine heart, thou mayest;" and if he had not professed to believe that Jesus Christ was the Son of God, Philip would not have baptised him, Acts viii. And concerning the counseling of the church, on the reception of applicants, we find that before the baptism of Cornelius, &c., Peter says: "Can any man forbid water, that these should not be baptised." Acts x, from which we infer that the church has a right to be heard on their reception. Suffice it to say, teaching goes before baptising—therefore the applicant must be instructed, and examined, and the church counseled, in order to his reception.

THE ADMINISTRATORS, FORM, AND MODE OF BAPTISM.

The subject for Baptism has been already described. I shall proceed to call the attention of the reader to the Administrators of this institution: they are doubtless such as are entrusted with the word of the ministry. This authority they derive from Jesus Christ, the great head of the church. It is their duty to publish the glad tidings of the Gospel to a lost and ruined world. The whole theme of their preaching will be, "Jesus Christ and him crucified." i. Cor. ii. 2. Though preachers have a right to preach the Gospel, and to administer the institutions, yet they must bear in mind, that they are amenable to the church for their conduct, and in no case proceed contrary to the counsel of the church. It is their duty, in transacting the affairs of the kingdom of grace to always take counsel of the church, when it can be done. He must not think, because he is a preacher of the word, that he is above every member, and can pursue any course he may see proper. It is certain that every member has an equal voice—that is, as much authority in managing the business of the church, as the preachers have. Whenever preachers are entrusted with all the power, (which is quite contrary to the Gospel,) in managing church business, the church is sure to become corrupted: therefore, let the church keep an eye upon their preachers, and see that they always proceed according to the Gospel of Jesus Christ; and it is the duty of the preachers not "to shun to declare the whole counsel of God." Acts xx. 27. That it is the duty of the preachers to administer Baptism, see Mat. xxviii. 19; though it is certain, in cases of great necessity, that helpers or private members, have administered this institution.

Illustration of baptism
from Peter Nead's
Theological Works

Dear reader, after pointing out to you the Administrators of this institution, I shall now treat, in a few words, upon that form which is to be used in the administration of this ordinance. It is certain that there is but one evangelical form to be observed in the administration of this institution, and that we have upon record in the xxviii. chapter of Matthew, 19 verse: "Baptizing them in the name of the Father, and of the Son, and of the Holy Ghost." I cannot perceive from reading the New Testament, that we have any authority to alter or change this form. It is certain that we have no more authority to alter or change this form, than we have to change the mode. . . .

That this is the primitive mode of this sacred institution, is very evident—which I shall now proceed to make appear; and as it is a disputed point, I shall be the more particular. In the first place, I purpose to prove, that when the first christians administered this ordinance, that they always did it in the water. I shall commence with the baptism of Jesus Christ, and shall cite the believer to what Matthew and Mark recorded concerning this matter. Matthew, iii. 13, 17. . . . And in Mark, i. 9, 10, 11. . . .

Here we have a full account of the baptism of our adoreable Redeemer. Yes, here the Evangelist gives us plainly to understand, that it was in, not at Jordan that John baptized Jesus; for they tell us, when he was baptized, he came straightway up out of the water, which could not possibly be, if he had not been in the water. Christ, being the head of the church, and the author of baptism should be looked upon and obeyed in preference to any man. Indeed, he gave us, not only the law of Baptism, but also the example. . . .

There are persons who acknowledge that it is very plain, that John, the Baptist, and others, did administer this ordinance in the water, and yet contend for pouring and sprinkling, from the supposition that it cannot be proven in what way John and the first christians proceeded with the candidate when in the water. I shall now undertake to prove, not only from what learned men have said on this subject, but also from the Testament itself, that the first christians did administer this institution by immersing the believer in the water. That immersion, or an overwhelming in the water, is the ancient mode of Baptism, is very obvious from the meaning of the word itself. I shall, therefore, call the attention of the reader to the signification of the word, as given by learned men—and shall commence with Martin Luther:

He writes thus—"Baptism is a Greek word, and may be translated a dipping—when we dip something in the water, that it may be covered with water; and though it be for the most part almost altogether abolished, for neither do they dip the children wholly, but sprinkle them only with a little water—they ought, nevertheless, to be wholly dipped, and presently drawn out again—for that the etymology of the word seems to require. I would have those that are to be baptized, to be wholly dipped into the water, as the word imports, and the mystery doth signify." Tome i. fol. 19. . . .

I might multiply quotations of the above nature, but the above with the circumstances attending the administration of the institution, as already given, are sufficient. So that we may take it for granted, that the proper signification of the word Baptism is immersion. . . .

That immersion is the scriptural mode of Baptism is very evident from those representations and figures which we have upon record in the New Testament. For example—the apostle Paul, in his epistle to the Romans, vi. 3, 4, 5. . . . In these verses, the apostle compares Baptism to a burial; and well he may do so, because there is a striking analogy between the burial of a corpse in the earth, and a believer in the water; for they are both covered, or immersed—one in the earth, and the other in water. If you pour a few handsful of earth upon a corpse, you cannot say that the corpse is buried—neither can you say that a believer is buried in Baptism, when only a few handsful of water are either poured or sprinkled upon him. . . .

There are great numbers who agree with me, and contend warmly for the mode of immersion, and yet do not administer the institution by a trine immersion, which is as obvious as that Baptism signifies immersion. In the first place, I contend, from the apostolic commission, baptizing them in the name of the Father, and of the Son and of the Holy Ghost, that if this institution be properly administered, the believer must be plunged three times in the water, in the name of the Father, and of the Son, and of the Holy Ghost. I ask the question, is there not a material difference between baptizing in the name and in the names of the Father, and of the Son, and of the Holy Ghost? I answer, there is a very great difference. To baptize in the name of the Father Son and Holy Ghost implies but one immersion—whereas, to baptize in the name of the Father, and of the Son, and of the Holy Ghost, implies a trine immersion. Notwithstanding this explanation some still contend there is no difference. They tell us, in immersing the believer, they pronounce the three names of the Most High, and that is all that is necessary.—Now, this would do very well, if Christ or the Apostles had said so. But Christ tells us to baptize in the name, and this can only be done by immersing the believer in each of those three high names.

That the Ancient Fathers understood by the charge, or commission, which Christ gave to his apostles, a trine immersion, is very evident from what they have written upon the subject. And those ancient Fathers whom I shall quote, shall be such as are held in high repute by those who administer Baptism by immersion. . . .

And again—I believe it ought to be done face forwards, and not backwards. We can read no where in the Bible, or Testament, of any of the institutions or appointments of God being observed by presenting themselves before God upon their backs. Nay, in all those various examples for the worshipping of the true God, in the Holy Scriptures, not one is to be found in which the posture of falling upon the back was observed. The attentive reader, by examining the scriptures, will find, that the posture of kneeling and falling upon the face, was observed by the old Fathers, Jesus Christ, and the apostles, in divine worship: and as we have no command, nor example, for the posture of falling upon the back, therefore I consider it not a divine posture;—and as Baptism is a great institution in which the attention of the whole Godhead is attracted by the believer, therefore, kneeling, and falling upon the face will be observed in the administration of this sacred ordinance.[5]

Within three years, in 1837, the Mennonites had their reply ready for circulation. It was a long book of some four hundred and sixty pages, twice as long as Nead's. It was in English, but most of the material had been translated from Mennonite writings in German including some of the material of Peter Burkholder. The translator was Joseph Funk, who lived on the western side of Rockingham County, Virginia, who also wrote the introduction.

The final round in this debate on baptism began in 1851 when Joseph Funk translated and published a book on baptism written by his grandfather, Henry Funk, more than a century before. Since the book was circulated in considerable quantities among the Brethren and others in Virginia, it was necessary for Brethren to counteract the impact of this Mennonite volume. Since Peter Bowman was dead and Peter Nead had moved to Ohio, the Brethren turned to John Kline. Unfortunately, Kline's native language was German, and his knowledge of English grammar was very limited. However, he put the ideas together, and Henry Kurtz, the editor of the "Gospel Visiter" in Ohio, edited and published the material, which appeared in 1856.

The writer of this little defence being impressed with the necessity of answering some, as he conceives, of the erroneous views exhibited in the little work, which he is reviewing, has done so, not from love of controversy, but simply from a sincere love of truth and of mankind. He believes, as every truth received in the love of truth is accompanied by a proper reward, so error, received and adopted instead of truth, will be followed by an adequate punishment, and hence he feels, if any seem to swerve too far from the path of truth, to call aloud and to bid them to pause and reflect.

There are thousands of simple, innocent and well-meaning people, who are either not careful or not capable enough to discern and distinguish pure Gospel-truth from the errors of popular sects and creeds. These are led astray by not taking heed to the word of God itself, but following such human works and creeds, of which the world is now full. Either designedly or accidentally they get hold of such books, and by reading their specious and false reasonings are led astray from the truth of God, as it is in Christ Jesus.

Such has been the case in a few instances with readers of the little work under consideration, and coming under the notice of the writer of this defence, he, as a minister of the Gospel, has felt it his duty to give the following treatise, in order to expose some of the main errors on the subject of Baptism, and to set forth the truth of Gospel-Baptism to an inquiring and Truth-seeking community.—That God may add his blessing to the humble labors of the writer, that they may accomplish his honest design, which he believes to be in unison with the design of the Lord, to save some from the errors of their ways, is the prayer of

A Lover of the Truth.

Rockingham, Va.
July 1856.

DEFENCE OF BAPTISM

A Review of a little work, entitled "A Mirror of Baptism with the spirit, with water, and with blood. By Henry Funk, minister of the Gospel in the Mennonite Church. First written in German, but now translated into the English, by Joseph Funk, and printed at his office in Mountain-Valley, Rockingham co. VA."

The writer of the above little work, as the whole production shows, had for his object, the establishment of the oft-refuted doctrine of water baptism by sprinkling or pouring, out of the Old and New Testament. And this the author intimates to be the object of his labor.

And in order to do this, he makes many quotations from the Bible, where the words pouring and sprinkling occur, but where these words have no more reference or relation to water baptism in the New Testament, than the offerings of bulls and goats of the Old Testament had. That there were under the Old Testament, divers baptisms (as rendered in the German translation,) or washings as rendered in the English, is not to be denied, for so Paul states in his epistle to the Hebrews, chap. 9: 10. But these, with all the sacrifices of "meats and drinks" and "carnal ordinances, imposed on them until the time of reformation," have entirely come to an end;—for they "could not make him that did the service perfect, as pertaining to the conscience." verse 9 "For if that first covenant had been faultless, then should no place have been sought for the second. For finding fault with them, he saith, Behold, the days come, saith the Lord, when I will make a new covenant with the house of Israel and with the house of Judah. Heb. 8:7,8. In that he saith, A new covenant, he hath made the first old. Now that which decayeth and waxeth old, is ready to vanish away." verse 13. This is the case with all the orders of the old covenant ceremonies of worship of the law of Moses;—they are all done with as having only been a "schoolmaster to bring us to Christ." Gal. 3: 24. "But after that faith is come, we are no longer under a schoolmaster." verse 25. Then we have no more to do with the ordinances of worship under the law of Moses.

But to show the great, and it is to be feared willful, dishonesty of both the writer and translator of the above little work, I will follow the subject of their figures and types which they make of the old covenant, and upon which they lay so much stress, in order to establish baptism by pouring and sprinkling.—They first, as they purport, want to show the baptism of the holy Ghost; secondly, the baptism of water; and thirdly, the baptism of the passion of Jesus. See contents above. Now as to the first of those subjects, I think it would be hard for my friends to show from the Old or New Testament, that the baptism of the Holy Ghost, or Spirit, was even practiced more than once, and that was at the day of Pentecost. Before and after this time, it was ever called the giving or receiving the gift of the Holy Ghost or Spirit, and not a baptism.

And now to show the weakness of the writers' idea, as this is one of their main pillars upon which they build, or base their proof for baptism by pouring or sprinkling, I will lead the mind of the reader to the spot where this baptism of the Holy Ghost was performed. We read Acts 2: 2-4. "And suddenly there came a sound from heaven, as of a rushing mighty wind, and it filled all the house where they were sitting. And there appeared unto them cloven tongues like as of fire, and it sat upon each of them. And they were all filled with the Holy Ghost, and began to speak with other tongues, as the Spirit gave them utterance."

Now the question arises, what part of the transaction shall we call baptism, or the figure of baptism? Is it all we read of in the above quotation? Or is it only the sound of the rushing mighty wind? or as Joel says, "the pouring out," that constitutes baptism? If so, then the writer is at a loss to understand language, or the matter therein comprehended. But we see "it filled all the house where they (the disciples) were sitting." If the matter, breath or essence (if you please so to call it) of the Holy Ghost, was poured out, it of course filled like a divine atmosphere all the house where they were sitting, and of course the disciples were all overwhelmed in it; and thus buried with or in the element or essence of the Holy Ghost at the moment of the baptism. This was soon over, as even water baptism also is.

Then before all the scene of the day or transaction of the operation was over, there was seen another important action described as follows: "And there appeared unto them cloven tongues like as of fire, and it sat upon each of them." It would seem that it must have been like a lambent flame sitting upon each of them. This is the 2d action or scene of the day, "And they were all filled with the Holy Ghost." This is the third action or scene of the day, that came from heaven as the work of God. And now it drives the apostles to action; "and they began to speak with other tongues as the Spirit gave them utterance." This shows that this last action was not shed on their heads, but on their hearts and minds; and even their whole souls were filled with it, which denotes their being filled with power from on high. See Luke 24: 49.

So here we see the element or essence (if we may so call it) of the Holy Ghost poured out (or sent) as Christ says John 14: 26, 15: 26, "and it filled all the house where the disciples were sitting." In this filled house they were all baptized or immersed. And now, being thus immersed, that is all surrounded (not only a little on the head of each of them) they were overwhelmed or buried, and baptized in the substance or effusion of the Holy Ghost, as Dr. Campbell and others have rendered the translation *in*, instead of *with* the Holy Ghost, as will appear hereafter.

But if our friends would rather have king James' translation, from which they so exultingly quote the word with the Holy Ghost, or with water, we can inform them that the preposition "with" can help them no more than to give the distinction or qualification of the particular substance between water and the Holy Ghost. So when John thus speaks "he shall baptize you with the Holy Ghost," he does not mean to say, he will put a little of it on your heads, but the action shows a different thing was done; for all the house was filled where they were sitting, and consequently they were all surrounded with the substance of the Holy Ghost. This makes it no less *with* that substance, than if only a particle of it had been shed on each of their heads. Any man of common sense must be able to see this. And of course, must also be able to see the fallacy of our friends' argument on the word "with," upon which they lay so much stress.

Now we see from what has been said on Acts 2: 2, that the apostles were baptized when they had been overwhelmed with the Holy Ghost. Now, for the second action of this great work, of qualifying the apostles for the great and important mission of going into all the world to preach the gospel to every creature, as it appears from verse 3. "And there appeared unto them cloven tongues like as of fire, and it sat upon each of them." Of course these unlearned fishermen and publicans must have tongues as of fire, so that their enemies cannot withstand them. This second action, although not baptism, yet it is no less necessary and important, as they were to be sent into all the world, and to all nations;—hence the necessity of the cloven tongues as of fire.

And, now to see in this third action, of the great work of qualifying the disciples—that of Verse 4, "And they were all filled with the Holy Ghost," which was equally necessary, that the endowment should not only be to have tongues to speak, but also hearts, minds and souls full of the Holy Ghost. For the Saviour promised that they should be filled with power from on high. Luke 24: 49. As touching the "tongues as of fire," and the filling with the Holy Ghost, much more might be said and quoted, both from the Old and New Testament, but the writer of this thinks it unnecessary, as he thinks that every dear unprejudiced reader, that will read with attention, will at once see the propriety, and the glorious beauty, of the order and harmony of the truth of God, & likewise the consistency of the whole tenor of the scripture and revelation of God. The many quotations which have been made by our friends from the ceremonies of the law of Moses, of the sprinkling of the blood of the sacrifices on the tabernacle, and of the sprinkling of the water of purification on the unclean, to support their doctrine of sprinkling and pouring for baptism, is certainly a failure.

I contend that the sprinkling of the blood, and of the water of purification under the law of Moses, was a figure of the sprinkling of the blood of Christ. "The Holy Ghost thus signifying, that the way into the holiest was not yet made manifest, while as the first tabernacle was yet standing: which was a figure for the time then present, in which were offered both gifts and sacrifices." Heb. 9: 8,9 "By his own blood he entered in once into the holy place, having obtained eternal redemption for us," verse 12. "How much more shall the blood of Christ, who through the eternal Spirit offered himself without spot to God, purge your conscience from dead works to serve the living God," verse 14.

It is strange, passing strange, that our friends who appear to have much esteem for the welfare of the souls of men, and who say so much about the subject of baptism and the true order of God, that they should be so much under the influence of prejudice, as to mistake so far the plain truth of the gospel, as to apply the sprinkling of the blood of the sacrifices and the water of purification to the water baptism of the New Testament! And in quoting from the Old Testament, they quote a part of the process of purification, but the latter part of it, which actually makes a figure of water baptism under the new covenant they omit. I cannot see the reason of this, unless it is because the part omitted did not suit their fancy doctrine.

For example, on page 70 of their work, they speak of the consecrating of Aaron and his sons, to the priesthood; and also of the purification of the unclean; and reference is made to Ex. 24: 4, and Num. 19: 18. In, the latter place, the whole law of purification is set forth. The reader should read the whole chapter. Our friends quote from verse 18, as follows: "And a clean person shall take hyssop, and dip it in the water and sprinkle it upon the tent, and upon all the vessels, and upon the persons that were there." But here they stop, when they should have continued the account of the process, which reads thus: "And a clean person shall sprinkle upon the unclean on the third day, and on the seventh day: and on the seventh day he shall purify himself, and *wash his clothes,* and *bathe himself* in water, and shall be clean at even," verse 19.

They likewise quote from Num. 8: 6,7, but the last part of verse 7, which speaks of washing their clothes, they omit. On page 80, they say; "thus we see in all the types and figures of water baptism, that the baptism with water was administered to believers by pouring or sprinkling the water on the head." This seems to be a remarkable discovery, indeed, for it was not known in the Christian world for some centuries after Christ. The subject of the purification of the law of Moses, shows, first, that it took an offering, and that the offering must be offered outside of the gate. For the preparation of the water of purification, a red heifer was taken without blemish, and its blood had to be sprinkled seven times before the tabernacle of the Lord. The heifer was burned and the ashes preserved, Num. 19.

Then running water was poured on the ashes, and it was for purification. And after it was applied to the unclean person who was to be purified, he then must *wash his clothes* and *bathe his body in water*. Now let us make the application of this type or the figure of the Old Testament and bring it over to the New. Jesus the true prophet and high priest of the new covenant was consecrated at the time of his baptism—when he was baptized by John in Jordan. So he here came to the gate, that is, the entrance of the gospel dispensation and was washed all over, and so entered, first, upon his prophetic office, and here gives a pattern for all those who wish to follow him, Mark 1; Matt. 3; Luke 3; John 1; like the high priest of the old covenant, see Ex. 29, and Num. 8, and 19.

And Jesus, as the great prophet, after he had delivered his father's will to man concerning their salvation, made an offering; and as the red heifer was offered outside of the camp, so Christ also was offered outside of the camp, that is on Calvary upon the cross, and his blood was shed for the remission of sin. His side being opened, blood and water came forth; the water may represent the water of purification of the law, and is laid up without the camp for the comfort of the poor sinner, who, when he is made to know his sins through the drawing of the Father, John 6: 44, and is made to see his unclean state, applies to God by prayer. He comes to some clean person of the church of the Lord, who will point him to the sacrifice made for him by the high priest, Jesus, and apply the blood and water which came from his side. By the sprinkling of this water of purification on the sinner, he is encouraged to a true repentance and faith, he comes to the entrance as a true believer, and is now washed in water by baptism for remission of sin, and thus pronounced clean.

But this washing in baptism cannot be accomplished with a handful, or a few drops of water. This I think will suffice, as touching the types and figures of the Old Testament as being applied to the practices of the New Testament. As touching the passage of the "sprinkling of clean water upon you" as given by the prophet Ezekiel 36: 25, it is very plain, that that is a work which the Lord will do at the time of the conversion of the Jews in the latter days, when they shall again be gathered into their land, and shall learn to know the Lord. That this passage refers to the time we have applied it, the context clearly proves. Let the reader read the chapter, and particularly verse 24, which reads thus: "For I will take you from among the heathen, and gather you into your own land." "Then will I sprinkle clean water upon you, and ye shall be clean: from all your filthiness, and from all your idols, will I cleanse you." Verse 25.

This shows that the prophet speaks of a time which has not been, but which has yet to come, and of a work which the Lord will do in due time,—a work which man cannot perform. But the work that man is to do, Christ speaks of in Matt. 28: 19, 20. "Go ye therefore and teach all nations baptizing them in the name of the Father, and of the Son, and of the Holy Ghost; teaching them to observe all things whatsoever I have commanded you: and lo, I am with you always, even unto the end of the world. Amen." This is an ordinance and a work, which ministers of God are to perform. And what a pitiful thing would it be, if the Lord had sent out ministers and would have given them "authority and to every man his work," and would have given them no true rule or example to go by, to perform that work or duty.

What a pity that professed ministers of the gospel of the lowly Jesus, should bring such a stain upon their Master, by representing him as being so careless, as to have given them no true landmark how to go, or do, as is indicated in the little work above alluded to. What a pity that professed ministers of the gospel, have to run over all the Old Testament, to seek for terms to contradict, or controvert, the plain order of the baptism of Christ, as given in the New Testament, and to change it into pouring or sprinkling, and that for no other purpose, than that to build up some fancy doctrine of their own.

I will now try to give the true order of baptism, as delivered by the Lord God, through the lowly Jesus himself. In order to do this, I will confine myself alone to the New Testament of our Lord Jesus Christ, the pattern and author of the way of salvation. I think we have no need to go to any other place or authority. For the baptism of the New Testament order never existed in the Old Testament time, but had its beginning at the commencement of the new era; and right there I will make my beginning. "The beginning of the gospel of Jesus Christ the Son of God," Mark 1: 1 John did baptize in the wilderness and preach the baptism of repentance for the remission of sin. verse 4. See also Matt. 3, and Luke 3: 3. This was he that prepared the way of the Lord, and made straight his path. I ask the question, how could it have been the "preparing of the way of the Lord and making his path straight," and yet be under the law? This "preparing of the way of the Lord and making straight his path," Mark says is the "beginning of the gospel of Jesus Christ the Son of God," and hence, not under the law of Moses as my friends endeavor to show.

John says, "But he that sent me to baptize with water, the same said unto me, upon whom thou shalt see the Spirit descending and remaining on him, the same is he which baptizeth with the Holy Ghost. And I saw and bare record, that this is the Son of God." John 1: 33, 34. This shows that John had received his mission directly from God; and of course he directed him how he was to perform the work which he was sent to do. For when Jehovah sends his ministers to accomplish a special work, he also gives them directions how to perform it. That John's ministry was not of the law of Moses is plain from what has been said; but I will give some more evidence. The Saviour says "the law and the prophets testified until John: since that time the kingdom of God is preached, by the gospel," Luke 16: 16 (German translation.) So then, as Mark says, "there was the beginning of the gospel of Jesus Christ the Son of God." Mark 1: 1. This is also what Peter says in the house of Cornelius; "that word I say ye know, which was published throughout all Judea, and began from Galilee, after the baptism which John preached," Acts 10: 37.

Paul intimates the same: When John had first preached, before his coming, the baptism of repentance to all the people of Israel. And as John fulfilled his course, he said, Whom think ye that I am? I am not he. But behold, there cometh one after me, whose shoes of his feet I am not worthy to loose. Men and brethren, children of the stock of Abraham, and whosoever among you feareth God, to you is the word of this salvation sent. Acts 13: 24-26. This shows that the apostles Peter and Paul look at John's mission as under the Gospel; for Paul here says "to you is the word of this salvation sent." Although when John preached and baptized, the Gospel was not yet finished, but the foundation of repentance and baptism was laid. And the doctrine of baptism as prepared by the command and direction of God through John, Jesus ratified, as being the order of God, by himself bowing under it, "and being baptized of John in Jordan," Mark 1: 9. And here for the first time he received the great plaudit, "this is my beloved Son in whom I am well pleased, ver. 11; Luke 3: 22. And lo, the heavens were opened unto him, and he saw the Spirit of God descending like a dove, and lighting upon him. Matt. 3: 16. What honor to the baptism of John! What testimony to both the baptism of John and the personage of Jesus, "this is my beloved Son in whom I am well pleased." Jesus also ratified the doctrine that John preached, by preaching it himself—he said "repent and believe the Gospel." Mark 1: 15. As to the mode or form of John's baptism, it of course was that which God gave him, in or at the time he sent him to baptize. And God gave it to John (so we believe) as it was formed by himself in heaven, even from the foundation of the world, to be the entrance of the way of the Lord, as an ordinance of the new covenant, "for salvation." Zacharias speaking of the child John, said he was "to give knowledge of salvation unto his people, by the remission of their sins." Luke 1:77.

And just as John received it from God, so he administered it to the people, and as he administered it to the people, so he administered it to Jesus, and as Christ received it from God through John, so he baptized those who were baptized by him. "And all the people that heard him, and the publicans, justified God, being baptized with the baptism of John." Luke 7: 29. "Jesus made and baptized more disciples than John, though Jesus himself baptized not but his disciples." John 4: 2. "After these things came Jesus into the land of Judea; and there he tarried with them, and baptized." John 3:22. That is, his disciples baptized under his direction and in his presence. It would be unreasonable and unscriptural to suppose that Jesus changed the form of baptism. Consequently, that very same baptism which he received from God his Father, in the same form he commanded his disciples to use it, only with the addition of the form of words, "In the name of the Father, and of the Son, and of the Holy Ghost," to be used when the actions, which constitute the ordinance are performed.

I repeat it, it would seem entirely unreasonable to suppose that Jesus changed the form of baptism which he received from his Father through John, who "came to prepare the way of the Lord," and to begin the Gospel, when most certainly he received it directly from God, for he was the messenger or voice "crying in the wilderness, Prepare ye the way of the Lord, make his paths straight." Matt. 3: 2. Now if John was to prepare the way of the Lord, it would be unreasonable to suppose that he was still acting under the law of Moses, which was unable to justify. "By the deeds of the law, there shall no flesh be justified in his sight." Rom. 3: 20. But John's baptism was a baptism of righteousness, for the remission of sins. And, therefore, it is more reasonable to suppose it was, as Mark says, "the beginning of the Gospel." For God had sent him to prepare the way of the New Covenant. And as we have stated above, Jesus submitted, and the Father testified that he was well pleased with him.

I think this is sufficient to show any unprejudiced mind, that John the baptist did not act under the law of Moses, but that he laid the foundation of the Gospel of Christ. And that the form of baptism, which he baptized with, was the same that Jesus baptized with, and also the same that the apostles used, although it was to be administered according to the form given in the commission. But that the baptism of John, and that of Christ and his apostles was the same baptism, is plain, and reasonable, and scriptural. And now to show forth the true form of water baptism, according to the truth of God's word, I will show, First, that the baptism of John, and of Christ and his apostles, was performed in the water. Secondly, that it was performed by immersing or dipping the subject under the water. And, thirdly, that in baptism, there are three actions, one in the name of the Father, and one in the name of the Son, and one in the name of the Holy Ghost. And now to my first proposition, that John the baptist, Jesus Christ, and the apostles, baptized in water.

"And there went out unto him, (John) all the land of Judea, and they of Jerusalem, and were all baptized of him in the river of Jordan, confessing their sins." Mark 1: 5. "And were baptized of him in Jordan." Matt. 3: 6. Here are two testimonies that John baptized the people in the river of Jordan. And now let us examine the baptism of Jesus. And "Jesus when he was baptized, went up straightway out of the water." Matt. 3: 16. Jesus came from Galilee, and was baptized of John in Jordan. Mark 1: 9. Here are two testimonies that Jesus was baptized in the water. We will now look at the practice of the apostles. I will give the plain testimony of Acts 8: 38. And he (the Eunuch) commanded the chariot to stand still: and they went down both into the water, both Philip and the eunuch: and he (Philip) baptized him (the eunuch). Now here is a plain testimony that the apostles baptized in the water. And this makes five testimonies in the New Testament, proving that baptism was performed in the water. This evidence is worth more than all the far-fetched reasoning or suppositions that can possibly be brought up from any other source. This is conclusive proof, that water baptism was performed by John, and by Christ, and by the apostles, in the water. This should certainly be sufficient evidence to convince all honest and unprejudiced persons. But now we come to the critical question with some, How did they perform the ordinance when in the water? Here the critic seems to exult, as though he had proposed a question not easily answered. And this question brings me to my second proposition, in which I shall show that baptism was performed by immersing, or dipping under water.

Here we must acknowledge, that our testimony is not as direct and conclusive as in the former proposition, yet we think it is satisfactory. The apostle calls baptism a burial: "therefore we are buried with him (Christ) by baptism into death: that like as Christ was raised from the dead by the glory of the Father, even so we also should walk in newness of life." Rom. 6: 4. Again, "buried with him (Christ) in baptism, wherein also ye are risen with him through the faith of the operation of God, who hath raised him from the dead." Col. 2: 12. Now here are two testimonies that Paul called baptism a burial. He likewise called it a washing. "But ye are washed." 1 Cor. 6: 11. Again, "He saved us by the washing of regeneration, and the renewing of the Holy Ghost." Tit. 3: 5. In these passages Paul calls baptism a burial, and also a washing. And making use of figurative language, says, that as Christ was buried in the grave, and rose again, so they, the Romans, were buried with him by baptism; as he was "raised by the glory of the Father, even so they should walk in newness of life." And to his Colossian brethren he says, "buried with him in baptism, wherein (that is in rising out of the water) also, ye are risen with him through the faith of the operation of God, who raised him from the dead." What can be plainer than the figure which Paul here makes use of? It plainly teaches that water baptism was performed by burying the subject under water. All must agree that the meaning of the word bury is, as Webster says, "to inter in a grave, to hide in surrounding matter." Walker explains it, "to inter, hide, conceal." What more then do we want to prove baptism to be an immersion or a dipping? For as Paul says, "buried with him by baptism," and "in baptism," he of course meant to convey the idea that they were interred, hid, or concealed & surrounded with water in baptism; and when possessing true penitency and belief they were also washed from sin; "for ye are washed" says Paul. And by their rising again from the water, made the likeness of the resurrection of Christ from the dead, and thereby making a figure, in which the old man is represented as being drowned.

This was the manner in which the first Christians spake of baptism, and they so understood and applied the language of Paul to the Romans and Colossians—the figurative language which we have been considering.

But say our friends in the work we are reviewing, "it was with water." This objection we have already completely answered, in a manner which we think should satisfy every reasonable, candid, and honest man. For if a man is baptized under water, is it not with water, as much and more so, than if only a little is poured on his head: It is with water, and no other element that he is baptized. Ask the woman who washed, what she washed with, and the reply will be, with water. And yet does she not immerse her clothes and put them under water? Ask the dyer what he colors with, and the reply will be, with dye; yet he puts his cloth into the dye. But to go a little further in exposing the argument on the phrase "with water," it seems that where king James' translation and Luther's give the word *with,* Campbell, Macknight, and Doddridge, and some others render the word *in the water, in the holy Ghost.* These translations have the preposition *in* instead of *with,* and this seems the most consistent. For as I have shown in my remarks on the baptism with the Holy Ghost, that the disciples were all surrounded with the material of the Holy Ghost, and of course were immersed in it. And as to the subject of the baptism of suffering, or as my friends see fit to call it, the "baptism of the passion," it is evident that Jesus was entirely surrounded, that is overwhelmed in the suffering sense.

Here I must take notice of the ridiculous idea advanced on page 92 of the little work alluded to, namely, that when the "Jews and Roman soldiers began to spit on the Saviour, the baptism of suffering began." What an idea! Does the spittle of those enemies of the Lord constitute baptism? Or are the enraged Jews become the administrators of the baptism of suffering? Strange indeed! The baptism of suffering, was over and past when the Saviour left the garden. And the suffering of the body was indicated when he underwent the baptism of suffering in the garden. The baptism of suffering did not last long, but was soon over. Water baptism too is soon over. But that which is indicated in it, the dying unto sin, and living unto righteousness is not soon over. In baptism, man renounces Satan, and yields himself to God, and now the temptations, and dying unto sin follow.

So in the baptism of the suffering of the Saviour in the garden of Gethsemane, in the same night in which he delivered unto the disciples the ordinances of feet washing, John 13: the Lord's supper, Matt. 26: Mark 14: Luke 22: John 13: 4, and also the breaking of bread, see the above chapters, and the new command of love, John 13: 34, 35, then he could say to his Father when on Mount Olivet, before he entered the garden of Gethsemane, "I have glorified thee on earth, I have finished the work which thou gavest me to do." John 17: 4. He had finished the work of delivering the order unto the new covenant to his disciples, by his own example as well as by his words, and he is now to undergo the suffering baptism; this is done or suffered in the garden of Gethsemane, to which he now hastens, and kneeling down, and falling upon his face, he calls upon his heavenly Father, and says, "if it is possible let this cup pass from me, but not my will but thine be done." Here I repeat, Jesus was all surrounded and immersed in sufferings; but prays a second, and a third time, saying the same words, "Father is it possible." But it seems it was not possible for the cup to pass. The decree of God requires a sacrifice, and none but his Son, his only Son can answer for that sacrifice. The Son yields in this suffering baptism, to the will of God his Father, and accepts his will fully.

At this critical moment an angel is dispatched from heaven to strengthen him. And now he rises a third time and comes to his disciples. Here there was no man as administrator to perform this baptism. None saw his suffering but the Father, and the angel who was sent to strengthen him, for the disciples were asleep. Now the suffering baptism is over, and

Jesus is taken by the bands of Roman soldiers and led to Annas and Caiaphas, where the effects of the avowal made in the baptism make their beginning. Just as in his water baptism, he avowed to fulfill all righteousness, and as soon as he rose out of the water, he was led into the wilderness to be tempted of the devil, so here, after his suffering baptism he was led by the soldiers and Jews first to Annas and Caiaphas, then to Pilate's judgment hall, then to the cross, till the whole effect of the indication made and avowed to in the garden was accomplished, and the offering for sin made; yea the painful death of the cross was the fulfillment of what the Saviour said in the garden, when overwhelmed in the suffering baptism, "my soul is exceeding sorrowful even unto death."

And I now proceed to my third proposition; and it might appear as though I had digressed from the subject, but I have been preparing to introduce my third proposition by replying to the erroneous idea of the suffering baptism as though it was done by the spittle of the Jews and soldiers. My third proposition is, that there are three actions in water baptism, as directed by the Saviour in the command, "baptizing them in the name of the Father, and of the Son, and of the Holy Ghost." Now if as has been proved above, baptism means an immersion or a dipping, then of course there must be an action "in the name of the Father," and also an action "in the name of the Son," and a third action "in the name of the Holy Ghost." This of course should be so to be obedient to the Master, for he commands so.

And in these actions we must have a form or position, for without position, we cannot act properly. Now in order to get a proper position in which to perform baptism, we will look to the Saviour for it, for in water baptism, the evangelists and apostles are silent as to position. And as we must have a position to act in baptism, we are more safe in taking the one the Saviour gave us in his baptism of suffering in the garden of Gethsemane, than in taking the position of man. "And he was withdrawn from them about a stone's cast, and kneeled down and prayed." Luke 22: 41. And he went forward a little, and fell on the ground, and prayed that, if it were possible, the hour might pass from him. Mark 14: 35. This he did the second and the third time. See Mark 14: 41. And this we have before shown was the baptism of suffering which the Saviour experienced. And the position, which he took, we see was that of kneeling, and falling on his face. We, therefore, hold (and good authority we have for so doing) that in water baptism, this is a legal, scriptural, reasonable, and decent form or position, and that we may safely take it, without any fear of a successful contradiction from man, or without any fear of adding improper forms to the gospel, for we have Christ's pattern for it.

It seems that the Saviour when suffering in the garden, prayed, and Mark tells us that he came a "third time," or a second, and a third time,—so then his baptism of suffering had three actions (and yet but one baptism,) so he teaches his disciples to baptize in the name of the Father, and of the Son, and of the Holy Ghost, making also three actions in water baptism. Here we see a beautiful harmony. And water baptism performed by three actions, is agreeable with the trinity of the Godhead, and the baptism of suffering, and with the whole order of the new covenant. And it seems surprising that every lover of the truth should not accept of it. Why should we run over the whole of the Old Testament rites, to seek for terms to establish a fancy doctrine, which is not found in the Bible—to prove the mode of baptism, while we have the subject so plainly taught in the New Testament, by the Saviour and the apostles "that the wayfaring man cannot mistake." But it is not pouring or sprinkling.

Dr. Martin Luther says, "baptism is performed by being sunk into the water that it will pass over us, and presently drawn out again; these two things, to be sunk under the water, and to be drawn out again, signify, the power and act of baptism." Form. Coae. page 453, New York German edition of 1848. See also the Edition printed in Germany, in 1790. It is to be lamented, that attempts have been made to destroy this testimony of Luther, by incorrect translations. A translation of the work just alluded to, by the Rev. Stirewalt, and printed by A. Hinkel, New Market, Shenandoah, Va. gives the words, "bringing into connection with the water, and taking away again," instead of the words expressing correctly the original, "sinking into the water that it may pass over us." Such attempts to change the meaning of authors to accomplish a certain purpose, should receive the severe rebuke of every honest man.

Let us also see what Menno Simon, the father of the Mennonites says:—"After we have searched ever so diligently, we shall find no other baptism besides dipping in water" *(tauchen in das Wasser)*. Menno Simon's works, 1539, page 24. His works, however, have since been translated, and reprinted, and this passage as well as others has been changed. And it appears that the followers of Menno and Luther would if they could put out of existence those noble testimonies for baptism by immersion, which those eminent men have given. But we are thankful we have them yet in the old copies of their works, and we intend to preserve them, for a testimony against those who would give spurious copies of those men's works to the world. If men, to promote their peculiar views, will change the meaning of the works of human authors, what would they do with the New Testament if they had the power? It is to be feared they would change that to something else from what it is, to darken the testimony of the truth, and blindfold the deluded people.

I have read the little work alluded to, again and again, but I am still of the opinion that pouring and sprinkling are not baptism. I think I have now sustained the propositions I proposed to prove. First, the baptism of the Gospel of Christ was performed in the water. Secondly, baptism was performed by putting the subject under the water. Thirdly, there are three actions in baptism. I will now follow up several of the erroneous ideas advanced to justify the illegal mode of baptism by pouring and sprinkling, in the little work already alluded to. Reference is made to 1 Cor. 10: 2, where the apostle says that they (the Israelites) "were all baptized unto Moses in the cloud and in the sea." By further reference to this occurrence, we find that they were "all under the cloud, and all passed through the sea," ver. 1. "And they went into the midst of the sea upon dry ground, and the waters were a wall unto them on their right hand and on their left." Ex. 14: 22. Again, David says, "He turned the sea into dry land; they went through the flood on foot." Ps. 66: 6. Paul says, "By faith they passed through the red sea, as on dry land." Heb. 11: 29.

But this being only a figure, we here see that it did not rain on them, but they passed through on dry ground. See the quotations above. And of course they were not made wet with water, notwithstanding they were all overwhelmed or surrounded with or in water, making a beautiful figure of baptism in the new covenant. So also in reference to the flood in the days of Noah. They that had faith to enter into the ark were saved "by water." Notice, Peter says, the like figure whereunto, even baptism, doth also now save us. 1 Pet. 3: 21. None we presume will contend that Noah and his family were saved because it rained on them, but rather because they believed God, and built an ark, and entered into it according to his command, and thus were in the ark saved by water, the water bearing up the ark, and it floating through and in the water.

This ark was the means that God saw fit to use in those days, to save Noah and his family. So is baptism now given as a means of salvation in the new covenant. "The like figure"—"not the putting away of the filth of the flesh"—not as some light-minded people say that those who baptize by going into the water and by putting the subject under the water, think to wash away sin by mere water—but baptism is, according to Peter, "the answer of a good conscience toward God, by the resurrection of Christ." These incidents all prefigure baptism in the new covenant. As the Israelites went through the Red sea and all surrounded by it, and were under the cloud and in the sea; and as Noah went into the ark being shut up in it, while it floated through the water, these both prefigure or represent baptism; for as the believer is baptized under water which signifies a shutting up or burial, so his rising or emerging from the water, represents the resurrection of Christ from the grave. And both of those occurrences, namely, that of the Israelites coming out of the Red sea, & Noah coming out of the ark and water, indicate plainly the true and evangelical baptism of the Gospel as we have shown.

But if water baptism were administered by pouring or sprinkling, there is no fulfilling of the figures, either of being "in the sea and in the cloud," or of being in the ark, and in the water, neither of the resurrection of Jesus, in coming out of the water—in all these there is no representation whatever, if baptism is performed by pouring or sprinkling, and of course there can be no benefit derived from it, although thousands of poor deluded and deceived mortals congratulate themselves upon having water sprinkled or poured upon them, as being baptized, and take to themselves a false hope of future salvation and happiness, forgetting that Jesus said that only those who "do the will of his Father which is in heaven" shall enter in, Matt. 7: 21. And, again, "many shall come in that day and say unto me, Lord, Lord, have we not prophesied in thy name? and in thy name have done many wonderful works? and in thy name have cast out devils? And then will I profess unto them, I never knew you: depart from me, ye that work iniquity." Matt. 7: 22, 23. Again, "then shall ye begin to say, we have eaten and drunk in thy presence, and thou hast taught in our streets. But he shall say, I tell you, I know you not whence ye are; depart from me, all ye workers of iniquity." Luke 13: 26, 27. "We have eaten and drunk in thy presence," these expressions show that they are under the impression that they have attended to the Christian duty of breaking bread, and of partaking of the cup of the Lord, and also that he had taught them in their streets. Take notice, they say in our streets, it is in that particular doctrine which they made choice of, and which they thought would do, because they believed it; but as it was not in accordance with the precept and command of the great prophet, Jesus, it of course must have been nothing but the invention and tradition of men; and, consequently the answer, I never knew you, or I knew not whence you are, depart from me all ye workers of iniquity. This makes it plain, that not every thing which is called religion, is agreeable to the word of God or within that day meet his approbation.

These characters seem to be those professors of religion who have changed the truth of God into a lie, and hold the truth in unrighteousness, Rom. 1: 18-25. And wherever we find persons holding the idea, that a little water is just as good as much, and that John's baptism was under the law of Moses, and that the Lord's supper, the holy kiss, and feet washing are not necessary, and that the breaking of bread, and the cup of blessing, or the communion of the broken body and shed blood, are the Lord's supper. Wherever we find these ideas advocated, we may know that the "truth of God is held in unrighteousness," and that the "truth has been changed into a lie." Awful to relate, but that this is actually too much the case, is proved by the little pamphlet or book so often referred to in this work. And whence comes all this? Why, on this wise. Man is operated upon by the Spirit of God, and by his word, and is shown the way of righteousness. But alas! The false teachers, and false writers or commentators, who are "blind guides" pervert the mind thus operated upon by the Spirit and word of the Lord, man's love to the truth of God is weakened, like old mother Eve's in the garden by the doctrine of the serpent, and consequently the "truth is changed in the mind of man into a lie"—and he now receives the lie in his heart to his condemnation. Thus it was in the garden of Eden, the serpent like those false teachers and false christians now, said ye shall not surely die, but God had said ye shall surely die, and thus the truth of God was changed into a lie—our parents received the lie and acted accordingly, and the consequence was the curse. So all those who hear and receive from those teachers and professed Christians, doctrines contrary to God's word, act accordingly, and turn away from the plain truth and ordinances of the Lord, to their own destruction and damnation.

The apostle says, "Because they received not the love of the truth, that they might be saved." "And for this cause God shall send them strong delusion, that they should believe a lie: that they all might be damned who believed not the truth." 2 Thess. 2: 11, 12. Again, the Lord Jesus shall be revealed from heaven with his mighty angels, in flaming fire, taking vengeance on them that know not God, and that obey not the Gospel of our Lord Jesus Christ: who shall be punished with everlasting destruction from the presence of the Lord, and from the glory of his power." 2 Thes. 1: 7-9. So it appears, that it is the duty of man, to see to it, that he is not deceived; for, says the Redeemer, "take heed that no man deceive you. For, many shall come in my name, saying, I am Christ; and shall deceive many." Matt. 24: 4,5. "For there shall arise false christs, and false prophets and shall show great signs and wonders; insomuch that, if it were possible, they shall deceive the very elect," verse 24. "Behold, I have told you before," verse 25. See 2 Timothy 3: 4-7. And, again, "Even as there shall be false teachers among you, who privily shall bring in damnable heresies, even denying the Lord that bought them, and bring upon themselves swift destruction. And many shall follow their pernicious ways; by reason of whom the way of truth shall be evil spoken of. And through covetousness shall they with feigned words make merchandise of you: whose judgment now of a long time lingereth not, and their damnation slumbereth not." 2 Peter 2: 1-3. This points out the practice plainly, as it is now pursued, in these our last days when men in the garb of preachers of the Gospel have brought in, and do still bring in, such doctrines as change the truth of God into a lie. The truth is that in many cases to hear them preach and exhort, you would suppose that truth was in every respect their object while they speak in general terms, but when they begin to practice or attend to the things which in general terms they seem anxious to impress on the minds of the people with great zeal, as the commandments of the Lord, you will see quite a different thing. For instance, you will see them pour or sprinkle a little water on the head of the subject for baptism—a little bread and wine taken and called the Lord's supper—feet washing and the true supper excluded and cast away as not necessary.

Dear reader, beware of such, for they are those of whom Christ speaks, when he says, "they say and do not." Such appears to be the case with many in these our days, as well as with the writer and translator of the little work alluded to. And the followers of such men are in the same condition as the leaders. Beware, dear reader, thou hast a soul to save, and no man can save it for you. Neither can the doctrine or opinion of thyself or of any other man save it. The doctrine and merit of Christ alone can save it. O then, turn away reader, from all doctrine, and from all teachers that would set aside or change any of Christ's institutions. In this little treatise here given you, you have a true form of baptism, laid down, and drawn from the New Testament, and established by Christ's examples and precepts, and also by the example and precepts of the apostles. You have also understood, if you have given attention to what I have said, that true evangelical repentance and faith are essentially necessary. And as the Saviour commanded his disciples to teach the people to observe all things that he had commanded them, we should be careful to observe them. We have Christ's command for washing feet in John 13; we have a notice of the Lord's supper, Matt. 26; Mark 14; Luke 22; 1 Cor. 11; and the commandment of love, or new commandment, John 13: 34,35; Rom. 16: 16; 1 Cor. 16: 20; 1 Pet. 5: 14. We have also the doctrine of self-denial taught us in these words: "He that would be my disciple, let him deny himself, take up his cross and follow me."

Is it possible that men who speak of the great necessity of obeying the commands of God, can in their practice deny those commands: And can they expect to be accepted with God by pursuing such a course? Is it possible that a man can be a true follower of the lowly Jesus and at the same time deny in practice, and speak lightly of some of his ordinances which he himself gave us? It would hardly seem possible. This, however, I will leave to the consideration of every reflecting reader. And, dear reader, as you should look upon your soul as of intrinsic value, if you see these truths, pass not by them heedlessly, but embrace them with heart and soul, though you probably will have to forsake a father, a mother, a wife, a husband, or children, or goods, or friends, or applause, remember all these can do you but little good in a dying hour or at the great day of judgment. Let nothing then in this "acceptable time and day of salvation," hinder you from seeking the Lord. Adhere to the simple truth as it is in Jesus, that will save your soul and make you happy both in time and in eternity. Whereas if you turn from the truth, and follow cunningly devised fables, (and the doctrines and inventions of men are often no better,) then after your days shall be gone, and your time shall come to an end, and you will have to close your eyes in death, oh! what then will be your doom?—Reader, my heart mourns at the thought of the danger you are in. Oh! what will be the condition of that soul, that has rejected the counsel of God given through Jesus? Where shall he appear who obeyed not the gospel of the Lord Jesus Christ? "He shall be punished with everlasting destruction from the presence of the Lord, and the glory of his power." Horrible is the thought that man, disobedient man, will have to take up his abode in a "lake that burneth with fire and brimstone, when the smoke of his torment shall ascend up for ever and ever." Will not man shudder, will he not turn from the error of his ways! "Turn ye, turn ye, O house of Israel, for why will you die."[6]

Evidently Joseph Funk was very much upset by John Kline's short pamphlet, for in about a year Funk, who was nearly eighty years of age, had written and published an answer to John Kline in a book of three hundred and nine pages. Much of the material was taken from the Old Testament, because Funk refused to accept Kline's proposal that the material in the debate be limited to the New Testament. As might be expected, the publication of "The Reviewer Reviewed" by Joseph Funk did not end the debate, and in 1858 John Kline wrote and the Kurtz press edited and printed a seventy-four page booklet entitled, "Strictures and Reply to The Reviewer Reviewed, being a further Defence of Baptism." The material was primarily a reiteration and expansion of the material presented two years before. Funk responded by writing another lengthy answer to the "Strictures," but it was never published. The final chapter was written in John Kline's diary, for he noted in October 1862 that he had gone "to see my old friend, Joseph Funk, and succeed[ed] in bringing about a better state of feeling on his part toward me. He became reconciled." Funk had been "somewhat ruffled in his feelings by my 'Strictures and Reply' to his published writings on baptism and feet-washing." Kline ate a meal with him and returned home. Two months later, Funk was dead.

Bowman, Nead, and Kline were writing in Virginia, but there were Brethren writing about baptism in other areas, too. For example, in 1854, Christian Wise published "A Defence of Christian Baptism by Trine Immersion" in Ohio. In contrast to the material used by John Kline, which was primarily Scriptural in nature, Christian Wise relied primarily on historical material for his defense of trine immersion as the proper form of Christian baptism.

By the 1850s when John Kline was writing pamphlets defending the Brethren ideas on baptism, other Brethren were beginning to defend their baptismal practices in spoken debates. One of the most active and successful of these Brethren debaters was James Quinter, who had first joined the Brethren from a non-religious background in eastern Pennsylvania in the early 1830s. His daughter, Mary, later described her impressions of her father's conversion.

In the surrounding community were the homes of brethren John Umstad, George Price, Samuel Supplee; and, although not in the immediate neighborhood, the home of Brother Isaac Price was not far away. These brethren, with Brother [Abel] Fitzwater, were among those who came into the Church during a religious revival in the community in 1831. As there was no Church of the Brethren in the neighborhood, they were baptized in the Coventry Church, near Pottstown. Through the efforts of these brethren meetings for public worship were held in the school-houses, and prayer meetings were held at their homes. During a meeting held in the old Green Tree school-house, [James Quinter] was convicted and his mind aroused upon the subject of his salvation. It engaged his thoughts deeply for a time, and one day as he was working at the barn he suddenly stopped, exclaiming, "I've got—I've got it," and ran to the house. "I've got it—peace with God!" He was baptized in the Coventry Church. He was at this time in his seventeenth year.[7]

In 1838, at a council meeting held at the home of George Price, James Quinter was called to the ministry. At the time he was teaching school, and education continued to be one of his major interests throughout his life. In 1842, he moved from his home in Montgomery County, Pennsylvania, to Fayette County, Pennsylvania, where he farmed, taught school and served as the pastor of a Brethren congregation. It was while he was located here that he became involved in a debate on baptism with a Lutheran minister in Blair County. Henry R. Holsinger, who heard the debate as a young man, later described his recollections of the event.

I attended a four-days discussion on baptism between Elder Quinter and Joseph Fitchner, a Lutheran preacher. The debate was held in the vicinity of Claysburg, Blair County, Pennsylvania, in the winter of 1853. In this discussion Elder Quinter showed his Christian manhood and strength of purpose to perfection. It was, in the estimation of the writer, a fiery ordeal, almost equal to martyrdom. It appeared as though Mr. Fitchner was determined to break down his opponent by provocation. He taunted him, mocked him, ridiculed him, and did everything that he thought might provoke Brother Quinter and throw him off his guard, but Brother Quinter appeared to be clothed with a coat of mail, proof against the darts of his enemy. Nothing but the grace of God could sustain a man under such trial.[8]

If this was Quinter's first public debate, it could have been an unhappy enough experience to have ended his public debating; however, that was not the case, and he engaged in a number of other public debates, including one with S. P. Snyder of Indiana who represented the Evangelical Lutheran Church. This debate was published in 1868 in Indianapolis. By the time of this debate Quinter had become an editor on the staff of the "Gospel Visiter." He became one of the most influential leaders in the church because of his editorial work, his educational activity, and his defense of the church's beliefs.

Another outstanding Brethren debater and defender of the church's beliefs, who was getting off to a strong start in the 1860s, was R. H. Miller, whose early life in the Church of the Brethren was described in the section on geographical expansion. By 1861, three years after he joined the church, it was reported:

a reformer preacher wants Robert to preach on baptism   he offered his meetinghouse to the brethern for that occation. . . . Robert is agoing to prove the Trine Immersion rite by history, then by Grammer, and then by Scripture, and then lastly by common good sence, and then prove by Scripture that the forward motion is nearer rite than the backward motion. they think he cant. he will deceave them bad when they hear him. he is an able debater in Scripture.[9]

Like Quinter, Robert H. Miller became one of the outstanding leaders of the Church of the Brethren, because of his able preaching in many Brethren congregations and at the Annual Meeting and because of his skill as a debater and defender of Brethren beliefs.

Brethren ministers like R. H. Miller, James Quinter, and John Kline were defending the Brethren belief in baptism by writing and by debating.

Many other ministers, who were neither able writers nor debaters, were putting Brethren baptism into practice in many different areas of the United States during these years. One illustration of such a minister was J. D. Haughtelin, who arrived in Iowa in 1857 and who spent a number of years as a minister in that area. Toward the end of his life, he recollected some of his baptismal experiences in an autobiographical sketch. Undoubtedly, similar stories could have been told by most Brethren ministers.

In his first experience in baptizing he drove sixty miles west across the, then bleak prairies of Western Iowa, in midwinter in an open buggy. Ice over two feet thick was cut to make a pool in a millrace. The weather was so cold that after baptizing about a half dozen applicants, his outer garments were frozen while walking about twenty rods. Later on he was baptizing when it was twenty below zero. He had to dip his hands in the water to keep them from freezing as the air was about fifty degrees colder than the ice water....

He baptized a brother with an internal incurable cancer. His physician said, "If the tumor don't burst it won't hurt you. If it does it may be fatal." His reply was, I would rather die in the act than omit it." He had to be *carried* into the river on a chair. After being baptized he *walked out,* and later on expressed himself as being greatly comforted. A pedo Baptist minister who was a witness to this baptismal scene said, "Haughtelin ought to be prosecuted for taking that man into the water."[10]

Finally, in the discussion of baptism Annual Meeting Minutes indicated that Brethren were having some difficulty maintaining strictly their form of trine immersion as the exclusive means of membership in the church, because there were those individuals who wanted to join the church on the basis of other forms of baptism.

BAPTISM
Y. M. 1821. Art. 6. Whether members (persons) might be received into the church, who have been but once immersed (without baptizing them in the manner we believe it ought to be done according to the gospel)? It was considered, that a threefold immersion is the true baptism; but if such persons would be content with their baptism, and yet acknowledge the Brethren's order as right, we would leave it over to them, and receive them with the laying on of hands and prayer.

Y. M. 1828. Art. 6. Whether a person may be received into the church, having been immersed but once? it is the counsel to be better that they should be baptized again in the true order....

Y. M. 1833. Art. 1. Whether we are to immerse at baptism once or thrice? It was considered, that we cannot deem any other baptism as valid according to the word of God, but a threefold immersion. . . .

Y. M. 1835. (Miami.) Art. 13. What is the order to receive applicants for baptism? It is necessary that there should be self-knowledge, repentance and faith, together with scriptural instruction, and then that it may be done with the counsel of the church. . . .

Y. M. 1845. Art. 4. Where is the proper place for asking the candidates for baptism concerning their faith in Christ—in or out of the water? Considered, that the most proper place for making a public confession of our faith in Christ, is in the water, immediately before baptism. See 1 Tim. 6:12.[11]

THE BELIEF IN THE LOVE FEAST

As in the practice of the ordinance of baptism, the Brethren were biblical literalists in their observance of the love feast. They believed in following as exactly as possible the practice of the service in the New Testament. On the last night before his crucifixion, Jesus ate a meal with his disciples in the upper room in Jerusalem and gave to that meal a special significance by certain actions. For the Brethren, there were three parts of the evening's events which needed to be included in the service. The first part was the washing of feet; in contrast to the overwhelming majority of Christians the Brethren believe that Jesus intended for his followers to engage in the washing of each other's feet, and they defended their belief on numerous occasions. One of the earliest such defenses in this period following the American Revolution was published in 1799 by Alexander Mack, Jr., the prominent Brethren elder in Germantown, Pennsylvania, and son of the first leader of the church. This material was included as a brief appendix in a book including the writings of his father and of Jeremias Felbinger, which was published by Samuel Sauer in Baltimore.

Grace and peace from God the Father through Jesus Christ be multiplied in you all. Amen.

Beloved brethren!

Being informed that some brethren are in difficulty about the washing of feet, which Jesus has commanded to his own, as though it had been performed between the supper and breaking of bread, and think it not rightly done, if feet are washed before supper; therefore I have been moved in the spirit, in love and simplicity to state the cause, why we do wash feet before supper. But at the same time I would say, it is our faith and intention, that if a brother or any other man could in love and moderation instruct us more perfectly according to the word of the Lord, otherwise than we do now point out, we would be willing to accept of it not only in this point of feetwashing, but also in other things, and would not at all rest upon old customs, but the word of the Lord shall be our only rule and guide.

In the first place let us see how the old, pious patriarchs used to observe feetwashing, before the law. Gen xviii. 4.   xxiv. 32.   xix. 2. Here we see quite clearly that the holy patriarchs performed feetwashing before the meal. We see also under the law in the figurative worship, that Moses had to set a big laver between the tent of the congregation and the altar, and put water there to wash withal, and Aaron and his sons, yea all their successors in the priesthood had first to wash their hands and feet, when they were to serve in the temple. Exod. xl. 31. 32. We can even notice, that feetwashing was customary under the law (among the people). See 1 Sam. xxv. 41.

Again, feetwashing was still a customary thing in the time of our Lord Jesus, when he himself preached the Gospel, if friends would show their love to each other, and this was always done before the meal, as we see, Luke vii. 44. Here the Lord Jesus told the pharisee, during the meal, that when Jesus had entered his house, he (the pharisee) had given him no water for his feet. But to come to the point itself, we see first that when the feast of the passover had come nigh, the Lord Jesus sent two of his disciples, namely Peter and John, which John is the same disciple who has described feetwashing, John 13, whom the Lord Jesus sent to prepare the passover, as Luke says xxii. 8-14. "And when the hour was come, he sat down and the twelve apostles with him." Mark xiv. 17. Matth. xxvi. 20.

Now these evangelists say nothing about feetwashing, but the evangelist John describes it John xiii. According to the greek text, as Reitz, the Low-dutch translators and Felbinger have given it, says John (verse 2) who himself had prepared the supper, he says, "when the supper was done," have the Hollanders, "when the supper was ready," according to Felbinger, and Reitz expresses it yet clearer by adding, "was ready prepared." Others given according to the Greek, as it is even in the Greek dictionary, "When the supper was made," or, "when the supper was existing."

Now the word as Luther has it, "after supper," or as the English translators have it, "supper being ended," is not according to the Greek, but thus we ought to read John xiii, 2. When supper was done, i. e. all prepared,—then Jesus arose from the prepared supper, as follows verse 4 &c. "he riseth from supper,—and began to wash his disciples' feet," even as they should now in lowliness, humility and love wash each other's feet.

That Jesus after feetwashing sat down again and did eat with his disciples, testifies not only John, as may be clearly seen verse 26, where he dipped the sop, and gave it unto Judas Iscariot, but also Matthew writes chap. 26: 23, that Jesus says, "He that dippeth his hand with me in the dish, the same shall betray me." Even so writes Mark, chapt. 14: 20. "It is one of the twelve that dippeth with me in the dish."

Here we see, that when John writes of dipping the sop, that this was done while they were eating, and that the feet were already washed, is still more clear, when Jesus says verse 21, 'Verily, verily, I say unto you, that one of you shall betray me.' And that feetwashing was over, and Judas was yet present, when Jesus said this, see Matt. xxvi. 21. and Mark xiv. 18. Here both evangelists testify that Jesus said this, while they were eating.

But since the other evangelists say nothing at all about feetwashing, and John writes nothing about the breaking of bread and its institution, it is necessary to look upon and understand the scriptures with a spiritual eye of love and submission. And if even all the translators had written as Luther did, 'after supper,' yet we would have to understand, "after supper was done or prepared." But now it is sufficiently plain, that when the supper was ready, or done, or made, or prepared, Jesus arose from the prepared supper, and washed even Judas' feet; but as soon as Jesus while eating, began to say, One of you shall betray me, then there was no rest nor stopping, until Judas was gone out.

Three evangelists state that while they were eating Jesus revealed Judas the traitor; but Luke is putting it back after the breaking of bread, when he says chapt. 22: 21. after the breaking of bread, "But behold, the hand of him that betrayeth me is with me on the table." According to the other evangelists this word does not belong after the breaking of bread, but to the time of eating the passover (supper), and for this Judas was clean according to the law in the outward body. Therefore Jesus could wash his feet, namely before supper. But if Jesus had instituted a particular preparation after supper, by the washing of feet unto the breaking of bread, and had washed the feet, and broken the bread also unto the traitor Judas, whom Jesus knew well, then we might also break and give the bread of communion to a known sinner, even if we knew, he had already joined a band of thieves and robbers, and that he intended that very evening to steal & murder. Yes, knowing all this, we might still break the bread of communion with him, because Jesus himself had done so, which however should be far from any true believer to think. Yea, I for my part would rather never break bread any more, than with such.

Now the blind scribes say, Judas had broken the bread of communion with Jesus, and remain stubbornly adhering to the letter of Luke, that

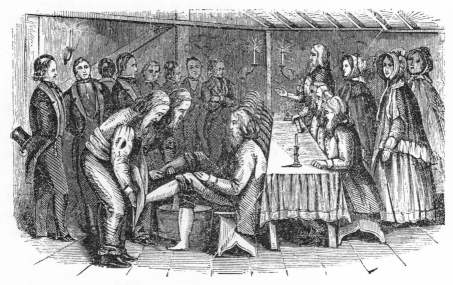

Illustration of feet washing from Nead's *Theological Works*

Jesus said only after the breaking of bread, "the hand of him that betrayeth me, is with me on the table," without being willing to use also the other evangelists. But thus the true lovers of wisdom should not be minded; for true wisdom, and her lovers, must be fashioned, as James teaches and says, chap. 3: 17. "But the wisdom that is from above is first pure, then peaceable, gentle, and easy to be entreated."

But generally it is the case, that when a person conceives something in his own mind, and retains such knowledge in his own will, then he is not easily instructed. He will dispute in his own wisdom about the shell, and let slip the kernel, and therefore, dear brethren, let us all be prudent, even especially with regard to feetwashing let us take care how we ought to be minded, that we should submit to each other in love and peace and humility.

For Christ indeed has given no especial command, *when* it should be done, whether before or after the meal. But he has commanded, that we should do it, and also should love one another. Christ has not said, that his disciples should be known at the washing of feet, or at the breaking of bread, but he said, "By this shall all men know, that ye are my disciples, if ye have love one to another." Oh! how should Satan mock us justly, if we were to quarrel with each other about the time, when the feet should be washed, and love were destroyed, yea even feetwashing and the breaking of bread entirely omitted and peace annihilated! This would undoubtedly please Satan, and make the doctrine of Jesus an object of derision with other men.

Therefore it is indeed of the highest importance, that we cherish love and peace among ourselves, and that each one resolves to pray to God for more wisdom. For I can write in truth and from experience this much, that in the beginning of baptism we have washed each other's feet with benefit and in love, after supper and after the breaking of bread. Afterwards we were enlightened and came nearer, and have washed one another's feet after supper, and *before* the breaking of bread, also with benefit. Finally, when Reitz had published (his translation of) the New Testament, and a brother had come among us, who understood *Greek,* and showed unto us in order, how Jesus had washed feet before supper, we were so simple and did so too, ever since, always before eating.

Now no brother will find fault with us, if we do not want to begin again at the hind end; no, so long as no man can give us better information, we should not be offensive to any one, if we do as we understand it. Yet I say, that if I should come to a fraternity, who would break bread, and the leaders of that fraternity could not understand it otherwise, but that the feet must be washed after supper, I would partake with them in simplicity, and in love and peace. However, I would lay my views before them according to scripture and wait in love, and have patience with them, until they should understand it so too.

For I am assured, that when the subject is considered quite impartially, and we remain in love and peace, we will be well convinced and persuaded, that it is as above shown, that Jesus rose from the prepared supper, and washed his disciples' feet, and then sat down and did eat, and while eating revealed the traitor, who then went out, and after that Jesus instituted the breaking of bread. Thus scripture accords with itself; the examples of the pious patriarchs before the law and those under the law, all correspond with it; and we will be able to sustain it with a good and peaceful conscience before God and men.

But if one was of the opinion, that feet must be washed after supper, I would not venture at all to maintain such opinion with a good understanding of the scripture, nor would scarcely any one be able to do it. For if we only examine the two evangelists Matthew and Mark, they both say one thing. First Matthew xxvi. 26. "As they were eating, Jesus took bread, and blessed it, and brake it &c." And Mark xiv. 22. "And as they did eat,

Jesus took bread, and blessed, and brake it—and said, Take, eat; this is my body." Here it is clearly to be seen, that between the eating of the passover (or supper) and the breaking of bread there was no change at all, or they would certainly have recorded it also. But because it (feetwashing) was done before eating, they have not mentioned it, but left out.

But John has described the washing of feet, and on the other hand left out the institution of the breaking of bread. Therefore the Scripture requires spiritual eyes, a spiritual mind and understanding; otherwise by the letter we would have nothing but trouble and dissension; if we without true illumination would try to hold fast to the letter in one place, in another place we would act contrary to it, without taking notice. Therefore, dear brethren, let us watch and be cautious, and above all preserve love; then we preserve light, as the Spirit of truth testifies 1 John ii. 10. "He that loveth his brother, abideth in the light, and there is none occasion of stumbling in him." Then our good Lord, who is pure, impartial love, can and will bestow little by little, what is yet wanting light or knowledge. I now conclude and beg again of all brethren to read and consider this in love and with a calm spirit, and remain your weak brother.[12]

In his "Primitive Christianity" published in 1834, Peter Nead also had a chapter on feet washing in which he explained why the Brethren engaged in the practice as they did.

FEET WASHING.

Baptism is not the only institution which Jesus Christ established for his church to observe; but in examining the Gospel, we find, that in the same night in which he was betrayed into the hands of sinners, he did establish three other institutions, to be all observed in order, at one meeting—namely, Feet Washing, the Supper, and the Communion; and writing upon these three institutions, I shall commence with Feet Washing, which was the first of the three instituted and observed by Christ and the apostles.

Feet Washing, is an institution which the major part of the professors of religion contend is no commandment. If Feet Washing be no commandment, then there is no commandment to be found in the Gospel. But it is evident that Christ gave as plain a commandment for the observance of this institution, as he did that we should repent for our sins. In the 13th chapter of our Lord's Gospel according to St. John, we can read of the establishment of this institution. I shall, for the satisfaction of the reader, insert in this place, so much of the chapter as is connected with this subject, and then paraphrase the same, agreeably to that light and knowledge which I have upon the subject. . . .

Again—If you will closely examine the 13th chapter of John, you may know from the same, that Christ washed the feet before supper. For instance—"So after he had washed their feet, and had taken his garments, and was set down again"—that is, at the table: (Now the feet were washed, and when Christ was set down again at the table, then they commenced the eating of the supper is plain from the 26th verse,) "Jesus answered, he it is to whom I shall give a sop when I have dipped it, and when he had dipped the sop, he gave it to Judas Iscariot, the son of Simon." . . .

Feet Washing has a spiritual meaning, and on that account many reject the observance of it. They tell us, that Christ only intended by this circumstance to teach his disciples humility. In part, I admit the assertion. But can that be taken as an evidence that it is not to be observed literally? If so, then Baptism and the Communion are not to be observed—for they also have a spiritual meaning. Where can you find in the Gospel a plainer command than the words of our Saviour to his disciples concerning Feet Washing? . . .

I have said that Feet Washing hath a spiritual import. In the first place, I believe it represents that brotherly chastisement, which the children of God are sometimes called upon to exercise one towards another. Christ told his disciples, that the spirit is willing, but the flesh is weak. . . .

Now, Feet Washing represents that course which we are to pursue. For instance—You observe, that in order to wash a brother's feet, you must bend or stoop yourself; and, secondly, your brother gives his feet into your hands, and then you can wash them. . . .

Feet Washing must be observed before supper—for every time the believer attends to this institution, he must call to mind, that now, in this present time, he must equip, or qualify himself, having the wedding garment of righteousness, so that he may be found in a state of readiness at the coming of his heavenly bridegroom, and enter in with him to the marriage.[13]

THE LORD'S SUPPER.

By the Lord's Supper, we are not to understand the bread and wine. The bread and wine no where in the Gospel, are called the Lord's Supper: and this is a point on which the majority of the professors of christianity will differ with me; yea, nearly all our learned divines, as they are termed will oppose the above assertion—for, as far as I know, they do term the bread and wine the Lord's Supper; and because they write and speak so, thousands are led to believe that it must be so. And, again, thousands and tens of thousands, no doubt have never heard anything to the contrary. I shall, therefore, be as particular as possible, in proving, from the word of God, that the bread and wine are not termed, in the Gospel, the Lord's Supper. The phrase "the Lord's Supper," is only to be found in one place in the Gospel, i. Cor. xi. 20. "When ye come together, therefore, into one place, this is not to eat the Lord's Supper," and because the apostle, in this chapter, also speaks of the bread and wine, it is inferred, that he has an allusion to the same, which I shall endeavor to show to the reverse.

A question presents itself—what then, are we to understand by the Lord's Supper? I answer, that meal which the faithful partake of, immediately after Feet Washing, and just before the Communion. What is it that constitutes that meal? I answer, that which is calculated to refresh the body. It is a common meal, but it must be observed as the Lord's meal, or Supper; because it is of his appointment. In the 13th chapter of John, we have an account of Christ eating a meal with his apostles, or, as it is termed a supper. John calls it a supper—some understand it, as a supper prepared for our Lord and his apostles, a day or two before the passover. And in as much as Christ partook of a meal at the time he instituted Feet Washing and the Communion, the apostles gathered their authority for eating a meal upon such occasions. Let that be as it may, it is evident that they did eat a supper upon such occasions; and that the same was termed by the apostle for Lord's Supper. Whereas, if they had no authority for so doing, the apostles would not have called it the Lord's Supper, but would have given them to understand, that the like ought not to be observed at such times. . . .

THE COMMUNION.

By the Communion, we are to understand, the bread and wine set apart as emblematical of the broken body and shed blood of our Lord and Saviour, Jesus Christ. The bread and wine, for the above use and purpose, is no where in the Gospel called the Lord's Supper. It is termed by the apostle Paul, the Communion: i Cor. x. 16. . . . and in the 11th chapter. . . .

The above quotation from Paul to the Corinthians, concerning the Communion, coincides with what the Evangelists have recorded upon that institution. . . . It appears very evident, that it was after supper that Christ celebrated the Communion with his disciples, and that there is a difference between the Supper and the Communion. Luke appears to be very explicit upon this point, when he says—"Likewise also the cup after supper." Paul refers to the same, when he says-"After the same manner also he took the cup, when he had supped." i Cor. ii chapter. . . .

Illustration of the communion from Nead's *Theological Works*

As it respects the proper administration of the Communion, we can learn from the Gospel, that the great head of the church, our dear Redeemer, in that doleful night in which he was betrayed into the hands of sinners, he took bread—that is, unleavened bread; for it appears reasonable, that it was of the bread which they partook in eating of the passover, without it can be proven that they had two sorts of bread upon the table at that time—for it was the days of unleavened bread—to represent his unleavened body, which was shortly to be broken upon the cross. It is wrong, and quite contrary to the ancient order, to make use of fermented, or leavened bread, in celebrating the Communion. Leavened bread is not a fit emblem of the sacred body of our adorable redeemer. The apostle Paul has an allusion to this bread, and the state in which the communicant ought to be at the time of the Communion: ... i Cor. v. 7-8. ...

After the bread is eaten, the administrator, or the brother at the head of the table, will proceed to prepare the cups for the Communion—and when a portion of the wine is poured into the cups, he again, with all the members, will rise upon their feet, and he, the administrator, will supplicate a throne of mercy, concluding with thanksgiving unto the Almighty for his blessings, especially for the cup, or wine, which has been selected for that sacred purpose; and all the members will unite with him in saying Amen. And when they have taken their seats again, the Administrator will present the cup to his right hand brother, saying the cup of the New Testament is the communion of the blood of Jesus Christ. The brother will take a sup and then say the same words to the brother on his right. So the cup will pass around, until it will arrive at that brother who is seated next on the left hand of the administrator. He will then give the cup to the administrator, who will also take a sup. . . .

I do not believe that the bread and wine, in the Communion, undergoes any change, so as to become the real body and blood of our Lord Jesus Christ. It is the same as it was before it was selected for that purpose. Many undertake to prove from what we can read in the 6th chapter of John, 53d, 54th, 55th, and 56th verses, that the bread and wine used in this ordinance are transubstantiated into the real body and blood of Christ. For my part, I understand the Saviour in these verses, in a spiritual and not in a literal sense. . . .

It is possible for members to disqualify themselves for the Communion, and that it is the bounden duty of all members, previous to their going to the Communion, to examine themselves. Upon examining ourselves, there is no doubt that we shall discover flaws in our characters. The very best christians are liable to err. . . .

Dear reader, you must see the great necessity of observing those institutions as they have been appointed; for a deviation from this rule will frustrate the design of what the Saviour had in view in giving these institutions to the church.[14]

When Peter Nead published a booklet on baptism in 1845, he also included "An Essay on the Lord's Supper" by his friend, fellow minister, and former neighbor (Nead was now living in Botetourt County, Virginia), John Kline. In his essay, Kline attempted to demonstrate that the meal which Jesus ate with his disciples was not the Jewish Passover celebration.

An Essay on the Lord's Supper
by John Kline

This is that institution which God instituted, through his Son Jesus Christ, as a remembrance in figure of that Heavenly Supper of which Christ speaks—"A certain man made a great supper, and bade many;" Luke xiv. 16, and "blessed are those servants, whom the Lord when he cometh shall find watching; verily, I say unto you that he shall gird himself, and make them sit down to meat, and will come forth and serve them, xii. 27, and they shall come from the East and from the West, and from the North and from the South, and shall sit down in the kingdom of God." xiii. 29. "That ye may eat and drink in my kingdom, and sit on thrones, judging the twelve tribes of Israel." xxii. 30—among other passages go to prove the above. That the Lord in the evening (or end,) of this world, will or has prepared such a Supper, for all them that love him and keep his commandments, as the above, is a fact (which cannot be denied.) We must reasonably conclude, that the Lord has something in his Church and in his ordinances of the new covenant, as an anti-type of that Heavenly Supper. And as the ordinance of the breaking of bread, and partaking of the cup, is an entirely different representation, to accomplish, in the mind, of the believer, namely, to remember the broken body of Christ, which was mangled, and lacerated by the lash, in Pilot's judgment hall, and by the nails and Spear on the Cross; and of his shed blood, which was shed for the remission of sins;—of this the Saviour says: "This do in remembrance of me." Luke xxii. 19. And Paul says, as oft as ye eat this bread, and drink this cup, ye do show the Lord's death till he come. i. Cor. xi. 26. So we see, that the communion or breaking of Bread, is not the Lord's supper. It becomes a subject of investigation, to see what is the Lord's Supper. Paul speaks thus of the Lord's Supper, "when ye come together into one place, this is not to eat the Lord's Supper." i. Cor. xi. 20. Why was it not the Lord's Supper, which the Corinthians held? he answers, for in eating, every one taketh before other, his own Supper, and one is hungry, and another is drunken, 21. This is plain, but he now shows that he wished them to eat a supper, for he says in the latter part of the same chapter. "Wherefore my brethren when ye come together to eat, tarry one for another." verse 33. Do not as you have done—"every one take before other his own supper;" but tarry, wait until the night, and then eat the Lord's Supper, as becometh Christians in love and union. Thus it is plain, that the Apostles had, and ate a Supper; and that the Bread and Wine, are not that Supper, is likewise plain; but that Paul called it, (that is the breaking of Bread and the partaking of the cup,) the communion is plain. "The cup of blessing which we bless, is it not the Communion of the blood of Christ? the bread which we break, is it not the Communion of the body of Christ?" i. Cor. x. 16. So when the believer, who does all the commandments, of the Lord, attends to this also, and in the attendance remembers the Lord's death, and suffering, he is spiritually in communion with the Lord's body, and consequently becomes partaker of his promises. But still, this is not the anti-type of the Heavenly Supper. We shall now see whether Christ has not given his disciples a litteral ordinance, by which the mind of the believer can be fed with heavenly things, while partaking of it, according to the word of God. Here it would be well to see the authority, by which Christ came. Moses says, Deut. xviii. 15, "and will put my words into his mouth, and he shall speak unto them, all that I shall command him," 18. "And it shall come to pass, that whosoever will not harken unto my words, which he shall speak in my name, I will require it of him, verse 19. And the Prophet Isaiah, says, "Behold I have given him for a witness to the people, a leader and commander to the people, lv. 4. So Christ was that prophet, and that commander of the people, and he himself declares, that the Father had sent him, and had given him a commandment, what he should speak, and what he should say," John xii. 49.

Now he, as the Commander, and legal Author of the New Testament, in the evening of the day before the day of the Preparation of Jewish Passover, after he had come to Bethany, six days before the Passover, John xii. 1; and after having eaten a supper in the house of Simon the Leper (still in Bethany) two days before the Passover. See Matt. xxvi. 6. Mark xiv." He now on the next day, that is, the day before the Passover, sends his disciples, Peter and John, to the city, that is, Jerusalem, to prepare, as they thought, the Passover. See Matt. xxvi. 17-19. Mark xiv. 12, 13, &c. Which however, could not yet be prepared according to the law, on that day, is as plain as can be, as it was the day before the legal day of the preparation of the Passover of the law, as I shall show hereafter. Now it is plain, that the disciples were under the impression that Jesus intended to eat the Passover according to the law, this year; but at the same time, they also knew that that day, in which Jesus sent them to the city to prepare, was not yet the day in which the Passover according to the law could be prepared, and eaten, but of course, the room, the place for lodging the night before, must be engaged, and procured, and the room cleansed from leaven, according to the law, and of course prepared a Supper, in that large upper room to which Jesus sent them. So when it was evening, Jesus and his disciples came and seated themselves at the table, see Matt. xxvi. 20; Mark xiv. 17, from which table, or supper he rose; John xiii. 4; and laid aside his garments; and took a towel, and girded himself: and now begins to wash his disciples' feet; now a new something makes its appearance, and all was astonishment with the disciples; this was something that Jesus never before practiced with his disciples; he now institutes some of those ordinances, which he had received of his Heavenly Father, of which the disciples, as yet, knew nothing, see 7 verse; what I do now, thou knowest not. So after he had washed his disciples' feet, and taken his seat at the table, see verse 12, he begins to eat, which is very plain; and now hear him—ye call me Master and Lord and ye say well, for so I am; 15 v. If you know these things, happy are ye, if ye do them, 17 v. He that eateth bread with me, hath lifted up his heel against me, 18 v. This of course, all transpired while they were eating; "now I tell you before it come, that when it is come to pass ye may believe that I am he. 19v. Verily, verily, I say unto you, he that receiveth me, receiveth him that sent me: 20 v. When Jesus had thus said, he was troubled in spirit, and testified and said; verily, verily, I say unto you, that one of you shall betray me; 21 v.: now see Matt. xxvi. 21; And as they did eat, Jesus said; verily, verily, I say unto you, that one of you shall betray me. See also Mark xiv. 18; one of you that eateth with me, shall betray me. Now it is evident that they were eating at this time, a meal or supper—not yet broken bread which Jesus after this broke to represent his body; but a supper, as John styles it; John xiii. 4; now, as the disciples became somewhat alarmed at the saying of the Saviour, that one of them should betray him, they began to make inquiry who this should be; when Jesus at last reveals him, by telling them, that the one that dippeth with him in the dish; Matt. xxvi. 23; Mark xiv. 20; and at last by dipping a sop, and giving it to Judas Iscariot. Judas was finally fully revealed. John xiii. 26. So Judas went immediately out, and it was night; 30 v. Now it is evident from John, that Judas went out from supper while they were yet eating, and so was not at the communion or breaking of bread. . . .

I have shown above, that the supper, which our Lord ate with his disciples, in the large upper room, in the city of Jerusalem, the night before he suffered, was not the Jewish passover; but I promised to give it here plain, which I intend to do here. Jesus after he had finished the supper, and breaking of bread, sung a hymn and went out, Matt. xxvi. 30, but yet talketh with his disciples through all the latter part of the xiii. c. of John, the 14, 15, 16, and 17, chapters, and in the 18th chapter again joins the rest of the Evangelists, in speaking of the circumstance of the garden of Gethsemane, where he is taken by the soldiers and led to the Palace of Caiaphas, from thence early in the morning to Pilate the governor, and to his judgment hall; but here a difficulty comes on the Jews:—they are not willing to go into the judgment hall, lest they be defiled, and then they could not eat the passover, John xvii. 28. This judgment hall was under the jurisdiction of the Romans; therefore, the Jews as they thought, would have become unclean, and consequently disqualified to eat the Passover that evening; you see then that the day, in which Jesus was condemned before Pilate, and crucified, was the day in which the Jews prepared, killed, and ate their Passover; see John xix. 14, 31, 42. Now Jesus was crucified, and died, just about the hour of the day, and on the same day of the month, and year, in which the Lamb, under the law, was commanded to be killed. How then could he have eaten the Jewish Passover that year?

That could not have been, nay, but he ate a supper with his disciples, but not that of the law, but still a supper, according to his good pleasure, and the directions of God his Heavenly Father, as also those other ordinances, that he established at the same time, washing of feet, and the breaking of bread, and while engaged in instituting them, he enforces the importance of them upon his disciples in these solemn words, an example have I given you, that ye should do as I have done to you, John xii. 15, and if you know these things happy are ye if ye do them, 17; and this do in remembrance of me, Luke xxii. 17, and just as he ascended to heaven, "all power is given me, in heaven, and in earth, therefore go teach all nations baptizing them, &c., and teach them, to observe all things whatsoever I have commanded you." Matt. xxviii. 19, 20.[15]

The love feast service was certainly one of the most important activities in the life of the church; and consequently numerous problems regarding the Brethren practice were taken to the Annual Meeting for guidance. The following minutes of the Annual Meeting are arranged chronologically from a number of Henry Kurtz' sections. The minutes are introduced by Kurtz' personal comments on the Lord's supper and on the love feasts.

By [the Lord's Supper] we understand, not the communion of bread and wine as it is understood and used by many denominations, but we understand by it that meal immediately preceding the communion, called in the New Testament *deipnon—supper,* the principal meal of the Hebrews, and taken by them in the evening; see Luke 14:12, &c., particularly 1 Cor. 11: 21, or that feast of charity to which Jude v. 12, is alluding.

By [the Love Feasts] we understand those festivals celebrated from time to time in our churches, at which there generally assemble ministers and members from all the surrounding districts, and sometimes from far and near, and where most of the ordinances of the house of God are administered, viz: Baptism, when there are applicants, and always feetwashing, the Lord's supper and the communion, &c. These generally attract great crowds, hence the following queries.

Y. M. 1812. Art. 2. Concerning feet-washing, inasmuch as it has happened sometimes that members are permitted to have their feet washed by other denominations, who also practice feet-washing at their breaking of bread, yet not quite according to the word as we can understand it, it is considered advisable that it should not be proper to take part in such imperfect exercises, &c.

Y. M. 1819. Art. 3. Whether we could break the bread (of communion) without having a supper? We hold, that we ought by all means in all the exercises (ordinances) look to the testimony of Jesus and his example; for the Lord Jesus, shortly before his suffering, when he instituted the Lord's supper, &c., after he had washed his disciples' feet, he did eat the supper with them, where he also dipped the sop, and gave it to Judas; see John 13:26. And Mark 14: 18, "And as they sat, and did eat, Jesus said, Verily I say unto you, One of you which eateth with me shall betray me." And v. 22, "And as they did eat, Jesus took bread, and blessed, and break it, and give to them, and said, Take, eat: this is my body, &c."

Y. M. 1822. (Miami.) Art. 3. Whether there should be something of the supper on the table at feet-washing, it was the unanimous agreement in the council of the great meeting, that it should not be.

Y. M. 1827. Art. 6. Whether there should be no other meat but mutton at the supper, was generally considered as most agreeable (to our feelings "gemuthlichste") to take mutton, as it has been always customary with the ancient brethren, yet to make no law herein, and to bear with one another. . . .

Y. M. 1832. Art. 2. Whether such may participate in the (Lord's) supper who are not members, if there is room? Considered, to leave it to the churches, when there is such room. (N. B. This is not to be understood of the communion of bread and wine.)

Y. M. 1833. Art. 4. Whether a person may be admitted to our (communion or) breaking of bread, who is not baptized according to Gospel (as we understand it)? Considered, No. . . .

Y. M. 1841. Art. 2. Whether the brethren practice feet-washing strictly according to the gospel? Considered, after much conversation and reflection, that feet-washing as practiced hitherto by the brethren is according to the word, and that the mode as far as we could learn until now, could in nowise be improved. . . .

Y. M. 1848. (Ohio.) Art. 21. Whether it would not be more according to the word in St. John's gospel, 13: 15, that a brother should both wash and wipe his brother's feet? Considered, that the brethren still think as they did seven years ago in this respect. See Min. of 1841, Art. 2 (above). . . .

Y. M. 1849. Art. 5. Some members think there is too much feasting at our lovefeasts, in providing so much for those who come to feast and make disturbance at our meetings. Considered, that we are to feed the hungry, if we are led by Christ's example; and the apostle says, "Therefore if thine enemy hunger, feed him; if he thirst, give him drink: for in so doing thou shalt heap coals of fire on his head." Rom. 12: 20. . . .

Y. M. 1849. Art. 35. Whether it would not be more consistent with the word, if at the communion the administrator would give the bread and cup to the sisters, and they divide it like the brethren among themselves, and the administrator to pass along to keep order? Considered unanimously, to go on in celebrating the communion as heretofore. . . .

Y. M. 1850. Art. 34. Would it not be better and more corresponding with the Gospel, if the brethren would hold the Lord's supper more in unison with each other; for it appears that some have bread and cheese, and some have meat and soup, &c. Considered, that uniformity would be better. . . .

Y. M. 1863. Art. 21. Whereas, there has obtained of late years some difference in observing the Lord's supper among different churches, some setting the supper on the table before feet-washing, while some do not till after—the latter being the old universal practice;—and whereas the proceedings of Annual Meeting of last year in the Art. 43, have grieved some of our brethren; and whereas, a conciliatory course should always be pursued when brethren have a preference as it regards the mode or way of observing an ordinance, so that it is properly observed—we therefore recall the decision of the Annual Meeting above referred to, and let the subject of the time of putting the supper on the table stand precisely where it stood previous to the decision of 1862, with the understanding that the churches may and should continue without making any change either way, until we have further light on the subject to bring about a more full union.[16]

Another insight into the Brethren love feast and its significance in the church is provided by a series of private letters, which were written primarily in the decades of the 1840s and in the 1850s from various Brethren congregations in the states east of the Mississippi River.

From Indiana in 1839:

i will allso inform you that I wase at A sacrement down in putnam 10 mils from her   we went down sunday morning and stad til monday   it commenced   on   satterday   an   held   til   monday   thare   was   fore prechers   thar two myers that preached one miller and one garvar[17]

From Maryland in 1840:

Mother and myself was a few weaks since at a lovefeast in Washington County the other side of Bonsborow   there was a great many people there   I dont think I seen so maney preachers together since I was at the yearly meeting,   Old br Daniel Garver was there and br John Cline and br Miller from virginia   br John Price and br John Umstead from pennsilvania,   br Emmert br Funk and the two br Longs and More br preachers I cannot mension,   br Cline and br Price spake powerfull, how we should keep close to the word of God and should it be that we should have to suffer Death for our faith in Jesus that we should not give way for we would then be removd from this land of trial, to the mansion of Everlasting rest.[18]

From Virginia in 1845:

there was a love feast in Franklin Co last saturday & on Sunday there was preaching   Elizabeth, Nathaniel & William Niniger went from here. Jacob, Sarah & Julia A Whitmore went from his house. Old Mrs. Cruse went with them   they all went in Mr. whitmores Carriage   they went over last friday and came back yesterday[19]

From Indiana in 1848:

there is talk of having a communion meting in this arm of the church in June   its thought Peter Nead will be hear if there is a communion hear but we are not certain yet if it will be or not.[20]

From Maryland in 1851:

I have not been to see Aunt Betsy Englar yet but I intend going before long   she intend having meeting at her house on Thursday next.   we have Lovefeast at Medow branch church on Tusday next & at the Beverdam on Thursday. your old friend Mary Stoner was immersed a few sabbeths ago but I think it will be some time before they Baptize him   he is a pretty hard case   people say he is not kind to her. . . .

I attended the lovefeast   I saw a number of our friends & a little of everybody   we had 10 strange preachers   2 of them where from Va. although I believe I cant remember their names   they had a number of meetings around us & I think they have done some good in our neighbourhood. I attended the meeting at your Aunt Betsy Englars   there was quite a concourse of persons assembled   they held their preaching in the Barn[21]

From Maryland in 1853:

Lord willing there will be a lovefeast meeting at "Pleasant Hill" near New Market on the 29th day and evening of September—and at Beaver dam on the 13th of October—and at "Meadow Branch" (near Royer's and Roop's) on the 16th day of October.[22]

From Indiana in 1853:

On the 25th of this month there will be a communion meeting in Owen County South of us 50 miles   Brother John Metzgar will be at our house on the 23rd to accompany the brethren down thare. the communion meeting commences on Dear Creak Carroll County the 11th October the 13th on Bachellers run and on the 15th on wild cat with Brother John Metzgar, and on the 27th of Oct. at our meetinghouse on Cornstock.[23]

From Maryland in 1855:

there was Lovefeast at the Pipe Creek church on last Sunday. Otho's Brother and I talked of going down but could not leave just at that time. he is a preacher. I suppose you know him his name is Cornelious Castle. we will not have Love feast here until fall   then you can come to it   we have a new Dunker Church in Brownsville   Mr. Bear, Mr. Slifer & Mr. Castle are our ministers. I was at Mr. Slifers last week & spent the day   he lives in Burkettsville.[24]

From Maryland later in 1855:

We had Lovefeast at our Dunker church on last Tuesday week   had quite a pleasant time   not very many strangers there   the Rev. Slifer & Bear stayed all night with us   I suppose you know them . . . we have had quite a revival in the Dunker church here this summer   a great many persons Baptized on most evry meeting day   the Baptizing is done at our dam   I expect the church has been built since you visited Brownsville   it is quite a comfortable Church   Otho and I talk of going down to Beverdam to Lovefeast the 18th of this month.[25]

From Indiana in 1858:

our communion meeting was on the 24th of October   there was a
large concourse of people hear   Some though not less than 3000 people
hear   we had meetings at 2 places in day time   in the woods near the
meeting Danial Nahar, Jacob Flory & Jacob Wagoner Spoke to the people
and in the Meeting house John Metsgar & John Shively Spoke. our Meeting house very much crowded at night   we had excellent preaching
hear   thare was 20 add[itional] members from wild cat down with us.
Some from Bachellors run church and Dear creak church above Delphi.[26]

*All of the above letters describing Brethren love feasts were written by
members of the church, who were reporting what had happened or would
happen from their particular perspective. Two accounts of the love feast
written by non-Brethren provide a different type of perspective. The first is
a relatively brief private letter, which was written by a young man with a
sense of humor to his girl friend.*

                                         New Market, Va.
                                         June 9th, 1857
[I have] been confined at home very closely, ever since I last wrote
you, leaving once . . . to gratify a curiosity which I had of seeing the
Tunkers partake of the passover, viz., lamb's soup—foot washing—holy
kissing. Indeed it presents a solemn and an imposing scene for any one to
behold & contemplate. However, I felt rather the worse of my trip. For
they do not partake of the *passover* until sometime after night. Knowing
this, I did not start to the meeting, nine miles distant until late in the evening, & not having the precaution to sup at home I became so hungry by the
time (12 o'clock) a general invitation was extended to the audience to partake of refreshments, that I made myself as much a *sheep* as the meat was
sheep for I indulged by far too freely. Our supper over, I mounted my
horse & gave him the rein, as the cloudy sky & darkness of the night, made
it impossible for me to see it. Tho I reached home in safety, I felt rather
sleepy & Sheepy all next day. Hence concluded to stay up all night & eat
too much lamb's soup & mutton wasn't what it is cracked up to be.[27]

*The second account was written by a German journalist, Julius Her-
mann Moritz Busch, who traveled in the United States in 1851-1852. The
report of his travels was published in Germany in 1854 and included a detailed account of his visit to a love feast at the Lower Stillwater congrega-*

tion near Dayton, Ohio. Peter Nead, who had just moved to Ohio in 1848, was the presiding elder. Busch was given a copy of Nead's "Theological Writings," which had just been published in 1850; he was evidently favorably impressed by Nead and the Brethren.

It may occasionally happen to the traveler who journeys from Southern Pennsylvania or Maryland through Virginia to Ohio and Indiana that he comes upon a farm along the road leading to his destination which, despite its generally American character, reminds him of Germany by various features and peculiarities. He may meet there people who seem to be set down from another time. A black felt hat with noticeably wide, completely flat, brim does not seem to go with a curiously-cut, ordinarily grey or dark brown tailcoat with standing collar and only one row of buttons, resembling Grandfather's costume when he married Grandmother. But what a greater contrast to this and to the appearance of the neighbors of Anglo-Saxon derivation are the long flowing locks of hair and the foot-long patriarchial beard which curls down from chin and cheeks!

However, if this traveler enters the clean and comfortable homes of these strangely dressed men, he then finds them and theirs to be an upright, simple, hospitable race, who live a harmless life in modest prosperity. The head of the house will seek to convince him, as soon as the conversation turns to religion, that only the baptism of adults is scriptural. An American friend, to whom he recounts the encounter with these people, will tell him that they are called "Dunkers" or "Dunkards" in English, and that they make up a brotherhood which counts as its members a large part of the German farmers from the woods of Pennsylvania to the praries of Iowa and Missouri. . . .

The Dunker Character

The Dunkers, as mentioned earlier, have no history after the time of Beissel's departure. But if the latter (who approached the Shakers in their mystic doctrines) have dried up to a frail twig which will soon wither completely, the former have developed into one of the largest branches on the American tree of sects. In general, they are considered to be an industrious, sober, charitable people, who walk the way of the Lord irreproachably, do good as far as it is possible for them, and instruct their children in the fear of the Lord. Of course, their dogmatic theology is as crudely hewn, awkward and rustic as their Pennsylvania Dutch, as is not otherwise to be expected. Also the living faith and glowing devotion which yet during this century expressed itself in a mighty revival has been replaced, according to their own testimony, in the hearts of many souls by lethargy and indifference. This is explained by them as owing to the circumstance that the majority of the brethren have become wealthy and that some of these have married those of other faiths.

So much for the character of this German Baptist brotherhood in the backwoods of North America. The following sketch is a picture of their churchly life which I had the opportunity to learn virtually from the ground up.

An Ohio Dunker Meeting

About six miles from Dayton, a few hundred steps off the road to Salem in a clearing in the endless woods stands a long, low brick house covered with shingles, which is enclosed by a typical worm fence with a circumference of about one American acre. In front of it is found a spring under some trees, next to which has been built a rough bench. It is a meetinghouse of the Dunkers, who settled in great numbers in this area, as is true for the entire valley through which the Mad River and both Miamis run.

It was on October 7 [1851] that I attended there one of their meetings, to which they often come from many miles distance in order to hear the Gospel preached and to hold the Lord's Supper with feetwashing. . . .

It must have been nine o'clock when I arrived at the meeting house. In the woods in front of the fence a peddler had set up a bar, and in his vicinity were found under the trees many coaches and horses, belonging to people who, like myself, had come without belonging to the brotherhood. Among them the genus "Loafers" (here, as in every other place in Uncle Sam's land composing at least a fourth of the male youth) was present in numbers. Inside the fence, however, there teemed the long-bearded figures and beaver-tailed coats of the "Brethren," whose numbers increased by the minute. They walked about hand in hand, and all newcomers gave and received the "brotherly right hand" and the "holy kiss." It must be said that the latter ceremony was practiced only between brother and brother, or sister and sister.

Along the fence behind the house a square of buggies, market carts and riding horses was formed, which had brought the believers of both sexes. From one door of the meetinghouse, which opened onto a small veranda, flamed an open fire around huge pots and kettles, attended by women in white caps and aprons, and a blue pillar of smoke spiraled from the chimney. On a stone near the spring was placed a metal cup with which those who had no interest in refreshing themselves from the peddler's barrel of whiskey could slake their thirst.

Suddenly all moved toward the entrances, and in a short time the house was so filled with Dunkers and onlookers that several latecomers had to stand beside the door, which was almost completely taken up by a colossal deacon with a long brown beard, the largest and most handsome male figure which I encountered in America. The room was a rectangle, with nine windows and three doors. Its low board ceiling was supported by four roughly-hewn timbers as pillars, and it probably contained at this time between three and four hundred persons. Neither choir nor chancel, organ nor altar, nor burning candles were to be seen in it, and therefore the room was more to be compared with a large farmhouse room [*Bauernstube*] than to a German church. . . .

The First Session

The worship service began with an English hymn from the second part of the *Harfenspiel der Kinder Zions*. Following this anything but pleasant-sounding singing was a prayer in German by a preacher with a whining voice. During this the profane fire crackled in an unmannerly fashion through the open kitchen door and was also accompanied—a not unusual occurrence in American churches—by the unashamed and frightful crying of one of the infants which had been brought along. After the one praying pronounced the Amen, one of the bishops read a chapter from Jeremiah, and that from an English Bible, whereupon several German verses were sung. These were read line for line by a preacher for the congregation, a circumstance which is possibly based upon the fact that only a few of those present still owned a songbook in their mother tongue. It also happened that more parts had been sung to the English hymn, and from this one does not seem to go far wrong in assuming that the transition process which all German settlers undergo who leave Pennsylvania is already more than two-thirds completed among the Dunkers in the west. . . .

Then followed several more preachers who spoke with more or less talent, mostly in English, some in German, almost all disturbed by the screaming infants and the noise of the fire which cooked their noonday meal and therefore, seemed to have the right to speak a word along with them. All of them concluded their remarks with the naive sentence that if they had not brought anything to the benefit and edification of the brotherhood, they at least hoped that they had not said anything harmful.

It was then three o'clock, and perhaps nine or ten speakers had appeared, when the presiding bishop ended further oratory as he directed those present to leave the house. It was time for the midday meal and the room had to be prepared for that. Since there was not enough space for all to be fed at once, as soon as it was ready the elderly and the women should eat first. The others, with which he also intended to mean those not belonging to the brotherhood, would find their portion at the second course. . . .

The praying, singing, and preaching began once more. It continued until the growing darkness reminded of the rites which were intended for the evening. Then tin insect lights were placed on the tables, a hymn was sung which dealt with that which was to take place, and the passion story was read according to the Gospel of Mark. Then two brethren, who had rolled up their sleeves and bound long towels around their bodies, carried in a tub, in which the male members of the group were to wash their feet. The same occurred on the sisters' side with two deaconesses.

During this holy practice one of the bishops spoke about its meaning, in that he considered depicted there not only the obligation of humility through the kneeling and bowing of the one who washed, but also equally a symbolic correction of the brother through the extension of his feet to be washed and the act of purification. Each was to admonish the other to forgiveness for transgressions as preparation for the Lord's Supper, which was seen by the speaker as the symbol of the meal of the believers at the time of the second coming of Christ on the evening of the world.

Upon the feetwashing followed then the supper in the form of an ordinary evening meal during which the congregation, as had happened during the midday meal, after grace ate from tin bowls with tin spoons, first soup, then meat, bread and butter.

All of these ceremonies were no longer disturbed and mocked by the noisy fire and the strong-lunged infants, but unfortunately by far worse guests. Namely, as thanks for the midday meal given them freely, the gang of loafers outside made it their business to interrupt the love feast of the harmless Dunkers in the most cunning ways. Some yodeled and croaked through the doors. Others outside sang with all of their voices the street song:

I come from Salem City
With my washbowl on my knee. [English in original]

Still others shot with pistols at the windows near where the women sat, and others circled the house in troops imitating the scream of wild turkeys. In short, it was an uproar as if a wild horde or a men's choir traveling to Blorberg had bivouacked outside on the lawn. This was more than youthful high spirits; it was outright baseness, at which a lamb's patience could have learned to bite. This notwithstanding, the tone of voice in which Bishop Nead, the presiding elder, finally forbade them the tumult hardly contained anger. Whoever cannot appreciate the mildness of this disposition, can at least pay the respect of astonishment.

Following their theory of biblical literalism, one might seem to be justified in the expectation that the Dunkers would understand their communion following the supper as the partaking of the true body and blood of Christ, and thereby accept the teaching of transubstantiation. However, this is not the case, as Peter Nead's address demonstrated with which he introduced the rite. He explained this as the possibility of an inward experience of the communion of all brethren in faith and in love. After this meditation, which concluded with the admonition that any member of the congregation who had any misunderstanding with any other brother or sister should be immediately reconciled or refrain from participating in the table of the Lord, the kiss of love passed from mouth to mouth. Then a bishop arose and pronounced a prayer upon the bread, which had been brought in the meantime. This consisted of unleavened bread, baked in such a way that they could be easily broken into equal sizes. The prayer ended with a loud "Amen," joined in by the entire gathering.

Now the administrator of the sacrament broke a long strip from the bread, turned to one who sat next to him on the right, and said to him: "Dear brother, the bread which we break is the communion of the body of Jesus Christ," whereupon he broke off a piece and gave it to the one addressed, who laid it before him. The latter then took the long strip, with which he performed the same for his neighbor on the right as had the administrator. After all had received bread in this fashion, the presiding bishop now announced that the bread was broken, and that when they then ate they seriously remember its meaning as "shadowing forth the bruised and mangled body of our dear Redeemer." [English in original]

After the distribution of the bread, the presiding bishop prayed over the wine, which was brought in in two green flasks, and was drunk out of tin cups. It was red wine. The cup went around the tables in the same manner, during which one said to the other in English or in German: "Dear brother, the wine which we drink is the communion of the blood of Jesus Christ." The congregation then sang an appropriate hymn.

The entire ceremony closed with a prayer after which Nead invited the brethren coming from a distance to a breakfast to be held in the meeting house on the following morning. Then all left, and I started my homeward journey illuminated, as wished for, by the stars.

Epilogue

Some weeks later I followed the repeated invitation of Bishop Nead, to visit him at his farm, extended to me upon departure. Here I learned to know in him not only a childlike, loving spirit, but also a man much more informed in theological matters than I had anticipated. He had formerly pursued the tanning trade and had only moved here from Virginia three years before. His book on the beliefs of his sect is for me one of the most valuable memorabilia of all the souvenirs gathered in beautiful Ohio.[28]

THE BELIEF IN THE HOLY KISS

Always related to the love feast, but not limited to it in Brethren practice, was the holy kiss or salutation. Peter Nead also had something to say on the holy kiss in his book, "Primitive Christianity," although not much was written on the subject by Brethren during these years.

THE HOLY KISS.

It is the duty of brethren to salute one another with an Holy Kiss. The inspired apostle Paul, in his epistle to the Romans, xvi. 16, hath given the law for this practice: "Salute one another with an Holy Kiss"—and in i. Cor. xvi. 20: "Greet ye one another with an Holy Kiss"—and likewise the apostle Peter hath commanded the observance of the same: ii. Pet. v. 14. "Greet ye one another with a kiss of charity." The literal observance of this command, is simply to touch with the lips; and I will venture to say, that we have not, in the Bible or Testament, a plainer command of any thing, than that of the observance of the Holy Kiss. The apostle does not say when or how often we shall salute one another. From this I take it for granted, that it ought to be frequently observed. Whenever brethren give one another the right hand of fellowship, at times of meeting for divine service, and when a member is received by Baptism—that is, upon his coming up out of the water, those upon the shore or bank ought to give him the right hand of fellowship, accompanied with the salutation of the Kiss; and especially when we observe Feet Washing, and just before we celebrate the communion, this can be done in an orderly manner, so as to cause no confusion. Whenever brethren wash and wipe a brother's feet, he ought immediately to give the right hand, accompanied with the salutation of the Kiss; and after the Lord's Supper has been partaken of, and just before the celebration of the Communion, it ought again to be observed—which can be done without causing any interruption. The members being all seated at the table, let them commence at one end of the table and so pass along, until every member has been saluted with hand and Kiss. Oh! how solemn and important is the observance of this duty upon such occasions. The members being invited to call to mind the death and sufferings of their Lord and Master, and now knowing how soon they may be called upon to

Giving the holy
kiss, from Nead's
Theological Works

seal with their blood the testimony of the truth, as it is in Jesus; it therefore becometh the members to bind themselves with hand and Kiss, to be
true to one another—not to forsake one another in times of tribulation—
but as John says, to lay down their lives for the brethren.

We are informed by Godfred Arnold, in his Portrait of the First
Christians, that they (the first christians) at their lovefeasts, saluted one
another twice, with hand and Kiss,—it is highly probable at the time of
Feet Washing, and between the Lord's Supper and the Communion, as we
have already observed. The spiritual import of this performance is spiritual
affection, and is intended to promote mutual love among the fraternity. It
has been supposed to have been used by men and women separately—that
is, brethren to salute brethren, and sisters to salute sisters. There can be no

impropriety in a brother giving a sister the right hand of fellowship, nor for a sister to give a brother the right hand of fellowship.[29]

In addition, the Annual Meetings of this era discussed the use of the holy kiss a number of times. Henry Kurtz added his own introduction.

Scriptural foundation for the same: Rom. 16:16, "Salute one another with an holy kiss." 1 Cor. 16:20, "Greet ye one another with an holy kiss." 2 Cor. 13:12, "Greet one another with an holy kiss." 1 Thess. 5:26, "Greet all the brethren with an holy kiss." 1 Pet. 5:14, "Greet ye one another with a kiss of charity."

Y. M. 1797. Art. 4. It was in union concluded, that the holy kiss and the kiss of charity should not be neglected, since in some places it is almost entirely omitted; but according to the words of the apostles, we should prove ourselves on all occasions as disciples of Jesus, and be steadfast in brotherly love; and notwithstanding all disgrace, we should not be ashamed of the word of Christ.

Y. M. 1810. Art. 4. Concerning when brethren or members get at variance or in difficulty with one another, no one is allowed to refuse to the other the kiss for himself, without counsel of the church, unless there has been committed an obvious crime.—Art. 5. Concerning when a member has been put back from the communion, and some from kindness or relationship continue to salute such with the holy kiss, before they are received again by the church, was considered as a fault, and should be by no means.

Y. M. 1828. Art. 8. Whether the holy kiss should be observed at feet-washing and the breaking of bread? Considered, that it is right and proper.

Y. M. 1831. Art. 3. Whether it could be approved of when the brotherly kiss is so often omitted, even at meetings and love-feasts? Considered, no, not at all. . . .

Y. M. 1843. Art 2. Whether a brother may refuse the kiss to a brother who has committed a fault, for instance, getting intoxicated, ere he has been brought before and judged by the council of the church? Considered, that though a member could not be required to salute a brother with the kiss, while in a state of intoxication, it is still our duty first to tell the fault unto the church, and to await its decision, before we withdraw ourselves from a member. . . .

Y. M. 1853. Art. 39. Would it not be more consistent with the gospel and the practice of the apostles, to extend the kiss, termed the holy kiss and the kiss of charity, to each other only when coming together and separating from each other, and not at feet-washing, and at the communion? Or did our Lord and Master indeed institute such a thing in that night in which he was betrayed? Considered, that we feel perfect liberty in the gospel to continue as we always heretofore have done.

Y. M. 1856. Art. 27. Does Christian fellowship, according to the gospel, forbid, or require, or leave it optional for brethren, when meeting in cities, towns or at public gatherings, when extending the salutation of the hand, to accompany the same with the salutation of the holy kiss? Considered, optional.[30]

THE BELIEF IN ANOINTING THE SICK

Another distinctive belief of the Brethren was the anointing of the sick as a means of bringing about healing. Peter Nead included a relatively brief statement on this subject in his discussion of Brethren theology.

ANOINTING THE SICK WITH OIL IN THE NAME OF THE LORD

This is a performance which has become almost extinct in this our day; and oh, what a pity! seeing that it is connected with such great promises. Our beloved brother and apostle James hath written thus upon this subject: "Is any sick among you, let him call for the elders of the church, and let them pray over him, anointing him with oil in the name of the Lord: and the prayer of faith shall save the sick and the Lord shall raise him up, and if he have committed sins, they shall be forgiven him." James v. 14, 15. And when our Lord sent the seventy disciples it was a part of their commission to perform this holy work, as we can read in Mark iv. 13: "And they cast out many devils, and anointed with oil many that were sick, and healed them." Now, this is the privilege of the afflicted sons and daughters of men; and if they do not embrace this opportunity, it is their own fault. Now, all those who desire to have this holy work performed upon them ought to be perfectly reconciled unto the will of God—in particular as it respects their recovery from a bed of affliction. Yes, they ought to make a complete surrender of themselves into the hands of the Lord; and it is the bounden duty of the children of God to visit the sick and administer to their relief as far as lieth in their power; and it is the privilege of the sick, as we have already remarked, to call or send for the elders of the church; and if it is their desire to be anointed with oil, let two of the elders, in the fear of Almighty God, perform this holy work, by applying oil (sweet oil is generally used) to the head of the sick, in the name of the Lord; after which, the elders will lay their hands upon the top of one another on the head of the sick, and then supplicate a throne of mercy, calling upon the name of God, through Jesus Christ, to forgive and pardon the sins of the sick, &c.; and the prayer of faith shall be heard.[31]

Henry Kurtz also provided a good explanation of this practice as an introduction to the Minutes of the Annual Meeting which related to this topic.

ANOINTING THE SICK.

On this head thus read the word of God: "Is any sick among you? let him call for the elders of the church; and let them pray over him, anointing him with oil in the name of the Lord: and the prayer of faith shall save the sick, and the Lord shall raise him up; and if he have committed sins, they shall be forgiven him. Confess your faults one to another, and pray one for another, that ye may be healed. The effectual fervent prayer of a righteous man availeth much. Elias was a man subject to like passions as we are, and he prayed earnestly that it might not rain: and it rained not on the earth by the space of three years and six months. And he prayed again, and the heavens gave rain, and the earth brought forth her fruit, &c." James 5: 14-18.

This "anointing of the sick," based on the Scripture given above, is, as far as our limited knowledge extends, not practiced by any of the modern denominations, except by the Roman and the Greek Churches under the name "Extreme Unction," and it is therefore necessary to explain our position as simple followers of Christ and primitive Christianity in respect to this matter. We find also that at least in one case the Saviour declared, that wheresoever his gospel should be preached it should be also mentioned what had been done to him in this respect. From this we infer that our Lord and Master deemed this an act worthy not only of remembrance, but also of imitation. He also instructed his disciples among other things to "anoint the sick," and we cannot doubt that they obeyed this instruction. And now since we cannot exercise this act any more on the person of Christ himself, we simply obey what James had recorded, namely, when one of the very least of the members of Christ calls upon the elders of the church, the member being sick, and desirous for that anointing, we feel it our duty to obey that call. We believe if it is done and received in faith, the Lord will accept it as if done unto himself, and he will bless it either to raise the sick again from his sick-bed, or, what is far better, raise him or her up to glory.

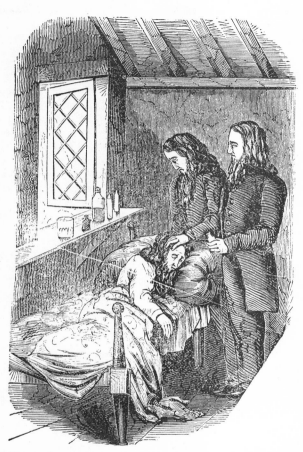

The anointing,
from Nead's
Theological Works

Y. M. 1797. Art. 5. From James 5: 14, &c., the brethren testified unanimously, "that the sick who desire and call for it, should be anointed, according to the word of the holy apostle, in the name of the Lord." ...

Y. M. 1827. Art. 1. About the ordinance of anointing the sick, the manner of proceeding has ever been, first to sing a few verses, and with a united prayer to turn to God. Then (there should always be two brethren) the one reaches forth his hand, and the other poureth the oil on it, and the first puts the same on the head of the sick, and says the words which the Apostle James teaches (chap. 5: 14), "Thou art anointed in the name of the Lord," and thus three times, but the words only once said. Then both brethren lay their hands upon the head of the sick, and pray over him. For it is not considered to be intended only as inward unction, but an outward anointing, whereof the apostle speaks, as mentioned before.[32]

The purpose and observance of the anointing service by Brethren was characteristic of their desire to follow the practices of the early Christian church as outlined in the New Testament. This desire was also seen in the Brethren belief in baptism and in the love feast service, which were maintained as much as possible as they had been done in the time of Jesus Christ. In other words, the goal of the Brethren was a literal following of the New Testament. To follow such a goal made the Brethren different from other Christian groups, such as the Mennonites, although a full understanding of the differing practices of the Brethren and of the Mennonites would require a careful study of their respective beginnings. At any rate, the Mennonites of the nineteenth century did not emphasize a literal following of the New Testament to the extent that the Brethren did.

Because the Mennonites were German and because they lived in the same areas as the Brethren, the Brethren defenders of the faith in the years down to 1865 concentrated their efforts on the Mennonites, as demonstrated especially in the writings of Peter Bowman and John Kline. Peter Nead, who had been both a Lutheran and a Methodist before becoming Brethren, was somewhat more cosmopolitan in his writings in referring at least indirectly to other religious groups. Regardless of which religious group was drawing their attention, the significant point is that the Brethren were producing a number of capable defenders of their distinctive beliefs during these years.

IV. POLITY AND ORGANIZATION

INTRODUCTION

An excellent, concise description of Brethren polity and organization was prepared in the 1840s by Philip Boyle, a Brethren minister in Maryland. Many of the points which he made will be examined in greater detail in this chapter, although not necessarily in the order in which he discussed them.

Each congregation has from two to three preachers, and some more. In travelling and preaching there are in general two together; and very frequently one speaks in German, and the other in the English language, to the same congregation. None of their ministers receive any pecuniary compensation for any services they perform pertaining to the ministry; they preach, officiate at marriages and funerals among all who call upon them, without respect to persons: though their ministers will not perform the rites of matrimony, unless they can be fully satisfied that there are no lawful objections in the case of either of the parties to be married.

Their teachers and deacons are all chosen by vote, and their bishops are chosen from among their teachers, after they have been fully tried and found faithful; they are ordained by the laying on of hands and by prayer, which is a very solemn and affecting ceremony. It is the duty of the bishops to travel from one congregation to another, not only to preach, but to set in order the things that may be wanting; to be present at their love-feasts and communions, and, when teachers and deacons are elected or chosen, or when a bishop is to be ordained, or when any member who holds an office in the church is to be excommunicated. As some of the congregations have no bishops, it is also the duty of the bishop in the adjoining congregation to assist in keeping an oversight of such congregations. An elder among them is, in general, the first or eldest chosen teacher in the congregation where there is no bishop; it is the duty of the elder to keep a constant oversight of that church by whom he is apointed as a teacher. It is his duty to appoint meetings, to baptize, to assist in excommunication, to solemnize the rites of matrimony, to travel occasionally, to assist the bishops, and in certain cases to perform all the duties of a bishop. It is the duty of their teachers to exhort and preach at any of their regular stated meetings; and, by the request of a bishop or elder, to perform the ceremony of baptism and rites of matrimony.

It is the duty of their deacons (or, as they are sometimes called, visiting brethren) to keep a constant oversight of the poor widows and their children, to render them such assistance as may be necessary from time to time; it is also their duty to assist in making a general visit among all the families or members in their respective congregations, at least once a year, in order to exhort and comfort one another, as well as to reconcile all offences that may occur from time to time. It is also their duty to read the Scriptures, to pray, and even exhort, if it may appear necessary, at their regular meetings of worship.

The general order of these people has been to hold their meetings for public worship at dwelling-houses; but in some of their congregations they have now erected meeting-houses, or places expressly for worship. Some of them are built very large, without a gallery or a pulpit.

They, as yet, have but one Annual Meeting, which is held every year about Whitsuntide, and is attended by the bishops and teachers, and other members, who may be sent as representatives from the various congregations. At these meetings there is, in general, a committee of five of the eldest bishops chosen from among those who are present, who retire to some convenient place, to hear and receive such cases as may then be brought before them, by the teachers and representatives from the various congregations, which are (or at least the most important of them) afterwards discussed and decided upon, and then those several queries with the considerations as then concluded, are recorded and printed in the German and English languages, and sent to the teachers in all the different congregations in the United States, who, when they receive them or as soon as convenient, read them to the rest of their brethren. By this course of proceeding, they preserve a unity of sentiment and opinion throughout all their congregations.

Some of their ministers manifest a great deal of zeal in their Master's cause; and although some of them are poorly circumstanced in the world, yet they, at their own expense, leave their families for several weeks in succession, and some even longer, to preach the Gospel to others. They have had a general revival amongst them within the few last years past; many have been convicted and converted under their preaching, and the cause of religion seems to be progressing among them; and what might seem strange to some, is, that they baptize by immersion, and that at any season of the year.[1]

THE ANNUAL MEETING

The Annual Meeting or Yearly Meeting, as it was frequently called during this period of time, became a very important part of the polity of the church. As with any governing body, the development of a body of precedents was a significant aspect of the work of the Meeting, and the Meeting frequently cited past decisions. The individual who did more than anyone else to collect and preserve the minutes of the Meetings was Henry Kurtz, who served for a quarter of a century from 1837 to 1862 as the clerk of the Meetings. In 1867, seven years before his death, Kurtz published a "Brethren's Encyclopedia," which included all of the available minutes, arranged in topical form, together with extensive comments based on Kurtz' own understanding of these decisions. His two sections on the Annual Meeting and on the Yearly Meeting provided an excellent illustration of his combination of personal comments and minutes.

ANNUAL MEETING

This is an *ancient* institution, almost as old as our brotherhood in this our land America, though not exactly under that name; or rather, more correctly speaking, it is an institution as ancient as the gospel. It is a *peculiar* institution, not at all like the synods, conferences, ecclesiastical associations, assemblies or conventions of the present day among the various denominations of Christian professors. It is a *highly prized and cherished* institution in our brotherhood, as a reunion not only of ministers and official members, but of the church at large, open to all the brethren and sisters who feel disposed and able to attend it. Hence multitudes from far and near, not only of members but also of outsiders, come together on such occasions. This latter feature threatening to defeat its original object, has been the frequent subject of thought and reflection of earnest and sober minded brethren, and has also been the cause of some changes in conducting the same, heretofore adopted, and still contemplated for the immediate future.

SCRIPTURAL FOUNDATION OF THE CHURCH
AND HER AUTHORITY

When our Lord and Saviour Jesus Christ had asked his disciples, Matt. 16: 13-20, "Whom do men say that I, the Son of man, am?" they said, Some (say that thou art) John the Baptist; some, Elias; and others, Jeremias, or one of the prophets." "He saith unto them, But whom say ye that I am. And Simon Peter answered and said, Thou art the Christ (Messiah), the Son of the living God. And Jesus answered and said unto him, Blessed art thou Simon Bar-jona: for flesh and blood hath not revealed it unto thee, but my Father which is in heaven. And I say also unto thee, That thou art Peter (Greek, *petros*); and upon this rock (Greek, *petra,* i. e. not the man, but that confession made,) I will build my church; and the gates of hell shall not prevail against it. And I will give unto thee (the disciples, or the church as a unity) the keys of the kingdom of heaven: and whatsoever thou shalt bind on earth shall be bound in heaven; and whatsoever thou shall loose on earth shall be loosed in heaven."

That this authority was given to the church and not to the individual, is further evident from the express words of our Saviour on another occasion, Matt. 18: 15-18, where he gives direction how a brother is to deal with his brother in case of a private trespass against him personally, and says at last, "TELL IT UNTO THE CHURCH!" and adds presently after, "Whatsoever ye (as forming the church) shall bind on earth shall be bound in heaven; and whatsoever ye shall loose on earth shall be loosed in heaven."

How this authority was exercised not only toward private members, but also toward the ministers, and the apostles themselves, even Peter, when any thing was done that needed explanation and seemed to some wrong, we find an example, Acts 11: 3. (Please read all from the beginning of the chapter v. 18.)

But the example related, Acts 15: 1-35, appeared to our ancient brethren as the main foundation for holding such general councils or annual meetings, and this apostolic example was their avowed pattern; see hereafter, Y. M. 1837, Art. 3.

THE ORIGIN OF ANNUAL MEETINGS

From our forthcoming History of the Brethren in America, which shall be published as soon as possible, if the Lord will spare us yet so long, we will find that the first company of our Brethren, having arrived in 1719, almost 150 years ago, held their *first* love feast in Germantown, Pa., on Christmas-day, December 25, 1723, and previous to this, we are informed, *"they had important work. They remembered difficulties, which had oc-*

curred in Crefeld (Germany) *already. They were indeed a branch of a church, but not yet a church* (sufficiently organized and established) *that could assume* (the authority) *to administer the sacraments* (ordinances). *But the chief difficulty was, that there were still differences among themselves, and they only of late had commenced to come together. After all these difficulties had been worked through in the spirit, they at last agreed to gratify them* (the new converts, who desired baptism and being received into fellowship, and also to hold the love feast)." So then we have a record not only of the first church visit, the first meeting for public worship, the first baptism and the first love feast, but also of the first council meeting and in fact the first general council or yearly meeting ever held in this country; and it is presumable that the love feasts were connected and preceded by such council meetings the day before love feast, and that these council meetings being attended by members and ministers from every church, were sufficient for every purpose during the first thirty or forty years, while the churches were confined at first within a territory bordered only by the Delaware river on the east and the Schuykill on the west, and at a later date by the Susquehanna on the west. But as the churches multiplied, and extended into New Jersey on the east and beyond the Susquehanna on the west, and even into Maryland, &c., and it thus becoming impracticable for all the churches to be represented at every ordinary love feast, it became a necessity to set apart every year a certain time, and appoint from year to year a place for such a general council. This was done, as far as we can learn, a little after the middle of last century, and consequently a little over a hundred years ago. The first council meeting had been held, as we have seen, about Christmas, the presumed birthday of the Saviour, but now a more proper time was chosen in fixing Pentecost of every year, the birthday of the church, for the big meeting, as it was called even to a recent day of our own recollection. With regard to the place, it was concluded at a late day, that the big meetings should be held alternately, one year east of the Susquehanna, and the next year west of that river. The churches spreading further west and south, the Allegheny mountains were considered as the dividing line for a time in this respect, and still more recently the Ohio river was named as such line.

HOW THE YEARLY MEETINGS WERE HELD

That they were at first held in the most simple manner, even as our ordinary council meetings have been held up to our own times, is evident from all the testimony we could gather. Brethren met on Friday morning before Pentecost, and opened as usual by singing, exhortation, prayer, and, perhaps, reading the Scriptures. Having met in the fear of the Lord, and invited him to preside over the meeting, and prayed for the Holy Spirit to guide and direct all hearts, they considered the meeting ready for business. Cases were presented and decided, questions asked and answered, all by word of mouth, as in ordinary council meetings; there was no clerk chosen nor minute taken, and hence it is that our records are so meagre for the first twenty-five or thirty yearly Pentecostal meetings.... When any important case or cases had been presented, it was answered afterward by letter to the church or churches that had presented them....

FIRST CHANGE

When in course of time it came to pass, that among many questions also improper ones were asked in the presence not only of a great number of brethren and sisters, but also of strangers, it was counseled and concluded, that five, seven or more of the oldest ministers should, after opening the meeting, retire to a private place, where those who had questions to ask, or cases to present, might present them; while at the same time younger ministers might exercise themselves in preaching, and edify the people. This order prevailed up to our own time, as many elder brethren can testify as well as the writer. Some few of those questions were privately answered, others were answered by letter to the church concerned, and only questions of general interest were reserved for public discussion. There were some advantages, and some disadvantages in this change, and it is hard to tell on which side was the preponderance. Before the change, we believe, the council consumed but one day (Friday) in most cases; on Saturday was public worship during the day, and in the evening love feast, and on Lord's day (Pentecost) morning solemn worship, at the close of which the whole meeting was considered ended, and the people departed to their own homes about noon. Upon the whole this first change worked well, and was a judicious one. It seems to have given general satisfaction to the church for a great number of years even up to A. D. 1830 and 1831, where the writer was an eye and ear witness; to his certain knowledge, this improved yet simple manner of holding our yearly meetings still prevailed. Thus far no change or extension in the time has taken place. The meeting commenced Friday morning, and broke up on Lord's day noon. We will try to set before our readers a simple description of what we witnessed at those two first Y. M's. we ever attended, among, perhaps, more than thirty such meetings at which we were present within thirty-six years past.

On Friday morning at an early hour meetings commenced as usual. When worship was over, one of the oldest brethren made a brief statement, according to which it became the duty of the elders of the church where the

Y. M. was held, to nominate those brethren who should receive the messages, &c., and conduct the business of the meeting. This nominating was done simply thus: the brother stepped up to what may be called the ministers' table, and with a sweep of his hand pointed out those seated behind that table as his and the church's choice, without naming them, and told them to follow him to a private place. When these arose in order to retire, some one mentioned that during their absence the congregation might be edified by preaching, which was done by those younger ministers who felt disposed or were called upon to do so, one by one, until the elder brethren returned to the congregation, and business meeting was commenced, and continued, if necessary, till Saturday noon. Then, after dinner, public worship began again, and in the evening the great love feast and communion was held, and on Lord's day morning (Pentecost) the solemn worship of God commenced at an early hour, and continued till noon, when the great congregation was dismissed, and dispersed after partaking of some refreshments. Thus the ordinary time consumed by those meetings had been only two days and a half. . . .

Y. M. 1813. "It has been also again requested of, and counseled by the old brethren, that the great (annual) meeting should be continued in the order as it has been heretofore declared and laid down by the old brethren, namely, that the ministers and overseers of the churches, every one in his own district and church, should in good time lay it before the church, how some should be willing to go to the big (annual) meeting, and that the church should assist them if possible, that some may be able to go, so that from all parts, and if it could be from all churches, some may come to that meeting; and those that will come, should endeavor to arrive on Thursday evening so near to the place of meeting as to be able to be at the place Friday morning at 9 o'clock, that the business may go on without hindrance."

Y. M. 1837. Art. 3. "How is it considered, to make a better arrangement in holding annual meetings according to the pattern of the apostles (Acts 15)? The unanimous counsel of this meeting and desire of the old brethren is, to follow the track of the apostles as closely as possible. Therefore the council meeting ought to consist of the elders and all the members of that church which receives the meeting, and of such teachers, ministers or (private) members, who may be sent as delegates from other churches. It is considered necessary, that every church, or where the distance is too great, several churches together, should send two, three or more delegates to the annual meeting. The yearly meeting is to take place as heretofore on Pentecost or Whitsuntide, and the council meeting to be held on Friday and Saturday before, to which the delegates ought to arrive in the neighborhood on Thursday evening. The public meeting to begin on

Sunday, when love feast will be held, and the church is at liberty to invite thereto also neighboring churches as usual. The proceedings of the council meeting should be immediately recorded in writing and as much as possible communicated to all the churches." (The minutes of this meeting were printed and published for the first time this year by order of the brethren assembled.)

Y. M. 1847. Art. 1. "Whether we could not amend our plan in holding our yearly meetings, so that the business might be conducted more quietly and orderly? Concluded in regard to our yearly meetings, that the brethren meet on Saturday before Pentecost, and have public meeting till Sunday evening. Love feast to be held either on Saturday or Sunday evening, at the option of the church where the Y. M. is held. On Monday the council meeting to begin and continue until all the business is transacted or disposed of. The council to consist of delegates, not more than two to be sent from each church, with a written certificate, containing also the queries to be presented (by the church whom they represent) to the yearly meeting. The delegates to constitute a committee of the whole to receive and examine all matters communicated to the Y. M., and to arrange all the queries and questions for public discussion, and after they are publicly discussed, and the general sentiment heard, then the delegates are to decide, and if two-thirds or more of the delegates agree, let the decision thus made be final. But if the nature of the case be such that two-thirds do not give their consent, then let it be delayed (postponed) until it receives the voice of at least two-thirds of the legal representatives. The yearly meeting to be attended by as many teachers and members as may think proper to do so, and the privilege in discussion to be free and open to all who may desire to participate in the same as heretofore."

Y. M. 1848. Art. 29. "The committee to whom the letters concerning our yearly meetings had been referred, reported as follows: No less than twelve letters from all parts of the church had been presented in regard to this important matter, and after reading and weighing them all, and taking also in view the general state of feeling and experience of this present meeting, we propose the following in the fear of the Lord: Considered, that this yearly meeting is as anxious and unanimous in the desire of following in the track of the apostles (Acts 15) as our beloved brethren were eleven years ago at the Y. M. in 1837. We find however, by experience, that the change of the time holding the council after public meetings doth work well, removing from us the great crowd of strangers. We are also satisfied, that the sending of delegates or messengers from all the churches is necessary and proper, as also, that all the elders who come to us, ought to be members of the meeting, whether sent or not. A general committee of five or seven elders is to be appointed as heretofore, and as many special committees as may be deemed proper or necessary, in order to dispatch business. But as to voting, we hold that it will be best to aim always at unanimity, and dispose of business as hitherto. Should the meeting not be able to agree in any one point, let it be postponed to a future meeting. In addition, it was proposed that all the churches should be admonished to use every diligence in sending each year two delegates, or at all events one, to yearly meetings."

"The above was unanimously adopted (by the whole meeting) *without a dissenting voice."*

Y. M. 1851. Art. 9. "Would it not be better to alter the plan of holding our annual meetings, so as to have no public preaching, but only a church council meeting? Considered, that at this time we could make no more alteration but this, that instead of meeting on Friday, and having public meeting on Saturday and Sunday, we will come together on Saturday evening, and meeting to commence on Sunday morning, and to be no communion meeting at the place of the annual meeting. The council meeting then to commence on Tuesday morning (after having prepared for business on Monday)."

Y. M. 1857. Art. 21. Would it not be better in deciding upon all subjects brought before our annual meeting, to refer first to the word of God, instead of first referring to the old minutes? We think it always safest to refer first to the word of God. (So it is thought and believed that our old brethren also did, and by consulting them we may be directly led to the word of God on the point in question.)

Y. M. 1860. Art. 1. Inasmuch as we publicly denounce (human) church discipline, and claim the New Testament Scriptures as the only rule of our faith and practice, is it, then, consistent with our profession to make a direct observance of the minutes of the annual council a test of fellowship? Answer.—The decisions of the annual meeting are obligatory until such decisions shall be repealed by the same authority.

Y. M. 1863. Art. 6. Would it not be expedient and consistent, that the brethren forming the standing committee of the Annual Meeting of the brethren should open and examine all questions sent in by the several churches, and assort them, and thereby save an amount of unnecessary labor and time spent, as there are frequently two, three, and even more queries of the same import and meaning sent in, and acted upon and separately reported hitherto by different committees at the same conference, which we think could be avoided in a great measure? Considered, it is expedient.

Y. M. 1864. Art. 36. It having been agreed upon at a former time that our Yearly Meetings should be held alternately in the East and West, the Allegheny Mountains being considered the dividing line, it is requested that this meeting change the line to the Ohio River. This request was granted. . . .

Y. M. 1865. Art. 1. Could not this Annual Meeting make some change in the manner of holding our Annual Meetings, which would be advisable and acceptable to the brotherhood? Answer.—This meeting feels the importance of a change, but not to make any change too hastily, it appoints the following committee to take this matter into consideration, to propose the result of their wisdom and labor to the next Annual Meeting for its acceptance or rejection. D. P. Sayler, Philip Boyle, Benjamin Moomaw, Andrew Detrick, J. H. Umstad, John Wise, H. D. Davy, Jacob Hershey, John Miller, Hiel Hamilton, Christian Long, John Metzger, David Brower, and Frederick P. Loehr. . . .

Y. M. 1866. Page 1-3.—The deferred business of last Annual Meeting being the first business in order before the council, the committee appointed at that meeting to devise some plan for holding our Annual Meetings which will be more satisfactory to the brotherhood, was called upon for its report, and submitted the following:

INTRODUCTORY REMARKS

The authority for holding General Conference Meetings is founded on the 15th ch. of the Acts of the Apostles, and a strict compliance with the example therein is advisable. By reference to said scripture, we learn that the question in dispute, and upon which the disciples differed, was not referred to a general council until all efforts had failed to settle it in the church in which it originated. . . . Here seems to be authority to send questions upon which the brethren differ in their judgments to a General Council, and that the bishops ought to go, and also to have certain others with them. . . . Here we see that those who were sent were brought on their way by the church. So should we do. That is, help such to go that we send. . . .

THE ANNUAL MEETING

We recommend that the Annual Council be formed by the delegates sent by the District Meetings, and by all the ordained elders present; that the Meeting be held at the place designated by the Council the preceding year, to commence on the first Tuesday after Whitsunday, the previous Lord's day (Whitsunday) to be spent as it has hitherto been by the brethren, in worship at such places in the vicinity in which the meeting is to be held, and shall be desired, and as may be judged most profitable; that there be no public meeting for worship where the Council Meeting is held, though the meeting should be opened with devotional exercises, and the reading of the 15th ch. of Acts, and likewise closed with devotional exercises; that the Meeting shall be held alternately in the East and in the West. . . .

THE ORGANIZATION OF THE ANNUAL MEETING

The bishops and elders of the church holding the Annual Meeting, shall select from among the bishops present the standing committee. Virginia, Maryland, Pennsylvania, Ohio, Indiana, and Illinois, shall each be entitled to three, if present, and two, if present, from each of the remaining states in which churches are established, and whenever said states shall contain ten bishops each, they also shall be entitled to three. The standing committee shall choose its own officers, and these shall be a moderator, two clerks, and a door keeper. It shall be the duty of the moderator to keep order among the members of the committee, and also in the public meeting. He shall not permit two brethren to speak at the same time, and he shall decide who is entitled to the floor. He shall also keep the speakers to the question, and declare the query passed, after general consent, by silence. It shall be the duty of the first clerk to keep a faithful record of all the queries and answers, and prepare them for publication. It shall be the duty of the second clerk to read distinctly all papers as often as requested. It shall be the duty of the door keeper to take charge of the room in which the committee meet for business, and shall allow no intrusion in time of session.

As soon as the standing committee has been named, they shall retire to a private room for organization, and the reception of the queries presented by the delegates from the District Meetings (or churches), after which all proper queries shall be read by the General Council Meeting for adoption or amendment, and sub-committees be dispensed with.

The proceedings of the Annual Meetings shall be published, and it is earnestly recommended that all the overseers of churches, whether ordained or not, have them faithfully read and observed in their respective charges. And if it be represented to the Annual Meeting, that this recommendation is disregarded, it shall be the duty of the standing committee to appoint faithful brethren, whose duty it shall be to visit said churches, and see that the Minutes are properly read and observed, and to set in order things that are lacking. The above is unanimously recommended to the Annual Meeting by the Committee.

Signed by the Committee. D. P. Sayler, Henry Koontz, of Md., Benj. Moomaw, of Va.; David Detrick, of Tennessee; John H. Umstad; John

Wise, of Pa.; H. D. Davy, James Quinter, John Hershey, of Ohio; Jacob Miller, Hiel Hamilton, of Indiana; Christian Long, John Bowman, of Illinois; David Brower, of Iowa.

(Three members of the committee not being present, John Bowman, Henry Koontz, and James Quinter were appointed to fill their places.)

This report being read before the General Council, was adopted by the following resolution:

Resolved, That we try the committee's report for at least a sufficient length of time to give it a fair trial. . . .

[Having been asked what plan we considered best to follow in conducting Yearly Meetings, we will in humility repeat what we said to the committee a year ago in substance when on the subject: "Finding that the committee, as all the brethren from the earliest period of their history in this country, were inclined to follow the example of the apostles in their first general council at Jerusalem (see Acts 15), in the conduct of our Yearly Meetings, with which we were most cordially agreed, we merely suggested, that by observing as strictly as possible that illustrious example and the principles inculcated by the gospel, such as 1, Simplicity; 2, Liberty; 3, Order; 4, Subordination of our reason to the word of God in its letter and spirit in all matters of difference; 5, A due regard to the conclusions of former Yearly Meetings; 6, A sincere love of the brethren consistent with the love of God, and Truth and Righteousness; 7, A constant aim for union in the body of Christ, the church, &c., &c.;—that these items would suffice without any lengthy plan, or many particular rules and regulations, which would only tend to curtail the liberty with which the committee that conducted the meeting, and the church that received the meeting, ought to act.][2]

Another individual in addition to Henry Kurtz who attended many of the Annual Meetings during these years was John Kline of Virginia. In his diary, he commented on many of the Annual Meetings in the years from the 1830s to his death in 1864. Three of the Annual Meetings which he attended and described in his diary are included in this section because Kline provided a different perspective regarding the events of the Meeting. The first was held in his home congregation, the Linville Creek Church of the Brethren.

THURSDAY, May 4, 1837. Preparations are being made to-day for the Annual Meeting. The brethren and sisters are all alive with desire to make all the visiting brethren and sisters as comfortable as possible during the meeting. . . .

SUNDAY, May 14. Yearly Meeting begins. Introductory sermon by Elder George Hoke, of Ohio. Text—"And it came to pass, that while they communed together and reasoned, Jesus himself drew near, and went with them." Luke 24:15. . . .

MONDAY, May 15. Yearly Meeting opens at the Linville's Creek church. Brethren Henry Kurtz, John Garber, Umstead and Price spoke in exposition of the Word and doctrine in the forenoon meeting, which opened at 8 A. M. Brother Price took the lead, and spoke from 1 Peter 1:12. . . .

Brother Price was followed by brethren John Garber, Henry Kurtz and Umstead, all bearing testimony more or less extended. The services were brought to a close, and an intermission was given. In the afternoon queries were taken in.

TUESDAY, May 16. The meeting was continued to-day. Seven queries were disposed of. Love and harmony abound.

WEDNESDAY, May 17. The meeting was brought to a close to-day. The business being all disposed of, it broke up in the afternoon by the singing of the hymn:

"Blest be the dear uniting love
That will not let us part;
Our bodies far apart may move,
We still are joined in heart."

O my God, I pray that we, as thy dear people, may ever be thus joined in heart; that we may ever be of one mind and speak the same thing; that thy Spirit may fill us and guide us into a clear understanding of thy revealed will that we may not err therein; that we may keep all pride and emulation of the flesh out of our hearts; that each one may esteem another better than himself with all lowliness and meekness; with long-suffering; forbearing one another in love; endeavoring to keep the unity of the Spirit in the bond of peace; till we all come in the unity of the faith and of the knowledge of the Son of God unto a perfect man; unto the measure of the stature of the fullness of Christ. Amen!

THURSDAY, May 18. Some of the Brethren from a distance start home to-day. Set things in order at the meetinghouse. While thus engaged our thoughts would turn to the pleasant season of brotherly communion we had just passed through. I can but wish and pray that the same spirit of love and union may pervade every meeting yet to be held in the Brotherhood, through all time, to the end of the world. . . .

SATURDAY, June 7, 1851. Meeting in the grove near the Brick meetinghouse, on Middle River. Many people gathering. Acts 3 is read.

From present appearances there will be a very large concourse of people at this Annual Meeting.

SUNDAY, June 8. Meeting in the meetinghouse and also in the grove.

MONDAY, June 9. The Yearly Council opens. Take in the questions. Transact some business. Good order prevails, and a spirit of love and union abounds. If by these meetings we can foster and preserve the unity of the faith and order of our beloved Brotherhood, so that wherever we may go among our Brethren we may be able to see eye to eye and face to face as to the doctrines we preach and the order of Christian life we uphold, our highest aim will have been reached. It may be that as time goes on and knowledge is increased new things will come up demanding consideration; but I sincerely hope and pray no departures from what we now regard with so much love and unanimity as the will of the Lord will ever take place.

TUESDAY, June 10. All the queries and business items left over from yesterday are taken up and disposed of to-day. The Annual Meeting breaks up in good feeling, but with the sad forecast that some present to-day will never attend another Yearly Meeting. Be it so. In heaven no farewell tears are shed. It is not the parting that makes one sad. It is the how and the where and the when we shall meet again that break up the fountains of our hearts. . . .

MONDAY, May 5, 1856. This day I start to the Annual Meeting, which is appointed to meet about fourteen miles from Freeport, in Stephenson County, on the extreme north border of Illinois, and about three miles from Brother Young's. After being exposed to many dangers and detentions, and one wreck on the way, I arrived safe at the place of meeting on . . .

SATURDAY, May 10. Stay at Brother Young's first night. A great concourse of people on the ground.

SUNDAY, May 11. We have a very fine day. Preaching at several points. An immense assembly to-day.

MONDAY, May 12. Meeting is organized. Committees formed. Go to rooms and take in queries. Stay all night on the meeting grounds. Rain all day and cold.

TUESDAY, May 13. Begin to discuss questions. Rain all day and night, and unpleasant. Stay all night on the meeting grounds.

WEDNESDAY, May 14. Continue the discussion of questions. Close at half past five o'clock. Stay again on meeting grounds. Although we have some differences of opinion among us on minor points of order and usages, I am happy to know that in all great matters of doctrine and practice we are one. Whilst the meeting was in progress I was made to think of what Solomon says in the book of Proverbs about the locusts. "The locusts," says he, "have no king, yet go they forth, all of them, together in bands." We have no human king over us as pope, cardinal or bishop, with well-assumed authority and dignity; yet we hold together. We acknowledge allegiance to but one king, and he is out of human sight. He is the King of glory. But of him we can say with an apostle: "Whom having not seen we love; in whom, though now we see him not, yet believing, we rejoice with joy unspeakable and full of glory."[3]

The "Old Hay Homestead" near Trotwood, Ohio
where the Annual Meeting was held in 1862

DISTRICT MEETINGS

One of the new developments in the polity of the church which was just being implemented at the end of the period under consideration in this book was the district meeting. A good insight into its development is provided by the Annual Meeting Minutes of the 1850s and the 1860s. In this case, Kurtz arranged the minutes under two headings, District Meetings and Missionary, and the minutes ought to be read chronological- ly in order to understand the reasons for the organization of such district meetings. Also, the Annual Meeting's caution in making such changes is well illustrated in this particular development.

Y. M. 1852. Art. 8. Whether the commission of our Lord and Saviour Jesus Christ, Matt. 28: 19, 20; Mark, 16: 15, does not require of the church to send brethren to preach the Gospel, where the name of Christ is not known? Considered, that the brethren acknowledge the great commission of Christ to its full extent, and that it is the duty of the church, the ministers and every private member, to do all that is in their power to fulfill that commission in accordance with apostolic practice.

Y. M. 1856. Art. 22. A letter from Virginia urging that this Y. M. devise a plan, how the church could fulfill the command of the Saviour, Matt. 28: 19, more effectually, so that the Article 8, on our Minutes of 1852, should not remain a dead letter. This meeting recommend the subject to the serious consideration of all the churches.

Y. M. 1856. Art. 23. A proposal of forming districts of five, six or more adjoining churches for the purpose of meeting jointly at least once a year, settling difficulties, &c., and thus lessening the business of our General Y. M.; we believe this plan to be a good one, if carried out in the fear of the Lord.

Y. M. 1858. Art. 58. Whereas, there is a strong desire among the brethren in various places to have a more general exertion made on the part of the church to have the truth more universally spread; and, whereas, the subject has been frequently talked of without any definite plan being proposed; we, therefore, have concluded by way of introduction, to offer the following outlines of a plan, subject, however, to such amendments as may from time to time be thought best. That is, let each State where there is a respectable number of brethren, form a district; let the brethren then hold their annual meetings; let each of these divisions (districts) have its treasury; let the churches that feel favorable have their treasury; let the churches be called upon as often as may be necessary to cast in their mite as a free-will offering. Then let these contributions be put into the district treasury, and let the district meeting appoint ministering brethren, say two or more, if necessary (such as are willing to go), to travel through the respective States for one year, their expenses being paid, and such provision made for their families as may be thought necessary. What does the annual meeting think of this proposition? Considered, that we think it not good to adopt this proposition; but we believe it is a subject worthy the serious and prayerful consideration of the brotherhood, and we recommend the brethren to give it such consideration.

Y. M. 1859. Art. 28. Seeing the great necessity of having the gospel as held and practised by the brethren more extensively spread and known, we desire that the brethren in this annual council reconsider Art. 58 of Minutes of 1858, and adopt it with such amendments as in the fear of the Lord may seem best.

As it was recommended by the last annual meeting to make the subject of spreading the gospel one of prayerful consideration, it appears it was done; and several churches have expressed their wish to this annual council meeting, to have it take a favorable action upon the subject. The following is the conclusion this annual meeting has come to in relation to what is referred to in this article.

This meeting recommend and give liberty to any of the districts or States to make a move on the subject of spreading and sustaining the gospel as preached and understood by the brethren, so that the same may be done in the order of the gospel. And we recommend to those churches who may adopt this, to make a report to the next annual meeting upon their success. And in view of the importance of the subject, we appoint the following brethren as a committee, to propose some plan by which the brotherhood in general may take a part in this good work; said plan to be reported to the next annual meeting: DANIEL P. SAYLER, JOHN KLINE, JOHN H. UMSTAD, SAMUEL LAYMAN, JOHN METZGER, and JAMES QUINTER. DANIEL P. SAYLER is the corresponding member of the committee.

Y. M. 1864. Art. 13. As the annual meeting has recommended the holding of district meetings, we wish to know from it, whether it would be advisable to make a record of the proceedings of such district meetings? Ans. We would advise to keep no record of proceedings but what is to be submitted to the annual meeting. . . . Art. 31. Since the yearly meeting favors district meetings for the purpose of adjusting local difficulties, and lessening the labor of the yearly meeting, would it not be advisable to form regular districts meetings in each State, and close them with lines, that individual churches may know to what district they belong? And if so, should not this Y. M. appoint brethren in each State to form such districts in their respective States, and close them by making such lines? Ans. Yes, but we will leave the districting of the States to the churches in the respective States.

Y. M. 1866. We recommend that each State form itself into convenient district meetings. These meetings shall be formed by one or two representatives from each organized church, and we recommend that each church be represented in the district meeting, either by representatives or by letter. We think it best to hold those meetings in simplicity, and as much like the common council meetings are held as possible. A record of the district meetings may be kept, but not published. They should endeavor to settle all questions of a local character. But those of a general character, or those that concern the brotherhood in general, should be taken to the annual meeting. And all questions that cannot be settled at the district meetings, should be taken to the annual meeting. In taking questions from the district to the annual meeting, they should be correctly and carefully formed. And all queries from district meetings should be accompanied with an answer. But in case those meetings cannot agree upon any questions, then they shall be referred to the standing committee, and this shall form answers to the questions before they be read before the general council. And it is considered very desirable, and indeed necessary, that in all cases, in answering questions both in district and annual meetings, some Scripture authority, or reason, be given for the decision, though it should be done as briefly as possible.

No business can come before district meetings until it has passed through the church in which it originated. It is understood that any member falling under the council of the church, and being dissatisfied with the decision, may appeal to the annual meeting by presenting a petition signed by a number of the members of the church. Nothing in this arrangement shall be so construed as to prevent any member from presenting himself before the standing commitee of A. M. to offer anything that cannot be brought before it in the manner prescribed, and the committee shall hear his case, and dispose of it according to its judgment.[4]

The churches of Virginia were evidently providing some leadership in getting such district meetings established, as indicated in Article 22 of the Minutes of 1856. The Minutes of a "general council meeting" which was held in the Valley meetinghouse in Augusta County, Virginia, in 1859 indicated both the need for such meetings at the district level and the desire not to conflict with the authority of the Annual Meeting.

The committee appointed by the general council meeting held at the Valley meetinghouse in Augusta County, Virginia, on March 11 and 12,

1859, report, that this meeting appoint another meeting of the same kind, to be held at some central point, between this time and the spring of 1860, in which all the churches favorable to holding general council meetings (District Meeting), shall be represented, if possible.

This meeting also recommends that B. F. Moomaw, Peter Nininger of Botetourt County, Martin Garber of Augusta, Solomon Garber of Upper Rockingham, and Jacob Miller of Lower Rockingham, be appointed a corresponding committee to invite all the churches in Virginia, Tennessee, and North Carolina to represent at said meeting at time and place of appointment, that we may determine what can be done for the great cause of the Gospel.

This meeting is further of the opinion that the many calls from the various parts with the extensive spread of the Brotherhood, demand that some systematic regulation should be made to facilitate this great cause. (Wherefore,) this meeting recommends

1. That it shall be the duty of such conferences to grant similar meetings, for the purpose named, to applicants from the various parts of the territory represented in these general council meetings as in their wisdom they may deem proper.

2. It shall be the privilege of any of the churches in the bounds above stated to make application for such meetings when desired.

3. Said meetings shall in no way supersede Annual Meeting, but they shall be assistants thereto, by discussing and settling all differences so far as possible, in order to lessen the labor of Annual Meeting. Also they shall labor to keep love and union in all the churches. But,

4. These meetings shall not have the power to finally settle questions of general doctrine. This duty shall devolve upon Annual Meeting alone. Signed by

Daniel Thomas	John Kline
Abraham Garber	Daniel Brower
Martin Cosner	Peter Nininger
Jacob Miller	John Harshberger
John Wine	John Wine
Solomon Garber	Martin Cosner[5]

A letter of 1863 from B. F. Moomaw to John Kline reported another meeting held in Virginia. Although this particular meeting evidently carried some implications of being a southern Annual Meeting during the Civil War when very few southern Brethren attempted to cross the battle lines to attend the Annual Meetings in the northern states, it also served to strengthen the basic idea of holding district meetings. At any rate, the

Brethren in Virginia were clearly moving in the direction of organizing into districts. In 1866, immediately after the end of the Civil War, the Brethren congregations in Virginia were divided into the First District, which included the congregations in southern Virginia, and the Second District, which included the congregations in the Shenandoah Valley of northern Virginia. In this way the Brethren had established a new level of organization in their church government.

Botetourt City, Virginia
May 1, 1863

According to promise, I this evening seat myself to write a few lines to you. And first I will inform you that by the kind providence of God, I arrived safely at home on Thursday evening after I parted from you at Harrisonburg. Found my family and also the brethren well for which I thank our heavenly Father. On the next day pursuant to appointment, we met the brethren in council meeting. The surrounding churches were generally represented, including the churches in Washington County, Tennessee, and I had to regret that the churches generally were not more extensively represented. We had truly a fine meeting. The two days set apart for council were entirely consumed in discussing Scriptural and doctrinal questions. And while we had animated debates on several subjects, entire harmony and love marked the whole meeting. So much so that the brethren assembled unanimously agreed that we of the South would (God willing) hold annually a general meeting of the kind. So long at least, as we were deprived of the privilege of holding general conference with the brotherhood at large. For the furtherance of this object Brethren D. Thomas, A. Naff, D. B. Klipper, and myself were appointed a corresponding committee to arrange the time and place for the meeting next year, which I think probably the brethren in Franklin County will take. We had preaching each night at several places and also on Lord's day.

The question concerning putting members in bond occupied a considerable portion of the first day, discussed freely pro and con and decided that the exhortation of Paul to the Corinthian Church was a law with its penalties defined and still so stands to the church. Another question as to how long a gross offender should be kept separated was decided, until the honor of the church is vindicated; he gives satisfactory evidence of contrition and humiliation to all and redeems his christian character by an exemplary life. As to publishing hymn books, it was decided as you suggested. I hope that you may at an early day be able to procure a copy that we may get a supply printed. They are much needed.

Another question, whether the one baptism spoken of by Paul

(Ephesians, 4th chapter) was the baptism of water or of the spirit. There was no decision formally called for, but I think it was decided in the mind of the church, as being that of water.[6]

THE LOCAL CONGREGATION

In many ways the most basic unit in the polity of the Church of the Brethren is the local congregation, for Brethren have been more congregational in their polity than episcopal or presbyterian. The governing body of the local congregation has been the council meeting, which had tremendous power in the nineteenth century over the lives of the members of the church. For example, the first item in the minutes included in Kurtz' section entitled, "Church Council," made it clear that any member who rejected a decision of the local council meeting was no longer to be considered a member of the church.

CHURCH COUNCIL

Y.M. 1845. Art. 8. How is it considered, if a brother will rebel against the counsel held at council meetings, and say it is an abomination to God? Considered, that such a brother should be visited and exhorted, and if he would not hear and obey the admonition, he could not be held as a brother.

Y.M. 1856. Art. 9. How is it considered, where there is a church with a bishop and two speakers, one authorized to baptize, &c., and the other not, and a case of difficulty occurs between two members, and is brought before the church, those three ministers being present; but the two first being relatives to the parties, they authorize the third to attend to the case, and present it before the church; the question is, would it be considered legal? Considered legal.

The apostle informs us, that though things may be lawful, they are not always expedient. The position of the old brethren was accordingly, and they would in such a case have called brethren from other churches to act in it.

Y. M. 1857. Art. 13. What right have any two or three churches to reconsider the action of another church, and that without any representation from the church upon whose decision they sit in judgment, and then reinstate members which said church had excluded? Answer.—We consider that one branch of the church has no right to restore a member to his place in the church, when he had been excluded by another branch of the church, without the concurrence of the church which excluded him.

[Y.M. 1862.] Art. 55. Which is the most advisable in holding council meetings, to ask each individual member for his consent, or to take silence for consent? Answer.—In all weighty matters it is best for each member to answer.[7]

Sometimes the problems that developed in a local congregation were too great for the local council meeting and its leaders to settle. Then the leaders of the congregation were expected to call in leaders from neighboring (or adjoining) congregations to settle the problems. By the end of this period in 1865, the Annual Meeting had taken over the responsibility of assigning leaders to go into local congregations to settle problems. For example, in 1851 the Annual Meeting sent a committee to Tennessee to try to settle a major division which had occurred in that area. The committee, which was not identified, sent a report to the "Gospel Visiter."

We the committee sent by the Annual Meeting of Pentecost last to assist the brethren in East Tennessee to settle the difficulties existing amongst them, having been with them and doing all that could be done or that was necessary to do, and being this far on our way home, and having leisure this evening; concluded to write a few lines to you to let you know how we found them and how we left them &c. . . .

The members were glad to see us and received us with the highest marks of love and kindness and this the more on account of the hope entertained of the speedy adjustment of the difficulties into which they had fallen. The state of things was truly lamentable. So much had they gotten confused, that they hardly knew how to proceed. They had council after council and nothing permanently effected. They had not been able to commune for 2 years. However those members who had withdrawn from the church, had been again received into the church as private members. But debarred from exercising in their office, on account of which a large majority of the members were dissatisfied, and were not permitted by those who had the over-sight of the church, to lay it before the church, for them to decide.

We arrived in Tennessee on the 5th inst. and as it happened they had a church meeting appointed on the 6th. when the majority of the members was present when according to our instructions, the matter was laid before the church, that is, Whether those brethren should or should not be restored to their office, when it was decided in their favor by a vote of 41 to 6, and they were received joyfully. The meeting was then adjourned till

Monday the 8th when we went into a critical examination of the whole church in order to find, if possible, where the fault lay, and we found that the cause was principally in the Elder brother, on account of him exercising undue and unnecessary authority over the body. So the case was again laid before the church whether they were willing he should continue to rule over them in his office, or whether he should be reduced to a level with the other ministering brethren, and the result was that he was suspended from his office by a voice of 50 to 7 and in this situation we left them to all appearance well satisfied, even the old brother expressed himself altogether satisfied with the decision. So we think the prospect is now good for peace, at least they had, before we left, made arrangements for two communion-meetings, in that district.[8]

Something of the way in which one of these Annual Meeting investigating committees operated was described in a letter from an individual in Maryland who was evidently a member of a neighboring congregation. This 1865 committee was composed of H. D. Davy, J. P. Ebersole, John Wise, and Joseph R. Hanawalt.

McKinstrys Mills, Maryland
October 16, 1865

The Committee that was to come to Beaverdam came according to arrangement and such an investigation of Matters I never before heard in any council meeting   they went back 12 years & brot up every thing that had been said and done of an evil nature since or in that time   the committee heard them through very patiently then made Dnl P. Saylor acknoledge his fault & ask the pardon of the church and the old Brethren. Made the old Bro Jacob Saylor and Isaac Pfoutz do the same to D. P. S. and the church reinstated Samuel Pfoutz in church & deaconship   reinstated George Pfoutz in church but took of[f] his deaconship   reinstated Upton Waltz and settled up matters finally and very Satisfactory to all as far as I have learned   there was many individuals concerned & implicated. I think now things will go better there   they will have a lovefeast I think next Saturday week   our lovefeast was the 7inst.   one at New Market the 19 and 20 inst.[9]

In addition to dealing with the many problems of the members of the local congregation, a committee was needed to draw up specific geographical boundaries between congregations. Sometimes when there were too many Brethren who were too spread out for the leadership to provide for efficiently, a congregation would be divided. An example of this action occurred in Maryland in 1855 in the very old Beaverdam congregation.

January 6, 1856

the Beaverdam congregation has laid of[f] their congregation into 3 churches or congregations the upper or north called the Monocacy congregation the middle the beaverdam & the lower or southern the bush creek congregation and we the pipe creek congregation has made a move to divide theirs   the congregations are getting to large for counselling   the members are so scattered it is hard to get them together   to keep matters more right we must make the congregations smaller[10]

Another responsibility of the local congregation was the maintenance of membership lists. Related to this responsibility was the transferring of memberships when Brethren emigrated from one congregation's territory to another congregation's territory. Several examples of such transfers of membership are included here as illustrations. Obviously, there was no standardized form and each congregation's clerk used his or her own ideas in the preparation of the document.

Frederick County Maryland
17th day March 1816

Grace love and peace of God the Father and our lord Jesus Christ with all what is good that may pertain to this life and the life to Come with a harty greeting   The reason of these few lines is because our beloved brother John Bonsak intends to move from us to you   we therefore write to you that we are in love and peace. We therefore hope you will take him up into your Church   We hope and trust that you will take him up as a brother and member in your Church namely

Philip Englar	David Wampler
William Stove	Jacob Snader
John Garber	Samuel Pfoutz
	Jacob Switzer[11]

Franklin County, Va.
Nov. 11, 1826

Beloved Brethren in the Lord, Daniel and David Miller:
We take this opportunity of writing you informing you of our welfare. Our families and the members of the church in general are well, for which we

have great reason to thank God for his kind Providence toward us. We remember our love to you and to the members of your church; further we will inform you of the brother and sister about moving to you. Brother Jacob Ronk and Hanna, his wife, are in peace and love with all the members as far as we know, and we hope you will receive a blessing with all the sanctified on high. So much from us, the undersigned in the name of Christ.

Isaac Nave.   Jacob Nave.
John Bowman.   Saml. Flora.
John Ikenberry.[12]

State of Ohio, Montgomery County to wit, the Brethren neare Dayton assembled this 27th day of October in the yeare of our Lord 1850 Send this Epistle Greeting, to the Elders and Brothers wheresoever this may be presented; this is to certify that Susan Hire the wife of Brother Wesley Hire has been duly received into Church fellowship with us and that she is in peace and Union with all the members as far as we have Knowledge,   we now Commit them to your charge and oversight and humbly Commend you with them to the Lord our Great Shepherd and to the word of his Grace which is able to build us up and to Give us an inheritance among all them wich are sanctified

Sighned in behalf of all the members present by

Peter Nead   Abraham Flory
Philip Wampler   William Stoner
Jacob Wolf   John Cripe
John Denlinger[13]

CALLING MINISTERS

A very important aspect of the organization of the church was the calling of ministers. As Philip Boyle indicated in the introduction to this chapter, there were three levels of leadership within the church: the deacon, frequently considered the first step in the ministry in the nineteenth century; the preacher, who was frequently called a teacher; and the elder or bishop. He also pointed out that the deacons and preachers were elected by the vote of the local congregation, while the elders were ordained "after they have been fully tried and found faithful." The Annual Meeting of 1848 described the pattern to be followed in calling ministers.

Y.M. 1848. Art. 4. How to forward a brother to the ministry as speaker according to the gospel? Considered, that the church is exhorted to prayer to guide them in a proper choice, not discussing the subjects with each other, but keeping their thoughts before God only; two ordained elders to be invited by the church to hold the election, who shall preside (at the election) and declare the one having the highest number of votes as chosen; the brother so chosen, having declared his willingness to fulfill the duties laid on him, is then received with hand and kiss.[14]

Several examples of the election of leaders by the local congregations of the church may be cited to illustrate how it was done. From Virginia in 1845:

we have choosin 2 preachers Namely Benjamin Moomaw and Andy McClure. Great many people was at our big Meeting as meny as I ever saw at the New Meeting house.[15]

From Illinois in 1852:

Yesterday I heard from Illnois whare the gishes went   Samuel Brits received a letter from Some of them which Stated that there was an Election held thare and Rufes Gish and his Cousin George Gish ware put in for Speakers in their little church in Ilinois   they are generly well thare.[16]

From Tennessee in 1859:

The Brethren of Knob Creek Church met in Church councill To hold an Election in order to advance on to the ministry September the 3th 1859 and the same fell upon Brother Henry Garst

In presents of Brethren
John Nead
Henry Brubaker
Garret Baily

Washington Dove   H. Garst
11111   11111,11111,11111,11

From Tennessee again in 1859:

November the 5th 1859

The Brethren of Knob Creek Church met in Church Councill and there in fear of god advanced the following Brethren to the office of Deaconds Samuel Miller and Christian Bashore

Done in presents of
John Nead Elder
John Lair
Henry Garst
M. M. Bowman
D. B. Bowman

From Tennessee in 1861:

Knob Creek August 3nd 1861

The above named Church met in Church counsil and there in the presents of the undersigned   Brethren approved the folling brethren when placed to the office of Decont Joseph Bowman

David Solenberger
In the presents of the
Following Brethren
John Nead Eld
M. M. Bowman
John Lair
Henry Swadley
Henry Garst
Austin Hylton

From Tennessee in 1864:

Knob Creek Washington Co. Tennessee August 6 1864

The Brethren assembled at knob creek went into an election in the fear of the Lord to set apart a Brother to the ministry and the lot fell upon Br Joel Sherfy,

Joel Sherfy 11111,11111,11111,111
Joseph Bowman 11111,11111,1
Peter Bashor 11111,11111,1
William Clark 11
Frederick Sherfy 1

Signed by the Elders and Brethren
John Lair Elder

Henry Garst Elder
M. M. Bashor
Conrad Bashore
Henry Swadley[17]

The call to the ministry sometimes came to a young person unex-
pectedly, when one really did not feel personally capable of accepting such
a responsibility. Enoch Eby, who eventually became a very prominent
leader in the church, recalled the personal struggle which he endured as the
result of his call to the ministry.

With all these disadvantages, and limited knowledge and experience, I
was called to the ministry by the Aughwick church, in May 1851, at the age
of twenty-two years and six months. And with it came sore trials and temptations. Although I consented to be installed, I spent the first night in
sleepless tossing and rolling, over the floor weeping bitterly, with the
prayer of Jesus on my lips, "Father, if it be possible, let this cup pass from
me." This I shall never forget. My unholiness, my poor qualifications, in
every sense, my care of family, but little education, no experience in public
speaking,—all stared me in the face. On the other hand, was the high calling standing between God and man, to warn sinners. All pressed me sore.
Finally, the thought came; the Lord will not require more than he gives me
ability to do, and I surrendered at once.[18]

One of the activities expected of Brethren ministers was that they
should travel extensively, preaching in homes, schoolhouses, and meeting-
houses, and ministering in every way possible to the spiritual needs of the
scattered Brethren, and their friends and relatives who were potential
members of the church. The diary which John Kline maintained described
many of his trips. One such journey in the year 1845 has been selected
because it illustrates well this kind of activity.

Thursday, October 16. Daniel Miller and Daniel Yount, in company
with myself, start to Hampshire County, Virginia. We get to Jacob
Warnstaff's, in Pendleton County, Virginia, where we stayed all night.
Friday, October 17. We have meeting at Bethel church. Matthew 11 is
read. Cross the South Fork mountain and stay all night at Chlora Judy's. I
am not surprised that these people are fond of hunting. Several deer
crossed our path in front of us to-day.
Saturday, October 18. Meeting at Chlora Judy's. Romans 6 is read.

Magdalena Rorabough is baptised. Brother Daniel Miller spoke in the German on the twelfth verse of the chapter read; and I interpreted to such as could not well understand German, following him. Text: "Let not sin therefore reign in your mortal body." ...

After dinner we all go to Isaac Shobe's, where we have night meeting and stay all night.

Sunday, October 19. We have meeting at Brother Jacob High's. Acts 3 is read. Also night meeting at Parks's where we stay.

Monday, October 20. Meeting at Solomon Michael's, where we stay all night.

Tuesday, October 21. Meeting at Joseph Arnold's, on Patterson's Creek, in Hampshire County, Virginia. I spoke to-day on 2 Timothy 1:13. Text: "Hold fast the form of sound words." ...

Wednesday, October 22. Love feast to-day. Matthew 23 is read.

Thursday, October 23. Meeting. Matthew 13 is read. Brother Daniel Miller goes to the Greenland Gap. I stay all night at old Brother Arnold's.

Friday, October 24. I and Daniel Yount start for home. We dine at Sister High's, and all night at Vanmeter's.

Saturday, October 25. Dine at Elijah Judy's and stay all night at Isaac Dasher's on the South Fork, Hardy County.

Sunday, October 26. Meeting at Rorabaugh's. John 10 is read. I baptised Lydia Shireman. Stay all night at Rorabaugh's.

Monday, October 27. Preach funeral of Joseph Reel's daughter. Age, seven years and nine months. Stay all night at James Fitzwater's in the Gap.

Tuesday, October 28. Reached home.[19]

For all of the time that Brethren ministers spent in attempting to meet the spiritual needs of their scattered members, they received no remuneration. In fact, it was a matter of principle that Brethren ministers were to make their living in other ways than by their work for the church. One interesting reference to this principle was written by a Brethren woman in Maryland who knew a Baptist minister who was receiving pay for his preaching.

December 1, 1844

we have a teacher boarding with us who is a Baptist preacher by the name of Adam Basisk, a young man ... he tends to a congregation beyont taney town where he is gone to day, where he gets twenty-five dollars for the quarter for Preaching and teaches school through the week near us,   he says he would not think it rong to take a thousant dollars a year for preaching,   O my heart feels sometimes sick when I think of such a murchendise as is made of the scriptures,   we have some very close conversations   I will leave him in the hands of God who knoweth all things[20]

WOMEN MINISTERS

Although there undoubtedly were not many women in the Church of the Brethren of the early nineteenth century who desired to become ministers, we know of at least one, Sarah Righter, the daughter of a minister in the Philadelphia congregation. The very excellent records of that congregation reveal something of her early life in the church.

1826—Nov. 12 Miss Righter, John Righter's daughter
    Baptized by Peter Keyser.[21]

She herself had the opportunity to set forth her ideas in a letter written in 1835.

Lower Merrion, April 1, 1835
May Grace, Mercy and Peace be with thee and all those who love our Lord Jesus Christ- to whom be praise now and forever, Amen. 40 years you have been, professing Jesus—if when you were baptiz'd, you put on Christ, and never put him off—you must by this time have come, not only to the fullness of the stature of manhood of Christ, but also to a fatherly age. At this day Bro. Paul's testimony is very true, "Ye have ten thousand instructors in Christ but not many Fathers. The tempter has tried you, yes, Satan himself is transform'd to an Angel of light, and no marvel, if his ministers are too, who if it be possible will deceive the very elect. Through a number of your friends, you have heard of me as sustaining an extraordinary character, feeling it my duty to make known even publicly, the unsearchable riches of Christ. You remind me of the Savior's parable of the woman having 10 pieces of silver, and losing one piece, doth light the candle, and sweep the house, and seek diligently till she find it, and when she hath found it, she calleth her friends and neighbors together saying, "Rejoice with me, for I have found the piece which I had lost." So they rejoice in heaven over one sinner, that repenteth, and so you have heard of me, that as a repenting woman I call on my dying friends, to see "the pearl of price" I have found, "the unsearchable riches of Jesus Christ my Lord."

Well, well, my dear brother, may our dear Redeemer give me grace to be faithful, that you may never hear any worse report of me than this. You once thought this liberty I use an assumption not belonging to the female character, because the Head of the Church, in sending out into the world, chose his first heralds from your sex. My dear brother, I shall ever acknowledge the head of the woman to be the man, and the Head of every man is Christ. He did not send many men, and gave them no authority to forbid any that should do works in his name and kingdom. You recollect when the apostles return'd they said, they saw one casting out devils in his name, and forbid him, because he followeth not with us. But he said, "Forbid him not, no man can do a miracle in my name, and speak lightly [or in the least] of me." They forbid him, because he went not with them when he might have as strict command to go home, and shew the people, how great things the Lord had done for him, as they had to go shew the kingdom of God to the cities of Israel. I believe man to have been first in creation, but I also believe woman was made to be an help meet for or equal to him, having a soul and body, capable of helping him, in his natural, and spiritual world, the companion of his joys and sorrows, in heaven and on earth, who looks up to him as for her power and protection, and on whom he is bound to look with feelings of care and love, so as to secure that confidence to himself which belongs to his high station. I am happy to say, that at this dark age of the world, I have met with men, who are always the same faithful friends in temporal and spiritual things, but believe me these are the fewest, who are brethren indeed, in every time of need, especially when the truth is suffering, and many are asham'd to defend it. I believe my character is not so uncommon as that of "Anna the prophetess" of great age, the widow of 84 years, which took the liberty of staying in the temple to serve God, with fastings and prayers night and day. Simeon was singing his dying song with the infant in his arms, in the presence of the many who came daily to the temple, and no doubt there were many there at that time, who knew the time was then when the Child (wise men came from far to worship), must be offer'd to the Lord. They came looking for redemption in Israel, and she coming in that instant, as he did, so she gave thanks, and spake of him to all who look'd for redemption in Israel. Let me say, Christ has not only honored your sex, but he has comforted mine. When he has to come into the world, he sent his angel, not to Joseph, but to Mary, face to face, to tell her she was "bless'd among women" and by the Holy Ghost gave her words to magnify God with Elizabeth in a loud voice, in the very city of the priests, where Zachariah dwelt. When he came first in the temple his spirit moved the lips of Simeon and Anna, and some historians whose sects oppose a woman's testimony, call her the first herald of the gospel, and say she went from house to house, and to the towns of Israel, proclaiming to them that Christ the Messiah had come. And when he burst the bars of death, his few disciples are in fears and tears—at home, but Mary seeks him—living or dead, and finds him alive and receives his dear command to go and tell his disciples and Peter too, that he is risen from the dead, and the resurrection of our Savior, believe me, I rejoice to tell to saints and sinners, for this living fact holds up the kingdom of the living God, the kingdom of heaven. Happy woman! methinks, many often sat silent to hear her tell, what she saw and heard that joyful morning, when beside his tomb her Master stood and as he call'd her Mary, dri'd her tears away, and put such tidings in her lips, as heavenly angels wonder'd at with joy. But when the day of Pentecost was fully come, you know they were all together with one accord in one place, the number of the disciples was 120 (men and women) in prayer and supplication they waited for the promise to endue them with power from on high, and cloven tongues like as of fire sat on each of them, and they were all filled with the Holy Ghost, and spake with other tongues as the spirit gave them utterance, even so that none of their many enemies could dispute Peter's testimony when he said to them, This is that which was spoken by the prophet Joel, "And it shall come to pass in the last days I will pour out my spirit on all flesh and your sons and your daughters shall prophesy." And that this gift continued in the church, just as they receiv'd the Holy Ghost, I am well convinced, and was the gift of the Holy Ghost, to some women at Corinth, to whom Paul wrote, to prophets male and female, how they should dress, when either of them pray'd or prophesied. Let Paul explain prophesy. "He that prophesieth, speaketh to edification, exhortation and comfort," and the gift of speaking to edify, to exhort and comfort is not given at the schools, nor at any time we please, nor by the power of man. Therefore, I conceive it would be very inconsistent in an apostle, who had laid his hands on men and women, and pray'd over them, that they might receive the Holy Ghost, to quench the gift of the Spirit of God, because it was given to a woman— in answer to prayer—when at that time it may not be given in such measure to more experienced Christians. God always gave his gifts freely where they were willing to use them, and I believe in Christ Jesus male and female are one, just as Jew and Gentile are made one. Every one should do as much as they can to glorify God with the different gifts of the Spirit of God. You once thought in reference to the church the apostle said "Let the women be silent." Now in two places in the scriptures they tell me, Paul says so—but there is much in the Old Testament about holy women, in the old and new church of Moses and of Christ. Now if all the rest of the scriptures prove that Paul in these two passages forbids all women to speak by

Sarah
Righter
Major

the spirit of God, to edify, exhort and comfort the church of believers, and convince the unbelieving men and women of the truth, then it might be so believed. But if the rest of the testimony proves the contrary, then Paul in these two letters is not understood. I believe he very honorably would not suffer any woman to come in and teach doctrines she never received from Jesus or his apostles, as many believing women do oppose their wise men, and do as they please in word or deed. Again he will not suffer them, to talk in meeting, nor ask questions, who have not wisdom enough to know when to ask their husbands, they know not the time to speak, know not what to speak.[22]

Sarah Righter's compulsion to preach the Gospel led her from Philadelphia to other areas where there were Brethren. For example, in the winter of 1839-1840 she spent time in Maryland, a ministry which was described in two letters written during that period of time.

Pipe Creek, Maryland
February 22, 1840

mother often complains, but just now she is setting by me buisy a sew-
ing without the need of any spectukles, she has had rather better health this
winter then common, for had bin visiting a good part of the winter about
with our Dear Sister Sarah Righter who has bin spening some time with us
this winter   she has left our neighbourhood this several weeks past   I
think she is up about Middletown, ... I think she will not get home for
several weeks yet or not till spring,   I would not pretend to tell you how
many meetings she had while with us,   she spoke in New Windsor, in
Woodsberry, in Union town a couple times, in New Market several times,
in Frederick town a couple times, in the poor house, in Cregers town, in
Machanicks town several times, in different meeting houses, in private
houses by day and by night, declaring the word of God to a dying and guilty world with all the fervency that ever I heard a Mortal express   she
looks weak and pale, one would hardly think that it would be possible that
she had the strength to speak that she has, but none but God can support
her. I often wish you were here, but perhaps you will come to see us before
she goes home so that you can hear her, as we expect her to speak not far
from here in a few weeks.[23]

Pipe Creek, Maryland
July 12, 1840

we received a letter from our Dear Sarah,   she got home to there
love feast which was the 14 of May,   she sends love to all and to the poor
and Needy

. . . .

St Sarahs case was brought forward at the yearly meeting,   If I understood correctly it was settled in this way, that in her own parts she can
speak when ever they think proper, but other Churches, that is the br in
other parts or districts durst not send for her unless that family of the
church in which they live are in union ... I feel sorry that it is pind down
so close, and yet I rejoyce that God did not permit her to be entirely put to
silence,   May God carry on his work where ever he sees best and O may
the professing Children of God not prevent it.[24]

*Nothing was recorded in the minutes of the Annual Meeting of 1840
regarding the matter of women preaching in the church. However, the
question was raised on at least two different occasions during the life of
Sarah Righter.*

TEACHING BY SISTERS

Y. M. 1834. Art. 17. Concerning a sister's preaching. Not approved of; considering such sister being in danger, not only exposing her own state of grace to temptation, but also causing temptations, discord and disputes among other members.

Y. M. 1859. Art. 7. Does the gospel admit of female preaching? And if it does, shall they not have authority from the church under whose jurisdiction they are?

Answer.—As Paul recognizes a distinction, in Rom. 12: 6, 7, between teaching, ministering, and prophesying, and as he evidently approves of females prophesying, 1 Cor. 11: 5—we then think that a female cannot teach or preach, according to 1 Cor. 14: 34; 1 Tim. 2: 12, in the ordinary acceptation of those terms, yet we cannot under all forbid them to prophesy.[25]

In 1842 Sarah was married to Thomas Major, a minister in the Philadelphia congregation, and a year later they moved to Ohio, where they lived for most of the remainder of their lives. They traveled together, visiting many churches. How they handled questions related to her preaching was described by J. H. Warstler, who had heard her preach in northern Indiana.

I had the pleasure of seeing and hearing Sister Major only once. A number of years ago she in company with her husband, Elder Thomas Major, paid a short visit to some of the churches of Northern Indiana. I had heard of her years before, perhaps before she was married, but never saw her, and of course my anxiety to hear her preach was great; in fact, there was quite an interest manifested by many others to hear the "woman preacher."

When she entered the churchhouse of Solomon's Creek congregation she took her seat down in front of the stand while Elders Shively and Major (her husband) went up on the stand and, after some little talk and arrangement among themselves, Brother Major invited her up, and she took her seat at his right side. In dress she was neat and plain,—a very plain bonnet, which she soon laid aside, and a little shawl around her neck and over her shoulders extending down the back and over the breast. Her face showed marks of age and care and labor. She was the picture of meekness and humility, completely subject to the will of her husband.

After the opening exercises she was invited by Brother Major to preach. She arose, and slowly announced her text, an old, plain simple one.

I was disappointed. I expected something new, at least something out of the ordinary course of texts, and here was one of the common ones. I was disappointed in a text, but was interested in the preacher, and I gave attention. It did not take long to discover that out of the common came forth the sublime. I could see a wonderful unfolding of the text. I think I am safe in saying that I never heard a text so expounded, illustrated and so transformed into newness of life as was done in that discourse. The sermon was a masterpiece of workmanship. I came to the conclusion that the Scriptures of Divine Truth are a gold mine, and it is our work to bring the gold forth. Then I learned also that the old, old story may be always new.

> 'Tis old, yet ever new;
> 'Tis old, yet ever new;
> I know, I feel 'tis true,
> 'Tis old, yet ever new.

Sarah Major was one of two sisters who labored publicly in the ministry of the Brethren church. It was no wild fancy of imagination of hers that called her to assume the important responsibilities and labors of the sacred office of the ministry. She was, it seemed to me, specially and divinely set apart for the Lord's work.

It was a question of much concern among the Brethren of her day whether she should be allowed to continue to preach. The elders finally concluded that she should be silenced, and a committee was appointed to go to her and so inform her. The committee went but those brethren could not command her to preach no more, and they returned home without fulfilling their mission, and that settled forever the question of her preaching the Gospel. One of the members of the committee was James Tracey, of Indiana, who, when he returned home and was asked about their work, said, "I could not give my voice to silence one who can out-preach me."[26]

In 1857 the Majors moved back to Philadelphia, according to a letter of transfer granted by the Fall Creek congregation in Ohio and found in the records of the Philadelphia congregation.

We the undersigned do Certify that Thomas Major and his wife Sarah R., are respectable Members of the Society of German Baptists of Fallcreek and permit us to add that our Brother Thomas has been Elected or chosen to be Bishop or Elder in said church among us, and in this character he and his wife Sarah have appeared and approved themselves to our entire satisfaction.

Fall Creek March 8, 1857

Eld. C. Samuel Parker
Dec. Isaac Morris
Dec. David Ockerman
Dec. James P. Jasperson
Dec. John Barker
Thomas Nance
Joseph L. Parker
Nathan Smith
John Ockerman

Daniel Hisser Clk.[27]

While the Majors were living in Philadelphia, Henry R. Holsinger participated in the same worship service with Sarah Major in the Philadelphia church. He reported some of his reactions regarding the experience.

I had the satisfaction of sharing the Philadelphia pulpit of the Tunker Church some time during the sixties of the nineteenth century with Sister Major. It was my turn to preach in the forenoon, and I confess guilty of a feeling closely akin to humiliation, at the thought of being in the same stand with a woman preacher. In the evening Sister Major preached, and I now humbly acknowledge that I was very much ashamed of myself and of my effort, but most of all was I dissatisfied with myself because of the prejudice confessed to above, but which I am thankful to have the assurance I had carefully concealed. She preached an excellent sermon. Her style was simple, her manner perfect, and every gesture in place.

At the Sunday-school she was called on to address the children. The Sunday-school was held in the gallery. Sister Major arose, and walked around the pulpit opening in the floor of the gallery, to a point opposite the writer. She stood for a moment, looking about as if to decide as to whether she was occupying the proper spot, when she said, "Years ago to-day, at this very hour of the day, I stood in this same spot; I was converted to Christ, and felt the assurance of my sins forgiven," or words to that effect, as I am quoting from memory, after a lapse of thirty odd years.[28]

How long the Majors remained in Philadelphia is not clear, for they eventually returned to Ohio, where Sarah died in 1884. James Quinter wrote a poignant obituary.

The life and labors of Sister Major were such as not only justify, but also deserved something more than a simple obituary notice. Having been acquainted with her for more than fifty years, we shall endeavor to give a short sketch of her life. She was born in the county of Philadelphia, and near the city, on the 29th of August, 1808, and died on the 18th day of September, 1884.

Her father, John Riter, was a minister in the Philadelphia church of the Brethren. He had two daughters; Sarah, the subject of our memoir, and Mary. These were his only children. Mary survives her sister, and was with her at the time of her death. The attachment of these sisters to each other, was such that made the death of Sister Major a sore affliction to her Sister Mary. Nothing but the counteracting influences of her deep Christian experience, kept her from the deepest grief.

Sister Major was converted and joined the church of the Brethren in her eighteenth year. She was awakened to a consciousness of her sins and danger, under the ministry of Harriet Livermore, a female preacher of considerable notoriety in former years. She preached some among the Brethren in Philadelphia and Germantown. Soon after Sister Major's conversion, she felt that she was called by the Lord to preach. Her feelings in regard to the subject were for awhile suppressed, and suffered much distress of mind during that time. She appreciated, in some degree, the labor and responsibility of bearing public testimony to the truth, and her young and inexperienced heart trembled at the thought of assuming that responsibility, yet the conviction that it was her duty to warn the people of their danger, remained. Her great distress of mind was observed by her family and friends, but they knew not the cause. At length her father becoming concerned about her, pressed her to acquaint him with the cause of her trouble, and she finally yielded to his earnest and repeated solicitations, and opened her mind to him. He then acquainted Bro. Peter Keyser, the principal minister of the Philadelphia church with the circumstance. In him the young and troubled sister found a warm sympathizer, and judicious counselor in her struggles to overcome her fears, and to take up her cross. There were some in the church who could not appreciate her feelings, and of course they could not sympathize with her, and, therefore, instead of encouraging her, they discouraged her. The stand that these took, produced some little trouble in the church, and this increased the difficulties in the way of our sister. But being a young woman of energy, and of strong convictions, and having the grace of God to help her, she was finally able to overcome the difficulties in the way, and to make an attempt to do what she felt it was her duty to do. She began her public ministry at home in Philadelphia, in a very humble manner.

Bro. Israel Poulson, of the Amwell Church, in the state of New Jersey, learning the state of mind of Sister Major at that time, took quite an interest in her, and encouraged her in her work. He invited her to visit his congregation, and she did so, and this was the first place that she spoke in public outside of Philadelphia. After she commenced to bear testimony in public, the sphere of her labor grew and that rapidly. Though she had considerable prejudice to contend with in our Brotherhood, such was her modesty, her humility, her discretion, and her exemplary life, that as she was known she was loved. Generally, if not universally, wherever she went once to preach, she was invited to repeat her visit. Some brethren went to hear her preach with a little prejudice, but, when they had heard her, that prejudice was greatly diminished, if not altogether removed.

Sister Major was a remarkable woman. It was said, and that justly, by one of the preachers that bore testimony at her funeral, that she was "an uncommon woman." She was not an educated woman; that is, she had no more than a common school education. But she had a good and discerning mind. She read considerable, and observed what she read, and probably the good and correct language that she used when presenting her thoughts in her public speaking was more the result of careful reading, than of her knowledge of grammar, though she was not ignorant of the rules of grammar. She had good taste, good judgment, and fine feelings.

In her public speaking, she, at times, produced considerable influence. When she became deeply interested in her subject. she was fluent and sometimes eloquent. Her appeals to her hearers were often very effectual, and especially to those of her own sex. And not unfrequently was the strong man seen to wipe the tear from his eye, even when endeavoring to conceal it, under her stirring appeals to conscience. The members of the church generally, were much edified by her ministry. And we believe that in the revelations of the future, it will be found that aliens were brought to Christ through her ministry, and will constitute the crown of her rejoicing in the day of the Lord.

Sister Major did not attempt to present the truth in a systematic way. There was not much method in the plans of her sermons, but she would generally get out of her texts much of what was contained in them. She would also put into them much from other texts, and in this way would generally make an edifying discourse.

But much of the influence exerted by Sister Major for good, was done through her private talk, and her exemplary life. She was a very consistent Christian. She had been gay and fashionable before her conversion, but after that she observed the principles of the Gospel in dress as well as in other respects, and was modest and simple in her apparel. She sympathized with the unfortunate and wretched of every condition. She took much interest in the improvement of the colored people, and when an opportunity was afforded, labored to instruct and encourage them. In the last years of her life, she took much interest in the cause of temperance, and labored to promote it.

In 1842, the subject of our memoir was married to Bro. Thomas Major, who was a minister at the time of their marriage. This union seemed to be very satisfactory to both. In 1843, Bro. Major exchanged property he had in Philadelphia, for some land in Scioto County, Ohio, on which he moved. After some four years, he sold that and bought a farm in Highland County, Ohio, in the Fall Creek church. A few years ago, he moved into Greenfield, Highland County, Ohio, and here he is still living within the bounds of the Fall Creek church.

When Bro. Major moved to Scioto County, Ohio, just commencing business and housekeeping, he and sister Major did not travel much for some little time. But they commenced holding meetings in the community in which they lived. There was no church of the Brethren there. After they moved into the Fall Creek church, their labors greatly multiplied, and they traveled and labored much in the ministry to the edification of the churches and the people. Though much of their time and labor was devoted to the service and cause of the Lord, they prospered in their business, and attained unto easy circumstances in life, so much so, that they could retire from business, which they did several years ago.

In May, Brother and Sister Major took a journey east, to visit their children and friends. They have three children, two sons and one daughter, all married and filling respectable places and callings in the world. The daughter lives in Washington City, one son in Boston, and one son in Chilicothe. They visited their daughter in Washington, but did not get to Boston. In Philadelphia Sister Major took sick. They returned home in August, and she continued to decline until her death. She felt in her affliction that her work was done, and she patiently, hopefully, and meekly submitted in death, as she had done in life, to the will of her divine Master. The blessed cause of Christ continued to be dear to her heart to the last, as was manifested in her reference to it.

We feel that in the death of our sister, the church on earth, or that part of it which is on earth, has lost a worthy member, and an efficient worker, and that too at a time when every talent and power is needed that can be put under contribution, and made to subserve the cause of Christ. But we do pray and hope, that a double portion of her spirit may fall upon many that survive her, and that the good work in which she was such an efficient helper, may advance with increased rapidity and success. And we further pray that her godly life and faithful admonitions may be retained in the memories of her children and friends, and have a good and sanctifying effect after her death; that it may be said of her, as it is of Abel, "she being dead yet speaketh."[29]

BUILDING MEETINGHOUSES

After their arrival in America in 1719, the Brethren were hesitant about building church buildings. In fact, it was not until 1770, fifty years later, that the Brethren erected their first meetinghouse in Germantown, Pennsylvania. One of the reasons for their hesitation was the fact that the New Testament Church which the Brethren were following as a pattern had not erected any church buildings. Even in the nineteenth century, after dozens of Brethren meetinghouses had been built, the Brethren continued to question on the floor of the Annual Meeting the propriety of such action.

MEETING-HOUSES

Y. M. 1828. Art. 12. Whether we may build meeting-houses? Considered, to leave it over to every church to do as they deem good.

Y. M. 1855. Art. 14. Is it conforming to the world to build meeting houses? Ans. No; if built without unnecessary ornaments, and only for the worship (and service) of God.[30]

Certainly one of the oldest meetinghouses and one of the earliest urban meetinghouses built by the Brethren was built in Philadelphia in 1817. The congregational records provided a very detailed account of the building of this meetinghouse.

At a meeting of the members of the Church of Christ In Germantown commonly called German Baptists residing In Philadelphia convened the 22nd day of the first Month (January) one thousand eight hundred & seventeen For the purpose of taking into consideration the necessity as well as expediency of purchasing a small lot of ground and erecting thereon a plain house of public worship of Almighty God they feel themselves justified in making an Essay at least to discover whether an undertaking of that kind will be practicable. They feel great satisfaction as Well as encouragement from the generous overtures which Many respectable Individuals have made to them, some directly and others Indirectly by which they were primarily stimulated to take the subject into consideration; and upon mature deliberation have unanimously agreed to make an essay as before mentioned; In Justification of which they offer the following circumstances as an apology for calling upon and soliciting the voluntary and generous aid of their friends.

1st.—For more than two years they have met and Worshipped in a school room hired by them for that purpose which has proved too small and otherwise Inconvenient.

2nd.—From the great increase of audience and uniform attention to the means of Grace a revival and subsequent increase may be safely calculated on.

3rd.—They are very confident that the utmost exertions of their own resources will prove inadequate for an Undertaking of the kind or a completion of the Work if begun—They intend having the foregoing printed and also a list of all subscribers' names & preserved among the archives of the Church so that at any future day it may be seen what every person contributed.

In the Name of the Lord Jesus

We the Subscribers do hereby associate ourselves into a Society or Church under the style, or title, of the Church of Christ in Philadelphia; commonly called German Baptists, to worship God agreeably to the Scriptures (according to the best of our Judgment) and to cultivate the principles & practice of Christianity in ourselves & others.

The Scriptures, which are able to make us wise unto Salvation through Faith, we acknowledge to be our rule, both in Matters of Faith & practice, in all things looking unto Jesus, who is the head of the Church, and the light of the world. . . .

And as it appears needful for the Society to have a house to meet in, for Religious worship, we agree to make an Essay to purchase a lot of ground, and erect a house thereon for that purpose, and appoint trustees, to whom the property when purchased shall be conveyed, in trust for the use of the Society, and if any vacancy shall take place among the said trustees, when appointed, by any one, or more of them being removed by death or resignation or other cause, the Society shall assemble, and appoint another Member, or Members, to the office which shall have become vacant, and if circumstances should occur to render it expedient, in the Judgment of the Church, to dispose of the whole, or any part of the lot or building, Two Thirds of all the members concurring in the Opinion of its expediency, the Society shall then give authority in writing signed by the Members, to the trustees for the time then being, to sell and transfer the same, and to make & execute proper and sufficient deed or deeds for the same, and the money thence arising shall be disposed of as the Society (or such proportion of them) shall direct.

In the deed of the lot to the Society, we wish it to be explicitly understood, that the Conveyance be made to the trustees, and their successors in office, in trust Nevertheless, for the use, and benefit of the Church of Christ in Philadelphia commonly called German Baptists, who have no other confession of faith than the New Testament.

Philadelphia, March 1st, 1817

Peter Keyser
Jacob Zigler
Jas. Lynd
Christn Lehman
John Heisler

John Fox
her
Catharine X Langstroth
mark
Deborah Lehman

At a meeting of the subscribers and contributors, for purchasing a lot of ground and building a meeting house, for the use of the Church of Christ in Philadelphia (commonly called German Baptists) held March 19th, 1817, for the purpose of considering the expedience of progressing in the undertaking—When after hearing the report of the funding committee, stating that nearly Five Thousand Dollars are already subscribed, and considerable more is calculated on; it was resolved unanimously, that it is expedient to proceed in the undertaking. Whereupon James Lynd, Geo. Gorgas, Jacob Zigler, Jos. Gorgas, and John Rink, were appointed a committee to procure a lot of ground suitable for the purpose, and report at our next meeting.

Adjourned.

At a meeting of the contributors &c as above, held March 24th for the purpose of hearing the report of the committee appointed at our last meeting (all present) the committee for procuring a lot of ground report, that they have purchased from Jesse Stillwaggon, a lot of ground situate between Crown and Fourth Streets, a little south of Callowhill Street, 45 feet front on Crown Street, and running that breadth to Fourth St., say between 75 and 86 feet deep for Four Thousand Two Hundred and Fifty Dollars.

It was unanimously agreed that it is expedient to proceed without delay to the Collection of the subscriptions, or so much of them as to enable the lot committee to meet their engagement with Jesse Stillwaggon.

The expediency of appointing a Treasurer was likewise considered and agreed to, who may receive the amounts collected from time to time whereupon James Lynd was unanimously appointed.

It was likewise considered expedient now to appoint Trustees, to whom the lot of ground shall be conveyed in trust for the use and benefit of the Society; whereupon Peter Keyser, Jacob Zigler, Senr., James Lynd, John Heisler, John Fox, Jacob Zigler, Junr., Christian Lehman, George Gorgas, Joseph Gorgas, Christopher S. Langstroth, Michael Keyser, and John Leibert, were appointed for that purpose.

A building committee was likewise appointed to procure a plan of the contemplated building, to engage workmen, and collect materials, to whom all accounts shall be rendered and examined by them and passed to the Treasurer for payment: The Committee appointed are Jacob Zigler, Senr., Jas. Lynd, Geo. Gorgas, John Heisler, Jos. Gorgas, Peter Keyser, and John Rink.

Adjourned.

At a meeting of the building committee April 11th (all present)—

The subject respecting the dimensions and situation of the meeting house was considered and unanimously agreed, that the house be built on the Crown St. side, and as near the street as may be deemed convenient, say within Five feet, and that we build on the whole front, say Forty Five feet on Crown Street, and Forty feet deep.

A committee was appointed to enter into an agreement with John Fox and Jacob Zigler, jr. respecting the carpenters work, or such parts thereof

Crown Street
meeting house,
Philadelphia

as we contemplate giving them, the committee were Geo. Gorgas, John Rink & Peter Keyser....

Proposals from several bricklayers were received, whereupon it was resolved, that the proposal offered by Shaffer & Ritter, is considered the most favourable: (viz) To lay the brick at 2.67 cents per M, and the stone at 75 cents per perch; and make an allowance in their bill for the use of the church.

James Lynd, Joseph Gorgas and John Rink were appointed a committee to procure Brick and Stone for the Meeting House.

It was resolved likewise that the height of our building be Twenty Four feet in the clear, from the lower floor; and that the cellar be Seven feet deep in the clear.

Resolved, likewise, that Joseph Gorgas, Geo. Gorgas, Jacob Zigler, Senr., and Peter Keyser be a committee to procure lumber.

Resolved that Jacob Zigler, Senr., John Heisler, and Jos. Gorgas be appointed a committee to employ a person to dig the cellar. Michael Senderling was proposed.

Joseph Gorgas was appointed to procure lime for the building.

Adjourned.[31]

In Virginia the earliest meetinghouses were evidently built in the decade of the 1820s. Somewhat later, one of the leaders in Virginia, John Kline, suggested an explanation for the building of meetinghouses.

MONDAY, January 1, 1844. I feel sure that the work of the year cannot be entered upon more suitably than by making arrangements for building a house of worship unto the Lord. The need of a house of this kind has long been felt among the Brethren on Lost River. We have here, as elsewhere, "not shunned to declare the whole counsel of God" publicly, as Paul says he did among the Ephesian brethren, "and that from house to house." But it is best to have a stated place of worship, and with this in view we have this day made arrangements to build a meetinghouse, to be known as the Lost River meetinghouse. Celestine Whitmore, Jacob Mathias and Silas Randall have been elected trustees; and Celestine Whitmore, one of the number, has been elected master builder.[32]

The Lost River meetinghouse was located in present-day West Virginia, some miles west of John Kline's home. In another area of Virginia, near Roanoke, a group of Brethren in the 1850s signed their names on a subscription list to make possible the building of a new meetinghouse.

Subscription List for Building a Church, December 8, 1855.

We the undersigned do hereby agree and bind ourselves to pay to the Dunkard Church in Botetourt the Sum annexed to our Respective Names for the purpose of building a meeting house in the Neighbourhood of Bonsacks

Subscribers names	$	cts
B. F. Moomaw	100	00
John Bonsack	100	00
D. H. Plaine	50	00
Jacob Bonsack	50	00
Mortimer Oaks	10	00
Saml G. Wood	30	00
[illegible]	5	00
William Moore	5	00[33]

Pennsylvania and Virginia were of course not the only states in which the Brethren were building meetinghouses. A letter from Indiana in 1843 reported that the funds had been secured and the builders employed for the building of a Brethren meetinghouse.

Cornstock Grove, Montgomery County, Indiana
August 27, 1843

I will now inform you that we are about to put up a Dunkard Meeting House on my land in Site of the old cornstock Meeting house   myself, Daniel Graybill, & William Byrd are the Trustees to conduct the building the house   it is let for $500.00   it is to be frame 40 by 50 ft.   Old Daniel Himes boys David & Daniel that once lived on Jacob Stoners land are the undertakers of the house   they are to complete it by the first of September next   we talked of building one for Several years   at least I drew up an article for that purpose and now we will Succeed I expect[34]

THE TRANSITION FROM THE GERMAN LANGUAGE TO THE ENGLISH LANGUAGE

In 1785 nearly all Brethren spoke the German language as a native language. During the next fifty years, many of them learned to speak and write the English language, although some of them never learned to use it

correctly, as many of the letters quoted in this book clearly indicate. In other words, for a number of years many Brethren were bilingual, using German as a native language and English as a second language. They were being forced to learn English because that was the prevailing language of American society; even though the Brethren wanted to have as little intercourse as possible with their non-Brethren neighbors, it was necessary to conduct business and legal affairs with non-German speaking officials.

As Philip Boyle indicated, at least two Brethren ministers usually traveled together, and one of them preached in German and the other preached in English. Such an approach raised some questions and the matter was discussed at the Annual Meeting at least twice.

LANGUAGES, USING DIFFERENT, AT MEETINGS

Y. M. 1841. Art. 4. Whether it is proper for teachers to speak both German and English in meetings, when there are only a few English members, the majority of the church being German? Considered, that it is right and our duty to preach the gospel to every nation as far as we are able, yet so that in such a case not too much time ought to be taken up in English.

Y. M. 1845. (Indiana.) Art. 5. How is it viewed, when there are persons and members in a meeting, some not understanding the English, and others not the German (language), and there are some members still opposing the use of both languages? Considered, that the commission of our Saviour, Matt. 28: 19, commands us, and the love of Christ constrains us, 2 Cor. 5: 14, to preach the gospel to all nations, and in every tongue as far as we are able. See also Y. M. 1841, Art. 4.[35]

PROTRACTED MEETINGS, CAMP MEETINGS, SUNDAY SCHOOLS

In addition to being influenced by their neighbors to learn the English language, Brethren were also being pressured to adopt some of the new religious methods being used by other sects and churches. One of these new methods was the use of protracted meetings, perhaps better known as revival meetings, during which one or more preachers conducted meetings each evening for a week or longer. The Brethren were very dubious about the propriety of such meetings and placed various restrictions on their ministers. Samuel Murray, who was preaching in Indiana, reported: "We were only allowed to preach three times at the same place, then we had to move to another place." The Annual Meeting considered this problem on two different occasions.

MEETINGS PROTRACTED

Y. M. 1842. Art. 2. Whether it will be for the edification of the church of God, to hold protracted meetings, and to introduce mourning benches, in imitation of the new measures adopted by different sects and denominations? The brethren generally considered that it was advisable to be very cautious, and at all times to keep good order, in accordance with the doctrine and example of the apostles, and not to introduce such innovations, like mourner's benches, &c.

Y. M. 1858. Art. 31. Is it contrary to the Gospel for brethren to hold meetings for a number of days in succession in one place, in order to preach the pure word of God, and to administer the ordinance of baptism to those who believe the word and receive it? Considered, not contrary to the gospel, if the believer is proceeded with according to the gospel, and the order of the brethren as given by the Y. M. of 1848. Art. 3. Art. 50. Is it agreeable to the gospel to hold a protracted meeting, say for one week or ten days in succession? Ans. As to the phrase "protracted meetings," we know nothing of it in the gospel; but as touching the frequency of the saints meeting together, we find no limits in the gospel, so that they are held in the order of the house of God.[36]

In addition to introducing such things as the mourner's bench, the Methodists were also playing a prominent role in the development of the camp meeting. The Brethren also were discouraged from attending camp meeting by the Annual Meeting. The objection seemed to be based on the idea that such programs emphasized too strongly the emotional side of religion, while the Brethren wanted any person becoming a Brethren to "count the cost" carefully.

CAMP MEETINGS, ATTENDING

Y. M. 1848. Art. 11. Can it be considered prudent or profitable for members to frequent camp meetings or protracted meetings from time to time? Unanimously considered, not to be profitable for members to do so.[37]

To what extent Brethren were interested in camp meetings is hard to determine. A careful study of a number of primary and secondary accounts of the camp meetings of the early nineteenth century failed to indicate any participation or attendance by Brethren. However, three letters from three different sections of the country revealed at least isolated instances of Brethren attendance at camp meetings. The first two were written by Brethren, and the third was written by a non-Brethren.

Putnam County, Indiana
September 8, 1839
i will now inform you that I wase at a camp meting, the 24 and 25 of augest   it commenced on satterday and held over til weday or thursday[38]

Carroll County, Maryland
August 28, 1845
there has been a great many meetings ... the lovefeast was last Sunday week   there was a great many Persons there and 3 camp Meetings at the same time   we went to the love feast on sunday and on tuesday we went to Methodist camp and John & Elizabeth E. went to Winebrenner camp   they continued these Meetings about ten days but I did not go there at all but some of the[m] went again last sunday and some went to Beaver Dam and I and cousin ann went to Quaker Meeting   while there I thought of what Jacob said when he went that he thought he made more noise than any other one in the house.[39]

[Shenandoah Valley, Virginia]
Sept. 3rd, 1868
Camp meeting was much more largely attended this year than before not only on Sabath and monday but from the commencement untill the close.   there was a general interest manafested large congregations daily & of all denominations & a mong the rest a great many tunkers & indeed if I could read there countenances right I think they looked like they would not care to cast in there lots with us.   Some of them at least one mennonite did join our church   dont remember her name[40]

A third new development of this era was the Sunday school. In this case, the Brethren at the Annual Meeting quite clearly changed their minds in the two decades from the 1830s to the 1850s, as outlined in the following decisions.

SUNDAY-SCHOOLS

Y. M. 1838. Art. 10. Whether it be right for members to take part in Sunday-Schools, Class Meetings, and the like? Considered most advisable to take no part in such like things.

Y. M. 1857. Art. 11. How is it considered for brethren to have Sabbath-Schools, conducted by the brethren?

Ans.—Inasmuch as we are commanded to bring up our children in the nurture and admonition of the Lord, we know of no scripture which condemns Sabbath-Schools if conducted in gospel order, and if they are made the means of teaching scholars a knowledge of the scriptures.

Y. M. 1862. Art. 1. Is it agreeable to the order of the brethren to hold Sabbath-Schools? And if so, how should they be conducted?

Ans.—The decision of the Annual Meeting of 1857, is re-admitted.

Art. 31. Will the brethren at Annual Meeting consider it right to establish Sunday-Schools, and if they do consider it right, will they also consider it right for members of the church and their children to attend Sunday-School celebrations?

Ans.—We consider it right to have Sunday-Schools if conducted by brethren, but not to have celebrations.[41]

By 1865 Brethren congregations were beginning to establish Sunday schools, although the desirability of having such a program in the church had not yet been settled.

PROVIDING FOR POOR MEMBERS

Still another way in which the society in which the Brethren lived provided a challenge was by its insistence that those people who were too poor to take care of their own needs should be provided with the basic necessities of life. If the church would not accept the responsibility, then the local government would provide for the needs of the poor. The Church of the Brethren of the eighteenth century had taken care of its own poor people, and the church of the nineteenth century proposed to continue that policy. The Annual Meeting dealt with the matter on a number of occasions.

PROVIDING FOR THE POOR

Y. M. 1812. Art. 3. Concerning a woman whose husband is dead, and having several children and no property, and her hands too weak to provide for them, was considered that the church should provide for her, and at the proper time to put out the children in good places, and to good people, and thus supply their wants.

Y. M. 1851. Art. 20. Whether it is according to the gospel to let any of our poor members go to the county poor house? Considered, that we know of no passage in the gospel authorizing this, but of many, where the duty of the church is expressly enjoined to support their poor members, and if not able, to ask aid from neighboring churches.

Y. M. 1852. Art. 18. Whether members have a right by the gospel to go begging for money through the different churches? Considered, that they have no right according to the gospel, and where there are poor members that are in a suffering condition, it is the duty of the church in which they live, to see to it and to supply their wants, and if that church is not able to support them, the church has a right to apply to the neighboring churches for help, and not the brother that is in want. . . .

Y. M. 1857. Art. 12. How is it considered if a poor brother becomes insane, and void of all reason, so much so as to become dangerous and very troublesome, and a place can scarcely be obtained for him in a private family upon any condition: a poor house being in the county, are the brethren bound to keep him according to the gospel, or are they permitted to deliver him to the trustees of the poor to take charge of him? Answer. A member of the church should not be put into the poor house if it can possibly be avoided.[42]

A specific illustration of how Brethren implemented these policies was provided by a case history in Virginia in 1812.

AGREEMENT BETWEEN THE BAPTIST CHURCH
and
ANNA SHERFIG AND CHILDREN

A contract: the agreement made, concluded and made binding in the following manner and form between the Baptist Church in Shenandoah and Rockingham counties, and especially with the oldest servants in the aforesaid church, namely, Benjamine Bowman, and Martin Gerber, and John Glick, and John Kagey, and Joseph Bowman, and Jacob Gerber, and as said before with the entire church already mentioned, of the one part, and with Anna Sherfig, widow, of Shenandoah County, State of Virginia, and with her oldest children who are of age, namely, John Sherfig, and Josua Sherfig, and Magdalene Sherfig, and Salome Sherfig, of the other part,

Witnesseth: Whereas the said Anna Sherfig has been complained of and has promised that she will move from the place and that the children will be put out as soon as her deceased husband, namely Abraham Sherfig, has directed in his last will and testament, so it has seemed well to be charitable and merciful with her, and it has thus been mutually agreed that she shall be allowed to give a proof (of her good intentions) in the following manner and form: that with the consent of the children who are of age, she may remain dwelling upon the place for a period of time, and farm the place according to the agreement, and bring up her children in the order and fear of God; she may thus dwell a year or two longer than her deceased husband's will says, if she can come off in peace and according to the agreement with her children. If, however, one or several of the children are not willing to follow, then shall the church have full right and put her off as her husband's will provides; but if the family comes into disorder, then the said church shall have the right to break up the household, according to their judgment; or if the children who are of age shall complain because of their inheritance or the magistrate should also be opposed, then the executive, with the advice of the church would have to break up the household and do as the will says; or if it should also fall too heavily upon her, the mother of the family, then she shall have the right with the advice of the church to break up her home if she wishes to do so; and while some of the deceased and said Sherfig's children are small and cannot earn their food and clothing and the said mother is unwilling to bring them up and provide them with food and clothes, and neither the magistrate nor the said church will assume the care or guardianship of the little children, then the church must see to it that it is just to permit her something for the place besides her third. If the third of the grain which they cut at the last harvest was not enough to maintain the children and bring them up, then the church has decided, in the hope that the magistrate would not oppose, to leave her use all the grain which she had gathered at the last harvest on the aforesaid place to maintain her family in the manner as said, and all the grain which is sowed upon the said place she shall have for her use as already mentioned.

   ... It is further agreed that neither the mother nor the children shall sell wood from the above mentioned place without the consent of the church, and they shall keep the place well fenced and especially in good order. If they wish to clear land, they shall do it with the consent of the church. The said Josua shall keep no more stock on the place than he necessarily requires on the place to secure all the articles of this instrument. All the instruments of both parties are written, and all are signed with their own hands; and the three oldest of the children named within together with their mother named within seal it with their own seal, this day, the twenty-seventh of November, in the year of our Lord one thousand eight hundred and twelve.

   In the presence of
   Samuel Bowman
   David Bowman
   George Wever
   William Good

Yohones Kagey
Joseph Bowman
John Scherfig (seal)
Joshua Scherfig (seal)

William Good

Michael Wine

Benjamine Bowman

Martin Gerber

John Glick

Salomy Scherfig

or Miller (seal)

Magdalena Scherfig

(seal)

*In a later generation, in 1845, a well-known Virginian named John
Kline commented in his diary on the church's proper treatment of the poor.*

FRIDAY, July 25, 1845.... How best to help the poor has been a
matter of much thought with me. If we give to such as are able to work and
support themselves, but do not, we rather encourage them in their habits of
idleness. If we do not give to them, they complain that we care but little for
them, and do not feel toward them as we should. I think the best way to
help such is to encourage them to honest labor by aiding them to procure
situations in which they can support themselves. If they then fail to provide
for their families, I think they should be visited by a committee and instructed in regard to what Paul says: "He that provideth not for his own,
especially those of his own house, hath denied the faith, and is worse than
an unbeliever." Paul never aimed this stroke of condemnation at any who
are not able to provide for themselves. I am glad to think that we have but
very few poor members who are not able to help themselves. These are the
ones of whom the Lord said: "The poor ye have always with you, and
whenever ye will ye may do them good." In respect to such he also said: "It
is more blessed to give than to receive."[44]

*John Kline's attitude toward the poor people was typical of the
Brethren approach to polity and organization; they wanted to follow a
practical approach as much as possible. Whether it was the organization of
the Annual Meeting at the national level or the congregational council at
the local level, or the calling of ministers or the preaching by sisters, the
Brethren were essentially not very concerned with an extensive theoretical
background, but rather they seemed to want to organize in the simplest
way possible in order to get the job done. And the evidence as measured by
growth in membership and by new congregations organized seems to indicate that they were getting the job done.*

V. SEPARATION FROM SOCIETY

During the nineteenth century Brethren in many respects separated themselves from the society in which they lived, because they believed to do so was to choose the Christian way of life. Perhaps their approach should be described as nonconformity, since the Brethren were convinced that a Christian ought to be different from a non-Christian and that this difference ought to be manifested outwardly. By the 1830s this policy was well established in a number of different ways. In that decade Peter Nead included a short chapter in his book, "Primitive Christianity," entitled "Non-Conformity to the World." This chapter provided a theological basis, as the Brethren understood it, for the policy of separation from society.

NON-CONFORMITY TO THE WORLD

Jesus Christ declared in his high priestly prayer to his Father,—that his disciples are not of the world. "They are not of the world, even as I am not of the world." John xvii. 16. The true disciples of Christ, are of God. John says, "We are of God."

The people of God are a distinct and separate people, from the world—that is, they are of another character and party, engaged in a calling which is opposed to the sinful maxims, customs, and practices of the world; yea, in many things, which not only the unconverted, but lamentable to say, many of the professed disciples of the meek and lowly Jesus, do not discover any impropriety; and thus contend and plead for the unnecessary fashions of this sinful world. How often do we hear them say—there is no necessity to be so particular in our customs, dress &c. Here I would remark that is a great pity, and is certainly a great injury to the cause of Christ—that there is so little uniformity in sentiment and more so in practice on the subject of self-denial in the brotherhood; oh! that the people of God, were of one mind and judgment. It is certainly their privilege, and bounden duty, to be in the unity of the spirit, as the apostle writes to the Ephesians. "I therefore 'the prisoner of the Lord' beseech you that ye walk worthy of the vocation wherewith ye are called, with all lowliness and meekness, with long suffering, forbearing one another in love. Endeavoring to keep the unity of the spirit in the bond of peace." Eph. iv. 1, 3. And so Christ prayed to his Father "that they all may be one; as thou, Father, are in me, and I in thee, that they also may be one in us; that the world may believe that thou hast sent me." John xvii. 21. Thus it is very evident, that the people of God should be united, and be as uniform in their customs and habits as possible, that there be no difference of character among them. Now all those who plead for the foolish and giddy fashions of the world let them be professors of religion or not, must surely have a proud heart, and not willing to walk in the path of self-denial—and it would be well for them seriously to reflect upon what Christ declared, in Luke xvi. 15. "And he said unto them, ye are they which justify yourselves before men, but God knoweth your hearts; for that which is highly esteemed among men is abomination in the sight of God." The riches, honors, and pleasures of the world, are very tempting, and that the people of God be not overcome, let them be humble, keep down at the feet of Jesus, and they are safe. It is very dangerous and certainly unbecoming in the people of God to imitate the world in its costly and unnecessarily adorning of the body, such conduct is indicative of a high mind.

It would be well to bear in mind, that everything that has a tendency or is calculated to keep alive and exalt the corrupt nature in man, should be abandoned. The people of God have a right to use the world, but not to abuse it—as the apostle Paul writes in the first epistle to the Corinthians, vii. 29-31; "But this I say, brethren, the time is short. It remaineth, that both they that have wives, be as though they had none; and they that weep, as though they wept not; and they that rejoice, as though they rejoiced not;

and they that buy, as though possessed not; and they that use the world, as not abusing it—for the fashion of this world passeth away." The world can be abused in many ways. If we spend our money, or the gift of Providence, for that which is of no real advantage to soul or body, it is an abusing of the world; and Oh! how much time and money are spent, merely to attract the notice of the eye—the gratification of the flesh; whereas it becometh sinners to be found at all times in an acceptable state to present our bodies as well as our souls, a living sacrifice unto God, as the apostle writes, Rom. xii. 1,2; "I beseech you, therefore brethren, by the mercies of God, that ye present your bodies a living sacrifice, holy and acceptable unto God, which is your reasonable service. And be not conformed to this world; but be ye transformed by the renewing of your mind, that ye may prove what is that good and acceptable and perfect will of God." Again, the apostle tells us to "let our moderation be known unto all men." Phil. iv. 5. That it is our duty to observe plainness—Hear what the apostles Paul and Peter say upon the subject—"In like manner also, that women adorn themselves in modest apparel, with shamefacedness and sobriety not with broidered hair, or gold, or pearls, or costly array." 1 Tim. ii. 9. "Whose adorning, let it not be that outward adorning of plaiting the hair, and of wearing of gold, or of putting on of apparel." It should always be borne in memory that our bodies were originally taken from the earth, and will return to the earth again. This solemn truth should teach us humility, and not pride in our bodies, but to bring them under subjection to the will of God. The church of Christ should be distinguished from the world in the inward and also the outward man. Christ tells us, that the tree is known by its fruits; Mat. vii. 16. When we can discover no difference in conduct between the world and those who profess not to be of the world, we conclude that the difference is in the name only, which in this respect is worse than nothing. The most of the world's recreations are sinful—an abuse of time, and should be abandoned. We admonish our fellow pilgrims to the land of promise, to seek those things which are above, where Christ sitteth on the right hand of God. (See Col. iii.) And as John the beloved disciple exhorts, "Little children, keep yourselves from idols" 1 John, v. 21.[1]

One of the many idols from which Brethren were to be separate was the institution of human slavery which the Brethren found in the English colonies when they arrived in America in the second decade of the eighteenth century. By the 1780s Brethren had accepted a policy of rejecting anything that involved slavery in any form, and they continued to emphasize this policy in the years down to the Civil War in the decade of the 1860s.

SLAVERY

From the beginning of the church in Germany Brethren expressed their opposition to human slavery. In Europe this belief had not been a problem of any kind, since human slavery was virtually unknown in northern Europe by 1700. In America, however, Brethren encountered a different situation, for human slavery was widespread, even among their Quaker neighbors in Pennsylvania. Like most Germans, however, Brethren usually found work in occupations where human slaves could not be profitably employed. Even after the Brethren began to move into the colonies south of the Mason-Dixon line, where slavery was more widespread, they generally settled on relatively small family-sized farms in the mountain valleys which could be farmed without slaves rather than on the large plantations owned by the English which required slave labor.

By a combination of hard work and thrift the Brethren generally prospered, and prosperous Brethren were sometimes tempted to invest their money in Negro slaves. At any rate, the Annual Meetings of these years discussed various problems related to slavery on a number of occasions.

Y. M. 1782. Concerning the unchristian negro slave trade, it has been unanimously considered, that it cannot be permitted in any wise by the church, that a member should or could purchase negroes, or keep them as slaves. . . .

Y. M. 1797 (Virginia.) It was considered good and also concluded unanimously, that no brother or sister should have negroes as slaves, and in case a brother or sister had such, he (or she) has to set them free. And in case a person is drawn by the grace of God, who has negroes, and desires to be received into the church, then it is to be laid before him (or her) before being received by baptism into the church, that it is the brotherly and united counsel, that brethren and members having negroes for slaves, and thinking that they could not at once emancipate them, may hold them so long as the nearest church may deem that they had earned the money, and then according to the counsel of the church to let their slaves go out free with a good suit of wearing apparel (frei kleid) as is given to a white serve. And if they (the slaves) have children, they shall stay with the brother as servants, until they are twenty-five years old; he is to have them taught reading and writing, and bring them up in the fear of the Lord, and when they enter upon their (26) twenty-sixth year, to let them go out free with a good suit of clothing (frei kleid). Further it is considered, if a brother, contrary to this conclusion, would purchase negroes, and would not emancipate them, he would have to be considered as disobedient, and we could have no fellowship with him until he sets them free.

Y. M. 1812. Art. 5. Concerning the slave trade and slaveholding, it was considered, that it is a most grievous evil, and should be abolished as soon as possible.

Y. M. 1813. Art. 1. With regard to the slave trade and slaveholding, it was unanimously considered, that it is wrong, and that it belongs to the iniquities of Babylon, making merchandise of souls of men (Rev. 18: 13), and that it is carried on by the spirit of this world, and is contrary to the good and holy Spirit of God, by whom all the faithful souls, dedicated to God, are ruled, and led into all truth, and are to come out according to the counsel of God, of Babylon, not touching the unclean thing, that they be not partakers of her sins, and receive not of her plagues. Hence it is unanimously and in union considered, that no member, neither brother nor sister, shall purchase or sell negroes, and keep none for slaves; members should also with all diligence restrain their children from it, as far as it is possible, while they are yet out of the church. . . . And if there are any who have not bought, but inherited their negroes, they are to be liberated as soon as the church consider it right and proper. . . .

Y. M. 1837. Art. 10. How is it considered, if a brother buys and keeps slaves, and also sells them again? Considered, that it could in no wise be justified in a brother according to the gospel.

Y. M. 1845. Art. 3. In regard to hiring slaves, it was considered, little better than purchasing and holding slaves, and that it would be best for a follower of Jesus Christ to have nothing at all to do with slavery.

Y. M. 1851. Art. 14. Whether it would be contrary to our profession and the doctrine of Christ, to make contributions to, or become members of the American Colonization Society, with the view of the furtherance of the liberty of the African race? Considered, that a person may contribute to the Society, but not become a member. . . .

Y. M. 1853. Art. 9. Concerning slavery. How shall any branch of the church proceed in case an individual wished to become a member who is in possession of a slave or slaves, and the law of the State in which they reside is such, that they cannot manumit them in safety without transporting them beyond its (the State's) limits, and as we are aware that the several States where slavery does not exist are contemplating and passing strenuous laws prohibiting their emigration thither, &c.? It seems indispensably necessary for us to adopt some other plan than hitherto practiced, in order that the church should be kept clear from the evils of slavery, and that such persons may be enabled to come into Christ's kingdom. The questions involved were considered too important to be decided upon at once, and therefore (it was) concluded, to intrust this matter to a committee to report thereon as soon as possible. The committee to consist of the following brethren: Joseph Arnold and B. Moomaw, of Va.; John H. Umstad, Sam. Lehman, Isaac Price and David Bosserman, of Pa., and D. P. Sayler and Henry Koontz, of Md. . . .

Y. M. 1854. Art. 1. Report of the committee appointed last year on the subject of slavery (see Min. 1853, Art. 9). The question having been, How shall any branch of the church, etc.? (see above). Agreeably to the ninth query of Y. M. 1853, concerning slavery, the committee appointed to report on the same have had this subject under serious consideration in the fear of the Lord, and do report as follows:

First. Under no circumstances can slavery be admitted into the church.

Secondly. In all cases, where a holder of a slave or slaves wishes to become a member in the church, he be required to manumit all his slaves before baptism, upon the following conditions: the males to go out free at the age of twenty-one years, and the females at the age of eighteen years. All those over and above these ages when manumitted, are to be paid by their former owner such a sum, either in money or goods, as may be judged right by the church in which the case may occur, and which is considered as the best judge, being acquainted with all the circumstances, as a compensation for their services over age. This will enable the manumitted to emigrate to a land of liberty, and will relieve the conscience of the liberator from the burden of taking with him to the bar of God the wages of oppression. This report was adopted after a lengthy discussion by the meeting.

Y. M. 1863. Art. 5. What should be done with a brother who would preach that slavery was right according to the Scriptures, and cause discord among the brethren? Inasmuch as the brethren always believed, and believe yet, that slavery is a great evil, and contrary to the doctrine of Christ, we consider it utterly wrong for a brother to justify slavery either in public or private, and that he should be admonished, and if obstinate shall be dealt with according to Matt. 18.[2]

The two lengthy decisions of 1853 and 1854 came at a time when the crisis over slavery was reaching a climax in the United States, and cumulatively the decisions put tremendous pressure on the Brethren, especially in the South. In Virginia, for example, two council meetings in 1855 and 1856, which probably involved a number of congregations, attempted to meet the demands of the Annual Meeting.

Rockingham County Va.
March the 2nd day 1855.

We the Breathren of Augusta upper and lower Rockingham Shenandoah and Hardy having in general council assembled ourselfs in the Church on linvils creek and having under consideration the following questing that is conserning thouse breathren that are holding slaves at this time and have not complied with the reqquestion of the annual meeting of 1854 first query   We have come to the following conclusion that is that they make speady preaperation to liberate them eather by emancipation or by will that this eavil may be banish from amongst us as we look upon slavery as dangrous to be tolerated in the church and is attended to create disunion in the brotherhood and a great injury to the cause of Christ and the progress of the cnurch   So we unitedly exhort our breathren humbly yet ernestly, and lovingly to clear themselss from this principel of slavery that you may not fail and come short of the glory of god at the great and notable day of the lord and further more as considering Breathren hiring of a slave or slaves and paying wages to those owners we dont approve of the same and is attended with eavil and combined with slavery and taking hold of the same eavil wich we can not incurage and should be banish and put from amongst us and can not be tolerated in the church

Breathren present

Benjamine Bowman	Abraham Knupp
Daniel Yount	Martin Miller
John Kline	Solomon Garber
John Wine	Joseph Miller
John Harshberger	Jacob Miller
George Shaver	Daniel Thomas
Daniel Brower	John Brindel
Jacob Brower	David Kline
Selestine Whitmore	John Miller
Christian Wine	Martain Garber
John Neff	John Wine

At a Counselmeeting held at the Linvill Creek Meetinghouse the 11th of Sep. 1856, the brethren taking into consideration the slave question come to the following conclusion that no member ought to be received by baptism into the church as a member until they first have manumited or freed all slaves or slave over-which they have a lawfull controll as slave which manumission is to be effected by putting on record in the clerks office of the county a letter of freedom, with an agreement to assist them with the means for transportation provided they cannot be tolerated enough with their masters after their freedom to earn the proper amount for transportation.

We do not hereby wish to force them from their former masters if they wish to stay with them after they are 21 years of age, then the master may agree with them as with other free persons and pay them their wages or take care of it for them.[3]

The list of those Brethren present at this council meeting in 1856 has not been preserved, but one of those present was John Kline, for he commented on the meeting in his diary.

THURSDAY, SEPTEMBER 11, 1856. Council meeting at our meetinghouse. Decide the question as to what the churches here in the slaveholding States should require of any slaveowner desiring to come into the church. A very delicate matter to act upon in the present sensitive condition of public feeling on slavery. But it is the aim of the Brethren here not to offend popular feeling, so long as that feeling does not attempt any interference with what the regard and hold sacred as their line of Christian duty. Should such opposition arise, which I greatly fear will be the case at no distant day, it will then be seen that it is the fixed purpose and resolve of the Brotherhood to "obey God rather than men." It was decided in council that every slaveholder coming into the church must give up his or her slaves as property; and yet not turn them off houseless and homeless, but allow them to remain, and labor, and be fed and clothed as usual, until suitable and lawful provisions can be made for their complete emancipation.[4]

Nearly a decade earlier, John Kline had preached on the eastern side of the mountains in Virginia, where slavery was much more widely accepted than in his home area. He described some of his reactions in his diary.

SUNDAY, July 4, 1847. Meeting in the Methodist meetinghouse. John 4 is read. I spoke as best I could on the Water of Life and kindred topics, but in this country we feel sadly the want of encouragement and sympathy which we are used to in our own houses and congregations. Our doctrinal views and practices as a denomination are not well understood in Albemarle County, Virginia. The prevailing denominations here are Baptists and Methodists. We have one consolation, however, even here. We can preach the Gospel to the poor, and they are ready to hear it. But there is one barrier between us and the wealthy classes which will continue, God only knows how long; and that barrier is African slavery. Many, seemingly good and reasonable people, in this country justify themselves in their own eyes, even on scripture grounds, for taking part in and encouraging the holding of slaves. I fear, however, that the god of this world has blinded their eyes, so that seeing they see not and hearing they understand not. . . . I do believe that the time is not far distant when the sun will rise and set upon our land cleansed of this foul stain, though it may be cleansed with blood. I would rejoice to think that my eyes might see that bright morning; but I can have no hope of that.[5]

In Tennessee also a number of Brethren faced the problem of slavery, and one of them, John H. Bowman, signed a document in 1853 by which he agreed to free his slave, Jim, after eleven years of work. Bowman's relation to other Bowmans in Tennessee, including M. M. Bowman who witnessed the document, is not known, but very likely, John H. Bowman took this step because of pressure from the Brethren.

Know all Men by these presents that I John H Bowman of the County of Washington and State of Tennessee do hereby grant order and direct that my Black Man Jim or James Shall be free for Life after he Serves me Eleven years from the first day of March One-thousand Eight Hundred and fifty three after making up all loss time that he may loosse and paying all Doct Bills &c and I also order and direct that Wm Clark Henry Swadley and Samuel Sherfy Shall be my lawfull Trustees in trust to See that the Said Jim or James Shall be free for life after the manner here in mentioned and in Case the Said Bowman Should die the Said Jime is to be Hired out to Some man he may chose for the Sum of Eighty four dollars and Sixty five cents for Annum and the man that hires the Said Jim must find his clothes and all the money of the Said Jims hire is to be Equally divided between my Children at the End of Said time as they may come of age and all the time that he has or will labour for the Said Bowman he is allowed Eighty four dollars and Sixty five cents toward his freedom and no instrument of Writing what ever Shall Supercede or change this instrument of Writeing April 30-1853
Sealed With my Seal and Delivered in the
Presence of

John H. Bowman   Seal

Test
M. M. Bowman
John Nead[6]

Tennessee was also the setting for an interesting incident which illustrated both the strong Brethren convictions regarding slavery and the strong feelings of many Southerners on the subject. Samuel Garber was a Brethren minister who had lived a number of years in Tennessee before moving to Illinois about 1840. In 1858 he and his family spent some time in the East visiting relatives; he had married Mary Long from the Hagerstown, Maryland, area. He spent much of the time preaching.

In the fall of 1858 he [Garber] went to Tenn. and was there but a short time when he was asked to preach a sermon on the text taken from Isaiah 58-6. He having just come to this part of the country knew little of the aggitation there regarding slavery accepted the text which had been refused by a minister living there. It was known that my father was to preach from this text so the Sherriff & officers came to listen to the sermon during the preaching of which they could scarcely keep their seats. Immediately after church the Sherriff & officers surrounded him and arrested him & asked him to make his appearance in court the same day; but he refused saying he would appear any day but Sunday. Thursday was set his appearing. The Sherriff having known Father when he lived there was so effected over the matter that his hand trembled so when he tried to sign the paper for the arrest that he had to get some one else to sign for him. During the week it was published in the papers that Father was to be tarred & feathered and ridden on a rail. A slave holder who sent one of his slaves on a mule with the news & what was to be done with Father lost his slave valued at a thousand dollars as the mule on which he was riding became frightened at something & threw the negro off & he broke his neck by the fall. Father appeared on Thursday & was told that his case would be tried when court opened in September. He was out on $500.00 bail. The brethren were much woried about the matter, tho Father never lost a minute's sleep over it, that they urged him to leave which he finally consented to do and the church payed his bail.[7]

One way to avoid such problems was to move to a free state, just as Samuel Garber had done about 1840, when he went to Illinois. Many Brethren took such action, and they wrote letters to their friends and relatives in the South urging them to emigrate to a free state. From Indiana in 1837:

We understand by your Letter Father Harshberger has also Sold the Old Plantation, and that Joseph Brubaker has Some Idea to go to Tennisee. Dear Brother & Sister I would advise you, and Every body Else that would sell their Land in a Slave State Never Never to by Land in a Slave State again   My Dear friends [if] you once lived in a free State, and Could See and feel the Differance that there is in a free State, you would Never wish your Selves in a Slave State again. But when you are in a Slave State, you Daily See the abominuble Traffic of Slavery, and the Cruel treatment that is Inflicted upon them, and Draged too and frow, Like the Broute of the field, and you Come to be rather hartened to it, and you do not See the Grate abomination. My Dear Brother & Sister, when I think of these things it makes me Shudder to think, What will be the case with those that are Gilty of this Grate Man Soul Selling Traffic. If you was to live in a State where Slavery is not admited It would become more Sencible to you and would See the Grate Evel much Plainer[8]

From Indiana in 1843:

This is to inform you that we are all well at this time, also hope that these lines will find you enjoying good health, happiness, and prosperity. Tho as for being contented in mind I dont think you can be for this reason, our country is so much superior to that of yours.   our Country is not infested with Slaves[9]

From Iowa in 1854:

wee are all highly pleasd with the Country and our home   one off our old neighbours from tennessee Came to see us   he was hear weeke before Last   you have seen him   it was John Blair that ust to wagon to Linchburg   he says he Cant Content him self in tennessee no Longer   he is a going to sell as soon as he Can and move right hear   he says he studied all the way out hear how wee was fixt and what kind off a home wee had but he found it all so much better then he   had anny ideia that he wants to Come and settel hear in a free Country   wee have not seen the first negro since wee are in the state[10]

Probably some Brethren in the South who did not emigrate to a free state considered such an action seriously, but then found more compelling reasons why they should remain where they were. For example, Jacob Faw, the elder of the Fraternity congregation in North Carolina wrote in 1853:

Sometimes I am almost inclined to contemplate about going to a free state where the brethren is more prosperous but it don't seem like I can ever leave this country as long as there is any church here, and as long as I am here.[11]

Since some Brethren continued to live in areas of the country where there was a considerable number of blacks, a different problem developed when a black person applied for membership in the church. Probably, such a development did not happen very often, but when it did, it was important enough to demand the attention of the Annual Meeting, which considered the matter on at least three different occasions.

Y. M. 1835. Art. 1. How it is considered, to receive colored persons into the church? (The object of the question was not, whether they should be received at all, but whether they could or must be received or treated altogether like white members.) It was considered, that inasmuch the gospel is to be preached to all nations and races, and if they come as repentant sinners, believing in the gospel of Jesus Christ, and apply for baptism, we could not consistently refuse them. But inasmuch we receive our fellow members with the holy kiss, and there is a repugnance in some of our white members to salute colored persons in this manner, the colored members should bear with that weakness, and not offer the kiss to such weak members until they become stronger, and make the first offer, &c. Otherwise, if they (the colored members) prove faithful, they should be considered on an equality of full membership.

Y. M. 1845. Art. 2. In regard to receiving colored members into the church, it was considered, to leave it to the counsel of every individual church, as it is done in all cases; but if colored persons are once received as members into the church, the members should be at liberty to salute them in like manner as (we do) white members; at the same time having patience with those who may be weak in the faith, and cannot do so. The assembled elders, however, consider it as the more perfect way, to which we all should strive to come, namely, that love which makes no distinction in the brotherhood in this respect. See James 2:1-10.

Y. M. 1849. Art. 31. How are we to conduct with colored members at communion? Considered, that this ought to be left to the individual churches, in which such members are, only that they ought not to be debarred from the Lord's table on account of their color.[12]

The major problem was of course the salutation or holy kiss, which has been described in the chapter dealing with the beliefs of the church.

A fascinating account of a black man who became a member of the church has been preserved. It is the story of Samuel Weir, who eventually became a minister in the church.

THE LIFE OF ELDER SAMUEL WEIR
A COLORED BROTHER

INTRODUCTION

The following sketch of the life of this humble servant of God, was obtained, in part, February 23, 1887, when Brethren William D. Mallow, Henry Frantz and the writer, gave a visit to the aged brother at his home in Frankfort, Ross County, Ohio, and during the time of his last affliction.

It may differ in minor points from accounts given previous to this but we feel that the statements here offered are correct, being obtained directly from the old brother himself, or from those who were fully acquainted with the statements made. Of his birth, we learn an earlier date for it than before given, and from a note written in a small Testament, which was found after his death, and which is supposed to have been presented to him by a brother or sister soon after Sammy's baptism in 1843.

HIS BIRTH

Samuel Weir was born a slave, in Bath County, Virginia, April 15, 1812. In his second year his family, with their master, William Byrd, moved into Botetourt County, of that State, where he remained a servant of Mr. Byrd until twelve (12) years of age. At this age, and in the year 1824, he was sold at a private sale to a Mr. Andrew McClure for the sum of two hundred and eighty dollars. He then lived with and served Mr. McClure till the winter of 1843. When nearly thirty years of age the following event occurred, which, although a sad one, yet it resulted in good— the conversion of a father and mother, the freeing of a slave and then in his conversion also.

A little son of the master, and the favorite of the family, was, about this time, thrown from a horse and killed. The event at once marked a change in the lives of both the father and mother, and soon afterward they made application to the Dunkard Brethren for membership. They were told that the Brethren did not receive any one who held slaves, and that they could not be received until they would first give freedom to Sammy, their only slave. Such terms of Christianity were at that time and in old Virginia, thought to be severe, for it was then that members of the church thought to justify Slavery by the Gospel, and to oppose Slavery then was thought to be a sin. But the terms named by the Brethren to this penitent father and mother, were accepted by them, and Sammy was set free.

Mr. McClure had been, in the fullest sense, a worldly man, as I learned from Brother B. F. Moomaw, of Virginia, but kind to his family and also to his servant, laboring with him in the field, and as a servant of all. And the fact being known to the Slave Traders and drivers, that he would be required to give up his slave upon coming to the Brethren, these did much to obtain Sammy by purchase, offering for him the sum of fifteen hundred dollars. But it was refused with a declaration that he was now opposed to the sale of humanity, and that the slave should go forth a free man. So freedom was given him, but he remained with the family, laboring as before, until an opportunity offered to send him safely to a free state.

About this date, brother Peter Nead, of Virginia, began preaching in Botetourt County, and during his ministry there, Brother and Sister McClure were baptized in February, 1843.

Soon after their baptism, in 1843, Sammy met a Methodist minister and wife, and of this interview, Sammy gives us the following: "Sam, is it true that McClure and his wife joined the Dunkards?" I told him it was true. He said, "Why Sam, we have been fishing for them this long time, but we did not get them." I told him they did not fish in deep enough water. "And that sets you free, does it?" I told him I was free. The wife then spoke up and said: "Well, Sam, I wish to God that all men were Dunkards, for that would do away with this awful curse of Slavery."

The great and serious changes in the family and that in his own life, had a marked effect upon the mind of Sammy also, and soon after the baptism of the brother and sister, he too made application to the Brethren for membership. He now felt that he owed his love and service to God during his life; for the sudden death of the little son, the conversion of the father and mother to the Gospel of Christ and, above all, the freedom now given to himself, were enough to lead him to the one Savior of all; and Sammy felt that to give himself and his life to the service of God was no more than was due, and he loved the church that had given him his liberty. He applied to the Brethren for membership, and was baptized by Brother Nead on Sunday, May 14, 1843. And, he being the first colored member received by the church in that part of Virginia, it was soon a question as to how he should be received by the Brethren after baptism—whether with the right hand and kiss of charity, or with only the right hand of fellowship. See First Thes. V, 26. But after some consideration by the church, it was decided to receive him with the right hand of fellowship, but without the salutation; and in this manner he was received as a member.

We have in this case, both with Sammy and his former master, a spirit of submission worthy of our imitation. Sammy, although a free man, remained with and worked as a servant for his former master—and that, too, without a murmur—for eight months after being set free, and when baptized and in full relation with a royal priesthood; he was willing to be received on any terms his white brethren were ready to take him.

And his master, but now a brother, although in but moderate circumstances in wealth, refused a large sum of money for the servant, now one of the most valuable; and not only gave him his freedom, but a good suit of clothes, a valuable horse, a saddle and bridle, with money and all things necessary for Sammy in his journey to Ohio; and they parted as Brethren, with their best wishes and prayers for other's welfare, They met no more in this life.

And Brother B. F. Moomaw, of Virginia, yet alive, coming to Ohio in October of that year (1843), it was decided by the Brethren in Virginia, that Sammy should come under his guidance and protection to Ohio. It was urgent, too, that he should come that year; for the laws of Virginia at that time held all liberated slaves liable to be sold again into slavery, if found within the State one year after being free. And it was all important, too, that he should have a guide and protector during his journey; for some who had been set free before, and who had started without protection to the free States did not reach them, and were never again heard from by their friends, who supposed that the lost ones had been captured and sold again into slavery.

Brother Moomaw and his valuable charge came away from that part of Virginia in the latter part of October, and coming at the rate of thirty-five miles per day, reached the Ohio River, then the Jordan to slaves, and the line of the Slave and Free States. They crossed at the mouth of the Big Sandy on Sunday, October 29, 1843, when Sammy and his faithful guide passed over from slave territory into the land of freedom.

Upon reaching the Ohio shore, Brother Moomaw said to him: "Sam, you are now a free man and on free soil, where you can enjoy your freedom as all other free men." We can only think that we imagine what the feelings of this humble believer were, but none of us can know them, and much less can we describe them.

Brother Moomaw speaks thus of the event: "He did not, while on the way, seem to be affected in the least, but now, it appears to me, that his whole being was affected, and that he now felt as he had never felt before."

It was another era in Sammy's life. He was now a free man and on free soil, and his heart swelled in gratitude to God for his deliverance. And none but pardoned sinners can ever know or share in the feelings of a liberated slave.

From the place of crossing they came down the Ohio River, reached the home of Brother Thomas Major, living then in Scioto County, Ohio, on Monday. But Brother Major being away from home, they were received and cared for very kindly by Sister Sarah. This was Sammy's first meeting with Sister Major.

On Wednesday, November 1st, they reached the home of old Brother John Moomaw, in Twin Valley, a few miles north of Bainbridge, Ross County, Ohio, where they remained until the next Sunday morning, November 5th, when they left that part and came north twelve miles, to the Brethren's meeting at the Bush Meeting House, on Paint Creek, three miles west of Frankfort, in the same county. Upon their arrival at the church, they were met by the Brethren, among whom were Elders Robert Calvert, John Cadwallader and John Mohler. . . .

It was soon decided to receive Brother Sammy into the Paint Creek Church, and over which body Brother Calvert was at that time the Elder in charge. It was also decided that Brother Calvert should act as a Guardian for Sammy for at least one year, and see that he obtained a home and all wants be provided for. And Sammy being the first and only colored member in that church, and in that part of the State at that time, the one great question was, "Where can we find a Home for him?" When this was offered, an old brother, William Bryant, a minister, and one of the most zealous, came up and said: "I will find a home for him if he will come and live with me." Upon hearing this offer, the council decided that Sammy should go and make his home at Brother Bryant's. . . .

Sammy lodged that night with Brother Jacob Everman, near the Fairview Church, in Fayette County, and on the next day went to his new home at the residence of Brother Bryant, on Paint Creek, some six miles above Frankfort. And here, at this home, he lived and worked as a farm hand for almost two years. Of the home and treatment received at Brother Bryant's, we feel that it must have been fully satisfactory to Sammy, for in speaking of the family and also Brother Bryant, he seemed to regard each one as a member of his own household. And Sammy's character, some conception may be had from the respect ever shown him by the family of Brother Bryant, and also from a statement made by Brother Bryant himself, who said, "I regard Sammy as an example to me in many things, but especially so in that of religion."

It was here that Sammy's education began, and none but the hand of God could have so well directed events to the gaining of that end, as is shown in this case. When consulting with him as to his education, we learned that he, with the thousands held in Slavery, had by law been denied the benefit of learning to read or to know even a part of the alphabet; and now, upon being set free, and especially after coming into the church and a new State, for a home among strangers, Sammy felt the need of an education more that ever before. It was all-important to him, and to acquire this, was to mark one of the most important changes of his life, and it was to destroy the last effect of slavery with him. But this great change in his life did not begin until after his arrival in Ohio, in the winter of 1843-44, and when he was upwards of thirty-one years of age.

Of the many changes in his life, he spoke with pleasure, but especially so, of that of his education. I give the event in his own words: "We were all sitting around the fire one night, when I said, 'I wish I had had a chance to go to school when I was young.' At this, old Mother Bryant spoke up and said, 'Sammy, you are not too old to learn, and you can learn yet; and if you will say you will try it, I will have Katy to learn you.' This Katy was their little grandchild, Catherine Long, then ten years of age, who at that time was living with the family. I said I would try it, and Katy went and got the book, and we commenced. We got along very well at times, but not very fast, for she would often get out of heart, and sometimes very angry at me, because I did not learn faster; and then she would tell me that I was nothing but a black Negro, and that she could do nothing more for me. The work would then stop, but on the next night, after she had been to school and I to my work, with the old alphabet leaf in my pocket, and we had all come together again, and supper was over, and Katy in a good humor again, then I would say, 'Now, Miss Katy, please try again; I will do better this time.' So she would get the books and begin, but sometimes I did no better than before. But we worked at it that way all winter, and I learned my letters. After this I went to school two winters, and to a colored teacher over in Highland County, where I studied spelling reading and arithmetic, but I could never make any headway in writing. I stopped going to school too soon, for when I found that I could read the Bible I felt satisfied, and I gave up all other books but that. The Bible has been my delight, and I have read it through several times." . . .

From Brother John Mohler, of Clermont County, Ohio, we learn that Sammy, while attending school in Highland County, about 1845, boarded at the home of Elder John Mohler, the father of our informant, and who, at that time, lived on Clear Creek, some eight miles north of Hillsboro. We learned from Sammy, and also from Brother Mohler, that the teacher was a colored man named Jacob Emmings, and a minister in the Baptist Church; and it is to him that Sammy owed the completion of the education obtained by him, and also the beginning of his works as a minister. His life is one of great variety, and this was another change and the great one, but it was not all.

Of the beginning of his public ministry—a work he seemed slow to engage in at first—he spoke thus: "My teacher in Highland County was a Baptist preacher, and at their meetings, where I often went, he would urge me to get up and talk. At last I told him I would try; but when the day came I felt so very weak that I thought I could not, and did not get up. But I did not feel well over it, and I then thought I would never do so any more."

This was in 1845 or 1846, and, being the only colored member then in that part of the State, and the sentiment among the whites not favorable for admitting the colored people into the meetings with the whites, Sammy was compelled to meet mostly with his own race, and they always of other denominations. It was under these circumstances—and they were the most discouraging—that his work in the ministry began; but with a firmness and a zeal that many of us do not yet possess, he won his way over every obstacle. He was spoken well of by many people of other denominations; he had there none of his own to go to hear him. And well should his zeal be commended, for he, with none to stand by, to cheer and support him, still labored on for the one Master, whilst scores of white ministers, with friends and help on every side, have given up both faith and work, and have gone down in despair.

Of his election to the ministry, he said: "I had been preaching around at the meetings of the colored people, and of other churches for four or five years; so when the Brethren heard that I was trying to preach, they told me to come out from town, and preach a sermon for the whites at the Bush Meeting House. And they said if they then thought that I could preach, they would put me at it earnest. The minister, Joseph Kelso, also asked me to come, and I told him I would. So one day when I was present, he gave it out for me, and some five weeks before-hand. When he gave it out, I thought everybody tried to look me in the face, but I thought it was nothing that I should be ashamed of."

SAMMY'S SERMON AND ELECTION

"The meeting was held in August, 1849, and there was a great crowd present, and all of them white but myself. I spoke thirty-nine minutes by Kelso's watch, and from the words in Hebrews ii, 1-2; and I have never seen prettier behavior in all the preaching I have done than I had that day."

After the trial sermon was delivered, the members present were asked if they were willing that the colored brother should take part in the ministry, and their voices were unanimous in his favor. He was then given his charge as a minister, and instructed to go to his own race and hold meetings wherever opportunity was offered.

Of his work and life as a minister, he said little, but that little expressed much in the life of a minister, and especially so with one placed as he was; for his public life was at that time, and in his situation, well calculated to bring out all of the variety found in the brief period of one man's life. He said: "I then preached just wherever I could find a place, and they would argue with me, and they do yet. I would tell them what the Word said about these things, and then they would say, when they saw that I wanted what the Word said: 'Why, Sammy, it is only some of your notions of it.'" . . .

[However] of his knowledge of the Bible, the whites say there was no one in the village or neighborhood who was better acquainted with the reading and sense of the Scriptures than was Sammy; and if any question or dispute arose among his neighbors as to a Bible subject, he was their reference, and his decision satisfactory.

Thus it continued until in August, 1865, when Brother Harvey Carter and Martha, his wife became satisfied that Sammy's teaching was nearest in accordance with the Words of Jesus, and they made applications to Sammy for baptism. Arrangements were at once made for a meeting at Frankfort, Ross County, Ohio, where Sammy and the applicants all lived, and Brother Thomas Major and Sister Sarah, then of Highland County, were sent for. This brother and sister attended at the meeting in August, 1865, and Brother and Sister Carter were baptized in Paint Creek, near Frankfort.

The event occurring just at the close of the Rebellion, and while the feeling was yet excited on the subject of Slavery, the great question of trouble, it made the reception of these colored people into full relation, and into the same church with the whites, a cause for some stir, but that soon passed away. It was a matter for a sinful world to talk of, and to find fault with, but it was a cause of thanksgiving to God by Sammy; for he then felt as he had never felt before—he was no longer alone in his work for his Master.

In October, 1865, a Love Feast was held by these few members in Frankfort, and embracing but five members; two whites and three colored—Brother and Sister Major, Sammy, and Brother and Sister Carter. It marked a new era in Sammy's life and also with his race, for it was the first feast held by the colored Brethren in the State of Ohio, and for all that we can say, it was their first one on the Earth. But it was a feasting on the Body which was broken for the Races, and this feast marked a new point in the extent and goodness of the great salvation.

Sammy was given authority to baptize and to solemize marriages by Brother Thomas Major, when at a meeting of the Brethren at Fairview, some miles west of Frankfort in the year of 1872. He then continued meetings in and around Frankfort, and also at or near Circleville, on the Scioto River, with an increasing interest, and the reception of some by baptism, and one or two colored members from Virginia by letter.[13]

In addition to Thomas Major, who had been baptized and ordained as a minister in the Philadelphia congregation, another Brethren minister in Ohio who ministered to the spiritual needs of a black congregation was Philip Younce, who had been born and reared in North Carolina. The following account was written by John Swinger, Sr.

Eld. Philip Younce was born in Ashland [Ashe] County, N. Car., in October, 1792, and died about the middle of April, 1864, aged 72 years. He was married to Margaret Burket, of North Carolina, and was elected to the ministry in North Carolina. He was the only English minister in that church at that time.

John Younce, their oldest child, was born in North Carolina. They came to Ohio some years after Wayne's treaty with the Indians at Greenville, Ohio. They told about them taking a wash tub of sweet cakes and giving them to the Indians, when they would take Johnny and carry him around and call him the "white papoosey."

Eld. Younce preached the first sermon that was preached in Franklin township by our Brethren, in a round log cabin.... Sometimes he would hold church in a barn or in a grove, as his congregation was small, because there were only a few people living in this county at that time, yet he preached over a large territory in Western Ohio. At that time there was a colored settlement three miles west of West Milton, Ohio. They asked him to preach for them, and he did so for a number of years. I heard him say once that the color did not go deeper than the skin. I never saw him discouraged nor out of humor. He would always have a smile and a pleasant word for everybody; no matter whether they were young or old, white or black, and he was always a firm friend to the Red man of the wilderness.[14]

An excellent summary of the Brethren beliefs and practices regarding slavery was prepared in 1853 by Philip Boyle, a well-informed Brethren elder in Maryland, who had been called upon by various individuals outside of the Brethren for information about the Brethren. In this case he received a request from Lewis Tappan of the American Anti-Slavery Society for information about the Brethren position on slavery. Boyle was thoughtful enough to send a copy of his response to Tappan to the editor of the "Gospel Visiter," Henry Kurtz. Kurtz, of course, commented on

Boyle's statement at some length. In fact, Kurtz' comments were longer than Boyle's statement. Taken together, they provide a valuable insight into Brethren attitudes toward blacks.

SOMETHING ABOUT SLAVERY
Copy of a letter from the Secretary of the American and Foreign Anti-Slavery society to a brother in Md.—

New York   June 25th 1853.

Sir: You will oblige me very much by giving me, as early as you can, a brief statement of the doctrine and measures of your religious denomination with reference to American Slavery and especially what has been done on the subject since May 1851, distinguishing between the years 1851-2 and 1852-3   I shall be glad also of the name or style of your denomination, so as to insure entire accuracy on my part. If some other gentleman of your denomination can furnish the information more readily than yourself please inform me, and give his postoffice address.

I want it for the body or appendix of the Annual Report of the *American and Foreign Anti-Slavery Society,* but your name will not be mentioned in connection with it without your consent, if at all.

Yours very respectfully,

Lewis Tappan.

The following is the answer to the same.

Friend— Yours under date of the 25th of June was received this morning. I now hasten to answer the same as follows:

1. The first members of our denomination in this country migrated here from Germany. We have therefore been styled *"German Baptists,"* in order to distinguish us from the other American Baptist denominations. We have for ourselves assumed the name *"Brethren"* from Matth. xxiii.8. hence we are now called *German Baptist Brethren.*

2. We hold no other creed or discipline separate and apart from the Gospel.

3. As to our doctrines and measures with reference to *American Slavery* I will briefly state that slavery is repugnant to the doctrines and principles of the Gospel, see Matth. vii. 12. hence we hold no slaves, neither do we hire any: and we conceive it to be our conscientious duty to declare with meekness our sentiments upon *this,* as well as upon every other subject which comes within the province of the Gospel ministry: and I feel happy to state that the course we have pursued has had a very

salutary influence upon a great number of our slave-holders: and I sincerely wish that all who profess to be under the government of the Gospel
would "go and do likewise."

In a political as well as in a moral point of view slavery is a great evil,
however, it must be remembered that this right which the slaveholder
claims, was guaranteed by the Constitution of the United States. But this
does not compel us to hold slaves, the slave-holders know that we consider
it wrong for us to do so, and as a proof we hold none: he admits that we
are sincere in our pretensions, but contends that he has a *right* to hold
slaves, and as a proof he does so: and he looks upon them as we do
upon our cattle, and should any of them run away he has the same right to
pursue them as we have to go after our cattle, and it does not matter
whether they stray to Va. or to Pa., it does not lessen our right to pursue
them,.and so in the other case, and if the laws of the United States protect
us in the exercise of our rights, should they not also protect the slaveholder in the exercise of his rights? Hence we look upon the Compromise Bill of
May 1851, as being in accordance with the constitution of the U. S. and we
do feel ourselves in good faith bound as good citizens to submit to the re-
quisitions of its laws, and to exhort all others to do so. See Rom.xiii. 1-5.

We as a people feel to sympathize deeply with our colored population,
& consequently advise all who may in sincerity desire to adopt measures,
with a view of mitigating their condition, to consider the subject seriously,
and in all cases to speak and express their sentiments with *calmness,* and in
respectful terms.

We conceive it to be our Christian duty, frequently, to bring the case
(of the poor slaves,) before Him, who, can work, and no man can hinder,
hoping that he through his allwise providence may hasten the time, when
their rights will be considered by all, and when it will be said their redemption is at hand.

I remain sincerely your friend and well-wisher.

P.————

(We have avoided as much as possible to introduce that exciting and
perplexing question about *Slavery* into our columns. Not that we thought,
the question in itself unnecessary or unimportant;—not, that we felt
callous and indifferent about those millions of our fellow-beings, who are
held in perpetual bondage in this our boasted land of liberty;—not that we
were afraid of speaking out our mind on a subject, which to men of the
world may be a matter of doubtful disputation, but which to a christian,
who sincerely believes and tries to practise the principles of the Gospel, is a
matter very easily decided.

No, no; far different reasons and motives brought us to this conclusion, to say as little as possible on the question under consideration in the foregoing article. Our readers, who are in possession of our first volume, will remember or find them there on page 159, and for the sake of those, who cannot refer to it, we will merely state, in the fewest words possible, why we did feel it our duty to pursue this course, to wit,

1. Because the question has unfortunately become a political party-question, and has caused passion, animosity, and hatred, with all its concomitant evils.

2. Because the Gospel-Visiter circulates chiefly among those, who are sufficiently enlightened by the Gospel to understand and decide this question for themselves.

3. Because in setting forth the doctrines and principles of the Gospel we believe to present a more efficacious remedy for every moral and social evil, than by any party-measures of man's invention whatever.

But, while we thus deprecated unnecessary and uncalled-for discussion on this subject, we felt free to confess our own convictions, and to state the views and practice of our brethren in that respect at the same time, as the following brief extract from the same article (vol. 1. page 159) may testify.

"With them (the brethren) the question, Whether slavery be right or wrong?—is no question at all. While slavery existed yet in every state of the Union, and almost every denomination took part in it, the Brethren stood aloof, and declared, not by words only, but by their constant practice, that '*to hold any of their fellowmen in perpetual bondage was a* GREAT WRONG, & *should never be committed by a* FOLLOWER OF CHRIST. There are now living hundreds, and perhaps thousands of our brethren in the so-called Slave-states; but we verily believe, they all agree with the sentiments of their brethren of old, and with us in the so-called free-states, and discountenance slavery by their example."

Hence if a brother should have been tempted to buy and hold slaves, the church would have taken him immediately under dealing according to the Gospel, and if he would defend and persist in his course, he would have been disowned. When a person, holding slaves, made application for membership, he or she was at once instructed, that this was inconsistent with the Gospel, and that an arrangement was necessary, to liberate his slave in due time, and if he should have failed in the faithful performance of the arrangement, made under the cognizance of the church, and become refractory, he would likewise be disowned. Such were the measures to carry out the principles of the Gospel, and to keep the church pure from the evils of slavery.

We are truely rejoiced, that the testimony of our beloved brother from Md. fully corroborates with this, and inasmuch as he resides in a slave-state, in the midst of slave-holders and slaves, his testimony will be of much more weight, though it will scarcely be satisfactory to our Anti-slavery friends. They probably expected an exposition of the evils of slavery in the strongest terms, and here they find but a simple avowal of principles in the mildest language possible.

This is, in our humble opinion, as it should be, though we believe, that if that letter of the Secretary of the American and Foreign Anti-Slavery Society had been addressed to some brother North of Mason's and Dixon's line, he would have received a somewhat different answer. But whether we live North or South of that line, and though we have been holding and practising Anti-Slavery-principles from the time of our ancestor's coming to this country, we should be neither *Anti-Slavery* nor *Pro-Slavery* in the present acceptation of the terms. We should rather hold out the olive-branch of love and good will toward all men, until SLAVERY with all its evils shall be among the things that were, but are no more. Ed.)[15]

On the one hand Brethren were vigorously opposed to human slavery and did everything they could to prevent the members of the church from owning, hiring, or trading slaves. In that position Brethren were different from the society around them in many of the areas in which they lived, for there was much sympathy with slavery not only in the South but also in much of the Ohio River Valley. On the other hand, however, the Brethren were not at all eager to have black persons as members of the church, and consequently very few blacks became Brethren in the years before 1865. In that regard Brethren were not very different from the society around them, since most of the Christians in the United States in 1860 were members of segregated churches. The Brethren had neither the desire nor the leadership to established segregated congregations.

POLITICAL ACTIVITY

Even though slavery was considered an evil institution by the Brethren, it was protected in a number of states by the laws enacted by the state legislatures and by certain actions of the national government. For this reason as well as for other reasons Brethren believed that participation in political "electioneering and elections" was wrong for them. On a number of occasions the Annual Meeting was asked to deal with this matter.

ELECTIONEERING AND ELECTIONS (POLITICAL)
Y. M. 1813. Art. 2. Further, it has been considered in union concern-

ing electioneering, namely, giving votes for officers or men for the assembly or congress, in order to elect them to their several offices. Inasmuch as the appearance of the times into which we have come are grievous (it was the time of the war with England), and inasmuch as party spirit has risen so high in the kingdom of this world, that men and even the heads of government, are among themselves at variance, therefore it has been viewed in union, that it would be much better if no votes were given in at elections for such officers (by the brethren); for so long as there is such division of parties, we make ourselves suspicious and unpropitious on the one side, on whatever side we may vote. Thereby every one that desires to be defenseless (or non-resistant) may readily see what might be best (for him to do). Moreover, is (not only) our land and (but also) almost all empires engaged in war (in Europe especially); hence it was considered to be best to give in no vote, else we might perhaps assist in electing such that would afterward oppress us with war. To pray diligently for our government we believe to be our duty, and to call upon the Lord we think will be most acceptable.

Y. M. 1849. Art. 33. Is it safe and proper for the humble followers of Jesus to go to the elections, and take an active part in the political affairs of the country? Considered, as it was always the advice of the older brethren, and as the anointing (1 John 2: 27) will teach every sincere follower of Jesus, that it would be safest in regard to political elections to remain as neutral as possible, and rather than go to the election, to commit the matter in prayer to the care of Him who setteth up and removeth rulers.

Y. M. 1853. Art. 17. Concerning going to political meetings and elections. Considered best not to attend any such at all, inasmuch the true Christian belongs to another kingdom.

Y. M. 1864. Art. 1. In no less than four papers the question is presented, whether it is right and proper for a brother to go to or take part in political elections, it being specially stated that it had caused hard feelings and disunion? Ans. We have been led to think that at all times it would be best and most consistent with our profession, and specially most proper and safe in the present critical state of things, to have nothing at all to do with politics, and entirely to abstain from voting. See 2 Cor. 6: 14-17.

VOTING, (Political.) See "Electioneering,"

Y. M. 1866. Art. 1. A number of questions being presented upon the subject of voting and some asking for a repeal of former minutes, the following resolution as an answer to the questions, was adopted:

Resolved, That we think it most expedient not to repeal any minutes touching voting; that this Annual Meeting recommends to the members of the church to refrain from voting, fearing that by voting we may compromise our non-resistant principles. But we recommend forbearance towards those who vote, not making voting a test of fellowship, hoping that in time they will see with the body of the brethren upon this subject.[16]

Brethren were not to participate voluntarily in politics or election campaigns in any way, nor were they to accept any kind of "worldly office," even if there was an attempt to impose it on them. This refusal to participate in the responsibilities of government even included serving on juries.

JURIES, SERVING ON

Y. M. 1841. Art. 11. Whether it is becoming for a member of the church of Christ to act as a juror in the courts of our country? Considered, that it would be best not to serve at all even in civil cases, but by no means (can a brother serve) in criminal cases.

OFFICES, HOLDING WORLDLY

Y. M. 1789. Art. 3. Further it has been discussed and unanimously deemed good and evangelical, that all brethren in all places should shun all worldly offices, so as not to serve in any of them, provided it is possible to be relieved from them, such as Supervisor, Overseer of the Poor, Collector, Constable, Assessor, or also Juryman, &c. Yet it is considered, with some difference, such as Supervisor or Overseer of the Poor, might be served perhaps with least objection; provided, there is no suing or something else contrary to the Word of the Lord. If a brother should be elected to one of these offices contrary to his will, then only that what he would have to do contrary to the gospel, should be rebuked in love and compassion, according to the word of the Lord.

Y. M. 1834. Art. 9. Concerning the office of Supervisor and other worldly offices, was considered, that brethren should keep themselves clear of them as much as possible.

Y. M. 1844. Art. 3. Whether a brother may go to the Legislative Assembly as a representative of the people, agreeably with the gospel? Considered, that though we look upon the higher powers of this world as being of God for the protection of the pious, &c., and desire to be thankful to God for the benefits we enjoy under our government, and feel it our duty to pray fervently and daily for the same, (still) we cannot see how a follower of the meek and lowly Saviour can seek or accept an office of this kind consistently with the gospel he professes. See Matt. 20: 25-28; Mark, 10: 42-46; Luke, 22: 25, John, 17: 16, &c.

Y. M. 1857. Art. 39. Is it consistent with the gospel for brethren to serve in the capacity of any of the civil officers under our government; and is there any material difference as to state, county, or township officers? Answer. We consider it wrong for brethren to accept of any office which requires them to administer an oath, or to use physical force in performing the duties of that office.[17]

A long-standing principle of the Brethren was their refusal to use the courts to settle differences, because they believed such things ought to be handled by the church itself. However, there were numerous situations in which the Brethren wanted to use the courts, it seemed; and frequently such situations were taken to the Annual Meeting for a decision.

LAW, TAKING THE BENEFIT OF

Y.M. 1822. (Miami.). Art. 2. Whether it is right for a brother to take the benefit of the law, was considered, that when a brother is so imprudent that he falls under the power of law, he is not to have privilege to take the benefit of the law, but to seek counsel from the church. Yet it would be always best to seek counsel before a member comes so far.

LAW, USING IT AGAINST DEBTORS

Y. M. 1810. Art. 2. Concerning brethren who use the law for collecting debts, was considered, that it is unbecoming for brethren to do so, that it cannot be permitted, and if they should do such a disallowed thing, they are to be left over to the counsel of the church.

Y. M. 1833. Art. 2. Whether there is any difference in using the law for our own benefit or only as executors or administrators? Considered, there is none in reality; it is wrong for ourselves, it is wrong if we do it for others.

Y. M. 1849. Art. 28. Whether a brother, who considers himself injured by any public improvement, such as a turnpike or a rail road passing through his land, can without a violation of the gospel make use of the provision of the law, which government has enacted for the recovery of damages in such cases? Considered, as the matter has been fully stated that it would not be a violation of the gospel to make use of the provisions of the law in such cases.

Y. M. 1852. Art. 3. Have we a right to help making the political government, and to serve as officers; also to put the law in force against any of our fellowmen in any case whatever? Considered, that the brethren should be careful, and not betray their profession in helping to make and serve the civil government, and if they give in their vote, they should do it in a quiet and peaceable manner, without taking part in electioneering, and return immediately from the ground: that brethren should hold no office under the civil government, that would cause them to betray their faith; and as respects using the law against our fellow creatures, brethren should use lenity and Christian forbearance toward our fellowmen, and not compel them by the law, unless forced so to do by stern necessity. But before so doing they should always take the counsel of the church.[18]

A specific example of the way in which Brethren used the mediation of a disinterested third party from the church to settle disputes which might have otherwise ended in the courts was cited in the diary of John Kline; he also commented on the advantages of keeping such cases out of the courts.

TUESDAY, February 17, 1846. Make an amicable adjustment of complicated business matters between the widow Judith Detrick and Abraham Detrick. It is pleasant to straighten between members of our body business matters which present a somewhat crooked and tangled appearance, when all the parties are willing to have things adjusted through the mediation of disinterested Brethren. How much better this than to go to law! The tendency of private adjustments by arbitration is to heal over breaches of friendship and love between members; but going to law before the world is almost sure to widen them. I am glad to be able to add, here, that I say this, not from any experience with law that I have ever had in my own case, or in that of any of the Brethren; but I speak it from what I have observed in others who have gone to law.[19]

In a more general way, John Kline added his observations on the relation of Brethren to political life in America, when he wrote in his diary on Washington's birthday in 1849 his ideas of patriotism.

THURSDAY, February 22, 1849. Hear the distant report of cannon in commemoration of the birth of George Washington, which is said to have occurred on the twenty-second day of February, 1732. It is presumable that those who find pleasure in public demonstrations of this sort are moved by what they regard as patriotic feelings and principles. Let their motives and enjoyments spring from what they may, they have a lawful right to celebrate the anniversary of his birth in any civil way they may choose. But I have a somewhat higher conception of true patriotism than can be represented by the firing of guns which give forth nothing but meaningless sound. I am glad, however, that these guns report harmless sound, and nothing more. If some public speakers would do the same, it might be better both for them and their hearers. My highest conception of patriotism is found in the man who loves the Lord his God with all his heart and his neighbor as himself. Out of these affections spring the subordinate love for one's country; love truly virtuous for one's companion and children, relatives and friends; and in its most comprehensive sense takes in the whole human family. Were this love universal, the word *patriotism,* in its specific sense, meaning such a love for one's country as makes its possessors ready and willing to take up arms in its defense, might be appropriately expunged from every national vocabulary.[20]

Taking an Oath

One of the problems for Brethren in political activity and the use of the courts was the taking of an oath in which the individual swore to uphold the government, to tell the truth, etc. The Annual Meeting dealt specifically with this question on only two different occasions in consecutive years in the 1820s.

Y. M. 1821. Art. 4. How far a brother has liberty in giving testimony to speak the truth before a magistrate, since there are different forms presented to brethren, was considered, that by no means a brother should take the liberty to raise his hand (or kiss the book), but to obey the counsel of the Gospel; to affirm yea that is yea, and nay that is nay, "for whatsoever is more than these cometh of evil."

Y. M. 1822. Art. 5. Concerning the form or manner of swearing oaths to save our consciences for the gospel's sake, whether we could answer with yea such a form, viz: "And this you do under the pains and penalties of perjury." It has been considered, that if a brother were oppressed or troubled herein, let him consider or seek counsel, whether there is no other form for us.[21]

Peter Nead explained why the Brethren were opposed to the swearing of an oath in political and court life.

Swearing, or Being Under an Oath

The subjects of Christ's kingdom must not swear or be under an oath. Hear the law of the King upon this subject: Mat. v. 33-37, "Again ye have heard that it hath been said of them of old time, thou shalt not foreswear thyself, but shall perform unto the Lord thine oaths: But I say unto you swear not all all, neither by Heaven for it is God's throne, nor by the earth for it is his footstool, neither by Jerusalem, for it is the city of the great King. Neither shalt thou swear by thy head, because thou canst not make one hair white or black, but let your communications be yea, yea, nay, nay, for whatsoever is more than these cometh of evil." And the apostle James writes thus in his epistle, v. 12. "But above all things, my brethren, swear not, neither by heaven, neither by the earth, neither by any other oath; but let your yea be yea, and your nay be nay, lest ye fall into condemnation. This is so plain that it needs no comment. But it is astonishing that so many who profess to be subjects of Christ's kingdom, do overlook, or wilfully transgress this plain commandment; and furthermore, there is no necessity for the children of God to be under an oath. The Government, as far as I know, under which we live, is so kind as not to compel the conscientious to swear or be under an oath; an affirmation, yea, yea, or nay, nay, is all that the Government will require. Therefore, it is a violation of the law of Christ, for his followers to be under oath. The followers of Christ ought to be men of truth, so that their word may be received without an oath.[22]

MASONS AND OTHER SECRET SOCIETIES

The Brethren refused to allow the members of the church to join societies that would compete in loyalty with the church, especially if these groups had secret rituals which might have religious overtones. Essentially, Brethren were suspicious of the motives and values of such societies, and members of the church were not to be contaminated by such "worldly" groups. The Annual Meeting examined such membership a number of times.

FREE-MASONRY, &c.

Y. M. 1804. Art. 5. What is to be done with brethren who join the Freemasons? Though we are not sufficiently acquainted with this (secret) association to judge in the case, still there are revealed many trifling things, frivolities and unfruitful works, so that it is considered to be highly improper for brethren to be members in their association, or to have fellowship with their works. Therefore it has been unanimously concluded, that in case there are brethren defiled therewith, they should be admonished in heartfelt love, and informed, that if they wanted to be (remain) in fellowship with these (masonic) brethren, we could have no fellowship with them; but if one were contaminated with this, and would repent from the heart (and renounce all further fellowship with that association), in faith and hope, he might be received again in the name of Jesus Christ.

Y. M. 1848. (Indiana.) Art. 5. Whether brethren, and especially teachers (ministers) can consistently with the gospel and our holy profession attach themselves to the Freemasons and the society popularly called the Sons of Temperance; and if not consistent, how is the church to proceed in such a case? Considered, that whereas the Holy Spirit testifies by the apostle Paul, 1 Cor. 11: 39, "He that eateth and drinketh unworthily, eateth and drinketh damnation to himself, NOT DISCERNING THE LORD'S BODY,"—and, whereas, we are informed in holy writ, that the Lord's body is his church, of which we desire to be members, as he is the Head; from such and other considerations and declarations of the word of God, the brethren have always believed, and still believe, that it is not only unbecoming and wrong, but highly dangerous for brethren to attach themselves to such secret societies or any association of this world, and if they should do so, they should be visited in love, as the advice was forty-four years ago in a yearly meeting at Pipe Creek, and admonished to withdraw themselves from such; and if they should acknowledge their fault before the church, the members might bear with them. But in case of a minister of the word having gone so far as not only to attach himself to such secret societies, but also to act as their chaplain and orator, it was considered, that such a brother ought to be silent in the church, until the members should feel renewed confidence in him again.[23]

A specific illustration of the group called the Sons of Temperance in the church came from an unidentified "Brother in Pennsylvania" who wrote to the editor of the "Gospel Visiter" in 1851.

We are now troubled with the question of receiving members who are sons of temperance. We have received none yet, who did not withdraw from them, nor are we likely to do. But some think we have no right to refuse them baptism on that ground, as we cannot prove it to be the work of the devil. Indeed some say they cannot see any harm in the institution. A few of our members have joined the sons of temperance. I think not any of them have communed with us, after joining, because objection was made by the Brethren. But a very troublesome question has arisen, What shall we do in the case?—Can we excommunicate them for that which we cannot prove sinful: We know not whether it be good or evil intrinsically, and our Brethren I suppose take no part in their processions,—wearing the collar and badge &c.—But they meet them sometimes, pay their dues, and means to look to them for support, attendance & comfort in time of sickness &c.

Again, can a person be a member and yet not a communicant? One who absents himself voluntarily for a long while, we cut off on that ground, if there be no other reason for so doing. But here is a case of involuntary absence, their presence not being acceptable to all. Besides some do and some do not salute such Brethren. I know of no other way, but to make a clean work of the matter and say, a membership with those, who form a league under shade of night and pledge of secrecy, can stand in no connection of union or church-followship with us.[24]

A new group in the 1850s which had both political and religious implications was the Know Nothings, more properly known as the Native American Party because of its objection to immigrants, Catholics, and other such "non-native" groups. The Brethren were of course opposed to its secrecy, as the Annual Meeting of 1855 noted.

KNOWNOTHINGS

Y. M. 1855. Art. 3. How is it considered, if a brother or brethren belong to the party of "Know Nothings," so-called, and take an active part in it, trying to persuade brethren to join said party? Considered, that no brother, who is a member of the so-called Know Nothings, or any other secret society, can be a member of our communion.[25]

The evidence does not indicate from what section of the country the query to the Annual Meeting which elicited this response had come, but in Maryland, a local congregation was struggling with the problem of members who had become associated with the Know Nothings.

January 6, 1856

we have the Knownothing members belonging to our Church now arraigned for trial which is to be settled tuesday if possible   this is the second day of trial   the subjects are Brother M. Barthlow and Brother L. Hammond   they are pretty stubborn   I fear they will be expelled unless they be come more penitent by next meeting day—[26]

Cleary, the evidence supports the conclusion that the Brethren of the nineteenth century were vigorously opposed at both the national level of the Annual Meeting and at the local level of the congregation to having members in the church who were members of secret societies which might compete with the church for the loyalty of its members.

BUSINESS AND BANKING

During this period of time most Brethren made their living as farmers. But even farmers could not remain completely aloof from the world of business and banking, because farmers had to sell their products in the marketplace, and they had to purchase the products which they did not raise or make. Frequently, in making purchases of land and products, Brethren farmers needed to borrow money, either from other Brethren who had money to loan or from bankers. When they borrowed money, they had to pay interest on it, and they had to repay the loan. Most Brethren were scrupulously honest, and the expression that "A Brethren's word is as good as his bond," was widespread. However, sometimes Brethren got into financial difficulty for a variety of reasons, including unexpected weather conditions, exorbitant interest rates, unscrupulous bankers, gouging land speculators, and poor business judgment. Such problems were taken to the Annual Meeting. Henry Kurtz arranged these decisions under several different headings.

BONDS OR NOTES, BUYING AND SELLING
Y. M. 1810. Art. 1. About brethren who intend selling bonds, it was considered, that it should not be done without the counsel of the church.

Y. M. 1817. Art. 6. Whether we may sell a note (or bond) or not? Considered, that no member should sell a note without the consent of the debtor.

Y. M. 1827. Art. 7. With regard to selling bonds, it was considered, that none should be sold by which poor people might be oppressed; but since circumstances are so different, the church should be counseled (asked for counsel in any case).

Y. M. 1864. Art. 16. Is it right and according to the gospel for a brother to invest money in government bonds? Ans.—We consider it not wrong to do so.

BORROWING FROM BANKS
Y. M. 1847. Art. 8. Whether it may be proper and agreeable with the gospel for a brother to borrow money from banks or speculating money-

lenders, for the purpose of buying and droving cattle, sheep and horses, or for buying wheat or other produce, and transporting the same to the Atlantic cities or other public markets, for the purpose of making gain or profit? Considered, that we in general council (assembled) would advise any (and every) brother not to engage largely in trading, as there is great danger, both in a temporal and in a spiritual point of view. See 1 Tim. 6: 9, 10.

INTEREST FOR MONEY TAKING

Y. M. 1783. Art. 2. Concerning taking interest, it is considered, that no member should take interest for his money, inasmuch in the law of God it was expressly forbidden, and Christ says that the Scripture cannot be broken (John 10: 35); and inasmuch the dear and chosen vessel and faithful apostle Paul says, that Christ became the end of the law, and yet the word of God and also divine knowledge teaches, that in order to become partakers of Christ it is required to deny ourselves entirely of all those things which are contrary to the word and command of God: therefore, we exhort again heartily and unitedly, that such members who might be involved in this point, should think of better things, and have more regard and respect for their denied Lord Jesus and his truth and wish them faith and the grace of God heartily.

Y. M. 1822. (Canton.) Art. 10. Whether it be right for a follower of Jesus to take interest, was considered, that neither the law nor the gospel gives us such privilege, and that it should not be among the membership.

Y. M. 1837. Art. 9. How is it considered, if members take more than lawful interest? Considered, that this ought to be by no means, and if a brother should do so, he ought to be visited, and if he would not take advice, we could not be satisfied with him.

DEBTS, ABOUT BRETHREN GETTING INVOLVED IN

Y. M. 1804. Art. 3. About such brethren, who so easily and heedlessly involve themselves in debts, and do not seek counsel, until they do not know any more how to counsel or help themselves; then they want at last counsel, when they desire and need help. It has been unanimously deemed good, that every church where such brethren live should endeavor diligently to instruct such brethren also in temporal or bodily things, that they should act considerately, and make no more debts than they can pay; and when at times their circumstances should be such that they can pay; and when at times their circumstances should be such that they could not see through, they should seek counsel of prudent brethren, and even the whole church is in duty bound to give counsel when requested; and if the counsel of the church should be sufficient, it is also her duty to assist as far as possible in a case of necessity. At the same time such should not expect or hope that the church would feel bound or willing to assist much.

Y. M. 1862. Art. 30. What shall we do with brethren, of whom the world complains to the church for neglecting to pay their debts, and for causing disappointment to their creditors? Ans. If the brethren can and will not pay their debts, they should be dealt with according to the gospel as offending members.[27]

In a local situation a member of the church in Maryland advised his brother in Virginia regarding possible investments and in his letter commented on the value of government bonds and bank stocks.

Carroll County, Maryland
March 1, 1866

In regard to your investments, I would say I cannot see any impropriety in investing in Government bonds, or *National bank stocks.* there is a kind of gambling carried on by the brokers in all kinds of stocks at the stock boards in the city, especially when the money market is excited, but of course we as bond holders have nothing to do with their nefarious transactions   the bonds bear 7/30 interest in currency and six per ct in gold, and it is collected at the nation[al] banks by cutting off the coupon and presenting it at the bank every six months.   my bank stock affords me 10 per ct interest and free from government taxes as also are the bonds.

I cannot conceive anything wrong in it and it pays better than anything else. If you get a bank at Salem I would take stock if I were you.   you can sell it whenever you wish to.   the brethren here are amongst the largest bank stock and bond-holders. I gave Doc a pamphlet containing the national bank law when he was here.   borrow it of him and examine it.   it must and will become our only currency except coin.

There is quite as much gambling in western lands as anything else. I will not invest there unless I remove there, that I may seperintend my lands myself.[28]

Also locally, an individual who was not Brethren, John S. Wise, the illustrious son of a noted Virginia Governor, provided an insight into Brethren business practices in a description of Rocky Mount, Virginia, during the time of the Civil War.

Everybody traveled on horseback. By midday the country folk began to stream in. Up and down the street a gradually increasing line of saddle-horses were "hitched." Women, old and young, arrived, all of conventional dress, and with horses singularly alike. Their bonnets were the long-slatted poke-bonnets; their riding skirts, of coarse cotton. Alighting at the horse-blocks, they untied and slipped off the skirts and tied them to their saddle-bows, revealing their homespun dress. Their horses were broad-backed, short on the leg, carried their heads on a level with their shoulders, and moved with noses advanced like camels. They had no gaits but a swift walk, a gentle fox-trot, or a slow, ambling pace. When they had "hitched the critturs," these women went poking about the stores, or the tavern kitchen, or the private houses, with chickens or butter, or other farmyard produce, seldom speaking further than asking one to buy; and when their sales were effected and little purchases made, they went away as silently as they had come.

The men came by themselves. Their principal occupation seemed to be horse-trading. At times, the neighboring stables, and even the street itself, were filled with men leading their animals about, and engaged in the liveliest of trading. A considerable proportion of the population belonged to a religious sect known as Dunkards. In appearance, they were solemn ascetic. The men wore long, flowing beards, and their homespun dress was of formal cut. Their doctrinal tenets were opposed to slavery and to war. Whenever political or military discussions arose, they promptly withdrew. They were very strict temperance men, and decent, orderly, law-abiding citizens, but horse-traders! It must have been a part of their religious faith! A Dunkard was never so happy as when he was horse-trading!

There were others to whom temperance was not so sacred as to the Dunkard. By three or four o'clock, the tavern bar was liberally patronized.[29]

EDUCATION

Just as it was necessary for Brethren to engage in some business activities in order to market their farm products, so Brethren agreed that it was necessary to secure a minimum of education in order to engage in religious activities. Consequently, there seemed to be little debate among the Brethren regarding the acceptance of a "common school" education which was the basic elementary education provided by most of the states during these years. However, the pattern of separatism from worldly society led the Brethren to object vigorously to the securing of a more advanced education at the high school or college level. The issue was brought to the Annual Meetings of 1831 and of 1852. Somewhat different reasons for the same conclusion were given.

Y. M. 1831. Art. 1. Whether it was considered advisable for a member to have his son educated in a college? Considered, not advisable, inasmuch as experience has taught that such very seldom will come back afterward to the humble ways of the Lord.

Y. M. 1852. Art. 12. How is it considered by the brethren, if brethren aid and assist in building great houses for high schools, and send their children to the same? Considered, that brethren should be very cautious, and not mind high things, but condescend to men of low estates. See Rom. 12: 16.[30]

This issue was evidently controversial enough that its discussion was kept out of the new "Gospel Visiter" for several years. At any rate, one of the earliest major discussions was offered by the editor in the March 1854 issue.

TO OUR YOUNG ASPIRANTS AFTER LEARNING

Are Academies, Colleges &c., safe places for young brethren and brethren's children?

A question similar to this came up at last yearly meeting in Maryland (Art. 28.) and was answered as follows:

"Considered, that we would deem colleges a very unsafe place for a simple follower of Christ, inasmuch as they are calculated to lead us astray from the faith and obedience of the Gospel."

Since that time we have received communications on the subject from different quarters, expressing different views. One from a respectable friend, who has near and dear relations in the brotherhood, and is apparently well acquainted with the brethren's views, and favorable to their doctrine;—yet, being an intelligent, well-educated and withal a college-bred man, he finds fault with us as preventing ourselves from acquiring an education, or affording our children the necessary means of a liberal education. He then goes on to set forth the advantages and benefits of colleges, and endeavors to remove the objections which might be raised against them. Upon the whole the article was well written, and well deserving a place in any publication, not altogether based upon conscientious principles. So it remained on our table for a considerable time "sub judicio."

Another communication we received from one of our beloved and highly esteemed elders, whose praise is in all the churches, wherever he is known. He stated, that he was in difficulty about his youngest son, a youth of 19 years old, who had been pleading with him for permission to go to the Academy; that he had been opposed to it, giving his reasons, and, alluding to what had been said last yearly meeting. . . .

Yet being aware, that some of our young men here and there, the children of brethren, become dissatisfied with the humble way and manners of their parents, to make an honest living by the labors of their own hands, and desirous of acquiring learning or what is called a liberal education, in hopes that thereby they might be enabled to obtain a more easy and respectable living, we feel it our duty to say something on this important subject in this public manner.

Dear youth, allow one who sincerely loves your souls, and is desirous from the inmost of his heart for your temporal and eternal happiness, to present to you a few considerations on the query at the head of this article. Ponder them well, and if you find them true and wholesome, try to act upon them, and consider that whether you do so or not, you will have to abide the consequences, and he with his brethren and your parents will have cleared their skirts.

First we would wish you to consider the answer of our brethren, (in yearly meeting and in the fear of the Lord assembled from all parts of our country,) as we have given it above on the subject in question. Do they condemn learning, and those places where it is usually acquired in toto?— No. Do they presume to condemn without reason or understanding, whereof they affirm? No, no; sad experience has taught them, what they say. There have been brethren's children, who might have become bright ornaments in the church; but they wanted more, they wanted to be shining lights in the world by obtaining a liberal education, and where are they now?—

We could point to some half dozen living instances of the kind, as evidences of what our brethren affirmed, who were led thus astray from the faith and obedience of the Gospel. And it is almost asmuch a miracle of grace, as the conversion of Paul, when one of the learned and college-bred becomes an humble follower of Jesus with us, and indeed we have but little hope for these, who desire and insist upon obtaining that, what is against the will and better judgment of their parents, and against the counsel of the church, that such an immediate and wonderful act of grace will be enacted in their behalf while they pursue a perverse course. . . .

Our Saviour told us to judge of the tree by its fruits. This tree of knowledge stands in the midst of the world, it is supported by the world, and will finally perish with the world. Those who taste its fruit, are enchanted by the spirit of the world, and woe unto him, so as to have left no room nor relish for that heavenly wisdom, which proceeds from the tree of life. Pride, ambition, his academical honors, his college-friends, his very dependence upon the world for a living, &c. &c. form so many chains to bind him to the world, that it is next to impossible, to reclaim him from it, and to permit him to become an humble follower of Christ.

While these are the deleterious fruits of that tree, the leaves of the same are not quite so dangerous, if you are careful to reject the rotten ones, (bad books) and make a judicious use of the sound, (good books). If you are truly desirous after useful knowledge, you can find all, that you can wish to learn, all that can be learnt in academies, colleges, seminaries &c.— in books, at home, under your parent's roof. If you only read a little every day, and study over it and make it your own while at work, and in the evening sit down, and write, without looking again into your book, what you have learnt, and thus go on, every day adding a little to your stock of knowledge, you will improve yourselves better, and at the same time be more useful to the world, as if you had spent your best years within the walls of a college. More anon. Dear young friends, reflect upon these things, and believe me to be your sincere wellwisher.[31]

As Kurtz indicated, he had been refusing to publish articles supporting a more advanced education than that of the common schools. However, by December 1854, he had changed his policy to the extent of publishing a short article, "On Education," the author of which was identified only as H. B. W. In his comments on the article, Kurtz conceded that it and some other articles similar to it had been on hand "partly over a year." He also added:

We did not then, nor do we now agree with the author and advocate of colleges in general, believing still with our brethren, that colleges are very unsafe places for simple followers of Christ, or their children,—yet, when those two other communications came to hand, after much reflection we were brought to the conclusion, that they ought to have a fair hearing through the columns of the Visiter. This we have done without intending to make any remarks at this time, further than this, that circumstances have come to our knowledge within a year or so, which require us to take the subject of which the foregoing articles treat, into the most serious and prayerful consideration, and we would like to hear the sentiments of other brethren ere long. There are far more of our rising generation (brethren's children) thirsting after a more liberal education, than our common schools afford, and more actually attending academies and colleges, notwithstanding the advice of our Elders to the contrary, than we were, and many of our brethren may be still aware.[32]

In the January 1855 issue Kurtz published an article opposing the need for an advanced education by the Brethren, written by a pseudonymous author, who called himself Rufus. He did concede the value of a "good, common school education."³³ The issue of education and schools was evidently not discussed in the "Gospel Visiter" for more than a year until March 1856, when James Quinter wrote a letter to the editor, a part of which dealt with "our contemplated school." Kurtz added his comments in parentheses.

Upon serious reflection upon our contemplated school, some ideas have been presented to my mind, which I offer to you for your consideration. One important desideratum is, well qualified teachers—teachers possessing both literary and moral qualifications. It has occurred to my mind, that if there are brethren among us, possessing qualifications sufficient to enable them to discharge the duties of teachers in such an institution, perhaps they would not feel free to abandon other callings in which they are now engaged. I have therefore thought, it would be proper to send one or two of our young brethren to school, to qualify them for teachers. Two perhaps would be better than one. I would prefer poor young men, young men who look for success in life, to their own exertions, and the blessing of heaven. I have a person now before my mind, who might answer for one. . . .

I merely submit these thoughts to you for consideration, thinking that something of this kind might further an object we both think important and desirable, as an auxiliary for the advancement of Gospel truth.

(The last mentioned object requires a few words of explanation from us. Years ago we could find many brethren, who had received only a common-school education, engaged in teaching school, where the Bible and the New Testament was read, and probably both English & German was taught. But now so much is required of school-teachers, that many of those old teachers cannot pass examination any more, and others have taken their places, who need the Bible no longer, and our children are deprived of a vital element of education, namely the moral and religious.

This want is supplied by some or most religious denominations by Sunday or Sabbath-schools; but even this is denied in a great measure to our children for want of teachers. Hence the idea, which struck us both, though unknown to each other at first, to establish a school to educate young brethren for school-teachers.)³⁴

Kurtz explained his own position in more detail in the June 1856 issue. Clearly, his ideas were changing.

Our common public school system is a noble institution. The state provides thus for the education of all our youth. Children of the poor as well as of the rich enjoy its privileges without expense to their parents, excepting for books.—The common school is free to all children (at least of white color,) whether their parents are native citizens, or emigrants from foreign countries, and children, whose native language is English, can obtain there an education sufficient for all the ordinary purposes of life.

However this is not the case with children, whose mother-tongue is other than English, who neither understood nor spoke English previous to their going to school. What others learn understandingly, they learn mechanically. They learn to spell words without knowing their signification; they begin to read sentences without comprehending them; they write, or rather imitate writing, without being able to express one single thought of their own on paper. Do we wonder, why so many of these children, when they become men and women, are so deficient in learning, as scarcely to be able to write their own name? . . .

We trust all parents agree with us, that our children ought to have a good common school education. This, we find, children of german parents cannot get in an english school, simply because such a school is merely intended for children, who understand and speak english already, and who are to learn to read, write &c. in that language, hence we have come to the conclusion, these many years, that german children ought to have a german-english, french children a french-english school &c. in order to learn english, with the help of their native language, understandingly.

For this purpose we need in the first place school-teachers, who are qualified to teach such schools. They should be able, not only to speak, read and write the english language properly, and to pass an examination in all those branches, as required by our existing school-laws,—but also to speak, read and write the native language of the children; not only to give the signification of an english word in german, and of a german word in english, but to read from an english book in german, and vice versa. This is looked upon by many as a very difficult matter, but it is easily acquired by even young children with proper tuition and practice, as we can testify from actual experiments.

But we need something more than mere teachers of spelling, reading &c. for our children; we need Christian teachers, Godfearing men, who love the Bible, and will inspire our children with love for the same; who will not exclude the Bible from the school, and thus withhold from our children the divine lessons of religion and morality which are calculated more than any thing else to enlighten their understandings, to ennoble their minds, and to prepare them for all the vicissitudes of their after-life, to make them good citizens, good neighbors, and better still, if the influence of the Bible takes once by grace full possession of their hearts, good Christians and happy heirs of immortality.

Such teachers we need for our children.[35]

The lengthy material in favor of a Brethren school written by Quinter and by Kurtz had stirred opposition, and in September 1856, Kurtz published a detailed response from Rufus. Two of his objections were described in the following selection:

It would be a higher one than our Common Schools, else the qualification could be obtained there; and besides, such institutions are progressive,—it might start with teachers of limited education, and progress on till it would combine all the sciences taught in the very highest schools in the country, and yet be the same institution, and still pass under the same name. I have no doubt, but this was the case with the first high schools among other denominations, adding one branch to the other—one science to the other—till they gained the fame and renown in which they are now held by their respective admirers. It may be said, we need learned men among us. True, I admit all this; but, is "the Lord's hand shortened?" Is he not the same yesterday, to-day and forever? When he needed a Moses to lead his people out of Egypt, did He establish a school among His people to qualify him? Or when an apostle was needed, that possessed a good education, we find of no preparation being made in the church for his qualifications: but the instrument was ready, and answered the purpose too. . . . This is one of the strongest grounds of objection that I have against the project: if started in the name of the brethren, and under their superintendence, of course every brother would have to be admitted that would ask for it, under the design of becoming school-teachers; now we know temptations are manifold, is there not then danger, that a new door might here be opened for the tempter, to reason with some of our young ministers on this wise: the brethren have a school of their own; it is true the design is to qualify school-teachers; but your education is too limited for the ministry, it will not hurt you to go a session or two; you can even say the object is to become school-teachers; thus giving the secondary object, if one at all, for the primary one. And from this it may slide over into the custom of other denominations; to qualify them before they are chosen to the ministry.

James Quinter wrote the response for the editors. He did not attempt to answer the objection that such schools would also train ministers.

We are, not at all, surprised to receive such a communication as the above, upon the subject of which it treats. Neither does it by any means offend us. Looking at the subject of education and the means to promote it from different stand points, as we shall be likely to do, since the circumstances under which we have been placed or the influences which have surrounded us, as well as our habits of reflection differ so much; and different persons will be likely to take different views of the subject. In the absence of any positive law of God either for the institution or the prohibition of such a means for the promotion of the moral and intellectual improvement of our youth, we should prayerfully examine the subject in the light of an impartial judgment, and of solid arguments, and by the help of fair inferences drawn from the letter and spirit of the divine word. . . .

We shall state some considerations which have had a tendency to impress our minds with the propriety, and indeed with the necessity, of increased facilities among us, for affording our youth additional opportunities to what our common schools give, for obtaining education. Powerful efforts have been made within the last few years to awaken a more general interest upon the subject of a liberal education. These efforts have been in a measure successful. And there is now a much more general inclination manifested to acquire knowledge, than there was some years ago. This increased interest upon the subject of education has shown itself among our brethren, as well as in other religious denominations, and throughout the country generally. And what shall we do under the circumstances of the case? This is a question which is urged upon our consideration at the present time, and which assumes a degree of singular importance.

Shall we as a religious denomination throw ourselves into a hostile position against the onward march of intellectual improvement? Some might be ready to assume such a position, but I think the church would not. And what if it would? Its opposition would avail but little. It might pass resolutions at its annual councils against the brethren giving their children any thing more than a common school education, but many could not reconcile submission to such resolutions with their sense of duty, and could not be governed by them. Others might submit, and oppose their sons as long as they had authority over them, but such sons, should they have an inclination for learning, as soon as they were free from parental authority, would labor to acquire an education, and would then labor under disadvantages.

If our youth now desire any thing more than a common school education, they are compelled to resort to institutions not under that pure christian influence which we as parents should want our youth placed under, and thus by failing to afford them the helps desirable for pursuing their studies, we may in some degree endanger their spiritual welfare. And not only so, but we are in danger of losing the influence and talents of many of our youth as they will not be likely to feel the same respect for, and attachment to, our denomination, should they not find in us an inclination to sympathize with them in their desires for mental culture, and a readiness to afford them suitable opportunities for obtaining that culture, that they would if they found the church ready to encourage them, and to take them under her sheltering wing, and to feed them with useful knowledge. . . .

Knowing that such is the state of things among us, and feeling a deep concern for the welfare of our youth, and a growing attachment to the holy doctrines and practices of Christianity, as held by our beloved brethren, we confess we feel no little desire to see the church affording her youth every opportunity necessary for the promotion of their happiness and usefulness. We think that it is not only right that the church should encourage institutions in which our youth may acquire useful knowledge, but we think it is her duty—a duty she owes to her God, to herself, and to the rising generation, to encourage and build up such institutions. . . .

We will give a short sketch of such an institution, as we want to see started among us if any is started. And we would kindly say to br. Rufus, "give place." We would then expect such an institution to be under the influence of spiritually minded brethren. We would want religious teachers—teachers who would have a regard to the religious as well as to the intellectual improvement of the students,—consequently the students would have religious counsel administered to them. We would have the Bible daily used in the institution. We would have the students to board in a religious family—and have them led daily to a throne of grace and heaven's blessings invoked upon them. In short, we would have the school to resemble a pious family, under such rules as would discountenance whatever is evil, and encourage whatever is good.

Now would it be dangerous for youth, to have them placed under such circumstances? It may be said, to bring a school under such regulations, could not easily be done. But do we think it would be impossible? If we do, then we doubt the practicability of the principles of Christianity. It is true, it requires energy and perseverance. But these are required in our family devotions, and in all our relations in life, in which we reduce Christianity to practice. . . .

We should always try to distinguish between the abuse of a thing, and its proper use. How has it been with our common schools. How immoral have many teachers been! And what bad conduct have many youth learned at the common schools! But will we repudiate the common schools altogether? By no means. They have been much improved. . . . We have not been trying to prove the necessity or utility of education. We are happy to find that br. Rufus does not deny this. Our object has been to show, that as our youth desire to acquire knowledge, we should afford them suitable opportunities.[36]

From the "Gospel Visiter" the debate about a Brethren school now turned to the floor of the Annual Meeting, where it was considered in 1857 and 1858.

Y. M. 1857. Art. 19. What are the views of the present annual council in regard to the contemplated school that was alluded to some time since in the Gospel Visitor? Answer. It is conforming to the world. The Apostle Paul says, "Knowledge puffeth up, but charity edifieth."

Y. M. 1858. Art. 51. We desire to know whether the Lord has commanded us to have a school besides our common schools, such as the one contemplated in the Gospel Visitor. If we are, ought we not to have one soon; and if it is not commanded of the Lord, ought we to have one; and is it right to contend for or against such an institution publicly through the press, since our different views may become stumbling blocks before the world; and if it is once decided, ought we not to keep forever silent about it? Answer. Concerning the proposed school in the Gospel Visitor, we think we have no right to interfere with an individual enterprise, so long as there is no departure from gospel principles.[37]

With this announcement from the Annual Meeting of 1858, Kurtz and Quinter began to seek an opportunity to open a school. Such an opportunity did not develop until 1861 when a brick school building was offered for sale in the community of New Vienna, in Clinton County, which was in southern Ohio. The Brethren of the Fall Creek congregation, which was evidently the closest Brethren congregation, offered to buy the building and make it available to Kurtz and Quinter. The offer was accepted and James Quinter moved to New Vienna to become the superintendent of the school, which became known as an Educational Institute, according to the following notice in the February 1862 issue of the "Gospel Visitor."

The third Session of this Institution for young ladies and young men, situated on the Marietta and Cincinnati Rail Road, will commence on the last Monday of March, 1862. Competent Teachers are employed, and it will be the aim of these and all connected with the Institution to merit a liberal share of patronage.

Boarding can be obtained in the village at about $2.25 per week.
Tuition from $3.00 to $6.00 per Session of eleven weeks.
For further information address the undersigned at the above place.[38]

*The timing of the opening for such a school was not good, because of
the disturbed state of the country due to the Civil War. As the result of
war-related problems, the school was forced to close in June 1864.*

*Actually, the school at New Vienna had been preceded by a school es-
tablished by a member of the Church of the Brethren in Pennsylvania, S.
Z. Sharp, who had opened a school in April 1861, according to his own account.*

In 1861 the auspicious moment came for starting the first high school
taught by a member of the Church of the Brethren. In the beautiful valley
of Kishacoquillas, about twenty miles north of Huntingdon, Pa., and ten
miles north of Lewistown, was located Kishacoquillas Seminary. It was
built in a strong Presbyterian community by that church. It was not popular then for ladies to attend the same college with gentlemen, hence a
Ladies' Course of college grade was provided in this school for ladies who
wished to graduate. Young men also were prepared to enter the freshman
or sophomore classes in college. The school had started with a large attendance, and for several years was well sustained, but by some mismanage-

Kishacoquillas
Seminary

New
Vienna
Academy

ment it failed financially and was bought by one of the creditors for one-sixth of what the building originally cost, and was sold to S. Z. Sharp.... His brothers furnished him the money and he purchased Kishacoquillas Seminary. April 1, 1861, he started a summer normal term for teachers, with thirty-six students in attendance. This number was increased during the year to seventy-two. As assistant, Prof. Davenport, a graduate of Columbia College, New York, was employed. He was a "world trotter," and, becoming stranded at Lewistown, was willing to work for a low salary to get a start again. He proved to be an expert teacher and took charge of Latin and higher mathematics. His wife was a finely educated lady and taught music. An old German artist of great ability, who had come to the country from New York to escape the heat of summer, was persuaded to teach oil painting. His terms were reasonable, as money was no object to him, because he could paint a picture at any time and sell it for $100. A devout Presbyterian lady left her pleasant home in McVeytown and took charge of the boarding department. Thus thoroughly equipped, the school began with a spirit and enthusiasm that meant success. Young ladies came to complete their course and graduate, and young men came to prepare themselves to enter college. The patronage from Brethren's families was considerable. In the catalog issued we find such familiar names as Amich, Bashore, Bolinger, Brumbaugh, Custer, Hanawalt, Myers, Smith, Snowberger, Swigart, Rush, and Zuck.

S. Z. Sharp

The bright prospects of the school were soon darkened when on April 12, 1861, Fort Sumter was fired on by the Confederates and the Civil War was on with all its horrors. It aroused the restless spirit of Prof. Davenport, who obtained a commission to raise a company and enter the army. Some of the students enlisted and left the school. Prof. Davenport's place was ably filled by Rev. S. H. McDonald, a Presbyterian minister, a ripe scholar, a graduate of Princeton University and for a time an instructor in that institution.

With the coming of the war, the price of provisions rose rapidly. The terms for boarding for the year had been published before the school started, and could not be changed, and the results was that boarding had to be given at a loss. At the end of the year the expences had exceeded the income. The brothers of the principal furnished more money. He increased the price of boarding but it became a momentous task to conduct a school with borrowed money when it was daily sinking deeper into debt. The price of provisions soared higher than ever. Every known device of economy had to be practiced to save the life of the school. The principal taught ten hours a day, to get along with less help. The genius of a skilled stewardess was taxed to the utmost, and then that sometimes failed. . . .

Although special attention was paid to the normal department for the preparation of teachers, yet there was maintained the high scholastic standard which was set when the seminary was first started. Besides the sciences and higher mathematics, there were taught Latin, Greek, German, music and painting. Several young ladies were graduated, and a number of young men were prepared to enter the freshman and sophomore classes in college.

The religious training was not neglected. The labors of each school day were begun by reading of Scripture and prayer, and when the time came for retiring in the evening the students were called to the chapel and the labors of the day were closed by Scripture reading and prayer.

Preaching services also were conducted whenever circumstances favored. Eld. Graybill Myers, Eld. William Howe, and Samuel Myers were among the ministers of the Church of the Brethren who preached here.

During the fourth year the expenses were more than met. During the fifth year, when the price of boarding was up and the price of provisions had come down with a crash, the seminary realized a handsome profit above expenses.

The school was now in a prosperous condition, but the strenuous labors of the three previous years bore heavily upon the health of the principal's wife, and a change was advisable. The seminary was sold to Prof. Martin Mohler, brother of our well-known evangelist, J. M. Mohler. Members of the Church of the Brethren continued to patronize this school until Juniata College was started.[39]

Thus, by 1865 at least two different schools of the high school level had been established with Brethren teachers and with the encouragement of the church in that location. These years have been considered the preparatory period in the development of Brethren education, which would continue to develop in a significant way in the years from 1865 to 1900.

PUBLIC THEATRES, SHOWS, AND FAIRS

Brethren were to be seen in public as little as possible, and certainly they were not to go voluntarily to places of recreation, such as the theatre or the fairground. Such attendance was a serious enough infraction of the church's rules to merit disciplinary action, according to the Annual Meeting of 1859.

Y. M. 1835. (Miami.) Art. 3. How it is considered when brethren go with their children to shows? Considered, it should not be.

gy. M. 1859. Art. 14. What shall we do when brethren, and even speakers and bishops, attend yearly the county fairs?

Answer.—Such brethren should be admonished not to attend such places, and if they still persist in doing so, they should be dealt with according to Matt. 18.[40]

PERSONAL APPEARANCE

Brethren were expected to shun participation in human slavery, in political activities, in secret societies, in business, and in high school education, and to avoid attendance at theatres and fairs. These requirements dealt with the relation of Brethren to their society. Also, Brethren were expected to maintain certain personal standards regarding their clothing, their jewelry, and their homes, which would set them apart from non-Brethren and thus make possible their nonconformity to the world.

John Kline pointed out that this nonconformity was based on religious grounds, rather than on a simple desire to be separate from other people.

FRIDAY, May 20, 1842. Got home this evening [from Annual Meeting]. Often will my thoughts return to the churches attended and the homes visited. I could not help cautioning the Brethren in some of the congregations against the inroads of pride and fashion. The younger members, particularly, need to be instructed in regard to these things, that they may avoid conformity to the world in dress and other things; not because the church, as such, opposes them in it; but because the Word and Spirit of the Lord opposes them in it. The love of Christ, that is, our love for him and his people, and the way of holiness, lead to a life of self-denial for his sake. The new nature in Christ does not crave the vain and often hurtful fashions of the world. It is best, for both body and soul, to dress plainly, but comfortably; and to live, in every respect, according to the same rule. The godliness that is profitable unto all things, having promise of the life that now is and also of that which is to come, is not conformed to this world.[41]

The Annual Meetings of the nineteenth century considered many aspects of the whole problem of nonconformity to the world in personal appearance. The following Minutes are rearranged in chronological order from three of Henry Kurtz' topics: "Conformity to the World," "Discipline of Children," and "Fashionable Garments."

Y. M. 1789. Art. 2. Inasmuch as many of our children and young people fall into a coarse life, and a great occasion of it seems to be a want that there is not sufficient diligence used in instructing the children according to the word of the Lord given by Moses in Deut. 6: 7, where we read: "And thou shalt teach them (these words which I command thee this day) diligently unto thy children, and shalt talk of them when thou sittest in thy house, and when thou walkest by the way, and when thou liest down, and when thou risest up;" and also, the apostle Paul says, Ephes. 6: 4, that parents should "bring them (their children) up in the nurture and admonition of the Lord;" it is our opinion (and advice) that there should be used more diligence to instruct our dear youth and children in the word of truth to their salvation, and that it is the special duty of the dear parents, as well as of the pastors and teachers, to be engaged herein, inasmuch as the apostle teaches, "Feed the flock of God which is among you, taking the oversight thereof" (1 Pet. 5: 2); and inasmuch as the children of the faithful belong to the flock of Christ, just as naturally as the lambs belong to the flock of sheep; and inasmuch as the word can be brought nearer to the hearts of children in a simple conversation or catechization, or however it may be called, than otherwise in a long sermon, so that they apprehend the word of divine truth, believe in Jesus Christ, and accept his doctrine and commandments, and walk therein to their eternal salvation—hence we admonish in heartfelt and humble love all our in God much beloved fellow members, dear fathers and mothers of families, as also pastors and teachers, our in God much loved fellow laborers, in the dear and worthy name of our Lord Jesus Christ, who has given himself unto death for us, that we should die to ourselves, and live to him forever, that they would use all possible diligence, that our dear youth might be provoked to love God, and to appreciate his word from their childhood. Do not spare any labor and toil to convince them by our teaching and by our life, not after the manner, which is almost too common now-a-days, where the young are made to learn something by heart, and then to rehearse it in a light (thoughtless) manner, and then are permitted to go on in a life as thoughtless as before—but that they may give themselves up to God in an earnest life. The great Rewarder of all good will undoubtedly well renumerate you; for those that have done right shall live forever, and the Lord is their reward, and the Most High provides for them; they will receive a glorious kingdom and a beautiful crown from the hand of the Lord. Sap. 17: 17.

Y. M. 1804. Art. 8. Further, it has been discussed about the evil, offensive to God and the holy angels in heaven, and also to the faithful souls on earth, namely, about the new fashions which are in vogue with the world, and there are here and there even believers who obey the lust of their eyes, and herein conform themselves to the world, especially the young, having gone so far astray that the Lord has cause to complain that almost all flesh have corrupted their way. Therefore, it has been deemed good, that the bishops and ministers, as well as all fathers and mothers of families, should use all diligence to resist such things, that they may not spread further, but rather might be done away; especially when there are persons desiring to be received into the church, it should be laid before them, that such is contrary to the doctrine of salvation, and that it is their duty to deny themselves, and when they are willing to lay such things aside, then we may baptize them cheerfully, hoping that they will continue to receive further instruction, &c.

Y. M. 1817. Art. 2. Concerning conforming to the world in wearing fashionable clothing and everything that is high, without exception, it was considered, that when a member should herein be found guilty, he should be admonished, and if the admonition would not be heeded, we could not hold such in full fellowship, inasmuch the Saviour says, "That which is highly esteemed among men is abomination in the sight of God." Luke 16: 15.

Y. M. 1840. Art. 7. Concerning the lamentably prevailing evil, that members conform themselves so much to the world in building, house furniture, apparel, &c., and even in sleighing have bells upon their horses? It was considered, that all brethren and members, and especially ministers, should withstand and labor against this growing evil, and that anything unbecoming for brethren should be avoided.

Y. M. 1846. Art. 10. About pride in its various forms, which is creeping into the church, it is thought highly necessary that the yearly meeting instruct and urge it upon all the overseers of the church to see especially to that matter, and protest strongly against all manner of superfluities and vanity, such as building fine houses, having paintings, carpeting and costly furniture, &c., together with the adorning of the body too much after the fashion of the world. We believe that we should deny ourselves, and abstain from these things, especially the laborers in the word, who are called to be examples of the flock.

Y. M. 1857. Art. 10. How is it considered for brethren, and especially ministering brethren, to adorn their children with earrings, breast pins, finger rings, and jewelry in general, and send them from home to have them taught music, and to procure pianos for them? Ans. Brethren should not do so.

Y. M. 1861. Art. 3. Inasmuch as the brethren have decided in conference, that members who would not conform to the order in dress as generally practiced by the old brethren and sisters, that they could not have the privilege to the communion. But as this does not restrain them into the order, we wish to know whether the church has the right to deal with them as offenders, when they will not conform in dress or to wearing caps, and leave off wearing hoops? Considered, that such members should be admonished, and that warmly too, to lay aside all superfluities, and conform to the order of the church. Otherwise they must and will be regarded as disobedient members. See Rom. 12.

Y. M. 1866. Art. 27. Inasmuch as pride and an inclination to follow the fashions of the world are still increasing among us, in wearing fine apparel, frock and sack coats, dusters, shawls, &c., with the hair parted off to one side, or shingled and roached, mustaches, &c., the sisters also wearing fine apparel, going without caps, wearing hoops, hats, veils, overcoats, jewelry, &c., and as admonition in some cases has not effected anything, cannot this yearly meeting propose some plan by which this growing evil may be arrested? Ans. We think members of the church conforming to the fashions of the world as above stated, should be admonished again and again, and if they will not hear the church, the Saviour has given directions in Matt. 18, how to deal with them—Art. 47. The following resolution was proposed to the annual meeting by a district meeting, with a request that it be adopted: Resolved by this annual meeting, that the churches throughout the brotherhood enforce plainness of dress, and a plain manner of wearing the hair and beard, upon the preachers and officers of the churches. By plainness of dress we mean the common order of giving shape to dress as practiced by the old brethren and sisters generally, and by plainness of hair we mean the hair parted on the top of the head, or all combed back in a plain manner, or combed straight down all around the head, and not having the hair and beard trimmed according to the custom of the world. Considered, that the annual meeting unanimously adopt this resolution, according to Rom. 12: 2; 1 Pet. 1: 14, 1 John 2: 15, 16; and that all preachers and officers that follow the fashions of the world in the foregoing particulars, violate the order of the gospel by doing so, and render themselves liable to be brought under the council of the church.[42]

The Annual Meeting was also concerned specifically about the wearing of jewelry by members of the church.

JEWELRY FOR MEMBERS TO WEAR

Y.M. 1853. Art. 8. How shall we proceed in case we have a love feast, and a sister or sisters come from another congregation to our love feast who wear (gold) ear-rings or *jewels,* whether we have a right to take them in council, and if not willing to lay it (them) off, whether we are privileged to keep them from the communion-table? The committee was decidedly of opinion, that as it is positively forbidden by holy writ, see 1 Pet 3: 3, 1 Tim.

2: 9, it should not be tolerated except in cases of actual necessity (for medical reasons); and that the church where such members propose to participate in the communion, has the right (if it is not the duty rather) to take them into council, and if they are not willing to be admonished, to advise them to withdraw until they are willing to sacrifice those forbidden things.

Y. M. 1864. Art. 7. When the apostles prohibit the wearing of gold and pearls 1 Tim 2: 9, 1 Pet. 3: 3, are gold watches to be included? Ans. As the carrying of gold watches may and is likely to lead to pride, we think it advisable not to wear them[43]

The male members of the church were expected to have beards, especially if they were leaders such as deacons or ministers.

BEARDS

Y. M. 1804. Art. 4. Whether upon request a brother might be ordained as a bishop, who shaves off his beard? It was considered, that inasmuch God made man with a beard; and again, God commanded his people in the law not to cut off the beard; it was especially required of the priests of God not to mar the corners of the beard; and also Christ, our Master and precursor, together with his disciples, has left us the example herein—in consideration of these and other scriptures and examples, it (the ordination) could not readily be done in a sound faith and with an unoffended conscience.[44]

Related to the whole concern for personal appearance was the prohibition of photographic portraits. Members of the church were not to have their pictures taken by the new process of photography. Apparently, there was a concern about the sin of idolatry.

PORTRAITS

Y. M. 1849. Art. 17. Whether brethren can be allowed to have their likeness or profile taken? Considered as not advisable.

Y. M. 1857. Art. 15. Is it really considered a sin according to the gospel, for members of the church to have their likenesses taken? Answer. Members of the church should not have their likenesses taken.

Y. M. 1858. Art. 52. Is it right for a brother to go about taking likenesses with a Daguerrean apparatus? Considered, that it is not right. See. Rom. 1: 23; Deut. 27: 15.[45]

*In addition to the actions of Annual Meeting regarding personal
appearance, the newly-formed district meetings were also taking steps to
enforce the patterns of personal nonconformity, according to the minutes
of a district meeting held in northern Illinois in 1863.*

Church Council held at Cherry Grove, 1863

According to previous appointment the German Baptists held their
Annual District Council at Cherry Grove the 27th   1863.   the meeting
was opened by singing & prayer. Bro. S. Lehman was appointed
moderator, Bro. Garber Secretary & Bro. Long Clerk. They proceeding to
business the following was considered.

What is to be done with members if they still persist in having their
likeness taken in the face of minutes of 1857. It is considered an evil and
members persisting in it shall be treated as disobedient.

Is is right for members to wear coon skin coats, sheep skin coats &
caps. If it is worn for comfort—Advised put it away if for pride

Is it right for sisters to wear Shakers & collars—Considered among
the superfluities.[46]

*In spite of all of the decisions of Annual Meeting and of the district
meetings, it seems probable that some Brethren were renouncing the
patterns of separation and of nonconformity in personal appearance and
were accepting the styles of the more fashionable members of society. At
least, that conclusion may be drawn from the following letter.*

Ladoga, Indiana
August 12, 1865

I only stopped in Dayton 4 days & did not enjoy myself much at that
place as John insisted that I was obliged to put on hoops at that place &
when I left I left the hoops there. I could not bear the idea of putting them
on after having taken them off, although most of the sisters in Maryland at
the Brownsville church wear them. I was fretted to find the church at
Brownsville look so much like the world that one could not tell them from
them in appearances. We have a large church in this place & it is very
much like our church in Virginia. I have been to church once since I've
been here & heard brother Robert Miller preach a delightful sermon.   he
is an excellant preacher & a good man.[47]

HOMES

Personal pride could lead to a rejection of the required patterns of personal appearance among the Brethren; it could also lead to special furnishings in one's home, such as carpets, and decorations on one's buildings, such as lightning rods. The Annual Meeting was asked to rule on both of these items.

CARPETS

Y. M. 1827. Art. 8. How it is considered to lay carpets in (our) houses? It was considered, that it belongs to the grandeur (highness) of this world, and that it will not become a follower of Jesus to garnish his house in this manner, but rather that he should adorn his house as may be considered with lowliness.

Henry Kurtz noted in 1867 regarding carpets:

While such improvements were yet new, and only found in the houses of the great and rich in the world, it was proper for brethren to advise as above; but after such improvement had become a common thing, and it was a convenience generally known, there was no further objection to their introduction. Thus it was almost in all cases.

LIGHTNING RODS

Y. M. 1851. Art. 7. Should brethren have the privilege to put up lightning rods? Considered, that we would not advise brethren to do so, nor would we say to those who have them, to take them down; but advise all our dear brethren to bear with each other in such matters, and try to put their chief trust in God.[48]

ALCOHOLIC BEVERAGES

In a day when most farmers on the American frontier converted some of their grain into alcoholic beverages for their own use and for sale because it was cheaper to transport than the grain, Brethren vigorously opposed the patterns of society by rejecting the making, selling, and using of any kind of alcoholic beverage. The Annual Meeting was forced to deal with this problem frequently, because of its prevalence in American society and because of its impact on the Church of the Brethren.

ARDENT SPIRITS, making, selling and using of

Y.M. 1783. Art. 1. At this great meeting a unanimous conclusion was laid down with regard to the very offensive evil which has endeavored to gain ground in the church, and by which already much mischief has been done, while the brotherly counsel has been repeatedly given, that distilleries (of ardent spirits) in the church (among members) should be put away. And since there are still from time to time more erected, it has been at this time unanimously concluded, that those brethren who have distilleries should be earnestly admonished to put them out of the way, and when they have been admonished in sincere love once and again, and they would not obey the counsel of the church, and not put away this loathsome idol, we could not break the bread of communion with them, and have to withdraw also the kiss and church council from them, until they are willing again to hear the church, as they have promised also at first at their baptism, before God and many witnesses.

Y. M. 1804. Art. 1. Whether it should or would be allowed to a brother or sister to keep public tavern by or with a license, was unanimously considered, that it could not be allowed, because we are convinced that it cannot be done without disorder, and is rather a hindrance to a godly life and quietness of spirit? It has been deemed good in union, that if a brother or sister should undertake to keep tavern, they should be visited in friendship, and in love and seriousness, and in the name of the church be dissuaded and warned from it, and shown unto them what disorder and harm is likely to result thereof. Further it was concluded, that if a brother or sister would not hear, accept or obey such counsel and admonition, then we would have to consider such as disobedient, and could not have fellowship with them. Yet the sisters, who are bound in such matter by the urging of their husbands, and would gladly be relieved from it, but cannot without the consent of their husbands, they should be held less guilty.

Y. M. 1835. Art. 9. How is it viewed for brethren to sell grain to distillers? Considered, that it should not be, especially if grain is scarce and high in price. Besides, it was mentioned of the abuse and harm which comes from what is made by the distiller, and that brethren should take no part in it, and by no means use distilled liquors for a common beverage, nor offer it to those that work for them. . . .

Y. M. 1837. Art. 11. How it is considered, when a brother keeps a brewery, and makes strong beer? Considered, that it could not be directly forbidden to a brother, but ought to be left to his own conscience, and to advise him that the safest would be not to carry on such a business, from which may arise so many and great disorders.

Y. M. 1841. Art. 14. Concerning the use of ardent spirits, it was considered, that it is a great evil, leading to vice and crime, to destruction of peace and property, and to the ruin of body and soul, and that members of the church of Christ ought to refrain from use of it except as medicine.

Y.M. 1842. Art. 4. How it is considered, if a brother or sister signs the pledge of total abstinence? Considered, inasmuch as our churches have always testified against intemperance, and even against the free use, the making and selling of ardent spirits, it is not advisable for members to put their hands to the pledge, or to meddle with the proceedings and excitements of the world on the subject.[49]

One of the very remarkable documents regarding alcoholic beverages during this period was a sermon preached by a Brethren minister, John A. Bowman, in the Baptist church in Blountville, Tennessee, near his home on his forty-fifth birthday, June 20, 1858. The sermon was preached by the request of Landon C. Haynes, a prominent attorney; what makes the sermon so unusual was that it was printed, for the printing of a sermon was a mark of pride, which of course was very unbecoming for a Brethren minister.

SERMON

The following is the substance of a sermon delivered by John A. Bowman, in the Baptist church in Blountville, Tennessee, June the 20th, 1858, to a large and attentive audience, on the subject of *Christian Temperance.*

"Know ye not that they which run in a race run all, but one receiveth the prize. So run, that ye may obtain.

"And every man that striveth for the mastery is temperate in all things. Now they do it to obtain a corruptible crown; but we an incorruptible."— I. Corinth., chap. ix.—24,25.

We presume that this large and intelligent congregation is fully apprised that we intend to deliver a discourse upon Christian Temperance here to-day, and we remark that it is not our intention to please men— "For if I yet please men," saith Paul, "I should not be the servant of Christ"—neither is it our intention to rake any one more than the truths contained in the word of God will justify. And, furthermore, ye are well aware that christian temperance proclaimed in its purity, according to the holy scriptures, will rake the last one of us present here to-day, because none of us are so perfect in all things, but what there is a work for each one of us to do; so that there is no sitting down upon the stool of "do-nothing-with-any-one," the professor as well as the non-professor.

The portion of holy writ which we have selected as our text or foundation of remarks, represents christian temperance to consist in being temperate in *all* things, and not in one item alone. We are also apprized of the necessity of this christian virtue, which we may term the quintessence of christianity, in order to obtain the prize, which is an incorruptible crown of righteousness that fadeth not away.

All who have made a profession of religion are represented in scripture as running a race. Paul, in writing to the believing Hebrews, admonishes them to lay aside every weight, and the sin that doth so easily beset them, and run with patience the race that is set before them, ever looking unto Jesus the author and finisher of our faith; hence the clause in our text, "So run, that ye may obtain." The christian is also represented as striving for the mastery, not in one thing only, but in all things. We have already seen that he must lay aside every weight and the sin that doth so easily beset him; that is, overcome every evil propensity, as it is written in Revelations, "Unto him that overcometh will I grant to sit with me on my throne, even as I also overcame, and am set down with my Father on his throne." The Lord overcame the world and the devil, and was crowned triumphant and victorious; and as his mission into the world was to destroy the works of the devil, therefore the gospel which he introduced to bring life and immorality to light is compared by John, his forerunner, to the axe that is laid at the root of the tree—"and every tree that bringeth not forth good fruit, is hewn down and cast into the fire;" so the christian professor need but examine the word of God, and he will at once see that the gospel strikes at the root of all evil, which he will have to overcome and obtain the victory over before he has any promise of the crown of righteousness and a seat upon the throne of God and of the Lamb; and as "all scripture is given by inspiration of God, and is profitable for doctrine, for reproof, for correction, and instruction in righteousness, that the man of God may be perfect, thoroughly furnished unto every good work." And Paul further remarks to Timothy: "Because thou hast known the scriptures from a child, they are able to make thee wise unto salvation, through faith in our Lord Jesus Christ."

Now is any more wisdom than this necessary to man? We answer no. If the scriptures are able to reprove, correct, and instruct in righteousness, which will make man wise unto salvation through faith and obedience, what more is required to crown him with that incorruptible crown of righteousness that the apostle declared was in reservation for him, and not for him only, but for all them that love his appearing?

Temperance, my friends, is a doctrine strongly inculcated by the divine apostles, and their lives were so replete with this, as well as every other christian virtue, that Paul could say as he did to his Corinthian

brethren,"Be ye followers of me, even as I also am of Christ." And when
Felix, a Roman governor, sent for Paul, and heard him concerning the
faith in Christ, we are informed by St. Luke, in the Acts of the Apostles,
"And as he reasoned of righteousness, temperance, and judgment to come,
Felix trembled, and answered: go thy way for this time, and when I have a
convenient season I will call for thee." St. Peter, in the first chapter of his
second epistle, exhorts the christian believer to "give all diligence, and add
to his faith, virtue; and to virtue, knowledge; and to knowledge,
temperance; and to temperance, patience; and to patience, godliness; and
to godliness, brotherly kindness; and to brotherly kindness, charity. For if
these things be in you, and abound, they make you that ye shall neither be
barren nor unfruitful in the knowledge of our Lord Jesus Christ. But he
that lacketh these things is blind, and cannot see afar off, and hath
forgotten that he was purged from his old sins."

Paul also remarks, in his Epistle to the Galatians, fifth chapter, that
the "fruits of the spirit is love, joy, peace, long suffering, gentleness,
goodness, faith, meekness, temperance: against such there is no law. And
they that are Christ's have crucified the flesh, with the affections and lusts."
Now, from these testimonies, and many more that we might produce from
the word of God, it must be evident to every unprejudiced and reflecting
mind, that christian temperance is a doctrine of the bible, and that it doth
not consist in our being temperate in one thing alone, but in all things. A
man may be very temperate in a few things, and very intemperate in other
things; which, according to the doctrine held forth by St. James, would
make or leave him still an intemperate man. "For whosoever shall keep the
whole law, and yet offend in one point, he is guilty of all. For He that said,
do not commit adultery, said also, do not kill. Now if thou commit no
adultery, yet if thou kill, thou art become a transgressor of the law." Just
upon the same principle the same gospel that commands temperance in one
thing, commands temperance in all things; and whosoever shall be
temperate in all, and yet offend by being intemperate in one point, he is
guilty of the whole; or, in other words, an intemperate man, according to
the gospel of Christ, which Paul affirms to be the power of God unto salvation unto every one that believeth.

But the main question before us is, What is temperance? and what are
the principal items of christian temperance? My friends, the word temperance, like many other words, is variously defined, to suit the taste and fancy of the definer: while the dram-drinker, whose lust after wine and strong
drink on the one hand, defines it moderation; contending that according
to scripture, it is no harm to drink a dram daily, so as a man doth not become drunken; while, upon the other hand, some contend for teetotal

abstenance from all intoxicating drinks. These positions remind us of St. Peter at the time the Saviour washed the disciples' feet when he said: "Lord, thou shalt never wash my feet." But Jesus told him plainly, "If I wash thee not, thou hast no part with me." Peter no sooner heard this declaration, than he fell into the opposite extreme, and said: "Lord, not my feet only, but my hands and my head also," now willing to do more than his Lord and Master required of him. But we see that the fancy of Peter could not be gratified; for the Redeemer replied: "He that is washed, needeth not save to wash his feet, but is clean every whit." Now is not the same course perceptible among the children of men. In many things they do not wish to do what is right and what the Lord requires; and when they cannot succeed in that way, they are then ready to do more than their master's will. Now, one is just as bad as the other in the sight of God; for both are contrary to the will of God, and cannot receive his divine approbation; for we read that "not every one that saith unto me, Lord, Lord, shall enter into the kingdom of heaven; but he that doeth the will of my Father which is in heaven." Again, "I testify unto every man that heareth the words of the prophecy of this book; if any man shall add unto these things, God shall add unto him the plagues that are written in this book: and if any man shall take away from the words of the book of this prophecy, God shall take away his part out of the book of life, and out of the holy city, and from the things which are written in this book."

Now, from these testimonies and many others, we see that nothing but the will of the Lord will do. Let our intention be ever so good, we must bow to His word. We shall then assume the position, that temperance, according to the scriptures, consists in the necessary use of all things; and that intemperance consists in the unnecessary use of anything whatever. For we believe that this position is not only a medium between the two extremes already noticed, but will fully comport with the word and will of God; and shall now proceed to make some remarks with regard to some of the principal items of christian temperance; and as drinks, especially spirituous liquors, occupy a prominent position, we shall first notice their necessary and unnecessary use.

First, all intoxicating drinks are produced by fermentation; and all men must acknowledge that God, through his infinite wisdom, power, goodness and foreknowledge, ordained the law of fermentation. And again it must be confessed, that such a being as God, with and by his almighty power, could have ordained that the juice of the grape, or the juice of the apple, or any other substance, should not ferment as easily as to ordain that it should; for we read that "all things are possible with God," and "with God there is nothing impossible." So wine is nothing more than the fermented juice of the grape; and by the process of distillation, the spirit that any fermented substance contains is extracted from a large body and reduced to a small quantity; and in this way all pure spirituous liquors are produced. Although there are some who contend that wine, the juice of the grape, has no intoxicating qualities about it until age and some process of the art of man produce it; but to all such we would say, hear the word: "Others, mocking, said these men are full of new wine. But Peter, standing up with the eleven, lifted up his voice, and said unto them, ye men of Judea and all ye that dwell at Jerusalem, be this known unto you and hearken to my words: for these are not drunken, as ye suppose, seeing it is but the third hour of the day.—*Acts,* c. 2. Here we have a plain testimony that new wine, in the days of the apostles, possessed intoxicating properties long before the art of distillation or production of spirituous liquors in the form we now have them, existed. Even long before Christ's mission here on earth, we see in our bible that wine and strong drink intoxicated the children of men when drank to excess. We are admonished in Proverbs to "give strong drink unto him that is ready to perish, and wine unto those that be of heavy heart." And Paul saith to Timothy: "Drink no longer water, but use a little wine for thy stomach's sake, and thine often infirmities." And we see that the Saviour, at his last supper, instituted the communion with bread and wine as a commemorative institution of his death and sufferings. So from these testimonies we may safely conclude that wine and strong drink, or spirituous liquors, have their necessary use. But when man drinks dram upon the top of dram when in good health, is he not using it unnecessarily. What use has a man for a dose of medicine when in good health? Did you ever know a man to send for a doctor unless he was sick? Did you ever know a physician who was in his right mind, and understood his calling, to administer a dose of medicine to a well man? We answer, no. Let the christian professor, then, ask himself these questions: What advantage will spirituous liquors be to me? Am I sick? If so, will spirits be a remedy for my case? If so, then you are at liberty to use such a portion as is necessary to accomplish the desired effect; but no more, lest you become intemperate in the use of spirits, using them when and also in larger quantities than will be advantageous to the health of the body or mind. For by the habitual use of any intoxicating drinks, the mind, the will, and the body, all become impaired, and will sink the creature man, who bears the image of his Creator, down upon a level with the brute creation. Oh, ye drunkards, who become drunken, and with your fierce temper disturb the peaceful home! behold, we entreat you as a lover of your immortal soul, think of the tears that have trickled down the cheeks of the wife, the companion of thy bosom; the object of thy early love; the tender-hearted and consoling comforter of all thy troubles, and the chief administrator unto all thy wants; how canst thou trouble her very soul, break her heart, and bring her body down with sorrow to the grave? Reform; do so no more; break off from such evil habits, that peace, love, joy, and social happiness may be restored at thy fireside, and thy children may greet thee with smiles on their lovely faces, and not with tears of sorrow streaming down from their eyes over their innocent little cheeks, like the offspring of some unfeeling tyrant. Remember thou must die: ere long, your body must mingle with its mother dust, and the soul wing it flight to a region now unknown unto you; and if unprepared, walking in drunkenness, rioting, and all such manifest works of the flesh. Paul declares that such shall not inherit the kingdom of heaven. Oh, dreadful thought! to be banished from the peaceful presence of God and the Lamb, and all the heavenly hosts of angels, and the spirits of just men made perfect, and take up an abode in hell with the devil and his angels, "where the worm dieth not, and the fire is not quenched."

And now, christian professor, it is your duty to let your light shine before men, so that others may see your good works, and be constrained to glorify the name of our Father which is in heaven; therefore, use neither wine nor strong drink, nor any spirituous liquor unnecessarily, and no more in quantity than is necessary; that you lay a bright example in this before all who drink to excess; and let your moderation be known unto all men, in the use of spirits as well as in everything else.

The Sons of Temperance, as a worldly organization, have no doubt accomplished much good in reforming many habitual drunkards; but as this institution is only engaged in one item of reformation, we cannot look upon that organization as of a christian character, but as a moral institution of the world; and as far as its influence has succeeded in improving the morals of society, that much praise is due to it; and we hope that it may succeed in reforming every drunkard in our community, for all such are a pest to society, and unfit for the christian church, until a thorough reformation is perceptible in all things inimical to the will of God.

We have said that the necessary use of a thing is temperance, whether it be spirituous liquor or any thing else that is not strictly forbidden in the word of God. But we cannot believe that liquor is like the negro's rabbit, good for every thing; or like the quack's nostrums, a perfect king cure-all; but has its place in and among the medical antidotes and stimulants, and ought to be so used by the christian professor, in order to be strictly temperate in accordance with the word of God. But liquor temperance is but a drop in the bucket when compared with christian temperance, for this reason: it is only one item of reformation, while christian temperance embraces all things.

We shall next take up the superfluity of dress, or, in other words, the unnecessary adorning of the body, as another item of intemperance that has its millions of adherents; and, alas! alas! for the professors of the religion of the Lord Jesus Christ, we fear that hundreds and thousands even who profess the name of Christ, are not even like the moderate dram drinker, but more like the drunken sot, indulging into the very extremes of excess in the forbidden things of time and sense. What saith Paul? Hear him: "I beseech you therefore, brethren, by the mercies of God, that ye present your bodies a living sacrifice, holy, acceptable unto God, which is your reasonable service, and be not conformed to this world; but be ye transformed by the renewing of your mind, that you may prove what is that good, and acceptable, and perfect will of God." "Mind not high things, but condescend to men of low estate." "In like manner also, that women adorn themselves in modest apparel, with shamefacedness and sobriety; not with broidered hair, or gold, or pearls, or costly array; but (which becometh women professing godliness) with good works." And again, Peter speaking of women's adorning, saith: "Whose adorning, let it not be that outward adorning of plaiting the hair, and of wearing of gold, or of putting on of apparel; but let it be the hidden man of the heart, in that which is not corruptible, even the ornament of a meek and quiet spirit, which is, in the sight of God of great price."

Dear friends, who profess the name of Christ, have you ever reflected seriously upon the declarations of the apostles? Have you never considered that you were laying a bad example before the sinner or non-professor by the wearing of gold, by indulging in the foolish and ornamental fashions of the day, or by clothing your body in rich and costly array? Is this condescending to men of low estate? Is this not minding high things? Has not the apostle forbidden the wearing of gold, and pearls, and costly array; and how can you consider that you are presenting your body a living sacrifice, holy, acceptable unto God when arrayed in all the lust of the eyes and the pride of life? Hear what St. John hath to say concerning this matter: "Love not the world, neither the things that are in the world. If any man love the world, the love of the Father is not in him. For all that is in the world, the lust of the flesh, the lust of the eyes, and the pride of life, is not of the Father, but of the world. And the world passeth away, and the lust thereof; but he that doeth the will of God abideth for ever." But many endeavor to justify their pride under the cover of decency; but, my friends, this won't do; decency is a christian virtue, while pride is the offspring of hell. What advantage is derived from the wearing of jewelry, and in being

clad in costly array, or in the indulgence of all the ornamental fashions of
the day? Doth it promote the health of the body? Doth it invigorate the
constitution? Or, doth it contribute anything to the comfort and ease of the
body? All must answer no. Well, then, all this superfluity is unnecessary,
inasmuch as we can be decent without it; and as there is not benefit derived either bodily or mentally from the wearing of such things; and why is
it that so much of the fruits of a proud heart exhibits itself not only among
the children of this world, but even among the professors? Is not the love
of money, which St. Paul terms "the root of all evil," at the very bottom of
all this evil? For as all men follow some occupation for a livelihood,
whether agricultural, mechanical, professional, or speculative, all have an
eye to their income, and wish to fill their coffers with the cash. It is right
that all men should follow some occupation for means of subsistence; for
Paul saith: "For even when we were with you, this we commanded you,
that if any would not work, neither should he eat. For we hear that there
are some which walk among you disorderly, working not at all, but are
busy bodies. Now them that are such we command and exhort by our Lord
Jesus Christ, that with quietness they work, and eat their own bread." And
it was also said to Adam, "in the sweat of thy face shalt thou eat bread, till
thou return unto the ground; for out of it wast thou taken; for dust thou
art, and unto dust shalt thou return." And again: "If any provide not for
his own, and especially for those of his own house, he hath denied the
faith, and is worse than an infidel." And the apostle saith to the believer,
"Provide things honest in the sight of all men." Hence, the christian
professor may see what is his duty in all things. But many of the
mechanical art, with some of the speculators, remind us of Demetrius the
silversmith, and men of like occupation of Ephesus, in the days of Paul.
The sacred historian informs us that through the preaching and miracles of
the divine apostle, "that many believed, came, and confessed, and showed
their deed; and many who used curious arts brought their books together
and burned them, to the amount of fifty thousand pieces of silver; so
mightily grew the word of God and prevailed." So this Demetrius, who
made silver shrines for the goddess Diana, the great idol of the Ephesians,
called together the workmen of like occupation, and said to them: "Ye see
and hear, that not alone at Ephesus, but almost throughout all Asia, this
Paul hath persuaded and turned away much people, saying that they be no
gods which are made with hands. So that not only this our craft is in
danger to be set at nought, but also that the temple of the great goddess
Diana should be despised, and her magnificence should be destroyed,
whom all Asia and the world worshippeth. And when they heard these saying, they were full of wrath, and cried out, saying, great is Diana of the

Ephesians!" In like manner do many of the children of men, in this our day, have their gain by the same craft to supply the magnificence of the people in the gratification of the lust of the eyes and the pride of life, which is not of the Father but of the world, by the manufacture and sale of jewelry, silks and satins, embroideries, and every species of frippery; saying, O, how handsome this, that, or the other, as the case may be, will make you look; causing poor dying mortals to idolize themselves as a Diana upon the temple of fame, with all the magnificence of a deity. Is this not saying in substance "Great is Diana of the Ephesians!" Remember, christian professor, it is your privilege to grow in grace and in the knowledge of the truth, as you grow in days and in years. But St. James saith: "God resisteth the proud, but giveth grace unto the humble." How, then, can we expect to find grace to help in every time of need, when we are proud, high-minded, not willing to forsake every folly as well as every vice, and step down into the valley of humility—that glorious and christian pathway of our Redeemer. Sinner, remember thou, too, must die, and appear in judgment, and give an account of all your deeds; and the drunkard's hell will be the proud man's hell, as well as the hell of all them that do wickedly, with all the nations that forget God.

Again, it is not only the object of the liquor maker, and the jewelry maker, *etc.,* to cry out, great are these things. But the speculator is, perhaps, more engaged in this cause than any; for it is a well known fact, that the greater the consumption of any article, the greater the demand; and the greater the demand, the more enhanced the price; and this affords a considerable traffic, by which they have their gain. No wonder, then, that such are so intent to introduce new fashions and every thing else to increase the magnificence and demoralization of mankind. Therefore the merchant should be temperate, and not introduce these ornamental and unnecessary things, and be content with moderate gain, restrain his own extravagance; live temperately in all things; and it will not require such exhorbitant profits to keep him going: and the farmer, the lawyer, the doctor, the mechanic, the teacher, and the minister in the sacred desk (as it is termed), should all let their moderation be known unto all men, in their prices, fees and bills. Let each one inculcate temperance in all things at home, and it will not require so much to keep them going; so that all can walk by the golden rule of the Redeemer, which saith: "Therefore all things whatsoever ye would that men should do to you, do ye even so to them: for this is the law and the prophet."

But another item of intemperance is vain and unprofitable conversation. "The tongue," saith St. James, "is a little member, and boasteth great things;" and is compared by the apostle to "a fire, a world of iniquity, that defileth the whole body, and setteth on fire the course of nature; and is set on fire of hell." He further represents it as "an unruly evil, full of deadly poison," and a member of the body that cannot be tamed: "Whilst men have put bits in horses' mouths, and caused them to obey and turn about their whole body; and every kind of beasts, and of birds, and of serpents, and things of the sea is tamed, and hath been tamed, of mankind." "Therewith," saith the apostle, "bless we God, even the Father; and therewith curse we men, which are made after the similitude of God. Out of the same mouth proceedeth blessing and cursing. My brethren, these things ought not so to be;" and then asks the question, "Doth a fountain send forth at the same place sweet water and bitter? Can the fig tree, my brethren, bear olive berries? either a vine, figs? so can no fountain both yield salt water and fresh." Now, my friends, is this not a desperate picture of the tongue. Well may it be said that it is an unruly member, for it runs oftimes at random; is engaged in lying, backbiting, slandering, and cursing; much engaged in lying for the sake of gain. Oh, these things ought not so to be. This is gross intemperance. The christian professor must bridle his tongue, or else his religion is vain. Hear what the apostle saith: "If any man among you seem to be religious, and bridleth not his tongue, but deceiveth his own heart, this man's religion is vain." But the apostle gives us to understand who is able and doth bridle his tongue, when he saith: "If any man offend not in word, the same is a perfect man, and able also to bridle the whole body." Oh, how careful ought each and every one of us to be who profess the name of Christ! what holy persons, in all manner of conversation! and strive for the mastery over our unruly tongue. Well did the poet say:

"The tongue, that most unruly power,
Requires a strong restraint;
We must be watchfull every hour,
And pray, but never faint."

But, my friends, we are not only as christians to be temperate in liquor, dress, and conversation, but also in eating and drinking; in sleeping and exercise, and in all manner of action and behaviour with and towards one another. It is said by the apostles in their Epistles, "wives, submit yourselves unto your own husbands, as is fit in the Lord." "For the husband is the head of the wife, even as Christ is the head of the church: and he is the saviour of the body. Therefore, as the church is subject unto Christ, so let the wives be to their own husbands in every thing." "Husbands, love your wives, even as Christ loved the church, and gave himself for it." "So ought men to love their wives as their own bodies; he that loveth his wife loveth himself; for no man ever yet hated *his* own flesh, but nourished and cherished it, even as the Lord the church." "Children, obey your parents in all things, for this is well pleasing unto the Lord." "Honor thy father and mother (which is the first commandment with promise), that it may be well with thee, and thou mayest live long on the earth." "And ye fathers, provoke not your children to wrath, but bring them up in the nurture and admonition of the Lord." Yes, converse with them about the goodness of God; pray for them at the family altar often; speak to them about the foolish and forbidden things of time and sense; endeavor to restrain their evil passions and every propensity that is in opposition to the will of God, that the smiling countenance of your Heavenly Father may rest upon you both in time and in boundless eternity. "Servants, be obedient to them that are your masters according to the flesh, with fear and trembling, in singleness of your heart, as unto Christ; not with eye-service, as men pleasers, but as the servants of Christ, doing the will of God from the heart; with good will doing service, as to the Lord, and not unto men; knowing that whatsoever good thing any man doth, the same shall he receive of the Lord, whether he be bond or free." "Let as many servants as are under the yoke count their own masters worthy of all honor, that the name of God and his doctrine be not blasphemed. And they that have believing masters, let them not despise them, because they are brethren; but rather do them service, because they are faithful and beloved, partakers of the benefit. These things (saith the apostle) teach and exhort." "If any man teach otherwise, and consent not to wholesome words, even the words of our Lord Jesus Christ, and to the doctrine which is according to godliness, he is proud, knowing nothing, but doting about questions and strifes of words, whereof cometh envy, strifes, railings, evil surmisings, perverse disputings of men of corrupt minds, and destitute of the truth, supposing that gain is godliness: from such withdraw thyself." "Art thou called, being a servant, care not for it? but if thou mayest be made free, use it rather. For he that is called in the Lord, being a servant, is a free man: likewise he that is called, being free, is Christ's servant." "Masters, give unto your servants that which is just and equal, (forbearing threatening,) knowing that ye also have a Master in heaven." "Abstain from all appearance of evil." "Follow peace with all men, and holiness, without which no man shall see the Lord." "Be perfect; be of good comfort; be of one mind: live in peace, and the God of Love and Peace shall be with you."

Now, my friends, this is something like temperance, when carried out in all things. But we must all acknowledge that we come short in many things, in laying aside every weight, and the sin that doth so easily beset us. Much is yet to be overcome; many imaginations are yet to be cast down;

and high things, that exalt themselves against the knowledge of God, as well as many thoughts that are yet to be brought into captivity unto the obedience of Christ.

And now, my friends, only consider what a vast sum of money is spent in our land for the unnecessary use of wines and spirituous liquors, and the useless and forbidden ornaments of the body, in jewelry, and apparel, and other magnificence, and the unnecessary use of cigars and tobacco; would not all this, if thrown into one pile, educate every son and daughter, and relieve every destitute widow and orphan, and all the afflicted, and spread the glorious gospel into every heathen clime on earth? All must acknowledge that it would. We then invite all to come to the church of Christ, which is the best temperance society on earth, because it is founded upon temperance in all things; and whoever is a subject of this body is a citizen of the kingdom of heaven—a member of the general assembly and church of the first born, who are written in heaven, full of love, joy, and peace; for the love of God is shed abroad in their hearts by the Holy Ghost; and the prerequisites necessary to initiate a son or daughter into this church, body or kingdom, is, *First,* Faith: "For without faith it is impossible to please him: for he that cometh to God must believe that he is, and that he is a rewarder of all them that diligently seek him."

Secondly, Repentance: "Let the wicked forsake his way, and the unrighteous man his thoughts: and let him return unto the Lord, and he will have mercy upon him; and unto our God, for he will abundantly pardon." "Bring forth fruits meet for repentance, by forsaking all vice and folly, as an humble penitent at the feet of Jesus, like good old Mary, having no merits of their own to plead; for the Saviour invites all such to come unto him, whom he declares he will in no wise cast out."

Thirdly, And be baptised into Christ, and put him on as the only prophet, priest and king. Behold the high station that the subjects of the kingdom occupy! They are called the sons of God; it is said they shall judge the world; they have the promise of being kings and priests of God, and to live and reign with Christ a thousand years, or during that glorious and long wished for period, the Millennium, when all jars and divisions shall be done away; when all envy and strife shall cease; when the devil, who now goeth about like a roaring lion seeking whom he may devour, shall be cast into the bottomless pit, and a seal set upon him that he shall deceive the nations no more, until the thousand years are expired. Oh, my friends, will not this be a glorious day! No inducement to sin; no child of misfortune will be found; no destitute widows and orphans; no sons and daughters of affliction; no sectarianism; no jars and divisions; no envying and strife— for the whole earth shall be filled with the knowledge of the Lord, as the waters cover the great deep. Yes, the kingdoms of this world shall become the kingdoms of our Lord and of his Christ, and he shall reign forever and ever; "and the saints shall possess the kingdom." That little stone that Nebuchadnezzar saw in his dream cut out without hands, and smote the great iron image of iron, clay and brass, and brake it in pieces; and the stone that smote the image became a great mountain, and filled all the earth, will then be fulfilled. "And it shall come to pass," saith the prophet, "in the last days, that the mountain of the Lord's house shall be established in the top of the mountains, and shall be exalted above the hills; and all nations shall flow unto it. And many shall go and say, come ye, and let us go up to the mountain of the Lord, to the house of the God of Jacob; and he will teach us of his ways, and we will walk in his paths: for out of Zion shall go forth the law, and the word of the Lord from Jerusalem. And he shall judge among the nations, and rebuke many people; and he shall beat their swords into plowshares, and their spears into pruning hooks: nation shall not lift up sword against nation, neither shall they learn war any more."

It is also declared by the prophet Micah, that "they shall sit every man under his vine and under his fig tree, and none shall make them afraid, for the mouth of the Lord hath spoken it; for all people will walk every one in the name of his God." "In that day, saith the Lord, I will assemble her that halteth, and I will gather her that is driven out, and her that I have afflicted; and I will make her that halted a remnant, and her that was cast afar off a strong nation; and the Lord shall reign over them in Mount Zion henceforth even forever." We are also informed that the brute creation will be restored to a state of innocence; the ferocity of the lion, with other beasts of the forest, will become harmless and inoffensive; the poisonous sting of the asp, and the fangs of the deathly reptile will no more be the dread of the children of men. For Isaiah, the son of Amos, saith: "The wolf, also, shall dwell with the lamb, and the leopard shall lie down with the kid; and the calf, and the young lion, and the fatlings together; and a little child shall lead them. And the cow and the bear shall feed; their young ones shall lie down together; and the lion shall eat straw like the ox; and the sucking child shall play on the hole of the asp, and the weaned child shall put his hand on the cockatrice's den; they shall not hurt nor destroy in all my holy mountain: for the earth shall be full of the knowledge of the Lord, as the waters cover the sea." We are further told that "the moon shall be confounded, and the sun ashamed, when the Lord of Hosts shall reign in Mount Zion, and in Jerusalem, and before his ancients gloriously." Yes, my friends and christian professors, then it is that christian temperance will pervade the whole earth in its fullest extent. Then let us labor for these great objects before us, "while it is called to-day, least the night cometh wherein no man can work."[50]

TOBACCO

Like alcoholic beverages, tobacco was forbidden; Brethren were not to raise it or use it, according to the Annual Meeting decisions of this era.

Y. M. 1817. Art. 1. Concerning the abuse of Tobacco, it was in union considered, that if a member should be contaminated with it, such should be admonished to quit it, and if it would not be told, such a member could not be elected to any office in the church.

Y. M. 1827. Art. 12. Concerning members who engage in the raising of Tobacco? Considered, that members should have nothing to do with such things, by which so much mischief is done, and so many men (and women too) are led captive, as in the case with Tobacco.

Y. M. 1864. Art. 9. Inasmuch as all that our annual meetings has hitherto done to suppress the excessive or intemperate use of Tobacco in smoking and chewing, has virtually proved a failure, could not this meeting adopt some method by which the excessive use of this growing evil could be suppressed in our brotherhood?

Answer—As the use of Tobacco is offensive to some brethren and sisters, and the excess of it an evil, we advise and counsel brethren not to use it in time of worship so as to be either filthy, or offensive to others; and we think our ministering brethren should admonish their members not to indulge in the excessive use of it in any way, because it is wrong to do so.[51]

EXCOMMUNICATION, DISFELLOWSHIPPING, AVOIDANCE, BAN

Many of the decisions of the Annual Meeting regarding human slavery, political activity, suits in court, secret societies, business, theatres and fairs, education, personal appearance, alcoholic beverages, and tobacco included provisions in various forms indicating that those Brethren who refused to accept the standards regarding nonconformity to the world would no longer be considered members of the church. They became involved in a process of excommunication or disfellowshiping, by which they were removed from the membership of the church. In the most serious cases, these ex-members were subjected to avoidance, or the ban, which meant that the members of the church were to have nothing to do with such ex-members.

This whole procedure was explained in a lengthy introduction by Henry Kurtz and in a number of Annual Meeting decisions. Obviously, this whole matter was a very important part of the enforcement machinery of the church, by which it attempted to maintain its standards of separation and nonconformity.

AVOIDANCE, OR EXCOMMUNICATION

Avoidance is a term not known or used in the ecclesiastic terminology of the greater part of so-called Christian professors of the present day, outside of our fraternity and a few other communities of a more ancient date. For this reason we have added another term, which is more in general use by ecclesiastical writers, though not strictly a scriptural term. We will give the definition of both terms by the lexicographer Webster: "Avoidance: the act of avoiding or shunning. *To avoid* is to shun; to keep at a distance; to avoid the company of a certain person." Excommunication in an ecclesiastical sense, is defined by the same author as "the act of ejecting from a church; expulsion from the communion of a church and deprivation of its rights, privileges and advantages; an ecclesiastical penalty or punishment inflicted on offenders. Excommunication is an ecclesiastical interdict (or prohibition) of two kinds, the lesser and the *greater*. The lesser excommunication is a separation or suspension of the offender from partaking of the eucharist (communion); the greater is an absolute separation and exclusion from the church and all its rights and advantages." ...

We are compelled to differ from [him], when [he] speak[s] of ejecting, expelling, which imply the use of physical force, as being so contrary to the spirit and law of Christ, that no Christian could entertain such an idea, much less perform such an act. Hence the Brethren prefer the simple term "avoidance" to the Jewish word "ban" or "anathema," or to the Roman term "excommunication." The reason is, because avoidance is a simple, plain word in our own language, readily understood by all, and not subject to misapprehension, as words taken from other languages, and having acquired a signification foreign to the letter and spirit of the gospel, and what is still more, because it is a scriptural term. True, the substantive noun does not occur in our common version of the Bible, but the verb and root of the substantive, avoid, occurs in the following passages: 1 Sam. 18: 11..., Prov. 4: 15..., Rom. 16: 17..., 1 Cor. 7: 2..., 2 Cor. 8: 20..., 1 Tim. 6: 20..., 2 Tim. 2: 23..., Titus 3: 9, 10 ...

From these passages it is sufficiently clear what the general idea of avoidance is, namely, to avoid, shun and keep at a distance from evil, from physical or moral evil, and from evil men; and from two of the passages,

Rom. 16: 17, and Tit. 3: 10, it is evident that they refer expressly to the ordinance under consideration.

But we must bring our remarks to a speedy close. That the main law of Christ concerning avoidance is recorded in Matt. 18: 15-20, and in 1 Cor. 5 from beginning to end, but more particularly verses 9-13, has been mentioned already, and will be repeated again in the following articles of counsel of the Brethren at yearly meetings. A critical and prayerful examination of these and other passages, together with a careful study of the history of the churches and of mankind, has convinced the writer of the correctness of the views and practice of the brethren in this respect, and that they can be defended against every objection of a candid believer of the word of God. . . .

We now merely add to those above our definition and description, derived from the word of God and the once universal practice of our brethren.

The ordinance of avoidance is an institution of the Lord Jesus Christ for the preservation of the purity and unity of the church, and for the bringing to repentance and restoration of fallen members. In cases of private offences and minor faults, which upon acknowledgment and submission to the counsel of the church might be readily forgiven and remitted, if the offender obstinately refuses to do so, and thus will not "hear the church," then, if admonished once and again, the church has no choice but to submit herself to the necessity and duty to pronounce the sentence expressed in Matt. 18: 17, i. e. she must avoid in part such stubborn members, by not admitting them to communion or church council, and not saluting them as members. This avoiding in part was called by some suspending, and Cyprianus of the second century called it putting back, and so do our brethren to this day. But in cases of crimes and such heinous sins as enumerated 1 Cor. 5: 11, and other places, a different course is to be pursued. Here confession and acknowledgment will not suffice, nor a putting back or avoiding in part would answer the purpose of justice and mercy: hence Love and Wisdom divine devised and ordained "not to keep company with such, no not to eat," and to this our ancient brethren from the time we have any record of them, and many that live to this day, without adding or taking away a single word (for they tremble at God's word, Rev. 22: 18, 19) gave their most humble yet willing assent and obedience, took up the cross as cross-bearing children of God should do (and there is undoubtedly a cross in this ordinance, and not a pleasure), and this they call full avoidance. Why the Lord did not institute this while yet personally on earth, the answer may be, may it not have been one of those things which the Lord had to tell the disciples, but they could not bear it then. What Paul said and did, he did it in the name of Christ, and consequently as if the Lord had said and done it himself.

From the testimony of the Brethren in 1713 (fully 150 years ago). See "Groundsearching Questions" in Alexander Mack's writings [:] ... Qu. 22 ... Qu. 25. ... Qu. 26. ...

Y.M. 1794. Art. 6. Concerning the ban, we would very readily deny ourselves so much for our brethren's sake, so as to drop the Jewish word "ban." But the ordinance of the Lord Jesus and his holy apostles we cannot give up even for our brethren's sake, namely: "If any man that is called a brother be a fornicator, or covetous, or an idolater, or a railer, or a drunkard, or an extortioner: with such a one no not to eat," 1 Cor. 5: 11. Here we see clearly that Paul does not mean only the eating in (the Lord's) supper, but all eating (in his company). This is shown in the foregoing verse very plainly, when it says, "yet not altogether with the fornicators of this world, &c." Otherwise we might eat the bread of communion with the fornicators of this world, which certainly he cannot have meant at all. ...

Y.M. 1822, Canton. Art. 11. How shall the church conduct itself toward those members that have been separated from the church? Considered, first, when a member is separated from the church as far as from the kiss, breaking of bread and church council, such ought to be diligently exhorted according to the evidence of the apostle, but could not be called brother. But when such would not receive the admonition of love, and should fall into more grievous sins, the church has to put them in avoidance, and have no company with them, according to the word of the apostle.

Y.M. 1822, Miami. Art. 1. When a member is put in avoidance, how far is his companion in wedlock to be held as a member? It was considered, that she may be held as a member, yet so as not to break the bread of communion.

Y. M. 1837. Art. 6. Whether the sense of the words of the Saviour, Matt. 18, "Let him be unto thee as a heathen man and a publican!" is the same as the sentence of the apostle, 1 Cor. 5, "Have no company with him," &c. It is understood by the meeting almost unanimously, that the expression of the Saviour, "Let him be unto thee as a heathen man and a publican" excludes a member only so far as from the church council, from the kiss and from the breaking of bread, but that the intention of the apostle when he speaks of the vicious (gross sinner), "Have no company with him," and after noting the (sins, crimes) vices, adds yet, "with such a one (you ought) no not eat!" that we ought to avoid such altogether, according to the (obvious) sense of the word.

Y.M. 1840. Art. 4. About the difference among brethren in regard to avoidance; since some seem to know or observe nothing at all of an avoidance, others take the liberty to eat with and greet as brethren those that are put in avoidance, which causes oftentimes temptations and great grief in those who feel themselves in duty bound, according to the word, to observe the avoidance strictly? Considered, that it is truly to be lamented that such a want of uniformity has crept in by degrees among the brethren in such a most important matter, and that it should be the ardent desire and earnest endeavor of all brethren and members, and especially of all ministers and housekeepers, to come again into full union in observing this evangelical and apostolic ordinance, to accomplish which may the ever faithful Chief Shepherd and Bishop of our souls grant his grace and the assistance of his good and holy Spirit.

Y.M. 1843. Art. 5. When a brother is put in avoidance, according to the words of Paul, 1 Cor. 5, and his wife and children, being members in the church, have company with him, as it happens in a family, how is the church to treat them, or whether there is a difference between the wife and the children, who are yet under the lawful ages, and how we are to do when there is a difference of opinion about the withdrawing of the hand from those that are in avoidance? Considered, though we are always truly sorry when such a case occurs where we must put a member in avoidance, and feel sincere compassion for those who suffer immediately under it; yet we cannot set aside this apostolic ordinance, and do really believe that the more strictly it is observed by all the members, and especially by the nearest relatives, the more powerful it would operate to the salvation of the fallen member. But in case a wife would not withdraw from fellowship with her husband (being) in avoidance, it was always considered, that such a member could not break the bread of communion while so doing; and we do consider, that the children are in the same predicament, either to withdraw fellowship with the parent in avoidance, or not to break bread. And in regard to withdrawing the hand, it was considered, that when the church concludes to withdraw even the hand, the members should all unite in observing the same.

Y.M. 1850. Art. 20. If a member commits a fault, whether the church has the power according to the gospel, to put that member in avoidance without the assistance of another church? Considered, that if there is a bishop in that church, they have the power in the case of a private member.

But whether it is best and expedient to undertake such a solemn work, where family connections might interfere much with a fair and impartial trial, without the assistance of another church and other bishops, the church should seriously consider and decide in the fear of the Lord—a church like that of Philadelphia (Rev. 3: 8), where true brotherly love dwells; where the door is open for her sister churches at any time to enter; where humility acknowledges of but little strength, and is therefore willing to avail herself of all the help her sisters, though they have but little strength too, may afford.

Art. 33. Whether members who have been put in avoidance, can be released without their request? Considered, that they cannot.

Art. 35. If a brother transgress so as to be deemed guilty of avoidance, should he not be cited to appear before the church in the presence of the witnesses, to hear the testimony given? Considered, that he ought to be particularly requested to attend.—

Art. 36. In case such member be found guilty, by whom should he be informed? Considered, that this is a duty incumbent on the ordained brethren.

Art. 37. If it is proved by two or three brethren (witnesses) that a brother has been drinking to excess, yet not so much as to disable him from keeping on his feet; but has often before been charged, and also before been set back or put in avoidance, and still denies the charge; would he not come under the class of drunkards, or would it be prudent to hold him as a brother, or should he be expelled by the proof of four or five witnesses, though not members of the church? Considered, that no member should be put in avoidance without positive proof from members that he or she has been guilty of one of those mentioned by Paul, 1 Cor. 5: 11.

Art. 38. Have we a sufficient right according to the gospel, to put a man in avoidance who has already been put back from the kiss, the communion and the council, and disowned as a brother? Considered, that the church has the power to do so.—

Art. 40. Whether an ordained brother, who has been once in avoidance, can be restored again to his full office? Considered that a brother can be restored again to his full office by the voice of the church (as in a choice).[52]

Like all persons, Brethren were human and subject to human weaknesses, such as owning slaves, participating in political activities, wearing fine clothing, drinking alcoholic beverages, and using tobacco. At any rate, these activities were all considered weaknesses by the Brethren, for they were "worldly" and the Brethren were not of this world. Various actions were taken to maintain the practices of the church based on separation from the world, including actions separating members from the fellowship of the church.

VI. WAR AND MILITARY SERVICE

INTRODUCTION

During most of the years from 1785 to 1865 the United States was at peace, and therefore war and military service did not make a major impact on the Brethren. The major exception was the time of the Civil War from 1861 to 1865 at the very end of the period. Other briefer and less important exceptions were the War of 1812 and the Mexican War, neither one of which had much effect on the Brethren. The Civil War did make a major impact on the Brethren, and much of the material in this chapter is related to the Civil War.

Throughout this period, Brethren were consistently opposed to their participation in war and military service. This opposition was both historic and religious. Brethren had been opposed to military service from the beginning of the church in Germany, and their opposition was based on their interpretation of the New Testament. What they condemned during these years was not war itself, but Brethren participation in war. The material in this chapter should help to clarify the positions taken by Brethren.

THE YEARS BEFORE THE CIVIL WAR

Most of what was taking place in the church related to war and military service in the years before the Civil War is summarized in Annual Meeting decisions. The major problem was the annual muster day, held in every United States community. All of the able-bodied men gathered for a day which included primarily drinking, gambling, and other festivities, as well as a short period of military practice. In some ways it seemed harmless, and there were penalties for not participating. The Annual Meeting insisted, however, that it was not harmless.

MUSTERING

Y. M. 1789. Art. 5. Further it was discussed and unanimously considered, that no brother should permit his sons to go on the muster ground, much less that a brother go himself.

Y. M. 1815. Art. 2. See "Non-resistance;" also, "Warfare."

Kurtz' entry at this point is puzzling, for at no place in his entire volume was Article 2 from the 1815 Annual Meeting quoted: however, Kurtz evidently knew that there was an Article 2. M. G. Brumbaugh, writing at the end of the nineteenth century, discovered and quoted the missing Article 2:

2nd. It has been discussed by us concerning the war matter, and it is agreed by all the brethren that if a brother or brother's sons who consider themselves according to the teaching of the brethren "defenseless" and prove themselves to be such and wish to obey the teachings of the Brethren—when these shall be hard oppressed with the payment of fines they shall be assisted by the brethren according to the teaching of the apostle—let one bear the burden of another, thus you will fulfill the law of Jesus Christ.[1]

Y. M. 1817. Art. 5. Whether brethren or their children may go on the muster ground or not? The counsel was, that no member may go there, and prevent also their children from going on that ground, and not willingly permit it to them, as long as they are under parental authority; should a brother do so, he could not be in full fellowship with the church; for the Saviour said to Peter, "Put up thy sword into his place, for all they that take the sword, shall perish with the sword."

Y. M. 1835. Art. 5. How it is considered when brethren go to muster and drill. Considered, that it is contrary to our baptismal vow, contrary to the Word of God, and contrary to the professed principle of the church, and can by no means be permitted or tolerated.

Y. M. 1840. Art. 9. Whether it could be permitted for brethren to attend a mustering in the militia? Considered, that mustering is a preparation for war; and since we by the gospel of Jesus are called unto peace and to a non-resistant state, it would in no wise be proper (consistent) or allowable for a brother to learn war. Isa. 2: 4. Mic. 4: 3.

Y. M. 1859. Art. 23. In those States where muster fines are high, and where the fines are the only means whereby the military musters are kept up, would it not be better for brethren to muster a few times, and thereby cause the military system to be abolished, than to pay an oppressive fine and thereby keep up the regimental muster? Ans. It would not, inasmuch as our Lord and Saviour teaches non-resistance in his gospel throughout. And when we go to musters, we there learn the art of war, and the most appropriate method of shedding our fellow-creatures' blood. See 2 Cor. 6: 17, John 18: 36.[2]

Kurtz also found two entries in the Minutes dealing with the subject of non-resistance.

NON-RESISTANCE
Y. M. 1845. (Virginia.) Art. 5. In regard to our being altogether defenceless, "not to withstand the evil," but "to overcome evil with good," the brethren consider, that the nearer we follow the bright example of the Lamb of God, who willingly suffered the cross, and prayed for his enemies; who, though "heir of all things," had on earth "not where to lay his head,"—the more we shall fulfill our high calling, and obtain grace to deny ourselves for Christ and his gospel's sake, even to the loss of our property, our liberty and our lives.

Y. M. 1855. Art. 4. Has a brother a right to defend himself with a deadly weapon at the appearance of his being in danger? Considered, that he has not, inasmuch as the Saviour says to Peter, "Put up thy sword into his place; for all they that take the sword, shall perish by the sword." Matt. 26: 52.[3]

A specific illustration of the problem for the Brethren of mustering in peacetime was found in Botetourt County, Virginia, when a group of more than forty Brethren men signed a petition in 1799 to the Virginia Legislature, requesting that they not be fined for their failure to attend muster and suggesting that they would be willing to spend an equal amount of time working on the public roads.

TO THE HONBLE THE SPEAKER
AND MEMBERS OF THE LEGISLATURE OF THE
STATE OF VIRGINIA
The petition of a number of Inhabitants of the County of Botetourt known by the name of GERMAN BAPTISTS respectfully represents.

That the members of our Church have at all times and in all countries, been forbid by their conscience to take up arms against their fellow man. Observing as we trust we do, a conduct void of offense toward all men we are by the same principles forbid all legal strife and contention—When differences arise among us they are settled by the rulers of our Church. We support our own poor and suffer none of them to become burthensome to any but to ourselves.

To live in this peaceable and inoffensive manner, we consider among our first duties. Notwithstanding laws have at various times been passed to compel a departure from these our religious opinions, they have in no instance produced other effects than fines and amerciaments. We humbly hope that in this our country, the boast of which is the uninterrupted enjoyment of civil & religious Liberty no part of the community will be impoverished by perpetual fines for refraining to do an act which their consciences abhor. To this end we pray that ourselves with others similarly circumstanced may in future be exempted from fines for not attending musters. Should your Honbly body deem it improper for us to employ that part of our time to our own emolument, which is employed by others in attending musters, we will chearfully be employed in labor of public utility and beg leave to suggest that the improvement of public Roads in our respective neighborhoods might be most beneficial.

In allowing us to commute our labor for public benefit, instead of military duty, or granting such other relief to your petitioners as their case requires, they as in duty bound will ever pray etc.

Samuel Hershberger
Jacob Ritter
Lorens Bodner
Jonadan Ladner
William Stover
Christian Houts
Michel Frans
Christian Frans
Nicolas Beckner
Matthias Snider
David Gist
Joseph Arnolt
Philib Simon
Hannes Griebiel
Niclaus Sietz

Jacob Heistand
Uly Rienhart [?]
Hannes Reinhart
Christian Hershberger
Micel Minnic [?]
Durst Ammen
Daniel Becner [?]
Christian Kinszy
Abraham Kinszy
George Stover
Johseph Noffzinger
Hadrian Bisz
Jacob Frans [?]
Leonhard Houts
David Zolleberger

John Beckner
Nole [?] Durke [?]
Lehmen [?]
George Lemen
John Neff
Jacob Noftsinger
John Myers
Boug Lisz [?]
Adam Critz
Jacob Brot [?]
Abraham Brot [?]
Paul Zigler
Hannes Heiner

[Dated: Dec. 13, 1799][4]

*As events developed in the late 1850s which led eventually to the out-
break of the Civil War, Brethren became increasingly involved for several
reasons. One was that they were opposed to military service. Another was
that they were just as vigorously opposed to human slavery. And a third
was that on occasion they were located in areas where the action was taking place. The latter two factors were combined in John Brown's raid on
Harper's Ferry, Virginia, in October 1859. That Brethren were sympathetic
with John Brown's goal of freeing the slaves was obvious; in fact, it has
been reported that on the evening before the raid, John Brown had
"preached" in a Brethren meetinghouse.5 The report may be questioned,
since Brethren were reluctant to allow anyone except a Brethren minister to
use their meetinghouses. That there were Brethren in the area was indicated
in a letter, the first part of which was written by the wife and the second
part of which was written by the husband, from Brethren in the immediate
area to their friends in Virginia.*

November 6, 1859

Well David we had a Lovefeast the 2nd of this month at Brownsville
notwithstanding the greate excitement that prevaled in our valley during
that week occasiond by the insurrection at Harpers ferry   it was the
smalest lovefeast I ever attended there.   people were affraid to leave their
homes to attend the meeting.

... Otho and I took a ride day before yesterday across our back
mountain ... and saw the rendezvous of the Harpers fery desperadoes &
the place that they had deposited their guns   it is the most dismal &
gloomy looking place I ever saw   just a fit place for robers and
murderers   I really felt badly in passing through that Valley   we went
on to the Ferry from there, which was about 4 miles from Capt Brown location   he had entered quite a suitable place amongst quite an ignorent
class of people. . . .

Our little Valley was thrown into quite an excitement a few weeks
Since, the cause of which you have been informed.   the morning on
which the attack was made at Harpers ferry a messenger was dispatched
from the Seat of war in every possible direction to give the alarm. One
came through our valley and reported that the abolitioners had taken
posession of the armry and all the U. S. arms, and killing our men. Many
of our Citizens repared to the scene of action at the earliest opportunity
but by the time they arrived the Charlestown troops had driven the
desperadoes back from the bridge of which the[y] had possession   the attack was made about ten oclock and the sound of musketry was distinctly
heard from that time untill dark   we was all considerably alarmd fearing
an attack from the negroes. I with several other persons stood guard for

two nights, moved our families to Brownsville, and guarded the town. The excitement has pretty well subsided and evrything is again quiet.[6]

As the year 1861 began, John Kline, the prominent Virginia minister, commented in his diary regarding the current situation and his ideas about the future.

TUESDAY, January 1, 1861. The year opens with dark and lowering clouds in our national horizon. I feel a deep interest in the peace and prosperity of our country; but in my view both are sorely threatened now. Secession is the cry further south; and I greatly fear its poisonous breath is being wafted northward towards Virginia on the wings of fanatical discontent. A move is clearly on hand for holding a convention at Richmond, Virginia; and while its advocates publicly deny the charge, I, for one, feel sure that it signals the separation of our beloved old State from the family in which she has long lived and been happy. The perishable things of earth distress me not, only in so far as they affect the imperishable. Secession means war; and war means tears and ashes and blood. It means bonds and imprisonments, and perhaps even death to many in our beloved Brotherhood, who, I have the confidence to believe, will die, rather than disobey God by taking up arms.

The Lord by the mouth of Moses, says: "Be sure your sin will find you out." It may be that the sin of holding three millions of human beings under the galling yoke of involuntary servitude has, like the bondage of Israel in Egypt, sent a cry to heaven for vengeance; a cry that has now reached the ear of God. I bow my head in prayer. All is dark save when I turn my eyes to him. He assures me in his Word that "all things work together for good to them that love him." This is my ground of hope for my beloved brethren and their wives and their children. He alone can provide for their safety and support. I believe he will do it.[7]

The Harshbargers in Indiana did not see things from quite the same perspective as John Kline, although they agreed that bloodshed would be wrong.

Cornstock, Montgomery County, Indiana
January 21, 1861

Now Br. David about the times and Signs in our country, it is deplorable to think off how in Kansas the Sufering that is thare for want of some Nurishment to Subsist on.   we a few of our church made a Small collection for the brethren in Kansas   by order of the church I sent it to them last weak   I hear the churches North are a contributing for their relief also.

But this is nothing.   look to the North, then to the South and see how they stand at this time in hostile array against each other   the South wants their due, and the North says no, no more territory for you Southerners   all rong in my opinion   if we cant live no more in this good old union in peace let us devide peacibly and have no blood shead   make a treaty before any blood is shead   if they fight 5 years there will have to be a treaty made and thousands of lives lost and the matter harder to settle than it would be now   I told them as soon as I hear that Lincoln was brought before the people by the North a Sectional Candidate I knew if he was elected the South would Secede from the union   he was not a union man   the speach he made in Springfield Illinois saying the union could not exist as it is it must all be either Slave or all be free. I told them it would not do to talk that way to the South.   they wont bare it   they are the hot abolitionists   Said we will soon git them back again   there is a great menny men hear that Supported Lincoln would not do it now   he could not git Indiana now   I always was opposed to a Sectional Man for office   I voted for Douglas and if Douglas or Bell would of been elected there would been none of this trouble   Now let me tell you if any fighting will be done and any volenteer companys made up hear they will all be abolitionists that will turn out first   this you know   now if there Should be a draft made Douglas Democrats will hardly go to fight the South   Some think a magority will go South   Some say they wont fight.[8]

From Maryland came still another Brethren perspective in the frenzied months of early 1861, just before the war began.

Burkettsville, Frederick County, Maryland
March 23, 1861

I have however not forgotten you, nor your neighbourhood, it being the first place after leaving home where I met Brethren. I afterwards met many at many other places yet at no other place was I more kindly received than at yours. Not having seen any of you before except Bro. Moomaw, yet it did not require a long time before I felt perfectly at home among you.

The best news I have to impart is that we are in the enjoyment of good health, myself and children, also your relations residing in our church. I saw Bro. Bartholow and his wife last Sunday. They were well, and contemplate going to the Annual Meeting, at least Some of them if not the Elders, some of the younger of the family.   they have an idie of extending their journey as far as you. How far do you live from the place of our Meeting, which is to take place in May next.

You have perceived no doubt in the Visitor a disposition to change the place of Meeting, owing to the great excitement in your state upon the Slavery subject. I received a letter from Bro. Neff who informed me that the Brethren in his section held a Council lately, and among other things spoke of the desired change, and concluded that the apprehension of the Eastern Brethren upon that subject was not well founded.

But since then I have been reading the proceedings of the Conference of Methodists now assembled at Staunton, and from their excited debates as published, I fear that the Pub[l]ick mind there will be a Condition not most favorable to the Meeting of our Brotherhood, in the same vicinity so soon thereafter. I perceive that the new chapter to the Discipline of the Methodists, as it was enacted at Buffaloe meets with no favour, at Staunton. Neither does it meet with much favour with a similar conference now in session at Chambersburgh, Pa. The substance of that chapr is that Slavery is a Sin.

Have you read the Rev. Vandykes Sermon upon the subject of slavery. It is widely circulated in the South. It is very good upon that subject. It denies that Slavery is Sin, only its abuse is sin. I wish you could get it and read it.

I still entertain the hope of being at the Annual Meeting where I hope to see [you] and many other persons with whom I am acquainted.

Br. Neff gave some directions with respect to those intending to make the trip from here by private conveyance, from which it appears that it will require part of four days to perform the trip from here.

Many of the Washington County Brethren and Sisters Contemplate going. From Frederick and Carrol I am not advised. Bro. Saylor and Bro. Koontz are going together.

... We have no collision yet between the North and South yet, and I hope we will not have any. I think if politicians would remain at home and let well enough alone, things would come out right again.

Those conventions held in different states seem to be of very little account. Calculated only to keep the publick mind excited. In our State our Gov. refused to convene even the Legislature, and he has been sustained by the people, yet a self constituted convention sent a committee from here to confer with your State Convention. Their first Communication was not agreeable to all of your delegates I perceive.

With regard to church matters I have nothing very encouraging to write. We have made but few additions to our numbers, since I saw you. The public mind has been so much engrossed here with political matters, that there appears to be little room for anything else.[9]

In April 1861 the Civil War began. Two Brethren diarists, one in the Confederacy and one in the Union, entered their impressions of the opening events of the war. In Virginia, John Kline wrote:

SUNDAY, April 21, 1861. Meeting at our meetinghouse. Great excitement on account of secession and war movements. The volunteers are being called out to enter the field of war, and God only knows what the end will be. There is great commotion everywhere in the realm of thought and sentiment, men's hearts failing them for fear, the sea and the waves of human passion roaring.[10]

In Illinois, John J. Emmert wrote:

April 23, 1861—President Lincoln orders out 75000 men to quell the rebellion at Charleston.
April 27, 1961—130 men in Carroll Co. inlisted for the war.
April 29, 1861—Great war excitement
May 24, 1861—Great preparations continue to be made for the War
May 31, 1861—Bought some things in town- took in survey of the volunteer parade and returned in the rain.
June 18, 1861—The Regiment of Volunteers camping at Freeport left this morn for Alton.[11]

The first major event for the Brethren after the beginning of the War was the holding of the Annual Meeting late in May. As previously scheduled, it convened at the Beaver Creek congregation, near Harrisonburg, Virginia. The "Introduction" to the Minutes described to some extent the prevailing conditions and problems created by the War.

Minutes of Yearly Meeting
Beaver Creek, Rockingham, Va.
May 20th, 1861.
Pursuant to appointment made on Pentecost last, at the Annual meeting in Washington county, Tennessee, the brethren met in Annual Coun-

sel, at Beaver Creek meeting-house, Rockingham, Va. A very large congregation having asembled, public preaching was commenced on Sunday morning, at the time, and conducted at three different places, the meeting-house, in the tent, and in the grove: at each of which places the people assembled in dense crowds, as far as speakers could be heard understandingly, and still there were many who did not get any benefit of the preaching, for which there seemed to be an ardent desire, so much so, that all the meeting-houses in the surrounding country and villages, were opened for our use, and pressing invitations given to the brethren, to occupy them. It was therefore to be regretted that there were not more ministering brethren present. The brethren here had also made extensive preparations for the bodily comfort of those who should be with them, and seemed to lament much that the brethren from distant countries were not with them to share in their hospitality, as well as in the spiritual feast they had anticipated. Nevertheless, as there were many brethren and sisters present, we enjoyed a feast of fat things together, forgetting, for the time-being, the confusion of the political affairs without, owing to which, many of the churches composing our common fraternity, were not represented. But not wishing by any means, to change the regular usage of the church, whereby the fraternal bond of our common brotherhood might be affected, we have, therefore, with those Elders and brethren, who have assembled, after having dedicated ourselves to God, concluded to proceed with the business before us, in the regular way.[12]

John Kline, who served as the moderator of the Meeting, also commented on the prevailing national situation at the time of the Meeting in entries in his diary.

SUNDAY, May 19, 1861. Meeting in the Beaver Creek meetinghouse and at two other places near by. A very great concourse of people on the ground. The spiritual peace and composure of heart, however, usually manifest in the Brotherhood on all former occasions of this kind, is sadly interfered with now by the distracted state of our country. But the weather is pleasant, and we hope to have a good meeting. Preaching in the meetinghouse to-night, and also in Dayton, Virginia. . . .

WEDNESDAY, May 22. Get through with business by eleven o'clock, and the Annual Meeting breaks up, most of those present from the North as well as from the South carrying awey with them heavier hearts than they ever before have borne from a meeting of this kind. Many prayers were offered in the course of its progress in the behalf of our country. The

Shekinah of God's care may be gloriously waving over our heads now, and we are not able to see it. The Red Sea is before us, but Jehovah will part its waters for us to go through unharmed.[13]

SECURING EXEMPTION FROM MILITARY SERVICE

Since Brethren were conscientiously opposed to military service on religious grounds, one of their earliest concerns after the beginning of the Civil War was to secure exemption from military service in the armies of the Union and of the Confederacy. Consequently, the Brethren exerted extensive pressure on the civil and military authorities, especially in the South where there was more uncertainty about governmental willingness to recognize religious grounds for exemption from military service.

Certainly, one outstanding leader of the church in the South during the years of the War was John Kline from the Linville Creek congregation in the Shenandoah Valley of Virginia, who served as the moderator of the Annual Meeting throughout the War from 1861 to 1864. He maintained an extensive correspondence with many persons, including John Letcher, the Governor of Virginia. Some of the letters have been preserved and are included in this section. However, one of Kline's early letters to Letcher is available only in the summary in his diary.

WEDNESDAY, January 30, 1861. Write a letter to John Letcher, Governor of Virginia, in which I set before him in a brief way the doctrines which we as a body or church, known as Brethren, German Baptists or Dunkards, have always held upon the subject of obedience to the "rightful authority and power of government." We teach and are taught obedience to the "powers that be;" believing as we do that "the powers that be are ordained of God," and under his divine sanction so far as such powers keep within God's bounds. By *God's bounds* we understand such laws and their administrations and enforcements as do not conflict with, oppose, or violate any precept or command contained in the Divine Word which he has given for the moral and spiritual government of his people. By *government,* to which we as a body acknowledge and teach our obligations of duty and obedience, we understand rightful human authority. And by this, again, we understand, as the Apostle Paul puts it, "the power that protects and blesses the good, and punishes the evildoer." The general government of the United States of America, constituted upon an inseparable union of the several States, has proved itself to be of incalculable worth to its citizens and the world, and therefore we, as a church and people, are heart and soul opposed to any move which looks toward its dismemberment.[14]

Letcher replied promptly to Kline's letter, and in his letter indicated that Kline had discussed a proposal for exempting the Brethren from military service—a proposal which was not mentioned in Kline's own summary of his letter.

Richmond, Virginia
February 1, 1861

I received your kind letter this evening, and am gratified to find that our views upon public questions are so nearly in accordance. I have never doubted, that I would in the main, he sustained by the reflecting and conservative men, in all sections of our State, and I am now receiving numerous evidences, of the correctness of that opinion.

We have many men in the North and South, who are anxious to see the Union destroyed. By far the larger number, are reckless adventurers, without property, who have nothing to lose; and no revolution in the country or its business can therefore injure them. They think they may in a war better their condition, and they are therefore disposed to take chances, and run all hazards.

I would be glad to see the arrangement in regard to military service, suggested in your letter adopted. I think it entirely reasonable, that those who have conscientious scruples, in regard to the performance of militia duty, should be relieved by the payment of a small pecuniary compensation. There are enough of others who take pleasure in the performance of such duties.

It is gratifying to hear that my old friends in the Tenth Legion sustain me now, as in other days. I appreciate a compliment from such people most highly.

I have great hopes that the controversy now unhappily existing between the North and the South will be eventually settled, to the satisfaction of the conservative men of all parties.[15]

The Southern Army in the early stages of the Civil War was raised primarily by local community recruiting, in calling out the militia units, which were supposed to include all of the able-bodied men. By the summer of 1861, this type of local pressure was creating some problems for the Brethren, and John Kline again wrote to John Letcher. Incidentally, this letter was copied directly from the original, without any editorial changes, and thus reveals something of Kline's knowledge of English, which was a second language for him.

John Kline,
from mural painting
by Medford Neher

Bowmansmill Rockingham Va
July 22d 1861

I take up my pen to drop a few lines to you, though feeling a delicacy, knowing that you must evidently be over burdened with business, and sad questions and requests, but seeing things as they pass I feel presed to through in a little might, of queries and if possible advice. it is so now here with us that almost all men capable to labor, save a few aged and invalid are called away, and who is to take care of those at home is a mistery to me, and who is to prepare the ground for seeding, and seed for another year, is equally so. In your last Proclamation, third clause, you speek of overseers, on the subject of which there is a difference of opinion, some think that it only means overseers, who have the control of slaves, if that is the meaning, there seams to be some thing partial in it, which ought not to be, but, if it means all overseers of farms as the word actualy expreses, then it would leave one man to each farm, and in that case, the people could shift along pretty well, with the feamale and children who all can help, with the invalids that are here who also can help a little, and likely a pretty fair crop may be put out for another year, for without that, it is evident that we cannot git along very long without starvation. It seems to me that the proceedings of some of our officers is entirely too rash, many men in our parts who are absolutely not proper subjects for field or soldier services, are not exemted, who must soon give out in a soldiers life, while at home, with due care to themselves they might be usefull, and do considerabl service. others who have small families, and wifes, who are in a state of utro gestation, expecting to go to bed in a few weeks, or month, it seems that in such cases, it is cruel to take away the husband from them, (other cases have been that men concientious of bearing arms were bound, and forced, to go, against the feeling of their faith, and the Solemn Vow, that they have made to their God, to be true to the Doctrine of the saviour and Prince of Peace, who declares, that, "they who would be his Disciples, must deny themselves, take up their cross, and follow him dayly," and again that they should not retaliate "evil for evil" and, "that they should love their enemies, do good to them that hate them" asf.

It looks a little like as if our men or officers desire to compel those to brake that Solemn affirmation of the heart to God, recollect that those men ar in other respects the most law abiding, and willing tax paying citizens, in our commonwelth, they are not of the rude careless, and unworthy citizens, of the land, and whether such proceedings, with those, of God avowed people, will not go far to bring down his indignation, upon our cause is a question with me, and to me it is evidend that without the smiles of the providence of God, we cannot succeed, with the odds in number against us, as we have. I make those sugestions not as an enemy to our cause, but as a wellwisher or lover of justice, and equty, but I hold, as thouthands before me did, that, where the laws of earthly governments cross the laws of God, it is more safe to obey God than man. It is evident as things appear now, that we have engaged in a fearfull strugle. I pray God, that he may so overule things, that it may come to an amiacabl adjustment without the sheding of so much Blood. please if you can do any thing inbehalf of our cause of relieve, to do so, and write to me soon, if I ask not too much at your hands. I however am aware of the troubles in which you are, and of the many questions and requests that are made to you. this leaves us well thank God, except my overseer A. Knopp he is unwell. I hope when this comes to hand it may find you and family well. plese give my respect to wife, and mother in law.[16]

One of John Kline's neighbors, Christian Wine, who was also a Brethren minister, wrote to the governor in the fall of 1861 to discuss the problems connected with the departure of the able-bodied men, including his son, with the militia units and the related problem of a shortage of farm labor, which would make it possible to plant the fall crops. He suggested that money payments be accepted by the government in lieu of the service of these men.

Bowmansmill Rockingham Va
September the lt 1861

I take up my pen to write a few lines to you. I am a man of common occupation, a farmer, and have a son grown, who attends to a great part of my buisness, as I am often from home, on Ministerial calls. I can hardly spare my Son for the Army, though he has reasently been sumened by his Captain. I feel willing to make full recompence to government by way of fines, or taxs for his time, if that can be accepted, which our officers say Cannot be accepted, and the law says it can at least as far as I know it. please let me know what you say about it by return mail.

PS. we are in a deplorable conditions as a great bulk of labor is on hand, seed time and all its attendends of preparing the ground and no hands to do it. all are at Winchester apparently doing nothing. could not Money be entended at least to such that desire so much to be at home and are so much needed in their families?[17]

John Kline was also having difficulty securing someone to take care of his farm, while he was away from home, who would not be required to serve in the militia. In November, he outlined his problem to the governor.

Bowmansmill Rockingham Va
Nov 22 1861

I take my pen to drop a few lines to you, rather of nessesaty, its age and the extensive labors that fell upon me in the ministry of the church, and as my wife also being partially insane, I found myself under the imparitive nessesaty to employ an overseer of my farm, as of course, my ministerial duty often calls me from home. the most suitable person I could get was Abraham Knopp Jun., who was drafted in the first draft of the Militia Col Dovels Regment. he then was sick and could not go. afterward at the general call his young son John A. Knopp went to Winchester to fill his own call, and remained their til they were all discharged, at which time I sent a certificate that Abram Knopp was my overseer and that they should exemt him according to your proclimation, but it was [refused] by the officers, and now as he got tolarable well again from his sickness, they have sent for him again which call he filled by sending his young son in his place to avoid trouble, and I again sent a certificate to the officers who are at Randesvous. this evening my certificate was returned without being granded, which leaves me in a critical situation and I though to write to you at once, and see whether you would not do some thing for me, and my overseer, on the subject I could send you the certificate, with its qualification before the proper officer, but I think it unnessesary as I think you know anough of me, as I hope, to have confidence that I would not deceive you, which I would not do under any circumstance. Please give this the earliest attention, and write to me forthwith and I shall for ever be gratefull to you. and so I remain yours with the highest esteem

While he was writing, John Kline decided to mention another person in his neighborhood who was also having a problem keeping an overseer.

I saw in the papers of the berievement of your little child on which account I had considerable sympathy for you and companion I was also solicided by the widow Turner of James Turner of Brocks Gap who has a considerable family of young women and small children to take care of. one of her sons Isaac, single is in camp, the other one Joseph maried, lives with hir on the place, whom she has employed as hir overseer, which has not been accepted by the officers, why I know not. it would be hard for hir to get along without him, as they have their milling and other things a distance off and some young boys who ought to have some one with them to train them to labor. Please take this also into consideration, and grand him his exemption, if it is not inconsistand with your good feeling which however I know is always humane[18]

As the War dragged on into the winter of 1861-1862, the need for some more efficient means of getting men for the Southern army increased, and the probability of the enactment of some kind of draft also increased. This prospect frightened the Brethren and encouraged them to put as much pressure as possible on the civil and military authorities to exempt Brethren from such a draft. In December, 1861, John Kline discussed in his diary his efforts on behalf of the Brethren.

FRIDAY, December 20, 1861. Write to John Hopkins, to John C. Woodson, and to Charles Lewis. I can but entreat these men to stand in defense of our Brethren, and try to devise some plan by which they can be exempted from the necessity of bearing arms. I feel sure that if we can be rightly understood as to our faith and life, there will be some way provided for their exemption. The Brotherhood is a unit, heart and hand against arms-bearing. These things I make known to these men; not, however, in any spirit of defiance, but in the spirit of meekness and obedience to what we in heart believe to be the will of the Lord. Many have already expressed to me their determination to flee from their homes rather than disobey God.[19]

The letter that John Kline wrote to Charles Lewis has been preserved.

Bowman's Mill, Rockingham County, Va.
December 16, 1861

I arrived home safe and have been looking to hear from you. . . . I now desire to approach you on another subject which I would like you to consider and use your influence with the generals and other officers in the army. The subject is this: We German Baptists (called Tunkers) do most solemnly believe that the bearing of carnal weapons in order to destroy life, is in direct opposition to the Gospel of Christ, which we accept as the rule of our faith and practice. To this we have most solemnly vowed to be true until death. Hence we stand pledged to our God to carry out that which we believe to be his commandment. By his apostles he speaks plainly in Romans 12: 17 to end of the chapter: "Recompense to no man evil for evil. Provide things honest in the sight of all men. If it be possible as much as lieth in you, live peaceable with all men. Dearly beloved, avenge not yourselves, but rather give place unto wrath: for it is written, Vengeance is mine; I will repay, saith the Lord. Therefore if thine enemy hunger, feed him; if he thirst, give him drink: for in so doing thou shalt heap coals of fire on his head. Be not overcome of evil, but overcome evil with good." In many other places also, the Lord has spoken on this.

We feel bound to pay our taxes, fines, and to do whatever is in our power which does not conflict with our obligation to God. Whenever God speaks we think we should obey Him rather than man. But in this unholy contest, both law and all former precedents of making drafts have been set aside. The privilege usually granted Christian people to pay a fine has been overruled and set aside, and they are compelled to take up weapons of carnal warfare to drill and if need to be to shoot down their fellow man. This is not only revolting to them, but a positive violation to their solemn vow to their God. This is without precedent in a land of Christian liberty. Who the prosecutor of this outrage on our constitutional rights is I know not, but that it is so is clear. That it has been driven by some one is also clear. This state of things the much abused Abe Lincoln would have much deplored. For I am credibly informed that he issued a proclamation that no conscientious Christian should be forced to war or to take up arms.

Thus it should be in a land of Christian liberty. None but those who have a disposition or desire to rear up a hierarchy or despotic government could feel otherwise. None that have a spark of the spirit of Washington or Jefferson in their hearts would desire to compel their fellow countrymen to take up arms against their conscience, and to force them to kill their fellow man. Let any one look at and read the fifteenth section of the Constitution as before the convention: "Nor shall any man be *enforced, restrained, molested,* or *burdened* in his *body* or *goods* or otherwise *suffer* on account of his religious *opinion* or *belief.* This I understand is unchanged. Neither should it be. Therefore, a great breach of the constitution has been practiced on us for we have been enforced, restrained, and molested because of our religious belief and opinion.

Please give this matter your earnest attention and tell it or read it to your fellow officers, and if expedient, to Gen. Jackson.[20]

Colonel Lewis evidently had something to do with the status of John Kline's farm overseer, because Lewis was mentioned in a letter which Kline wrote to the governor in February 1862. The letter also reflected the confusion in the postal system during a time of war as well as Kline's continuing efforts to secure sufficient labor supply to maintain his business.

Bowmansmill Rockingham Va
feb the 15t 1862

I take My pen once more to drop a few lines to you, to inform you that I have recved your answer of 21 last to mine, through your aid Mr. R. H. Collett. I feel thankful to you, for your promptness in answering my letters and also for the interest you take in my business. You stated in your last that the Sec of war had declared my overseer exempt and hoped that before your letter would reach me, I would have received the Inteligence from him, this I am sorry to say has not been the case. I presume that his letter either to me or Col Luis must have been lost, for I have a letter just received from Col Luis, stating, that he has not received any thing on the subject. so if the Sec has send the Certificate it must have been lost. I had send through Col Luis the necessary qualificaded papers to the Sec, I have to day written to the sec which letter I expect will go in the same package to Richmond. please use your influence with the Sec for me, in which letters I also plead with the Sec to detail to me George W. Moyers, my foreman, to make ties for Manassas Gap Rail Road, of which I have become a Contractor, and by Mr. Moyers being taken away from me, I am behind with my contract and also I have beseached the Sec to exemt John A. Knopp son of my overseer, who had been kept from school the past year on account of some uncontrolable circumstances his father then intended to send him this year and now he has been to the army for some 6 months, and still remains at Martinsburg, his father, with myself feel very anxious that he should have a reasonable position of education. he is a lad of some fine qualities, and it would be great pitty if he could not git a reasonable education. please use your influence in behalf of him. I now must close on this subject and hope that the God, whom I serve, may Smile down upon us, and upon this our onced hapy, but now troubled land, and may he, in whose hands are all the destinies of Nations, so overule maters that a speedy Secesion of the troubles may be brought about, to the satisfaction of all. this is my dayly prayer may the Lord Grand yours in the bond of friendship and affections

Yesterday and the few days previous the farmers that are at home and have horses were ploughing. to day that is this morning the snow is pouring down and is now some inches deep and looks as it might keep on to day. there is much sickness in and through the Valley, such as Pneumonia Plurisy typhoid fever and of course many death

this however thank the Lord leaves us all reasonable well hoping it may find you all well   Give my best respect to Mrs. Letcher and her mother and retain a portion for yourself

We have received some sad inteligence from Roanoke Island   if true and so from other places   I hope it is not true[21]

The last statement about the Confederate defeat at Roanoke Island raises an interesting question about John Kline's loyalty to the Confederacy, even though it was fighting in defense of slavery, a practice to which the Brethren were vigorously opposed.

On March 29, 1862, the state of Virginia enacted a law which granted exemption to the Brethren and other groups who were prevented from participating in military service by their religious beliefs. They were to pay $500 plus 2% of the assessed value of their property.

That whenever upon application for exemption to the board of exemption it shall appear to said board that the party applying for said exemption is bona fide prevented from bearing arms, by the tenets of the church to which said applicant belongs, and did actually belong at the passage of this act, and further, that said applicant has paid to the sheriff of the county or collector of taxes for the city or town in which said applicant resides, the sum of five hundred dollars, and in addition thereto, the further sum of two per cent of the assessed value of said applicant's taxable property, then the said board, on the presentation of the receipt of said officers for said moneys, and after the said applicant shall have taken an oath or affirmation that he will sustain the confederate government, and will not in any way give aid and comfort to the enemy of the said confederate government, then the said board shall exempt the said applicant: provided, that whenever said party may be unable, or shall fail to pay the said sum of five hundred dollars, and the tax of two per centum on their property, he shall be employed (when liable to militia duty) in the capacity of teamster, or in such other character as the service may need, which does not require the actual bearing of arms: and provided further, that the persons so exempted do surrender to the board of exemption all arms which they may own to be held subject to the order of the governor, for the public use.[22]

In addition to the pressure exerted by the Brethren, and other groups such as the Friends and the Mennonites, one possible source of pressure on the authorities in Richmond was a letter written by T. J. (Stonewall) Jackson, a major-general in the Confederate Army, about a week before the enactment of the law. He was writing to S. Bassett French, a military advisor of the governor.

Mount Jackson, Va.
March 21, 1862

There are three religious denominations in this military district who are opposed to war; eighteen were recently arrested in endeavoring to make their escape through Pendleton to the enemy. Those who do not desert will, to some extent, hire substitute; others will turn out in obedience to the Governor's call, but I understand some of them say they will not "shoot." They can be made to fire, but they can very easily take bad aim. So, for the purpose of giving to the command the highest degree of efficiency and securing loyal feelings and co-operation, I have, as those non-combatants are said to be good teamsters and faithful to their promise, determined to organize them into companies of 100 each, rank and file, and after mustering them with the legal number of company officers into service assign them to the various staff departments without issuing arms to them; but if at any time they have insufficient labor, to have them drilled, so that in case circumstances should justify it arms may be given them. If these men are, as represented to me, faithful laborers and careful of property, this arrangement will not only enable many volunteers to return to the ranks, but will also save many valuable horses and other public property in addition to arms. Please inform as to the Governor's decision as to whether it is obligatory on me to assign them officers. All I have pledged myself is that as far as practicable I will employ them in other ways than fighting but with the condition that they shall act in good faith with me and not permit persons to use their names for the purpose of keeping out of service.[23]

Unfortunately for the Brethren and their allies in the struggle to secure exemption from military service to the South, no sooner had they secured the desired recognition from the Virginia government than the control of the military draft was taken out of the hands of the states and placed in the hands of the Confederate government by a law enacted on April 16, 1862, by the Confederate Congress. This new measure permitted the securing of substitutes but made no provision for religious exemption from the draft as did the Virginia measure. Interestingly enough, even some sources which were not normally sympathetic with the cause of the Brethren were disturbed by the difference between the Virginia and the Confederate draft laws. The "Daily Richmond Whig" of June 30, 1862, noted:

Scattered over certain portions of Virginia are a well-known sect called "Dunkards." These Dunkards, in the act of the Legislature calling out militia, were exempted. . . . Under the conscript act which is now being put into operation these men will have to enter the army, no provision being made by Congress for their exemption. It seems hard they should be made to pay and fight, too, but as the law now stands there is no help for it.[24]

As might be expected, Brethren leaders now began to exert pressure on the Confederate Congress to secure redress. For example, John Kline wrote to the local representative in the Confederate Congress, John B. Baldwin, urging him to secure acceptance by the Confederate government of the Virginia law which Brethren had worked diligently to secure.

Bowman's Mill, Rockingham County, Virginia
July 23, 1862
I seat myself in behalf of my Brotherhood, the German Baptists, so-

called Tunkers, to drop a few lines in order to give you a correct view of our faith toward our God, and, in consequence of that, our unpleasant standing in and under our government which we now live.

As there is now a session of Congress of the Confederate states on hand of which you are a member and the special representative of our immediate district, I wish to enlist you to advocate our cause in that body. I wish to be short as possible. I will, therefore, at once inform you that we are a noncombatant people. We believe most conscientiously that it is the doctrine taught by our Lord in the New Testament which we feel bound to obey. Having made in our conversion a most solemn vow to be faithful to God in all his commandments, it is and should be regarded by us as the first in importance and above all made by man to man or to earthly government. Hence we feel rather to suffer persecution, bonds, and if need be death than break the vow made to our God.

Yet, as touching things and obligations, which in our view do not come in conflict with the law of God, in whatever way our government may demand of us we feel always ready and willing to do. Such as paying our dues and taxes imposed upon us and assisting in internal improvements, our profession binds us to do. Paying unto the government that which is due it, but that which is due to God we wish to give to him. Through his Son and the apostles, he says "recompense to no man evil for evil." To him we feel to render obedience and therefore are bound not to take up carnal weapons to destroy our fellow man whom he teaches us to love.

We have noticed that those who have been made prisoners and paroled, their oath is regarded by the government. They are let alone and no one presses them into the army. This obligation is only made to man. Why then should not that solemn obligation be regarded by our government, which we have made to our God without any earthly interest whatever? Why not leave that class of men at their homes who can not, for conscience sake, make soldiers to kill others, that they may make provisions for the sustenance of life, which is as necessary to any government as soldiers?

It seems that the late Conscript law made by the Confederate Congress, whether so intended or not, is made use of to overrule or nullify our state law. This law was made by our State Legislature to exempt us from military duty provided each one pays a tax of $500 and two per cent on all taxable property. This, though as oppressive as it is, we were willing to pay hard as it went with some. Now as we are informed through the above cited conscript act of Congress, we are again to be troubled. Our rights given to us by our kind legislature, for which privilege we have paid so dearly, is to be made null and void.

Please use all your powers and influence in behalf of us, so that the Conscript law or all other Confederate laws be so constructed that Christian conscience be so protected that the south shall not be polluted with a bloody persecution.

We as a people try to be as little burdensome to the government as possible. We believe that all the precepts and ordinances of our Lord should be equally regarded and should be practically obeyed according as given to us by the Master. We believe it to be our duty, out of love, to contribute to the poor and needy, and consequently we maintain our poor members and let none of them become dependent upon the country parish. Yet we pay our parish levy as all other citizens. These are some of our tenets given in general terms. In brief, we take the New Testament for our guide and Jesus Christ the man of our religious faith.

Please give this, our request, a candid consideration. At least so much as to write to me your opinion. If we cannot get protection of our Christian liberty in the south, the home of our nativity, we will be compelled to seek shelter in some other place, or suffer bonds and persecutions as did many of our forefathers. For we can not take up carnal weapons of warfare and fight our fellow man to kill him.[25]

In responding to Kline's letter, Baldwin evidently evinced a genuine concern and sympathy, and suggested that the Brethren take steps to prepare a petition to the Confederate Congress. The suggestion was followed and a petition was prepared.

To the Senate and House of Representative of the Confederate States of America.

The Undersigned members of the Tunker and Menonite, churches, in the state of Virginia, respectfully and humbly represent, that at the late session of the state legislature of Virginia, that body passed a law exempting from Military Duty the members of our churches upon each member paying the sum of $500 and 2 per cent upon all his taxable estate. This exemption was based upon the long established creed of faith, of our churches against bearing arms, and is as *we think, we feel,* the *command of God.* While we know there is a strong popular feeling against such doctrine, yet it is none the less dear and sacred to us, who believe it. The question which we represent to you, is not one of persuasion, in favor of our peculiar doctrine, but a prayer, that you may Exercise that same charity, and respect for our opinions, and faith, that we freely accord to others, there are many forms of religious creed and various are the doctrines of Religious faith, but there is no arbiter on earth. God alone is to Judge. But there is a coincidence in civilized society, in its universal respect, for the conscientious conviction, of all Christian Churches, with this feeling and in this spirit we appeal to you to *pass a law, ratifying the act of the legislature of Virginia, on this subject.*

It may not be amiss to state here, that under the excitement of the hour, indiscreet, and inconsiderate persons have preferred the charge of disloyalty against our Churches, this charge, has not the semblance of truth in fact, and has doubtless originated from our faith against bearing arms. We would further state, that those of our members, embraced in said act of the general assembly of Virginia, have already payed the penalty of $500 & 2 per cent, to the officers of the state, and thus fulfilled our contract, and have complied with the law. We only ask Congress, so far, to *respect our rights, our consciences, and the act of the state of Virginia, as to ratify the same.* And we will ever pray.[26]

This petition was presented by Baldwin in the Confederate House of Representatives on September 1, 1862; also, a similar petition was presented by B. F. Anderson, the representative of the Brethren in southern Virginia.
Another factor which helped to influence the minds of the members of the Confederate Congress was a pamphlet entitled, "Non-Resistance, or the Spirit of Christianity Restored," written by William C. Thurman in 1862. Samuel Cline, a Brethren leader in Augusta County, reported that Baldwin, who was from Staunton, wrote to him and asked him to send the best thing that he had on the subject of pacifism; Cline responded by sending Thurman's pamphlet. After the passage of a religious exemption act by the Confederate Congress, Baldwin reported to Cline "that Thurman's pamphlet did the work."[27] What did Thurman write in this pamphlet that made it so valuable?

INTRODUCTION
When gliding on with the smooth tide of popular opinion, all seemed to lend a smile—I knew not a foe. But since the time has come which tries men's souls as to whether they are really the servants of Christ—all turn against me.... But having had no idea of preparing a work for the press, when first I took my pen, I intended only to write out these for my own benefit to guide my feet into the straight and narrow way which leads unto

life; and to put it in a form suitable to leave in the hands of my dear mother and loved friends, that they might know my life was lost for Christ's sake, should the want of a provision in our law for those who think "We ought to obey God, rather than man," cause me to have to share a place with the Christian martyrs.

AN INQUIRY AS TO WHETHER THE CHRISTIAN MAY USE THE SWORD

Though I have during the last ten years so often declared the use of the sword to be incompatible with the Gospel dispensation, and all retaliation for injuries received contrary to that meek and lowly spirit of Christ, which, if a man have not, he is none of his (Rom. 8: 9), since those whom we regarded as faithful servants of our Lord and Savior Jesus Christ, leaving the quiet fold of "The Prince of Peace," have resorted to the use of the sword, and are as deeply involved in this bloody war as those who have made no pretension to the Christian religion; it becomes necessary to give the matter a second investigation and see if it may not be possible that we have been in error; seeing the wise and learned are against us. But if, on a more thorough investigation of the matter, it is discovered that we are not mistaken as to the teaching of our Lord and his apostles, we must cling to the truth and follow their footsteps, though opposed by all the world.

And since the larger body, even of the Christian church, is at the present day governed and controled more by the force of custom than the Bible, we should be but little biased by the opinion of others in our investigation: and calling "no man father upon the earth," Matt. 28: 9, we shall endeavor to follow the teachings of Christ and his apostles only; for the "holy scriptures are able to make us wise unto salvation," 2 Tim. 3: 15, and not the wisdom of man, "for the world by wisdom knew not God." 1 Cor. 1: 21.

That the Christian religion should be neither propagated nor defended by the use of the sword, is a settled question, at least among all Protestant churches. The only point of controversy is, as to whether those who, "putting off the old man with his deeds," have been "born of the Spirit" of "the Prince of Peace," whose kingdom is not of earthly possessions.

But, since all admit that we are not to use the sword in the cause of Christ, nor even as a means of self-defense where it is drawn against us because of our religion; why should it be a question of controversy as to whether we may use the sword in defense of earthly things? Is there in all the Bible the least appearance of authority for supposing the Christian to have a better right to use the sword in defense of that which he is required to forsake,—Matt. 19: 21, 27, 29; Luke 12: 33; Acts 2: 45, 4: 34,—than to obtain that for which he has forsaken all? Matt. 13: 46. And is it not strange that this doctrine, which is too absurd to be worthy of controversy, has become so universal?

Our Lord has positively forbidden retaliation. "I say unto you, that you resist not evil." Matt. 5: 39. But this being too humiliating for the carnal mind, which "is not subject to the law of God," man in his wisdom, since the Christian religion has become popular, ingeniously shields himself from obedience to this soul-humiliating law of Christ by saying that this prohibition is to be restricted to those evils only which are imposed on us because of our religion: in proof of which they refer us to the words of Paul: "But if any provide not for his own, especially for those of his own house, he hath denied the faith, and is worse than an infidel." 1 Tim. 5: 8. And thus they "by good words and fair speeches deceive the hearts of the simple." Rom. 16: 18. But is it not strange that they have so completely deceived the hearts of the simple as to make them believe that while they have no right to defend by force of arms that which is of more real worth than all the world, they may yet defend that which is of so little worth that our Lord regarded it as even unworthy of thought (Matt. 6: 25): yea, requires us to forsake. Luke 14: 33. "For all these things do the nations of the world seek after." Luke 12: 30. The express language of him who has become "the Author of eternal salvation unto all them that obey him" (Heb. 5: 9) is this, "I say unto you, that ye resist not evil." Matt. 5: 39. And I appeal to the honesty of every intelligent man to say what there is, either in the language as used by our Lord, or in the connection in which these words are found, from which we may draw the least inference that it is to be restricted to those injuries only which are imposed because of our religion. If this had been our Lord's meaning, would he not have said so? And since he has not said so, who is wise enough to know that this was his meaning? . . .

But "he who is born of the Spirit" is no more "of the world" (John 17: 16); hence "the weapons of our warfare are not carnal" (2 Cor. 10: 4); for "if any man be in Christ, he is a new creature, old things are passed away, behold all things are become new." 2 Cor. 5: 17.

"If," says the Prince of Peace, "my kingdom were of this world, then would my servants fight, . . . but now is my kingdom not from hence." John 18: 36. So they fight not. Hence when the land of their fathers, their native home and country, was invaded by the Romans, they were forbidden to take up arms, but, leaving all earthly treasures behind, were required to "flee to the mountains." Luke 21: 21.

This, by the world, would be considered ignoble, unmanly and cowardly. He who would at the present day carry out the spirit of this precept would be despised as one unworthy to live; "for the carnal mind is enmity against God, for it is not subject to the laws of God, neither indeed can be." Rom. 8: 7. Therefore he that would at a time like this have worldly friends, is compelled, in disobedience to Christ, to take up arms. "Whosoever therefore will be a friend of the world, is the enemy of God." James 4: 4.

The Mosaic dispensation, being that of justice between man and man in case of injuries, the law enjoined retaliation: "life for life, eye for eye, tooth for tooth" (Exod. 21: 23, 24) was required. But the Christian dispensation being that of grace, all retaliation is forbidden. Hence the Prince of Peace in giving his law, refers to the Mosaic thus, "It hath been said, An eye for an eye, and a tooth for a tooth: but I say unto you, that you resist not evil," by returning evil for evil. "But whosoever shall smite thee on thy right cheek, turn to him the other also." Matt. 5: 38, 39.

That the apostles taught this same doctrine, we notice that Paul, more than thirty years after, enjoined the same precept upon the church at Rome, saying: "Recompense to no man evil for evil." Rom. 12: 17. And again he enforces this law, saying: "Dearly beloved, avenge not yourselves, but rather give place unto wrath: for it is written, Vengeance is mine, I will repay saith the Lord. Therefore, if thine enemy hunger, feed him; if he thirst, give him drink; for in so doing thou shalt heap coals of fire on his head. Be not overcome of evil, but overcome evil with good." Rom. 12: 19-21. Peter also enjoins the same law, "Not rendering evil for evil, or railing for railing: but contrariwise, blessing: knowing that ye are thereunto called that ye should inherit a blessing." 1 Pet. 3: 9.

We will now inquire as to the example of Christ, in regard to this his own law of nonresistance. We learn from Matt. 26: 6, 7, that the Jews spit in his face, and buffeted him; and others "smote him with the palms of their hands": "who, when he was reviled, reviled not again: when he suffered, he threatened not, but committed himself to him that judgeth righteously." 1 Pet 2: 23. Instead of retaliation, or resisting those who were about to slay him, he prayed, saying, "Father, forgive them; for they know not what they do," Luke 23: 34, thus "leaving us an example, that ye should follow his steps." 1 Pet. 2: 21. "Now if any man have not the Spirit of Christ, he is none of his. Rom. 8: 9.

The example of the apostles in obedience to this law of the Prince of Peace, is as follows: "Being reviled, we bless; being persecuted, we suffer it; being defamed, we entreat." 1 Cor. 4: 12, 13. When "buffeted," they bore it. 1 Cor. 4: 11. When beaten, instead of retaliation, they rejoiced "that they were counted worthy to suffer shame" for Jesus' sake. Acts 5: 41. When Paul and Silas received "many stripes," instead of exhibiting a spirit of revenge, they "prayed and sang praises unto God." Acts 16: 25.

"Seeing that many glory after the flesh," says the apostle Paul, "I will glory also." But in what did he glory? In those things in which the world glories? No! Just the reverse. He gloried in that he had "five times received forty stripes, save one." 2 Cor. 11: 24. . . .

But, perhaps we are going on too fast; let up pause and think a moment. These words are either true or untrue. Our Lord either meant what he said, "Except ye repent, ye shall all likewise perish" (Luke 13: 5), we believe he meant just what he said. And are those who use the sword to share the same fate with those who do not repent? As all must perish who are saved by Christ, so none can be saved by him who refuses to obey him. Hear his express language: "Not everyone that saith unto me, Lord, Lord, shall enter into the kingdom of heaven, but he that *doeth* the will of my Father which is in heaven. . . . Therefore, whosoever heareth these sayings of mine, and doeth them not, shall be likened unto a foolish man, which built his house upon the sand, . . . and it fell, and great was the fall of it." Matt. 7: 21-27. Now, one of the "sayings" to which our Lord had reference, was this: *"I say unto you, that ye resist not evil."* Matt. 5: 39. Now I ask, Can we use the sword without disobedience to our Lord? So the use of the sword must be one of those carnal ordinances with "which all that use are to perish with the using." Col. 2: 22. "For all they that take the sword shall perish with the sword." Matt. 26: 52. "He that killeth with the sword must be killed with the sword. Here is the patience and the faith of the saints." Rev. 13: 10. "For with the same measure that ye mete withal it shall be measured to you again." Luke 6: 33. . . .

That the first Christians, as foretold by the prophets, did cease from war, Paul says, "We do not war after the flesh." 2 Cor. 10: 3. That they use neither the sword, nor any other carnal weapon of warfare, he declares "the weapons of our warfare are not carnal." 2 Cor. 10: 4. . . .

The lamb-like subjects of the Prince of Peace are required to love even their enemies, which celestial love consumes and destroys forever the spirit of war; for that meek and lowly spirit of love, which "beareth all things" (1 Cor. 13: 7), "worketh no ill to his neighbor." Rom. 13: 10.

When this Prince of Peace made his appearance on earth, he was introduced to the people of God by "a multitude of the heavenly host praising God, and saying, Glory to God in the highest, and on earth peace, good will towards men." Luke 2: 13, 14. Therefore "the kingdom of God is righteousness and *peace*" (Rom. 14: 17), the very reverse of war and wickedness.

"God hath called us to peace" (1 Cor. 7: 15), not to strife; for the Christian's God, into whose image and likeness he must be transformed, is "the God of love and peace" (2 Cor. 13: 11), and not "the god of battle." In war there is "hatred, variance, emulation, wrath, strife, envyings, murders." And "they which do such things shall not inherit the kingdom of God." Gal. 5: 21....

"But the wisdom that is from above is first pure, then *peaceable,* gentle, and easy to be entreated; full of mercy and good fruits; and the fruit of righteousness is sown in *peace,* of them that make peace." James 3: 17, 18.

The Christian is required to "follow *peace* with *all men,* and holiness, without which no man shall see the Lord." Heb. 12: 14. And can those who take just the opposite, that is, follow war and unrighteousness, ever see the Lord?

In war there is a continual retaliation, or returning of evil for evil. But the Christian can "recompense to no man evil for evil" (Rom. 12: 17); hence he cannot go to war. In war men avenge the evils imposed by other nations, which the Christian is forbidden to do. "Avenge not yourselves, but rather give place unto wrath."

In war men overcome their enemies by pouring on them more evil than they are enabled to return or withstand.

But the little flock of Christ must take a path leading just in the opposite direction. They must *"overcome* evil with good." Rom. 12: 21.

Do not those who meet on the battlefield hate each other? "Whosoever hateth his brother is a murderer, and ye know that no murderer hath eternal life abiding in him." 1 John 3:15....

But, says one, when the soldiers inquired of John as to what they must do, he did not tell them to ground their arms, but to "do violence to no man." To this we answer: Had these words been delivered by one of the apostles to the Christian church, after the opening of the gospel reign of peace, the question would have been settled, and I never would have raised my pen to prove that the Christian has no right to use the sword.

But we must remember that these words were spoken *before* the Prince of Peace had issued his law for the government of his church; and they were addressed, not to the Christians, but to Roman soldiers, who, if ever they became Christians at all, did not till at least nine or ten years afterwards. Therefore we ask, What has this to do with the question at issue? We have never said it was wrong for the people of the world to use the sword.

That the powers that be, the kingdom of the world, may use the sword, Paul in allusion to such, says, they bear "not the sword in vain." Rom. 13: 4....

But it is asked, Are we not required to be "subject unto the higher powers"? To this we answer yes. But we are nowhere required to be subjects *of* the higher powers. The devils were subject unto the apostles through Christ. Luke 10: 17. Were they also subjects of the kingdom of Christ? If men, ceasing to add to the Word of God, or ceasing to believe the apostle meant something he has not said, would hold fast to the form of sound words (2 Tim. 1: 13), as used by the apostle, they would not "wrest the scriptures unto their own destruction" (2 Peter 3: 16), by saying the apostle here gives license to the subjects of the kingdom of Christ to take up arms when required to do so by the government under which they live. The apostle does not say: Let the Christian be a *subject* of the powers under which he lives. His express language is: "Let every soul be subject unto the higher powers" (Rom. 13: 1), which, being in the plural, embraces all powers; hence lays us under as much obligation to be subject to all other powers as to the one under which we live. And since we cannot be the subjects of all higher powers, this proves that be being "subject unto the higher powers" he did not mean that we must be the subjects of those powers.

And if we are not the subjects of the powers of the earth, then we are under no obligation to bear arms. For example: The prisoners you take in war are "subjects unto," but not subjects of, your government. Hence you do not require them to bear arms. Or if a stranger from another kingdom sojourns among you, he is subject unto, but not a subject of, your kingdom; hence is under no obligation to take up arms in time of war, until he takes the oath of allegiance. Many such are now in this country; some at the call of the government have entered the army as soldiers, others have refused, but those who have refused have in this resisted no law of the higher power, seeing they are not the subjects of your government....

Here it may be asked, Since the higher powers, acknowledging as it were the existence of no such kingdom as that of the Prince of Peace, do require their subjects also to take up arms, how shall we reconcile Paul's liberty to the Christian, "Let every soul be subject unto the higher powers," with Christ's unconditional law, "Resist not evil"? To which we answer, if by the expression, "be subject unto the higher powers," the apostle meant an active obedience, then it would be irreconcilable; but that he meant only a passive subjection is clear from the text itself. For he, speaking in the plural, lays us under as much obligation to be subject unto all powers, as to the one under which we live. And this, you know, would be morally impossible, had he meant an active subjection; for if in obedience to one of the powers of earth, I take up arms and resist another, then I am not subject to the one I resist. And since we are positively and unconditionally forbidden to resist any of the higher powers, we can only be subject to them all in a passive sense. The subjects of the Prince of Peace, as pilgrims and sojourners in a strange land, must be "subject unto the higher powers" of earth; but they must not be subjects of those powers.

It is true, we are born subjects of the government under which we live; but as he who is dead has ceased to be a subject, so he that is dead with Christ from the rudiments of the world, has lost his citizenship, and is no longer a subject of the kingdoms of earth, though passively he is subject to them all. By regeneration and the new birth, he has been translated from the kingdom of this world unto the kingdom of Christ, the Prince of Peace. And as those who were baptized unto Moses had no more to do with the kingdom of Egypt, but were under obligation to fight the battles of the kingdom of Israel, so those who are "baptized unto Christ," having left the kingdom of this world, are under obligations to fight no battles, save those of the Prince of Peace: the weapons of whose warfare are not carnal. 2 Cor. 10: 4. . . .

Reader, ponder well and bear in mind that since the Prince of Peace has positively and unconditionally forbidden his subject to resist evil, all the authorities and powers of earth cannot repeal that law. And yet, until that law is repealed, the resisting of evil on the part of the Christian is open rebellion to Christ, his King, though by all the powers of earth combined he may be required to do so. Hence when, by the authority of the world, the Christian takes up arms, he tramples the authority of Christ, his King, beneath his feet, and makes the authority of man superior to that of Christ,—he becomes the servant of him whom he obeys. Rom. 6: 16.

One law of Christ our King was this, "Go ye into all the world, and preach the gospel." Now when Nero, emperor of Rome with all the authority and power of his kingdom, required the apostles to cease to do this, they chose rather to obey God than man.

Another law of Christ our God, as given in terms yet more positive, by using the expression, "I say unto you" is, "that ye resist not evil." Matt. 5: 39.

And since "he that saith, I know him, and keepeth not his commandments is a liar, and the truth is not in him" (1 John 2: 4), had we not as well renounce the religion of Christ at once, as to refuse to obey him? We are to be "subject unto the higher powers" in all things that do not conflict with the clear law of Christ. But since "no man can serve two masters" (Matt. 6: 24), when the higher powers require us to do that which our Lord has forbidden, "we ought to obey God rather than man." Acts 5: 2.

But we are often asked questions like this: Was not George Washington a good Christian? To this I answer, "I know nothing by myself" (1 Cor. 4: 4). If you prefer the example of Washington and other good men to that of Christ, I have only to say, "calling no man father upon the earth" (Matt. 23: 9), I choose rather to follow the example and obey the precepts of Christ and his apostles *only*.

If, by the new birth, Washington had entered within the pales of the new covenant dispensation, then he did violate the laws of heaven in resisting the higher powers. But I know no law forbidding those to use the sword who do not belong to the new covenant dispensation of peace. For the "higher power" is as properly "the minister of God, a revenger, to execute wrath upon him that doeth evil" as the peaceable lambs of Jesus are the ministers of Christ to "teach all nations" (Matt. 28: 19) "the way of peace." All we contend for is, that the two kingdoms, the kingdom of the world and that of Christ, be not blended together. . . .

Is there a minister of the Gospel under the canopy of heaven who does not admit the the precepts and example of Christ and his apostles are to the Christian a living *law?* Then why deny what you preach? If honest, you are compelled to admit that Christ and his apostles did both by example and precept, teach the doctrine of nonresistance; insomuch that when everything dear to them on earth was being destroyed, their near relatives, friends and neighbors were falling "by the edge of the sword and led away captive into all nations" (Luke 21: 24), so far from being permitted to take up arms to resist the desolating foe, they were commanded to "flee into the mountains," and that under a law too strict to allow a man even to "return back and take his clothes" or "anything out of his house." Matt. 24: 16-18.

And if they "took joyfully the spoiling of their goods," why may we not suffer loss for Christ's sake? "Knowing in yourselves that ye have, in heaven, a better and enduring substance." Heb. 10: 34. . . .

The Gospel of Christ is "the Gospel of *Peace.*" Eph. 6: 15. "As it is written, How beautiful are the feet of them that publish the gospel of peace." Rom. 10: 15.

In conclusion, we admit that this doctrine of nonresistance is humiliating to the flesh; but ponder well, and then answer the following question: From the example and precepts of Christ and his apostles, what appears to have been the object of the Gospel: Was it to moralize, raise and exalt the people to a more elevated sphere, that they might be the happier during the present life? *Or was it to prepare a people for heaven at the sacrifice of every earthly thing?*[28]

An interesting compliment to Thurman's work from a non-Brethren source appeared in "The Friend," a journal published in Philadelphia.

Being a non-resistant in principle, he refused to take up arms, and was exempted by the authorities at Richmond, Virginia. He afterwards wrote and published this Tract on the subject of non-resistance. Copies were sent to the members of the Richmond Congress, and it is said the arguments used had much influence in inducing them to pass a law exempting from military service those who are conscientiously opposed to bearing arms. The arguments are presented in a sober, devout, strain, and are almost entirely scriptural. . . .[29]

The result of all the cumulative pressure was the enactment of an amendment to the law of April, 1862, which included a provision for exemption from military service for religious reasons.

VII. Friends, Dunkards, Nazarenes, and Mennonites.

All persons of the above denominations in regular membership therein on the 11th day of October, 1862, shall be exempt from enrollment on furnishing a substitute, or on presenting to the enrolling officer a receipt from a bonded quartermaster for the tax of $500 imposed by act of Congress and an affidavit by the bishop, presiding elder, or other officer whose duty it is to preserve the records of membership in the denomination to which the party belongs, setting forth distinctly the fact that the party on the 11th day of October, 1862, was in regular membership with such denomination.[30]

Brethren had now secured the exemption they sought, and they turned to the task of raising the funds necessary to compensate for the exemption. Not all of the young men being drafted could raise $500, and much of the money was contributed by older members, such as John Kline. The following note was found in his memorandum book of 1862-1863.

December 30th, 1862

I paid to Mr. Woodward, the Receiver of fines, $500 for each of the following persons:

Harvey Fifer	George W. Ritchie
Philip Baker	William Ford
Samuel R. Wine	George Rodecap
Adam Ritchie	John A. White
George Smith	Adam Andes
James W. Fitzwater	John B. Kline
William Spitzer	Isaac Kline
Henry W. Moyers	George Kline
Jacob Fitzwater	Samuel Kagey[31]

Also, the diary of John B. Crenshaw, a leader of the Society of Friends in the Richmond area, refers to the payments made to secure the exemption of Friends and Brethren.

1862 10th month 18th.... We paid the tax for five Friends and three Dunkards, $4000....
1862 10th month 20th.... Met some of the Virginia Dunkards brought here as conscripts, some of whom had paid the $500 tax into the State Treasury. At their request I drew up a petition to the Secretary of War, asking that those who had paid the tax might be allowed to return home until the legislature meets, when they hope to be allowed to draw the money from the State treasury to pay the Confederate treasury.[32]

John Kline agreed with John B. Crenshaw that it was certainly not right for the Brethren and Friends to be required to pay $500 to both the Virginia and the Confederate governments for exemption from military service. On November 17 John Kline wrote a rather strongly worded letter to the local authorities who were trying to collect a second $500 for the Confederate government.

I take this opportunity to write you concerning a letter that I saw yesterday from your hand to Mr. Andes, on the subject of fines imposed on our Brethren in order for them to be exempted from military duty. There seems to be something wrong. Why press those who have paid to the State? Cannot the Confederate Government as well indulge the State until she will pay it over as the individual who paid? Why trouble and harass those who have paid their fines and have their certificates from the sheriff? Or, why trouble even those of our members who have not yet paid and are desirous to pay as soon as they can? Even before the government has designated a proper person to receive the fines this has been done by the scouts. It seems to me you could save yourself and us a great deal of trouble by telling the scouts not to bother those who could establish their membership by one or two neighbors or members until the proper arrangements are made. When that is made by the government, the State may be ready to refund and we may have the necessary arrangement to meet the difficulty. There are many who are not able to pay their heavy fines. Others have to make this up and it is not done in a few hours or even days. All we ask is to have a little time and to be let alone for a while. Why this running the people who have by law been exempt, the distance of from two to twenty-five miles to Harrisonburg and again to a justice to certify to that which every one knows to be true?[33]

In the southern Virginia Brethren settlement in the Roanoke area Brethren were also having some difficulty securing the exemption from military service to which they were entitled by both state and Confederate laws. B. F. Moomaw, a prominent Brethren leader in the Botetourt County congregation, described both the problem and the solution.

The Brethren in Roanoke have been until lately much annoyed by the quartermaster in that county, refusing to allow them the benefit of the exemption. At length, however, I reported him to President Davis. He sent the case to the Secretary of War. He ordered him (the quartermaster) to report to Richmond and give an account of his conduct. I afterward met him in Salem, when he made a furious assault on me, cursing and threatening violently. I calmly told him I disregarded him; despised his threats; that he must understand that he could not intimidate me and when he interferes with our rights I will attend to him. Since that time the Brethren have been unmolested.[34]

Certainly, in dealing with the government during a time of national crisis, the separatistic Brethren could expect to have problems. Sometimes these problems were complicated by the fact that Brethren had to deal with two different governments: a state government, like that of Virginia, and a national government, like the Confederate government. But in spite of all of the problems, the Brethren still had much for which to be thankful, as B. F. Moomaw indicated in a letter to John Kline.

Botetourt City, Virginia
December 16, 1862

You may be surprised at my writing to you so soon again. The object is to inform you that the brethren here seem to be so deeply convicted of the duty resting upon them of making a public manifestation of their gratitude to God for his special providence in so overruling the hearts of the late Congress of the Confederate States of America, as to release us from military service. While we agree with those brethren who say that the heart of every brother and sister should be drawn out in secret to God, yet we think, inasmuch as it was a public exhibition of his special providence, we should make a public demonstration of our gratitude. We have, therefore, set apart New Year's Day as the time to attend to this duty and heartily invite all those churches that feel so disposed to cooperate with us. You will please, after you read this, pass it to the Shenandoah Brethren.

I will here inform you that our military authorities are so construing the exemption bill as to deprive those few brethren that are in the army under the conscript act, from its benefit. I have just written to the Secretary of War upon the subject. If his answer is unfavorable, I will petition congress for an amendment, as soon as it convenes.

The cause of the Lord is still onward. We received five members by baptism last Sunday. We are tolerably well. Thank God for his mercy! May you be sharing like blessings.[35]

For the remainder of the War, the Brethren were exempted from military service on the basis of the action of the Confederate Congress of October 1862. However, the Confederate Congress reviewed and modified the draft law periodically, and every time it engaged in such a review suggestions were made to eliminate the religious exemption clause, which of course frightened the Brethren. B. F. Moomaw reflected that concern in two letters to John Kline in the fall of 1863.

Botetourt City, Virginia
September 2, 1863

Yours of the 13th ult. was duly received, which like all such communications from brethren, was like a calm to our troubled souls, for there is nothing in these times of sorrow to make the heart glad except our spiritual associations and those messages of love from brethren whose spirits are congenial with our own. You speak of the Governor's message to the Legislature as being fraught with mischievious design toward the brethren. You and I discover from the expressions of some of the members of that body that they are fully prepared to carry out his inhuman recommendation, and thus inauguarate a system of persecution, the like of which is only known to the dark ages of the religious world. But this measure is not passed yet from latest accounts and I still hope in the kindness of an overruling providence who has hitherto so signally protected his people, and if it be the will of God that we should be protected, he will still find instruments in the councils of the country to disappoint the intention of our enemies. I hope that there are still enough who cherish the blessings of religious freedom to control the final action of the Legislature. May God in his mercy so order it.

But the question that I would ask if the Legislature be so lost to every sense of Christianity as to require our brethren to go into the army, what is to be done? I will here give you the reflections of my own mind upon the subject and await an answer. We have in every case complied with the requirements of the government, because we could do so without a departure

Benjamin F. Moomaw

from our principles, but if they now require us to go into the army without any alleviation, what shall we do? What can we do? Shall we not unanimously petition for permission to leave the country with, or without property?

I forgot to say to you in the proper place that I think that our friend, J. T. Anderson of Botetourt, is chairman of the Committee on Military Affairs, if so I hope that he will exert a salutary influence in our favor.

Botetourt City, Virginia
December 27, 1863

Through the mercy and grace of God, our kind and heavenly Father, myself and family and the brethren generally are well for which we return our grateful thanks for his unmerited favor, and hope that when this comes to hand it may find you enjoying the same blessing. The object of my writing at this time is to inform you that by the appointment of the brethren, Bro. B. F. Byerly and myself intend, God willing, to start to Richmond tomorrow to try to cooperate with those friendly to our cause to make some arrangements to help our brethren out of the military service. We intend to present before the authorities the manner that we have lived, as loyal citizens complying with every requirement of the law; paying our commutation, our tax in kind; what we have done for the destitute and suffering soldiers and the quantity of produce that we are making, according to the number of hands employed, etc., giving some instances. Such for example, as this: one farm employing one substitute, one exempt on religious grounds, and their boys, has listed to the commissioner 1100 bu. of wheat,

1200 bu. of corn, 200 bu. of oats, 100 bu. of potatoes, 4500 lbs. of pork, 4500 lbs. of beef, etc. If nothing can be done in this we are authorized to request a peaceable passport out of the country, constantly averring that we cannot nor will we fight. If you have any thing that you think will favor the cause or wish to communicate with me, you can address me at Richmond. I should be glad to hear from you.

We held an election yesterday for two ministers. The lot fell upon Bro. Jonas Graybill and John C. Moomaw. While we are thus engaged, be engaged yourself and exhort the brethren to be engaged with the Lord for us, that we may still lead a quiet and peaceable life in all Godliness and honesty.[36]

The Brethren were successful in persuading the government not to make any changes in the conscription law. Moomaw's letters are probably most interesting because of their proposals that the Brethren attempt to leave the country, if the government attempted to force them into the army. Was he bluffing or would the Brethren actually have attempted to leave?

Most of the Brethren living in the Confederacy were in Virginia, but there were smaller numbers of Brethren in Tennessee and in North Carolina. Little is known about the status of the Brethren in North Carolina, although they were very probably profiting from the fact that there were a considerable number of Friends in that state, who generally secured rather generous provisions for the religious groups that were opposed to military service. The only known reference to the North Carolina Brethren is found in the Crenshaw diary: "10th month 22d. At Camp Lee found that the Friends had gone home, except young Gordon, who was too sick to go; also the North Carolina Dunkards. The Virginia Dunkards are not yet through with their cases."[37]

In Tennessee, Brethren were numerous enough to create problems for the authorities, as indicated in a letter written in February 1863.

Leesburg, Tennessee
February 24, 1863

Brother Lovegrove [?] was here yesterday and he seams to be in sum trubble about his sons   thay are booth in the church and there finds are paid but sum time ago the marshel demanded all of there sirtificats which they all gav up which he sent [to] Knoxvill to Col blake for approval or to obtain a finnel discharge   now the inroling officer refuse to Sine and thretin them with arest and Say the Law is repeld and they in tend to have us in fild yet   now as for my part I have no fears   yet they may put us to sum trubbles   will you bee so kind as to send me a form of the discharges the brethren have in thoere as it mite be sum satisfaction to sum of the brethren[38]

The leaders of the church in Tennessee finally decided that the only way to secure satisfaction of their grievances was by the preparation of a petition to the Confederate Congress and by the sending of a representative with this petition to Richmond. This action in 1863 was described many years later in the 1890s by P. R. Wrightsman, who was the young man selected to go to Richmond. He also described some of his experiences on the trip.

In framing an Act for the relief of nonresistants, the Confederate Government, upon the payment of a tax $500 each into the public treasury, relieved our Brethren for the time; but in the latter part of the war when the South needed all the men in her borders, the local authorities arrested many of our Brethren and shut them up in prison and in the stockades in various places, even after they had paid the $500 penalty. This very much tried our Brethren in East Tennessee. So a council meeting was called at Limestone church, and a petition was drawn up to send to the Confederate Congress, asking that our brethren be released from military service, as we were and always had been opposed to bearing arms. Nearly all the members of our church signed the petition. It then became a matter of anxious concern who would carry this petition to Congress and represent our claims. All our older brethren shrank from going to Richmond where Congress was in session. I was away at school; yet it was decided to send me though a youth as I was. The deacon brethren came to see me and to report their mission. I regretted to leave school and pleaded with them that older brethren should go, but they replied that it was the act of the church. I replied that I was willing to do anything in my power for my brethren in prison. "If you and the church will aid me in your prayers, I will go."

Accordingly I prepared myself with provisions for the journey and started from Limestone depot. I had not traveled far until a minister came on the train. I believe he was from North Carolina. After leaving Jonesboro, he came and sat down on the same seat with me. So far as I could see we were the only civilians on the train, the remainder were all soldiers. He asked me if I were a minister, and I replied that I was. He then asked me to what church I belonged, our faith and practice, to which I replied. When I mentioned the fact that we were a peaceable people and opposed going to war, he said, "Do you not think we all ought to fight for our glorious Confederacy?" I replied that Christ taught us not to resist evil. "Yes," said he, "but this war is an exception." I replied, "Christ made no exceptions, but says, Love your enemies; bless them that curse you; pray for them that despitefully use you and persecute you."

Failing in this he tried another line of reasoning: "Do you not believe General Washington was a good man; and that God used him to set up this government?"

"Now," said I, in return, "do you believe God used General Washington to set up this government?"

"Yes," he replied.

"Then what do you think God will do with you for trying to tear down what he built up?"

He never answered me, but arose and went into another car.

During our conversation the soldiers were all around eagerly listening. But when I put my last question to him some of the soldiers made some threats; but I felt the Lord was with me. I was not in the least alarmed, and continued my journey without further interruption.

At the proper time I went to the House of the Confederate Congress, presented my petition and made my plea stating among other things that our people were always a peace people; it is no use to take them to the army, for they will not fight. They would be just in your way. They are the best subjects in your government, for they stay at home and mind their own business. They are mostly farmers, raise grain and your men come and take it. In this way we feed the hungry. Our people never molest your men, but are loyal and law-abiding citizens. If you will let us stay at home, we will be loyal citizens to the powers that are over us. We humbly plead for your acceptance of our petition.

Alexander H. Stephens was then consulted; and finally my petition was accepted, and officially endorsed with the word "Granted."

With a heart overflowing with gratitude to our dear heavenly Father, I came on to my home at Limestone, Tenn. Brother M. M. Bashor met me at the depot and urged me to continue on to Knoxville on the same train, as some of our brethren had been taken off while I was at Richmond. So I continued my journey eighty-four miles further to Knoxville. I went to see Col. E. D. Blake, commander of conscripts and prisoners and showed him my papers. With an uncouth remark he told me to go out to the stockade and get my men. I went, entered the stockade, and got my brethren out of prison. We all went home like happy children. This was in the summer of 1863.[39]

In this manner Brethren worked out an arrangement with the government in Tennessee as they had done in Virginia.

In the North, Brethren did not seem to have as much difficulty working out arrangements for exemption from military service, perhaps because

*both state and national governments were well established at the begin-
ning of the War in 1861. For example, the state constitutions of Pennsylvania, Indiana, Illinois, Iowa, and Kansas all made provisions for exempting the Brethren from militia duty upon the payment of an amount
considered to be equivalent to such service. The constitution of Ohio
placed the matter in the hands of the state legislature to decide. On the
basis of existing laws in most of the Northern states the question of draft-
ing those individuals who were opposed to military service evidently did
not arise in 1861.*

*However, the Federal Militia Act of July 17, 1862 followed by General
Order #99 on August 9 provided for the mustering of the state militia as
called by the President. Nothing was said about religious exemption, and
the various groups opposed to military service sprang into action. In Iowa
the Mennonites, the Friends, the Dunkers, and the Amana Inspirationists
petitioned the governor and the General Assembly for exemption from
military service. Samuel J. Kirkwood, the governor of the state, in a
message to the legislature on September 3 supported the petition.*

There are in this State some religious bodies who entertain peculiar
views upon the subject of bearing arms, and whose religious opinions conscientiously entertained, preclude their so doing. Their members are among
our most quiet, orderly, industrious and peaceful citizens, and their sympathies are wholly with the Government in this struggle now going on for
its preservation, yet they cannot conscientiously bear arms in its support. It
appears to me it would be unjust and wholly useless to force such men into
the army as soldiers, and yet it would not be just to the Government or to
other citizens that they should be wholly relieved from the burdens that
others have to bear. I suggest, therefore, that these persons who cannot
conscientiously render military duty, be exempted therefrom in case of
draft, upon the payment of a fixed sum of money to be paid to the State.[40]

*The legislature refused to accept the governor's recommendation,
however, and eventually approved a measure permitting the furnishing of a
substitute or the payment of $300.*

*In Indiana the governor of the state, O. P. Morton, wrote to the
Secretary of War, Edwin M. Stanton, requesting guidance on the amount
to be paid in lieu of militia duty.*

Indianapolis, Indiana
September 24, 1862

The constitution of the State of Indiana contains the following provision:

No person conscientiously opposed to bearing arms shall be compelled to do military duty, but such person shall pay an equivalent for exemption, the amount to be prescribed by law.

Our Legislature has omitted to fix any equivalent for such exemption. This omission can be supplied by you under section 1 of the act of July 17, 1862. Will you please fix the amount and advise me of it as early as possible.[41]

Stanton assigned the matter to the Assistant Adjutant-General, C. P. Buckingham, who in turn wrote back to Morton for his recommendation. Morton suggested "not less than $200. per man," which was accepted as a proper amount. Consequently Brethren in Indiana evidently had a relatively small sum to pay in exchange for their exemption from military duty.

Next door in Ohio, where there were also many Brethren, the problem was handled in about the same way. David Tod, the governor of the state, reported to Edwin M. Stanton in October.

Columbus, Ohio
October 5, 1862

Without any well-defined authority therefor, I have exempted all State and county officers, also members of religious denominations whose creed forbids taking up arms, upon payment of $200 each; all of which I ask you to approve. I purpose using the money thus obtained in hiring substitutes and in caring for the sick and wounded, through Quartermaster-General Wright.[42]

In Ohio, as in Indiana, there evidently were no serious problems for the Brethren.

In Pennsylvania, where there were more Brethren than in any other state, the state constitution provided for exemption from military duty for religious reasons and required a payment which usually took the form of a levy upon one's property. Just to make sure that these provisions would continue to be honored during the War, a Brethren congregation in Adams County, Pennsylvania drafted the following petition and delivered it to the government.

We the members of the German Baptist Church in upper Canawago Adams Co. Pa. Do In the 1st Place acknowledge us indebted to the most high God, who created Heaven and Earth the only good Being, to thank him for all his great Goodness and Manifold Mercies and Love through our Savior Jesus Christ, who is come to save the Souls of Men, having all Power in Heaven and on Earth.

To the Honorable the Governor of Pennsylvania We Send Greeting two of our Brethren Elder Adam Brown & Saml. Longenecker as a Committee to wait upon the Governor of the State of Pa. In particular in allowing those, who, by the Doctrine of our Savior Jesus Christ are persuaded in their Consciences and who do not find Freedom of Conscience to take up Arms. And Every Prayer according to Article Sixth Space 2 of the Constitution of the Commonwealth of Pennsylvania. Those, who Conscientiously Scruple to bear arms, Shall not be Compelled to do so: but shall pay an equivalent for personal Service. We, according to Christ's Command to Peter, to pay the tribute and to render unto Cesar those things that are Cesar's, and to God those things that are God's although we think ourselves very weak to give God his due Honour, He being a Spirit and Life and we only Dust and Ashes.

We heartily Pray the testimony we lay down before our worthy Governor and that We are not at Liberty in Conscience to take up Arms. But pray to God to govern all Hearts of our Rulers to meditate those good things which will pertain to Our and Their Happiness. Amen.

The above Declaration signed by the Elders and Teachers of the Society of German Baptists of Upper Canawago Church, Adams Co. Pa. Presented to the Hon. the Governor of Pa. given under our hands this 29th day of August A. D. 1862.

Elders and Teachers	Deacons and Members
Adam Brown	Daniel Baker
Daniel Langenecker	Peter B. Kaufman
Andrew Brugh, Jr.	Peter Trimmer
Samuel Longanecker	Israel Brown
Jacob P. Lerew	[?] Sowers
Adam Hollinger	Cornelius R. Burkhalter
John B. Zeigler	Daniel D. Firestone
	John Trimmer
	John Brough
	Daniel Sowers[43]

Fortunately for most of the Brethren in Pennsylvania, they were well represented in the United States House of Representatives by Thaddeus Stevens. Typical of Stevens' convictions on their behalf was this part of a speech he made on February 24, 1863:

There are in all countries exemptions for conscience sake, and it is right that there should be. In my own county a very large number of our best citizens, our most loyal men, are conscientiously opposed to bearing arms. They are willing to pay their taxes; they would be willing to pay this amount to procure substitutes, but I do not believe that they should be forced to violate their conscientious and religious scruples which have existed from their birth, and which have descended to them from posterity.[44]

In spite of Stevens' convictions, however, when the United States government passed its first conscription law on March 3, 1863, there was no provision for exemption on religious grounds. Those individuals who were drafted could secure substitutes or they could pay $300.

Sec. 13—*And be it further enacted,* That any person drafted and notified to appear as aforesaid, may, on or before the day fixed for his appearance, furnish an acceptable substitute to take his place in the draft; or he may pay to such person as the Secretary of War may authorize to receive it, such sum, not exceeding three hundred dollars, as the Secretary may determine, for the procuration of such substitute; which sum shall be fixed at a uniform rate by a general order made at the time of ordering a draft for any state or territory; and thereupon such person so furnishing the substitute, or paying the money, shall be discharged from further liability under that draft.[45]

During the following year extensive pressure was exerted on the United States Congress, especially by the various Meetings of the Society of Friends, to make provisions for religious exemption from the draft. As a result, when a new law was enacted in February 1864, it did include such a provision.

That members of religious denominations, who shall by oath or affirmation declare that they are conscientiously opposed to the bearing of arms, and who are prohibited from doing so by the rules and articles of faith and practice of said religious denominations, shall when drafted into the military service, be considered noncombatants, and shall be assigned by the Secretary of War to duty in the hospitals, or to the care of freedmen, or shall pay the sum of three hundred dollars to such person as the Secretary of War shall designate to receive it, to be applied to the benefit of sick and wounded soldiers: *Provided,* That no person shall be entitled to the provisions of this section unless his declaration of conscientious scruples against bearing arms shall be supported by satisfactory evidence that his deportment has been uniformly consistent with such declaration.[46]

Very likely Brethren were quite pleased with this new legislation.

Finally, in this section dealing with Brethren efforts to secure exemption from the conscription laws in the North, it is informative to follow the actions of one member of the church, William Knepper, in Franklin County, Pennsylvania. He evidently secured exemption from the Pennsylvania laws on medical grounds, but then when that exemption did not hold in the eyes of those administering the United States law of March, 1863, he had to pay the $300 in "Commutation" money.

Chambersburg, Franklin County, Pa.,
September 25th, 1862.

It is hereby Certified, that I have this day duly Examined William Knepper of Quincy township Franklin County, Pa., and find that he is rendered incapable of performing Military Duty by reason of deficiency of vision chronic

A. H. Senserry, M. D.
Examining Military Surgeon of Franklin
County, Pa.

I concur in the above.
J. Brotherton, M. D.

Form 31

CERTIFICATE OF NON-LIABILITY TO BE GIVEN BY THE BOARD OF ENROLLMENT

We, the subscribers, composing the Board of Enrollment of the Sixteenth District of the State of Pennsylvania, provided for in section 8, Act of Congress "for enrolling and calling out the national forces," approved March 3, 1863, hereby certify that William Knepper, of Quincy Twp., Franklin county, State of Pennsylvania, having given satisfactory evidence that he is not properly subject to do military duty, as required by said act, by reason of Paying Commutation, is exempt from all liability to military duty under the present Draft.

C W Eyrter
Provost Marshal, and President of Board
of Enrollment.

WAR AND MILITARY SERVICE

Jm. L. McIlherring
Member of Board of Enrollment.

R. S. Seiss
Surgeon of Board of Enrollment.

Dated at Chambersburg, Pa,
this 16th day of October, 1863.

Note.-This certificate is to be given in all cases where it is applicable, according to the 2d, 3d, 13th, and 17th sections of the act of Congress referred to above.

No. 486 Office of Receiver of Commutation Money,
16th District of Penna.

Received at Chambersburg on the 17th day of October 1863 from William Knepper Quincy Twp Franklin Co Pa who was drafted into the service of the United States on the Twenty Ninth (29th) day of August 1863, from the Sixteenth (16th) Congressional District of the State of Pennsylvania the sum of Three Hundred (300) Dollars, to obtain, under section 13 of the "Act for enrolling and calling out the National Forces, and for other purposes," approved March 3d, 1863 discharge from further liability under that draft.

Ed Scale
Receiver of Commutation Money.[47]

WAR CONDITIONS AT HOME

Especially in modern times wars have increasingly tended to become total wars, involving all of the population. The Civil War involved the Brethren at home in many ways in addition to the pressure exerted by the government to secure manpower for the armies. George Snapp, a young minister in the United Brethren Church, which was a type of German Methodism, served a circuit in Rockingham County, Virginia, during a part of the War. He described in a diary some of his wartime experiences and some of his contacts with members of the Church of the Brethren.

Mond. morn. we started for Churchville some 20 miles distant where the Methodist were holding their Ann. Conference, the mud making it very difficult traveling. . . . Tues. morn. weather lowering, all met at conf. room about 9 Oclock; this being the first Methodist conf. I ever had the privilege of attending, I felt anxious to see how they did business and how a methodist conf. looked.   they did not wish to be wanting in parlimentary rule. I did not find that gravity and order which was expected, there seemed in their policy a greater disposition to please men, than God.   this day there was some discussion of politicks which produced considerable enthusiasm, in the conference. I was much astonished at this, indeed there was manifest much sectionalism, and but little universal love which is the bond of perfection, the conf. took an action here this day denouncing all its members within the federal lines an eternal separation from the North and a perpetual allegiance to the South and its divine institution. also a solemn ratification of something called the Staunton platform by a unanimous vote of the eclesiastical body. When a little dutch-man's name was called he got on his tip toes and exclaimed, "Mr. President, I wish I could not only say aye with my lips, but deep down in my heart *aye*." these things deeply pained my poor heart, and I could say with one of old, "O! What folly in Israel." these things made a sad impression on my mind which will never be erased. conf. closed this afternoon. there was in attendance nearly all of this branch of the methodist ministry in the confederacy, and the church was crowded with spectators from day to day not withstanding the inclemency of the weather. . . . Sund. Mar. 21 road some 6 miles and reached my 1st appointment which was 10 Oclock at Union Schoolhouse. on reaching the place, I found it occupied by a comp. of soldiers which had been camping there some several weeks. I told them there was an appointment for preaching there that day. they said they had herd nothing of it, but would be glad to hear preaching and would right up the house if I would stay and preach to them. I declined and said as no congregation had met there, possibly there were arrangements made at some other place in the neighborhod for preaching. I went one mile farther on to Bro. Wm. Thackers and preached in his house to a small congregation from Psa. LXXXIV and 1,2. . . . in the evening I mad my way to my sunday appointment at Mt. Tabor Church. found the church occupied by soldiers, and in a filthy condition. some were amuseing themselves with the chess board, etc. went to Abram Longs and staid all night. Sunday, April 5th Easter, this day, snowy. before leaving today, went up stairs and talked with several Confed. Soldiers, who were sick, in regard to their souls. they made little reply. one of them died soon after. as the church was not in a condition for holding meeting I went to the appointment which was next in turn at Mountain Valley 5 miles distant at 3 Oclock P.M. Stopped for dinner at old Bro. Stricklers. found this a very kind christian family. preached at the church and went to the next appointment about 6

miles distant, at Bethlehem Church on the Vally turnpike and preached at
night. tolerable congregation, but they did not know that the last time I
was in this house I was held with many other citizens as a prisoner of war.
neither did I wish to tell them. went to the widow Pickerings and staid all
night. Monday went to Bro. Howes new situation in the afternoon. went to
old Mr. John Clines, preacher in the Dunkerd church, living on Linville
Creek and staid all night. afternoon very high wind with rain and snow. I
felt very much at home here like I always do with my guard house friends.
was very kindly received and entertained here. after supper while sitting in
his room around the fire, several of his neighbors came in and one of the
number was the post master from the office near by with several letters,
and a little package very carefully enclosed with many rappings of paper.
the sight of all this seemed to lift the kind old man up very much. he spoke
freely of his augmented eclesiastical and medical engaguements, etc., while
he opened and read the letters. then he commenced opening the little
package, (with its heavy postage unpaid), eager to ease the excited mind
when lo! and behold, a deck of cards were in his hand. it mad the innocent
old man blush considerable. I felt sorry for him but said to him O! dont
mind that, they have got into good hands. yes he says I'll know what to do
with them. Tuesday went to old Mr. Keisers living on Shenandoah river
and spent most of the day. he is preacher in the Baptist Church, O. S. and
a very strong Union Man. the time was spent very pleasantly. he spoke
much and wept over the evils of this war and the suffering condition of our
Zion of God. the old man seemed much cast down; when I left he was
much affected and said he hoped to meet me in Heaven. May the Lord
bless him, Amen. in the evening went to Mr. Phillip Hollers and staid all
night. this man is a dunkerd and also one of my guard-house friends. here I
found two others of the same class. we had a very pleasant time together.
they told me that a neighbor of theirs, Mr. Beery, said it would go with the
South like it did with a swarm of bees of his. he said about the commencement of the war, he had a swarm of bees that seceeded. They swarmed at a
very unseasonable time, he hived them, but they did not do well at all. they
did not work right. some time afterward they came out again in great confusion and flew about in the air until a great many of them fell down on
the ground and died. the remainder of them went back into the old hive
from whence they came out first and that was the last of it. so he said it
would be with the southern Confederacy. . . .

Friday. Aug. 7th heavy showers. Afternoon, started out on a pastoral
visit. went through Harrisonburg and thence towards Edom. night over-
taking me, and with some difficulty in the dark, I made my way to the
house of Jos. Richey's where I expected to find a United Brethren family

and a nights lodging. After hollowing some time, a man came out to the fence and spoke in a low whisper. (having lost his speech in the army.) asked what I wanted. I told him I would like to stay all night with him. he said his wife and child and himself were all sick and he could not keep me. I had already become vexed and began to think strongly my case was a pretty bad one. being an entire stranger and in an entire strange neighborhood, I asked what should be done. he told me gout to the road and go on about one quarter of a mile farther and take off to the left and the first house I reached I could stay all night, where a Mr. Myres lived. I thought it an uncertain business to undertake to hunt a strange place in the dark night, but reached the place without any difficulty. I hollowed and asked if I could stay all night. was answered with, "I reckon," which was enough for me. was kindly received by the old lady and her daughters, the old man having gone to bed. I made out to get my horse away myself. the first thing I wished to was if they were religious and what church they belonged to. they said they were of the Dunkerds. soon found them very nice, kind, and hospitable, as I believe all the Dunkerds are. felt perfectly at home.[48]

Another way in which Brethren in the South were affected by the War was the loss of the men of military age by emigration. A considerable number of young Brethren fled from the South to safety with friends in the Ohio River Valley. How many were involved will never be known. Some of those who attempted to escape were not so fortunate and were captured. One group of more than seventy, not all of whom were Brethren however, was captured in present-day West Virginia and taken to a prison in Richmond. Joseph Miller, who was one of the group, explained what happened.

In the early part of March, 1862, having been informed that all the men subject to military duty would be called to arms in a very few days, Brother David M. Miller and myself concluded to do something to keep out of the war. We heard of some Brethren and others intending to go west, and we made preparations to go too, being hurried by our wives, who feared we would be arrested and taken to the army before we got started. So we lost no time in preparation.

After traveling about twelve miles, we fell in company with about seventy others—Brethren, Mennonites and others. The conclusion among us was to cross the line to West Virginia. So with the Shenandoah Mountain before us, we proceeded, going part of the way during the night. The next day we traveled on west, and the next night we lodged at a friend's house, resting on the floor. The next day we arrived at Petersburg, W. Va. Now a good many persons came out to see us cross the South Branch of the Potomac River, it being fifty yards or more wide, and more than half our company were on foot, so that in crossing some horses had to go three trips before all had passed over the stream. It seemed to be a great curiosity for the people to see us cross the Branch and to go through the town.

Soon after passing this place came the trouble, as we then thought, but it seemed that the good Lord did not think as we did; he prepared a better way for our escape than we had marked out for ourselves. After going through Petersburg, he sent two men to cause a halt in our journey, one in front, and one in the rear. The man in front made use of some hard words, but the man in the rear was kind. We halted, and at their solicitation we turned back to Petersburg. They took us into a large upper room and as we passed in by the door we were asked individually whether we had any arms. When the question was put to me, I answered, "Yes." "Let us see it," said he. I showed him my New Testament, the Sword of the Spirit. He said, "that is very good; you can keep that." I do not think there were any arms found in our company, except one or two small pistols, and they were not with the Brethren. We were furnished a snack for dinner.

One brother Mennonite, who had talked of going back before we got to Petersburg, and I had encouraged him to go on, said to me, "What are you going to do now?" I replied, "Stand still and see the salvation of the Lord."

My brother, D. M. Miller, and I had near relatives in Hampshire county, about thirty miles further on, and we expected to lodge with them until we could go back home; and the Lord let us all go within a few miles of the line between the Northern and Southern armies, then turned us back by the hand of two men. How good he is; but we could not see it at that time. We wanted to go on.

We were next ordered to leave the upper room and travel south towards Franklin, the county seat of Pendleton county, West Virginia. We were guarded by eight or ten men. Not reaching Franklin that day, we lodged with Mr. Bond, where one of our company (not a brother) got away. A brother and myself had all chances to get away that night, but we had no desire to leave the brethren. The next night we lodged in the court house in Franklin, sleeping on the floor, and guarded. At this place, six or seven others, that had been captured as we were, joined our number, making in all about seventy-eight. During the night, six of us were taken out one at a time, and asked where we were going, and the reason why. We told them the truth, that we were going away only to keep from fighting, that it was contrary to our faith, and contrary to the Gospel to fight and kill our fellow-man,—entirely wrong to do so. We were not abused. At this place one brother lost his horse and his clothes.

The next day we went twenty-four miles to Monterey, the county seat of Highland county, Virginia. Then next morning we started for Staunton, Va., distant fifty-two miles. We had a barrel of crackers and a few pieces of bacon on a wagon. It took us two days to go through and over the foot-hills and to cross the Shenandoah Mountain; and while we were going over the mountain, one brother got away. In going up the mountain pathway on foot, some one else riding my horse along the main road, we were scat-tered very much. It seems that the guards had confidence in us. Brother Cool and I were walking together, and I was showing him where I was ac-quainted. We had got so much scattered that no one was in sight of us in front or rear. Brother Cool said, "Let us slip." I replied, "I do not feel to do so." We continued on the way till we came to an old vacant house where we lodged for the night. The officer of the guards said, "Gentlemen, I will trust to your honor tonight." Then he and the guards went away about half a mile to get their lodging. After they were gone, Brother Thompson said to me, "Some of the brethren talk about running off to-night; what do you think about it?" I said, "I do not like that." Said he, "Suppose we send for the guards?" I said, "Do so," and they were soon there, drew us into line and counted us. They had so much confidence in us that they thought we would stay without being guarded, but Satan might have made us all dis-honest that night had we not been watchful of ourselves and on our guard.

The next day we went to Staunton, Augusta Co., Va., and lodged in the courthouse. We got plenty to eat. The guards were overheard saying, "Don't tell them that they have to go to Richmond to-morrow; they will not sleep well." It would have disturbed us some, if we had known it; for we did not yet know that Richmond was the place the Lord had directed us to go.

In the morning after breakfast, with some crackers in our pockets, and a little sadness in our hearts, we started on the train for Richmond, distant 120 miles, leaving our horses and saddles in the care of some one else. We were all day and part of the night on the way to Richmond. After reaching our destination, we were put into a large room in a machine house with a small stove. There was about three yards in one corner to which we had no access. The officer said, "Gentlemen, this is the best we can do for you to-night; make yourselves easy." This was the most unpleasant night for me on the trip. The weather being cool, with no fire and no bed, some of us walked nearly all night. Next morning breakfast came about 9 o'clock, but it came plentiful. We staid in that house one night only, then we were moved to a more comfortable house, and furnished with bedding and provisions.

In a day or two twelve of us were taken before Judge Baxter, and he said, "Gentlemen, I will ask you a good many questions, and if I ask any that you cannot answer, you need not say anything." He then asked many questions concerning what we had been doing during the war, and whether we had been in the service. He also asked us whether we had fed the soldiers and their families. We answered all his questions save one, and the judge was kind enough to answer that for us; which was, "Would you feed the enemy, should he come to your house?" He said, "We are commanded to feed our enemies." This was a correct answer. Before dismissing us the judge said that we would be sent home soon to work on our farms.

Just at this time the Confederate Congress was in session in Richmond, and some of the members of Congress came in to see us. Some of them wanted us to volunteer to drive teams; but we told them we left home to keep out of the war, and that we did not propose to go into the army service. Others wanted to know all about our faith, and we gave them all the information about our religious belief that we could. They also found out that twenty-five of our people were in prison in Harrisonburg, who had been arrested as we were, and that many others had gone through the lines, and we were told they got the question up in Congress, "What would we better do with these men? They raise more grain to the hand than any farmers we have, and they are nearly all laboring men, and we need them at home as much as in the Army. Would we not better make some provision for them, or they will all leave the country? If we force them into the army, they will not fight."

These things were brought to us in the guardhouse. So the question was considered in Congress, and they reached the conclusion to lay a fine on us, and send us home. The fine was fixed at five hundred dollars each. This may look like a large sum, but the Brethren at home soon sent the money to us, and we paid it, and went home. The poor brethren as well as the rich had their fine paid. It was not long after that till a good horse sold for a thousand dollars which paid two fines. This fine paid in 1862 cleared us during the war, which lasted three years more.

We were in Richmond thirty days. A few days before we left Richmond, six of us were taken before Judge Baxter again. He treated us very kindly, and expressed his sore regret that we had been kept there so long, when we should have been at home on our farms. He said the delay was on account of the press of business, and that we would soon be sent home, which came to pass. We were joyfully received at home by our families and the brethren. We were absent from home in all thirty-seven days. Our horses were kept in Staunton and put into service, but we received pay for them from the government. No money was taken from any of our company, and upon the whole we were kindly treated.[49]

Seventy-four men reached Richmond and were imprisoned in Castle Thunder, which was being used for political prisoners. They were interviewed, as Miller reported, by S. S. Baxter, an official of the Confederate War Department. He issued three reports. The first listed twenty-seven men who evidently were not church members and were therefore prepared to serve in the army. The second and third reports dealt with the remaining forty-seven and his recommendations regarding them.

Richmond, March 31, 1862.
Report of S. S. Baxter of prisoners examined by him

I have examined a number of persons, fugitives from Rockingham and Augusta Counties, who were arrested at Petersburg, in Hardy County. These men are all regular members in good standing in the Tunker (Dunkard) and Mennonite Churches. One of the tenets of those churches is that the law of God forbids shedding human blood in battle and this doctrine is uniformly taught to all their people. As all these persons are members in good standing in these churches and bear good characters as citizens and Christians I cannot doubt the sincerity of their declaration that they left home to avoid the draft of the militia and under the belief that by the draft they would be placed in a situation in which they would be compelled to violate their consciences. They all declare they had no intention to go to the enemy or remain with them. They all intended to return home as soon as the draft was over. Some of them had made exertions to procure substitutes. One man had sent the money to Richmond to hire a substitute. Others had done much to support the families of volunteers. Some had furnished horses to the cavalry. All of them are friendly to the South and they express a willingness to contribute all their property if necessary to establish our liberties. I am informed a law will probably pass exempting these persons from military duty on payment of a pecuniary compensation. These parties assure me all who are able will cheerfully pay this compensation. Those who are unable to make the payment will cheerfully go into service as teamsters or in any employment in which they are not required to shed blood. I recommend all persons in the annexed list be discharged on taking the oath of allegiance and agreeing to submit to the laws of Viriginia and the Confederate States in all things except taking arms in war....

April 2, 1862
Supplemental report on the case of
the Tunkers (Dunkards) and Mennonites.

Since my last report I have seen the copy of the law passed by the Legislature of Virginia on the 29th of March, 1862. It exempts from military duty persons prevented from bearing arms by the tenets of the church to which they belong on condition of paying $500 and 2 per cent. on the assessed value of their property, taking an oath to sustain the Confederate Government and not in any way to give aid or comfort to the enemies of the Confederate Government, with the proviso that if the person exempted is not able to pay the tax he shall be employed as teamster or in some character which will not require the actual bearing [of] arms, and surrender any arms they possess for public use. I renew my recommendation that these persons be discharged on taking the oath of allegiance and an obligation to conform to the laws of Virginia.[50]

On the basis of Baxter's recommendations and of the action of the Virginia legislature on March 29, 1862, the imprisoned Brethren and Mennonites in Richmond were released after about one month in captivity. Thus, a major crisis in the life of the Brethren in Virginia had been overcome, since there had been a very real possibility that the group might be executed for treason.

At the same time Brethren were dealing with a similar crisis in Rockingham County, where a second group of about eighteen was imprisoned after trying to escape and being captured in present-day West Virginia. J. M. Cline recounted his experience during this incident.

We started after night from Brother Jacob Miller's, and rode all night. On the next day we came to the camp of the pickets. We rode on as unconcerned as possible, trusting in Providence; but after passing the camp about a mile some of our number said, "Look out! yonder they come after us." We increased our speed a little; but some of the brethren called on us to stop, as a number of the party could not ride fast. So we all checked up, except one or two that rode on and got away. I think the most of us could have gotten away, but we had each other's welfare at heart. We knew, if some of us should get away, it would only make it worse for the rest. We were then in sight of Moorefield, and we were consulting how we could get through the place. Some thought we could go around through the mountains, but we did not have the pleasure of getting into or around Moorefield. As soon as we all stopped, more of the pickets came up, and we were taken back to picket camp where they kept us till next day. In the evening they took all our money and everything we had from us. Some of us never received anything back, while I believe some did.

They put us all in a room, where we lay on the floor with our budgets for a pillow. But we had worship before we retired. We prayed for our release, and for our captors. The next day they brought us over through the mountains to Woodstock. They let us ride on our own horses, and at different places we saw chances to make our escape, but the thought was with us all the time that if some of us do make our escape, it will only make it harder for the rest.

At last we got to Woodstock, and we were then relieved of our horses, saddles and bridles for good. We could see them from our prison windows, riding our horses around. The next day they walked us up to Mt. Jackson with our budgets to carry the best way we could. At Mt. Jackson they put us into a large upper room. We did not omit having worship, and some of the guards were seemingly affected. For a day or two this was our lodging place, but we were then brought to the upper end of town, and put in a little room with guards around the doors. A part of the time we had to go nearly up to the river where there was a large barn to load wagons. This was generally after night. Sometimes two or three guards would take all of us, and we would string out far enough that they could not see us all. They would call to us to keep closer together, but we often got far enough apart to get away, if we had tried to do so.

At last the time came to move us up to Harrisonburg. They marched us up the pike to the Bethlehem church without anything to eat that day, but sometime in the night they got us something to eat. The next day they brought us up to Harrisonburg, and some of us nearly gave out on the way. A man by the name of Miller had charge of us as well as the guards, and to show his authority, he would every now and then say, "Close up the prisoners!" He even got so vicious as to command the soldiers to stick them with the bayonet. When we would meet any person, he would say, "Close up the prisoners!" This he did to show his authority. But he came to a bad end at last. I think he never did any good.

When we arrived at Harrisonburg, we had the honor of having our home for about two weeks in the courthouse. Here we were fed principally by friends who brought us boxes and baskets of good things to eat. After we were there a few days we all got a kind of epizootic and had it not been for Brother John Kline, it did seem that we could not have lived. It did seem that the Lord had him to come there to take care of us. As a physician he took care of us in our sickness, and as a minister he preached for us several times at night, and on each Sunday.[51]

As Cline noted, a fellow-prisoner in Harrisonburg was John Kline, the most prominent Brethren leader in this area. The group of eighteen was captured late in March 1862 and evidently arrived in Harrisonburg about

April 1. John Kline was arrested and brought to the same place of im-
prisonment in the county court house on April 5. In his diary, he described
his two weeks of imprisonment.

SATURDAY, April 5, 1862. This forenoon I am about home. In the afternoon I am taken to Harrisonburg and put in the guard house. My place is in the large jury room of the court house, up stairs, with others who are captives with myself. Rain this evening.

SUNDAY, April 6. Rain and snow all last night, and continues on so all day. Have preaching in our captive hall. My subject is "Righteousness, Temperance, and a Judgment to Come." I aimed at comforting my brother captives and myself with the recollection that Paul was once a captive like ourselves, and that in this state of imprisonment he preached upon the text which I have selected for this day....

TUESDAY, April 8. Rain and snow continue as on yesterday. Our room very uncomfortable.

WEDNESDAY, April 9. Still cloudy, with rain and snow. We have some pleasant conversations in the prison, with books and papers. But all the public prints are so filled and taken up with war that they give me but little enjoyment. The minds and spirits of nearly all the prisoners are so broken down by the state and prospects of the country that interesting and instructive conversations can hardly be held.

THURSDAY, April 10. The following beloved brethren and dear sister came in to see us to-day: John Zigler, John Wine and Christian Wine, Benjamin Miller, Joel Senger, and Catharine Showalter, daughter of Brother Jacob Miller and wife of Brother Jackson Showalter. The sight and presence of these brethren refreshed us much; and the dear sister carries sunshine with her wherever she goes. Last night and this morning regiment after regiment passed through town on their way down the valley in the direction of Winchester.

SUNDAY, April 13. We have meeting to-day. I speak from Matt. 11:28, 29, 30: "Come unto me, all ye that labor and are heavy laden, and I will give you rest: take my yoke upon you, and learn of me; for I am meek and lowly in heart; and ye shall find rest unto your souls: for my yoke is easy and my burden is light."

MONDAY, April 14. To-day our two brethren, John and Joseph Cline, are released from imprisonment, and start for home to-night.

TUESDAY, April 15. I am not well. The dampness of our room and the lack of comforts in the way of bedding and fuel have given me a cold from which I am very hoarse to-night.

WEDNESDAY, April 16. There is talk that we are to be removed to

New Market. The talk is correct. We leave here at twelve o'clock, and come to Bethlehem church where we stay all night. This church is between nine and ten miles northeast of Harrisonburg on the valley pike leading from Staunton to Winchester.

THURSDAY, April 17. Start for New Market; but after getting on two miles hear the cannons at Mt. Jackson. We turn and go back to Harrisonburg. News comes of the retreat of Jackson's army. Front of the Federal army at New Market. Jackson halts for the night at Lacy Springs.

FRIDAY, April 18. Great excitement and confusion in town. General Jackson with his army passes through in his retreat, and the Federal troops are hourly looked for. Gabriel Heatwohl, Joseph Berry and myself are released from the guard house. I dine at Samuel Shacklett's; then walk out to Samuel Niswander's three miles, and ride from there to Jacob Miller's, where I stay all night.

SATURDAY, April 19. Brother Benjamin Bowman brings me on my way home nearly to Christian Wine's. I walk the short distance to Brother Wine's; get a horse of him, and come home.[52]

While John Kline was imprisoned, he used some of his time to write a letter to the editor of the "Rockingham Register," which had reported critically the imprisoning of the Brethren and others. Evidently, Kline's letter was never published by the "Register."

In your isue of the 11th inst. I see an article headed, Union men taken, in the article several names are mentioned, who was known to have *strong Union proclivities,* otherwise the article makes no nominal charge against us, which of course it was out of your power to do, but the article carries with it a strong insinuation as though we had used our influence against the confederacy, if this has been so, why not come out and point to the place where, or when, and what the act or deed, and if this cannot be done, which I know it cannot, then why shut us up in the guard house? Why make such false insinuations against good and inocent citizens and publish them to the world? Why contrary to the Constitution, take up men without their accusers making affidavit that the thing charged was to their knowledge true? but all that is now nessisary is for some vague friend to raise a falsehood and tel it to some of his Captains, who have no better principle than themselves, and law and Constitution is at an end. if this is the kind of laws that we are continding for, then may the Lord save us from it, but I think by the quivolous movement so far transacted there has been more done to make Union men and against the south then all the in-

Rockingham County
Courthouse at the time
of the Civil War

fluence of the union men ever did, because they were inactive. This influence is active, first because near all those men that are taken are known
to be *inocent,* second it shows to the world that those who are engaged of
arresting such men on nothing but falsehood and misrepresentation, are
acting under a cowardly fear of being overcome, and thirdly, it is keeping
all such out of employ, and usefullness, at home preventing them from
making provition both for man and beast, fourth it is keeping just so many
men out of the army as are engaged of guarding those, and weakening the
army that much, and fifth it makes a considerable expence upon the
government which all could be avoided, besides many other privations and
usefullness both to their families and neighborhood.[53]

*Even though John Kline's letter to the editor was not published, he
had had the opportunity to express his sentiments in writing; also, his writing the letter evidently did not work against his securing his freedom, for
only three days after he wrote the letter he was released. His release was related to the imminent arrival of Northern troops. Quite probably his
guards did not want to be around when the enemy arrived.*

The Brethren in Tennessee also found it desirable to flee from their homes on occasion to escape from military service. P. R. Wrightsman was a young man during the War, and in 1864 he was drafted, according to his report.

In February of 1864 I was conscripted. Learning of their coming after me, some of my neighbors, with myself, fled to the mountains in the night. With snow knee-deep, and provisions on our backs, we plodded up the mountainside.

At break of day we halted and prepared something to eat. Here we remained, in the snow-capped mountains, for a number of days. When we received word that the soldiers were coming after us, we went to the settlement, and hid until the panic of excitement passed away. I then returned home.[54]

Wrightsman was evidently successful in escaping the pressure of the draft.

Another approach used by some of the Brethren in East Tennessee was to take refuge with the Brethren in southern Virginia. B. F. Moomaw reported in September 1863:

There has been, and still is a number of Refugees in the county from East Tennessee. But the Federals are falling back towards Knoxville and some of the refugees are going back.

B. F. Moomaw also reported in this letter of September 2, 1863, to John Kline concerning the death of John A. Bowman of Tennessee.

I suppose you have before now heard of the melancholy death of poor John A. Bowman of Tennessee. He was killed in his own stable some three weeks ago under the following circumstances. A man was discovered about to take his riding horse. He approached toward him and when coming pretty near, the man ordered him not to approach but John still advanced expostulating with him and finally took hold of the horse when he shot him through the abdomen and then clave his skull with the butt of his gun. So ends his eventful life and it is thought will end his church.[55]

Moomaw's final statement about "his church" refers to the fact that a division had developed among the Brethren in Tennessee in the years before the Civil War. Bowman had been excommunicated from the church for defending himself in a court case, after he understood that he had the permission of the church. Eventually, a dispute had arisen over the issue, and he ended up establishing a schismatic church. This was the way things stood at the time of his death. However, James R. Gish and Henry Garst were dissatisfied and appealed to the Annual Meeting of 1866, which appointed an investigating committee. The Annual Meeting accepted the committee's conclusion that Bowman had been unjustly excommunicated and that all of those whom he had baptized after being excommunicated would be accepted as Brethren without re-baptism.

Bowman's death was probably the most tragic event in the life of the Brethren in Tennessee, but there were other incidents, according to the report of P. R. Wrightsman.

Being a minister as well as physician, my business called me over considerable territory. In the spring of 1862 Southern soldiers came to my house searching for firearms, none of which I kept except a plantation rifle. This they took without pay. They came from time to time for three years and took my crops and horses. When the soldiers came for the last horse they rode up with threats and curses. Their language and manner impressed me that they came with intent to kill me. Part of the squad went to the field for the last horse and part remained with me under their charge. I just stepped inside the stable, stood with my hands upwards, and prayed to my heavenly Father, saying, "Dear Father, save me from these men. Have mercy upon them, and turn them from their evil course, and save thy servant."

I never exercised stronger faith in prayer than at that time. It seemed as if I was speaking face to face with my blessed Lord. When I stepped out to the soldiers I felt that God had answered my prayer, for I could see the Satanic look going down out of their faces like the shadow of a cloud before the bright sunlight.

The soldiers then said to me, "Mr. Wrightsman, can we get some bread?" "O yes," said I, "we are commanded to feed the hungry." I went at once to the kitchen and requested my sisters to cut off a large slice of bread, and butter it for each one of them. They did so and I took it out into the yard and handed a slice to each. They thanked me for the bread, bowed their heads, mounted their horses and rode away, taking my last horse with them, however. Feeling sure the Lord had saved my life, I felt happy, "thanked God and took courage." This occurred in the summer of 1863. . . .

In the autumn of 1864, our church at Limestone, Tenn., had prepared

P. R. Wrightsman

to hold a love feast, as all seemed to be quiet just at that time. So on the fourth Saturday in September we started for the church with provision necessary to hold the meeting. But, behold! there on our grounds around and near the church, was a regiment of soldiers. Many of our members were frightened, and some of them urged the dismissal of the meeting. I told them, "No, let us go on with the meeting. Perhaps the Lord has sent them to this place to hear the Gospel." This delayed our decision. In the meantime the colonel heard of our dilemma and at once sent us word to go on with our meeting, that nothing should be molested, but that we should be protected. So we went on with the services, invited the soldiers into the church and our house was crowded. It proved to be one of the best love feasts that I ever attended,—the best of order and attention prevailed. Not a thing was molested, all behaved well, and many requests were made for us to come to their part of the country after the war and preach for them. But, alas! many of those poor men no doubt fell on the field of battle.[56]

Another account of the War in Tennessee in the winter of 1862-1863 indicated something of the wartime inflation as well as the difficulties of freight transportation because of the disruption caused by the War.

Washington County, Tennessee
January 5, 1863

I have to confess, that I have been to negligant in not answering yours, but had concluded of not writing before I had procured your molasses and being unwell at a time I had set to attend to it and harder to get then I had immagened with out paying such a price $3.00 per gallon and Mary intended to send you them 2 gallons that she had told you but under the presant circumstances there cant be no freight sent   No doubt you have heard of the affairs in Tenn. before this time how the Federals have dashed in here 3 regiments of mounted cavalry and burning 2 rail road bridges across Holstein and Watauga Rivers and taking them prisoners that were guarding the bridges but I intend to send you the molasses if the repairs are made soon if it is only them 2 gallons and you can inform me whether you would be willing to give those prices.[57]

An item in the papers of David H. Plaine, to whom this letter was being written from Tennessee and who lived in the Roanoke, Virginia, area, demonstrated the inflation that had gripped the Confederacy by the beginning of 1864.

Sales Sundries Made by William H. Jones for and on account Mr. David H. Plaine

1864						
Jany 20	Cash	2	Bushels Onions		$25	50.00
21	"	1	Can Lard 59½ 5½ 54 lb		$4	216.00
22	"	1	Bucket Butter 37 lb		$5	185.00
28	"	1	Bag Dried Apples 27 lb			25.00
Febry 8	"	1	Bag Raspburys			5.00
10	"	7	Doz Eggs		$2½	17.50
17	"	1	Box Butter 15 lb		$6	90.00
"	"	7	Bushels Potatoes		$10	70.00
"	"	2	Shoulders Bacon 41 lb		$5	205.00
29	"	½	Bushel Onion		$25	12.50
....						
Febry 19		2¼	Yards Gingham		$10	22.50
"		3	Gallons Molasses		$40	120.00
20		4	Pounds Coffee		$15	60.00[58]

Poor families were particularly hurt by the inflation in the South. To some extent, at least, Brethren showed a concern for these people and their problems. For example, the following was reported in the "Rockingham Register," which was not usually very sympathetic with the Brethren:

Some time ago when flour was selling from twenty- to twenty-five dollars at the mills I happened to notice a poor man hand over to one of the Tunker friends two ten dollar notes for a barrel of flour, and he returned him one of the tens. The same evening I saw a poor woman hand this same man money for a barrel of flour and I inquired afterwards how much she paid and I found she only paid ten dollars. I came directly to the conclusion that this man certainly is a loyal man to his country, although I never heard him open his mouth about his loyalty.... I am satisfied that this was not an exception to the general rule, but only one case out of many that I could mention where molasses, apple butter, corn, dry fruit and a variety of other necessaries of life have been sold to the poor and the refugees for less than half or one-third less than others.

In the same article, it was also reported on a related topic that the Brethren

... never turn away any that are in want, where they have it possibly to spare ... and ... the refugees ... who have been driven from their homes by the fiendish Yankee enemy, could hardly have remained amongst us if it had not been for the kindness of the Tunker and Mennonite friends.[59]

The Brethren themselves learned what it was like to be treated as refugees as the result of the campaign in the Shenandoah Valley in the fall of 1864. It all began when Jubal A. Early, a Confederate commander, launched a surprise raid on the Washington area in July 1864. U. S. Grant, the Union commander who was attacking Robert E. Lee and his Confederate army in Virginia, was embarrassed by this attack on Washington and issued orders to a Union General, David Hunter:

Monocacy Bridge, Maryland
August 5, 1864

In pushing up the Shenandoah Valley, where it is expected you will have to go first or last, it is desirable that nothing should be left to invite the enemy to return. Take all provisions, forage, and stock wanted for the use of your command; such as cannot be consumed destroy. It is not desirable that the buildings should be destroyed; they should rather be protected, but the people should be informed that so long as an army can subsist among them recurrences of these raids must be expected, and we are determined to stop them at all hazards. Bear in mind the object is to drive the enemy south, and to do this you want to keep him always in sight. Be guided in your course by the course he takes.[60]

Hunter was replaced a few days later by Philip H. Sheridan, who now commanded the Union army's invasion of the Shenandoah Valley. Two major Union victories in the Winchester area in September opened the Valley to the Union army. Evidently, the Union army generally concentrated on the destruction of livestock and grain products until the death on October 3 of John R. Meigs, one of Sheridan's engineers, who was shot near the town of Dayton. Sheridan ordered the burning of all houses within five miles. Before the orders had been completed, they were recalled, but certainly, a number of Brethren families living in this area suffered extensive destruction. Joseph Bowman, one of the Brethren living in this area, described the destruction.

A great many of the brethren and neighbors had all their buildings burned. There was a little town called Dayton, two miles and a half from where we lived, which was burned and all the houses & barns within two miles around it. Our buildings were not burned but my sister's and nearest neighbors were. Oh! brethren, it is hard to leave our homes, and our brethren and friends, and to leave our property behind and suffer the troubles we had to undergo since this war. I had good property there, upwards of two hundred acres of land. My father and mother lived with us and are with us now. My father's name is John Bowman; he is in the seventy-fifth year of his age, and we are now in a strange country, and have but a little to go upon, and everything is high. Our consolation is that we are among the Brethren who have been very kind to us for which we desire to be thankful.

The widespread destruction of the property of the Brethren encouraged a considerable number of them to accept Sheridan's offer to "furnish one team and wagon to each Union sympathizer to transport his belongings and family beyond the boundaries of the Confederacy." In other words, the Union army would escort them to safety. In his report of the incident, Sheridan noted that from "the vicinity of Harrisonburg over four hundred wagonloads of refugees have been sent back to Martinsburg. Most of these people were Dunkers."[61] Joseph Bowman was one of these Brethren, and he seemed to indicate that a large number of the members of the Garbers congregation, which was probably the hardest hit by the destruction, had accepted Sheridan's offer.

We lived in Rockingham Co., near Harrisonburg, in brother Solomon Garber's church. There were seventy-one or seventy-two members left their homes out of our district, besides friends and children. There were three speakers in our church, and two come out: brother John Eberley, and John Flory. There were five deacons and three came away: brother Samuel Miller, Joseph H. Harshburger, and Myself.[62]

That this number of Brethren refugees from the South created some problems for Brethren in the North was indicated in a letter from Indiana in 1865.

Ladoga, Indiana
August 12, 1865

Most of the refugees from the Valley church were in this vicinity & they flocked together so much that people did not like to hire one of them of a Sunday at places where they hired. I am [told] that 25 or 30 came to stay all day just to be together. At Mr. Pefleys 30 came to see their hired man & a few got ashamed and went to old brother Kesler's (a near neighbor.)[63]

Brethren in the South were generally quite fortunate that they lived through the Civil War with the loss of nothing more than property. However, there were two notable exceptions: the first was the death in Tennessee of John A. Bowman, which has already been explained; the second was the death in Virginia of John Kline, the influential churchman and physician from the Linville Creek congregation, north of Harrisonburg. He was shot from ambush by local Confederate bushwhackers on June 15, 1864. The local report was published by the "Rockingham Register" on June 24.

The Rev. John Kline, of Linvill's Creek, in this county, an aged Tunker preacher of considerable prominence, and a man of great influence with and in his church, was shot and killed near his residence, about eleven o'clock on Wednesday morning of last week. He had gone to a neighbor's in the direction of Turleytown, we learn, to clean a clock, and was on his return when the tragedy occurred. He was shot in the groin and breast with four balls, and is supposed to have been instantly killed. He had some money and his watch on his person when he was killed,—these were not disturbed by the party by whom he was slain.

He was known as an uncompromising union man, and during the early part of the war had been arrested by order of Gen. Jackson for disloyalty. He had however been honorably acquitted, and was pursuing "the even tenor of his way," passing frequently by permission of our authorities within the Yankee lines to preach and hold other religious services. He was a man of the strictest integrity in his business transactions, and was highly esteemed in his church, whose membership will mourn his death as the removal of one of the pillars of the church. The motives which induced some assassins to waylay and kill him will probably be never fully known and understood; but the cause of his death doubtless had some connection with the troubles that now afflict the country, occupying as he was believed to do, a position of antagonism in feeling to the Confederacy. Whilst our people differed with Mr. Kline in the erroneous views which he entertained, yet all good citizens must deplore such a lawless wreaking of vengance upon the person of an unarmed and feeble old man.—Such things show how rapidly we are drifting into scenes which must be full of terror to us all.[64]

The "Gospel Visiter" carried the news of Kline's death in its issue of August 1 in two letters from West Virginia.

Greenland, Hardy co., W. Va.
June 21, 1864

Last night a reliable brother came to my house from near Harrisonburg, Rockingham co. Va., who informed me that the news was amongst the brethren and others of that part of the country, that brother Elder JOHN KLINE was found dead, lying in a road not far from his house, shot with four balls. A rebel soldier said, that he was shot for traveling West carrying news and helping people to get out of the S. Confederacy. We understand, the rebels shot him intentionally. I have given this as I received it, and I think this time his death is only too true. If not, we will let you know immediately.

I wrote you last week of the death of br Elder JOHN KLINE, which is now confirmed from every source. We hear it from the Union army, from rebel citizens, and from a rebel paper.

All of this information led the editor, Henry Kurtz, to comment:

Little did we think, when we met our beloved above named on Thursday May 12 last at the lovefeast in Bear Creek meetinghouse, O., sat and

John Kline's grave

labored with him side by side in sweet communion, and rejoiced together in the mercies of the Lord, and in the institutions and privileges of his house, and indeed spent almost a whole week (to the close of last yearly meeting in Indiana) together;—we repeat—little did we think, . . . that we would so soon have to record his death, and what is more grievous still, his sudden, violent and cruel death, being shot down without a moment's warning by the hands of murderous rebels.—But we hope and trust, he was ready to depart with the prayer of the first martyr, Stephen: "Lord, lay not this sin to their (his murders') charge!"[65]

John Kline's death was certainly a terrible loss for the church during a time of crisis, and it indicated, as the editor of the "Rockingham Register" pointed out, how rapidly the South was "drifting into scenes which must be full of terror" for all of the civilian population, including the Brethren.

THE ANNUAL MEETINGS DURING THE WAR

The Annual Meetings of 1862, 1863, and 1864, which were held during the War, met in the northern states of Ohio, Pennsylvania, and Indiana, respectively. However, John Kline from Virginia served as the presiding moderator at each of these meetings, as well as the first wartime meeting in Virginia. His election as moderator was one indication of his widespread respect and influence in the church of his day, and of the seriousness to the church of his death in June 1864, rather shortly after his return from the Annual Meeting in Indiana. Surely his death was related to his travels, as suggested in the first letter from West Virginia reporting his death.

However, John Kline was concerned about taking proper procedures to secure permission to cross the lines for religious reasons, and the evidence indicates that he was carrying passes to permit such action from both armies at the time of his death. One indication of his concern was a section of his letter to the Governor of Virginia in November 1861.

NB   I desire to call your attention to another item. you know that I am a minister of the Church of God (called German Baptists, or by nickname tunkard.) Next Whitesuntite our Anuel meeting will be held in Ohio Montgomery County at which place I with others of our breth, desire much to attent. how it can be affected that we can get there under existing circumstances is the question? if you can see any way please give me information, if I do not ask too much. I have thought we could probable get there   but how to get back seams to be the difficulty for we want to get back again to our own land, if we go. truly, my dear governor we have thrown ourselves into a great dificulty, and whether the good that will result from it will come near to damage money and property and loss of life, that has already been spent and lost, remains yet to be lrnt.[66]

Unfortunately, the Governor's response to this request has not been found. It is quite probable that the Governor looked upon the request with favor, for Letcher and Kline were evidently well acquainted, judging by the nature of their correspondence. At any rate, it is clear that John Kline attended the Annual Meeting of 1862 in Ohio, for he served as the Moderator.

Although the recorded Minutes of the Annual Meeting of 1862 indicate that some seventy different items were discussed, not a single item touched on the War in any way. Had no problems arisen from the War thus far, or were the problems too sensitive to be discussed and recorded?

John Kline was again elected as the moderator of the Annual Meeting of 1863, which met in Pennsylvania. S. Z. Sharp, who later spent many years serving in various Brethren educational institutions, was a young man at the time of the Meeting in 1863. Many years later he recorded some of his recollections of the Meeting and of John Kline.

The first General Conference I attended was during the Civil War in 1863. It was held in Blair County, Pa. All the people gathered under a tent, which was not a large one. Only a small number of young people attended. There were only fourteen members on the Standing Committee. Bro. John Kline, who was one of the most prominent elders in the church, was elected Moderator. . . .

When Eld. Kline opened the meeting, he requested that no one ask him any questions concerning the South, as it was then in a dreadful condition, and it was dangerous to discuss it. He had come to the Conference through the Confederate lines on horseback, by picking his way through the mountains in bypaths. About a year later he was shot and killed by a Confederate, on the supposition that he had revealed some of the secrets of the South. Owing to the high esteem in which Bro. Kline was held, in all the Valley of Virginia, his murder was condemned by the public press generally.

Not long after this, I was drafted into the army but was released, as a conscientious objector, by paying a fine of $300. While many professed Christians met each other on the field of battle, and thrust the bayonets into each other's hearts, our Brethren, North and South, met each other with the right hand of fellowship and the salutation of the kiss of peace.[67]

Evidently some of John Kline's concern regarding the discussion of war matters was reflected in the first item in the recorded Minutes of 1863:

Article 1. How are we to deal with our brethren who have enlisted and gone to the army as soldiers or teamsters, or those who have been drafted, and are gone to the army? We think it not expedient to consider (or discuss) these questions at this time. Still it is believed, and was expressed, the gospel gave sufficient instruction.

One other article in the Minutes touched on the matter of slavery and took a much more forceful stand.

Article 5. What should be done with a brother that would preach that slavery was right according to the Scriptures, and cause discord among the brethren? Inasmuch as the brethren always believed, and believe yet, that slavery is a great evil, and contrary to the doctrine of Christ, we consider it utterly wrong for a brother to justify slavery, either in public or in private, and that he should be admonished, and if obstinate, shall be dealt with according to Matt. XVIII.[68]

Unfortunately there is no indication where this brother, who was preaching that slavery was right, lived, but it is clear that the church's stand on slavery had not changed.

A pass through the lines of the type that John Kline might have been carrying was prepared for the Annual Meeting of 1864 for a member of the church living in Page County, Virginia.

Near Newtown Frederick County Va
    May the 5th 1864
    We the undersigned do hereby certify that we are well acquainted with Samuel P. Forrer of Page county va   he is a good Loyal citizen and is a reliable man   he is a member of the German Baptist church (commonly called Dunkers)   he wishes to attend the Anual Meeting of the Above Society held in Wayne county Indiana commencing the 15th of May 1864
                                    John Brindle
                                    Daniel Brindle[69]

The Annual Meeting of 1864 took a strong stand on the relation of the church to the Civil War in two different articles.

Article 28. Is it according to the gospel, and the order of the brethren, to receive and baptize into the church such as are in the military service, bearing arms in this war, or to go into the camps and baptize such, and let them remain in the service, or should they not first get a full discharge before they can be received into the church by baptism? Answer: We can not encourage such proceedings; but in case of extreme sickness, and when there is a promise to shed no more blood, we will let the churches applied to decide what shall be done; but let the principles of the church be acceded to by all candidates.

Article 35. As our national troubles, consequent upon the rebellion now existing in our country, have caused considerable difficulty in our church, and have tried our non-resistant principles, and have caused several questions concerning the payment of bounty-money, voting, etc., to come before this council-meeting, what counsel will this Annual Meeting give upon these subjects. Answer: We exhort the brethren to steadfastness in the faith, and believe that the times in which our lots are cast strongly demand of us a strict adherence to all our principles, and especially to our non-resistant principle, a principle dear to every subject of the Prince of Peace, and a prominent doctrine of our fraternity, and to endure whatever sufferings and to make whatever sacrifice the maintaining of the principles may require, and not to encourage in any way the practice of war. And we think it more in accordance with our principles, that instead of paying bounty-money, and especially in taking an active part in raising bounty-money, to await the demands of the government, whether general, state, or local, and pay the fines and taxes required of us, as the gospel permits, and, indeed, requires. Matt. XXII: 21; Rom. XIII: 7. And lest the position we have taken upon political matters in general, and war matters in particular, should seem to make us, as a body, appear to be indifferent to our government, or in opposition thereto, in its efforts to suppress the rebellion, we hereby declare that it has our sympathies and our prayers, and that it shall have our aid in any way which does not conflict with the principles of the gospel of Christ. But since, in our Christian profession, we regard these gospel principles as superior or paramount to all others, consistency requires that we so regard them in our practices.[70]

One of John Kline's last letters was written on June 4 with a postscript on June 13, reporting to the "Gospel Visiter" his safe return from the Annual Meeting of 1864 in Indiana. Coming across the mountains of West Virginia, he reported that "we had some fears of getting in contact with scouts, but happily none made their appearance." Concerning conditions in Virginia, he found things quite unsettled.

Times are very squally here now. The northern army have gone up the Valley under Gen. Hunter, and where they now are we cannot tell. . . . Our wheat harvest looks very promising, but whether we will be able to gather it in, seems to be doubtful, as there are scarcely any hands to work. All are either gone North and West or are in the army; few left at home and but little hope of any coming back. I do hope, and my ardent prayer to my God is, that he will so interfere, that this awful and unnecessary war might be closed, and peace and amity restored. I herewith send you my hearty greeting both to you and all the Israel of God, and so remain your well-wishing brother until death.[71]

Two days later, he was dead!

THE AFTERMATH OF WAR

The Brethren, like everyone else, rejoiced that the War had ended. Also, many Brethren were able to rejoice because they had been spared from the physical destruction and the bloodshed of the War. This type of reaction was described in a letter from Maryland written in the summer of 1865.

McKinstrys Mills, Maryland
June 25, 1865

The long wished for has come at last. I have longed to have a letter from you ever since the war commenced, and lo yesterday it came. I was very glad to think the time has again arrived that we can again commune our thoughts to each other by letter.

We have fared remarkably well, considering the critical times we have been compelled to pass through. as you say in carnal things we have lost but little just here, but in some portions of the state they have been run over by the Rebel army several times, and all taken that they could carry off. Harry Gilmore made a raid through here last july and took a good many good horses from us, but other wise the loyal people have not been injured. but sometimes we were in fear and dred that our State would Secede and if it had we would all lost our all in regard to property, for there was those among us ready at any time to fall on us and plunder us, as soon as the time was at hand, but thank God it did not come and we still are safe and in possession of our homes and our families   God be praised that it is as well with us as it is.[72]

Something of the same rejoicing that the War was over was combined with some sour notes about the War and the Freedmen in a letter from Indiana written to friends in Virginia.

Cornstock, Montgomery County, Indiana
August 12, 1865

It gives me pleasure that I once more have an opportunity to address a letter to you   you may think I could have at any time done so. I have riten to you during the rebellion, but no go. it was returned to me again from Washington City. I also received one letter from Nathaniel, which I answered. if it had not been for the boys that come from thare, I should not of heard how you was treated by the Soldiers, in that raid through your country. I well knew before the war commenced if it did commence it would cost the Country both North & South menny valuable lives on both sides, besides the innumerable amount of property destroyd by the armys on ether side, and after all done the Negro is in a worse condition than when a slave before the war.

Sister Susan, it would be a great gratification to me to see you now, and talk with you all. I seen Joseph Kiser at the anual Meeting in Illinois   they were all tolerable well at that time. I also seen John Moomaw at that meeting. the last inteligence I got from you I received of him   I received a letter from G. W. Tillotson N. York saying anything I wish to know from you, he would answer immediately, but I never received the answer from him to my letter. I know no better way to find out all than to come in myself and see & hear for my self if they will let me come   During this war my Son Saml. was drafted twice & William once, but nether of them went to See the Eliphant.... it cost us all a good deal to keepe 5 from going to the Slaughter pens in the South. I Suppose Joseph Layman has told you all about us hear, or at least some of the refugees has told you how we are all gitting along hear. we have the Sorryest crop of wheat hear this year we ever had   I think the rain spoiled it bad   for us after it was cut & in shock & now the high tax, tax to pay for the Negro, or at least to git him free, and enslave the white for the black, and now they dont know what to do with them   government will provide for them if the white race will have to suffer for it.

Dear Sister, Jacob Amen Son Benjamin F. Amen will be hear to Night. he was taken prisoner an taken to kamp Chase Ohio and after his releas he come to pay us a visit in the west   he Starts home monday and he kindley carrys this letter to you for me.[73]

In contrast to Brethren in the North who could rejoice because there was virtually no physical destruction, many Brethren in the South had had their houses and barns destroyed during the War. The Annual Meeting of 1865 heard the plea of two Brethren from the South and agreed to raise funds to aid the southern Brethren in reconstruction.

Contributions for the brethren in Virginia and Tennessee: Bro. Wrightsman, from Tennessee, and Bro. Mumaw, from Virginia stated to the meeting that the brethren in those states need assistance, and that they must suffer unless they get assistance; whereupon the meeting appointed D. P. Sayler as a receiver to receive contributions for the relief of said brethren.[74]

A personal report of this matter was written shortly after the Annual Meeting by a brother from Maryland with relatives in the area of Virginia from which Mumaw came.

McKinstrys Mills, Maryland
June 25, 1865

I had heard from you through Bro. Jno. Mumaw at our Anual Meeting. I saw him there, heard his name mentioned by some of the older Brethren in the congregation, and then watched him untill he went out, followed him and found he was from Roanoke, had some conversation with him, but he seemed rather backward in conversing. he told me you were all well and still among the living. he seemed to be somewhat desirous of keeping back that I wished to know. there was also a brother there from Tennessee, as a representative of the Brethren from that State. Mumaw gave himself as a representative of churches from certain portions of Virginia. he Mumaw represented the people of Va. in your section as in a starving condition, and from this representation there was a collection taken one morning among the Breth. at the breakfast table, and several hundred dollars given, to be sent to their aid. the Brethren when assembled for council, then agreed that all the churches that was willing should be notified of the fact, and advised to hold a collection in behalf of the Brethren of the south, and a committee appointed to receive and forward the monies to them. Daniel P. Saylor was appointed to receive and forward from the East. Bro. Mumaw promised Bro. D. P. S. to come this way and receive and take the money to Virginia. he also promised me to come here if he could possibly do so. he expected to come sometime in July.[75]

Brethren congregations evidently responded well to this appeal. One Maryland congregation, Pipe Creek, accepted this challenge as indicated in the following letter.

This is to inform you that the brethren here at Pipe Creek, were among the first to respond to the appeal made through our last Yearly Meeting, in behalf of the needy in the South. On the 28th day of June the Church here sent its first contribution to the receiver. He was then told "that the church would do more"—and it has since done more by a third contribution, which the church here in the exercise of its descretion, sent directly to the needy in the South.[76]

Another Maryland congregation reported that it had raised over two hundred dollars by October 1865. Altogether thousands of dollars were contributed in this way for the relief of suffering Brethren in the South. In the spring of 1866, David H. Plaine, a Brethren minister in the Roanoke area, wrote a letter of appreciation to D. P. Saylor.

Bonsacks, Virginia
April 16, 1866

Many brethren and others in some sections especially the lower valley of Va. sustained heavy losses in stock & and other property but very few lives comparatively have been sacrificed in this unholy carnage, thank the Lord. Much inconvenience & anxiety of mind has been experienced by the brethren. The people are going to work with a right good will especially the liberal part, to rebuild the destroyed places. A few rolling years will blot out from the escutcheon of time the last vestage of carnage, so revolting to civilization & Christianity & these dread scenes will live only in the pages of history.

I will yet say that instead of separating the ties of friendship between the brethren North & South, as among other sects, it had only tended to effectuall[y] rivet the bonds of love & union & the noble sentiments expressed by our dear brethren of the North in opening their hands wide in contributing to our necessities, will ever demand from us grateful acknowledgement & while the emergencies were not so great as represented, yet that does not detract from such evidence of heartfelt sympathy that prompted such noble deeds and though many a heart was made to bleed with sorrow and many a family circle bathed in tears of sorrow, & many a loved one laid upon the grassy field of carnage.[77]

Apparently the raising of funds by Brethren in the northern states for the relief of suffering Brethren in the southern states was a worthwhile experience for those who lived through the Civil War period.

One final aspect of Brethren activity in the Civil War period was the concern for a return to normal relations between the seceded states and those that had not seceded—a process known by the term, Reconstruction. In the fall of 1866 with important Congressional elections on the political horizon, several Brethren in Rockingham County, Virginia, issued a printed broadside which had strong, political overtones. Although they stated specifically, "We are no politicians!" what they were saying certainly was political in nature. Such a political character makes the document especially interesting.

AN APPEAL!

To the Brethren in Pennsylvania:

The undersigned, members of the denomination of Christians known as Dunker Brethren, would respectfully address their brethren in Pennsylvania, in the interest of peace and brotherly kindness. We reside in Rockingham county, Virginia, and though perhaps, unknown to you we would ask you to hear us. We always were Union men and wanted to see the old flag triumphant. But we thought when the war would be over and the Union army triumphant, we would be back in the Union and at peace with the people of the North. It seems, however, that such is not the case. We are still out of the Union, and Oh! the suffering and misery of this people! You could but behold it, you would never, never support a policy which is so cruel and unjust. We are no politicians! Heaven forbid that we should be! But we desire peace and brotherly love and reunion. We cannot live without these. Will you deny us these blessings? We are innocent of the blood of your people, yet we are made to suffer. Have we not suffered enough and has not the whole South been dreadfully punished? Hence we would appeal to you to vote against the RADICALS, or if your party ties are too strong, not to vote at all. If you love us as we love our brethren everywhere you will not be deaf to this appeal! Farewell!

J. C. MILLER,
J. G. MOYER,
JOHN HAWMAN,
JACOB HOCHSTETLER.

Rockingham county, Va., Sept. 22, 1866.[78]

The "Appeal" was probably not successful, for the Radical Republicans won the Congressional election of 1866 and succeeded in putting into operation their plan of Reconstruction, which involved a long, slow process of healing the wounds created by the War. However, as David Plaine had reported earlier in the year 1866, "The people are going to work with a right good will . . . to rebuild the destroyed places." With that spirit the wounds of the War would be healed, especially for Brethren who had been particularly fortunate that their church had not been split into northern and southern divisions as had happened to the Baptists, the Methodists, and the Presbyterians. All in all, Brethren seemed to have come through the War in good condition.

VII. PUBLICATIONS AND DEVOTIONAL WRITINGS

INTRODUCTION

Much of the material in this chapter is related to the printing of religious material written by members of the Church of the Brethren, although some unpublished devotional writings will be included. Also, the publications in this chapter are taken from hymnbooks and religious periodicals, rather than from religious books, since the books have generally been discussed in other chapters according to their subjects. Although religious periodicals did not appear until after 1850, at least partly because the religious ideas of the Brethren discouraged such publications, hymnbooks were in continuous demand and were being printed throughout this period.

THE YEARS IMMEDIATELY FOLLOWING THE AMERICAN REVOLUTION

During the 1770s the press and equipment of Christopher Sauer, Jr., the prominent Germantown printer and Brethren minister, were confiscated and sold by the Americans because Sauer was accused of being a British sympathizer. Whatever the merits of the case, the action brought to an end a printing press which had produced a steady stream of religious material, such as Bibles and hymnbooks, and secular material, such as newspapers and almanacs, which were read and appreciated by the Brethren as well as by other Germans in colonial America. It must be remembered that the Sauer press was strictly a private venture and was not in any sense a church-sponsored or church-owned press. But its closing was a serious loss for the Brethren.

Brethren did find other printers from whom to purchase some of their basic necessities, such as hymnbooks. For example, in 1791 the first Brethren hymnbook in the English language, entitled "The Christian's Duty," was printed in Germantown by Peter Leibert, a Brethren minister who had purchased the Sauer press and had opened a printing office in 1784 after the end of the War in cooperation with his son-in-law, Michael Billmeyer, a Lutheran. The partnership dissolved after three years, and Leibert concentrated on the printing of books while Billmeyer turned to journalistic productions. Leibert printed several other items of interest to the Brethren, and Billmeyer printed hymnbooks, such as "Das Kleine Davidische Psalterspiel," for the Brethren.

Another successor of the Sauer press in a sense was established by Christopher Sauer, Jr.'s son, Samuel Sauer, who was printing material for the Brethren at Chestnut Hill, a short distance from Germantown, in the early 1790s. Later in the decade, he moved to Baltimore where he printed the "Psalterspiel" in 1797. He also printed a number of other items of interest to the Brethren. Finally, the Brethren also turned to the German language press at Ephrata, where Salomon Mayer printed a "Psalterspiel" in 1795 "In der Neuen Buchdruckerey," and where Johannes Baumann printed a book of poetry and of hymns by Jacob Stoll in 1806. In such ways Brethren were able to get some printing done after the closing of the press of Christopher Sauer, Jr.

HYMNBOOKS

In general practice hymnbooks were privately owned by Brethren and brought to worship services of the church. However, since many of the members evidently did not own hymnbooks, hymns were frequently lined by a leader with the congregation following. One evidence of personal ownership is that most of the old hymnbooks dating from this period of time have personal names written in them. The Brethren published three hymnbooks in the English language between 1791 and 1867, and a German language hymnbook in 1826, which will be considered in this chapter. Undoubtedly, many Brethren continued to prefer the German language hymnbook, "Das Kleine Davidische Psalterspiel," which had first been published by Christopher Sauer, Sr., in 1744 at Germantown. It contained five hundred thirty-six hymns selected from a European hymnbook, entitled "Davidsches Psalter-Spiel," which was first published by the Inspired group in 1718 and which included nine hundred two hymns. Some of the hymns in the 1744 Germantown edition were evidently by Brethren authors. "Das Kleine Davidische Psalterspiel" was reprinted more than a dozen times in America during the next century, indicating something of its continuing popularity with Brethren and with other German groups.

The first Brethren hymnbook to be printed in the English language was entitled "The Christian's Duty, Exhibited in a Series of Hymns," published in 1791 in Germantown by Peter Leibert. He had learned the printing trade as an apprentice in the Sauer shop, and then had purchased the Sauer equipment after its confiscation by the Americans during the American War of Independence. About 1791, Leibert's son, William, became associated with him. Perhaps one of their first productions, although it came out in the name of the father, was "The Christian's Duty." The hymnbook had both an Introduction and a Preface which help to explain why it seemed necessary to publish such a hymnbook at this time, although nothing was said about the fact that the hymns were in English rather than in German.

Introduction

Inasmuch as it both pleased the most high God, to enlarge the Place of our Tent, and the Curtains of our Habitation; it behoveth us to render thanks and praise to that beneficient Being, in whose Hands is the Life and Breath of all things; and, who doth according to his will in the army of heaven, and among the Inhabitants of the Earth, and none can stay his Hand, nor say unto him what doest thou. Tho' the Heaven is his Throne, and the earth is his Footstool, yet unto Man he saith, "whoso offereth Praise glorifieth me; and to him that ordereth his Conversation aright, will I shew the Salvation of the Lord. Let us therefore serve the Lord with Gladness, and come before his Presence with Singing. Enter into his Gates with Thanksgiving, and into his Courts with Praise." Psalm 50.23. and Psalm 100.2,4.

Preface

Dearly beloved Brethren, and fellow Heirs of the Grace of God; the Apostle exhorts us, "to let the Word of Christ dwell in us, richly in all Wisdom, Teaching, and Admonishing one another in Psalms, and Hymns, and spiritual Songs, singing with Grace in your Hearts, unto the Lord." You are therefore here presented with a Choice Collection of *Hymn's,* of the most approved Authors, suitable to almost every Circumstance of Life, which we are call'd to pass through, and corresponding with the Tenor of the Gospel, and adapted to commemorate the Birth, Life, Death, Resurrection and Ascension of our Saviour, and his Session at God's Right Hand, and his Intercession there; the Commission of the Apostles on Baptism, and the Lord's Supper, and the Second Coming of Christ, without Sin unto Salvation.

My Brethren, in the Performance of this noble Part of Worship, we Should have our Minds devoutly fix'd on God, who heareth Prayer, and inhabiteth the Praises of Israel; not raising our Voices only, but endeavoring to sing with the Spirit, and with the Understanding also: lest we be found among the Number of them over whom God laments, saying: This People draw near to me with their Mouths, and with their Lips do honour me, but their Hearts have they removed far from me, and their Fear towards me is taught by the Precept of Men. Let us therefore strive to offer in an acceptable Manner, the Sacrifice of Praise to God continually, that is the Fruit of our Lips, giving Thanks to his Name.

The Reason for printing this Hymn Book is: because of the Inconvenience arising from having several Sorts of Hymn Books in Meeting at once, it was therefore thought prudent to remove this Inconvenience, by collecting the most approved Hymns, of the several Books, and reducing them into One small Octavo, with a complete Index, which is wanting in the Hymn Book which we have latterly used; altho it was otherwise truly excellent.

Dearly beloved, let us be encouraged to look forward, to that happy Period, when "all the Kings of the Earth shall praise the Lord"; when they shall hear the Words of his Mouth, yea, they shall sing in the Ways of the Lord, for great is the Glory of the Lord. When he shall turn to the People a pure Language, and they shall serve him with one Consent, when they shall come and sing in the Heights of Zion; and flow together to the Goodness of the Lord. Under these Considerations and cheering Reflections we may freely say with David: "Let every Thing that hath Breath praise JEHOVAH." Hallelujah!
Germantown, May 18, 1791.[1]

Some indication of the nature of the hymns included is provided by the topical index to the hymns, which has the heading: "Suited to particular Subjects or Occasions." The number of hymns listed under each subject was provided by Nevin W. Fisher.

1. For the Nativity of Christ (5 hymns)
2. The Life of Christ, with his Characters and Representations (23 hymns)
3. The Passion of Christ (15 hymns)
4. The Resurrection of Christ (4 hymns)
5. The Ascension of Christ (2 hymns)
6. The Intercession of Christ (1 hymn)
7. The Effusion of the Spirit (2 hymns)

8. On Baptism (9 hymns)
9. For washing of Feet and the Lord's Supper (3 hymns)
10. Holy Fortitude (9 hymns)
11. Morning Hymns (6 hymns)
12. Evening Hymns (6 hymns)
13. For New-Year's Day (4 hymns)
14. Praise to the Redeemer (14 hymns)
15. The Mystery of the Cross (4 hymns)
16. On the Fall of Man, or Depravity of Human Nature (8 hymns)
17. Longing after Christ (15 hymns)
18. Supplicatory Hymns (30 hymns)
19. Christian Consolation (11 hymns)
20. Conversion (10 hymns)
21. The Wonders of Redeeming Love (5 hymns)
22. The Blessedness of the Gospel (14 hymns)
23. The Pilgrimage of Saints (5 hymns)
24. On the Kingdom of Christ (9 hymns)
25. Invitation to Praise and Repentance (19 hymns)
26. Faith and Obedience (11 hymns)
27. Judgment Hymns (8 hymns)
28. The Frailty of our Life (11 hymns)
29. Funeral Hymns (7 hymns)
30. On Death and the Resurrection (10 hymns)
31. Before Sermon 1st (2 hymns) After Sermon 2d (3 hymns)
32. The Being and Perfection of God (10 hymns)
33. On the holy Scriptures (3 hymns)
34. On Charity and Uncharitableness (5 hymns)
35. For the Hope of Israel (8 hymns)
36. Penetential Hymns (17 hymns)
37. Brotherly Love (7 hymns)
38. Spiritual Poverty (7 hymns)
39. Resignation to Providence (5 hymns)
40. To the Trinity (3 hymns)[2]

Quite possibly many of these hymns used by Peter Leibert had been taken from a hymnbook published in 1784 in Philadelphia by Elhanan Winchester, the Baptist-Universalist minister, entitled "A Choice Collection of Hymns, From Various Authors, Adapted to Publick Worship: Designed for the Edification of the Pious of all Denominations; but more particularly for the use of the Baptist Church in Philadelphia." At any rate, whatever the source, "The Christian's Duty" provided a valuable worship asset for Brethren and was reprinted several times down to 1825.

The publication of "The Christian's Duty" did not meet all of the needs of the Brethren for hymnbooks, for there were still many Brethren who preferred to use the German language. Also, the editions of "Das Davidische Psalterspiel" by the years of the nineteenth century had become very large and bulky, and were consequently inconvenient for traveling. There was a demand for a small, condensed German language hymnbook. As a result a group of Brethren in Maryland, possibly led by Philip Boyle, compiled a collection of hymns from the "Psalterspiel," from other hymnbooks, and from unpublished sources, and published "Die Kleine Lieder Sammlung" at Hagerstown, Maryland, in 1826. In their Foreword the unidentified compilers outlined their reasons for publication and their sources:

Dearest Friends, Brethren, and Fellow Pilgrims on the way to Blessed Eternity!

Here the *Kleine Lieder-Sammlung* is published for the first time. There is no intention, however, to discredit the well-established *Psalterspiel,* but on the contrary to heartily recommend to all God-loving house-fathers and house-mothers that they use it as often as possible in their families. This book also shows that the *Psalterspiel* is held in respect by the fact that most of the songs were taken from it; incidentally, various other songs have been added from other hymnbooks and a few from manuscript so that it can be called a very impartial hymnbook. It is for the convenience of the travelers and especially for those of our dear young people who still have the desire to honor their mother tongue. And as there is apparently everywhere a lack of hymnbooks for public worship, we hope to remedy this situation through this small hymnbook.

Now, you beloved young hearts and God-loving souls! here you have a small book with beautiful songs—a well-seasoned flower garden—use it often at your meetings; let the meaning of the rhymes penetrate into your hearts, so that it will help you to your eternal blessedness.

There was a special interest in keeping the book small. Therefore only the best-known songs and from some only the most moving verses were selected, and some of the most beautiful songs, especially in the *Psalterspiel,* could not be shortened because of their dignity and continuity and because of their length could not be included in this format.

May the Lord bless this humble work for his praise and to fulfill his word as he said: Is. 12:5, "Sing unto the Lord; for he hath done excellent things: this is known in all the earth." and: Psalm 149:1, "Sing unto the Lord a new song, and his praise in the congregation of saints."

"Let everything that hath breath praise the Lord. Hallelujah!" Ps. 150:6.[3]

This hymnbook evidently was in great demand, not only in the East but also in the West, for in the same year, 1826, Henry Kurtz, who had just moved to Ohio, was responsible for the printing of another edition of "Die Kleine Lieder Sammlung" at Osnaburgh (present-day East Canton), Ohio. At that time, Kurtz was not a member of the Church of the Brethren, for he was not baptized until 1828; the publication of this hymnbook possibly represented one of his early contacts with the Brethren in Ohio. The book must have continued to be in great demand, because nineteen different printings up to 1850 have been identified.

Quite possibly Kurtz was more directly responsible for the publication in Canton, Ohio, in 1830 of "A Choice Selection of Hymns," which was specifically identified with the term, "First Edition." However, until a copy of this hymnbook is located, it will not be possible to determine whether or not Henry Kurtz was involved, since the publisher is identified as John Saxton. The edition of 1833 was specifically identified as a second edition, printed at Osnaburg, Stark County, Ohio, and "printed and sold by Henry Kurtz." One of the purposes of this book was to condense "The Christian's Duty," which like the "Psalterspiel" had become quite bulky. Evidently this purpose was satisfactorily achieved, for the hymnbook was printed at least thirteen different times, including four printings in Pennsylvania and Maryland.

The 1833 edition had two hundred twenty-three hymns. By the time of the 1852 edition which was published by Kurtz at Poland in Mahoning County, Ohio, there were two hundred ninety-three hymns, a "Table of First Lines" arranged alphabetically, and "An Index or Table to find a Hymn suited to particular subjects or occasions."

Awakening Hymns (4 hymns)
Being and Perfection of God (2 hymns)
Brotherly Love (3 hymns)
Before Preaching (8 hymns)
Baptism (5 hymns)
Christ's incarnation (5 hymns)
His Character (8 hymns)
His Representations (6 hymns)
His Sufferings and Death (6 hymns)
His Resurrection (3 hymns)
His Ascension (1 hymn)
His Intercession (3 hymns)
His Kingdom (6 hymns)
Christian Consolation (13 hymns)

Charity or Love (2 hymns)
Communion Hymns (4 hymns)
Conversion (6 hymns)
Death in general (5 hymns)
of children (2 hymns)
of young persons (1 hymn)
of the pious (4 hymns)
Depravity of Man (3 hymns)
Evening Hymns (6 hymns)
Fall of Man (2 hymns)
Faith and Obedience (6 hymns)
Feet washing (1 hymn)
Frailty of life (10 hymns)
Gospel—its blessings (14 hymns)
Holy Scriptures (3 hymns)
Holy fortitude (7 hymns)

Heaven (6 hymns)
Hope of Israel (5 hymns)
Invitation to praise (4 hymns)
Invitation to repentance (12 hymns)
Judgment (6 hymns)
Longing after Christ (12 hymns)
Lord's Supper (2 hymns)
Marriage (1 hymn)
Morning Hymns (5 hymns)
Mystery of the Cross (4 hymns)
New Year (2 hymns)
Pentecost (1 hymn)
Praise to the Redeemer (14 hymns)
Penitential (2 hymns)

Parting and dismission (13 hymns)
Redeeming Love (5 hymns)
Resurrection (2 hymns)
Resignation to Providence (1 hymn)
Sabbath, or Lord's day (5 hymns)
Supplicatory Hymns (23 hymns)
Saint's pilgrimage (5 hymns)
Spiritual poverty (2 hymns)
Stony heart (1 hymn)
The Trinity (1 hymn)
Winter (1 hymn)
Youth prayer &c. for, (2 hymns)
Invitation (5 hymns)[4]

As a publisher Henry Kurtz was, of course, interested in selling these hymnbooks wherever he could, and quite possibly he secured agents to represent him in this business. At any rate, two letters written by Philip Boyle related to the distribution of hymnbooks.

New Windsor, Carroll County, Maryland
October 2, 1849

The hymn books could not be forwarded from Pittsburgh until brother Kurtz went on there in person, and as the cholera was prevailing his family were not willing for him to go to Pittsburgh till it had abated. However they came to hand this week, and I intend this week to re-box those that are to be sent to you, and send them to Baltimore next week, to be forwarded according to the instructions of Bro. Moomaw who instructed me to send them to the care of *Richard Tyree* Lynchburgh, Va. He did not write this man's name as plain as it should be and I perhaps have not got the proper name. However, it will go on to Lynchburg, Va. and if you authorize some of the agents to keep a close eye you will get it even if the name is not properly written.[5]

New Windsor, Carroll County, Maryland
August 4, 1853

Our Br. Henry Kurtz had ordered a large lot of Hymn books to be brot on to this year's annual meeting, but they did not come till after the Y. M. adjourned; he has employed me to dispose of them. Please make an effort *immediately* in connection with the Brn. with you, and in the adjoining

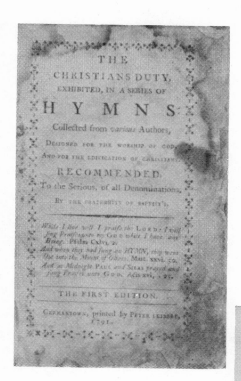

Title page of
The Christian's Duty,
hymns published in 1791

Die kleine

Lieder-Sammlung

oder

Auszug aus dem

Psalterspiel der Kinder Zions,

zum Dienste inniger, heilsuchender Seelen,

und insonderheit

zum Gebrauch in den Gemeinden der Brüder,
zusammengetragen in gegenwärtige kleine Form
und mit einem dreifachen Register versehen.

"Ich will den Herrn loben, so lange ich lebe,
und meinem Gott lobsingen, weil ich da bin."
Psalm 146, 2.

Stereotyp-Auflage.

Poland, Mahoning County, Ohio.
Zu haben bei Heinrich Kurtz.
1850.

Title page of
Die Kleine Leider-Sammlung,
hymns in German, published in 1850

congregations, to ascertain whether there would not be some wanting, and how many? and let me know; be particular in stating *how*, and where I shall send them. He has ordered me to sell the *single* at $3 and the *double* hymn book at $6.00 per doz. Br. Kurtz needs the money, and will now have to lay out of it till he can get it; please use your influence in his favor.[6]

The reference to the single hymnbook very likely was to "A Choice Selection of Hymns," while the double hymnbook was the English language hymnbook bound with "Die Kleine Lieder Sammlung." For example, there was an 1853 edition of the English language hymnbook bound with an 1850 edition of the German language hymnbook, published and sold by Kurtz.

In the history and development of Brethren hymnody, it has seemed necessary to have a new hymnbook about every quarter of a century. The one exception in the nineteenth and twentieth centuries has been the period from the decade of the 1820s to the decade of the 1900s, during which time there was only one new Brethren hymnbook, which came out in 1867. It was the first hymnbook to receive the authorization of the Annual Meeting. The Minutes indicated something of the process of agitation which led to action.

Y. M. 1849. Art. 38. Whether our hymn book now in use could not be improved by a better selection? Considered, that the hymn book we have answers our purpose very well.

Y. M. 1858. Art. 23. What does the Annual Meeting think of taking the prepatatory steps for producing a new hymn book? Referred to next annual meeting.

Y. M. 1860. Art. 9. We the brethren assembled in general district council at the Valley meetinghouse in Botetourt Co., Va., desire that the brethren in the annual council meeting of 1860 devise some plan or way to remodel, or enlarge by appendix, our hymn book, so as to satisfy the wants of the brethren. Ans. To comply with the above request, this annual meeting appoints a committee of five to make a new hymn book, with the understanding that as many of the hymns in the present book as possible be retained. The following brethren constitute the committee: James Quinter, O., Samuel Garber, Ill., John Metzger, Md., John H. Umstad, Pa., John Kline, Va.

Y. M. 1861. Art. 14. That we are in favor of postponing the revision of our hymn book. Considered, since a committee was appointed by last yearly meeting to attend to this business, and circumstances preventing their action, we are in favor of extending the same committee to consummate the work assigned them at their earliest convenience.[7]

These were the years of the Civil War, and it was very difficult for the committee to get together; consequently, James Quinter seems to have done most of the work on the new hymnbook. He wrote and signed the "Preface" to the new book, when it appeared in 1867.

PREFACE

Singing the praises of God may justly be regarded as an important part of the worship we offer to him, and it was enjoined by divine authority upon both Jews and Christians. The relation that the Hymn Book stands in to singing in the Church, is such, that gives it a place next in importance to the Bible, among Christians. And as the Hymn Book is an important auxiliary in promoting Christian worship and edification, the propriety of having one scriptural in its character, convenient in its arrangement, and varied and full in the hymns it contains, will be apparent to all. It has been the object of the compiler to make such a book. How far he has succeeded, those who make themselves acquainted with it, can best judge.

There has existed an impression among us for years, that our Hymn Book should be revised and improved; and this impression has grown with the growth of the Brotherhood. To meet the want of the Church in this respect, the Annual Meeting held in Tennessee, in 1861, appointed a committee to compile a new Hymn Book. That committee consisted of the following brethren: James Quinter, of Ohio; Samuel Garver, of Illinois; John Metzger, of Indiana; John Kline, of Virginia; and John H. Umstad, of Pennsylvania. But the members of the committee living so far from each other, found it very inconvenient to co-operate together to accomplish the work committed to them, and confided it to the undersigned. We felt the responsibility great when we commenced the work, but had we anticipated that responsibility as we afterward felt it, and the difficulties attending the undertaking, we would have declined it, could it have been done in accordance with a sense of duty. It has given us a considerable amount of perplexing labor. But the thought that in our humble labors we were serving the Church, and through it the glorious Head of the Church, our Heavenly Master, mingled some pleasure with our anxiety. The compiler regrets that remoteness of residence did not permit the other members of the committee to render more assistance in the important work, thinking that could their experience and judgments have been brought to bear upon it, greater satisfaction might have been given to the Brotherhood. But he assures his brethren that he has spared no labor, or pains, or expense that his circumstances made available, to compile a Hymn Book that in his humble judgment would best meet the wants of the Church. In collecting materials for the work, his library of works on Hymnology grew to nearly one hundred volumes. The most of these afforded some hymns. The books, however hitherto in use among the brethren, have formed the basis for the new book, and a large proportion of the hymns in those books has been retained. The compiler is aware that upon the idea as to the number of hymns a Hymn Book should contain, a difference of opinion obtains. Some, in looking at a Hymn Book as being designed especially for public worship, and finding that the number of hymns used on occasions of that kind is somewhat limited, think a larger number of hymns is objectionable. But when it is remembered that the Bible and Hymn Book constitute the library of some Christians; that the latter is the only book of sacred poetry they possess; that it is not only used as a book to sing from, but is also read and studied with pleasure and profit, the propriety of having some hymns beside those that are popular in the congregation, will be acknowledged. Some Christians who sing but little, and indeed some, who sing none at all, enjoy themselves very much in reading their Hymn Book, and regard it as an excellent companion in retirement. Hymns are lyrical discourses generally addressed to the feelings; and though usually used to express feelings, they may also produce them, and this may be done by reading them as well as by singing them, though not in the same degree. The Hymn Book now offered to the Brotherhood is in size, a medium between the two prevailing extremes.

Had the compiler consulted his own taste alone there have been hymns admitted which would have been omitted, and some omitted which would have been inserted. He has tried to keep before his mind the consideration, that he was compiling a Hymn Book for the use of the Brotherhood and not for a few individuals only.

The doctrinal character of the hymns has not been disregarded, and it is hoped that nothing will be found in the book that will materially conflict with the teachings of the gospel.

In the arrangement of the hymns, those of the same general character are brought together. This is more natural and more convenient than the arrangement that is founded upon the letters of the alphabet with which they commence. And a proper acquaintance with the arrangement adopted, and the help of the Alphabetical Index of Subjects, any one wishing to select a hymn adapted to any occasion, can readily do so. The Scriptural Index will also be found useful in selecting hymns.

It is recommended that in naming hymns to be sung, the number of the hymn, and not the page, be given. As two or more hymns may commence on the same page, if the page is given, the number also must, at times, be given, and when both the number and page are given, they may become confounded in the mind. To give the number of the hymn is sufficient.

The compiler thankfully acknowledges the suggestions, counsel, and selections with which he has been favored by the brethren, and though he is well aware, his work is not perfect, he hopes it will give general satisfaction to the Brotherhood. As the result of much anxious and prayerful labor, it now goes to the Churches with his prayer to God that he may bless it, and make it minister to the promotion of the spirit of Christian devotion in all the departments of worship, and thereby exert a holy influence upon the Churches, and through them upon the world, and thus contribute in some degree to advance the cause and kingdom of Christ.

JAMES QUINTER

Covington, Miami Co., O.—March 28, 1867[8]

"The Brethren's Hymn Book" was published by Quinter at Covington, Ohio, and was bound in leather. One of the significant differences between this hymnbook and previous hymnbooks was the inclusion of the names of the authors of the hymns, whenever they were known. The names were included after the first line of the hymn in the alphabetical index of hymns, but there was no index of authors.

Many members of the church still preferred the use of the German language, and consequently, a query was sent to the Annual Meeting of 1868.

Article 18. Whereas, there is difficulty in introducing the new hymnbook among the brethren where the German language is yet used, as there are none that contain both English and German hymns, would it not therefore be advisable to revise the German hymnbook and make a small collection of the choicest German hymns, and combine them with the English book, and thus have some books containing both English and German hymns, to meet the wants of our German members and avoid the necessity of having more than one book in the church? Ans. We consider it advisable to do so, and appoint the following brethren as a committee to select a number of German hymns, not exceeding two hundred, to be added to so many of the English books as it is necessary to supply the wants of the German brethren: Paul Wetzel, Henry Kurtz, F. P. Loehr, and D. M. Holsinger.[9]

Henry Kurtz evidently took the lead and by 1870 had prepared "Neue Sammlung von Psalmen, Lobgesangen und Geistlichen Liedern." He also wrote the Foreword for the new German hymnbook.

FOREWORD

Beloved friends and fellow pilgrims, brethren and sisters in the Lord, peace be unto you.

The "Little Davidic Psalter of the Children of Zion", had been honored for more than a century in our brotherhood, as its first American collection of hymns and was in general use. It was supposedly printed for the first time by our dear brother Christopher Sauer, in Germantown, Pennsylvania, who has long since falled asleep, and contained in the last edition 634 songs, and many among these of twenty, thirty, and one of over a hundred verses even. Thereby, however, it had become very clumsy and inconvenient to carry along on journeys, and for this reason the honorable brethren in the vicinity of Hagerstown, Maryland, some forty years ago, drew up "The Little Collection of Songs", which we at the present time are still using and which at the beginning contained only 140 songs, later however, it was increased to 175, and still in many respects, a lack was felt. Because also the first English songbook had become too large, so followed "The Little Collection of Songs", also a small English book of the same size and form, and both were very frequently bound together in one, and found rather general approval outside of the regions where the English language prevailed exclusively, and the complaint of the lack and the call for a better, more complete hymnal became loudest. Subsequently appeared several years ago "A Collection of Songs, Hymns, and Spiritual Songs, et cetera, Covington, Miami County, Ohio. published by James Quinter", which found quick adoption and free entrance into almost all the congregations, East and West, North and South, as it so richly deserved, an independent, and excellent work, which contained 818 songs. Now also a German work of similar character and form, so that it could be united with the previous volume, and would not be completely unworthy of its position, was suggested to this writer as early as 1867, and because he did not feel himself capable to undertake it alone, because of his advanced age, and then poor state of health, the following brethren were appointed to him as a committee in order to make a selection of 200 songs for this purpose: Paul Wetzel, F. P. Loehr, and Daniel M. Holsinger. This took place at the convention in August last year. Instead, however, of choosing only 200 songs, they found 325 and believed they had the right to put the majority in the place of the shortened songs, because indeed, in all the world two halves or three thirds count for a whole, and the committee felt itself convinced that only thus could they secure the approval of the brotherhood. In consequence of this, the manuscript was now drawn up, just as the book should be. Already in the English book it was often the case that smaller print was employed with certain hymns, for example, hymns No. 30, 21, 123, 139, and so forth, and so we thought also to do this where and when it was necessary in order to maintain balanced pages. Had this simple rule been observed from the beginning, the book would have taken another form. That the same had not been made known to the type setter is the fault of the author, who believed he had informed him verbally. Forgive him this sin, dear brethren, and do not despise thus the good that is in this little book. If we had had more space, it would have been also better in form and print. God's blessing be with you all.

In the name of the committee
Heinrich Kurtz

Columbiana, O. February 1870[10]

Actually the German hymnbook had only three hundred three hymns, which was still quite a few more than the two hundred that the Annual Meeting had authorized. In comparison the English hymnbook had eight hundred eighteen. Regardless of numbers, it seems clear that the Brethren had produced a very fine hymnbook; in fact, it has been called, "the most important Brethren hymn book of the nineteenth century."

HENRY KURTZ AND THE "GOSPEL VISITER"

Henry Kurtz played a significant role in helping members of the Church of the Brethren become more actively interested in the potential value of a religious periodical. Kurtz had been born in a Lutheran family in Germany in 1796 and then had emigrated to America in 1817. Since he had a substantial German education, he was soon employed as a schoolteacher. However, he had an interest in the Lutheran ministry, and in 1819 he was accepted by the Lutheran General Synod in Baltimore and took a pastorate in Northampton County, Pennsylvania. After marrying Anna Catherine Loehr in 1821, he accepted a call in 1823 to become a pastor in Pittsburgh. His sense of Christian zeal caused difficulties in his parish, and by the end of 1826 he had resigned. During his years in Pittsburgh he developed an interest in Christian communitarianism, which he now pursued more actively for a time. One of his contacts was with the Dunker colony of Blooming Grove, north of Williamsport, Pennsylvania, although their communitarianism was not typical of the Brethren.

In the winter of 1826-1827, Kurtz and his family moved to Stark County in northeastern Ohio, near the proposed site of a communitarian colony in which Kurtz was interested. The colony, to be called Concordia, was never actually established, and in this area Kurtz renewed acquaintance with the Brethren, whom he had perhaps first learned to know in

Artist's concept of
Henry Kurtz,
drawing by
Kermon Thomason

Northampton County. On April 6, 1828, Kurtz and probably his wife also were baptized as Brethren by George Hoke, a Brethren elder from the Canton area, and thus a new chapter began in Kurtz' life.

Since Kurtz had more education than most Brethren ministers, he was in many ways a valuable man. In 1830 he was elected to the ministry in the Church of the Brethren, and in 1844 he was ordained as an elder. In 1841 he was placed in charge of the Mill Creek congregation in Mahoning County, Ohio, and the following year he moved into that area. Most important, however, he was appointed as the clerk of the Annual Meeting in 1837, an office which he held every year except 1839, when he was in Germany for a visit, until 1862. In this capacity he learned a great deal about his newly-adopted church and its way of doing business. He was assigned the task of preparing and printing the Minutes on his own press which he had secured in the early 1830s, and he learned to know all of the influential leaders of the church.

During the 1830s and the 1840s Kurtz began to discuss with other Brethren the desirability of establishing a religious periodical which would appeal especially to Brethren and defend their ideas. The Brethren were very cautious and hesitant about such a venture, but finally in 1850 the issue was brought to the Annual Meeting for an open discussion. The response was noncommittal.

Y. M. 1850. Art. 21. Whether there is any danger to be apprehended from publishing a paper among us? This subject to lay over till next annual meeting.[11]

By the time of the next Annual Meeting in 1851, Kurtz had given Brethren something specific to discuss in the form of a trial issue of the "Gospel Visiter" which he had printed and mailed at his own expense to several hundred Brethren across the country. In this little paper, he explained at length why he thought such a paper was necessary in the church.

ADDRESS TO THE READERS—APRIL 1851.

Peace be unto you! Luke XXIV, 36. Dearest Brothers and Sisters, Friends and Fellow-Travellers to Eternity!

Peace be unto you! Not the peace, which the world may give, but that peace, which cometh from on high.

With this salutation we send the Visiter in the midst of you. Will you bid him welcome? We trust, that you are "not forgetful to entertain strangers, for thereby some have entertained angels unawares." Would you then send away a stranger, who comes to you in the name of JESUS, the Prince of Peace? No, certainly not, if you love his Master, & can possible make room for him. But you will ask, How may we know, that he is not an imposter? We answer,—By carefully examining and scrutinizing him in a spirit of candor according to the Gospel; by watching him closely, and by "trying his spirit, whether he is of God, because many false prophets are gone out into the world." 1 John IV, 1.

A long time has elapsed, since we sent out the queries, proposed in July 1849, to the printer,—and also his views on the subject of a publication of this kind. He wished to take the advice of his brethren, and the result of the consultation was, that a majority of churches heard from was in favor of the measure, or at least of a trial, that a respectful number subscribers (more than three hundred) and even payment for more than fifty copies were sent in.—Thus we felt encouraged.

On the other hand a variety of difficulties made their appearance.

From the minority of churches and a number of individual brethren, whom we both love and respect, objections were raised, and a difference of views were exhibited, that we felt loth to go on. Other disappointments following, we have postponed the beginning of the work from time to time, while we have been still urged on. We intended to submit the matter to the decision of the Yearly Meeting last spring; but in order to form a proper judgment, it would have been necessary to lay a few numbers before the brethren, and this was out of our power to do, on account of protracted illness in person and family.

But we cannot defer it any longer. We have prayerfully considered every objection; we have already felt the difficulties; we shrink from the responsibility. Yet there is one word of God staring us in the face, which will deprive us of our peace, unless we obey it. It is this. James IV. 17. "Therefore to him that knoweth to do good, and doeth it not, to him it is sin." Consider with us the following facts.

Thousands of presses are daily working in this our country, and are issuing a multitude of publications, some good, some indifferent, and some, alas! too many absolutely bad and hurtful. They find their way not only to every village, but we may say, into every family or cabin of our land. Every denomination almost publishes a paper of their own, holding forth and defending their peculiar tenets. Popular errors and the most ingenious counterfeits of truth are brought to our very doors, and our children are charmed with the same. Nay more; we have to look for such times, when, "if it were possible, the elect shall be deceived." Now if this be the case, should we not use every means in our power, to counteract the evil tendencies of our time, and to labor in every possible way for the good of our fellowmen, and for the glory of God and his truth as it is in Christ Jesus!

Some one will say: We have the Gospel, and that is sufficient for us. Truly we have abundant cause to be thankful to God, that he has given and thus preserved unto us the blessed Gospel, not only in the original language, but in so many different translations, that every one may read it in his own tongue. But we would ask: Are there now none among the many, who, reading their bible, if they were questioned like the Eunuch, "Understandest thou what thou readest?" would have to answer with him: "How can I, except some man should guide me."

Says another: Yes we must have preachers to expound the scriptures unto us, to teach, to exhort, to reprove and to warn the people according to the Gospel, but this must be done by their word of mouth, and not by writing and printing. Say we: Not so fast, dear friend or dear brother. Remember, that, if the first preachers of the Gospel had not preached by writing too, we would have no written or printed Gospel at all.

Seeing then, that we have apostolic example, of writing such things which may be profitable for doctrine etc., and that we are not to put the light under a bushel, but on a candlestick, so that it may give light unto all that are in the house, we trust no more need be said even about printing.

But we are asked: What do you want to print, and what is your object? We will try to answer in a few words. We are as a people devoted to the truth, as it is in Christ Jesus. We believe the church as a whole, possesses understandingly that truth, and every item of it. But individually we are all learners, and are progressing with more or less speed in the knowledge of the truth. For this purpose we need each other's assistance. But we live too far apart. If one in his seeking after a more perfect knowledge becomes involved in difficulty, which he is unable to overcome, this paper opens unto him a channel, of stating his difficulty, and we have not the least doubt, but among the many readers there will be some one, who has past the same difficult place, and can give such advice, as will satisfy the other.

Again—a brother is solemnly impressed with a view of Gospel-truth or Gospel-practice, which appears to him to throw additional light on some particular point. In his humility he mistrusts himself and wishes to see his view scrutinized and tried, knowing that we are in constant danger to mistake a false light for the true one. In his love to his fellowmen on the other hand, he desires to communicate to others, what he believes to be true. In either case this paper will open a channel, to have wrong views corrected, and right views promulgated.

While we would thus invite and crave the co-operation of our beloved brethren in this our undertaking, we would candidly state here, that in making our selections, we shall be guided by a sincere love of truth, and publish only what may appear to us most generally useful. No names of correspondents shall be published, as we neither wish to humble our erring brother, nor to tempt his vanity, if we approve of him. If our names are only written in the Lamb's book of life, we may be satisfied.

We have adopted a different name from the one first proposed, to speak its character in the least objectionable manner. May it ever be a Gospel-Visiter, that is a visiter in the power and spirit of the Gospel.

Finally our humble prayer is, that the Lord in his infinite mercy may grant his blessing to us and you all, and to this little work, so that none of us shall be ashamed in His coming, when He shall require of us an account of our stewardship.

PLAN OF THE PRESENT WORK
I. The main object is to exhibit and defend the pure and unadulterated

Gospel of our Lord Jesus Christ, as the power of God unto salvation, in the simplicity with which it was taught and practized by the apostles and the primitive church, with this twofold view:

1. To induce the young and thoughtless, the sinner and self-righteous, to fall in love with it, to come to it by repentance and to receive it in faith and obedience, in order to enjoy its great blessings and glorious promises.
2. To strengthen us and our fellow-believers in the faith once delivered to the saints, to the confirming of our hope, and perfecting us in love, so that we may more fully realize our Gospel-privileges.

II. The contents of the same may be comprised under the following heads:

1. Original or selected essays on important topics.
2. Notices and extracts of such books and writings as may be interesting to our readers.
3. Correspondence.
4. Articles for the edification, chiefly of the young, both in prose and poetry.[12]

Each issue of the "Gospel Visiter" would contain a section entitled, "Correspondence," the purpose of which the editor explained in this first issue.

CORRESPONDENCE, APRIL 1851.

Since our proposals went out, we have received more than fifty letters on the subject, by far the greatest number in favor of the same. Now, having made a beginning, it will be apparent to all, that it forms the most convenient and at the same time cheapest way of correspondence in all matters not strictly private, We will thus receive information equal to a dozen common letters every month for about 10 cents postage and all.

We trust the friends of it will exert themselves in sending names &c. so as to enable us to decide, how many we are to print. It will be like this present number, chiefly english, though there may occasionally be inserted some note or letter in the german, as thus far it seems a german paper could not be supported. We are not yet furnished with such a variety of type &c, as we ought to be for such a publication, but we shall spare neither pains nor expense, if sufficiently patronized, to make it appear better and better. We shall use this corner for the future, for acknowledging the receipts of letters and payment....[13]

The second issue of the "Gospel Visiter" was written before Henry Kurtz departed from his home for the Annual Meeting, which was held in 1851 at the Middle River congregation in Augusta County, Virginia. Although he seemed a bit apprehensive about what the Annual Meeting would say about the "Visiter," he did not believe that the Meeting would take steps to prohibit its publication.

CORRESPONDENCE. MAY 1851.

Since we issued the first number, of which we sent out only a very few to different sections, we have received a number of letters, but with the exception of one, none refers to our present undertaking. There may be two reasons assigned for this silence. Either those letters were written before the receipt of the Visiter, and consequently no reference to it could be expected, our long silence causing the matter to sink into oblivion. Or supposing our first paper had actually come to hand, our friends were so surprised at the sudden and unexpected appearance, we almost said apparition, that they did not know what to say about it, and expecting to see or meet us soon at the Yearly Meeting, they postponed the expression of their sentiments to that time. Maybe, some were afraid, that we were not in earnest, since nearly 2 years elapsed from the issuing of the proposal to the actual commencement, and that it would perhaps take us another such long period, to bring out the second number. To such we would say, that we are fully prepared to continue the publication regularly, provided we find an adequate support.

From the letter above mentioned as an exception, we make the following extract: I have thought of it (the Visiter), and have decided *in its favor.* It would prevent the evils, that have existed and still exist between the Eastern and Western part of the brotherhood. For the want of the knowledge of each other there is jealousy existing.—Differences (in doctrine or practice) should appear before every church in the fraternity, before a final decision is made in conference. Too hasty an action on any subject is not safe. Besides this, if a correspondence was published, it would prove to the brotherhood and to the world, that free inquiry and liberty of speech is granted among us without offence, which I consider as the safest rule to prevent error &c.

For our further encouragement we are informed, that all, who have seen the first number, are generally pleased with it, and we hope, they will continue to be so pleased, as our full determination is, to preserve a conciliatory spirit in the paper, and to do as much as we are able by the grace of God, to support such a character, and to advocate such sentiments, as may be conducive to that union and brotherly love, which is the distinguishing mark of the children of God.

Some brethren have thought, and probably do think still, that the question, whether such a publication shall go on or not, is to be decided by the Yearly Meeting. Permit us to say, that after what has already occurred, namely a diversity of opinion on the subject, we should not expect it now. There are difficult questions enough brought there without this. Under these circumstances we do not wish even, that the Yearly Meeting should decide in our favor. The thing ought to be tried first, and then, after a fair trial, the Annual Meeting may take it under consideration understandingly. For the Yearly Meeting now to forbid its publication, on the other hand, would appear so contrary to that principle of liberty, which we profess, and grant too at every meeting for worship, and which was enjoyed even with regard to printing, as the books of Br. Alexander Mack, sen. and jun., of Br. Benjamin Bowman, of Br. Philip Boyle, and last, but not least of Br. Peter Nead—testify. Consequently we cannot expect this either. If the advice of *Gamaliel,* Acts 5, 38, 39. was good, we trust, there is still greater wisdom guiding our beloved brethren at the Yearly Meeting, than his, and to their advice according to the word of God we shall always most cheerfully submit.[14]

True to Kurtz' expectations, the Annual Meeting of 1851 did not prohibit the publication of the "Gospel Visiter," but permitted it to continue publication for a trial period of one year.

Y. M. 1851. Art. 8. What is the opinion of the Yearly Meeting with regard to having a paper published under the title, "The Monthly Gospel Visitor?" Considered at this council, that we will not forbid brother Henry Kurtz to go on with the paper for one year, and that all the brethren or churches will impartially examine the Gospel Visitor, and if found wrong or injurious, let them send in their objections at the next annual meeting.[15]

A number of selected excerpts from the first volume of the "Gospel Visiter" during the years 1851-1852 revealed the variety of problems that the editor faced in getting such a periodical established. The major problem seemed to have been financial—getting enough subscribers to support the magazine.

CORRESPONDENCE. JUNE 1851,
Apology &c.
We owe to our dear readers an apology and explanation of the long

delay, which has happened in the issue of the present numbers, though a good many are aware of its causes, namely our attendance at the Yearly Meeting. Our partner not venturing to go on with the printing in our absence, accompanied us on our journey, and thus it come to pass, that 5 weeks nearly elapsed, before we could resume our work, and having also to do the printing of the minutes, we were still farther, thrown behind hand. We will try our best however, to come up again, and have the numbers appear as regular as we can, for the future.

We might have printed this number in advance, before we set out to the Yearly Meeting, had it not been for the uncertainty, under which we labored, not only in regard to the probable number of copies we ought to print, but also in regard, whether the Visiter would be permitted to live and go on his way rejoicing, or whether he would have to be sacrificed on the altar of brotherly love as a peace-offering. Many brethren expecting and wishing this question to be decided at the last Yearly Meeting, held back on that account. Much as we felt desirous, to see him live, all our hopes and promises of future usefulness in the brotherhood at large being centered in him, well-knowing that our traveling days would soon be over, and that there are scores, and perhaps we are safe in saying, hundreds of our brethren better able, both in body and mind, to preach the word by their living voice, we were trying as well as we could, to prepare ourselves to see him die in his very infancy. We may say in truth, that we never felt at liberty to make up our mind fully on any doubtful question of expediency beforehand, if it was to be decided by the Yearly Meeting, but to have our mind open for the convictions and teachings of that Holy Spirit which has been promised by our Saviour to his children, in the very hour when they need them.

Well, thanks to God, this uncertainty about the continuance of the Visiter is removed, so far as the Yearly Meeting could do it. The Brethren would not forbid us to go on with it for one year, and exhorted all the members to give it a fair trial, and if found injurious, to send in their objections at the next Annual Meeting. We ourselves would rather wish, if there is found anything wrong in the Visiter, to be informed of it right away, in order to correct what is wrong without delay. This is the advantage of a periodical, that any error or wrong committed in one number, can be corrected in the next, if the Editor is apprised of it, while if a book is printed and published, and perhaps sold by the thousand, and an error has crept in, the author has hardly any means left, to apprise his readers of the same. Should he even be humble enough, to publish his correction in other periodicals or papers, the owners of his book may never see those publications.

Many brethren at the Yearly Meeting, and even some, who had very strong scruples of conscience against the present publication before said decision, came forward and gave us or promised at least their active support together with their prayers. By the mail we are also receiving weekly a number of letters and remittances, all of which is very encouraging. We find prejudice is giving way, and our weak efforts to serve the truth and the brotherhood, are kindly appreciated. To all those, who have exerted themselves in behalf of the Visiter, our most heartfelt thanks.

We have sent the first numbers to brethren, who had not called for them, but whom we supposed, would perhaps be willing to receive and introduce the Visiter in their neighborhood. If we have made a mistake in this, we would wish to be informed of it, as the Visiter shall be no intruder. If not informed by the return of the numbers sent, or by postpaid letters, we shall, according to the general rule of all such publications, consider them as subscribers. . . .

We have promised in our conditions, that each number should contain from 16-24 pages, but were not able yet to come up to the latter number. We will do so however, and enlarge it still farther, and furnish better paper too, as soon as the number of subscribers will warrant it.

One word and request more Brethren and fellow-laborers in the Gospel especially: help us on not only with an outward support and with your prayers, but also with your communications. Though no earthly remuneration or worldly praise should follow, remember, the Lord will pay you, when He comes again.

Letters received. From Br. John Lutz with payment for 5. copies; from Br. J. Wise pay for 16. copies; from Br. Samuel Berkey, pay for 22. copies; from Br. Dan. M. Holsinger pay for 5. copies; from Br. George Wolfe with pay for 7. copies.

From a large number of letters we extract the following Commendations of the Visiter.

A dear brother from Virginia says: "Having read the first number, it is so far a welcome visiter with me. I think there can be a handsome subscription got here without fail, &c. &c. (Let them come; we shall be glad. Ed.)

A dear brother from Maryland writes: The second number of the Gospel-Visiter is before me, and I have no doubt, but my dear Br. at least looks for an acknowledgment of its receipt, at the hands of those brethren, to whom it has been sent, and I for my part can say, that the first number came to me, truly as its name would have it to be, a "Gospel-Visiter;" for being, as I was, shut up all winter and consequently cut off in a certain degree from my former communications with my brethren, written as well as verbally, thee can imagine my feeling of joy, when so an unexpected

"Visiter" greeted my thirsty spirit with joy and comfort; for I was filled with joy at the thought, that my breth. were not dead in regard to duty. And comforted in this, that through the medium of something (at least like the Gospel-Visiter) we could yet, although late in the day, more extensively contend for the faith as "once delivered to the Saints." I as one will pay for it at once, and try to support it, for I well know, that it is only in its infancy, and will grow. I will also give thee my opinion, respecting the character of the Gospel-Visiter. It should be just what its name would have it to be, a "Gospel-Visiter," and under no consideration to suffer anything of a controversial nature to go in its columns, and as its limits are narrow, its columns should be well filled with matter, both interesting and instructive, consequently long pieces should by all means be avoided, no one subject should fill much more than one column, rather less than more. It should be the aim of every contributor, to study brevity, and either write originally, or make choice selections. If this plan be pursued, although the "Gospel-Visiter" being of small dimensions, yet it can be made to contain a variety of subjects, which will be much more profitable, as long pieces are not generally read. Br. thou wilt bear in mind that this is not given as advice, only as opinion. Bear with me, and think of me, when it is well with thee.

(Reply. Thank you, dear Brother, for your kind epistle and friendly advice. We have tried, as you see, to mend our ways already, though we may not be able, always to avoid long articles. Pray for us.)

From an active Brother in Pennsylv.: I inform you with pleasure, that the strong prejudice which pervaded the minds of our leading Brethren here is measurably subsiding, and all who have read (which many do read) the numbers already out, say and admit, that they know nothing therein to condemn but much to admire,—therefore the frequent remittances occur.

From Illinois. After perusing it (the Visiter) through, I showed it to a number of the brethren, and it was much approved of by them. I have obtained a few names of the brn. that wished to take the first volume.

Beloved Brother, should I be spared, you may expect this only a commencement, as I intend to extend the circulation as much as I can. As I am fully of the belief for the want of such a work, we as a people have been very wrongfully represented, being too much unknown to the world.[16]

CORRESPONDENCE.   July 1851.

Note. We have nowhere tried ourselves to obtain subscribers for the Visiter, partly because we had but little time or opportunity, partly because we wish him to be such, as needs not our speaking for him. The following letters, lately received, seem to prove, that we have not entirely failed in this our wish.

From Virginia. Your packet, containing the Gospel-Visiter safely came to hand, and by carefully noting its contents, I am highly pleased with the work, hoping its contents may enlighten many. . . .

From Ohio. As respects your Visiter, it is heartily welcome and I trust there will be something worth mentioning done in its behalf, as soon as arrangements can be made. . . .

Another from Pennsylvania. There were two copies of the Gospel-Visitor came to this office for Br.___ but none since, and whether he wishes to take it or not I do not know. But if you have any prospect of continuing it I wish to take it. I fear you will get very little support in it from this region however. I have not yet met with any who are willing to remit the advance pay, or I should have written on sooner than this. I have a two dollar Ohio note laid by these three months intended for you, and was waiting to write for others as well as myself. I will now send it. Please place that much on your books to my credit. . . .

I should like to know too what the Brethren at Yearly Meeting said about the Visiter. They would not of course forbid its publication when done on your own responsibility, I suppose; but I mean what encouragement did they give to its publication?[17]

CORRESPONDENCE.   August 1851.

Our readers will perceive in this number, that we try to improve the external appearance of the Visiter, by getting a considerably better article of paper. If our subscription-list should increase sufficiently within 4 or 6 weeks, we would begin with the October-Number, to give 24 pages each month, and a farther increase of subscribers would enable us still to enlarge more.

From a letter from Pennsylvania. July 17, 1851. . . . I am not sorry for my visit to Ohio, for I have learned many things concerning the church. I wish you could feel to pay us a visit in the East. We have many things to contend against here, that is not so much felt in the West. We have much pride in our country and it has crept into the church in almost every quarter, and when it gets into the prominent members, it does much harm. Perhaps if you with some more of the old Brethren would visit us, you might assist in pulling down the strongholds of Satan; or perhaps if you would write an epistle to us to be read in the churches with us, it might be useful.

At least send us some good tidings that shall make our hearts glad. We all join in sending love to you all.

(Thank you dear Brother, for your kind invitation. My heart is inclined to make once yet a visit that far east, before I can travel no more, if for nothing else but to form a closer acquaintance, and to prove my humble love to all the brotherhood East and West, and North and South. God bless you and us with grace to know and do his will in all our going and coming in. Farewell.)[18]

CORRESPONDENCE   September 1851.
     Extract of a letter from Tennessee.
(Instead of the conclusion of the one in our last number, we give the following of a more recent date.)
     The object of my writing is on account of the Gospel-Visiter. I can assure you, that I greatly rejoice, that a work of that kind has commenced, which, if rightly conducted, will be calculated to promote the cause of truth and crown the church with inestimable blessings. Yet it appears that there are some Brethren opposed to the work; but we cannot expect that all our Brethren will have the same view of the matter. Some are opposed on the ground that money is at the bottom of this work; yet they are anxious to read the writings of those, who bear testimony to the truth. [(] I think that all ought to bear in mind, that printing requires labor, and paper, ink and type &c. costs money, and that the sum of one Dollar for twelve different numbers in the year is reasonable and scarcely sufficient to defray the expense of such a publication, when confined to the church alone in the different arms in the United States.)

     Notice. While we gratefully acknowledge the steady increase of our subscription-list, as stated monthly, we must still say, that not one half of those that promised their support from the first are yet heard from, and that even after so many subscribers have come in, our whole list does not yet come up, to what we counted on from the beginning, namely some 300. In order to give the friends of the Visiter time for renewed exertions, as to enable us, to enlarge it with next number, and to give ourselves time, to attend some of the appointments mentioned in this number, and also to go to Cincinnati for new type &c. our numbers for October and November will appear together perhaps not much before the middle of November.[19]

CORRESPONDENCE   October 1851.
     Since we have last issued our last Number, we have been sorely tried by untoward and unforseen circumstances, with a relation of which we will not trouble our readers. Only this much we must say, that we were unavoidably prevented to fulfil our promise of enlarging the Visiter yet, particularly as our subscription-list is yet too small to afford us the means for extra-labor and expense. We hope our readers will bear with us patiently.
     Having received a number of communications, and expecting still more, when winter-time will afford our correspondents more leisure, we

hope the Visiter will become more and more interesting and useful. To insure this, we would ask our readers but one thing & that is, not to be too
hasty either in approving or condemning ideas, that may occur in these
pages, and which may seem new or strange. Let us always be willing to
hear what may be said on the other side of the questions.[20]

CORRESPONDENCE   DECEMBER 1851

Two extracts of letters concerning the "VISITER."

Nro. I.

The numbers of the Visiter are truly among us. The piece headed
"Evidence of Christianity" is worth to me half what the paper costs me.
The Visiter is here with us (there are upwards of 20 subscribers) extensively
read in the church and out of the church, by old and young, male &
female. Therefore it ought to contain a variety of matter, a portion of
meat, duly seasoned, for every one. I think if only one brother in every
congregation could be stirred up to take the matter in hand, and reason the
case with the members,—the number of your subscribers might be
doubled, if not tripled. Below I give you the names of some new subscribers &c.

(Notwithstanding we receive weekly letters, expressing favorable
opinions concerning the Visiter like the above, yet we must say, that we feel
the want of some more such active agents, as we have in this and a few
other correspondents. The number of our subscribers is yet below Four
hundred, and while other printers would not begin such an undertaking
with less than five hundred, we have thus far gone on, and shall go on in
justice to our actual subscribers & in hope. Will not some take the hint of
our brother, and now try to enlarge our list of paying subscribers, so that
we may be enabled to enlarge the Visiter too? ED.)

Nro. 2.

(The following is of a different character, and we are glad to say, it is
the only one of its kind we received since the Visiter has made his
appearance. -It stands solitary and alone. We give it, without note or comment, to the discerning reader.)

I have received the first six numbers of the Gospel Visiter. As you
have sent them without my request, I had supposed for an introduction.
But in your apology in number 3. you inform all such that "according to
the usages of the children of this world" unless you are notified, we will be
held as subscribers, and eventually have to pay as such. Therfore I will occupy the station of the harmless dove, and say, I wish not to have the
Visiter any longer. Bear me in love, dear brother; were I not in impoverished circumstances, I should for your gratification have kept the paper for

a year. Likewise not having been favorable to its publication, and seeing no necessity for such an issue and in the mean while not having made any discovery to change my opinion, therefore I adopt this my asserted position. Permit me to say, that in my vicinity of the brotherhood there are many brethren and sisters, that coincide with me, &c.

––––––––––

We have been sending the Visiter from the beginning to a number of brethren, whose address we had, and of whom we hoped, they would bid him welcome, and assist us in its circulation, or if not favorable, they would inform us thereof. This last was done in one or two instances; a good many however have been friendly, and sent us lists of subscribers, but of many we never heard a word.

Still we continued to send, until October. The above letter and circumstances caused us to stop sending to any but paying subscribers, as we cannot afford with our small subscription to send several hundred copies every month of a work, that costs us a great deal of labor in body and mind, besides the heavy expenses for hands and materials, and at last to get nothing but such a harmless letter as the above. We repeat, we cannot afford this, and therefore hope no one will take offence at our stopping to send the Visiter. If a person is really poor in his outward circumstances, and yet desirous of having the Visiter, he may obtain it, by getting ten subscribers, free of cost except the trifle of postage. Nay, we will do more; to any church that hath sent or will sent pay for 10 subscribers, if we are apprised of the fact of a poor brother wishing also for the Visiter, we will send one for him gratis. But remember, we must all like the children of this world pay for what we buy, sell for money what we have to spare, and labor with our own hands, that we may have what we need, and also something to spare to the poor. Perhaps some have been waiting for opportunities, to send us word or pay. To those we would say, the best opportunity, and always at hand, is the mail. So far as we know all the money sent us by mail, has come safe. Send at once, then there is no need of keeping a long list of accounts, nor any need of that disagreeable task of dunning delinquent subscribers.

(With pleasure we communicate the following letter to our readers. It proves the increasing interest our brethren take in the welfare of the Visiter.)

From Maryland.

After a long delay, I take up my pen to write a few lines to you, informing you that we are still on mercy's side of our graves, in the enjoyment of reasonable health and many other blessings,—and for which we have daily cause to render a tribute of gratitude to God our Heavenly Father, who is the giver of every good & perfect gift.

I acknowledge the receipt of the Gospel-Visiter, have examined its contents, and I am now soliciting subscribers. I shall be able (I hope) to forward a number of subscribers to "the Gospel Visiter" hoping it will be able to sustain itself in the estimation of its readers, and afford a medium for communication to all who may feel a desire to improve the opportunity.

Had I been personally consulted, I should have suggested a few things to the publisher, and among others, the propriety of filling its columns as much as possible with original matter. This catering from the writings of others is objectionable, for various reasons. The names of the brethren are, (as I think with prudence,) withheld from being annexed to the articles which come from their pens. And it is thought that the names of all others should be excluded (at least,) if not their productions. And again if the brethren cannot write original matter sufficient to fill up its columns, I would advice delaying the publication, until this could be done. . . . I give this, as my sanguine opinions, and I am therefore ready to conclude,—that by the course suggested, the writing talent would become employed, the paper would be read with interest, would be enquired for, and thus find its way to the abode of many, who otherwise might remain ignorant of its existence, &c.

Dear brother, the responsibility you have assumed, is a heavy one; but if your motive is pure, God will impart his blessing, whilst the glory shall be His.

Should you adopt a course somewhat similar to the one above proposed. I would be willing to contribute my mite towards the matter, by trying my pen on some of the subjects that may present themselves to my mind as being necessary for discussion, &c.

May the grace of our Lord Jesus Christ be with you and yours. Amen.[21]

To Our Correspondents. January, 1852.

We have of late received several letters without the writer's proper name affixed to it, and in some cases have had to pay the postage on them. This is not as it should be. We must insist to know the writer's proper name, though we shall withhold it from the public, and we shall henceforth take no letter out of the office, which is not paid. Remember, a letter costs only three cents, if prepaid, while we have to pay five cents, if not prepaid. We prepay all our letters, and expect the same from our correspondents. Last mail-day we had to pay 20 cents for 4 letters, which might have been saved by each paying 3 cts. Think of this, dear friends & brethren.

THE GOSPEL VISITER FOR 1852.
NEW PROPOSAL.

When we set out in earnest upon the present publication, we did so under the solemn impression of our duty and responsibility, being fully aware of the difficulties of such an undertaking, especially taking in consideration the almost violent opposition, which had already then shown itself in different sections of our brotherhood. Believing that this opposition originated rather from prejudice and misapprehension, we hoped, that the actual appearance of the Visiter would by degrees remove the objections against it. This our hope has been realized in a good many instances, where strong opponents have become warm supporters of the Visiter; and our list of subscribers has been steadily increasing to this day. We consider this as a pleasing evidence, that we have not entirely failed of our aim.

Yet there are still some here and there, who do all they can in opposition to the Visiter. We received not long ago a letter without a name, for which we had to pay the postage, purporting to be from a brother, (though we never knew a brother, who was ashamed to show his face to his brother,) who asks us the very pertinent questions, "Whether our old brethren, or the apostles, or Christ ever were engaged in making money on any thing or not? Whether we have a right to get a living of the Gospel?" and wants an answer in the Visiter. He even goes so far, as to call our printing and publishing the Visiter a scheme to get money for bearing testimony to the truth.—We shall not stop at all to answer every silly question of nameless correspondents, who are too narrow-minded, as to comprehend good reason, and too close-fisted as to be willing to bear a part of their brother's burden, even in so small a matter as the postage. But we feel it our duty to be on a fair understanding in this respect with all our friends and candid readers. Some of these, though approving of our endeavors and willing to support them, think and say, "The price is too high for only 16 pages. There are publication of the same size, 16 pages monthly, circulating at 18¾ cents per annum. They have been looking for some time, that the Visiter should be enlarged to 24 pages &c."

These brethren understand perfectly, that "every laborer is worthy of his hire," and whatever honest business a man follows, he ought to live by it, whether it be by farming, in raising grain and stock, or whether it be by any trade, useful and necessary to mankind. They know, that no business can be carried on, unless it is paid for, and that even the farmer would soon stop operations, and try some other business, if he could not get a fair price for his produce. They know also, that our business is Printing, and that this business requires a great outlay, and therefore is always con-

nected with a greater risk, than almost any other business. They know lastly, that if we print the Gospel, or merely a Periodical on Gospel-principles,
we do not want pay for the Gospel, but for the labor of printing &c.

Now to those brethren and friends who know and understand this,
we would farther say that on consulting with experienced practical
printers we fixed our conditions, to publish every month from 16 to 24
pages at One dollar a year,   that is, to begin with 16 pages, and as soon
as 500 subscribers were obtained, to enlarge it to 24 pages. As soon as the
number of subscribers would have reached one thousand, we might have
enlarged it to 32 pages for the same price, and on a further increase of subscribers we should have reduced the price, so that 3000 subscribers should
have 32 pages a month for 50 cents a year; 7000 for 25 cts. a year and
10,000 for 20 cts. Try us, brethren, and we shall print as cheap as any
other printer can or will do, but we cannot print 500 at the rate we can
10,000.

This being understood, we must say that every reader, who will take
the trouble to count up the number of our subscribers, as we have given
them month after month, will find, that up to the present time the whole
number of subscribers, all told, is 428, consequently some 70 below 500.
Yet we would willingly continue to furnish 24 pages, as we do this time, in
hope of a further increase of subscribers. But upon trial, we now find, that
we cannot do it without confining ourselves all the day in the shop, to
assist and help along our young hands, and spend the nights in writing.
Still we have thought of doing a little more than justice to our subscribers,
conditionally, in some way until we can do better, and therefore we

PROPOSE,

1. If within two months one hundred new subscribers are sent, we shall
send two more No's extra for this first volume to all subscribers.
2. If within three months two hundred new subscribers come in, we
will add four No's to the Volume.
3. If Five hundred new subscribers are furnished within five months,
we will enlarge each number to 24 pages, & continue the first volume till
next December, furnishing new subscribers with back copies from the beginning, until exhausted, so that the first volume shall at least contain 320
pages, all at the price of One Dollar paid in advance.

To these conditions we shall strictly adhere, while life and health permits.

Consider! Now is the time!!

Remember that those who come first, will have most of the back
numbers!!![22]

List of Letters received by us since last Christmas [#122 through 183]. March, 1852.

... our dear readers will perceive, that the Gospel-Visiter is gaining daily new friends, and that we must now enlarge our monthly issue to 24 pages according to our own conditions. We rejoice at this:—but we do so with fear and trembling. For not only our labors and expenses will increase full one third,—but what is much more weighty on our mind, our duties and responsibilities are increasing likewise. Did we find difficulties, in making our selections for only 16 pages, so as to please our readers generally, how many more difficulties will we find, when we have still more selections to make, and still more readers to please! But we despair not. We are nothing but instruments in the hands of Him, who overruleth all for the best. The cause we plead is His, the glory we seek is His too. He has sustained us in every trial; His grace has enabled us to do what we did. Unto Him we trust for all, what we may need in future trials, so as to enable to do and to suffer His will in all things.

This, dear readers, is the fountain of our hope, that our labors shall not be in vain. We have already ample proofs of the blessing of God attending our weak endeavors. We have been blessed personally and individually in and through our work, for which we cannot be thankful enough throughout all eternity. But we have also evidences, that others of our fellow-pilgrims have been blessed in the perusal of the Gospel-Visiter. Could we spread those two hundred letters which we received since the first appearance of the Visiter, not only before our readers, but before all our dear brethren and sisters in these United States, who are yet prejudiced against any and every publication of our views and sentiments, but whom we do not love the less on that account,—we say, could we spread those 200 letters before them all, and the 200 pages of the Visiter too, that have by this time making their appearance, we believe every Thomas among our dear brethren would have to acknowledge, that the Lord is with us in this work, and that it might be dangerous for them to oppose it any longer. And if we are asked, what evidence have you beside your own belief and assertion of this fact, we would say, since it is impossible to enter into particulars, as follows.

We have now continued our periodical visits for twelve months;—we have conversed freely and unreservedly on many subjects, some of them at least being of a character, that they were not understood alike even among the brethren;—we have ventured to do all this in a language but imperfectly known by us, in which many of our readers can express themselves far more properly, far more happily to draw the attention of their hearers or readers, than we;—and what is the obvious result of this our undertaking? I mean, what is the result, not only obvious to us, but obvious to all who are willing to see? It is this, and we are confident, all our candid readers will agree with us, that we have through the means of the Visiter, though we are dispersed in twelve or more different states, become better acquainted with each other and with the sentiments of our old brethren, that were before us, in one short year, than we might have become in twelve years before, that we understand each other better, and love each other more than before;—that we all feel more strongly the benefit, the necessity and the blessedness of a true union in sentiment, in principles and in action or practice;—and may we not add, what we fondly hope and pray for, that we and all our dear readers have tried to become more prayerful, more watchful, and more consistent in our daily life and conduct with our holy profession. And now, dear brethren, this being the case, if not with all, yet with many, or even only with a few, as you will perceive in the following testimonies, will you say, This has been brought about by mere human agency? No, you cannot say that, because you know, mere human agency has always the contrary tendency, to separate, to divide and finally to destroy. We hope then, that you will be ready to admit, that this is the Lord's doing, and that if you be not willing to assist in the work of the Lord, you will be at least afraid to oppose it any longer....

To those dear brethren in particular, who have been or may be contributors to our columns, we must appeal most earnestly for a continuance of their favors, and for more frequent contributions. Small as the Visiter is, even with 24 pages, we have found by exact measurement, that our January No. contained as much reading-matter, as will be found in 36 pages of most other religions periodicals of the day, on account of its being printed with smaller type and less waste of paper by large margin. We agree with those brethren, that wish to see our columns filled chiefly with original matter. But this is impossible to do, unless we are more freely supplied by our correspondents with such articles, as may be proper for the columns of the Visiter. There are quite a number of our correspondents, of whom we should like to hear more frequently, who need not fear to send too often. Neither should those, whose articles do not appear immediately, or to which a short note of explanation &c. is appended, thereby be discouraged, to send communications. No, come, dear brethren, and help us in the good work as much as you possibly can; let all be done in love, in the love of truth, in the love of Christ and his brethren, and in love towards all mankind. In all our compositions let us try to please God, and then we may be sure to please His children, and benefit our fellow-men![23]

As Kurtz indicated both in some of the letters which he included in the

"Visiter" and in some of his own comments, the "Gospel Visiter" was not unanimously accepted among the Brethren. For that reason, the matter of its continuation was discussed by the Annual Meetings of 1852 and of 1853, and the final decision was not to interfere with its publication.

Y. M. 1852. Art. 4. In regard to the continuation of the Gospel Visitor, it was concluded that inasmuch as there is a diversity of opinion upon the subject, some in favor and others opposed, we cannot forbid its publication at this time, and hope those brethren opposed to it will exercise forbearance, and let it stand or fall on its own merits.

Y. M. 1853. Art. 3. In regard to Query 4th, of last year's Minutes concerning the Gospel Visitor. Inasmuch as the Visitor is a private undertaking of its editor, we unanimously conclude that this meeting should not any further interfere with it.[24]

Henry R. Holsinger and "The Christian Family Companion"

One of the young men who learned the printing trade as an apprentice of Henry Kurtz and who later established another periodical designed to appeal to the Brethren was Henry R. Holsinger from Pennsylvania. Holsinger explained that when he went "to live in the [Kurtz] family, in the autumn of 1856," he had been selected "as apprentice from a long list of applicants, because I was of 'German extract,' and could speak and read the language." Although Holsinger only remained about one year, he was a careful observer. Later he wrote some of his recollections of Henry Kurtz:

Elder Henry Kurtz was a German of the Teutonic caste. Anything that was not purely German might pass, but could not be set down as first-class.... Most of the editorials were written in German, and were translated into the English for the *Visitor*. He was an excellent German reader, and eloquent in prayer in his mother tongue, but hesitated and almost stammered in English. He was very religious in his forms, and held family worship every evening, and frequently in the morning, also. Under his charge I learned to exercise in prayer....

The melody [of his favorite morning hymn] was peculiar, and, of course, also German. Brother Kurtz was quite a musician, vocal and instrumental, and had an organ in the house, but rarely used it. I shall long remember one occasion on which I heard him perform and sing one of his favorites. I went to the house, where the editorial sanctum was, on business connected with the office. After entering the hall, I heard music, and finding the door ajar, I stopped and listened till the hymn was completed, much delighted with the strains. When I complimented him on his success, he explained that he had been tired of reading and writing, and had sought recreation and solace in the music. I prevailed on him to play and sing another piece for my gratification, which is the only occasion I remember that I was with him when the inspiration was upon him.

There was one German habit that Brother Kurtz had contracted which was a painful thorn in his flesh in his declining years. It was the tobacco habit. According to the flesh, he dearly loved his pipe, but he groaned in spirit to be relieved of the slavish bonds it had woven into his nature. And his experience furnished me with my strongest anti-tobacco sentiment. Poor old man! I would gladly have granted him full absolution, but his conscience would not. It was sad, and yet it was amusing to witness the pranks resorted to by this good man of mighty intellect and finished education. After dissipating with his pipe until dyspepsia and conscience came to his rescue, he would take the instrument of his torture to his wife, with the instruction, *"Now, gib mir sie nimmermehr."* ["Now, don't ever give me that thing again."] From the tone of her reply I'm very certain that she had received the same instructions before. Her reply was, *"Es Doart nicht lang,"* ["It won't last long"] and she knew what she was saying. Perhaps he held out faithfully a whole week, and sometimes possibly longer. The first time he went to the kitchen, he feigned sociability and business, and returned to his room without any farther advancement, to continue the warfare with the giant habit. After battling a day or two longer, he went again, ostensibly upon marital duties, but, in fact, with a view to the gratification of the baser passion. The mistake which he would invariably make before he was overcome would be in overdoing himself by unnatural smiles and courtesy. In this case he was told where he could find his old pipe, and he went his way rejoicing, although defeated and humbled.[25]

Holsinger and Kurtz parted ways because Holsinger was too ambitious. As Holsinger described the situation, "He endeavored to persuade Elder Kurtz, the editor and proprietor of the "Visitor," to change the paper to a weekly [from a monthly], and give him a place on the staff. But Elder Kurtz did not think the time had yet come when a weekly paper could be supported by patronage, or sustained by original contributions to give it dignity." Consequently Holsinger returned to his Pennsylvania home where he taught school in the winter and did farm work in the summer. For some eighteen months in 1863-1864, Holsinger published a secular newspaper, the "Tyrone Herald," but politics proved distasteful to him, and he decided to establish a weekly paper for the Brethren.

Holsinger had prepared himself carefully for such a venture, according to his own account, written in 1874.

I learned the printing business with Brother Henry Kurtz, in the office of the Gospel Visitor, in 1856-57. My first project then was the publication of the Morrison's Cove Journal, at Martinsburg, Pa., for which I had issued prospectuses, and secured upwards of 500 subscribers. But the financial crisis of 1857 spoiled the enterprise, for the gentleman who was to find the money to run it, thought it prudent, under the circumstances, not to invest. I had no money myself, so I betook myself to school teaching, and continued in the profession untill the spring of 1863. In the meanwhile, however, I made several attempts to raise the means to purchase a printing office, which I proposed to open at Martinsburg. In the spring of 1863 I learned of an old office for sale at Tyrone, I went to see it, and bought it for $300, in three annual payments, but concluded to operate at Tyrone instead of Martinsburg. Commenced operations at once, and in May issued the Tyrone Herald, which we continued untill November, 1864. The Herald started out as an independent paper, but during the political campaign of 1864, it became decidedly political, and took an active part in the election giving the soldiers a right to vote, the last election of Governor Curtin, and of President Lincoln. The political arena was taken from necessity, partly at least, but the sides from principle. We won, and earned a little money, but political work soured upon us, and before the campaign was ended we resolved to leave the field.

In the spring of 1864 we conceived the idea of publishing an independent church paper, to be issued weekly. At the district meeting of the middle district of Pennsylvania, we asked advice in regard to the project. The meeting publicly gave us permission to proceed upon our own responsibility, but privately many of the members present encouraged us in the enterprise. We then meant to call the paper the "Christian's Family Companion," but as that made the line a little too long of the letter we wished to use, we concluded to drop the apostrofix.

We thereupon issued a specimen number which we took to the annual meeting of 1864, held near Hagerstown, Indiana, and sent out through the mails, to such addresses as we could obtain. We also advertised in the Visitor. We then proposed to begin the regular issue by October 1st, but having the Herald on hand, and being in an important political contest, and having also engaged in school teaching, and besides the prospects not being very flattering, we concluded to postpone it until the beginning of the year. Accordingly we issued specimen No. 2, four pages, in which we announced that the paper was a fixed fact, and that we would now receive the money from all who wished to subscribe. This increased the confidence of the friends of the enterprise, and subscribers began to come in a little more rapidly.

After the results of the Presidential election had been announced we discontinued the Herald, and soon after we resigned the charge of the school, and began to make preparations for the prosecution of our new work. Some additional material and stock were required, to secure which we had to draw slightly upon our credit.

Promptly to promise, on the 1st of January, 1865, we sent out the first number of the Companion to less that 400 subscribers (memory says 384). In the first five numbers we acknowledge 252 cash subscriptions. The number gradually increased, and we closed the volume with over 1000 subscribers.[26]

In two different sections of the first number, Holsinger explained what he was trying to do and why it seemed necessary.

THE
"CHRISTIAN FAMILY COMPANION"

Is published every Tuesday, at $1.50 a year, by Henry R. Holsinger, who is a member of the "Church of the Brethren," generally known by the name of "German Baptists," and vulgarly or maliciously called *"Dunkards."*

The design of the work is to advocate truth[,] expose error, and encourage the true Christian on his way to Zion.

It assumes that the New Testament is the will of God, and that no one can have the promise of salvation without *observing all its requirements;* that among these are Faith Repentance, Prayer, Baptism by trine immersion, Feet Washing, the Lord's Supper, the Holy Communion, Charity, Non-conformity to the world and a full resignation to the whole will of God as he has revealed it through his Son Jesus Christ.

So much of the affairs of this world as will be thought necessary to the proper observance of the signs of the times, or such as may tend to the moral, mental, or physical benefit of the Christian, will be published, thus removing all occasion for coming into contact with the so called Literary or Political journals.

Introduction.

While, I think, I am fully sensible of my weakness and incapacity, to accomplish any great work, or to bring about a new era in the moral or literary world, and while I desire to have no aspirations, beyond those of an humble yet zealous Christian, and a respectable and useful member of society; and desire to assume no responsibilities, save those which the great Creator has placed upon every rational man, "duty to God and our fellow men," I am also conscious that, in fulfilling the duties which I have this day assumed, and in the prosecution of the work which I have this day begun, I am increasing my obligations to God and man, and that I am placing myself upon the record of time, among those who have aspired to greatness, and who have commanded influence and respect. I, therefore, enter upon these duties in all due seriousness of heart, and with a full and determined will. I believe I am making but a step forward in the path of life laid down in my childhood, and one which has been long desired and cautiously made; and the fact that it was only after thirty-one years of my life had been spent, that I was enabled to complete it, gives stimulus for forward movement. There is yet much to do. Of myself I can do little. By the grace of God I expect to fulfill my calling.

I desire to avoid repeating, as much as possible, any of the ideas advanced in the Introduction published in the specimen numbers, (which should be preserved with the first volume) and second No. of which can still be had; and inasmuch as the plan and object of my enterprize has been pretty fully set forth, there remains but little further to be said, by way of introduction.

It would be superfluous to lay down a long line for future action. All that has hitherto been done, must be accredited to the energy and capacity of the writer.—In the future the *Companion* will reflect, more, the number and character of its patrons, than the ability of its editor. I have built the ship and launched it, and shall make my best efforts to guide it alright, but it will require the tide of public favor to keep it in motion, and the gentle breeze of Divine approbation, to bring it safely into port.

With my present support, I shall be obliged to perform a great part of the mechanical labors of the printing office myself. To this I should not have the least objection, if I could at the same time manage to keep up the spirit and interest of the paper. There is perhaps more labor, anxiety, and attention required in the successful management of a public journal than the majority of our readers are aware. The regular and prompt appearance of our weekly issues will be expected, and to accomplish this, we may not unfrequently be obliged to make hasty selections, advance unpremeditated ideas, or admit unrevised correspondence.

With these few reflections, and with a full hope of being useful, and interesting, and of meeting with a living support, the *Companion* is sent abroad.[27]

Holsinger had evidently found a need among the Brethren, for his paper prospered, as he indicated in 1874 when he was retiring temporarily from the publishing field.

We then sold our old material and purchased an entire new outfit, and also bought an old power press. This was a big mistake, as we had better bought a good new press at once. However, we made it answer our purpose several years, by running it by horse power. The second volume closed with over 1500 subscribers, the third with above 2000, and printed by steam. In July of the fourth volume, we put in a new cylinder power press, took away the border from the paper, and enlarged it to sixteen pages, but reserved the first two and the last two for advertisements, but they have never been used. Volume four closed with about 3000 subscribers, and volumes five and six ran up to 4000 and upward. Since then we have been moving on in the even tenor—no not of *our* way, but at an even tenor, ranging at 4000 to 4500, other publications having somewhat divided the patronage.[28]

By the end of this period in 1865, Brethren had established two different magazines, the "Gospel Visiter" published monthly by Henry Kurtz and the "Christian Family Companion" published weekly by Henry R. Holsinger. The latter was more liberal and progressive, and in fact, Holsinger would eventually get into difficulty with the church for his progressivism, especially represented by his willingness to publish all kinds of letters to the editor. The most important thing, however, was that there were now regularly established, albeit privately owned, journals which provided a means of communication among the Brethren from the Atlantic to the Pacific.

DEVOTIONAL WRITINGS

During this period there is not much evidence of poetry being written by members of the Church of the Brethren. At the beginning of the period, Alexander Mack, Jr., was continuing to produce some poetry. A Brethren minister in Pennsylvania, named Jacob Stoll, published a book of poetry in 1806. At the end of the period, there were some illustrations of Civil War poetry. In 1796, Peter Leibert published a book in Germantown dealing with the validity and legality of war, which included some of the poetry of Alexander Mack, Jr., as an appendix. One of the poems is included in this section as an illustration of Mack's poetry.

Therefore, let God be feared in all the earth; for righteousness is so constituted that whoever associates himself with the pious will enjoy their benefits, and to whomsoever in all the world the fear of God is pleasing, to him will come the blessings of Salem's-tent.

Melody: The Bridegroom of the Soul

1.
God alone is good,
This gives us courage,
Our heart's delight and joy
The consoler and nourisher of good souls,
The flame of our faith,
God alone is good.

2.
God alone has power,
Deliberately He guides,
All the works of His hands
Submit to His omnipotent power,
The vigil of good angels
God alone has power.

3.
Jesus is the treasure
And the gathering-place
Of all the souls that love Him,
That practice themselves in love.
He who finds Him has found
Both gathering-place and treasure.

4.
Life in death,
Refuge in distress,
To embrace the beloved Jesus,—

That sweetens all pains,
It makes the Bread of Heaven,
Life in death.

5.
Say what is more rich
Than the poverty
Which, on the cross in Jesus' wounds,
With the robber, is found.
Christ's poverty
Makes us rich and free.

6.
He who tarries still
With the things of this world,
Cannot find this treasure
Nor freedom from sin
Which is always associated with
The things of this world.

7.
He who hates false living,
That evil guest
Which is to be nothing and to have nothing,
He will find God and all the gifts
That Heaven holds,
He who hates false living.[29]

Another prominent Brethren poet, about twenty years younger than Alexander Mack, Jr., was Jacob Stoll. Like Mack, he was a minister, the elder of the Conestoga congregation in Pennsylvania for a number of years. In 1806, when he was seventy-five years old, a volume of his poetry and other devotional writings was printed at Ephrata. The following hymns have been translated from the original German by Ora W. Garber.

Hymn Number 1
1.
I can hear a clear voice ringing
Which resounds o'er vale and hill;
Lovely as the shepherds' singing,
Gracious, charming, is it still.
2.
In the valleys' quiet fastness,
On the mountains round about,
One can hear it in the vastness
Calling to him, "Oh, come out."
3.
Why are you so long sojourning,
In the world with its allure?
Are you dreaming, not discerning
Your true fortune? Are you sure?
4.
Oh, the world brings naught but
sorrow
Which hell holds on grand display
In its dark room till tomorrow—
Till the coming judgment day.
5.
O dear soul, take counsel thereto
And reverse your course and pace,
For your Christ has come first to
you
Offering you His love and grace.
6.
Jesus, Thou my true salvation,
I would join myself to Thee.
Lameness is my life's low station;
Come, bring wholeness unto me.
(Jesus:)
7.
Come, then, I will heal your
weakness.

Let our pathways be the same.
In all patience, zeal, and meekness,
Gladly share with me my shame.
8.
Let my way of love be your way.
Follow me, nor draw apart.
I will lead you through heaven's
doorway
That you may, with your whole
heart,
9.
There rejoice in bliss unending
In that realm of soft, sweet rest.
Soul renewal I am sending.
Be prepared; by it be blessed.
(The Soul:)
10.
In Thyself then wilt Thou hide me,
Blessed Jesus, evermore,
On that pilgrim street to guide me
And prepare me to adore
11.
And to praise, with joy increasing,
In this noble time of grace
Till, in blissfulness unceasing,
I shall praise Thee face to face.

Hymn Number 6
1.
The day having come to its ending,
The darkness of night is now here.
May God then be praised, who was
sending
To me all I hold good and dear,
Whose mercy has shown

My soul, needy, lone,
A protector who always is near.

2.

Then into Thy care I am giving
Myself in the darkening night.
True friend of the souls of the liv-
ing,
Here under Thy strong, watchful
sight
Keep Thou my poor soul
Free from the control
Of my foes and their vast evil
might.

3.

Since it is not good to be spending
The deep-troubled time here alone,
Oh, grant me Thy presence unend-
ing,
Beloved Christ Child, Thou my
own;
And shield me, I pray,
By night and by day
With the brightness that comes
from Thy throne.

4.

O Jesus—my soul's life I've found
Thee—
I know Thou dost well understand
How my foes now completely sur-
round me
In this unfamiliar land.
My faith would they take
If it would but break.
Hold me then, O my God, by Thy
hand.

5.

Forgive all my sin, Thou who bore
it;
Blot out, gracious Lord, all my
wrong.

Let grace touch my heart and
restore it;
Empower me that I may be strong
To conquer my sin
And then enter in
Thy full life with that heavenly
throng.

6.

Strong champion in time of con-
tending,
Protector of Israel Thou,
To Thee, Thee alone, I'm com-
mending
Both body and soul here and now
Before those who aspire
To drag in the mire
My poor soul and to shatter my
vow.

7.

Dear Savior, I trust Thee securely;
Thou dost neither slumber nor
sleep.
To me, Thy vine-branch, then send
surely
True watchfulness that I may keep
Creating good things
Which my soul then brings
To discipleship rich, wide, and
deep.

8.

Then grant, Lord, that I may not
lose Thee;
O Jesus, supreme good Thou art,
Life's rock, the soul's fortress—I
choose Thee.
Send courage and strength to my
heart
That I hold Thee high,
While years hasten by,
As my present and eternal part.

9.

Amen, Lord, amen. O my Savior,
Speak Thy "yes" as Thou know'st
  to be best,
That I, in both word and behavior,
May praise Thy great name ever
  blest
  And give ceaseless thanks
  Within the glad ranks
Of the hosts in the heavenly rest.

Hymn Number 10

1.

Shepherd, Thou my soul art tend-
ing;
My life Thou dost understand.
Myself, then, I am commending
To Thee here in this strange land.
Free me of all vain pretense
And all else which gives offense.

2.

The true state of my whole being
Is not kept from Thee apart.
Thou art also clearly seeing
The corruptness of my heart.
All the perils threat'ning me
Are well known, O Lord, to Thee.

3.

In this difficult position
I do not know what to do.
Each wrong deed and each omission
Are before Thee in full view.
Every moment, day and night,
My life stands within Thy sight.

4.

Total is my degradation;
Nothing good in me is found;
I deserve complete damnation.
Unless Thy rich grace abound,

Animating me anew,
I am worthless through and
  through.

5.

Jesus, faithful shepherd, take me
Near to Thee, Thy little lamb.
Dwell within me and remake me
More like Thee than I now am.
Thou seest bonds about my soul;
Break them and assume control.

6.

Of Thy Spirit's power giving,
Grant unto me true faith's might.
Thyself in me working, living,
Help me exercise aright
Chivalry throughout my days.
Fit me, Lord, to live Thy praise.

7.

Dearest Jesus, life the dearest,
Thou dost fully know my strife.
My encircling foes Thou hearest
As they taunt my pilgrim-life.
They would take my hope away.
Steel my faith to meet that day.

8.

With Thy strength my life up-
holding,
Grant me earnestness and zeal.
In myself Thy works unfolding,
Let my life Thyself reveal,
That I live but to praise Thee
Here and in that world-to-be.

9.

Must the ills of life betide me?
Must I feel affliction's blight?
Then, O Jesus, stand beside me
Guiding me by day and night.
Grant me counsel, grant me power,
To endure till life's last hour.

10.

Jesus, for this I am pleading:
Be my life, my wealth, my own;
Give to me the grace I'm needing
That I honor Thee alone
Here in time unceasingly
And there in eternity.

Hymn Number 11

1.

Jesus, Thou the soul's dear treasure,
Come, oh, come. Be ever mine
And espouse me in full measure
That I may be ever Thine.

2.

Bring complete obliteration
Of that which is earthy still.
Lead me to glad dedication
Of myself to do Thy will.

3.

Lord, wash my corrupted being;
All my heavy guilt erase.
My life from its sin-stains freeing,
Send Thy favor and Thy grace.

4.

My whole heart unto Thee taking,
Purest jewel, Immanuel,
My whole being now remaking,
Candle-Flame, within me dwell.

5.

In this realm of time-bound story,
And in that of endless bliss,
I will spread abroad Thy glory;
Make me ready, God, for this.

6.

When death, then, life's cord shall
   sever
And my days on earth shall cease,

I can live with Thee forever
In that far-off land of peace.

7.

With the harp notes and the prais-
   ing
Of that throng already crowned,
Who their joyous songs are raising,
May my own glad song resound.

8.

Amen, Jesus, lambkin dearest,
Speak Thy "yes" to my request:
That I, O Thou love-flame clearest,
Praise Thy name in holy rest.

Hymn Number 13

1.

Jesus is my good, my goal,
Best of all eternal graces.
Through Him my uplifted soul
Makes its home in heavenly places.
He's the true light of my heart;
From him I shall not depart.

2.

Jesus I shall not forsake
While upon this earth I'm living.
All life-gains which I may make
I am gladly to Him giving:
My life's light that grows not dim—
I shall never turn from Him.

3.

Jesus is life's constant spring,
My faint heart ofttimes reviving.
To Him, sun of grace, I cling,
Light and warmth from Him deriv-
   ing.
I'll not put Him from my sight;
Of my life He is the light.

4.

O my Jesus, heavenly Bread,
Thou who my starved soul art
  feeding,
By whom I am comforted
When my foes have left me
  bleeding,
I can triumph but through Thee,
And from danger can be free.

5.

Bind me, Jesus, by Thy grace,
Close to Thee, my faith constrain-
  ing,
That I run life's ordered race,
To my rightful goal attaining;
That I win, through faithful strife,
To Thy praise, the crown of life.

6.

Close to Thee may I be bound,
In Thy faithfulness abiding,
On Thy narrow way be found
With Thy loving presence guiding,
Until Thee alone I gain,
Ever with Thee to remain.

7.

How shall I then, with delight,
Sing Thy praise, O King, forever,
In that land where is no night,
Lauding Thee and ceasing never?
Glory, thanks, and heartfelt praise
To the Lamb through endless days!

8.

Oh, what marvels meet one's glance
When to heaven he gains admission,
Where, before his countenance,
Pious faith is life's position,
Where the holy watchers throng
Full ten thousand thousand strong.

9.

I'll cling to Him till life's end,
And where heaven's pure light
  glances.
It is on Him I depend
In all troubled circumstances.
When my foes with strength assail,
My allegiance will not fail.

10.

By my Jesus I shall stay,
Ever to Him safely clinging.
I can walk my pilgrim way,
With the light that He is bringing,
Through grave perils lurking there
Of which one is scarce aware.

11.

Jesus is my life's true tree
Full of pure and noble fruitage.
Unbelief will cease in me
If I grant Him fullest rootage.
Here and there, whate'er befall,
He will be my All-in-All.

Hymn Number 14

1.

Dearest Jesus, Life the dearest,
Fountain of all blessedness,
Thou my dedication hearest,
Thou removest my distress
Bringing comfort, power, and grace.
Do not turn from me Thy face.

2.

O my Jesus, I shall love Thee
Best of all the friends I know
I shall love Thee and extol Thee
If Thy light within me glow.
My most precious gem Thou art;
I'll love Thee with all my heart.

3.

I shall praise Thee, my protector;
I shall praise Thee, O my shield.
Deeds will be my heart's reflector.
Not just words my lips may yield.
Teach me, Lord, that praise be
    found
In my heart, and thanks abound.

4.

And since Thou, my life's great
    treasure,
Hast been mine throughout my
    years,
Bringing life's profoundest pleasure,
Joy ofttimes displaces tears.
When I feel the greatest need,
Then Thy kindly hand dost lead.

5.

Dearest of all loves known to me,
Do not tire of me, I pray.
Let Thy gentle power flow through
    me
Evermore, day after day,
Radiating from above
Heavenly candelight's pure love.

6.

Draw me into that life station,
O my Jesus, in which nought
But Thy love gains penetration
In my heart of pureness wrought,
Where, in deep humility
I shall be found presently.

7.

Oh, that love—of loves the surest—
Shown in Jesus through God's plan!
Out of this warm love, earth's
    purest,
He became for man a man

And has played a patient part
With the evils of my heart.

8.

Therefore I am bound securely
To Him, ever to be true,
Every day and hour most surely
Held by Him in all I do
Till our spirits shall unite
And no changes are in sight.

9.

Praise the Lord, my entire being;
Praise His great and holy name.
All His far-flung works, agreeing,
Join in sounding forth His fame.
Hallelujah, great is He!
Let His name exalted be.

10.

Worm of earth, His love reviewing,
Let that goodness be extolled
Which He daily is renewing
And which He may yet unfold.
God be praised both now and then
In eternity. Amen.

Hymn Number 17

1.

Soul of mine, give praise to God,
Him whose nature is perfection
Of his own freewill election,
Him who gives you help divine.
Praise your God, O soul of mine.

2.

Soul, give praise unto your God,
Who in tender love is calling
Unto those whose yoke is galling,
Those who live through anguished
    days.
Soul, unto your God give praise.

3.

Soul, give praise unto your God,
Him whose chosen disposition
Lovingly meets man's condition,
Who from no man turns His sight,
Knowing his distress aright.

4.

Soul, give praise unto your God,
Who His love through Jesus gave
  you—
Him who lost His life, to save you,
On the cruel cross, that He
Your true Easter Lamb might be.

5.

Soul, give praise unto your God:
Who all peril has deflected;
Who has kept you safe, protected;
Who—how hard to understand!—
Proffered you His gracious hand.

6.

Soul, give praise unto your God.
Praise His name, the great and
  holy,
Who in Jesus Christ, the lowly,
Offered love to every race.
Soul, praise then your God of
  grace.

7.

Freely shall I thank Him then
For His grace which has caressed
  me,
Which has guarded me and blessed
  me
And has led me night and day.
Praise and thanks shall I display.

8.

May I bring my praise although
With earth's dust and worms I'm
  fated,
Till at last I'm liberated

And all strife and struggle cease
In the land of joy and peace.

9.

Where the "hallelujah" rings,
Where the saints chant ceaseless
  praises
And the host its thanks upraises,
There will I with constancy
Bring Him praise eternally.

10.

Go then diligently forth;
Disregard the world's restraining
Lest your love experience waning
And you reach not heaven's gate.
Go now forth; no longer wait.

11.

Pilgrim, do not be fatigued.
See you not, that height command-
  ing,
In its dazzling glory standing,
God's great city made of gold?
Pilgrim, be alert and bold.

12.

Enter through the narrow door.
Constant diligence maintaining,
From all earthly things abstaining,
Come at last to where he waits
In that city of twelve gates.

Hymn Number 20
1.

Oh, how is the time so urgent
Which God still allows us here;
And the world how vain, emergent,
Which can often interfere
With our footsteps, oft restraining
What love strives to be attaining,
Does not speed one on his way.
But may cause him much delay.

2.

Oh, how is the time so urgent,
Which God cannot give again;
And the world how vain, emergent,
Which is loved too much by man,
That we walk in dull neglecting,
Dreamily, with scant reflecting
On how long the time may be
Of God's vast eternity.

3.

Oh, how is the time so urgent,
Time so noble and so brief;
And the world how vain, emergent,
Clothed in sorrow, pain, and grief,
Bound by troubles which come
 thronging.
Therefore let your heart's deep
 longing
Go toward that eternal day
Where all sorrow fades away.

4.

Oh, how urgent is the present
Which God, out of mercy, gives;
And eternity how unpleasant
To the one who wholly lives
For this world with lures en-
 trancing,
Not with earnestness advancing
Toward that land of joy and rest,
Loving earthly things the best.

5.

How important and momentous
Are the days of life's brief span;
Teach me, Jesus, how portentous
Are these days to mortal man.
All my earthly days respecting,
None but Thee as mine electing
Here upon my pilgrim way,
May I bear the cross someday.

6.

Therefore give consideration
To time's ever-rapid pace,
Lest death end your life's duration
And you forfeit heaven's grace.
Though your earth-life you are now
 spending
You must go, in life unending,
Where the darkness is complete,
Where no moment can be sweet—

7.

Only bitter pain and fretting
In eternity's long span.
He who, all things else forgetting,
Follows Christ and lives His plan,
He who in His Lord rejoices,
Joining with that host whose voices
Are extolling Him, shall stand
Evermore at His right hand.[30]

An illustration of Civil War poetry was "A HYMN composed and sung by Brother John C. Moomaw on the day of fasting and prayer in 1861." It was preserved by the Crumpacker family.

1.

O Lord, we in thy presence are,
Fasting, we seek thee here in prayer.
Wilt thou then in our presence be,
And grant our souls to meet with
 thee?

2.

Our happy land, the exiles' home,
The scene of strife has now become.

O Lord, if it thy pleasure be,
From war and bloodshed set us
   free.

3.

Lord, thou hast been the widow's
   friend,
Then wilt thou e'en her sons
   defend?
Command the sword return again
Into its sheath and there remain.

4.

The spacious worlds are all thine
   own.
Sure thou dost rule, and thou
   alone,—
Then make the earth unto thee bow,
Nor say, "O Lord, what doest
   thou?"

5.

In days of old thou didst command
The rolling wave a wall did stand;
Thy people, Lord, thou then didst
   save,
Their foes then found a watery
   grave.

6.

Thy people in Assyria's day,
Besieged by Syrian forces lay;
They prayed, and thou didst hear
   their cry,
And sent an angel from on high.

7.

The angel of the Lord came down,

And took away the tyrant's crown,
His army all at break of day
As leaves in autumn's forest lay.

8.

Then, Lord, we to thee now draw
   near,
In confidence that thou wilt hear,
When we, thy people, pray to thee,
O Lord, from tyrants set us free.

9.

Roll back the mighty torrent wave,
That threatens to be freedom's
   grave,
And cause that all the world shall
   own
That thou art God, and thou alone.

10.

O may this happy land then be
From war and strife again set free,
That nations' strife and wars may
   cease,
In justice, right and endless peace.

11.

O Lord, destroy the cruel sword,
And in its stead supply thy Word;
Give grace to soften every heart
And grant thy mercies to impart.

12.

Our cause to thee we now resign,
Nor would we alter thy design.
In sweet submission all in one,
We say, "Our Father's will be
   done."[31]

A second illustration of Civil War poetry was "The Prisoner's Song," which was composed by the prisoners at Mt. Jackson; the chorus was added by John Kline while the group was imprisoned in the courthouse in Harrisonburg. Originally, there were nine verses, but only four were in-

cluded "with some changes in accent and rhythm," when it was arranged and set to music by A. D. Lair and J. M. Showalter.

1.
We are in prison, close confined,
But this not one of us should mind,
For Christ has told us in His word,
That we should always trust the
Lord.

2.
We know it is God's holy will,
Our fellow men we shall not kill;
That we should lead a Christian life,
And not engage in war and strife.

3.
But there is One who reigns on
high,
He always will to us be nigh,—

He will from prison us redeem,
If we will put our trust in Him.

4.
Then let us all the Lord obey,
And from the truth we'll never
stray;
Lo that we all may stand the test,
And when we die, go home to rest.

Chorus
We'll all go home as soon as freed,
A holy life with God to lead,—
Yes, we'll go home, and that to
spend
Our days in peace till life shall
end.[32]

Most of the private letters written during these years had something to say about religious concerns, as has been indicated by many of those already quoted. In addition, parts of the letters frequently dealt in general terms with the spiritual welfare of those who were writing and those to whom they were writing, for illness, suffering, and death were very real to people on the frontier, and religion seemed to provide the greatest source of security. A letter in 1839 from Indiana illustrated this type of concern.

Putnam County, Indiana
September 8, 1839
I have taken the pressent oppertunity of writen thes few indifrent lines to you to let you know that wee are all well hopeing and wishing thes few lines may find you all engoying god helth both to soal and boddy for which reason wee ought to be thank full to Almighty god for tender mercy towards us poor Mortals that he has sprd   us in the land of the Living that wee may praepare our selvs for that awfull Eturnety   thus saith the Lord set thy hous in order for thou shelt die and not Live thear fore let us try to follor his foot step and srve the Lord while wee sagor [?] hear below in this tourbelsom world   there fore this is no great pleasure in this

world   all is vain and soon vanish a way   would it profet us to gain the whole world and luse our soul or what wold wee give in our last Dying moments to hare that sweat voies say Come ye blessed of my father in herret the kingdom that is prepared for all true follows of the lamb[33]

From Maryland in 1840 came words of encouragement to serve the Lord and to follow him.

Pipe Creek, Maryland
July 12, 1840

my dear cousins you that are now in your youthfull blood now is your time to set out to serve the Lord,   the Grace of God that bringeth Salvation hath appeard unto all men, teaching them that den[y]ing unGodliness and all worldly lusts, we should have soberly and righteously and Godly in this preasant world,   no doubt but you have felt that small still voice, wispering to you, to prepare to meet your God,   O come to Jesus, read his word and obay it and you will be happy in time and in Eternity,   yes the greatest happyness we can enjoy is in the Lord   there is no substantial joys to be found in this world, only in God,   My son, the pleasures of Earth will soon fade away,   they bloom for a season but soon they decay but pleasures more lasting in Jesus are given, Salvation on Earth and a mansion in Heaven.[34]

This spiritual challenge was written by a man in Maryland to his brother in Virginia; eventually, the recipient of the letter not only joined the church as this letter suggested, but also was called to the ministry and served in that way for many years.

February 2, 1852

in reading the letter you sent to catharine I noticed that you gave her some good advice concerning her future state and it made me feel quite glad to find that your thoughts run in that channel at least sometimes would to god it were more so and the news would come that you and mary had made up your minds to serve the lord for I do think that if you would come that Mary would come with you and as you have a good education & possessed of sound mind what a usefull man you might be in the church besides saving yoursiff you might also be the means of saving others also.   remember it is appointed for man once to die and after this the judgement.   while we are in this world is the time to prepare for the next   if we spend all our time in gain[in]g the things of this world it will proffit us nothing in the end   therefore I as a brother and one that feels concerned for your eternal as well as temporal happiness would advise you to search the scriptures and try to serve the lord according to his word & will   you I judge have read enough of the scriptures already to know what you should do,   the scripture says first seek ye the kingdom of heavan and its righteousness and all the rest shall be added unto you   therefore you can percieve there is nothing lost by complying with Gods word but much to gain both in this world and in the world to come and I do feel assured that if you had once tasted of the mercies and good-ness of god you would wonder why you had stayed away so long and would never more want to go back to the weak and begarly element of this world.[35]

The final item in this chapter is a rather long unpublished biography, from which portions have been selected. It was written in the 1860s by J. C. Myers about his sister, Catherine Ann Myers, who had joined the Church of the Brethren after having been a Baptist. Since she did not live for very long after her change in church membership, the description of her illness and death was intended as a devotional and spiritual challenge to others.

Catherine Ann Myers was born near the village of Mt. Sidney in the north eastern part of Augusta County Virginia, on the 19th October 1833. She was the youngest child of Micheal and Ann Myers, whose ancestors had removed from Pennsylvania to the valley of Virginia toward the close of the past century. The parents of her whose humble life is sketched in this little volume, were in very common circumstances, too poor indeed to give their children the education they desired. Plain, honest and simple-hearted, they chose to bring them up, very much under the old fashioned Penn-sylvania rule of their ancestors. Being scrupulously honest in matters of right they never suffered them to do even the smallest act that was wrong. Although not connected with any branch of the Christian Church while their children were growing up; yet they never failed to read the Bible to them on the Sabbath, both in the German and English languages. Anxious to give them more religious instruction than they were capable of impart-ing they incouraged them to attend Sunday School and the preached word. Reading, writing, and to the Single Rule of Three in common Arithmetic was all the education they were able to give them. Their limited means thus compelled them to send a family of six children out in the world with nothing more than the elements of an English education. Thus, a crippled father, and a anxious mother, had to behold their children go forth, poor and ignorant from their homes, but always gave them this advice. *"Do not forget your heads and your books."* . . .

On the 19th day of September 1851, in the 18th year of her age she was baptised by Elder Thomas W. Roberts of Nelson County, then Pastor of Sacred Well Baptist Church. Side by side with her brother Samuel, she went down into the water and was buried with Christ by baptism. After she had arose from the liquid grave to walk with Christ in newness of life she beheld ten others going down two and two also to obey the Saviour's ordinance and obtain "the answer of a good conscience toward God."

No sooner had she entered the Saviour's moral vinyard, than she felt that she was not to do like the laborers he once described in his parable of an earthly vinyard. *"Stand there all the day idle?"* But, she felt that although now a member of the church, yet the great object of life was not accomplished. The church was not a cradle in which the saint was to be rocked to sleep. but it was rather a camp in which the soldier of the cross was to be drilled for usefulness in life. She felt conscious that it was the duty of every member of the church, male or female, young and old, rich or poor, to be engaged in *personal efforts* for the salvation of others. Although but a lamb in the church she saw that it was as necessary to have a Dorcas in the pew as it was to have a Paul in the pulpit. Impressed with these feelings she was ever found performing her duty as a private member of the church. . . .

No matter whether the church was in prosperous or in adverse circumstances she seemed the same meek and faithful diciple. Where the sun shine of prosperity gladdened and revived the garden of the Lord, she was there to share its joys, and when the dark Cloud of Trouble over-shadowed it causing its plants to droop　and some even to die, still she would be there to share in its adversity. Bodily infirmity and inclement weather of course sometimes prevented her attendance. Deacons who had not half so far to travel as she were often too busy to loose a part of one Saturday in each month to attend the meeting of the church while she would ride three or four miles to be there. Members, in health and vigor, nearer the church often found it more convenient to remain at home than to attend a church meeting while this frail diciple would be found at her post. Indeed, she seemed cheerfully to comply with every requirement of the church and often regretted that she had not the ability to do more.

From the death of her father on the 15th May 1852, she became more inclined to walk nearer the Saviour, and more ardently desired to be like him in feeling and disposition. This could be seen in her fondness for her Bible and the reading of every good book she could command. Her attachment to her books, her conversations and her deportment all seemed to say that her affections were permanently set in things above, and not on the transient things of earth. Singing of hymns and spiritual songs were also among the evidences she gave of the devotional frame of her mind. This last, was a regular and favorite mode of her's, in rendering praise to God. Singing his praises were among the first things you heard from her in the morning, and among the last things you heard from her at night.

On the 16th day of September she told the Compiler that she had for months some misgivings as to her Christian duty and had almost desided to change her church relation but before doing so desired his advice. Not having a record of what was said on that occasion he had to quote from memory alone but thinks he will not materially err by giving the following as her language.

It seems to me said she from the plain teaching of the Scriptures that the followers of Christ ought to observe feetwashing as an Ordinance of the church. But what shall I do when my church does not believe so? Must I remain in my church because I love it and at the same time feel some misgivings as to my whole Christian duty? Love to my church has struggled with me on the one hand and my duty fully to obey Christ called to me on the other. This conflict has distressed me more than it perhaps would some others; because I do not believe persons ought to go from one church to another, unless they have the best assurance that they are in error, and ought to change their church relations. These things continued to rob me of a good deal of religious consideration and prayer and often advice. But when once she clearly heard God's voice and saw his hand she endevored to follow where he led.

On the 17th September, or the day after the interview refered to her little niece, Virginia Alice Myers became prostrated with Scarlet Fever which terminated in her death in fourteen days. Upon this painful event she addressed the writer with the following note.

New Hope October 3rd 1862

Dear Brother

It is my solemn duty to write to you again upon the subject of death. Virginia is dead. She was taken with the Scarlet Fever the day after you left, and lingered on untill last Wednesday morning about 8 o'clock her spirit took its everlasting flight to that God who gave it. Her sufferings were very great during the two weeks she was sick but now she is at rest. I miss her very much. She was the last one to part with me when I left and the first one to meet me when I returned. As I stood by her grave a small voice whispered *my loss* is *her eternal gain*. I could not help thinking of the joy there was in heaven when her little spirit joined that of her father and grand mother, who so lately left her in the world of trouble. Ten months ago they were all *here,* but now they are *gone.* Three fresh mounds now mark their last resting place

"Alas the brittle clay.
That build our body first.
And every month and every day.
'Tis mouldering back to dust."

It is my intention to pay my Rockingham friends a visit next Tuesday if I meet with no Providential hinderances, I expected to attend a big meeting at Green Mount even two weeks ago, but could not go owing to the sickness and death of little Virginia. Two Baptist ministers joined the Dunkard Church at that place, one was Brother B[enjamin] F[unk]. The other Brother W. C. T[hurman]. Please excuse bad writing and mistakes, I generally write in hast. . . .

Having dissolved her connection with Laurel Hill Baptist church by a letter of dismission some time in the later part of September, she on the 4th October connected herself with the German Baptist church, usually known as Dunkards, and was baptised on the 5th by triune immersion by Elder John Miller of Augusta County.

On the 7th October, she left home for the purpose of carrying out the visit contemplated in the above letter. During the visit it would seem that her mind was often on a coming day set by her church for a Sacramental meeting. Being anxious for as many of her friends to be present on that occasion as could do so. She was induced to drop the following note to the writer of these pages, which was the last written communication he ever received from her.

Harrisonburg October 15th 1862

Dear Brother

I address you with a few lines to inform you that I left home on Tuesday after little Virginia was buried. I will return home the last of this month. There will be a Sacramental meeting at the Brick Church near New Hope, on the first and second days of November. Brethren F— and T— of whom I spoke in my last letter will be present. It was the wish of a friend that I should request you to come down then. This is also my wish. I anticipate a time of social and religious enjoyment. Ten days ago I changed my church relation. Come down if you can. I will be delighted to see you. If you cannot come then, you may find me at home any time after the first of November. Please excuse bad writing. I may perhaps do better in future. . . .

[From her Journal:]

Thursday morning January 1st 1863. Through our Heavenly Father's care, I am permitted to write a little concerning the year that has closed, and O, what sadness fills my heart, when I look back on the events of that year. Sad however as my heart feels, my sadness becomes almost swallowed up with solemnity. Thirteen months have not yet rolled away since it was my lot to endure many things, and to pass through several solemn transactions. One year ago on the 5th day of December last, it became my painful duty to follow my beloved mother to her grave. Soon after this, the Lord laid the hand of affliction upon one, and for months I was prostrated by sickness. On the 16th of April, while my body was languishing by reason of disease, my kind brother was brought a corps into the house, having died in the army a few days before. On the 30th September, death laid its cold and chilling hand on my little niece and consigned her to the grave. Alas for that family circle! Death has been there and robbed my beloved old home of a fond mother, a kind brother, and a sweet little niece: all within the short space of ten months. Poor broken circle! A brother's widow, and his little orphan son, are now all that compose that family circle. I myself, having left that home of my childhood and the friends of my youth, and come here to find a home in a strange land. Lord how mysterious are Thy ways!

My Brother David

In eighteen hundred and twenty six,
My little brother moaning lay,
Till God released him from all his
  pain,
And called him far, far away.

His cheeks felt the pure and cheer-
ful breeze,
Till he was nearly twelve months
  old,
Then cold and fatal croup was the
  disease
Which laid little David dead and
  cold.

So in the grave that brother was
  laid,
Ever, I saw his smile, and beaming
  eyes
His body in the land of deepest
  shade
His spirit recalled to the skies.

Lord, while he is lisping forth thy
  praise
Fill my poor heart with sacred love.
Help thy handmaid to walk in all
  thy ways
Til she may meet with him above.

My Sister Bettie

Once I had a little sister.
And a lovely child she was.
But e'er four summers rolled
    around.
She in her narrow grave was found.

I never saw my sister Bettie,
That blessing heaven denied.
For early she was called away,
To join the glorified.

Father and mother told me,
She was a lovely child
But now their voice is still.
They are sleeping by her side.

Oh! how often do I think,
Of that delightful day.
When I shall greet my little sister
Who long has passed away.

It was her custom during the winter months, as soon as the family were all assembled around the fireside at night, to strike up and sing some favorite hymn or spiritual song. When that was ended she would ask her two little nephews Scripture questions for their instructions. These questions, she continued to ask night after night, and answer them till the children could answer themselves, though one but four and the other seven years old. The questions she asked were generally simple enough to be understood by the young mind, and yet so useful and interesting as not to weary them. In closing her juvenile instructions, she would always sing them a little song, most frequently that song would be about angels, such as:

I want to be an angel,
And with the angels stand,
A crown upon my forehead,
A harp within my hand,
There right before my Saviour,
So glorious and so bright.
I'd make the sweetest music,
And praise him day and night.

I never would be weary,
Nor ever shed a tear,
Nor ever know a sorrow,
Nor ever feel a fear:

But blessed, pure and holy,
I'd dwell in Jesus sight,
And with ten thousand thousands,
Praise him both day and night.

I know I'm weak and sinful,
But Jesus will forgive;
For many little children,
Have gone to heaven to live,
Dear Saviour, when I languish
And lay me down to die,
Oh! send a shining angel
To bear me to the sky.

As soon as she was through teaching, and singing for her little friends, (as she called them) she would read her Bible till a late hour. The attachment she had for her Bible, and the manner in which she read it, would induce us to believe that she felt that she was holding an interview with her Maker, Lawgiver and Saviour, as to how she might honor them most, and reach heaven. She seemed to read it with humble and enquiring feelings, that she might learn from it and obey it. To all appearance she seldom read it without receiving an impulse heavenward, or catching some sacred truth which she stored up in her memory. The truths she gathered in this way were not permitted to remain idle, but they would often be repeated to sustain doctrain or any position she might assume. . . .

We now turn from her books to such correspondence only, as was addressed to her cousins, in the last six or seven months of her life.

Craigsville Va. December 23rd 1862
To Miss Suzzie H. R. Yount

It is of importance to me to hear from my friends, especially my favorites, and supposing you would like to hear from me I address you with a few lines this morning. I hope you will have a nice Christmas. I hope it will be your privilege to sit under the sound of one who will proclaim the glad tidings of the 'gospel, which is a glorious privilege for us to enjoy. Last Christmas I was at Barren Ridge at preaching. This Christmas I expect to spend at home reading my Bible. I have commenced to read through the Bible, and expect to confine myself to it untill I get through. I will confine myself to reading this winter if my health will permit.

I look back with solemnity on the year that is about to close. I have had many things to endure during the year. I lost friends, I was myself afflicted, but God gave me strength, to bear it all, and what the next year will bring forth God only knows. Perhaps it may be the last year for me, and many more. I must close for the present. . . .

Craigsville Va. January 13th 1863
To Miss Sallie J. Myers

I with pleasure address you with a few lines though I must be very brief, to inform you that I am well, I have enjoyed good health since I have been out here. I have not any exposure to injure my health. I have a good warm fire to sleep by every night. Well, I suppose you would like to know how I am pleased with the mountains. I like them very well so far.

I miss the Dunkards very much. I find plenty of Presbyterians here. They are very social people. Brother T— has not been out here to preach for us. I wrote to him but have as yet received no answer. . . .

Craigsville. March 2nd 1863

To Miss Sallie J. Myers

Your kind letter met with a cordial reception and demands a reply. I was sorry to hear of your mother's sickness. I wish I could come to see her. I feel under a thousand obligation to her for her kindness to me when I was sick. I hope she will soon be well again. I heard last week that she was improving. You say there was a good deal of sickness in the neighborhood at the time you wrote. Sickness is every where. I received letters from Rockingham County, and learn that Diptherie and Scarlet Fever are both very bad there. The Small Pox is within four miles of us. The Dr that has been attending them lives in sight of us, he is the only physician in the neighborhood and has never had it himself. Why is it that the people of our once happy country, have now to endure the horrors of war and pestilence? Is it because many have forgotten that they derived their existence from God? They look to their great leaders for counsel, instead of praying to God for pardon, and for light and knowledge. —

You say you had a pleasant time at Christmas, I wish I could have been with you at preaching and at Y— as I am sure you had a nice time. I heard from Brother T— since I wrote to you, he says it would afford him much pleasure to have the privilege of visiting this neighborhood on the glorious mission of preaching Christ's gospel. But, he cannot come untill after his return from the north. I expect to come down as soon as the weather gets warm. I want to get to Dunkard meeting again. I cannot come however till warm weather. I expect to teach school next Summer. Brother is building a school-house on his farm. Sister Victoria says your mother must come out here in the mountains as soon as she gets well enough to come. She thinks a trip out here would improve her health. My health has been very good since I have been out here with the exception of sore throat. I was very much threatened with Bronchitis at one time, but I soon recovered from it. I hope I will have my health very good when the weather gets warm. I weigh one hundred and sixty pounds, a *handsome weight,* —

I must close for the present. Give my love to all the family, and to all enquiring friends. Please tell me when there will be Church meeting at the Dunkard church. I want to come when it is. . . .

Craigsville. June 28th 1863

To Miss Sallie J. Myers

. . . I returned home safe, but felt very ill for several days after my return, but was soon well again. I was very glad to hear that Cousin Rebecah Yount had joined the church. I hope that many will see the importance of following her example. I would be delighted to hear of you joining the church. You may think like many, that you are young and it is time enough yet, but such thoughts are no consolation. Death is no respecter of persons. We are commanded to be always ready, for we know not when the grim messenger death will receive the warrant to close our existence here. What will give us consolation in the hour of death? Nothing but Jesus Christ whom we should serve through life. If we love and serve him we shall be happy forever in eternity. If we neglect to love and serve him, we shall be miserable forever in eternity too. . . .

In nothing was her fidelity to Christ, and her piety more strikingly exhibited than in her fondness for her Bible and her intense anxiety for the Salvation of others. The letters she wrote to her friends were seldom closed without directing their thoughts in some way to religion and its consolations. It was her custom, to view almost every subject, and almost every interest in the light of eternity. . . .

We now come to the last sickness she was called upon to indure in this world of sorrows. On Thursday the 10th day of July, she taught school as usual, enjoying as good health as she had at any time during the summer. On the evening of that day she enjoyed her supper with a relish more than ordinary, and returned to her room as well as usual. On Friday morning about half past 12 o'clock, she became suddenly attacked [with a] sickness at the stomach, followed by vomiting. . . .

Strange however to tell, that for twenty one days this stubborn disease did not reduce her in the least. At the end of that period she began gradually to die. Yet the remaining fourteen days she lived, she had sufficient strength to raise herself up in her bed even without aid. How she retained such strength for so many days, having taken little or no nourishment, may perhaps be a mystery to those in health and in their sins. But as God tempers the winds to the shorn lamb, so he sustains his believing child under affliction, and gives him strength for his days of suffering. In the strength of God she was enabled to endure to the end of her suffering days with patience and resignation, often dropping cheering expressions of the peace that filled her soul. The pleasing power of hope appeared to grow stronger and stronger, as strength declined and life gave way. For days, anxious friends watched her to see if they could discover signs of terror or agitation, any thing like the shrinking back of the soul from the grasp of death, but all was calmness and contentment. . . .

On learning her dangerous condition she did not seem to be alarmed in the least, or even disappointed in any of her plans or expectations. Submission to God's will at once took possession of her soul. Not one longing lingering look did she seem to cast behind on the fleeting world she was about to leave. Never cast down, never transmitted with fears, and never tempted to murmur or repine at her sufferings. The Saviour she loved, shed feelings of tranquility around her languishing bed, and brightened with immortal hopes her prospects for heaven. Her universal faith, and the smile of contentment that lingered on her face, seemed to cover and hide from the sight of mortals the sufferings of her body. Indeed, her faded countenance, oftener presented the expression of calm and resignation stronger than the pangs of the disease.

On Sunday morning, August 9th, she called the writer to her bedside, for the purpose of giving him instruction with regard to her burial with as much calmness and composure as ever she did any thing in her life. Said, "My days on earth are fast drawing to a close, and I will soon be numbered with the dead. I want you to bury me by the side of mother in that grave yard where so many of my friends are resting. Have my coffin made of walnut in a plain way, and lined with black callico. If you conclude to get a tomb stone for my grave, get one for mother's too. I want her to have one just like mine. Get Brother Isaac Long to preach my funeral at the Brick Church near New Hope. It is also my wish that Brother Abraham Garber be present and make some remarks in closing my funeral. And I want you to select some one to preach my funeral in this community, either here at the house, or at the church near the furnace."

The writer then asked her if she had any thing for him to tell Mr. Long when he should see him. "Yes" said she "I have. Tell him to tell the church that I bid them all an affectionate farewell, and I want them all to meet me in heaven. Tell them, when I was down there last, I expected to enjoy a happy season with them at their Communion meeting next Fall, but now I hope to enjoy my Communion above. Tell them I want every member to be faithful to the Lord, and meet me in a better world than this. My prospects are bright for heaven, and I feel that it will be gain for me to die." ...

On Monday night August 10th she requested that the evening worship be opened by reading the 103 Psalm. . . . She then looked at the company in the room for a moment, and said "Do me the kindness to sing for me some pieces I have so often sung myself."

Come sing to me of heaven,
When I am called to die.
Sing songs of holy ecstasy,
To waft my soul on high.

When cold and sluggish drops,
Roll off my marble brow.
Burst forth in strains of joyfulness.
Let heaven begin below.

When the last moment comes,
O watch my dying face.
And catch the bright seraphic
  gleam,
Which on each feature plays.

Then to my raptured ear,
Let one sweet song be given,
Let music charm me last on earth,
And greet me first in heaven.

Then close my sightless eyes,
And lay me down to rest.
And clasp and place my pale cold
  hands,
Upon my lifeless breast.

Then round my senseless clay,
Assembled those I love
And sing of heaven, delightful
  heaven,
My glorious home above.

The sound produced by singing of the last verse had scarcely died away, before she said,
  "Heaven delightful heaven
  My glorious home above."
Now sing

My heavenly home is bright and
  fair,
Nor pain nor death can enter there,
Its glittering towers, the sun out
  shine
That heavenly mansion shall be
  mine.

  Chorus
I'm going home, I'm going home.
I'm going home to die no more.
To die no more, to die no more.
I'm going home to die no more.

My Father's house is built on high,
Far, far above the starry sky,

When from this earthly prison free,
That heavenly mansion mine shall
  be

Let others seek a home below,
Which flames devour or waves o'er
  flow.
Be mine the happier lot to own,
A heavenly mansion near the
  throne.

Then fail this earth, let stars decline,
And sun and moon refuse to shine,
All nature sink and cease to be.
That heavenly mansion stands for
  me.

When this piece was ended, she said, . . . Now sing

Farewell vain world I'm going
home,
My Saviour smiles and bids me
come,
Bright angels beckon me away,
To sing God's praise in endless day.

I'm glad that I was born to die,
From grief and war my soul shall
fly;
Bright angels shall convey me
home,
Away to New Jerusalem.

And when to that bright world I fly,
And join the anthems of the sky,

O then my happy soul shall tell,
My Jesus has done all things well.

I hope to meet my brethren there,
Who once did join with me in
prayer,
Our mourning time shall then be
over,
And we shall live to die no more.

I'll praise my God while I have
breath
I hope to praise him after death,
I hope to praise him when I die,
And shout salvation as I fly.

She then spoke of the joys of heaven, and reminded all those who made a profession of religion, of the obligations they were under to the Lord, and exhorted them to be faithful to the Redeemer and meet her in heaven. And then she called such as made no profession, one by one to her bedside; and talked to them of the uncertainty of life and the certainty of death, and asked them to permit her as one near eternity to admonish them to prepare for death and judgement, and meet her in heaven.

On Tuesday night just before the hour of prayer, she spoke of her trials, the difficulties and the doubts, through which some Christians pass, and then requested the reading of the 42nd Psalm. After prayer she requested the singing of the following hymn.

Oh! how happy are they,
Who their Saviour obey,
And have laid up their treasures
above
Oh! what tongue can express,
The sweet comfort and peace,
Of a soul in its earliest love.

'Twas a heaven below,
My Redeemer to know;

And the angels could do nothing
more
Than to fall at his feet,
And the story repeat,
And the Saviour of sinners adore.

Jesus all the day long,
Was my joy and my song,
Oh! that more his salvation might
see,

He hath loved me, I cried.
He hath suffered and died
To redeem such a rebel as me.

Now my remnant of days
Would I spend in his praise,
Who hath died, me from death to
    redeem;
Whether many or few,

All my days are his due—
May they all be devoted to Him.

What a mercy is this!
What a heaven of bliss!
How unspeakably happy am I!
Gathered into the fold
With believers enrolled,
With believers to live and to die.

On Wednesday night, after the reading of the 46th Psalm, and prayer, she again commended Christ and religion to all in the house in a manner similar to that of Monday night. Calling friend after friend to her bed-side, she in the soothing tones of a departing Christian, talked to them of heaven and of God. Affecting admonition! Only those who heard it can fully appreciate it. This farewell discourse, like sunlight, drove sadness and gloom from the hearts of some, yet it caused others to weep and sob as if smitten in the dust. When she discovered that some of her friends were weeping she advised them not to grieve for her as there was a time coming when all must part, and she felt that death would be gain to her. With a countenance free from gloom, and with a voice calm and serene she requested the singing of her last hymn. "Sing for me," said she, "Believer's Departure, for if this be death, All is well—all is well."

What? this that steals, that steals
    upon my frame.
  Is it death? Is it death?
That soon will quench, will quench
    this vital flow.
  Is it death? Is it death?
If this be death I soon shall be
From every pain and sorrow free;
I shall the King of Glory see;
  All is well—all is well!

Weep not my friends—my friends,
    weep not for me;
  All is well—all is well!
My sins are pardoned, pardoned—I
    am free;
  All is well—all is well!

There is not a cloud that doth arise
To hide my Jesus from my eyes;
I soon shall mount the upper skies;
  All is well—all is well!

Tune, tune your harps, your harps,
    ye saints above;
  All is well—all is well!
I will rehearse, rehearse the theme
    of love;
  All is well—all is well!
Bright angels are from glory come.
They're round my bed, they're in
    my room.
They wait to waft my spirit home;
  All is well—all is well!

Hark, hark, my Lord, my Saviour
   bids me come;
All is well—all is well!
I soon shall see his lovely face at
   home;
All is well—all is well!

Farewell, my friends—adue, adue.
I can no longer stay with you.
My glittering crown appears in
   view;
All is well—all is well!...

She passed away on Friday morning, August the 14th, about half past 12 O.Clock, on the 35th day of her sickness to the very hour and in the 29th year of her age. As soon as death had done its worst, and left her body a lifeless corps, a profound silence filled the house. When all was still as the grave itself, an individual rose up at the bed side, and said, "Blessed are the dead which die in the Lord from hence forth. Yea, saith the Spirit, that they may rest from their labours and their works do follow them."...

On Saturday, her remains were removed to New Hope a distance of 35 miles, with the view of carrying out her request with regard to her funeral and burial. On Sunday morning at 10 O.Clock, Elder Isaac Long of Rockingham County, delivered to a large congregation, a solemn and impressive discourse on the words, "Finally, brethren, farewell. Be perfect, be of good comfort, be of one mind, live in peace, and the God of love and peace shall be with you." ii Cor xxiii-18. This solemn service was conducted with the use of the three hymns she had sung on Monday night before her death, and closed by Elder Abraham Garber in obedience to her request.[36]

The stories of the life and death of many other Brethren would undoubtedly have been just as inspiring as that of Catherine Myers, but fortunately for the historian and all of those who lived after her, her story was recorded by her brother. It was certainly a story of devotion and of dedication, and along with other evidence seems to indicate that the Brethren of the nineteenth century were capable of living devoted and dedicated lives.

CONCLUSION

The variety of the documents quoted in the preceding pages leads to the conclusion that the Brethren were engaged in many different kinds of activities in the years from 1785 to 1865. They were emigrating, like Daniel Leedy, who went from Virginia to Oregon with several stops along the way; they were writing, like Peter Nead, whose *Theological Writings* published in 1850 was widely read by the Brethren; they were attending Annual Meeting, like John Kline, who was Moderator of the Meeting for the last four years of his life in the 1860s; they were publishing periodicals, like Henry Kurtz, who introduced the *Gospel Visiter* in 1851; they were preaching sermons, like John A. Bowman of Tennessee; they were lobbying in the halls of government, like B. F. Moomaw of Virginia during the Civil War; they were influencing the formation of other religious groups, like Joseph Hostetler, who became a leader of the Disciples of Christ in Indiana; they were establishing schools, like S. Z. Sharp in Pennsylvania; and they were defending the beliefs of the Brethren in public debate, like R. H. Miller in Indiana.

The purpose of such a listing of activities, which is simply suggestive and not intended to be complete, is to counter the traditional interpretation of those historians who have written about this period of Brethren history, and have based their conclusions on the idea that these were the wilderness years or the dark ages.[1] That interpretation has emphasized such things as the lack of a periodical published for the Brethren in the years before 1851 and the Brethren objection to a high school or college education during these years. The Brethren were finding other ways to communicate, however, and they were securing an education. Also, they were doing other important things, like establishing new congregations and building churches in a number of states that had had no Brethren in 1785.

The basic strength of the Brethren during the years from 1785 to 1865 was demonstrated by their success in holding their ranks together in the face of threats from other religious groups and from the divisive issues of slavery and war. With the exception of the events in Kentucky about 1820, which are still not very well understood in terms of the number of Brethren involved, there were no major schisms among the Brethren between 1785 and 1865. That record is in marked contrast to the years following 1865 when the Brethren divided into three different groups in the 1880s. In 1865, however, when this period in the history of the Brethren ended, they were strong and united, and prepared to face the challenges of an industrializing United States.

NOTES

INTRODUCTION

1. Donald F. Durnbaugh, *European Origins of the Brethren* (Elgin: The Brethren Press, 1958) and Donald F. Durnbaugh, *The Brethren in Colonial America* (Elgin: The Brethren Press, 1967).
2. David Benedict, *A General History of the Baptist Denomination in America* (Boston: Manning & Loring, 1813), pages 434-435.
3. Joseph Belcher, "The German Baptists or Tunkers," *The Religious Denominations in the United States* (Philadelphia: John E. Potter, 1859), page 292.
4. Morgan Edwards, *Materials Towards a History of the Baptists in America* (Philadelphia: Thomas Dobson, 1792), page 145.
5. Benedict, *Baptists in America,* pages 434-435.
6. Timothy Flint, *The History and Geography of the Mississippi Valley* (Cincinnati: E. H. Flint, 3rd edition, 1833), volume II, page 216.
7. Frederick von Raumer, *America and the American People* (New York: J. & H. G. Langley, 1846) page 326, footnote. This book was translated from the original German by William W. Turner.
8. David Benedict, *A General History of the Baptist Denomination in America* (New York: Lewis Colby and Company, 1848), page 913.
9. Belcher, "The German Baptists or Tunkers," page 296.
10. Belcher, "The German Baptists or Tunkers," page 296.
11. *Statistics of The United States (Including Mortality, Property, &c.) in 1860; Compiled from the original returns and being the final exhibit of the Eighth Census, under the direction of the Secretary of the Interior* (Washington: Government Printing Office, 1866), pages 353-502.
12. Of the 163 Brethren churches identified in the Census of 1860, only 37 were located in the Confederate states and at least 5 of these were located in what later became West Virginia.

13. For a thorough study of Cassel and his collection, see Marlin L. Heckman, "Abraham Harley Cassel, Nineteenth Century Pennsylvania German American Book Collector," *Publications of the Pennsylvania German Society* (Breinigsville, Pennsylvania: The Pennsylvania German Society 1973), volume VII, pages 105-224. This study was accepted as a doctoral dissertation at the Graduate Library School of the University of Chicago.

I. GEOGRAPHICAL EXPANSION

1. B. E. Plaine to David Plaine, Bonsack Papers, Manuscript Division, Perkins Library, Duke University. Used by permission.
2. Lyman Beecher, *A Plea for the West* (Cincinnati: Truman & Smith, 1835), pages 11-12.
3. Miss F. A. Leedy, "Biography of Bro. Daniel Leedy," unpublished typescript, Brethren Historical Library, Elgin, Illinois.
4. Donald F. Durnbaugh, *The Brethren in Colonial America* (Elgin: The Brethren Press, 1967), page 189.
5. Adelaide L. Fries and others (editors), *Records of the Moravians in North Carolina* (Raleigh: North Carolina Historical Commission [State Department of Archives and History], 11 volumes, 1922-1969), II, 670. Used by permission.
6. Fries and others, *Records of Moravians,* II, 729.
7. Fries and others, *Records of Moravians,* II, 744.
8. Fries and others, *Records of Moravians,* II, 758.
9. Fries and others, *Records of Moravians,* II, 837.
10. Fries and others, *Records of Moravians,* II, 914.
11. Fries and others, *Records of Moravians,* V, 2324.
12. Fries and others, *Records of Moravians,* VI, 2662.
13. Fries and others, *Records of Moravians,* VI, 2909.
14. Fries and others, *Records of Moravians,* VI, 2920.
15. Fries and others, *Records of Moravians,* VII, 3129.
16. Fries and others, *Records of Moravians,* VIII, 3628.
17. Fries and others, *Records of Moravians,* IX, 4508.
18. Fries and others, *Records of Moravians,* IV, 1851.
19. Fries and others, *Records of Moravians,* III, 1114.
20. Fries and others, *Records of Moravians,* IV, 1804.
21. Fries and others, *Records of Moravians,* VI, 2624.
22. Fries and others, *Records of Moravians,* VI, 2636.
23. Fries and others, *Records of Moravians,* VII, 3405.
24. Fries and others, *Records of Moravians,* VIII, 3861.
25. Fries and others, *Records of Moravians,* VIII, 4194-4195.
26. Fries and others, *Records of Moravians,* VIII, 4210.
27. Fries and others, *Records of Moravians,* IX, 4737.
28. Daniel Peters, "The Brethren Church in Franklin County, Virginia," *Brethren Family Almanac,* 1909, pages 32-33.
29. Jacob and Sarah Faw to Wesley and Susannah Hyer, quoted in Amy Faw and

Linda Faw, *The Faw Family Record* (Chillicothe, Illinois: privately printed, 1955, revised, 1964).

30. F. P. Tucker, "Elder Jacob Faw—Biographical Sketch of an Exemplary Man— His Faith—The Dunkard Church," *The Union Republican,* Winston, North Carolina, June 16, 1887, page 1.

31. "The Petition of the Inhabitants of Ashe County. In Senate 18 Nov. 1802 Read & Referred to the Committee of Propositions & Grievances. By Order. M. Stokes, Clk." North Carolina State Department of Archives and History, Raleigh. Used by permission.

32. Fries and others, *Records of Moravians,* VI, 2967.

33. Quoted in Clayton B. Miller, "History of Flat Rock Church of the Brethren," unpublished manuscript in the editor's possession.

34. Bonsack Papers.

35. Copy of manuscript reproduced in D. L. Miller and Galen B. Royer, *Some Who Led* (Elgin: Brethren Publishing House, 1912), page 60.

36. Joseph and Catherine Brubaker to John and Susannah Bonsack, Bonsack Papers.

37. Henry Swadley to David and Mary Plaine, Bonsack Papers.

38. Geo. L. Willis, Sr., *History of Shelby County, Kentucky* (Louisville: C. T. Dearing Printing Company, Inc., 1929).

39. Madison Evans, *Biographical Sketches of Pioneer Preachers* (Philadelphia: J. Challen & Sons, 1862), pages 57-62.

40. W. W. Sweet, *Religion on the American Frontier, The Baptists, 1783-1820* (New York: Henry Holt and Co., 1931). Reprinted by Cooper Square Publishers, Inc., New York, 1964. Pages 185-200. Used by permission.

41. Otto A. Rothert, *A History of Muhlenberg County* (Louisville: Morton & Company, Inc., 1913), pages 57-58.

42. Francois Andre Michaux, "Travels West of the Alleghany Mountains, 1802," in Reuben Gold Thwaites, editor, *Early Western Travels, 1748-1846* (Cleveland: The Arthur H. Clark Company, 1904), III, 216-217.

43. Durnbaugh, *The Brethren in Colonial America,* page 189. David Eller, current- ly a graduate student at Miami University, has done extensive research on Stutzman's career in Indiana.

44. Evans, *Pioneer Preachers,* pages 62-64.

45. Samuel and Elizabeth Harshbarger to the Bonsacks, Bonsack Papers.

46. Samuel and Elizabeth Harshbarger to John and Susan Bonsack, Bonsack Papers.

47. Samuel and Elizabeth Harshbarger to John and Susan Bonsack, Bonsack Papers.

48. Jonas Graybill, "Elder William Gish," unpublished typescript, Brethren Historical Library.

49. Samuel Murray, "R. H. Miller," unpublished typescript, Brethren Historical Library.

50. Clipping from undated *Gospel Messenger,* R. H. Miller file, Brethren Historical Library.

51. John Click to David H. Plaine, Bonsack Papers.

52. Samuel and Elizabeth Harshbarger to David and Mary Plaine, Bonsack Papers.

53. William and Eliza Ann Moore to Davey and Mary Plaine, Bonsack Papers.

54. *The Gospel Visiter,* January, 1854, page 192.

55. John Wolfe, "Pioneer History," *Brethren at Work,* February 23, 1882, page 4.
56. John Clingingsmith, "Short Historical Sketch of the Far Western Brethren of the Dunkard Church ... to the year 1885," unpublished typescript, Brethren Historical Library. An abridged edition was prepared by W. W. Strickler and published as "History of the Far Western Brethren," *Brethren's Family Almanac,* 1890. The unpublished typescript is used in this volume.
57. J. H. Moore, "Life and Times of Eld. George Wolfe," *Brethren's Family Almanac,* 1893, pages 3-13.
58. Charles L. Wallis, editor, *Peter Cartwright's Autobiography* (Nashville: Abingdon Press, 1956), pages 179-180. Used by permission.
59. Clingingsmith, "Far Western Brethren."
60. John Sturgis, "Biography of Elder D. B. Sturgis," unpublished typescript, Brethren Historical Library.
61. H. R. Holsinger, *History of the Tunkers and the Brethren Church* (Lathrop, California: privately printed, 1901), page 397.
62. Jacob Negley, "Organization of the Coal Creek Church, Fulton Co., Ill.—Our first Acquaintance with Bro. George Wolfe, &c.," *Brethren's Almanac,* 1877.
63. Original in possession, 1969, of Mrs. Kathren Royer (Mrs. Q. A.) Holsopple, Yucaipa, California, copied by Harvey L. Long, copy loaned and used by permission of Samuel D. Lindsay.
64. John J. Emmert diary, Brethren Historical Library.
65. *The Gospel Visiter,* May, 1851, pages 26-27.
66. *The Gospel Visiter,* June, 1851, pages 43-44.
67. For further information on John Ham, see Roger E. Sappington, *The Brethren in the Carolinas* (Kingsport, Tennessee: Watson Lithographing Company, 1972), pages 61-64, 69-73.
68. John Wolfe, "Pioneer History."
69. Clingingsmith, "Far Western Brethren."
70. *The Gospel Visiter,* February, 1852, page 179.
71. Henry Kurtz, *The Brethren's Encyclopedia, Containing The United Counsels and Conclusions of the Brethren, at their Annual Meetings, carefully collected, translated (from the original German in part) and arranged in alphabetical and chronological order, accompanied with Necessary and Explanatory Notes, &c.* (Columbiana, Ohio: published by the author, 1867), pages 106-107. The full title is given because it explains that this book included all of the Annual Meeting Minutes, which Kurtz was able to locate. It was the first attempt to collect and publish all of these Minutes. It is used consistently in this volume, except in a few situations in which Minutes, which Kurtz did not have, have since become available.
72. *The Gospel Visiter,* April, 1851, page 9.
73. *The Gospel Visiter,* April, 1851, pages 9-11.
74. *The Gospel Visiter,* November, 1851, page 119.
75. *The Gospel Visiter,* February, 1852, pages 179-180.
76. *The Gospel Visiter,* April and May, 1852, page 232.
77. Kurtz, *Encyclopedia,* page 107.
78. John Sturgis, "Biography of Elder D. B. Sturgis."
79. Kurtz, *Enclopedia,* page 107.
80. Kurtz, *Enclopedia,* pages 107-108.
81. Kurtz, *Enclopedia,* pages 108-109.

82. Clingingsmith, "Far Western Brethren."
83. Clingingsmith, "Far Western Brethren."
84. Rufus Babcock, *Forty Years of Pioneer Life: Memoir of John Mason Peck, D. D., Edited from his Journals and Correspondence* (Philadelphia: American Baptist Publication Society, 1864), page 119.
85. Clingingsmith, "Far Western Brethren."
86. George Wolfe, "Biography of Eld. Geo. Wolfe Jun. & Wife," Abram Cassel Collection, Juniata College, Huntingdon, Pa. Used by permission.
87. K. O. Brubaker to "Dear Brother and Sister," Bonsack Papers.
88. Joseph and Catherine Brubaker to John and Susannah Bonsack, Bonsack Papers.
89. B. E. Plaine to David Plaine, Bonsack Papers.
90. *The Gospel Visiter,* December, 1853, pages 165-166.
91. *The Gospel Visiter,* February, 1855, pages 41-42.
92. Miss F. A. Leedy, "Biography of Bro. Daniel Leedy."
93. George Wolfe, "Biography of Eld. Geo. Wolfe Jun. & Wife."

II. RELATIONS WITH OTHER RELIGIOUS GROUPS

1. Philip Boyle, "Baptists or Brethren, German," in I. Daniel Rupp, *He Pasa Ekklesia: An Original History of the Religious Denominations at Present Existing in the United States* (Philadelphia: J. Y. Humphreys, 1844), pages 96-97.
2. Richard Eddy, *Universalism in America, A History* (Boston: Universalist Publishing House, 1891), pages 72-73.
3. Roland L. Howe, *The History of a Church (Dunker) with comments featuring The First Church of the Brethren of Philadelphia, Pa. 1813-1943* (Philadelphia: privately printed, 1943), page 147.
4. Thomas Whittemore, *The Modern History of Universalism* (Boston: published by the author, 1830), pages 415-416.
5. Whittemore, *Universalism,* pages 418-419.
6. Whittemore, *Universalism,* pages 440-441.
7. Eddy, *Universalism in America,* II, 396.
8. See Sappington, *Brethren in the Carolinas,* pages 54-76.
9. David Benedict, *A General History of the Baptist Denomination in America* (New York: Lewis Colby and Company, 1848), page 913.
10. Whittemore, *Universalism,* pages 430-431.
11. John F. Cady, *The Origin and Development of the Missionary Baptist Church in Indiana* (Berne, Indiana: printed by the Berne Witness Co. for Franklin College, 1942), note 25, page 19.
12. Richard Eddy, *History of Universalism,* volume X of *American Church History* (New York: Charles Scribner's Sons, 1903), page 441.
13. Eddy, *Universalism in America,* I, 39-41.
14. Eddy, *Universalism in America,* II, 386.
15. Clingingsmith, "Far Western Brethren."
16. Kurtz, *Encyclopedia,* page 190.
17. Kurtz, *Encyclopedia,* page 108.
18. Kurtz, *Encyclopedia,* pages 177-178.
19. Eddy, *Universalism in America,* I, pages 37-38.
20. The Committee Appointed by District Conference, *History of the Church of the*

Brethren of the Eastern District of Pennsylvania (Lancaster: The New Era Printing Company, 1915), pages 382-383.
21. Moses Miller, "The River Brethren," 1881, in the Abram Cassel Collection, secured from Carlton O. Wittlinger, the Archivist of the Brethren in Christ Church, Grantham, Pennsylvania.
22. Evans, *Pioneer Preachers,* pages 29-35.
23. Evans, *Pioneer Preachers,* pages 64-67.
24. Eddy, *Universalism in America,* I, pages 38-39.
25. Joseph and Catherine Brubaker to John and Susannah Bonsack, Bonsack Papers.

III. ORDINANCES AND BELIEFS

1. Donald F. Durnbaugh, "Vindicator of Primitive Christianity: The Life and Diary of Peter Nead," *Brethren Life and Thought,* Autumn, 1969, pages 196-223.
2. Peter Nead, *Theological Writings on Various Subjects: Or a Vindication of Primitive Christianity as Recorded in the Word of God* (Dayton, Ohio: New Edition, 1866), pages 18-31. The 1866 edition, which has been used consistently in this volume, included the entire *Primitive Christianity* of 1834.
3. Nead, *Theological Writings,* pages 9-18, 31-45.
4. [Peter Bowman,] *A testimony of Baptism, as practiced by the Primitive Christians, from the time of the Apostles* (Baltimore: Printed by Benjamin Edes, 1831), pages iii-v, 7-71.
5. Nead, *Theological Writings,* pages 45-89.
6. John Kline, *Defence of Baptism* (Poland, Mahoning County, Ohio: Office of the Gospel-Visitor, 1856), pages 1-16.
7. Mary N. Quinter, *Life and Sermons of Elder James Quinter* (Mt. Morris, Illinois: Brethren's Publishing Co., 1891), page 17.
8. Holsinger, *History of the Tunkers,* pages 383-384.
9. Samuel and Elizabeth Harshbarger to David and Mary Plaine, Cornstock, Montgomery County, Indiana, January 21, 1861. Bonsack Papers.
10. "Autobiography of J. D. Haughtelin, of Panora, Iowa," unpublished typescript, Brethren Historical Library.
11. Kurtz, *Encyclopedia,* pages 36-42.
12. Alexander Mack, Jr., "A Letter about Feet-Washing," translated and published in the *Gospel Visiter,* March, 1855, pages 65-67; April, 1855, pages 79-82.
13. Nead, *Theological Writings,* pages 127-133.
14. Nead, *Theological Writings,* pages 139-159.
15. Nead, *Theological Writings,* pages 386-393.
16. Kurtz, *Encyclopedia,* pages 54-55, 113-114, 125-126, 129-132, 132-133, 180-181.
17. Mary Noffsinger to Mary Bonsack, September 8, 1839, Putnam County, Indiana. Bonsack Papers.
18. Sophia Lightner to John Bonsack, July 12, 1840, Union Bridge, Maryland. Bonsack Papers.

19. Salome Bonsack to Mary Bonsack, September 16, 1845, Roanoke County, Virginia. Bonsack Papers.
20. Samuel and Elizabeth Harshbarger to John and Susan Bonsack, February 13, 1848, Cornstock Grove, Montgomery County, Indiana. Bonsack Papers.
21. M. C. Plaine to D. H. and M. Plaine, October 6, 1851, Bonsack Papers.
22. Philip Boyle to John Bonsack, August 4, 1853, New Windsor, Maryland, Bonsack Papers.
23. Samuel and Elizabeth Harshbarger to John and Susan Bonsack, September 5, 1853, Cornstock, Montgomery County, Indiana. Bonsack Papers.
24. Kate Castle to David Plaine, May 26, 1855, Bonsack Papers.
25. Kate Castle to David Plaine, October 1, 1855, Brownsville, Maryland. Bonsack Papers.
26. Samuel and Elizabeth Harshbarger to John and Susan Bonsack, November 6, 1858, Cornstock, Montgomery County, Indiana. Bonsack Papers.
27. A. G. Strayer to Bettie Ballow. John and Philip Winn Papers, Manuscript Division, Perkins Library, Duke University. Used by permission.
28. Donald F. Durnbaugh, translator and editor, "The German Journalist and the Dunker Love-Feast," *Pennsylvania Folklife,* Winter, 1968-69, pages 40-48.
29. Nead, *Theological Writings,* pages 135-136.
30. Kurtz, *Encyclopedia,* pages 124-125.
31. Nead, *Theological Writings,* pages 161-162.
32. Kurtz, *Encyclopedia,* pages 16-19.

IV. POLITY AND ORGANIZATION

1. Boyle, "Baptists—or Brethren, German," pages 95-96.
2. Kurtz, *Encyclopedia,* pages 9-16, 194-200.
3. Benjamin Funk, collator, *Life and Labors of Elder John Kline the Martyr Missionary* (Elgin: Brethren Publishing House, 1900), pages 66-67, 71, 78, 294, 373.
4. Kurtz, *Encyclopedia,* pages 87-89, 151-153.
5. D. H. Zigler, *History of the Brethren in Virginia* (Elgin: Brethren Publishing House, 1914), pages 71-72.
6. Zigler, *Brethren in Virginia,* pages 133-134.
7. Kurtz, *Encyclopedia,* pages 50-51.
8. *The Gospel Visiter,* December, 1851, pages 138-139.
9. B. E. Plaine to David Plaine. Bonsack Papers.
10. B. E. Plaine to David Plaine. Bonsack Papers.
11. Bonsack Papers.
12. Undated *Gospel Messenger* clipping, in R. H. Miller file, Brethren Historical Library.
13. From the collection of Donald R. Bowman, Brookville, Ohio.
14. Kurtz, *Encyclopedia,* pages 49-50.
15. John Bonsack to Mary Bonsack, September 1, 1845. Bonsack Papers.
16. Samuel and Elizabeth Harshbarger to John and Susan Bonsack, Cornstock, Montgomery County, Indiana, November 16, 1852. Bonsack Papers.

17. F. E. Mallott, "Glimpses from Early Church Records," *Schwarzenau,* July, 1940, pages 24-25.
18. Enoch Eby, "Brief Sketch of My Life," unpublished typescript, Brethren Historical Library.
19. Funk, *Elder John Kline,* pages 192-193, 195-196, 198-199.
20. Sophia Lightner to "Dearly Beloved Friends." Bonsack Papers.
21. Howe, *Philadelphia Church of the Brethren,* page 459.
22. "A Letter by Sarah Major," *The Gospel Messenger,* December 28, 1935, pages 13-14.
23. Sophia Lightner to "Dear Uncle." Bonsack Papers.
24. Sophia Lightner to "Very dear Uncle and Aunt and Cousins." Bonsack Papers.
25. Kurtz, *Encyclopedia,* page 186.
26. J. H. Warstler, "Sister Sarah Major," *Brethren's Family Almanac,* 1901.
27. Howe, *Philadelphia Church of the Brethren,* page 153.
28. Holsinger *History of the Tunkers,* pages 360-361.
29. *The Gospel Messenger,* Oct. 7, 1884, pages 641-642.
30. Kurtz, *Encyclopedia,* page 146.
31. Howe, *Philadelphia Church of the Brethren,* pages 23-33.
32. Funk, *Elder John Kline,* page 152.
33. Bonsack Papers.
34. Samuel and Elizabeth Harshbarger to John and Susan Bonsack. Bonsack Papers.
35. Kurtz, *Encyclopedia,* page 126.
36. Kurtz, *Encyclopedia,* pages 146-147.
37. Kurtz, *Encyclopedia,* page 47.
38. Mary Noffsinger to Mary Bonsack. Bonsack Papers.
39. Mary Bonsack to John Bonsack. Bonsack Papers.
40. Fannie [Burtner] to [Rev. G. H.] Snapp, Andrew Funkhouser Papers, Manuscript Division, Perkins Library, Duke University. Used by permission.
41. Kurtz, *Encyclopedia,* pages 183-184.
42. Kurtz. *Encyclopedia,* pages 172-173.
43. Zigler, *Brethren in Virginia,* pages 47-49.
44. Funk, *Elder John Kline,* page 191.

V. SEPARATION FROM SOCIETY

1. Nead, *Theological Writings,* pages 122-125.
2. Kurtz, *Encyclopedia,* pages 53, 101-104, 118.
3. Zigler, *Brethren in Virginia,* pages 86, 89.
4. Funk, *Elder John Kline,* pages 381-382.
5. Funk, *Elder John Kline,* pages 212-213.
6. Library, Bethany Theological Seminary, Oak Brook, Illinois.
7. Sarah Garber Lutz, "Biography of Samuel Garber," unpublished manuscript, Brethren Historical Library.
8. John and Elizabeth Beckner to John and Susanne Bonsack, January 17, 1837, Laporte Co., Indiana. Bonsack Papers.

9. Samuel and Elizabeth Harshbarger to John and Susan Bonsack, August 27, 1843, Cornstock Grove, Montgomery County, Indiana. Bonsack Papers.
10. Joseph and Catherine Brubaker to John and Susanah Bonsack, August 20, 1854, Story County, Iowa. Bonsack Papers.
11. Jacob and Sarah Faw to Wesley and Susannah Hyer, Faw and Faw, *Faw Family Record.*
12. Kurtz, *Encyclopedia,* page 53.
13. Landon West, *Life of Elder Samuel Weir* (Tuskegee, Alabama: Normal School Steam Press, 1897), pages 3-10.
14. John Swinger, Sr., "History of Eld. Philip Younce," unpublished typescript, Brethren Historical Library.
15. *The Gospel Visiter,* September, 1853, pages 87-90.
16. Kurtz, *Encyclopedia,* pages 100-101, 192, 168-169.
17. Kurtz, *Encyclopedia,* pages 122-123, 158-159.
18. Kurtz, *Encyclopedia,* pages 126-129.
19. Funk, *Elder John Kline,* page 201.
20. Funk, *Elder John Kline,* page 246.
21. Kurtz, *Encyclopedia,* pages 155-156.
22. Nead, *Theological Writings,* pages 121-122.
23. Kurtz, *Encyclopedia,* pages 115-117, 182.
24. *The Gospel Visiter,* July, 1851, pages 57-58.
25. Kurtz, *Encyclopedia,* page 125.
26. B. E. Plaine to David Plaine. Bonsack Papers.
27. Kurtz, *Encyclopedia,* pages 46-47, 47, 120-122, 68.
28. H. Plaine to David Plaine. Bonsack Papers.
29. Marshall Wingfield, *Franklin County, Virginia: A History* (Berryville, Virginia: Chesapeake Book Company [now Virginia Book Company], 1964), pages 22-23. Used by permission.
30. Kurtz, *Encyclopedia,* pages 87, 178.
31. *The Gospel Visiter,* March, 1854, pages 238-240.
32. *The Gospel Visiter,* December, 1854, page 151.
33. *The Gospel Visiter,* January, 1855, pages 10-11.
34. *The Gospel Visiter,* March, 1856, page 76.
35. *The Gospel Visiter,* June, 1856, pages 159-160.
36. *The Gospel Visiter,* September, 1856, pages 247-250.
37. Kurtz, *Encyclopedia,* page 178.
38. *The Gospel Visitor,* February, 1862, page 60, The spelling of the name was changed in December, 1856.
39. S. Z. Sharp, *The Educational History of the Church of the Brethren* (Elgin: Brethren Publishing House, 1923), pages 47-52.
40. Kurtz, *Encyclopedia,* page 188.
41. Funk, *Elder John Kline,* page 139.
42. Kurtz, *Encyclopedia,* pages 55-58, 86-87, 109-113.
43. Kurtz, *Encyclopedia,* page 122.
44. Kurtz, *Encyclopedia,* pages 42-43.
45. Kurtz, *Encyclopedia,* page 170.
46. John J. Emmert diary, Brethren Historical Library.
47. America Bonsack to Mary Plaine. Bonsack Papers.
48. Kurtz, *Encyclopedia,* pages 47-48, 129.

49. Kurtz, *Encyclopedia,* pages 20-23.
50. John A. Bowman, *A Sermon on Christian Temperance* (Bristol, Tennessee: Printed at the Office of the Va. & Tenn. News, 1859), pages 1-14.
51. Kurtz, *Encyclopedia,* pages 188-189.
52. Kurtz, *Encyclopedia,* pages 25-35.

VI. WAR AND MILITARY SERVICE

1. Martin G. Brumbaugh, *A History of the German Baptist Brethren in Europe and America* (Mount Morris, Illinois: Brethren Publishing House, 1899), page 492.
2. Kurtz, *Encyclopedia,* page 154.
3. Kurtz, *Encyclopedia,* page 155.
4. Robert Douthat Stoner, *A Seed-Bed of the Republic: A Study of the Pioneers in the Upper (Southern) Valley of Virginia* (Roanoke, Virginia: Roanoke Historical Society, 1962), pages 387-388.
5. William Couper, *History of the Shenandoah Valley* (New York: Lewis Publishing Co., 1952), volume II, page 823.
6. Catherine Castle to David Plaine. Bonsack Papers.
7. Funk, *Elder John Kline,* page 438.
8. Samuel and Elizabeth Harshbarger to David and Mary Plaine. Bonsack Papers.
9. Emanuel Slifer to David Plaine. Bonsack Papers.
10. Funk, *Elder John Kline,* page 440.
11. John J. Emmert diary. Brethren Historical Library.
12. *Minutes of Yearly Meeting* (independently printed, 1861), page 1.
13. Funk, *Elder John Kline,* page 442.
14. Funk, *Elder John Kline,* pages 438-439.
15. Zigler, *Brethren in Virginia,* pages 95-96.
16. John Kline to John Letcher. Archives Division, Virginia State Library. Executive Papers, Governor John Letcher, 1860-1864. Used by permission.
17. Christian Wine to John Letcher. Letcher Papers.
18. John Kline to John Letcher. Letcher Papers.
19. Funk, *Elder John Kline,* page 446.
20. Zigler, *Brethren in Virginia,* pages 99-101.
21. John Kline to John Letcher. Letcher Papers.
22. Edward Needles Wright, *Conscientious Objectors in the Civil War* (Philadelphia: University of Pennsylvania Press, 1931). Also available in a Perpetua paperback edition published by A. S. Barnes & Company, Inc., in 1961. This material is taken from pages 95-96 of the paperback edition. Used by permission.
23. United States War Department, *The War of the Rebellion: a compilation of the official records of the Union and Confederate armies* (Washington: Government Printing Office, 1880-1891). Reprinted by The National Historical Society, Gettysburg, Pennsylvania, 1971. Series I, Volume XXI, Part III, page 835. Used by permission.

24. Samuel Horst, *Mennonites in the Confederacy: A Study in Civil War Pacifism* (Scottdale, Pennsylvania: Herald Press, 1967), page 75. Used by permission.
25. Zigler, *Brethren in Virginia,* pages 115-117.
26. Zigler, *Brethren in Virginia,* page 118.
27. S. F. Sanger and D. Hays, *The Olive Branch of Peace and Good Will to Men: Anti-War History of the Brethren and Mennonites, the Peace People of the South, During the Civil War, 1861-1865* (Elgin: Brethren Publishing House, 1907), page 164.
28. Sanger and Hays, *The Olive Branch,* pages 166-187.
29. Wright, *Conscientious Objectors,* page 105.
30. War Department, *The War of the Rebellion,* Series IV, Volume II, page 166.
31. Zigler, *Brethren in Virginia,* page 125.
32. Fernando G. Cartland, *Southern Heroes: The Friends in War Time* (Cambridge, Massachusetts: The Riverside Press, 1895), pages 353-354.
33. Zigler, *Brethren in Virginia,* page 122.
34. Zigler, *Brethren in Virginia,* pages 131-132.
35. Zigler, *Brethren in Virginia,* pages 123-125.
36. Zigler, *Brethren in Virginia,* pages 135-137, 139-140.
37. Cartland, *Southern Heroes,* page 354.
38. Isaac Billhimer to David Plaine. Bonsack Papers.
39. Sanger and Hays, *The Olive Branch,* pages 89-92.
40. Wright, *Conscientious Objectors,* pages 51-52.
41. War Department, *The War of the Rebellion,* Series III, Volume II, page 587.
42. War Department, *The War of the Rebellion,* Series III, Volume II, page 650.
43. Unpublished manuscript in the Pa. State Archives, RG 26, Executive Correspondence, 1790-1951 (Box 43). Copied for my use by Grant Stoltzfus, a member of the Eastern Mennonite College faculty, Harrisonburg, Virginia, and a very dear personal friend, who died unexpectedly in July, 1974. Used by permission.
44. Wright, *Conscientious Objectors,* page 63.
45. Wright, *Conscientious Objectors,* page 64.
46. Wright, *Conscientious Objectors,* pages 82-83.
47. Library, Bethany Theological Seminary, Oak Brook, Illinois.
48. Funkhouser Papers.
49. Sanger and Hays, *The Olive Branch,* pages 66-73.
50. War Department, *The War of the Rebellion,* Series II, Volume III.
51. Sanger and Hays, *The Olive Branch,* pages 62-64.
52. Funk, *Elder John Kline,* pages 448-453.
53. Zigler, *Brethren in Virginia,* page 110.
54. P. R. Wrightsman, "Civil War Times," *Brethren Family Almanac,* 1915.
55. Zigler, *Brethren in Virginia,* page 137.
56. Sanger and Hays, *The Olive Branch,* pages 88-89, 92.
57. Henry Swadley to David and Mary Plaine. Bonsack Papers.
58. Bonsack Papers.
59. Horst, *Mennonites,* pages 128 (note 37), 94.
60. War Department, *The War of the Rebellion,* Series I, Volume XXXVIII, Part I, pages 18-19.
61. Horst, *Mennonites,* page 104.
62. *Christian Family Companion,* April 11, 1865.

63. America Bonsack to Mary Plaine. Bonsack Papers.
64. *The Gospel Visitor*, August 1, 1864.
65. *The Gospel Visitor*, August 1, 1864.
66. Letcher Papers.
67. S. Z. Sharp, "Reminiscences of Fifty Years Ago and Beyond," *The Gospel Messenger*, January 27, 1923.
68. Article 1 was not included by Kurtz in his *Encyclopedia*. For Article 5, see Kurtz, *Encyclopedia*, page 104. For Article 1, see *Minutes of the Annual Meetings of the Church of the Brethren: 1778-1909* (Elgin: Brethren Publishing House, 1909), page 218.
69. Indiana Historical Society Library, William Henry Smith Memorial. Church history—Brethren (German Baptists, Dunkards, etc.) Used by courtesy of the Indiana Historical Society Library. Copied for my use by John Scott Davenport, Lexington, Virginia.
70. *Minutes of the Annual Meetings*, pages 230, 231-232.
71. *The Gospel Visitor*, August 15, 1864.
72. B. E. Plaine to David Plaine. Bonsack Papers.
73. Samuel and Elizabeth Harshbarger to Susannah Bonsack. Bonsack Papers.
74. *Minutes of the Annual Meetings*, pages 244-245.
75. B. E. Plaine to David Plaine. Bonsack Papers.
76. Philip Boyle, New Windsor, Maryland, "Correspondence," *Christian Family Companion*, April 10, 1866, page 118.
77. Bonsack Papers.
78. Library, Bethany Theological Seminary, Oak Brook, Illinois.

VII. PUBLICATIONS AND DEVOTIONAL WRITINGS

1. Nevin W. Fisher, *The History of Brethren Hymnbooks* (Bridgewater, Virginia: The Beacon Publishers, 1950), pages 25-26. Used by permission.
2. Fisher, *Brethren Hymnbooks*, pages 28-29.
3. William R. Eberly, "The Printing and Publishing Activities of Henry Kurtz," *Brethren Life and Thought*, Winter, 1963, page 23. See also Emmert F. Bittinger, "More on Brethren Hymnology," *Brethren Life and Thought*, Summer, 1963.
4. *A Choice Selection of Hymns, from Various Authors, Recommended for the Worship of God* (Poland, Mahoning Co., Ohio: Henry Kurtz, 1852), pages 318-320.
5. Philip Boyle to John Bonsack. Bonsack Papers.
6. Philip Boyle to John Bonsack. Bonsack Papers.
7. Kurtz, *Encyclopedia*, page 119.
8. Fisher, *Brethren Hymnbooks*, pages 40-41.
9. *Minutes of the Annual Meetings*, page 272.
10. Fisher, *Brethren Hymnbooks*, pages 48-49.
11. Kurtz, *Encyclopedia*, page 173. The best study of the life of Henry Kurtz is Donald F. Durnbaugh, "Henry Kurtz: Man of the Book," *Ohio History*, Summer, 1967.
12. *The Gospel Visiter*, April, 1851, pages 1-3.
13. *The Gospel Visiter*, April, 1851, page 9.
14. *The Gospel Visiter*, May, 1851, pages 25-26.
15. Kurtz, *Encyclopedia*, page 173.
16. *The Gospel Visiter*, June, 1851, pages 40-42.

17. *The Gospel Visiter,* July, 1851, page 57.
18. *The Gospel Visiter,* August, 1851, pages 74-75.
19. *The Gospel Visiter,* September, 1851, pages 89, 92.
20. *The Gospel Visiter,* October, 1851, page 105.
21. *The Gospel Visiter,* December, 1851, pages 136-137, 140
22. *The Gospel Visiter,* January, 1852, pages 166-168.
23. *The Gospel Visiter,* March, 1852, pages 198-200.
24. Kurtz, *Encyclopedia,* pages 173-174.
25. Holsinger, *History of the Tunkers,* pages 353-354.
26. H. R. Holsinger, "Farewell Words," *The Brethren's Almanac for the United States,* 1874.
27. *Christian Family Companion,* January 3, 1865, pages 4, 8.
28. Holsinger, "Farewell Words," 1874.
29. Samuel B. Heckman, *The Religious Poetry of Alexander Mack, Jr.* (Elgin: Brethren Publishing House, 1912), pages 51, 53.
30. Jacob Stoll, "Four Hymns," *Brethren Life and Thought,* XVI (Fall, 1971), 227-232; Jacob Stoll, "Four Hymns," *Brethren Life and Thought,* XVIII (Spring, 1973), 71-76.
31. Sanger and Hays, *The Olive Branch,* pages 155-156.
32. Sanger and Hays, *The Olive Branch,* page 157.
33. Mary Noffsinger to Mary Bonsack. Bonsack Papers.
34. Sophia Lightner to "Very dear Uncle and Aunt and Cousins." Bonsack Papers.
35. B. E. Plaine to David Plaine. Bonsack Papers.
36. J. C. Myers Papers, Manuscript Division, Perkins Library, Duke University. Used by permission.

CONCLUSION

1. For a thorough and excellent discussion of the Brethren bibliography related to the interpretation of this period as the wilderness years or the dark ages, see Donald F. Durnbaugh, "A Study of Brethren Historiography," *Ashland Theological Bulletin* (Spring, 1975), 3-18.

INDEX

Rowland, Andrew, 28
Rowland, John, 70
Rowland, Joseph, 27, 30, 32, 61, 75
Rowrick, James, 28
Ruble, Adam, 32
Ruble, Jacob, 32
Ruble, Jonathan, 33
Rude, _____, 20
Rupp, C., 112
Rush, Benjamin, 104

Sauer, Christopher, Sr., 406
Sauer, Christopher, Jr., 405-406
Sauer, Samuel, 168, 406
Sayler, D. P., 84, 208, 209, 215, 221, 258,
   401, 402, 403
Saylor, Jacob, 221
Scale, Ed, 374
Schaeffer, _____, 112, 113
Schutz, _____, 18
Seiss, R. S., 374
Sell, Ann, 48
Senderling, Michael, 243
Senger, Joel, 384
Senserry, A. H., 373
Seventh Day Adventists, 9
Shacklett, Samuel, 385
Shank family, 29
Sharp, S. Z., 298-301, 397, 471
Shasser, James, 28
Shaver, George, 259
Sheafferites, 113
Sheets, Andrew, 28
Shepperd, Wm., 28
Sherfig, Abraham, 249
Sherfig, Anna, 249
Sherfig, John, 249, 250
Sherfig, Joshua, 249, 250
Sherfig, Magdalene, 249, 251
Sherfig, Salome, 249, 251
Sheridan, Philip H., 392
Sherfy, Frederick, 225
Sherfy, Joel, 31, 225
Sherfy, Samuel S., 31, 261
Shireman, Lydia, 227
Shively, _____, 233
Shively, Henry, 32
Shively, John, 186
Shobe, Isaac, 227
Showalter, Catharine, 384
Showalter, J. M., 455
Showalter, Jackson, 384
Sietz, Niclaus, 332
Simmons family, 29, 31

Simon, Menno, 136-137, 159
Simon, Philib, 332
Sisler, Michael, 69
Slavery, 256-276
Slifer, _____, 185
Slifer, Mary C., 69
Smith, Alexander, 48
Smith, George, 361
Smith, Nathan, 235
Snader, Jacob, 222
Snapp, George, 374
Snider, Matthias, 332
Snider, Peter, 32
Snyder, S. P., 166
Solenberger, David, 225
Sons of Temperance, 283, 315
Sowers, Daniel, 371
Spitzer, William, 361
Spogle, _____, 69
Sprogle, _____, 70
Stanton, Edwin M., 369, 370
Steiner, Abraham, 28
Stephens, Alexander H., 368
Stern, Hans, 112, 113
Stevens, Thaddeus, 371, 372
Stillwaggon, Jesse, 241
Stirewalt, _____, 159
Stocker, Michael, 28
Stoll, Jacob, 406, 444
Stone, Barton W., 114, 116, 119
Stoner, _____, 46
Stoner, Daniel, 49
Stoner, Jacob, 244
Stoner, Kate, 69
Stoner, Mary, 184
Stoner, William, 223
Stover, Anne, 121
Stover, George, 121
Stover, George, 332
Stover, William, of Tennessee, 222
Stover, William, of Virginia, 332
Strickler, N. R., 70
Sturgin, John, 28
Sturgis, D. B., 62-65, 84, 86
Stutzman, Jacob, 44
Summers, William, 115
Sunday schools, 247-248
Supplee, Samuel, 165
Swadley, Henry, 225, 226, 261
Swinger, John, Sr., 272
Switzer, Jacob, 222

Tanner, _____, 18
Tappan, Lewis, 272-273